The Awesome Power of Direct3D/DirectX

The Awesome Power
of Direct3D/DirectX

DirectX Version 5.0

PETER J. KOVACH

MANNING

Greenwich
(74° w. long.)

For electronic browsing of this book, see http://www.browsebooks.com

The publisher offers discounts on this book when ordered in quantity. For more information, please contact:

Special Sales Department
Manning Publications Co.
3 Lewis Street
Greenwich, CT 06830

Fax: (203) 661-9018
email: orders@manning.com

Library of Congress Cataloging-in-Publication Data
Kovach, Peter J., 1961
    The awesome power of Direct3D / DirectX / Peter J. Kovach.
      p.   cm.
    Includes index.
    ISBN 1-884777-47-3
    1. Computer graphics.   2. Three-dimensional display systems.
    3. Real-time programming.   4. Direct 3D   I. Title.
    T385.K68   1997
    006.6'93—dc21   97-17116
                                        CIP

Manning Publications Co.
3 Lewis Street
Greenwich, CT 06830

Copyeditor: Margaret Marynowski
Typesetter: Nicholas A. Kosar
Cover designer: Leslie Haimes
Cover illustration: Correia Emmanuel

Printed in the United States of America
3 4 5 6 7 8 9 10 – CR – 00 99 98

contents

dedication

This book is dedicated to the two most important women in the world to me—my wife Monica and my daughter Shannon. Thank you for putting up with my spending so much of my time on this book. Now it is time to play with my wonderful daughter and to enjoy life with my beautiful wife.

introduction

The purpose of this book is to help programmers learn how to program 3D applications for such uses as simulations, games, marketing, demonstrations, and computer animated videos. This book describes how to program graphics applications using Microsoft's Direct3D Software Development Kit (SDK).

Many of the books that are released today attempt to make it "easy" for the reader to create his or her first application by developing libraries of commands. These commands are in fact encapsulated command sequences that manage to hide the code design from the end user. Although for the casual experimenter such an approach can be a nice time saver, the end effect is that the user never learns how to properly code in the target environment.

Other books give you numerous little applets, each showing you how to use one, or maybe two, of the features available in the SDK. The problem with these is that they fail to teach you how to use the available commands *together* to create a *real* application!

My intent in this book is to provide you with the grounding necessary to develop serious 3D applications using the Direct3D SDK. By showing you how the various commands are to be used, and how they interact with one another, you will learn not just which are the commands available but why they do what they do and how you can best put them to use.

This book will show you how the library of 3D graphic commands in the Direct3D SDK can be used to produce a high quality, high performance, 3D application. A detailed Retained-Mode application is shown and the step-by-step creation process is discussed in detail. This main code example demonstrates how to construct a full first-person perspective walk-around demonstration game scenario in Retained Mode, including full, variable shape object, *collision detection*.

This first major 3D tutorial application is designed to teach the user how to create Direct3D Retained-Mode applications step-by-step. The user is lead from the creation of the DirectDraw and Direct3D interfaces through the addition of lighting, 3D object loading, mouse/keyboard control, joystick control, 3D object creation, 3D object/viewpoint animation, collision detection, sound, animated objects, shadows, and fog. At the completion of the tutorial, you will have gained the knowledge necessary to create complete Direct3D applications. Only your imagination and time will then limit or enable you to produce awesome 3D applications on your own home PC.

The remaining applications demonstrate critical areas such as shadows and full-screen mode. A second, shorter, tutorial covers the use of Immediate Mode to create an application. This tutorial shows you a step-by-step description of how to write your first Immediate Mode application. I will show you all of the code steps necessary, and there are a lot!

The book also provides a source CD containing the code defined in the body of this text. In addition, 129 excellent 3D objects in both DirectX and 3D Studio format (.x and .3ds) have been included for your use in developing Direct3D based applications. Many of these are better than the objects you would pay more than $100 for commercially. I have also included fifty-two superb textures which you can apply to these objects. A list of the objects, and the textures, included on the CD can be found in the appendix at the back of this book.

You will also notice that I mention 3D Studio several times in this book. This is because it is the easiest tool to use for generating both static and animated objects. These objects can then easily be converted to DirectX File Format using the conv3ds tool included as part of the DirectX SDK on the CD accompanying this book.

Skill level

Because this book takes an exhaustive look at the Retained Mode of the Direct3D SDK, and a detailed look at the Immediate Mode, it will appeal to anyone in the simulation and gaming/graphic world. It will assist any person who has the desire to develop new detailed, high speed, 3D simulations, games, or environments, including artists and designers.

To utilize the information within this book effectively in your own project, you must possess a reasonable knowledge of C and it helps to have a minimal familiarity with C++. This text assumes an intermediate level of experience in the area and does not attempt to teach you C/C++ basics. If you feel you need a refresher on C, you may wish to get a copy of a good C book such as *The C Programming Language* by Brian W. Kernighan and Dennis M. Ritchie.

This book is designed so that even the most graphically inexperienced reader can understand the subject matter. Advanced graphics programmers will learn the difficult nuances of Direct3D which will greatly assist their development efforts. It is intended that this book help entice the reader to begin or continue to view the development of a graphic application as an exciting endeavor rather than an overwhelming challenge.

Target audience

Professionals: Developers who like to have a reference library on hand to remind them of previously learned knowledge or to enhance their current level of 3D graphic expertise in the usage of Direct3D.

New professionals: Individuals who have recently entered the professional field in the graphics domain. This book will assist these users in learning a new, high performance, graphic library for use in programming advanced 3D applications.

Shareware or hobby programmers: Those who do not have much time for the research but enjoy doing the development. This book will provide a detailed understanding, as well as sample code, to program a 3D application using Microsoft's Direct3D.

A little about myself

I have been involved with computers since the advent of the personal computer. I have owned every type of home computer created, including the original Elf, Exidy Sorcerer, Pet, Apple, Macintosh, every Tandy machine made (literally), and numerous IBM machines/clones, from the 8086 to the Pentium family. I have also owned many of the workstation class machines such as the Silicon Graphics Indigo II Extremes, and so forth.

I have always been fascinated with computer graphics and have been developing systems and algorithms since the 1970s. I started my professional career developing autonomous vehicle and flight simulators for such vehicles as F-15s, F-16s, and Apache helicopters. Recently, I was the vice president of a national firm involved in the development of virtual reality exercise equipment and arcade systems. I am now spending much of my time writing 3D graphic applications and developing 3D animations.

I hope you enjoy this book and find it a valuable resource for your future software development efforts.

Feel free to contact me at kovach@imageman.com or at my website which can be reached from http://www.manning.com/Kovach. I would be happy to discuss the book, 3D animation, or any other graphic issues. I will also continue to post free Direct3D objects, textures, code samples, and tutorials on my website.

PETER KOVACH

acknowledgements

I'd like to thank several people for their help, input, feedback, and/or excellent content they have provided for this book:

Correia Emmanuel   The image you created for this book cover turned out truly beautiful. Your work is fantastic. Thank you also for the fifty-two textures you provided for the CD accompanying this book. They are a great basis for a texture library for game or other 3D software development.

Michael Gaertner   I started out helping you with Direct3D questions and in a very short time you were writing great Direct3D code. You picked this up fast! Thank you for the time you spent on the Retained-Mode code for this book. I enjoyed working with you to create a project that was very useful as a tutorial basis. Welcome to the U.S.!

Don Farr and Zygote   Thank you for your superb models. Your attitude and quality are impressive and an example in the 3D industry.

Kinetix   Thank you to everyone at Kinetix/Autodesk, Inc., for the excellent 3D Studio MAX and Character Studio tools. They are superb tools for the PC and make modeling fun!

Microsoft   Thank you to everyone at Microsoft for a wonderful 3D development environment. Many of the descriptions throughout this book are based on Microsoft sources.

Finally, thank you to everyone else mentioned at the end of this book, and on the accompanying CD, for the excellent models, or software, you have provided for the CD. You have helped create a superb library of DirectX and 3D Studio models for people to use in their development. I have become more and more impressed with the people I have met on the Internet while writing this book. I have met some new friends and also seen some excellent work done in DirectX and 3D Studio. Thanks for all of your time and generosity to your fellow 3D developers. Your models and code will help provide an excellent starting point for those beginning with Direct3D and be a nice addition to the libraries of those already experienced with Direct3D.

PART I

chapter 1

DirectX fundamentals

1.1 What is DirectX?

The DirectX Application Program Interfaces provide a direct interface to the hardware on the host systems of our software. This was achieved by removing the device-specific hardware dependencies which were previously part of almost any software development effort. DirectX has been designed as thin API layers providing access to all of the performance that the hardware can deliver. Beyond this, it also provides the benefits of device independence. This has the end effect of positively impacting test and support costs while supporting a wide hardware base. With rapidly growing support by the manufacturers of display adapters, sound cards, and input devices, software developers will be able to fully utilize the next generation of hardware.

DirectX provides performance capabilities similar or equal to those provided in DOS, but allows hardware to be fully utilized, resulting in a great overall increase in performance. The DirectX APIs are built on a hardware abstraction layer (HAL) which effectively hides the device-specific dependencies of the hardware from the developer. DirectX provides specifications for hardware accelerator features that are not currently available, and many of these are emulated in software through the hardware emulation

3

layer (HEL). Others of these poll the hardware and if the features are not available, they are ignored. In this manner, as hardware is upgraded, the software will be ready to take advantage of the new capabilities.

This feature is key to our development efforts because it provides our users with the ability to upgrade their hardware and each time gain the performance expected. In the past, we tended to have to develop our software for the majority audience, usually meaning the *least common denominator*, hoping that the owners of the higher performance systems would still be interested in purchasing our wares. Now, with the introduction of the HAL, we can finally write our applications for the highest performance systems, while providing functionality acceptable to the owners of the lower performance systems.

In order to make sure you have the most up-to-date release of DirectX, please visit the Microsoft web page at http://www.microsoft.com regularly. The DirectX 5 download page is at http://www.microsoft.com/directx/default.asp. This page is the Interactive Game Developers page, one you will probably wish to watch anyway. It contains links to various DirectX hint and fix pages, as well as the DirectX Download Page. You might want to download the DirectX Media SDK there which includes the new versions of DirectShow and DirectAnimation.

DirectX consists of six interfaces that are all directed toward the development of high speed, high quality games and applications in the Windows 95 environment. These components are:

- *DirectDraw.* This API enables direct access to bitmapped data in off-screen memory and fast access to the bit-block transferring and page-flipping capabilities of the user's hardware.

- *Direct3D.* This API enables direct low-level access to 3D graphics hardware. The higher level Retained Mode, the area we will focus mostly upon, provides a detailed library of commands for the development of 3D applications.

- *DirectSound.* This API provides hardware and software sound mixing and playback. The most interesting capability provided by DirectSound is the ability to play 3D sound. Three-dimensional sound generates positional sounds which seem to come from a particular location, rather than ambient sound, which cannot be defined as having a particular source in space.

This 3D sound feature of DirectX will have great usefulness in Virtual Reality applications and any first-person perspective game or 3D simulation. I will cover some of the basics of this API, for both 2D and 3D sound, in *Chapter 11, Creating your first application—adding sound.*

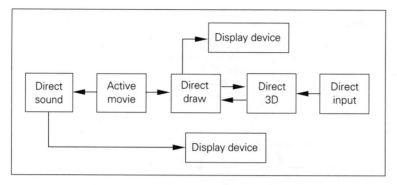

Figure 1.1 An example interaction of the Direct Modules

- *DirectPlay.* This API provides connectivity functionality enabling interactive gaming via a network or modem.
- *DirectInput.* This API provides joystick input capability for games, providing a growth path for future Windows APIs and drivers for hardware input. This is another critical API for game and simulation development. I will discuss this API in *Chapter 9, Creating your first application—adding joystick control.*
- *AutoPlay.* This feature provides the capability to easily run an installation program, or a game, directly from a CD.

Integration with Microsoft's ActiveMovie technology allows the developer to utilize video streams from such sources as MPEG video, QuickTime video, audio-video interleaved (AVI) video, and video capture devices to be mapped as textures to 3D objects in real time. The *avirm* application from Microsoft, included on the CD accompanying this book, shows you how to apply an AVI video as a moving texture on a 3D object.

Figure 1.1 shows how we could set up a movie to be played using ActiveMovie with DirectSound playing the audio and DirectDraw mapping the video frames as textures for use on a Direct3D object. Finally, Direct3D can utilize DirectDraw as the rendering target to display the completed final scene on the display device.

Figure 1.2 shows how the Windows system and the DirectX system interact.

1.2 How does Direct3D fit in?

Microsoft's Direct3D is one of the most promising development tools available to simulation engineers, game developers, and graphic designers for the PC platform today. This software development kit provides the ability to produce 3D graphic-based applications that begin to rival the performance previously only available on workstation class

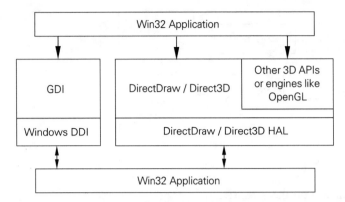

Figure 1.2 The DirectX, Windows, and overall systems relationships

machines. With the addition of some of the newest 3D graphic hardware, one million polygon per second performance and beyond has become a reality.

The purpose of this book is to describe how to program graphics application software using Microsoft's Direct3D SDK. Direct3D was developed for the IBM PC compatible market and is now owned, marketed, and enhanced by Microsoft, Inc. Direct3D was designed to provide a high performance library for software developers to use for the development of such applications as 3D games, virtual environments, and graphic demonstration software. The possibilities for development of virtual environments are great. Until recently, it has been basically unfeasible to develop realtime, quality, 3D virtual worlds on any system below the workstation class systems. Now, with the combination of Direct3D and the new generation of PC 3D accelerators, we are able to generate worlds that have accurate texturing, color, and special effects such as fog on personal computers. The line between *personal* computers and *workstation* class machines is rapidly disappearing.

This book was written to provide a complete tutorial on the use of the critical features of Direct3D. The focus will be upon the Retained Mode of the Direct3D API supplied as part of the DirectX SDK. I will also give full details on creating an Immediate-Mode application in chapters 16 through 18. DirectX was developed for the Windows Environment to help developers produce games in this user friendly environment rather than in the anachronistic DOS environment. Since the advent of Win32 and Windows95, game developers have begun to move toward the Windows environment. Up until these developments they had been stopped by the relative lack of support in terms of speed and general performance provided by previous versions of Windows.

Direct3D was developed to provide a high-speed, device-independent, set of software-based functions provided through both a high-level Retained Mode and a low-level

Intermediate Mode API. Retained Mode is written for applications which retain the graphic data, whereas Intermediate Mode streams the data directly to an execute buffer. Again, this book will focus greatly on the Retained Mode of Direct3D due to its applicability to the majority audience

Direct3D provides a complete suite of real-time graphics services which provide very fast software-based rendering of the complete 3D rendering pipeline (light, transform, etc.) and transparent access to the hardware acceleration capabilities available on the target PC platform. Direct3D provides support for hardware acceleration of such features as atmospheric effects (fog), perspective-corrected texture mapping, alpha-blending, mip-mapping, and z-buffering. These capabilities combine to provide an exceptional growth path for hardware and software developers as capabilities in both arenas continue to grow rapidly.

DirectDraw and Direct3D have been tightly integrated, with DirectDraw acting as the buffer management system. These capabilities enable DirectDraw surfaces to be used as 3D rendering targets and source texture maps. This book covers only the features of DirectDraw which are necessary to develop excellent 3D applications. I would recommend that any reader who is a serious developer pick up a reference which deals extensively with the DirectDraw capabilities. One book that covers DirectDraw basics and provides a DirectDraw Reference as well is *DirectDraw Programming* by Bret Timmins, which is published by M&T Books.

Through the integration which Microsoft has put into the DirectX, and ActiveX, technologies, Direct3D is able to bring capabilities such as video mapping, hardware 3D rendering in 2D overlay planes, and sprites to the home PC. This has resulted in a system which allows seamless use of 2D and 3D graphics and digital video in applications such as virtual reality, interactive video, and several other leading-edge technologies.

1.3 What it can do from a 3D perspective

The list of features provided to us with Direct3D is long and strong. The object classes and effects which I find the most powerful include

- Dithering
- Vertex Colors
- Orthographic and Perspective Projections
- Reflection (environment) and Video (.avi) Mapping
- Mipmaps
- Animation
- Real time object deformation

- Multiple movable colored light types (Ambient, Directional, Parallel Point, Point, and Spotlight)
- Ramp and True Color RGB (Red, Green, and Blue) Model
- Color Depth of 8, 16, 24, and 32 bits
- Full transparencies, including using alpha maps
- Mipmap texture mapping
- Perspective correct texture mapping, including multiple texture wrapping techniques and decals
- Picking support for user selection/control of objects
- Material types
- Shadows
- Depth cueing with atmospheric effects, including fog and haze
- Multiple Viewports, Devices, and Cameras
- Real-time Animation Keyframing

We shall cover all of the key features provided by Direct3D in the following chapters of this book.

1.4 Performance and device independence

In the next sections, we will learn about the efficiency of Direct3D, as well as the way in which DirectX has finally provided device independence to us developers and to the users of our software. The efficiency jump provided by Direct3D over past 3D libraries, combined with the removal of the hardware configuration nightmares for which software designers had to develop in the past, make the Windows 95 and DirectX combination a welcome arrival!

1.5 Why Windows is better than DOS

Microsoft has finally realized what 3D software designers have known for a very long time—Windows is better than DOS in terms of usability and interface capabilities and standards. In addition, with the new Plug-and-Play Windows95 hardware standard, Microsoft has provided an efficient upgrade methodology helping users to keep up easily with the rapidly changing hardware scene.

For those of us who are simulators or game designers, DOS has always been the default development environment. This was not due to our desire to use it; rather it was a forced choice due to the high overhead and low performance of the previous Windows environments. When we develop in the DOS environment, we are required to develop software attempting to work with a variety of hardware designed using a wide range of implementation techniques. This makes it very difficult to guarantee that our software will function on the many different hardware configurations.

Windows 95 is the Windows implementation that has finally addressed the needs of the game software developer. Beyond the efficient design of the DirectX family of SDKs, DirectX provides many performance enhancement features. These include the AutoPlay capability, which is designed to allow the distribution CD for software to execute an installation program or the game itself as soon as the CD is inserted into the user's PC. They also include the availability of the Plug and Play standard and the built-in Windows 95 communication services.

With these features, as well as many others provided in each of the DirectX components, DOS is no longer the operating system of choice for game developers. We now have a far more user friendly and capable system in which to develop our advanced 3D applications—DirectX.

1.6 Why Windows needs Direct3D

Software developers probably consider this to be a *very* key question. Microsoft has developed Direct3D, as well as the overall DirectX, to provide our Windows applications with real-time access to any of the hardware produced for PC platforms today. The interface provided by DirectX delivers a consistent interface between all new hardware devices and our software. DirectX as a whole was developed to provide real-time access to the hardware available on the target systems. It was also designed to provide a standardized interface between software developers and the designers of the hardware. This provides for far simpler installation and configuration, since much of the hardware detection and configuration is hidden from the users. This detection and optimal usage of hardware is also made much easier for us due to the design of the Component Object Model we will discuss shortly.

1.7 Hardware versus software

As discussed above, Direct3D was designed to utilize all of the hardware capabilities on our user's target platforms. In the past, we were forced to provide drivers for each of the hardware devices we wished to support, as well as tailor our application's performance based upon the features supported on each of the platforms. With DirectX and Windows 95, we can now provide support for any of the user's hardware choices easily.

Direct3D was built on top of the HAL, which was designed to hide the difficult device-specific dependencies normally found with hardware. With DirectX, we can query the hardware capabilities, and, for each of the required capabilities supported on the hardware, Direct3D can take direct advantage of the hardware acceleration. For any required functionality not supported on the user's hardware, software drivers provided in the Direct3D SDK will be loaded to fill the gap between the user's hardware and the desired capabilities. This means that Direct3D can provide both transparent access to the hardware acceleration capabilities of the users' hardware and use of the full 3D rendering pipeline functionality implemented in the Direct3D software when needed.

The Direct3D HAL has been tightly integrated with the DirectDraw HAL and the GDI display driver. This means that hardware developers now need to write only a single driver for acceleration of not only Direct3D applications, but also DirectDraw, Graphic Display Interface (GDI), and OpenGL applications as well. The HAL was created with the intent of supporting both hardware acceleration of the entire 3D graphics rendering pipeline today and future graphics accelerators as they become available.

For those capabilities not provided in hardware today, the Direct3D HEL was developed. It was designed as a companion piece to the HAL, and provides software-based emulation of the features not provided by the available hardware. Through the coupling of the HAL and the HEL, Direct3D can guarantee that the API services are available to all of our software and hardware users.

1.8 What form does Direct3D take?

Direct3D is supplied with two levels of support for both hardware and software based 3D rendering. The Direct3D high-level Retained-Mode API was developed for controlling 3D objects and managing 3D scenes. The Direct3D low-level Immediate-Mode API was developed for software designers who wish to port their previous DOS-based applications as easily as possible, but who still desire to utilize 3D engines or other code they have developed. These two approaches, as well as the 3D Object File Format designed for Direct3D, are discussed in this section.

1.8.1 Immediate Mode

The Direct3D low-level Immediate-Mode API consists of a thin polygon- and vertex-based API layer giving developers direct access, in a device independent manner, to the features of 3D hardware. Unlike the Retained-Mode API, the Immediate-Mode API does not provide a geometry engine so it expects the object and scene management to be handled by our application. The Immediate-Mode API allows developers an easy method of porting existing applications to the Windows environment. In addition, this API allows us to incorporate our own rendering and scene management modules while transparently adding the ability to fully utilize the new generations of 3D hardware accelerators.

1.8.2 Retained Mode

Direct3D's Retained Mode API allows us to incorporate 3D capabilities into our applications without the need for the intensive efforts to develop 3D geometry engines, 3D databases, or new object formats. Instead, the developer can load a colored, textured 3D object using a single API command. In addition, the developer can use other simple API commands to scale, rotate, light, or translate the object within the scene in real time. All of this is possible without knowledge of the internal structure of the data object (although it will help to understand it and you will learn about it later).

1.8.3 Direct3D file format

Direct3D uses objects conforming to the DirectX file format. These objects are fairly efficient in memory usage and provide very good object functionality—color, texture, animation, and so forth. One thing which has been quite conspicuously absent from Direct3D is a 3D editor allowing the software developer an opportunity to create his or her own objects. After all, without a tool to generate detailed objects to put in our 3D worlds, what do we have—some very basic geometric objects at best without a lot of hand graphing and data entry!

The DirectX File Format provides the developer with a file format fully capable of storing user definable objects, meshes, textures, and animation sets providing the facility to exchange 3D information between objects. Through the use of object-oriented techniques, a single instance of an object can be incorporated into a hierarchy, allowing for multiple references to a single data object, such as a 3D mesh, while requiring the data to be stored only once. This object format allows for the loading of 3D objects into an application, or the exporting of generated objects out of an application into a data file or another application. This will provide an excellent manner for developers to create objects and animation paths for use within an application or for sale for use in other titles.

The DirectX file format is just beginning to be considered for output directly by commercial software, due to the newness of Direct3D. To solve this problem in the short term, Microsoft has provided a tool named conv3ds, which takes as input a 3DStudio file and outputs a .x file. Currently, the easiest way to develop 3DStudio objects to convert for use in our Direct3D applications is to use 3D Studio MAX from Autodesk. I will discuss using 3D Studio to build objects in chapter 7. This tool provides very advanced modeling capabilities, including the incorporation of color, texturing, and animation information within the model. The .3ds file format was developed for 3D Studio and is thus native to this tool. Other options exist which allow the user to convert file formats from other tools first to the .3ds file format and then to the .x format. Although this is an extra step in conversion, and thus more time consuming, it can be a cost saving approach. I have included the shareware version of the best software conversion tool available, PolyTrans from Okino Computer Graphics (www.okino.com), on the CD accompanying this book.

To help address the need for 3D objects for our 3D virtual worlds in the short term (until I get my 3D editor done and out to everyone on my web page), I have included numerous objects on the CD which accompanies this book. These will save you the great deal of time (and skill) necessary to model them yourselves. Each of these objects was created using various tools, converted to the 3DStudio file format (if it was not already in that format, since many of the objects were created using the 3DStudio tool), and then converted to DirectX file format using the conv3ds tool provided with the DirectX distribution on the book's CD. Although this is a lot of steps to have to take to create a DirectX 3D object, it is really fairly simple and is the best approach for those who do not own 3DStudio and have not written their own conversion tool. You can save a step, and gain many nice capabilities, such as normal and face flipping, using the PolyTrans tool.

Each of the objects is in the public domain and thus you may use them as you see fit and to your heart's content. As you create new objects, feel free to email them to me! I will add them to my web pages which I have set up to allow people access to .x file objects, Direct3D help, and Direct3D example source. This web page can be reached from http://www.manning.com/Kovach. It will be updated regularly as I will continue to add new information, objects, textures, hints, and other useful data. Feel free to submit any 3D objects, textures, or ideas any time, and check the site regularly!

1.9 COM objects

The DirectX SDK consists of several interfaces based upon the Component Object Model (COM). These interface methods can be thought of and used exactly like C, or C++, functions. The component object model is the basis of an object-based system centered upon interface reuse. In addition, this model is the core of object linking and embedding (OLE) programming. COM is an object model at the operating system level from which interfaces can be built. COM interfaces are also referred to as *classes*. Each of the interfaces provides a set of *methods* which perform services for the object. New interfaces can be constructed using *inheritance,* allowing the new interface to use the methods of its parent's interface. The main difference from C++ or other object-oriented languages is that only the method definitions are inherited, rather than the actual code. The object which implements a COM interface must support all methods provided by that interface, as well as any interfaces from which it derives.

A number of the DirectX APIs are instantiated as a set of OLE objects. These objects allow communication with our applications through an *interface* to the hardware represented by them. The commands we may pass between our applications and the objects through the COM interface are called *methods.* Methods can be thought of like the *member function* in C++ programming (and the function in C programming). As an example of these methods, in Direct3D the `IDirect3DRM::CreateAnimation` method is sent through the IDirect3DRM interface to create an empty Direct3DRMAnimation object.

A program or other object can determine what services a second object can perform by knowing it is a COM object and what interfaces it supports. One of the methods inherited by all COM objects is the `QueryInterface` method, which lets the user determine which interfaces are supported by an object and create pointers to these interfaces.

The DirectX interfaces have been developed at a low level of the COM hierarchy. All of the main device object interfaces (IDirect3D, IDirectDraw, etc.) are derived from the OLE interface IUnknown. The creation of these main objects is performed via functions in the DLL for each object. The IUnknown interface has only three methods:

- `QueryInterface`. This method determines if an interface is present.
- `AddRef`. This method increments the reference count for each object that is created or newly associated with another object.
- `Release`. This method decrements the reference count for an interface when a pointer is deleted or disassociated from it.
- `AddRef` is automatically called by the method that creates the object, but `Release` must be called by the application whenever that object is destroyed. This `Release` method is equivalent to the free command in the C++ language. If this action is not performed, memory leaks may occur. A COM interface can be thought of as an abstract base class in C++. It defines a set of signatures and semantics but not the implementation. No state data are associated with the interface. In a C++ abstract base class, all methods are defined as pure virtual, meaning that no code is associated with them.

1.9.1 The vtable and the first argument in a method call

Both pure virtual C++ functions and COM interfaces employ a device called a `vtable`. A `vtable` contains a list of the addresses of all functions implementing the given interface. The `vtable` level of the data is hidden from the user in the C++ calling format. The `QueryInterface` method can be used by an object or program to verify the interface exists on an object, and to obtain a pointer to that interface. The program or object receives a pointer to the vtable when the object sends the `QueryInterface` message. This can then be used to call the interface methods implemented by the object. The private data used by the object and the calling client process are isolated in this manner.

The first argument of a method is the name of the interface or class which can be thought of as the *this* argument in C++. COM objects and C++ objects are completely binary compatible, so the compiler treats COM interfaces like C++ abstract classes and assumes the same syntax.

It is important for the software developer to understand how the Direct3D calling format differs in C from C++. Any COM interface method can be called from a C or C++ program. The key issues to understand when calling an interface method from C rather than C++ are:

1 The method's first parameter is always a reference to the object calling the method (in C++, the this argument).

2 Every one of the methods associated with the interface are referenced via a pointer to the object's `vtable.`

1.9.2 An example of the difference between a C and a C++ method call

As an example, the code below creates a `Light` associated with a Direct3D object through a call to the `IDirect3D::CreateLight` method. The Direct3D object associated with the new light is referenced by the `lpD3DRM` argument. The example calls `IDirect3DRM::CreateLightRGB` using C. In the call to the `CreateLightRGB` method, the object's `vtable` and the method from the `vtable` are dereferenced. The first parameter in any of the C methods is a reference to the Direct3D object invoking the method.

```
Light = lpD3DRM->lpVtbl->CreateLightRGB(lpD3DRM, D3DRMLIGHT_AMBIENT,
        D3DVAL(0.4), D3Dval(0.2), D3DVAL(0.2), &14));
```

To illustrate the difference, the method invoked through a C++ call would be as follows:

```
Light = lpD3DRM->CreateLightRGB(D3DRMLIGHT_AMBIENT, D3DVAL(0.4),
        D3Dval(0.2), D3DVAL(0.2), &14));
```

Remember that C++ dereferences the `vtable` pointer (`lpVtbl`) and passes the `this` pointer.

This book focuses on the C++ language format for method usage, but any example can easily be converted to run in C if you just remember the differences I have mentioned above.

1.10 What did we learn?

In this chapter we have learned about the components of the DirectX SDK with specific focus on the component of most interest—Direct3D. We have also learned about the COM and the difference between the C and C++ calling formats.

1.11 What's next?

In the next chapter we begin our tutorial on Direct3D. We will start with a discussion on the rather difficult, and quite long, set up functions we will need for all of our future Direct3D applications. So, let's get going!

chapter 2

The main window

2.1 Introduction

This chapter, along with the subsequent chapters, will show you all of the steps necessary to design your first Direct3D application. Like all new software development kits, operating systems, and libraries, learning the meaning of the commands is time consuming enough. When you also need to figure out how they work together, this effort can often become as fun as hitting your head against the wall (umm, that is meant to indicate *bad* for those that enjoy that type of thing).

I have found that a huge percent of the so-called tutorial type books end up either giving you a bunch of commands which are wrappers around the real code or a large amount of code with cursory explanations of what is happening. With the first approach, I have heard over and over from people that what they wanted was to know *how* to use the commands, in *context*, where any associated commands necessary to be used with them are shown. Instead, these books end up showing you how to use the author's library that hides the details and leaves the reader as uninformed in how to use the actual SDK or OS as when they started!

16

With the second approach, we may be given working code, even excellent working code, but again with no explanation of *why*, we end up with a major chore ahead of us to even learn how to modify the code to a minor extent, let alone develop new applications.

2.1.1 *The Retained-Mode tutorial format*

In the next several chapters ahead, I will present the philosophy of Direct3D commands and 3D concepts in general. You will be presented with routines and code segments in the order in which you should implement them for maximal efficiency in your code design. With every new segment, each representing new required functional blocks of code, I will not only explain the various Direct3D and Windows 95 commands, I will also explain their usage in *context*. By presenting the how and *why* of command usage and calling sequence, I hope you will find yourself at the end of these tutorial chapters with the understanding necessary to not just use the code examples with modification, but rather to jump into the detailed design of new Direct3D-based ideas.

You can break any 3D application down into six main functional blocks. These are:

1 Creating the Windows set-up code for any Windows Direct3D application (this chapter)

2 Creating an error handler (this chapter)

3 Creating the Direct3D main routine/message processing loop (chapter 3)

Figure 2.1 The tutorial application's main window

4 Setting up the models (and associated colors and textures), lights, and object positions (chapter 4)

5 Rendering the scene into the viewport (chapter 5)

6 Updating and rerendering the scene based on device (keyboard, joystick, mouse, etc.) input (chapters 6 and 9)

7 Creating 3D objects, including dynamic levels of detail (chapter 7)

8 Textures and materials (chapter 8)

By the end of this chapter, we will have your first application defined. The window it will produce will look like the screen shown in figure 2.1.

This window will only be the base window display. In the following chapters, we will begin to add the capabilities listed above.

2.2 Creating our application's main screen

A rather large amount of code is required to make our first application's window even visible on the screen. Although the number of lines of code may seem daunting at first, the thing to remember is that this set-up code is reusable, with minimal changes, for all of your applications in the future. I will be including code segments as we discuss each step of the process of creating our first application as we progress through this chapter. This same format will also be used in the remaining chapters. In this manner, you will be able to see all of the code in context, as well as each of the blocks separately when we discuss the commands in detail.

I have broken the code necessary for creating our first windowed application into two segments: 1) the generic Windows code and 2) the Direct3D-specific code.

There are really three ways of developing applications using Direct3D:

1 As a standalone, full screen, application

2 As a windowed application

3 As a Microsoft Foundation Class (MFC)-based application

We will be focusing on windowed applications for much of this book, but I will be discussing a full-screen application approach in chapter 15. I will also discuss how to write an Immediate-Mode application in chapters 16 through 18. For game writers, the full-screen mode is often the implementation method of choice, due to the removal of the windows overhead. Also, remember, everything you learn in the windowed application discussion is directly applicable to any MFC-based development efforts you decide to perform.

2.3 How to structure your Direct3D code

The code for this book is contained on the accompanying CD. The code for each chapter is held in a subproject in the main tutorial project which is stored in the *tutorial/makefile1*. You will notice that there are subfolders for each of the chapters in this directory. To build the project for a chapter, for now chapter 2, double click on the makefile1 icon. This will start Visual C++ (Microsoft Developer Studio). Now select the Chap2-Win32 Debug sub-project from the default project configuration window. Then you just need to select the Build chap2.exe option from the Build pull-down menu to build the project for chapter 2. Finally, when it is compiled, select the Execute Chap2.exe option from the Build pull-down menu item. You will use the same process for all subprojects for the remaining chapters covering Retained Mode in this book.

The project *chap1* contains all the code for this chapter's example. Load it up and take a look at it now, and we'll examine everything step by step. The number of lines of code may seem like a lot just to set up our program, but the thing to remember is that this code is reusable for any of our future applications. We will come back to it and add more functionality later on.

First, let's look at the structure of this program is set-up code. This will help us to make sense of the calling sequence and the reason that this is all necessary. The calling sequence is as follows:

```
WinMain
FirstInstance
AnyInstance
LoadAccelerators (System Function)
Loop until we quit
    PeekMessage (System Function)
    TranslateAccelerator (System Function)
    TranslateMessage (System Function)
    DispatchMessage (System Function)
```

We will walk through each of these functions in the following sections. First let's look at the includes and global variables.

2.4 The includes and the variables

The only reference to Direct3D I will be making in this chapter is the following line of code. The main reason I am doing this is that I wish you to remember that you should always set up your Direct3D application code this way! The first line referring to INIT-GUID is used because we need to define the storage for all of the globally unique identifiers

(GUIDs) in one module of our program. This is done by defining the symbol INITGUID before including windows.h, ddraw.h, and d3d.h. If you forget this, you will see a variety of link errors show up when you attempt to compile and link your code.

```
#define INITGUID
#include <windows.h>
```

One thing you need to remember is that you want to define INITGUID in only *one* of your modules. You will find yourself presented with errors during compilation if you forget this!

The next include is our custom application include file. This header file contains all of our function definitions, global variables, common types, and so forth. We will not be including Direct3D includes until the next chapter. You will see then that there are some ordering issues for inclusion of the files which you will need to remember.

```
#include "tutorial.h"
```

The remaining files define the standard windows, I/O, allocation, mathematics functions, and the function declarations for directory handling/creation:

```
#include <stdio.h>
#include <string.h>
#include <malloc.h>
#include <math.h>
#include <direct.h>
```

The name of our class is stored as a string. Microsoft tends to do this for the purpose of printing class information but you may find no need for this. I have just taken this up as a habit.

```
static char TutorialClass[32] = "TutorialClass";
```

The TutorInfo structure will contain all of the critical objects we need for creating, rendering, and viewing our 3D world. The objects include the camera, viewing frustum, color model, and others. For now, since we are creating just the window set-up code, we will only be defining a single variable, and we will fill in the remaining variables in the next chapter. Remember to use this structure to contain any application variables used throughout your routines if you want to keep from passing a large number of arguments between your various routines and member functions.

The minimized variable in the code segment below holds a boolean value you can set to indicate whether your window is minimized.

```
// Define a structure to hold the data associated
// with this tutorials window.
```

```
typedef struct _TutorInfo
{
 // Tells if the window is minimized or not
 BOOL minimized;
} TutorInfo;
```

The next global variable will hold the key objects associated with the window we will generate for our application. I will discuss this variable in detail in the next chapter.

```
// Initialize the tutor information structure
TutorInfo *info = NULL;
```

We next need to specify the various functions we will be defining. By using a forward declaration, we declare the calling structure ahead of time so we cannot mismatch our calling arguments. It also allows us to include the functions in any order in the code body. You would normally place these definitions in your header file, but I have chosen to use forward declarations to make the code layout slightly easier to understand for new C++ programmers coming from the C environment. For those of you who are long-time C++ programmers, realize that you can easily convert these to standard C++ header file format if you wish. As you can see, there are not many variables—yet! When we get into the Direct3D commands, there will be a number of variables (local and global) we will need to maintain.

2.5 The forward declarations

Our initial forward declarations will define only the three required routines for our Windows set-up code. I will be adding the forward declarations for our code as we add routines in the following chapters.

```
// Forward function declarations
static BOOL FirstInstance(HINSTANCE);
static BOOL AnyInstance(HINSTANCE, int);
long FAR PASCAL WindowProc(HWND, UINT, WPARAM, LPARAM);
```

Our first function is used to generate a message box for us to output any error messages necessary should our application ever produce an error. Certainly something we should strive against!

```
// Msg
// Create a message box to output any error notifications.
//
void __cdecl
Msg( LPSTR fmt, ... )
{
```

```
char messBuff[256];
wvsprintf(messBuff, fmt, (char *)(&fmt+1));
lstrcat(messBuff, "\r\n");
MessageBox( NULL, messBuff, "Tutorial Message", MB_OK );
}
```

This message box is in a standard format you will see in all of the Direct3D examples included on the Direct3D distribution. It works fine for our needs and thus I have defined it basically the same.

2.6 The main window

Now that we have the methods and globals defined, we are ready to define our main code. The `WinMain` function is always the main function of a Microsoft Windows based application. This function is called by the system as the initial entry point for our application.

The function definition is as follows:

```
int WINAPI WinMain(
    HINSTANCE    hInstance,       // The current instance handle
    HINSTANCE    hPrevInstance,   // The previous instance handle
    LPSTR        lpCmdLine,       // Command line pointer
    int          nCmdShow         // Show window state
);
```

The `WinMain` function acts as the main process loop. `WinMain` initializes our application and begins a message retrieval and dispatch loop. When the quit message is received, and our program terminates properly, `WinMain` exits our application and returns the value passed in the `WM_QUIT` message's `wParam` parameter. If the function terminates before we enter the message loop, it returns 0 (FALSE).

The function is defined as:

```
//
// This function is the main routine containing the message loop.
// Here we call the functions to create, initialize, and activate
// the program's main window and handle the various messages.
//
int PASCAL WinMain
    (HINSTANCE currentInstance, HINSTANCE previousInstance, LPSTR
    commandLine, int commandShow)
{
```

The first lines of this routine specify the local variables to be used.

```
MSG message;   // This variable is used to hold any error message
  int idle;    // Set to TRUE when the user is not requesting any
               // action through mouse or key input
```

```
int done = FALSE;          // Set to TRUE when we are ready to
                           // exit our application
HACCEL accelerators;       // Holds our accelerator list
```

The first thing we need to do in this routine is to either get or create an instance of our window class. If we must create a new window, we need to fill out the information on it and register it. See the FirstInstance routine to get an idea of what we are doing here. I will be discussing this code later in this chapter.

```
// If there is no previous instance set, register the window class
// for the application
 if (!previousInstance)
 if (!FirstInstance(currentInstance))
   return 1;
```

When we return from these calls, we have the Windows set-up information defined. Now we need to actually create the window, show it, and update the display. This is done in the AnyInstance routine.

```
// If we cannot do the remaining window set-up, return an
// error
 if (!AnyInstance(currentInstance, commandShow))
   return 1;
```

After we show the window, we load the tutorial accelerator table. The handle of the accelerator table is returned if the call is successful (otherwise NULL is returned).

```
// Load the accelerator table
 accelerators = LoadAccelerators(currentInstance, "TutorialAccel");
```

2.6.1 The message processing loop

With our window set up, we need to start our message processing loop. This is the main message processing loop which is used to handle all of the events which occur during the execution of our program. This loop is terminated when we receive a WM_QUIT message. The PeekMessage command is used to check a thread message queue for a message. If there is one it is placed in the specified structure.

The PeekMessage command structure is:

```
BOOL PeekMessage(
    LPMSG lpMsg,              // The pointer to the message structure
    HWND hWnd,                // Window handle
    UINT wMsgFilterMin,       // The first message
    UINT wMsgFilterMax,       // The last message
    UINT wRemoveMsg           // Removal flags
  );
```

For our purposes, we will store our messages in the variable `message`. By specifying the `hWnd` parameter as NULL, we are indicating that we want to retrieve the messages for any window that belongs to the thread currently making the call.

You will also notice that I have specified `wMsgFilterMin` and `wMsgFilterMax` as 0. By doing this, we are requesting that the system should perform no filtering and return all of the available messages.

In the final argument, I have set the `wRemoveMsg` parameter to `PM_REMOVE`. This is used to specify that we want the messages removed from the queue after they are processed.

The code we need to handle this is:

```
// Loop until we are done - either the user quits or an error occurs
 while (!done)
 {
idle = TRUE;
    // Check the thread message queue for a message and place it in
    // message if there is one.
    while (PeekMessage(&message, NULL, 0, 0, PM_REMOVE))
 {
    idle = FALSE;
    // If we get a quit message, drop out to quit
    if (message.message == WM_QUIT)
 {
    done = TRUE;
    break;
    }
    .
    .
    }
```

2.7 The accelerators

In the final major portion of our main functions, we need to perform three tasks: handle the accelerator keys, translate the messages, and send them to their appropriate location.

First we process the accelerator keys for our menu. This function translates a `WM_KEYDOWN` or `WM_SYSKEYDOWN` to a `WM_COMMAND` or `WM_SYSCOMMAND` message to the appropriate window procedure. `TranslateAccelerator` returns after the window proceedure processes the message. The command prototype is as follows:

```
int TranslateAccelerator(
    HWND    hWnd,           // Destination window handle
    HACCEL  HAccTable,      // Accelerator table handle
    LPMSG   lpMsg           // Address of message structure
);
```

The key arguments are

- **hAccTable.** The accelerator table loaded previously by either a call to `LoadAccel-erators` or the `CreateAcceleratorTable` function.

- **lpMsg.** A pointer to an `MSG` structure containing message information received from the thread's message queue using either the `PeekMessage` or `GetMessage` functions.

The code to handle this is:

```
// Process the menu and accelerator keys
if (!TranslateAccelerator(message.hwnd, accelerators, &message)) {
```

After we get the message, we need to translate the virtual-key messages into character messages. These messages are posted to the calling thread's message queue. They are read when the thread next calls `GetMessage` or `PeekMessage`.

The function prototype is:

```
BOOL TranslateMessage(
    CONST MSG *lpMsg;// Address of message structure
);
```

The `lpMsg` parameter points to a `MSG` structure containing message information from the calling thread's message queue. This message is retrieved through the use of the `GetMessage` or `PeekMessage` functions.

This function returns TRUE if the character message is posted to the thread's message queue. FALSE is returned if it is not posted.

```
// Translate the virtual key messages into
// character messages
TranslateMessage(&message);
```

Finally, we need to dispatch the message. The DispatchMessage function dispatches a message to a window procedure. This function returns a value specifying the value returned by the window procedure. This value is typically *not* useful for error checking.

```
    // Dispatch the message to the window proceedure
    DispatchMessage(&message);
  }
}
```

After all of this, you may be surprised to learn that we have now completed only the base portion of our main function. To make a truly effective program, we must develop a number of other routines and code segments to guarantee that our program executes properly. The remainder of this chapter will detail this code.

2.8 Implementing an error handler

Microsoft has provided us with a rather large number of possible error types. Although they are certainly events which we strive to never see, the reality of life is that during development we are bound to have a few show up. Since this is the case, we should always supply a good error message number to string routine so that we can present a useful description of the error to ourselves or our users.

On the CD accompanying this book, I have included the routine `MyErrorToString` in all of the sub-projects' tutorial*x*.cpp files. This code handles each of the possible errors and presents a text message describing each error in simple terms. This routine can be used effectively in all of your applications. There is no reason for you to rewrite this routine, since all of the possible Direct3D errors are handled.

The format of this routine is:

```
char* MyErrorToString(HRESULT error)
{
 switch(error) {
  // Each of the errors below is specified by Microsoft (C)
  // These are defined in the various Microsoft (C) documentation.
  case DD_OK:
   // Also includes D3D_OK and D3DRM_OK
   return "No error.";
  case DDERR_ALREADYINITIALIZED:
   return "This object is already initialized.";
  case DDERR_BLTFASTCANTCLIP:
return "Return if a clipper object is attached to the source surface
        passed into a BltFast call.";
  .
  .
  .
  default:
   return "Unrecognized error value.";
 }
}
```

The code provided on the CD contains an exhaustive list of the error messages provided by the DirectX SDK. This routine should be quite self-explanatory, and thus I will not attempt to go into detail on each of the possible errors. We just need to remember to do proper error checking and handling so that we can catch any of these occurrences before they do any additional damage.

2.9 The supporting functions

In the remainder of this chapter, we will walk through the supporting functions necessary to create our main window. First, we need to always create a function which defines and registers the instance of our window we are creating upon start-up. It is fairly simple but there are several fields in the WNDCLASS structure about which we should learn. This routine is called with the current instance of the window as an argument.

2.10 Defining our window

```
//
// Register the window class for the application. Also perform other
// desired application initialization
//
static BOOL FirstInstance(HINSTANCE this_inst)
```

The HINSTANCE type is listed as one of Microsoft's simple types. It is used to hold the handle of an instance of our window class.

```
{
  // Contains the window class attributes to be registered
  WNDCLASS windowClass;
```

The WNDCLASS is a structure containing the window class attributes that are registered by the RegisterClass function. The structure is defined as follows:

```
typedef struct _WNDCLASS {
  UINT            style;
  WNDPROC         lpfnWndProc;
  int             cbClsExtra;
  int             cbWndExtra;
  HANDLE          hInstance;
  HICON           hIcon;
  HCURSOR h       Cursor;
  HBRUSH          hbrBackground;
  LPCTSTR         lpszMenuName;
  LPCTSTR         lpszClassName;
} WNDCLASS;
```

All of the windows commands used in this routine are pretty much self-explanatory, as long as we have an understanding of the members discussed above. Because of this, I am listing just the code segment for your review, other than discussing a few minor issues.

```
// Status of the RegisteredClass call
BOOL  regClass;
//
```

```
// Fill the slots of and register the window class
//
windowClass.style = CS_HREDRAW | CS_VREDRAW;
windowClass.lpfnWndProc = WindowProc;
windowClass.cbClsExtra = 0;
windowClass.cbWndExtra = sizeof(DWORD);
windowClass.hInstance = this_inst;
windowClass.hIcon = LoadIcon(this_inst, "TutorialIcon");
windowClass.hCursor = LoadCursor(NULL, IDC_ARROW);
windowClass.hbrBackground = (HBRUSH)GetStockObject(WHITE_BRUSH);
windowClass.lpszMenuName = "TutorialMenu";
windowClass.lpszClassName = TutorialClass;
regClass = RegisterClass(&windowClass);

// Return the initialized object
return regClass;
}
```

The GetStockObject function is called to retrieve a handle to one of the predefined stock pens, brushes, fonts, or palettes. In our case we are grabbing the background brush.

We should only use the DKGRAY_BRUSH, GRAY_BRUSH, and LTGRAY_BRUSH stock objects in windows with the CS_HREDRAW and CS_VREDRAW styles. Other uses can cause a misalignment of brush patterns when the window is moved or sized. We should also remember that stock brush origins cannot be adjusted, and that HOLLOW_BRUSH and NULL_BRUSH stock objects are the same. It is not necessary to delete stock objects using a call to DeleteObject, but nothing will go wrong if you do.

The function prototype is:

```
HGDIOBJ GetStockObject(
 int fnObject // type of stock object
 );
```

That is all that is necessary to define and register our window class.

2.11 Creating our window

Now that we have defined our window, we need to specify the code to actually create it. This is performed for any instance of our window we create.

```
//
// Perform the set-up required for every instance of the application -
// Creation of the window and initialization of the data.
//
static BOOL AnyInstance(HINSTANCE thisInst, int cmdShow)
{
 HWND tutWindow;
```

The command to actually create our window is the Windows95 command `CreateWindow`. The prototype is:

```
HWND  CreateWindow(
    LPCTSTR lpClassName,   // A pointer to the registered class name
    LPCTSTR lpWindowName,  // A pointer to the window name
    DWORD dwStyle,         // A window style
    int x,                 // The window's horizontal position
    int y,                 // The window's vertical position
    int nWidth,            // The window's width
    int nHeight,           // The window's height
    HWND hWndParent,       // The parent or owner window's handle
      hMenu hMenu,         // The menu or child-window identifier's handle
    HANDLE hInstance,      // The application instance's handle
    LPVOID lpParam         // A pointer to the window-creation data
);
```

As you can see below, we will use mostly default values and just specify the windows size and program handle:

```
//
// Create the main window
//
tutWindow =
  CreateWindow
  (
  TutorialClass,            // The window class
  "Direct3D Tutorial",      // The window caption
  WS_OVERLAPPEDWINDOW,      // The style
  CW_USEDEFAULT,            // The initial x pos
  CW_USEDEFAULT,            // The initial y pos
  450,                      // The initial x size
  450,                      // The initial y size
  NULL,                     // The parent window
  NULL,                     // The menu handle
  thisInst,                 // The program handle
  NULL                      // The create parameters
  );
```

If the window was not created properly, we just want to return FALSE to indicate we have a problem.

```
if (!tutWindow) return FALSE;
```

If the window is created successfully, we want to show and update it. I will discuss it in a moment, but for now just remember that as with any windows program, after we create the window we desire we must properly show and update it. This is standard practice for all windows we create.

```
//
// Show and update the window
```

```
//
ShowWindow(tutWindow, cmdShow);
UpdateWindow(tutWindow);
```

And finally, we will return TRUE because everything went as we planned it!

```
return TRUE;
}
```

2.12 Message handling

The last routine we will need for our Windows-based Direct3D applications is the WindowProc routine. This is defined by Microsoft as the routine to process messages for our
main application window. We will use it to handle joystick, keyboard, device, and other
window events. This routine starts by storing the cursor for when we change it based on
user actions, and defines the window information structure we described at the beginning of this chapter

```
//
// Process the messages for the main application window
//
LONG FAR PASCAL WindowProc(HWND window, UINT message, WPARAM wparam,
        LPARAM lparam)
{
  static HCURSOR oldCursor = NULL; // Store the old cursor
```

The first thing we do is start our message-handling case statement:

```
// Handle the various message that we received
switch (message)
{
```

Next, we handle the window destroy message. All we will ever really need to do
here is to call the default PostQuitMessage function. This function is used to tell Windows that a thread has made a request to terminate.

```
// We are quitting and destroying the window
 case WM_DESTROY:
  PostQuitMessage( 0 );
  break;
```

The only other message we want to handle for now is the window paint message.
Each time the window needs to be repainted, the code we define here is called:

```
// Handle the window paint message and update the window
 case WM_PAINT:
   RECT r;
   PAINTSTRUCT ps;
```

To update our screen properly, we must first acquire the coordinates of the update region and then repaint it:

```
// Retrieve the coordinates of the smallest rectangle that completely
// encloses the update region of the specified window
if (GetUpdateRect(window, &r, FALSE))
{
```

The BeginPaint function prepares our window for painting and it also fills our variable ps with the painting information for our window. After we call this function, we can render to our screen. The process to perform 3D rendering will be covered in the next chapter, so for now I am just presenting a NULL set between the begin and end paint calls.

```
// The BeginPaint function prepares the window for painting and fills
// a PAINTSTRUCT structure (ps) with information about the painting.
BeginPaint(window, &ps);
```

The EndPaint call tells the system that we have completed painting to our window for now. We need to make sure we specify this whenever we are done updating the screen.

```
// The EndPaint function denotes the end of painting in the specified
// window (window). It is required to call the function for each call
// to the BeginPaint function, after all painting is complete.
EndPaint(window, &ps);
}
```

The only thing left to do is to call the default handler for any message we did not explicitly handle in this routine. This allows us to add functionality to our program later while not causing any problems with missing events in the interim. Some of the events for which we will be adding handling later are keyboard events and mouse events.

```
// This function calls the default window procedure to provide default
// processing for any window messages that an application does not
// process. This function is used to make sure that every message is
// processed.
default:
    return DefWindowProc(window, message, wparam, lparam);
}
return 0L;
}
```

Well, that is it for our windowed application set-up code. We will soon be getting into the discussion of Direct3D in earnest, but first, let's just compile our program and see what we get for all of this work!

To compile the program (if you have not already done so), just choose the chap1 subproject in the makefile project on your CD which came with this book. Select the Build menu and then select the Build chap1.exe option. The project will be built and a new executable will be created named tutorial1.exe.

2.13 The application window

Now that we have developed all of that code, what do we have? The answer is "visually, not much!" Run the executable you just created. The screen the program displays is the one I showed you earlier in this chapter.

As you can see, all we have displayed is an empty window with a Windows frame. After all of our work, you might have been hoping for a lot more. What we need to remember is that we have now generated most of the code structure necessary to create the Windows framework required for our 3D applications. That alone makes this code invaluable in terms of time savings from code reuse. By keeping this code generic, we will be able to use it over and over.

2.14 What did we learn?

In this chapter you learned what is involved in defining a Direct3D applications main routine (WinMain) and which global variables can be useful for our applications. As you saw, there is a fair amount of set-up code necessary just to get our base window visible and ready to be used.

We also created an error-handling routine we can use for all of our Direct3D and DirectDraw applications. As new features are developed by Microsoft, we can easily add them to this routine.

In addition, we also learned how to create a number of auxiliary functions which are necessary to create any of our Windows-based Direct3D applications and take best advantage of our hardware.

2.15 What's next?

Finally, we can get into what we came here for! The next three chapters will show you how to set up your 3D models, lights, and object positions and render your scene into the viewport, so you will be able to view the results of your hard work.

chapter 3

The Direct3D code and message processing loop

3.1 Introduction

This chapter details the code we must add to the application we began in the last chapter to make it a Direct3D application. Sample code demonstrating the code which must be added to our Windows routines to perform the Direct3D set-up is discussed

By the end of this chapter, we will have the window for our first application redefined as a Direct3D window. It will look like the window shown in figure 3.1.

If you looked at this window and said "But, it looks like the window we just created!" you are correct—it does. I have intentionally done this to show you how much code is necessary just to set up our window for rendering in 3D.

Please be patient, and you will see how the code discussed in this chapter will take us a long way toward our goal of a working Direct3D application. We will begin adding lights, objects, and special effects to our scene in the next chapter. I realize you have already taken a lot in, and this chapter will also cover quite a bit of difficult material. Just remember that once you have grasped this information, the rest of the chapters will be quite a bit simpler, in many respects, to understand (and the output of our code a lot prettier). So, let's cover the Direct3D required set-up process and we can celebrate at the end of the chapter.

3.2 Our new and modified data structures

The first thing we must do to create our Direct3D application is to add the include file which defines the GUIDs used by the Direct3DRM Windows interface. This include file is necessary for any Retained-Mode application.

```
#include "d3drmwin.h"
```

We also need to add the function prototypes for our new Direct3D-related functions. For now, we are only adding five routines. These five functions are designed to handle the main rendering and display of our 3D virtual world. In this chapter we are only covering the functionality necessary to create a basic Direct3D environment, so the functions will be somewhat sparse. We will flesh these out in later chapters, and I will discuss the meaning and usage of most of these functions later in this chapter also.

```
static BOOL Render(TutorInfo*);
extern BOOL CreateScene(TutorInfo*);
static BOOL RebuildDevice(HWND, int, int, TutorInfo*);
// Routine to create the DirectDraw Clipper
static BOOL CreateDevice(HWND, TutorInfo*);
static BOOL ResizeViewport(HWND, int, int, TutorInfo*);
```

Figure 3.1 The Tutorial application's main window

The first Direct3D objects we must define are the main Retained-Mode object and our Clipper object. I will be discussing the purpose and functionality of these objects later in this chapter:

```
// The Direct3D Retained-Mode main object
LPDIRECT3DRM lpD3DRM = 0;
// The DirectDraw Clipper
LPDIRECTDRAWCLIPPER lpDDClipper = 0;
```

3.2.1 Our TutorInfo structure

You will remember the TutorInfo structure from the last chapter. I originally defined it with only a single data element—the minimized variable. This variable was the only nongraphic element of our structure, and it was used to specify when our window was minimized. We now need to add the Direct3D-related variables which will hold the information on our scene, camera, output device, viewport, and color model. This variable is defined as a global structure, so that we can easily use it throughout the program since it is referenced so many times. The structure now looks like:

```
// Define a structure to hold the data associated
// with this tutorial's window.
typedef struct _TutorInfo
{
  // The objects to define the scene's and camera's
  // frame of reference.
  LPDIRECT3DRMFRAME scene, camera;
  // The output device for this tutorial
  LPDIRECT3DRMDEVICE device;
  // The viewport for this tutorial
  LPDIRECT3DRMVIEWPORT view;
  // The color model for this tutorial
  D3DRMCOLORMODEL model;
  // Tells if the window is minimized or not
  BOOL minimized;
} TutorInfo;
```

We will also need to define some variables for our mouse input. I will be discussing the usage of these variables later, but for now we just need to realize that these variables hold information on whether we are moving the mouse while depressing a button, and the mouse's previous location.

```
static int
  leftDrag = FALSE,    // Set the variable indicating that we are
                       // holding the left mouse button and dragging
                       // the mouse
  rightDrag = FALSE,   // Set the variable indicating that we are holding
                       // the right mouse button and dragging the mouse
  previousX,           // Holds the last read X position of our mouse pointer
  previousY;           // Holds the last read Y position of our mouse pointer
```

The next sections will detail the Retained-Mode set-up code we must produce for each of our Retained-Mode applications. I will be presenting both new code segments to place within our existing routines, as well as completely new routines.

3.3 Our new D3DRM set-up code

The first, and very simple, addition to our code is the allocation of space for the structure which will be holding the variables defining our world. The code is a simple `malloc`, as follows:

```
Info = (TutorInfo*) malloc(sizeof (TutorInfo));
```

3.4 Creating our main Direct3DRM object

The following code segment is added to the `WinMain` routine to create our main Direct3D Retained-Mode object. If we cannot create this, we have a serious problem and just drop out of our program. The object is necessary for us to create any of the other objects we will be generating for our Direct3D application. Our Direct3D Retained-Mode object is instantiated by a call to the `Direct3DRMCreate` function.

After the object is instantiated, our application must call the object's interface method to create any visual 3D objects we will use in our 3D virtual world. The calls to create our 3D objects will be covered in the next chapter. For now we will just write the code to create the Direct3D Retained-Mode object:

```
// Create an instance of the D3D Retained-Mode object.
replaceVal = Direct3DRMCreate(&lpD3DRM);
 // If we failed to create it, return an error.
 if (replaceVal != D3DRM_OK) {
  Msg("Failed to create Direct3DRM.\n%s", MyErrorToString(replaceVal));
   return 1;
}
```

3.5 Creating our DirectDraw Clipper object

Every application we write will use DirectDraw to display our graphics on the screen. Remember that we can choose to either use DirectDraw's full-screen exclusive mode or its windowed mode. Although the full screen mode has advantages in speed, it is much easier to debug code written in windowed mode and windowed mode allows us to create multiple views in our virtual world. I find it to be worth the speed hit to use windowed mode for many applications. Remember, good code design and optimization will help limit the effect of this performance loss.

The next DirectX object we need to focus on creating is the DirectDraw Clipper object. This will be used whenever we draw to our screen. Clipper objects can be created that are not directly owned by any specific DirectDraw object. These Clipper objects can be shared by several DirectDraw objects. By using the DirectDraw API function `DirectDrawCreateClipper`, we can create driver-independent clipper objects. We can call this function before we create any DirectDraw objects.

We need to remember that since these types of clipper objects are not owned by any DirectDraw objects, they will not be released automatically when we release our objects. Because of this we should remember to explicitly release these objects, although they will be released when our application is exited. Even though we can rely on DirectDraw to do this for us, it is a bit sloppy, so I would recommend making explicit release calls.

The code segment below shows how to create a DirectDraw Clipper object and prepare it so it is ready to manage our *clip lists*. Since we can attach our Clipper object to any surface, we can attach our window handle to it. DirectDraw manages clip lists using the DirectDraw Clipper object. When we do this, DirectDraw will update our Direct-Draw Clipper clip list with the clip list from the window when it changes. Our clip list will only be used for overlays by the HAL if the target overlay hardware supports clipping and destination color keying is not active. *Destination color keying* is probably a new concept to many of you. Destination color keying is used to specify a color, or color range, which will either be replaced, during blitting, or covered up, when using overlays, on our destination. The destination color key is used to indicate what may be written onto, or covered up, on our destination surface. When a destination surface has an associated color key, only the pixels matching the specified color key will be changed (during blitting), or covered up (when using overlays).

An overlay is occluded whenever another visual object is placed on top of it. Since much hardware today does not support occluded overlays unless they are destination color keyed, DirectDraw will turn off the overlay and ignore our clip lists when the overlay is occluded if it detects this type of hardware. The end result is that if we do not have hardware supporting destination color keying, the overlay will not be displayed when part of it becomes covered. An example of where this could be a concern would be if we used an overlay to represent a virtual cockpit which covered part of our 3D world view. If occluded overlays were not supported, and we popped up a window on top of our cockpit display, we would lose our overlay and only see the 3D world view in our window, with no cockpit displayed—not a very useful vehicle simulation!

DirectDraw calls the HAL to blit only the rectangles meeting the clip list requirements, even though the clip list is visible from the DirectDraw HAL. What this means is that if in our application the lower left rectangle of our surface were clipped and we requested DirectDraw to blit this surface onto the primary surface, it would direct the HAL to perform two blits. One blit would fill the lower right corner of the surface and the second one would fill the upper half of the surface.

One way to help efficiency is to share Clippers among multiple surfaces. Whenever we attach a Clipper to a surface using the `IDirectDrawSurface::SetClipper` method, that Clipper's reference count is incremented. No matter how many times in a row we call `IDirectDrawSurface::SetClipper` on the same surface, that Clipper's reference count will be incremented only once. Whenever the reference count of that surface reaches zero, the attached Clipper's reference count is decremented. The attached Clipper's reference count is also decremented whenever we detach a Clipper from a surface by calling the `IDirectDrawSurface::SetClipper` method with a NULL Clipper interface.

The calling sequence to create our Clipper object is actually quite simple:

```
if (!window) return FALSE;

//
// Create a driver independent clipper object for this window
//
if (FAILED(DirectDrawCreateClipper(0, &lpDDClipper, NULL))) {
  return FALSE;
}
```

When we have created the Clipper object, we next must set its hWnd. The hWnd will be used to obtain the object's clipping information.

```
if (FAILED(lpDDClipper->SetHWnd(0, window))) {
  RELEASE(lpDDClipper);
  return FALSE;
}
```

3.6 Defining our color model

The next thing we will always need to do is set our color model. The code to set the color model is:

```
// Set the D3DRMCOLORMODEL to RGB
info->model = D3DCOLOR_RGB;
```

The color model is used to specify how the color and specular interpolants are treated. A *spectral interpolant* is defined as the average of two vertex color values used to set a third vertex color component. A *vertex color* is the color associated with any of the vertices (corners) of our objects faces. When we use the RGB color model,

D3DCOLOR_RGB, the red, green, and blue color components will be used in interpolation. A color component is defined as the red, green, or blue portion of an RGB color. These values can range from 0 to 255.

If you wish to use the monochromatic lighting model (also known as the *ramp* lighting model), the system will use just the gray component of each light to calculate a single shade value. The monochromatic model uses levels of gray shading for lighting effects rather than using colored lights.

Direct3D interpolates each of the triangular faces making up an object face when it is rendered. The triangle interpolants are color, fog, specular, and alpha. Each of these interpolants is modified by the shade mode we choose. The effects are:

- *Flat.* Rather than interpolate, the system applies the color of only the first vertex across the entire face.

- *Gouraud.* The system linearly interpolates between the vertices.

- *Phong.* The system recomputes the vertex parameters for each pixel in the face.

As an example, in the Gouraud shading mode, if the blue component was .6 for the first vertex and .8 for the second, the blue vertex for the third would be .7 ((.6 + .8) / 2). When we use the monochromatic model, D3DCOLOR_MONO, only the blue component of the vertex color is used (to store the gray intensity), so only the one value is computed (interpolated).

Since device drivers can implement transparencies in two manners, by using stippling and texture blending, the alpha component of a color is treated as a separate interpolant. You can find which forms of interpolation your device driver supports by using the dwShadeCaps member of the D3DPRIMCAPS structure. The slots of this structure are used to describe the capabilities of each primitive type. It is described in the d3dcaps.h include file as:

```
typedef struct _D3DPrimCaps {
   DWORD dwSize;
   DWORD dwMiscCaps;              /* Capability flags */
   DWORD dwRasterCaps;
   DWORD dwZCmpCaps;
   DWORD dwSrcBlendCaps;
   DWORD dwDestBlendCaps;
   DWORD dwAlphaCmpCaps;
   DWORD dwShadeCaps;
   DWORD dwTextureCaps;
   DWORD dwTextureFilterCaps;
   DWORD dwTextureBlendCaps;
   DWORD dwTextureAddressCaps;
   DWORD dwStippleWidth;          /* maximum width and height of */
   DWORD dwStippleHeight;         /* supported stipple (up to 32x32) */
} D3DPRIMCAPS, *LPD3DPRIMCAPS;
```

3.6.1 Enumerating our drivers and showing our window

We also will need to enumerate the current drivers by calling `CreateDevice`. I will discuss this process in the next section, but understand for now just that this routine is used to set up our device by loading a hardware driver, if it exists, or otherwise by loading a software driver.

```
// See if we can create the Device
  if (!CreateDevice(tutWindow, info)) {
    return FALSE;
  }
```

The last steps we need to add are the calls to display and update our window. The calls we make to perform this are to `ShowWindow` and `UpdateWindow`. These functions are Microsoft Windows command calls and not Direct3D commands, but they are required for us to see our 3D world so I have waited until now to discuss them. The code performing the calling structure for the two commands will be added as follows:

```
//
// Show and update the window
//
Showwindow(window, cmdshow);
Updatewindow(window);

return TRUE;
}
```

The `ShowWindow` function is called to set our window's show state. The first argument specifies our window to be shown, and the second argument specifies how we wish it to be displayed.

```
BOOL ShowWindow(
  HWND hWnd,        // handle of window
  int nCmdShow      // show state of window
  );
```

The first time `ShowWindow` is called, the value of the `nCmdShow` argument should be the value of the `WinMain` function's `nCmdShow` parameter. After the initial call, this parameter may be set to any of the following values:

Value	Meaning
SW_HIDE	Hide this window and activate another window.
SW_MAXIMIZE	Maximize the window.
SW_MINIMIZE	Minimize the window and activate the next top-level window in the Z-order.

The `UpdateWindow` function is called when we wish to update the client area of our window. The update is performed by sending a `WM_PAINT` message to the window if the window's update region is not empty. The `WM_PAINT` message is passed directly to the window procedure of our window and the application queue is bypassed. If we ever call this function when the update region is empty, no message will be sent. The function prototype is:

```
BOOL UpdateWindow(
   HWND hWnd            // The window's handle
);
```

The `hWnd` parameter to the UpdateWindow function indicates the window which we want updated. This function returns TRUE if it succeeds; otherwise, it returns FALSE.

3.7 Creating the device and viewport

The main function for creating our device and Viewport is described below. It also sets up the scene and clipping plane. We will go into some of the routines it calls to perform this in detail both here and in the next chapter. For the nongeneric functions, we will just show the calling structure here and explain the arguments and structures passed, while going into their functionality in the following chapter. The general, all-purpose functions like the device and viewport creation segments will be discussed in detail here.

In the last section I showed where and when we made the call to our CreateDevice function, but not what it did. I will now show you what this code looks like in detail and explain what each step does. First, the function is defined as follows:

```
//
// Create the device and viewport for our application
//
static BOOL CreateDevice(HWND window, TutorInfo* information)
{
  RECT rectangle; // Define a rect structure variable
  int bpp;
  HDC hdc;
```

Now, as you learned earlier, we always need to create a `Direct3DRM` device for our application since it is the base object upon which we build the rest of our application's environment. Since we discussed the creation process for our Clipper object in detail earlier, we only need to realize that here we will be creating our device using this Direct-Draw Clipper.

Using the `IDirect3DRM::CreateDeviceFromClipper` method and specifying NULL for the `lpGUID` parameter is the way Microsoft recommends we create a

Retained-Mode device, because it always works—even when new hardware is installed. You then do not have to worry if both a hardware and a software device meet the default requirements, since the system will always acquire the hardware device. You should really only enumerate your devices rather than passing NULL for the lpGUID parameter if you have unique requirements. I have done this here to help you understand how to do this when it is necessary. The command sequence is:

```
// Get the rectangle for the client space of our window
GetClientRect(window, &rectangle);
// Try to create a Direct3DRM windows device by using a specified
// DirectDrawClipper object
if (FAILED(lpD3DRM->CreateDeviceFromClipper(lpDDClipper,
   FindDevice(information->model),
      rectangle.right, rectangle.bottom, &information->device)))
         goto generic_error;
```

The other parameters we will need to collect from our window are the Device Context and the bits per pixel. As I will show you in a moment, the bits per pixel value is used to set the best possible color and shading capabilities to provide the best rendering we can.

```
hdc = GetDC(window); // Get the windows device context
// Get the number of adjacent color bits for each pixel
bpp = GetDeviceCaps(hdc, BITSPIXEL);
ReleaseDC(window, hdc); // Release the device context
```

3.7.1 Setting our maximum rendering quality

Next we will set the maximum rendering quality which our device will be allowed to use when rendering on the surface of this device. This value indicates the shading mode we wish to use. All of our 3D objects can have their own quality values, but this call sets the *maximum* value we can use for any of these objects on this device.

Direct3D gives us three useful rendering qualities (shading modes) for our development purposes. When we use *flat shading*, Direct3D takes the color at one vertex and uses it across all of the other faces of the surface.

The code to set the default, highest level, rendering quality to flat shading mode is:

```
// Set the device render quality to unlit, flat
// We can change this per object
if (FAILED(dev->SetQuality(D3DRMRENDER_UNLITFLAT)))
   goto generic_error;
```

If you use this call, you must realize that you are locked into the flat mode since you specified that it was the highest level mode you wished to use (since the device will override the lower level object's settings, e.g., your various faces).

Figure 3.2 Using the flat shading model

The results of rendering a model using the flat mode is shown in figure 3.2.

Notice that this figure seems blocky. The reason for this is that the flat shading mode applies the same shade color to the entire surface. Because of this, the flat mode should be used when speed issues make it necessary to find time-saving steps, or when the rendering task you are working on does not require a highly realistic, more stylized, surface.

If you desire a more realistic surface, you should use a smooth shading approach. Gouraud shading allows you to render a surface much more realistically because the surface is smoothed by averaging the colors of the vertices across the surface.

The result of using Gouraud shading is shown in figure 3.3. Notice how the shirt and pants now look smooth and realistic rather than blocky. By the way, this model was created by the people at Zygote. They have created the best 3D models I have seen, their prices are good, and their people are incredibly helpful and nice. I have included one of their models, a model of an abominable snowman, on the CD accompanying this book.

Phong shading is not implemented in DirectX yet. It is intended to be added in a future release.

3.7.2 Color depth and other rendering settings

By checking the number of adjacent color bits per pixel, we can set the color and texture parameters, as well as the dithering, to the most realistic capabilities available to us from

Figure 3.3 Using the Gouraud shading model

our hardware. By using a case statement, we can check the possible values and set the quantity of our colors and shades to the maximum possible value.

A few things to remember about the monochromatic model (which you should use if you need maximal performance) is that it supports multiple light sources but their color content is ignored. Each of your light sources will be set to a gray intensity. The RGB colors at each of your object's vertices are interpreted as brightness levels. These are interpolated in Gouraud shading mode across a face between vertices having different brightnesses.

The number of colors you can use for your objects in a scene is limited to the number of free palette entries your system has. When there are no more available, the system's internal palette manager will use the color that is already in the palette which is closest to the color you requested. This model supports 8-, 16-, 24-, and 32-bit displays just like the RGB model, but it supports only 8-bit textures.

```
// Look at the bits for pixel and set the various
// parameters it affects
switch (bpp)
{
```

If we only have one adjacent color bit per pixel, we set the number of shades in the color ramp we can use for shading to 4 and the number of shades to be used for a

Direct3DRMTexture object to 4 also. Certainly this is not many, and we will not get very realistic color with such limited capabilities, but some is better than none!

```
case 1:   // If there is only 1 bit per pixel,
          // Set the number of shades in the ramp of colors for
          // shading to 4 (must be a power of two)
    if (FAILED(information->device->SetShades(4)))
      goto generic_error;
    // Set the default shades to be used for a
    // Direct3DRMTexture object to 4
    if (FAILED(lpD3DRM->SetDefaultTextureShades(4)))
      goto generic_error;
    break;
```

If we have 16 adjacent color bits per pixel, we set the number of shades in the color ramp we can use for shading to 32 and the number of shades to be used for a Direct3DRMTexture object to 32 also. Because of our better color capabilities, we can also set the number of colors to be used by our texture object to 64 and turn off dithering, since we do not need it anymore and it defaults to TRUE if we forget to set it.

```
case 16:
    // Set the number of shades in the ramp of colors for
    // shading to 32
    if (FAILED(information->device->SetShades(32)))
      goto generic_error;
    // Set the default colors for a Direct3DRMTexture object
    // to 64
    if (FAILED(lpD3DRM->SetDefaultTextureColors(64)))
      goto generic_error;
    // Set the default shades to be used for a
    // Direct3DRMTexture object to 32
    if (FAILED(lpD3DRM->SetDefaultTextureShades(32)))
      goto generic_error;
    // Sets the dither flag for the device to FALSE
    if (FAILED(information->device->SetDither(FALSE)))
      goto generic_error;
    break;
```

If we have 24 or 32 adjacent color bits-per-pixel, we set the same parameters as we did when we had 16, but we provide for greater color capabilities.

```
case 24:
  case 32:
    // Set the number of shades in the ramp of colors for
    // shading to 256
    if (FAILED(information->device->SetShades(256)))
      goto generic_error;
    // Set the default colors for a Direct3DRMTexture object
    // to 64
    if (FAILED(lpD3DRM->SetDefaultTextureColors(64)))
```

```
      goto generic_error;
    // Set the default shades to be used for a
    // Direct3DRMTexture object to 256
    if (FAILED(lpD3DRM->SetDefaultTextureShades(256)))
      goto generic_error;
    // Sets the dither flag for the device to FALSE
    if (FAILED(information->device->SetDither(FALSE)))
      goto generic_error;
    break;

  default:
    // Just set the dither flag for the device to FALSE
    if (FAILED(information->device->SetDither(FALSE)))
      goto generic_error;
  }
```

3.8 Creating our scene and viewport

The following calls to CreateScene, CreateViewport, and SetBack will be used in all of our applications. These are some of the main Direct3D functions we will concentrate on in this book and it will be critical that you understand their functionality. Remember that the information structure passed to our CreateScene routine contains the key object information, such as the model and scene.

```
    // Call our routine to create the scene
    if (!CreateScene(information))
        goto ret_with_error; // Return an error if we fail
```

A Direct3D *Scene* object is defined as a frame with no parent frame (a frame which is at the top of the frame hierarchy). The scene frame defines the frame of reference for all of our world's objects. We create our scene by calling the IDirect3DRM::CreateFrame method and passing the value NULL as the first parameter. Any frame without a parent is called a scene.

This is the first time I have mentioned a *frame* object, so let's define it. A Direct3D frame object is used to define any object's *frame of reference*. A frame is used to place all of our visual objects into our scene by specifying their positions relative to a reference (parent) frame.

The routine we will always use to create the scene object is our CreateScene function. This function is called to generate our scene by creating and loading the components of our scene—for example, the lights and objects. The shell framework we will generate for now will only need to create our scene and camera frames and return from the function. When you create your frames, you must remember that a child frame will always inherit its parent's motion attributes. This means that if the parent frame is rotating, the child frame will also. To create our scene and a child frame is as simple as the following:

```
//
// Create a simple scene.
//
static BOOL CreateScene(TutorInfo* information)
{
  // Create a new frame with no parent
  if (FAILED(lpD3DRM->CreateFrame(NULL, &information->scene)))
    {
      // If the create fails, return an error
      goto generic_error;
    }

  // Now, create a child frame for the main frame
  // we just created
  if (FAILED(lpD3DRM->CreateFrame(information->scene, &information->camera)))
    goto generic_error;

  return TRUE;
// If we get here, we had an error so just clean up and return FALSE
generic_error:
  Msg("A failure occurred while creating the scene.\n");
  return FALSE;
}
```

3.8.1 Viewport

One of the most important objects to create is the viewport. This is not because it is difficult to create, or for that matter truly interesting, but without it, we would not be able to see our 3D world!

A viewport is used to define the manner in which our 3D world (the *scene*) is rendered into a 2D window. This viewport is used to specify a rectangular area on a device into which objects will be rendered.

The Direct3D `CreateViewport` method is called to create a viewport on a device with the device coordinates (dwXPos, dwYPos) to (dwXPos+dwWidth, dwYPos + dwHeight). This action defines a 2D rectangular area on the device we just created on which to render 3D objects. In the call below, we are setting the window to start at (0,0) and end at the full width and height of our device. This will create a window filling the whole screen. As long as the viewport is created successfully, it will be returned in the information structure's `IDirect3DRMViewport` interface *view* slot. This viewport will then be used by our application to display the objects in the scene containing the camera, using the view direction and up vector of the camera.

3.8.2 Camera

A Direct3D viewport uses a `Direct3DRMFrame` object as a *camera*. The camera frame is used to define the scene to be rendered, as well as the viewing position and direction. The viewport renders only what is visible along the camera frame's positive *z*-axis. The up direction is defined along the positive *y*-axis.

You can think of the camera as your eye. When you look at something, you can only see so far up, down, left, and right without moving your eyes or head. This limitation of what you can view, of the whole world as well as your field of view (e.g., the angular range in both the horizontal and vertical planes), is specified in Direct3D, as well as other graphic systems using a viewport.

The `IDirect3DRMViewport::SetCamera` method is used to specify the camera for a viewport. The position, direction, and orientation of a viewport is set by this method for a camera's frame. The camera's settings are retrieved through a call to the `IDirect3DRMViewport::GetCamera` method.

```
// Create a viewport on the device with the position and
// direction of view specified in the camera structure
if (FAILED(lpD3DRM->CreateViewport(
    information->device,            // The device on which the viewport
                                    // will be created
    information->camera,            // The frame describing the view's
                                    // position and direction
    0, 0,                           // X, Y position of the viewport
    information->device->GetWidth(),  // Width of the viewport
    information->device->GetHeight(), // Height of the viewport
    &information->view)))           // Address which will be filled with a
                                    // pointer to a Direct3DRMViewport
        interface
    goto generic_error;
```

3.8.3 The viewing frustum

Once the viewport is created, we need to define the rest of our viewing *frustum* (see figure 3.4). The viewing volume for a perspective projection is a frustum of a pyramid—actually a truncated pyramid with the top cut off by a plane parallel to its base. The frustum is used to define the field of view I mentioned above, as well as the window into the world. Basically, you can think of the viewport as the screen of your monitor. If you drew lines from your eye to the four corners of the screen, and could continue into the virtual world residing in your monitor, these lines would specify what area of the virtual world you see (figure 3.4). Yes, there are things to the right, left, up, and down beyond the limits of that window, just as when you look outside through a window at home, but the window's edges keep you from seeing them.

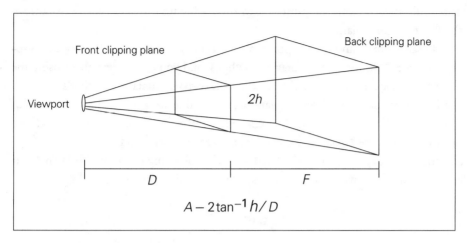

Figure 3.4 The viewing frustum

An interesting characteristic of perspective projection is *foreshortening*. Foreshortening is the term used to define the effect that the farther an object is from our camera, the smaller it appears in the final rendered image. The reason that objects which are closer to our viewpoint appear larger is that they take up a larger proportion of the viewing volume than objects that are located farther away.

Any of our objects which fall within the viewing volume defined by the frustum are projected toward the apex (top) of the pyramid. The camera (viewpoint) is at this apex. Objects which are closer to this viewpoint will appear larger than ones farther away because they occupy a proportionally greater amount of the viewing volume than those that are farther away (in the larger portion of the frustum). The reason this approach was chosen for graphic and animation systems is its similarity to the manner in which a real eye or camera works.

As long as our viewport is created properly, we can continue on to set the back clipping plane. The back clipping plane specifies the distance at which we no longer wish to render since it is too far from the eye-point to be useful. This is critical to ease the rendering load, since it eliminates the rendering of objects we consider to be at too great of a distance from the viewplane. The viewport's back clipping plane will be set at 5000.0 in the code segment below. You can set this parameter to any value you wish. I selected 5000.0 based upon the scale of the objects we will be building. You should experiment with this value to see how it effects your rendering speed with any new application you develop.

In figure 3.4, you can see that the camera (our viewpoint) is at the top of the pyramid. The z-axis runs from the pyramid's tip to the center of its base. The front clipping plane is at a distance D from the camera, and the back clipping plane is at a distance F from the front clipping plane.

You can set the front and back clipping planes using the `IDirect3DRMViewport::Set-Front` and `IDirect3DRMViewport::SetBack` methods, and you can retrieve them using the `IDirect3DRMViewport::GetFront` and `IDirect3DRMViewport::GetBack` methods.

The height of the front clipping plane has the value *2h* and specifies our field of view. You can set these values using the `IDirect3DRMViewport::SetField` method and reference them using the `IDirect3DRMViewport::GetField` method.

The angle of view, A, can be calculated with the following equation. You can use it to calculate a value for h when you wish to specify a certain camera angle

$$A - 2\tan^{-1} h / D$$

Finally, the viewing frustum is a pyramid only when you desire *perspective* viewing. If you wish to use *orthographic* viewing instead, the frustum is a cuboid. The projection types are defined by the `D3DRMPROJECTIONTYPE` enumerated type. You can use them with the `IDirect3DRMViewport::GetProjection` and `IDirect3DRMViewport::SetProjection` methods. For more information on the projection types see the `IDirect3DRMViewport` section in the Reference section of this book.

The code to set the back clipping plane is:

```
// Sets the position of the back clipping plane for the viewport.
  if (FAILED(information->view->SetBack(D3DVAL(5000.0))))
    goto generic_error;
  // Return TRUE indicating everything went well
  return TRUE;
```

At the end of our case statement, we just need to define the errors which will return FALSE as a function value if any of our set-up functions fail. As always, let's hope we never get there!

```
  // Let the user know an error occurred
generic_error:
  Msg("An error occurred while creating the device.\n");

ret_with_error:
  return FALSE;
}
```

3.8.4 Rebuilding the device

We will need to define a function to handle the regeneration of the device whenever the color model is changed or the window is resized. All of the parameters for the window must be reacquired. The reason for this is that whenever our window size changes, we also need to change the viewport size to match it. If we forget this, our world will disappear when we resize our window. This recalculation is one of the many reasons game developers in the past have avoided programming in Windows, and instead have stuck to the single-tasking DOS environment.

```
//
// Regenerate the device if the color model changes or the window size
// changes.
//
static BOOL RebuildDevice(HWND tutWindow, TutorInfo* information, int
        width, int height)
{
  HRESULT returnVal;
```

3.8.5 Dithering

The device's GetDither method must be called to retrieve the dither flag for our device. We then maintain it in the old_Dither variable for resetting our device when we recreate our window. Dithering is a technique used to increase the number of available perceived colors at the expense of spatial resolution. This is done by combining colors to create the effect of other colors.

To help explain how dithering works, imagine your system has only one bit for each of the R, G, and B colors so that only eight colors can be displayed—black, white, red, blue, green, yellow, cyan, and magenta. If you wanted to display a purple area on the screen, the hardware could fill in the desired area with a checkerboard of alternating red and blue pixels. If you are far enough from your screen, your eye will perceive it to be purple rather than a bunch of neighboring blue and red pixels. You can also make the color more reddish by adding more red and fewer blue pixels in the dithering process.

Figure 3.5 shows how you can dither black and white pixels to make various shades of gray. The two sets show dither patterns for 50 and 75 percent. If you look at these figures from a distance, the independent black and white pixels will blend together and form apparent shades of gray.

The code required to acquire the dither status is:

```
// Get the current dither flag for the device
int oldDither = information->device-> GetDither();
```

As with the dither variable, we also hold the device's quality value for resetting.

```
// Get the rendering quality for the device.
D3DRMRENDERQUALITY oldQuality = information->device->GetQuality();
```

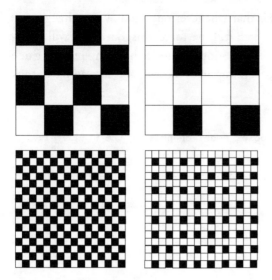

Figure 3.5 Dither patterns

Finally, we get the number of shades and hold them for resetting, also. Remember that we set these earlier based on our hardware and software capabilities. If in the future you add new hardware, these calls will allow an automatic recomputation of the shades.

```
// Get the number of shades available on the device
int oldShades = information->device->GetShades();
```

We can now free up our view and device so we can rebuild them and use the settings we saved above.

```
// Release the view and device
RELEASE(information->view);
RELEASE(information->device);
```

3.8.6 Recreating our device

The calling sequence is the same as when we originally created the device. We create our device, set the dither, set the quality, and set the shades as they were set before:

```
// Try to create a Direct3DRM windows device by using a specified
// DirectDrawClipper object with the size specified
returnVal = lpD3DRM->CreateDeviceFromClipper(lpDDClipper, FindDevice(
                information->model),
                width, height, &information->device);
// If the device did not get created properly, return an error
if (returnVal != D3DRM_OK) {
    Msg("Creating a device from HWND failed while rebuilding device.\n%s",
```

```
            MyErrorToString(returnVal));
        return FALSE;
    }

    // Sets the dither flag for the device to the previous value
    if (FAILED(information->device->SetDither(oldDither)))
        goto generic_error;

    // Sets the rendering quality of a device - The default value is flat
    if (FAILED(information->device->SetQuality(oldQuality)))
        goto generic_error;

    // Set the number of shades in the ramp of colors for
    // shading to the previous value
    if (FAILED(information->device->SetShades(oldShades)))
        goto generic_error;
```

Finally, we recreate our viewport to the full size of the screen, and set the clipping plane at 5000.0 again. The only other thing to do is to check for errors.

```
    // Get the width and height of the device
    width = information->device->GetWidth();
    height = information->device->GetHeight();

    // Create a viewport on the device with the position and
    // direction of view specified in the camera structure
    if (FAILED(lpD3DRM->CreateViewport(information->device, information->camera,
                0, 0, width, height, &information->view)))
            goto generic_error;

    // Sets the position of the back clipping plane for the viewport
    if (FAILED(information->view->SetBack(D3DVAL(5000.0))))
        goto generic_error;
    return TRUE;

    // If we get here, we had an error rebuilding the object
generic_error:
    Msg("A failure occurred while rebuilding the device.\n");
    return FALSE;
}
```

3.9 Obtaining the most capable device

The FindDevice routine is necessary for all of our applications and is the main routine used to locate a device having the highest level of desired functionality. The reason we will always want to call this routine is that it is the only way to guarantee that we are utilizing the maximum capabilities of our 3D hardware. If we do not check the device capabilities, we may end up not using hardware supported features and instead end up using software emulation, which will run substantially slower. Direct3D will attempt to get the most capable device.

The local variables we will use define the main DirectDraw and Direct3D objects, as well as device search structures which will hold the results of our attempts to locate a device for our application that will support our desired color model level.

The device search structures are defined by the D3DFINDDEVICESEARCH and D3DFINDDEVICERESULT types. The device search structure is used to specify the characteristics of a device we wish to find, and the device result holds the device our application finds after our call to the FindDevice method. Some of the capabilities we can request include GUIDs, color models, and texturing levels.

```
//
// Find a device (First try for a hardware device)
// for the received color model.
//
LPGUID
FindDevice(D3DCOLORMODEL colorModel)
{
   LPDIRECTDRAW lpDD; // The DirectDraw object
   LPDIRECT3D lpD3D;    // The Direct3D object

   // Specifies the characteristics of a device to find
   D3DFINDDEVICESEARCH devSearch;  // Identifies the device found
   static D3DFINDDEVICERESULT devResult;
   HRESULT error;
   HDC hdc;
   int bpp;   // retrieves device-specific information about
              // the specified device.
```

The first thing we need to do is grab the number of adjacent color bits per pixel. I discussed the concept of bits per pixel earlier. The reason for acquiring this information is that it has a severe impact on the quality of the output image. You may even decide that if a device has too low a color support capability, you want to just warn the user and exit. Although this would probably be a bad decision for commercial software, for your own software development or internal company usage you might decide that there is a minimum of hardware required before you want to run.

```
hdc = GetDC(NULL); // Get the window's device context

// Get the number of adjacent color bits for each pixel.
bpp = GetDeviceCaps(hdc, BITSPIXEL);
ReleaseDC(NULL, hdc); // Release the device context
```

Now we will try to create our DirectDraw object using the active display driver. The third parameter must always be NULL since it is just a parameter allowing for future DirectDraw extensions.

```
// Create the DirectDraw object
if (DirectDrawCreate(NULL, &lpDD, NULL))
```

```
    // If the create fails, return NULL
    return NULL;
```

3.9.1 *Checking if the system supports Direct3D*

We will also verify that our device supports Direct3D. If it does not, we need to let go of our DirectDraw object and return with the intent of exiting the program, since the user's system is not capable of Direct3D functionality. The first parameter we pass to `QueryInterface` to determine this is the interface identifier (IID) specifying the IDirect3DRM COM interface `IID_IDirect3D`. All of the available identifiers are named as `IID_InterfaceName`. As an additional example, the IID for the IDirect3DRMLight interface is `IID_IDirect3DRMLight`.

```
    // Determines if the object supports the D3D COM interface
    if (lpDD->QueryInterface(IID_IDirect3D, (void**) &lpD3D)) {
        // If not, decrease the reference by 1
        lpDD->Release();
        // and return NULL
        return NULL;
    }
```

3.9.2 *Getting the most capable device*

As long as DirectDraw and Direct3D are available as desired, we need to continue on and verify that the device capabilities we desire are available. The information we need to set up for this include the search structures which specify the desired color model. You can add any other required capabilities (texturing, etc.) you desire.

```
    // Allocate space for the device search structure
    memset(&devSearch, 0, sizeof devSearch);
    devSearch.dwSize = sizeof devSearch; // Set the size slot

    // Set the color model to mono or RGB
    devSearch.dwFlags = D3DFDS_COLORMODEL;
    devSearch.dcmColorModel = (colorModel == D3DCOLOR_MONO) ? D3DCOLOR_MONO :
            D3DCOLOR_RGB;

    // Allocate space for the search result structure
    memset(&devResult, 0, sizeof devResult);
    devResult.dwSize = sizeof devResult;
```

Once we have this information set up, we can call the `FindDevice` method to locate a hardware device which will work.

```
    // The results of the call are returned in the hardware and
    // software description slots of the D3DFINDDEVICERESULT structure
    error = lpD3D->FindDevice(&devSearch, &devResult);
```

If we cannot find an acceptable hardware device, we need to try to find a software device that will work. This will mean slower performance, but at least allows the software to run on the target platform. It will be up to you to decide if you wish to use software emulation, since you must determine at which point performance degradation from software emulation is below acceptable levels.

```
if (error == DD_OK) {
     // If we found a hardware device but it cannot support the current
     // bit depth, we need to drop back to software rendering.
     if (devResult.ddHwDesc.dwFlags
         && !(devResult.ddHwDesc.dwDeviceRenderBitDepth & bppToddbd(bpp))) {

         devSearch.dwFlags |= D3DFDS_HARDWARE;
         devSearch.bHardware = FALSE;
         memset(&devResult, 0, sizeof devResult);
         devResult.dwSize = sizeof devResult;
         // Redo the FindDevice with a software search
         error = lpD3D->FindDevice(&devSearch, &devResult);
     }
}
```

When we have retrieved the information we need, and set up the device, we just need to verify that everything went well and if it did, we return the GUID we have acquired.

```
// Decrease the reference count by one for the D3D object
lpD3D->Release();
// Decrease the reference count by one for the DD object
lpDD->Release();
if (error) // If we had an error, return NULL,
   return NULL;
else
   return &devResult.guid; // Otherwise, return the result
}
```

3.9.3 Finding the bits per pixel

Another function we will use a lot is the bppToddbd function. It is used to determine if the bits-per-pixel value is one of the acceptable values—1, 2, 4, 8, 16, 24, or 32. We call it when we want to make sure the desired rendering mode is available on our system—that the bit depth desired is available on our device. It consists of nothing more than a simple case statement, as follows:

```
static DWORD bppToddbd(int bpp)
{
  switch(bpp) {
  case 1:
    return DDBD_1;
  case 2:
```

```
    return DDBD_2;
  case 4:
    return DDBD_4;
  case 8:
    return DDBD_8;
  case 16:
    return DDBD_16;
  case 24:
    return DDBD_24;
  case 32:
    return DDBD_32;
  }
  return 0;
}
```

The most critical thing to add to our WinMain function is the code to render our scene, and this again is what we will be starting to implement in the next chapter. For now, we will just create the code which calls the rendering function in each iteration of our main processing loop. As long as the screen is not minimized and we have not specified that we are quitting, we can perform our rendering (and view our 3D world). The code sequence to check this is as follows:

```
// Check to see if we are minimized or quitting
// If either is TRUE, process the idle flag
if (!activeWindow->minimized && !Quit)    {
    if (idle) Idle();
    // Try to render the screen
    if (!Render())
    {
        // If rendering cannot be performed, quit
        // because of the error
        Msg("Rendering failed.\n");
        done = TRUE;
        break;
    }
}
```

The final code we need to add to our WinMain routine contains the calls to release all of our main objects.

The objects we need to make sure we delete are our scene, camera, view, device, main Retained-Mode object, and the Clipper object. We should always remember to destroy any objects we have created, to clean up after ourselves. These objects are held in the TutorInfo structure I showed you above. We will use the RELEASE macro, defined by Microsoft, in place of any call to the Release method of our objects. The reason we want to do this is that it forces us to verify that an object is instantiated before we try to delete it. The supplied Release method does not do this for us.

```
// Release all of the window's rendering objects
// RELEASE is defined in MicroSoft's rmdemo.h
// header file as:
```

```
//  #define RELEASE(x) if (x != NULL)
//       {x-> Release(x); x = NULL;}
RELEASE(activeWindow->scene);
RELEASE(activeWindow->camera);
RELEASE(activeWindow->view);
RELEASE(activeWindow->device);
RELEASE(lpD3DRM);
RELEASE(lpDDClipper);
```

3.10 Rendering of our Direct3D virtual world

Next, we will define the routine to render our scene into the viewport. The first call we
make is to our scene's Move method, which is used to apply the rotation and specified
velocity to all of the frames in the hierarchy we will be developing. This hierarchy specifies the objects in our scene and their relationship to one another. In this way, we reset
the scene when we have to redisplay it.

```
//
// Render the scene into the viewport.
//
static BOOL Render(TutorInfo *info) {
  // Applies the rotations and velocities for all frames
  // in the given hierarchy.
  // Change the velocity and rotation
  if (FAILED(info->scene->Move(D3DVAL(1.0))))
    return FALSE;
```

Once we have reset our scene, we want to clear the viewport by setting it to the
background color, and to re-call the viewport's Render and Update methods to redraw
the scene.

```
// Clears the viewport to the current background color.
if (FAILED(info->view->Clear()))
  return FALSE;
```

The Render method renders the frame hierarchy, specified by our scene object, to
the viewport. In the next chapter you will see how we render the scene. The Render
method of the IDirect3DRMViewport is called to render our frame hierarchy to the
viewport. All of the visuals on the scene frame, and any frames below it in the hierarchy,
are rendered.

```
// Renders the frame hierarchy to the given viewport.
// Only the visuals on the given frame (and any frames below
// it in the hierarchy) are rendered.
if (FAILED(info->view->Render(info->scene)))
    return FALSE;
```

The final thing we need to do to see our new scene is to call the Update method of
our device. This method copies the rendered image to our display. This method is also

used to provide a *heartbeat* function to the device driver. A heartbeat function is used to update our Direct3D world—the positions of our moving frames are updated, the scene is rendered to the display, etc.

Every time we call this method, the system calls a callback function, D3DRMUPDATECALLBACK which we define in our application

```
    // Copy the rendered image to the display
    if (FAILED(info->device->Update()))
        return FALSE;
    // Everything went well, so return TRUE.
    return TRUE;
}
```

3.11 The additions to our WindowProc routine

The final code we need to create for our set-up routines are the segments we wish to add to our WindowProc routine. First, we need to add a new variable to define the IDirect3DRMWinDevice interface, which is used to respond to the window messages we receive.

```
    LPDIRECT3DRMWINDEVICE windev;
    // The Direct3DRMWinDevice object is obtained by calling
    // the IDirect3DRMObject::QueryInterface method and specifying
    // IID_IDirect3DRMWinDevice, or by calling a method such as
    // IDirect3DRM::CreateDeviceFromD3D. Its methods are inherited
    // from the IDirect3DRMDevice interface.
```

3.11.1 Handling mouse events

The remainder of the code we will be adding to this function will be the additional case statements. First, we want to handle any mouse button events. If the user releases the left mouse button, we call a function to release the selected object and reset our cursor to the main cursor. We will discuss the object selection functions in chapter 5.

```
    // When the user releases the Left Mouse Button,
    // release the captured object and reset the cursor
    case WM_LBUTTONUP:
        ReleaseCapture();
        leftDrag = FALSE;
        if (oldCursor) SetCursor(oldCursor);
        break;
```

When the user releases the right mouse button, we turn off the drag flag, release the captured object, and reset our cursor. As with the left button, we will discuss this in chapter 5. For now, just remember that we should place any code here we wish to execute when a mouse button is clicked.

```
// When the user releases the Right Mouse Button,
// release the captured object and reset the cursor
case WM_RBUTTONUP:
    rightDrag = FALSE;
    ReleaseCapture();
    if (oldCursor) SetCursor(oldCursor);
    break;
```

3.11.2 Handling window activation

Whenever our window is activated, we need to determine if our Direct3D object supports the IID_IDirect3DRMWinDevice COM interface. If it does, the pointer to this interface will be placed into the windev variable. The reference count for the object is increased when successful, and we can then use the requested interface. If this interface is not supported, we will not even be able to create our window, so we will just drop out of our program since nothing can run.

```
case WM_ACTIVATE:
{
    if (SUCCEEDED(information->device->QueryInterface
            (IID_IDirect3DRMWinDevice, (void **) &windev)))
    {
```

As long as we are successful in our call, we will call the HandleActivate method for our interface. This method responds to our window's WM_ACTIVATE message. It is called to make sure that our active rendering window's colors are correct.

```
        // HandleActivate responds to a Windows WM_ACTIVATE message.
        // This ensures that the colors are correct in the active
        // rendering window.
        if (FAILED(windev->HandleActivate(wparam)))
                Msg("Failed to handle WM_ACTIVATE.\n");
        windev->Release();
  else }
        {
        Msg("Failed to create Windows device to handle WM_ACTIVATE.\n");
        }
}
break;
```

The final addition we will make to our input handler for now is exactly the same as the segment we just defined, except that we want to respond to our window's WM_PAINT message. The HandlePaint method must be called before we repaint any areas in our window, or it may repaint areas outside of the viewports which have been created on our device.

```
    Case WM_PAINT:
    {
```

CHAPTER 3 THE DIRECT3D CODE...

```
LPDIRECT3DRMWINDEVICE windev;

// The Direct3DRMWinDevice object is obtained by calling
// the IDirect3DRMObject::QueryInterface method and specifying
// IID_IDirect3DRMWinDevice, or by calling a method such as
// IDirect3DRM::CreateDeviceFromD3D. Its methods are inherited
// from the IDirect3DRMDevice interface.
if (SUCCEEDED(information->device->QueryInterface
    (IID_IDirect3DRMWinDevice, (void **) &windev)))
    {
        if (FAILED(windev->HandlePaint(ps.hdc)))
            Msg("Failed to handle WM_PAINT.\n");
        windev->Release();
    }
else
{
    Msg("Failed to create Windows device to handle WM_PAINT.\n");
}
}
break;
```

And that is it! We now have a working Direct3D framework upon which we can build a visual application.

3.12 What did we learn?

In this chapter, you have learned about the generic set-up code you can use for almost any of your Direct3D Retained-Mode applications. You have seen that a huge amount of code is required just to set up the environment for Direct3D rendering and animation. The great thing is that once you have learned how this code works, you can reuse it over and over with minimal, if any, modifications.

Because of this, I would recommend that you spend the time necessary to thoroughly learn the intricacies of the code. By doing this now, you will not only feel comfortable with the Direct3D objects and their use, but you will gain useful insight which will help you understand the code concepts we will be discussing in the remaining chapters.

3.13 What's next?

Now that we have our generic set-up code defined, we can get to the fun part! In the next chapter we will begin discussing the visual objects and methods of Direct3D. There is a great set of lighting options available to us in Direct3D, and they are the first visual objects we need to learn about since without them we would not be able to see our virtual 3D worlds. So let's get going to chapter 4!

chapter 4

Creating the lighting

4.1 Introduction

Yipeeee! *Finally* we have gotten to the part I am sure you are here for. We will at last get to see something on our screen. I know that the previous chapters have seemed like a lot of code just to get an application set up, but remember that you can reuse it for your future applications. In the next seven chapters I will be walking you through the truly interesting, and enjoyable, aspects of Direct3D. In this chapter we will be learning about lighting. We will then discuss object loading, keyboard and mouse control, object building, materials and textures, joystick control, collision detection, sound, animations, shadows, fog, other DirectX capabilities, and, finally, full screen applications and why you might wish to make them.

As you can see, we have a lot to learn, so let's just dive in.

4.2 Lighting overview

Two lighting models are available in Direct3D—*monochromatic* and *RGB*. The first model, monochromatic, also known as *ramp* lighting, uses each light's gray component to calculate a single shade value. The second model, RGB, uses the full RGB color content of the lights and materials to calculate the lit colors of our objects. I will elaborate on these concepts below.

There are five types of lighting available in Direct3D:

- Ambient
- Point
- Parallel point
- Spot
- Directional

These lighting types cover all of the lighting types you really need in a 3D application. The light types are all stored in the D3DRMLIGHTTYPE enumerated type. The possible values representing the above types are:

```
D3DRMLIGHT_DIRECTIONAL
D3DRMLIGHT_POINT
D3DRMLIGHT_PARALLELPOINT
D3DRMLIGHT_SPOT
D3DRMLIGHT_AMBIENT
```

Using combinations of these lighting types, you can create incredibly realistic virtual scenes rivaling the real world. Let's walk through each of these types and learn how we use them in Direct3D.

4.2.1 Ambient lighting

The first light type I will discuss is the *ambient* light type. Ambient light is defined as the light from a source that has been scattered by the environment to the point that its direction is no longer possible to determine. This light seems to be coming from *all* directions. When ambient light strikes a surface, it is scattered equally in every direction.

A real life example of ambient lighting would be the backlighting in a room. The reason it is considered ambient is that by the time the light reaches your eye, it has bounced off numerous other surfaces. When ambient light strikes a surface, it will scatter equally in all directions. Thus, to the eye, there is no apparent direction of the light.

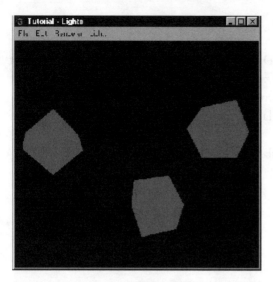

Figure 4.1 The effect of ambient lighting placed in a scene

Placing a low intensity ambient light in a scene creates the visual effect shown in figure 4.1.

The code to produce this type of ambient light is as simple as:

```
if (FAILED(lpD3DRM->CreateLightRGB(D3DRMLIGHT_AMBIENT, D3DVAL(0.1),
    D3DVAL(0.1), D3DVAL(0.1), &light2)))
    goto generic_error;
```

The arguments that the CreateLightRGB method takes to build the light are:

1 `ltLightType`. This value must be one of the lighting types available in the `D3DRMLIGHTTYPE` enumerated type. The `D3DRMLIGHTTYPE` is defined as:

```
typedef enum _D3DRMLIGHTTYPE{
  D3DRMLIGHT_AMBIENT,
  D3DRMLIGHT_POINT,
  D3DRMLIGHT_SPOT,
  D3DRMLIGHT_DIRECTIONAL,
  D3DRMLIGHT_PARALLELPOINT
} D3DRMLIGHTTYPE;
```

2–4 `vRed`, `vGreen`, and `vBlue` . The R, G, and B color components of the light. Their values should be between 0.0 and 1.0.

5 `lplpD3DRMLight` . The address to fill with a pointer to an `IDirect3DRMLight` interface

Based on this definition, you can see that our call requested the creation of an ambient light source having a bright white color and that it be placed in the `light2` variable.

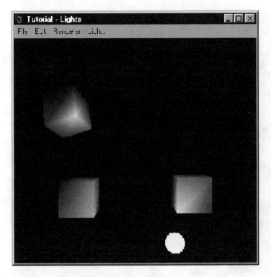

Figure 4.2 The effect of a point source light placed in a scene

4.2.2 Point source lighting

A *point source light* radiates light equally in every direction, starting at its origin. This type of light source needs to calculate a lighting vector for each facet or normal that it strikes (illuminates). It is more processor intensive, but it also is required in many scenarios where we desire realism.

Placing a point source light in a scene creates the visual effect shown in figure 4.2. The code to produce this point source light is:

```
if (FAILED(lpD3DRM->CreateLightRGB (D3DRMLIGHT_POINT, D3DVAL(1.0),
  D3DVAL(1.0), D3DVAL(1.0), &light)))
  goto generic_error;
```

This call creates a point source light having a bright white color and places it in the `light` variable.

4.2.3 Parallel point lighting

A *parallel point light* source is used when we wish to illuminate our scene with parallel light, and to acquire the light's orientation from the parallel point light source's position. This means that our parallel light source has both an orientation and a position. Two objects in a scene with a parallel point light source sitting between them will be lit on the side facing the position of the light source.

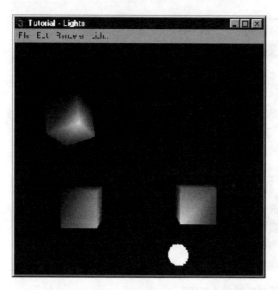

Figure 4.3 The effect of a parallel point source light placed in a scene

The effect of a parallel point source light being placed in a scene is shown in figure 4.3. The code to produce this type of parallel point source light is:

```
if (FAILED(lpD3DRM->CreateLightRGB
  (D3DRMLIGHT_PARALLELPOINT, D3DVAL(1.0), D3DVAL(1.0), D3DVAL(1.0),
        &light)))
  goto generic_error;
```

This call creates a parallel point source light having a bright white color, and places it in the `light` variable.

4.2.4 Spotlights

A *spotlight* source is used when we wish to produce a cone of light. This style of light illuminates only the objects within the cone of light. The cone is made up of two regions with differing intensities of light. The central portion of the light, known as the *umbra*, is the most intensely lit portion and acts as a point source. The outer portion of the light, known as the *penumbra*, surrounds the umbra and is a more dimly lit region which blends into the surrounding darkness.

Figure 4.4 shows the penumbra and umbra cones emitted from a spotlight.

The Direct3D `IDirect3DRMLight` methods `IDirect3DRMLight::GetUmbra` and `IDirect3DRMLight::SetUmbra` are used to get and set the umbra portion of the spot light we create. The Direct3D `IDirect3DRMLight` methods `IDirect3DRMLight::Get-`

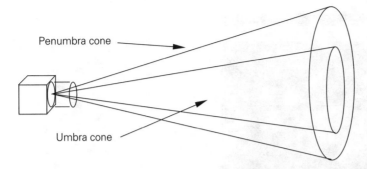

Penumbra cone

Umbra cone

Figure 4.4 The umbra and penumbra of a spotlight

Penumbra and IDirect3DRMLight::SetPenumbra are used to get and set the penumbra portion of our spotlight.

The effect of placing a spotlight in a scene is shown in figure 4.5.

The code to produce this type of spotlight is:

```
if (FAILED(lpD3DRM->CreateLightRGB(D3DRMLIGHT_SPOT,
    D3DVAL(1.0), D3DVAL(1.0), D3DVAL(1.0), &light)))
    goto generic_error;
```

This call creates a spotlight having a bright white color, and places it in the light variable.

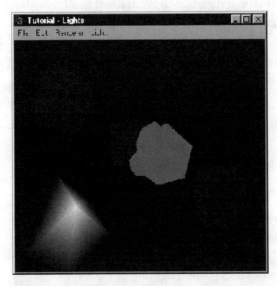

Figure 4.5 The effect of a spotlight placed in a scene

Figure 4.6 The effect of a directional light placed in a scene

4.2.5 Directional lights

The final light type provided by Direct3D is the *directional light* type. It is the best light source to choose for maximizing scene rendering speeds. A directional light source has an orientation but no position. This light type is designed to be attached to a frame, but illuminates all objects with the same intensity. It is used to simulate light sources such as the sun since it acts as if it were positioned at infinity.

The effect of placing a directional light in a scene is shown in figure 4.6.

The code to produce this directional light is:

```
if (FAILED(lpD3DRM->CreateLightRGB
(D3DRMLIGHT_DIRECTIONAL, D3DVAL(1.0), D3DVAL(1.0), D3DVAL(1.0), &light)))
goto generic_error;
```

This call creates a directional light having a bright white color, and places it in the `light` variable.

Each of these light sources will be useful to you for rendering Direct3D applications views. It is up to you to choose the most appropriate light type to simulate the lighting effects you desire. As an example, if you were to create a first person perspective scenario, you might wish to use a spotlight to simulate the light from a flashlight, and ambient lighting to simulate various levels of background lighting in the rooms.

Now that we have a basic understanding of the light types available to us in Direct3D, let's look at the ways in which we can add color to our lights and some of the structures to set our lighting parameters.

4.3 The color of light

The color components of light indicate something different than the color components of a material. With a light, the RGB values represent each color's percentage of full intensity. The values which can be given for the red, green, and blue components will usually run from 0 to 1. When all components of the RGB values for a light are 1.0, the light is set to its brightest possible white. If you specify the values to all be .5, the light will still appear whitish, but will be half the intensity of the first light, so it will appear more gray. If you set the R and G values to 1.0 and the B value to 0, the light will appear yellow.

You might have noted I said usually when I mentioned that the color components run from 0 to 1. The reason I stated it this way is that Microsoft allows each of the RGB components to fall outside of the 0 to 1 range to enable the use of advanced lighting effects (dark lights, etc.).

Although we will discuss them in more detail later, I'd like to discuss *materials* briefly as a point of comparison. With an object's materials, the RGB values indicate the reflected portion of the colors, and the diffuse component of the light's intensity is used as the shade. As an example, if we set the Red value to 0.0, the Green value to 0.5, and the Blue value to 1.0 for a material, it will reflect none of the Red light, half of the Green light, and all of the Blue light.

If we are using the *ramp* mode, and the material has a specular component, the shade will be computed as a combination of the specular and diffuse components of the light. The equation for this is:

$$shade = \frac{3}{4}(diffuse \times (1 - specular)) + specular$$

The computed shade value works with precalculated ramps of colors which are divided into two sections. The first $\frac{3}{4}$ of the ramp holds a ramp of the material's diffuse color and ranges from the ambient color to the maximum diffuse color. The last $\frac{1}{4}$ of the ramp holds a ramp ranging from the maximum diffuse color to the maximum specular color of the material. For rendering use, the shade value must be scaled by the size of the ramp. This value is then used as an index for looking up the required color.

The actual color presented to us from a rendered scene is derived as a combination of the lights in the scene hitting the object and the object's color. In the simple example (where we ignore all other light reflectivity in the scene) in which we only have one light with color components (RL, GL, BL) and an object with material color components (RM, GM, BM), the light we will perceive is computed as (RL*RM, GL*GM, BL*BM).

Also, remember that the lighting effects are additive, so if we have two lights with RGB components (.5, .3, .4) and (.2, .1, .3) at a point the scene's lighting at that point would be (.5+.2, .3+.1, .4+.3).

4.3.1 The direction of light

The D3DLIGHT structure's direction vectors define the direction from the model to the light source. These vectors should be normalized for our directional lights. The vectors are transformed into model coordinates using the current world matrix. Thus, they should be specified in world coordinates, so that the system does not have to convert the vector's coordinate system.

4.3.2 The range of light

Point lights and spotlights use the range parameter to specify the effective range of the light. Any object falling outside of this range is not affected by these light types. The intensity of these types is modified by a quadratic attenuation factor as follows:

$$\text{attenuation} = \text{attenuation}0 + \text{attenuation}1 \times d + \text{attenuation}2 \times d\,2$$

The d in this equation specifies the distance from the light to a vertex being lit.

4.3.3 Spotlight features

In Immediate Mode, spotlights also have members in the D3DLIGHT structure which specify the angles of the umbra and penumbra cones (dvTheta and dvPhi). The fall-off factor, dvFallof, is applied between the spotlight's umbra and penumbra cones.

4.4 Frames and how to use them with light objects

Well, now you know which light types are available in Direct3D, but we haven't talked about *how* to place them into our Direct3D scene. The basic concept of object positioning is actually quite simple, but to place a light and animate it, there are several things we need to remember.

First, we need to learn more about *frames*. We looked at these very briefly in chapter 3 when we created our scene. As you will remember, a *scene* is the highest level frame, and thus has no parent frame. This frame is the major component defining our view of the Direct3D world we build. It is used to define each object's physical frame of reference. A frame is designed to be used to position objects within a scene. Our objects are placed in the scene by specifying their position in space relative to a reference frame—the *scene* frame or any other frame that has been defined.

4.5 Visual object hierarchies

The frames in our scene are organized using a tree structure. Frames can have both a parent frame and one or more child frames. The scene is the top level frame of the tree and thus has no parent. It is known as the *root frame*. Child frames are created with positions and orientations relative to their parent frames. This means that whenever the parent frame moves, the child frame moves with it. The children or parents of any frame can be retrieved using the `IDirect3DRMFrame::GetChildren` or `IDirect3DRMFrame::GetParent` methods.

The position and orientation of a frame can be set relative to any other frame in a scene. Frames can be added and deleted from any of our parent frames. They also may be added to one frame, after we remove them from another, by calling the `IDirect3DRMFrame::AddChild` method. You can remove a child frame from a parent frame by calling the `IDirect3DRMFrame::DeleteChild` method.

Frames can be added as visual objects to other frames. This provides you the ability to reuse a specific hierarchy several times within a scene. These hierarchies are called *instances*. You will need to watch so that you do not accidentally create cyclic hierarchies by instancing a parent frame into its children. The `Direct3DRMFrame` interface will not allow you to create a cyclic hierarchy using its methods, but you could accidentally create one when you add a frame as a visual.

4.6 A quick graphics fundamentals overview

This section presents a quick overview of the transform matrices you should understand for the object manipulations (rotating, scaling, etc.) in the remaining chapters of this book.

Standard graphics conventions are used throughout the remainder of this book and within the Direct3D environment. Direct3D uses a left-handed coordinate system for the Retained-Mode graphics functions. This coordinate system can be remembered by thinking of the origin as the lower left-hand corner of the screen, the X-axis as the horizontal axis with the positive direction heading to the right, the Y-axis as the vertical axis with the positive direction heading upward, and the Z-axis as an axis with the positive axis entering into the screen and the negative direction heading outward from the screen toward the user. Figure 4.7 shows this axis configuration.

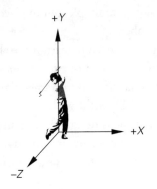

Figure 4.7 Object X-, Y-, and Z-axes in left-handed coordinate system

4.6.1 Object transformations

The three standard transformation functions consist of `Translate`, `Rotate`, and `Scale`. These three functions each transform an object by moving, rotating, or sizing it. Each of these transformations produce a 4×4 matrix (translation, rotation, or scaling) which is used internally to modify the object's point information. Each of these transformation matrices, and their resultant effect upon the object, are discussed below. First, let's look at the effect of a transformation on point (x, y, z).

$$[x'y'z'] = [xyz1] \begin{bmatrix} M_{11} & M_{12} & M_{13} & M_{14} \\ M_{21} & M_{22} & M_{23} & M_{24} \\ M_{31} & M_{32} & M_{33} & M_{34} \\ M_{41} & M_{42} & M_{43} & M_{44} \end{bmatrix}$$

This equation equates to the following operations to produce the point (x', y', z'):

$$x' = (M_{11} \times x) + (M_{21} \times y) + (M_{31} \times z) + (M_{41} \times 1)$$

$$y' = (M_{12} \times x) + (M_{22} \times y) + (M_{32} \times z) + (M_{42} \times 1)$$

$$z' = (M_{13} \times x) + (M_{23} \times y) + (M_{33} \times z) + (M_{43} \times 1)$$

These three operations show how the point (x, y, z) is transformed to the new point (x', y', z').

CHAPTER 4   CREATING THE LIGHTING

4.6.2 Translation

The matrix used to translate (move) a point, (x, y, z) by a specified amount in the X-, Y-, or Z-axes, with a resultant point of (x', y', z'), would be as follows:

$$[x'y'z'] = [xyz1] \begin{bmatrix} 1 & 0 & 0 & 0 \\ 0 & 1 & 0 & 0 \\ 0 & 0 & 1 & 0 \\ T_x & T_y & T_z & 1 \end{bmatrix}$$

This translation matrix could be implemented as an array in C++ as follows:

```
D3DMATRIX scale = {
    D3DVAL(1),      0,              0,              0,
    0,              D3DVAL(1),      0,              0,
    0,              0,              D3DVAL(1),      0,
    D3DVAL(Tx),     D3DVAL(Ty),     D3DVAL(Tz),     D3DVAL(1)
};
```

When an object is translated, the object is repositioned by the corresponding amount specified in the Tx, Ty, and Tz values of the translation matrix. The effect of this translation is shown in figure 4.8.

4.6.3 Rotation

The matrices used to rotate (spin) a point, (x, y, z) by a specified amount around the X, Y, or Z-axes, with a resultant point (x', y', z'), are described below.

The matrix for rotating an object about the X-axes would be as follows:

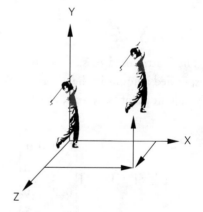

Figure 4.8 Effect of translating an object along the X-, Y-, and Z-axes

$$[x'y'z'] = [xyz1] \begin{bmatrix} 1 & 0 & 0 & 0 \\ 0 & \cos\theta & \sin\theta & 0 \\ 0 & -\sin\theta & \cos\theta & 0 \\ 0 & 0 & 0 & 1 \end{bmatrix}$$

The matrix for rotating an object about the *Y*-axes would be as follows:

$$[x'y'z'] = [xyz1]\begin{bmatrix} \cos\theta & 0 & -\sin\theta & 0 \\ 0 & 1 & 0 & 0 \\ \sin\theta & 0 & \cos\theta & 0 \\ 0 & 0 & 0 & 1 \end{bmatrix}$$

The matrix for rotating an object about the *Z*-axes would be as follows:

$$[x'y'z'] = [xyz1]\begin{bmatrix} \cos\theta & \sin\theta & 0 & 0 \\ -\sin\theta & \cos\theta & 0 & 0 \\ 0 & 0 & 1 & 0 \\ 0 & 0 & 0 & 1 \end{bmatrix}$$

Figure 4.9 shows the effect of an object when being rotated about the *Z*-axis.

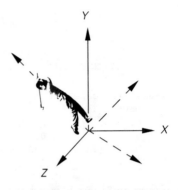

Figure 4.9 Effect of rotating an object about the Z-axis

4.6.4 Scale

The matrix used to scale a point (*x, y, z*) by a specified amount in the *X*-, *Y*-, or *Z*-axes, with a resultant point (*x', y', z'*), would be as follows:

$$[x'y'z'] = [xyz1]\begin{bmatrix} s_x & 0 & 0 & 0 \\ 0 & s_y & 0 & 0 \\ 0 & 0 & s_z & 0 \\ 0 & 0 & 0 & 1 \end{bmatrix}$$

If an object is just scaled in a single, or two, axes, the object will lose its original symmetric proportions. A simple example of this is the scenario where a square is scaled in the *X*- and *Y*-axes, but not in the *Z*-axis. In this case, the original square will be deformed into a rectangle.

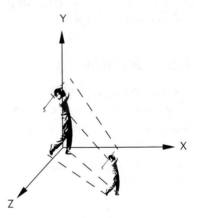

Figure 4.10 Effect of scaling an object in all axes

There is a lot more to understand about 3D graphic basics, and entire books are being written about the subject all the time. If you feel you need a 3D basics refresher course, I would recommend getting a good book on it, such as the excellent Graphics Gems series published by Academic Press. If you feel at all comfortable with the area though, don't worry, because I intend to make this subject as simple as possible. I will also be covering the main aspects of 3D, such as the frame transformations shown in the next section, as we need them.

4.7 Frame transformations

Now that we have covered the concept of transformations in detail, I will show you how they can be applied to control the position and orientation of a frame relative to its parent. This relationship can be thought of as a linear transformation that takes vectors defined relative to a child frame and converts them to vectors relative to its parent frame. These transformations can be represented by 4×4 matrices. The coordinates can be specified as four element row vectors $[x,y,z,1]$.

Whenever we transform a parent frame, all of its child frames are transformed also. If a child is several levels down in the tree, *all* of the transforms from the child frame up to the root frame are combined to generate a world transformation. This world transformation is applied to all of the child frames visuals for use in rendering the scene. The child frame coordinates are often called *model coordinates* and once they are transformed they are called *world coordinates*.

A frames transformations can be changed using any of the `IDirect3DRMFrame::AddRotation`, `IDirect3DRMFrame::AddScale`, `IDirect3DRMFrame::AddTransform`, and `IDirect3DRMFrame::AddTranslation` methods. All of these methods take a member of the `D3DRMCOMBINETYPE` enumerated type. This value indicates how we wish the matrix to be combined with the frames matrix.

The `IDirect3DRMFrame::AddRotation` method is called when you wish to add a rotation angle of `rvTheta`, about the axis (`rvX`, `rvY`, `rvZ`) to an object.

This method is defined as:

```
HRESULT AddRotation(D3DRMCOMBINETYPE rctCombine, D3DVALUE rvX,
  D3DVALUE rvY, D3DVALUE rvZ, D3DVALUE rvTheta);
```

This rotation modifies the frame's local transformation based upon the value of the `rctCombine` parameter. This parameter can have the following possible values:

• `D3DRMCOMBINE_REPLACE`. Replace the frames current matrix with the passed matrix.

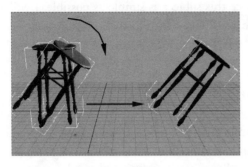

Figure 4.11 Object rotated and then translated

Figure 4.12 Object translated and then rotated

- D3DRMCOMBINE_BEFORE. Multiply the frame's current matrix with the passed matrix. The passed matrix precedes the current matrix in the calculation.

- D3DRMCOMBINE_AFTER. Multiply the supplied matrix with the frame's current matrix. The supplied matrix follows the current matrix in the calculation.

Remember that the order of the matrices in the computations is important since matrix multiplication is *not* commutative. Please look at figures 4.11 and 4.12. Figure 4.11 shows an object which was rotated first and then translated. Figure 4.12 shows an object that was translated first and then rotated. As you can see, there is a great difference in the end effect of the scene, based on the order in which we perform our transformations.

The IDirect3DRMFrame::AddScale method is called when you wish to scale a frame's local transformation by (rvX, rvY, rvZ). The rctCombine parameter can have the same set of values as the AddRotation method's rctCombine parameter.

The IDirect3DRMFrame::AddScale method is defined as:

```
HRESULT AddScale(D3DRMCOMBINETYPE rctCombine, D3DVALUE rvX,
  D3DVALUE rvY, D3DVALUE rvZ);
```

The IDirect3DRMFrame::AddTransform method is called when you need to transform a frame's local coordinates by a desired affine transformation. This method's rctCombine parameter can also have the same set of values as the AddRotation method's rctCombine parameter.

The IDirect3DRMFrame::AddTransform method is defined as:

```
HRESULT AddTransform(D3DRMCOMBINETYPE rctCombine,
  D3DRMMATRIX4D rmMatrix);
```

Note that I mentioned that this method takes an *affine* transformation matrix. An affine matrix is a 4×4 matrix with the last column being a transpose (0,0,0,1).

The `IDirect3DRMFrame::AddTranslation` method is used to add a translation by (rvX, rvY, rvZ) to a frame's local coordinate system. As with the previous methods, the rctCombine parameter can have the values `D3DRMCOMBINE_REPLACE`, `D3DRM-COMBINE_BEFORE`, or `D3DRMCOMBINE_AFTER`.

The `IDirect3DRMFrame::AddTranslation` method is defined as:

```
HRESULT AddTranslation(D3DRMCOMBINETYPE rctCombine, D3DVALUE rvX,
  D3DVALUE rvY, D3DVALUE rvZ);
```

A frame's rotation axis and transformation matrix can be acquired or modified using the following methods:

The `IDirect3DRMFrame::GetRotation` method can be used to get a frame's rotation axis relative to a passed reference frame. This method fills the passed variable's lprvAxis and lprvTheta with the frame's axis of rotation and rotation in radians. The lprvAxis parameter will be filled with the frame's axis of rotation. The lprvTheta parameter will be filled with the frame's rotation in radians.

The prototype of this method is:

```
HRESULT GetRotation(LPDIRECT3DRMFRAME lpRef, LPD3DVECTOR lprvAxis,
  LPD3DVALUE lprvTheta);
```

The `IDirect3DRMFrame::SetRotation` method can be used to change a frame's rotation axis. It sets the frame rotating by the passed angle around the passed vector (rvX, rvY, rvZ) each time the `IDirect3DRM::Tick` or `IDirect3DRMFrame::Move` methods are called. The method is defined as:

```
HRESULT SetRotation(LPDIRECT3DRMFRAME lpRef, D3DVALUE rvX, D3DVALUE rvY,
  D3DVALUE rvZ, D3DVALUE rvTheta);
```

The `IDirect3DRMFrame::GetTransform` method can be used to get a frame's transformation matrix as a 4×4 affine matrix. The matrix is returned in the rmMatrix parameter.

The method is defined as:

```
HRESULT GetTransform(D3DRMMATRIX4D rmMatrix);
```

The rmMatrix parameter is a `D3DRMMATRIX4D` type array which is thus actually an address. The `D3DRMMATRIX4D` type is defined as:

```
typedef D3DVALUE D3DRMMATRIX4D[4][4];
```

This array is organized as a [*row*][*column*] format.

Finally, the `IDirect3DRMFrame::InverseTransform` method can be used to switch between world and model coordinates. The method prototype is:

```
HRESULT InverseTransform(D3DVECTOR *lprvDst, D3DVECTOR *lprvSrc);
```

4.8 Frame motion

Each frame we create has a built-in rotation and velocity. A value of 0 for both of these attributes indicates that it is not moving. These attributes are used to move objects before each scene is rendered. You can also use these attributes to produce animated scenes, such as a universe where planets revolve around the main sun object, and moons revolve around the various planets.

You can use the `IDirect3DRMFrame::SetRotation` method to change the rotation to a new value when you desire. This method is defined as:

```
HRESULT SetRotation(LPDIRECT3DRMFRAME lpRef, D3DVALUE rvX, D3DVALUE rvY, ,
D3DVALUE rvZ, D3DVALUE rvTheta);
```

The arguments consist of:

- `lpRef`. The address of a `Direct3DRMFrame` object used as our reference
- `rvX`, `rvY`, `rvZ`. Specify the vector about which we want to rotate
- `rvTheta`. Specifies the rotation in radians

The `IDirect3DRMFrame::SetVelocity` method allows us to set the built-in velocity of the frame. Our frame will move by the vector [*rvX, rvY, rvZ*] relative to the reference frame each time the `IDirect3DRM::Tick` or `IDirect3DRMFrame::Move` methods are triggered.

This method is defined as:

```
HRESULT SetVelocity(LPDIRECT3DRMFRAME lpRef, D3DVALUE rvX,
 D3DVALUE rvY, D3DVALUE rvZ, BOOL fRotVel);
```

Again, it is important to remember that any children frames will inherit their parent frame's motion, so if you add a frame to a parent which is already moving, it will acquire these motion attributes also.

4.9 Callback functions

Each frame can have a callback function for use in handling animations more complex than can be handled by the motion attributes. This function is used to register a function to be called by the frame before the motion attributes are applied. In a frame hierarchy, the callback functions are called starting at the scene and moving down to the lowest level child frame.

One way you can use these callback functions is for attaching new positions and orientations acquired from a precalculated animation sequence (from a data structure or a file). The callback function can be added to a frame using the `IDirect3DRMFrame::AddMoveCallback` method and removed using the `IDirect-3DRMFrame::DeleteMoveCallback` method.

4.10 How to put it all together

At this point, you should understand how to add and create lights as well as other visual objects. But, you might be saying, "Peter, how do I actually write the code to effectively do this?" Well, although after all of the explanation above it may seem like it might be difficult, it is actually quite simple.

The function below is the main routine we can use to place lights in any of our applications. This function takes two arguments. The first argument holds the name of the light type we desire. This value can be `LIGHT_DIRECTIONAL`, `LIGHT_PARALLEL_POINT`, `LIGHT_SPOT`, or `LIGHT_POINT`. These are the lights which we can position in our scene.

You will notice a new object created and used in the code—a Direct3D *Builder* object. I will be covering this object first thing in the next chapter. For now just remember that it is used to load and hold our 3D objects representing spot or point type light sources.

```
//
// CreateLight
// This function creates a light of type Directional, Parallel Point,
//        Spot, or Point, and attaches it to the
// frame passed into the routine if it is not NULL
//
static BOOL
CreateLight(char* wparam, LPDIRECT3DRMFRAME frame2)
{
 LPDIRECT3DRMMESHBUILDER builder = NULL;
 LPDIRECT3DRMLIGHT light = NULL;
 LPDIRECT3DRMFRAME frame = NULL;
 HRESULT returnVal;

 // Create a mesh builder for use in building our camera object
 if (FAILED(lpD3DRM->CreateMeshBuilder(&builder)))
  goto generic_error;

 // If we wish to create an Ambient light,
 if (strcmp(wparam, "AMBIENT") == 0) {
```

```
    if (FAILED(builder->SetQuality(D3DRMRENDER_UNLITFLAT)))
      goto generic_error;
    if (FAILED(lpD3DRM->CreateLightRGB(D3DRMLIGHT_AMBIENT, D3DVAL(0.1),
      D3DVAL(0.1), D3DVAL(0.1), &light2)))
      goto generic_error;
}
// If we want to create a directional light,
else if (strcmp(wparam, "LIGHT_DIRECTIONAL") == 0) {
  // First load the camera model from the camera.x file
  returnVal = builder->Load("camera.x", NULL, D3DRMLOAD_FROMFILE,
    NULL, NULL);
  // If the camera model was not loaded properly, put up an error message
      and return
  if (returnVal != D3DRM_OK) {
    Msg("Failed to load camera.x.\n%s", MyErrorToString(returnVal));
    goto ret_with_error;
  }

  // Set the Quality of the builder (chapter 5)
  if (FAILED(builder->SetQuality(D3DRMRENDER_UNLITFLAT)))
    goto generic_error;

  // Create a Directional Light
  if (FAILED(lpD3DRM->CreateLightRGB
    (D3DRMLIGHT_DIRECTIONAL, D3DVAL(1.0), D3DVAL(1.0), D3DVAL(1.0),
      &light)))
    goto generic_error;
}
else
// If we want to create a parallel point light,
if (strcmp(wparam, "LIGHT_PARALLEL_POINT") == 0) {
  // First load the sphere model from the sphere2.x file
  returnVal = builder->Load("sphere2.x", NULL, D3DRMLOAD_FROMFILE,
    NULL, NULL);
  if (returnVal != D3DRM_OK) {
    Msg("Failed to load sphere2.x.\n%s", MyErrorToString(returnVal));
    goto ret_with_error;
  }
  // Set the Quality of the builder (chapter 5)
  if (FAILED(builder->SetQuality(D3DRMRENDER_UNLITFLAT)))
    goto generic_error;
  // Scale the object representing our light
  if (FAILED(builder->Scale(D3DVAL(0.2), D3DVAL(0.2), D3DVAL(0.2))))
    goto generic_error;
  // Create a Parallel Point Light
  if (FAILED(lpD3DRM->CreateLightRGB
    (D3DRMLIGHT_PARALLELPOINT, D3DVAL(1.0), D3DVAL(1.0), D3DVAL(1.0),
      &light)))
    goto generic_error;
}
else
// If we want to create a spot light,
if (strcmp(wparam, "LIGHT_SPOT") == 0) {
  // First load the camera model from the camera.x file
```

```
      returnVal = builder->Load("camera.x", NULL, D3DRMLOAD_FROMFILE,
           NULL, NULL);
       if (returnVal != D3DRM_OK) {
         Msg("Failed to load camera.x.\n%s", MyErrorToString(returnVal));
         goto ret_with_error;
     }
     // Set the Quality of the builder (chapter 5)
     if (FAILED(builder->SetQuality(D3DRMRENDER_UNLITFLAT)))
      goto generic_error;
     // Create a Spot Light
     if (FAILED(lpD3DRM->CreateLightRGB(D3DRMLIGHT_SPOT, D3DVAL(1.0),
       D3DVAL(1.0), D3DVAL(1.0), &light)))
      goto generic_error;
     }
   else
    // If we want to create a point source light,
    if (strcmp(wparam, "LIGHT_POINT") == 0) {
     // First load the sphere2 model from the sphere2.x file
      returnVal = builder->Load("sphere2.x", NULL, D3DRMLOAD_FROMFILE,
           NULL, NULL);
       if (returnVal != D3DRM_OK) {
         Msg("Failed to load sphere2.x.\n%s", MyErrorToString(returnVal));
         goto ret_with_error;
     }
     // Set the Quality of the builder (chapter 5)
     if (FAILED(builder->SetQuality(D3DRMRENDER_UNLITFLAT)))
        goto generic_error;
     // Scale the object representing our light
     if (FAILED(builder->Scale(D3DVAL(0.2), D3DVAL(0.2), D3DVAL(0.2))))
        goto generic_error;
     // Create a Point Source Light
     if (FAILED(lpD3DRM->CreateLightRGB
       (D3DRMLIGHT_POINT, D3DVAL(1.0), D3DVAL(1.0), D3DVAL(1.0), &light)))
        goto generic_error;
   }
   // Create a frame for our objects
   if (FAILED(lpD3DRM->CreateFrame(scene, &frame)))
     goto generic_error;
   // Position the frame
   if (FAILED(frame->SetPosition(camera, D3DVAL(0.0), D3DVAL(0.0),
        D3DVAL(10.0))))
     goto generic_error;
   // Add the builder as a visual
   if (FAILED(frame->AddVisual(builder)))
    goto generic_error;
   // Add our light
   if (FAILED(frame->AddLight(light)))
    goto generic_error;

   if (frame2)
     frame2->AddChild(frame);

   builder->Release(), frame->Release(), light->Release();
   return TRUE;
```

```
generic_error:
   Msg("A failure occurred while creating a new light.\n");
ret_with_error:
   RELEASE(builder);
   RELEASE(light);
   RELEASE(frame);
   return FALSE;
}
```

4.11 What did we learn?

In this chapter we learned about lights, frames, and basic animations. You now know how to create all of the light types available in Direct3D. As you have seen, the variety of lights available allows us to create almost any type of scene we could want. We can create incredibly realistic and complex scenes rivaling reality when we use the lighting effectively and in conjunction with one another.

You have seen how frames are used to add any visual object to our scene, including the light objects. They are also used to add motion attributes to these objects and to relate the objects to one another. You have also learned how to create a hierarchy of objects starting with the scene object, which has no parent frame and thus is the basis upon which all of our world's object frames are added.

4.12 What's next?

In the next chapter you will learn how to load Direct3D objects. These objects are in the DirectX (.x) format, which is a fairly complex and useful modeling format. You will also learn more details about the MeshBuilder object class which you probably noticed I introduced in the code above for generating lights. Well, if you thought "What's that?" when you saw the calls, it should become clear in Chapter 5. You will be using these objects whenever you create a new 3D component for your programs.

chapter 5

Loading an object

5.1 Visual object loading overview

In this chapter, we will cover the creation of a visual object by loading it from a file. This is a task that you will perform often in any serious application. Although we can model many objects mathematically and build them inside of our programs (I will show you this is detail in chapter 7), there are far more objects we will wish to use that are just not feasible to create *on the fly.*

Direct3D provides us a capability to load prebuilt objects into our virtual world. These objects are stored as .x objects. The DirectX file format is a custom format developed for Direct3D. Many of you will be familiar with other modeling tool file formats. The most common file format is the .3ds file format for Autodesk's 3DStudio also handled by the new 3DStudio Max. There are similarities between many of these formats, but there are also several unique features to the .x format. I have found it very important to know as intimately as possible the file format used by one's tool of choice. This will allow you to write your own tools to create, edit, parse, and so forth, any of the object files. The most important use, in terms of game development, is the ability to write programs which will algorithmically generate objects for your world and save them in the proper format for your tool.

Let's first look at a simple example of loading a .x file object. After that, we will look at a more complicated object having multiple parts and textures. Finally, I will show you many of the details of the DirectX file format This is something you may not have been able to find in the past, and the example file should show you all you need to know to use and create .x files.

5.2 Loading a DirectX file format object

At its simplest, loading a .x file object is very quick and easy. The code to perform this task is shown below. I will walk through the routine line by line and explain what we have to do to get the object into our scene and why.

The routine I will use to demonstrate the steps necessary to load an object is the LoadWell routine. This is one of the routines which will be in the 3D world simulations and games we are constructing. It loads a well object, sets its color, and adds it to the frame which was passed into the routine. So, let's dig into it!

The function takes a LPDIRECT3DRMFRAME object as input. This parameter holds the frame within which we wish to place the object (the well). In this demonstration case, this parameter is the *scene* frame object, but it can be any subframe you wish also. The function is defined as:

```
BOOL
LoadWell (LPDIRECT3DRMFRAME myFrame)
{
```

The next segment defines the object builder, the object mesh, the object's frame, and a result variable to receive the results of the function calls.

```
LPDIRECT3DRMMESHBUILDER obj_builder = 0;
LPDIRECT3DRMMESH  obj_mesh = 0;
LPDIRECT3DRMFRAME  obj_frame = 0;
HRESULT rval;
```

5.2.1 The Mesh and MeshBuilder objects

The first command in this routine is called to create a new MeshBuilder object, using the IDirect3DRMMeshBuilder COM interface. This IDirect3DRMMeshBuilder object is built upon the IDirect3DRMMesh COM interface. The IDirect3DRMMesh object is quite fast, and was designed to be used when building a mesh which changes a lot. This would happen when you morph an object from one shape to another—something you might find useful for game development!

The IDirect3DRMMeshBuilder object is slower than the IDIrect3DRMMesh object since the IDirect3DRMMeshBuilder object has to convert a MeshBuilder object into a Mesh object before it is rendered. Because of this, make sure you try to use the IDirect3DRMMeshBuilder for instances when your meshes do not change much. If you do this, the actual conversion will not effect your application much at all.

A nice aspect of both the IDirect3DRMMeshBuilder and the IDirect3DRMMesh objects is that they will split our mesh into multiple buffers whenever it is bigger than can be handled by the hardware to which we are rendering.

When you need to apply the same characteristics to multiple vertices or faces, you can use the IDirect3DRMMesh interface to combine them into a group. If you are building an object having the same texture, material, or other characteristic applied to multiple faces or vertices, you can group them using the IDirect3DRMMesh interface's methods. A key thing to remember is that if you share vertices between two groups, such as having two adjacent faces with different colors, you will need to include the vertices in *both* groups.

You can use the `IDirect3DRMeshBuilder::AddFace` or `IDirect3DRMeshBuilder::AddFaces` methods when you wish to add a single, or multiple, faces. When you wish to add a vertex to an object, you can use the `IDirect3DRMeshBuilder::AddVertex` method. If you want to calculate your object normals yourself, you can apply them as unit vectors. This will require a bit of math, so you might want to let the system do it for you. If you wish to see how to generate normals, please look at the `getNormal` routine in the x5.cpp file in the Chap11 folder on the CD accompanying this book. Finally, if you wish the system to calculate them for you, you should use the `IDirect3DRMeshBuilder::GenerateNormals` method. When you need to specify individual color, material, or texture properties for separate faces in your mesh, or for that matter *all* of the faces in a mesh if you have one group, you can use the `IDirect3DRMesh::SetGroupColor`, `IDirect3DRMesh::Set-GroupColorRGB`, `IDirect3DRMesh::SetGroupTexture`, the `IDirect3DRMesh::SetGroup-Material` methods.

Finally, you can set the mode (flat, Gouraud, or Phong) you wish to use for rendering the mesh by calling the `IDirect3DRMesh::SetGroupQuality`, method.

I will show you how to use each of these methods in detail as we need them in our program. For now, we will just be using them to load our prebuilt objects.

The prototype for the `IDirect3DRM::CreateMeshBuilder` method to create any MeshBuilder we need is:

```
HRESULT CreateMeshBuilder(LPDIRECT3DRMMESHBUILDER* lplpD3DRMMeshBuilder);
```

This call returns the value D3DRM_OK if it is successful, or else it returns one of the Retained-Mode Return values you learned about in chapter 2. If you wish to review the errors which can be returned, see the `MyErrorToString` routine in the tutorial.cpp file on the CD accompanying this book.

The parameter to this method, `lplpD3DRMMeshBuilder`, will be filled with a pointer to an IDirecr3DRMMeshBuilder interface if the call is successful. We will then use this MeshBuilder to load the representation of our well object.

The code to perform this task is:

```
// load mesh file
if (FAILED(lpD3DRM->CreateMeshBuilder(&obj_builder)))
  return FALSE;
```

5.2.2 Setting the color of the object

Since we just covered the color of light in the last chapter, let's also take a quick look at how we can set the colors of our objects. There are several ways to do this. I will be showing you how to load and build objects in this, as well as in the next few chapters, but understanding how to set their colors will help you create the most realistic games and simulations possible.

The `IDirect3DRMMeshBuilder::SetColorRGB` method sets the color of the entire IDirecr3DRMMeshBuilder object. There are also several other methods that you can use to set the color of your objects. These are `IDirect3DRMMeshbuilder::SetColor`, `IDirect-3DRMMesh::SetColor`, `IDirect3DRMMesh::SetColorRGB`, `IDirect3DRMFace::SetColor`, `IDirect3DRMFace::SetColorRGB`, `IDirect3DRMFrame::SetColor`, and `IDirect3DRM-Frame::SetColorRGB`. There are a large number of potential interactions, which can create some very unexpected results, when you use these methods to set the color of your objects. The `IDirect3DRMFrame::SetColor` and `IDirect3DRM::SetColorRGB` methods set the color of all the meshes in the frame. Because of this, if you set the color of a mesh, but you then use the `IDirect3DRMFrame::SetColor` or `IDirect3DRM::SetColorRGB` method on its parent frame to set its overall color, you will wipe out the color changes you made for your mesh—but only if you also set the `D3DRMMATERIALMODE` enumerated type to `D3DRMMATERIAL_FROMFRAME`. If you have not set the enumerated type, you will end up with no change made to your object.

The `D3DRMMATERIALMODE` enumerated type has three members:

- `D3DRMMATERIAL_FROMMESH`. The default value, it indicates that we want the material information from the mesh itself.

- `D3DRMMATERIAL_FROMPARENT`. The material, colors, and texture information will be inherited from the parent frame

- `D3DRMMATERIAL_FROMFRAME`. The material information will be acquired from the frame. This will override any information that the visual object may have had previously.

The other method I have found to be important is `IDirect3DRMMeshBuilder::Set-ColorSource`. This method is used to specify what color source your MeshBuilder should use. The two possible values that this method can take as a value of the source parameter, which is a `D3DRMCOLORSOURCE` type, are `D3DRMCOLOR_FROMFACE` and `D3DRM-COLOR_FROMVERTEX`. These are used to set your MeshBuilder color source to a face (`D3DRMCOLOR_FROMFACE`) or a vertex (`D3DRMCOLOR_FROMVERTEX`).

5.2.3 Loading the object

Once we have created the MeshBuilder object, we can go ahead and load our well object. The MeshBuilder's Load method takes a number of parameters. This method is defined as:

```
HRESULT Load(LPVOID lpvObjSource, LPVOID lpvObjID,
  D3DRMLOADOPTIONS d3drmLOFlags,
  D3DRMLOADTEXTURECALLBACK d3drmLoadTextureProc, LPVOID lpvArg);
```

The `lpvObjSource` parameter holds the file name for the object we wish to load (although it can also hold several other possible values). As we briefly discussed, DirectX uses a file format which has the naming convention of ourfilename.x. Thus, the name which we are passing, well.x, specifies that we wish to load our well object from the file named well.x.

The other parameter with which we need to concern ourselves is the third argument of the method, the `d3drmLOFlags`. This parameter holds the `D3DRMLOADOPTIONS` type describing the load options we wish to use when loading our object. There are many possible values to this type. This type is used by the `IDirect3DRM::Load`, `IDirect3DRMAnimationSet::Load`, `IDirect3DRMFrame::Load`, and `IDirect3DRMMeshBuilder::Load` methods.

The `D3DRMLOADOPTIONS` type is defined as:

```
typedef DWORD D3DRMLOADOPTIONS;
#define D3DRMLOAD_FROMFILE                0x00L
#define D3DRMLOAD_FROMRESOURCE            0x01L
#define D3DRMLOAD_FROMMEMORY             0x02L
#define D3DRMLOAD_FROMSTREAM            0x03L
#define D3DRMLOAD_BYNAME                 0x10L
#define D3DRMLOAD_BYPOSITION            0x20L
#define D3DRMLOAD_BYGUID                0x30L
#define D3DRMLOAD_FIRST                 0x40L
#define D3DRMLOAD_INSTANCEBYREFERENCE    0x100L
#define D3DRMLOAD_INSTANCEBYCOPYING      0x200L
```

The three flags I tend to use the most are the following:

Source flags:

- `D3DRMLOAD_FROMFILE`. This flag is the default setting.

Instance flags:

- `D3DRMLOAD_INSTANCEBYREFERENCE`. This flag indicates that we wish to check if an object having the same name already exists and if it does, we wish to use an instance of that object rather than creating a new one.
- `D3DRMLOAD_INSTANCEBYCOPYING`. This flag states that we wish to check if an object with the same name exists and if it does, we wish to copy it.

The instance flags do not affect the interpretation of the parameters. If we use the `D3DRMLOAD_INSTANCEBYREFERENCE` flag, the application can load the same file twice without creating a new object.

If you wish to see the other flags available, please take a look at the `D3DRMLOADOPTIONS` definition in chapter 37.

If an object has no name and we set the `D3DRMLOAD_INSTANCEBYREFERENCE` flag, it has the same effect as setting the `D3DRMLOAD_INSTANCEBYCOPYING` flag. The loader will make each unnamed object as a new one, even if some of them are identical.

The code to handle the loading of the well object is:

```
// Create a frame within the scene
rval = obj_builder->Load ("well.x", NULL, D3DRMLOAD_FROMFILE, NULL, NULL);
if (rval != D3DRM_OK)
{
  Msg("Failed to load well.x\n%s", MyErrorToString(rval));
  return FALSE;
}
```

Now, once our well object has been loaded successfully, we need to create a new mesh from the Direct3DRMMeshBuilder object. We must do this so that we have the mesh available to use for animation and modification in our program.

```
if (FAILED (obj_builder->CreateMesh(&obj_mesh)))
  return FALSE;
```

We also want to set the color of the object. As you have seen earlier, three 1.0 values indicate that we wish the object to have RGB components of 1.0,1.0,1.0.

```
if (FAILED(obj_builder->SetColorRGB (D3DVAL(1.0), D3DVAL(1.0), D3DVAL(1.0))))
  return FALSE;
```

You will need to call the `AddVisual` method of the IDirect3DRMFrame object to add a visual object to the desired frame. A visual object, such as a mesh, becomes visible when it is added, if it is in the view. The `AddVisual` method is defined as:

Figure 5.1 The appearance of the well.x object we loaded

```
HRESULT AddVisual(LPDIRECT3DRMVISUAL lpD3DRMVisual);
```

The code to add our visual object needs to take the mesh and pass it into the AddVisual method of our frame. You can add a mesh to several frames if you wish to display multiple instances of it. The code to add a visual to our frame is:

```
// add the loaded mesh into the frame
if (FAILED(myFrame->AddVisual ((LPDIRECT3DRMVISUAL)obj_mesh)))
 return FALSE;
```

And finally, before we leave the routine we need to remember to free all of the objects so we do not have a memory leak!

```
RELEASE (obj_builder);
RELEASE (obj_mesh);
return TRUE;
}
```

The result of this function is the addition of our well object to our scene. The well will appear as shown in figure 5.1.

5.3 Advanced object loading

As you can see, in its most basic form, there are very few lines of code to write if you want to just load an object. But what if you want to do more? This next series of routines will allow you to place an object in front of the camera, or at any *X, Y, Z* position.

They will also allow you to scale your loaded object to a desired scale factor, even allowing for variable scaling in each axis. It is surprising how you can make one object look quite different, almost like a new object, just by using different combinations of scaling factors! Imaginative uses of this capability will save you a lot of modeling time.

The first routine I will introduce is the `LoadObject` routine. I wrote this because I found it quite useful for complex programs to have a one command loader routine to load all of my objects, no matter what type they are!

The structure of this routine is:

```
int LoadObject(char *type, char *name, TutorInfo *info, float scaleX,
        float scaleY, float scaleZ, D3DVALUE x, D3DVALUE y, D3DVALUE z)
```

These arguments accept the type of object we wish to load (mesh, animation set, or frame), the data structure we use to hold all of our main visual objects, the *X, Y,* and *Z* scale factors, and the *X, Y, Z* position of the object. There are a lot of arguments, but it also makes our routine quite powerful. In one call we can load, scale, and position our object!

The routine is shown below and in the next section.

```
// This routine loads the various types of objects
int LoadObject(char *type, char *name, TutorInfo *info, float scaleX,
        float scaleY, float scaleZ, D3DVALUE x, D3DVALUE y, D3DVALUE z)
{
```

5.3.1 Loading textures

If we are loading a mesh object, we first need to create a MeshBuilder object and load the object into it. The `loadTextures` parameter to the `IDirect3DRMMeshbuilder::Load` method below is the callback function we define to load the textures for our object which require special formatting. I have just called the standard `IDirect3DRM::LoadTexture` method, but you can define any special routine you need here. The most common thing you will have this routine do is handle the loading of textures that are not in the .ppm or .bmp formats into a `D3DRMIMAGE` structure and then call the `IDirect3DRM::CreateTexture` method to create your texture from it.

```
HRESULT loadTextures(char *name, void *arg, LPDIRECT3DRMTEXTURE *tex)
{
 // Load standard .ppm and .bmp texture files
 return lpD3DRM->LoadTexture(name, tex);
}
```

The code to load a Mesh object is

```
// If we asked to load a mesh
```

```
if (strcmp (type, "MESH") == 0)
{
        LPDIRECT3DRMMESHBUILDER builder;
        HRESULT rval;
   // and we passed in a name
        if (name)
    {
    // Create a new builder
    if (FAILED(lpD3DRM->CreateMeshBuilder(&builder))) {
     Msg("Failed to create a builder for the new mesh.\n");
                 goto ret_with_error;
    }
    // Load the object
    rval = builder->Load(name, NULL, D3DRMLOAD_FROMFILE, loadTextures, NULL);
    if (rval != D3DRM_OK) {
     Msg("Loading %s failed.\n%s", name, MyErrorToString(rval));
         builder->Release();
       goto ret_with_error;
    }
```

Now that we have loaded the object, we need to position it in our scene. This call to PositionMesh, another one of our routines, places the mesh in our scene by creating a frame, adding the mesh to it, and setting its position. The call to this routine is

```
// Position the object where we requested
 if (!PositionMesh(builder, info, x, y, z)) {
   Msg("Placing the mesh in the scene failed.\n");
 builder->Release();
 goto ret_with_error;
 }
```

5.3.2 Positioning and scaling an object

The actual code for positioning and scaling objects is:

```
//
// Place an object in front of the camera.
//
static BOOL PositionMesh(LPDIRECT3DRMMESHBUILDER mesh, TutorInfo *info,
                  D3DVALUE x, D3DVALUE y, D3DVALUE z)
{
  LPDIRECT3DRMFRAME lpFrame;
  // Create a frame for our object
  if (FAILED(lpD3DRM->CreateFrame(info->scene, &lpFrame)))
    return FALSE;
  // Add the mesh as a visual
  if (FAILED(lpFrame->AddVisual(mesh)))
   return FALSE;
  // Place it at the requested x, y, x position
  if (FAILED(lpFrame->SetPosition(info->camera, x, y, z)))
   return FALSE;
```

```
    lpFrame->Release();
    return TRUE;
}
```

The `CreateFrame` method creates a new child frame for the parent frame, our scene. This child frame inherits the motion attributes of our scene when it is added. Any time you use the `CreateFrame` method to add a child to a parent frame, if that frame is moving, the child will move with the same motion parameters.

The `SetPosition` method sets the position of our frame relative to its frame of reference. It will place it a distance [rvX, rvY, rvZ] from the reference—in our case the camera. The prototype is defined as

```
HRESULT SetPosition(LPDIRECT3DRMFRAME lpRef, D3DVALUE rvX, D3DVALUE rvY,
        D3DVALUE rvZ);
```

After we have placed the object, all that is left is to scale it and release it. The `Scale` method of the Direct3DRMMeshBuilder object scales our object by the supplied values in the *X-*, *Y-*, and *Z-* axes.

The prototype for this method is:

```
HRESULT Scale(D3DVALUE sx, D3DVALUE sy, D3DVALUE sz);
```

Our calling structure, and the releasing of the builder object, is:

```
    // Scale the object to the requested scale
    builder->Scale(scaleX, scaleY, scaleZ);
     builder->Release();
      }
   }
```

5.3.3 *Loading the animation*

The next segment of the `LoadObject` function checks to see if we want to load an AnimationSet object. I will cover animation in detail in chapter 12, but to show the complete object loading process, I will include the call to the `LoadAnimation` routine in the next segment. An AnimationSet object is designed to be used to group Animation objects together, an act which can make the playback of complex animation sequences easier. This object is created by calling the `IDirect3DRM::CreateAnimationSet` method. The code looks like this:

```
    // If we asked to load an animation
    else if (strcmp (type, "ANIMSET") == 0)
     {
      if (name) {
      // Load the requested animation
```

The actual call to the `LoadAnimationSet` function we need to write is:

```
if (LoadAnimationSet(name, info) == FALSE) {
    Msg("Loading and placing of %s failed.\n", name);
  }
 }
}
```

Note that this routine takes two parameters. The routine prototype is:

```
static BOOL LoadAnimationSet(const char *filename, TutorInfo *info);
```

The two parameters are the filename we wish to load and the information structure containing the data structures describing our window, view, and so forth. The routine is:

```
// Load a .x object which was converted as an animation
static BOOL LoadAnimationSet(const char *filename, TutorInfo *info)
{
 LPDIRECT3DRMANIMATIONSET lpAnimSet;
 LPDIRECT3DRMFRAME lpFrame;
```

The first thing we need to do is to create a frame for our animation which is a child of our scene.

```
// Create a new frame for the animation
if (FAILED(lpD3DRM->CreateFrame(info->scene, &lpFrame)))
  return FALSE;
```

Now we can create our AnimationSet object. An IDirect3DRMAnimationSet object is created by a call to the `IDirect3DRM::CreateAnimationSet` method. The prototype of this method is:

```
IDirect3DRM::CreateAnimationSet (LPDIRECT3DRMANIMATIONSET
                                 *lplpD3DRMAnimationSet);
```

The parameter to this method holds the address which we want filled with a pointer to an IDirect3DRMAnimationSet interface when it is successfully created. The call is:

```
if (FAILED(lpD3DRM->CreateAnimationSet(&lpAnimSet)))
  return FALSE;
```

Once our IDirect3DRM::AnimationSet object is created, we need to load our AnimationSet from our data file. The load method is prototyped as:

```
HRESULT Load(LPVOID lpvObjSource, LPVOID lpvObjID,
   D3DRMLOADOPTIONS d3drmLOFlags,
   D3DRMLOADTEXTURECALLBACK d3drmLoadTextureProc, LPVOID lpArgLTP,
   LPDIRECT3DRMFRAME lpParentFrame);
```

The parameters to this method are:

- `lpvObjSource`. This parameter specifies the source of the object we want to load. This can be a file, resource, memory block, or stream, based upon the source flags you specify in the `d3drmLOFlags` parameter.

- `lpvObjID`. The object name or position you wish loaded. This parameter varies based upon the identifier flags you specify in the `d3drmLOFlags` parameter. If you specify the `D3DRMLOAD_BYPOSITION` flag, this parameter is a pointer to a `DWORD` value giving the object's order in the file. You can also set this parameter to NULL.

  Some of the most commonly used flags include `D3DRMLOAD_FROMFILE`, `D3DRM-LOAD_FROMRESOURCE`, `D3DRMLOAD_FROMMEMORY`, and `D3DRMLOAD_FROMSTREAM`.

- `d3drmLOFlags`. This parameter holds the `D3DRMLOADOPTIONS` type value which describes the load options.

- `d3drmLoadTextureProc`. Gives a `D3DRMLOADTEXTURECALLBACK` callback function which is called to load whatever textures are used by the object which require special formatting. You can set this parameter to NULL.

- `lpArgLTP`. Holds the address of your application-defined data to be passed to the `D3DRMLOADTEXTURECALLBACK` callback function.

- `lpParentFrame`. The address of a parent Direct3DRMFrame object. This parameter is used to prevent the frames which are referred to by the animation set from being created with a NULL parent.

This method defaults to loading the first animation set in the file specified by the `lpvObjSource` parameter. The actual code for our program is:

```
// Load the animation file
if (FAILED(lpAnimSet->Load((LPVOID)filename, NULL,
      D3DRMLOAD_FROMFILE, loadTextures,
      NULL, lpFrame)))
  return FALSE;
```

Once we have the frame, we may want to scale it to match the scene we are building. We need to define a routine to handle this, and the call to it is:

```
// Scale the frame
ScaleFrame(lpFrame, info, (D3DVALUE)8.0, (D3DVALUE)0.0, (D3DVALUE)0.0,
      (D3DVALUE)15.0);
```

The actual routine is defined as:

```
static BOOL ScaleFrame(LPDIRECT3DRMFRAME frame, TutorInfo *info, D3DVALUE
      ScaleFact, D3DVALUE x, D3DVALUE y, D3DVALUE z)
{
```

The routine takes the frame we wish to scale, our world information structure, a scale factor, and an *X, Y, Z* position.

The first things we need to do are define the local variables, our MeshBuilder, the object's bounding box, and a max dimension:

```
LPDIRECT3DRMMESHBUILDER mbuilder;
D3DRMBOX box;
D3DVALUE maxDim;

lpD3DRM->CreateMeshBuilder(&mbuilder);
```

The D3DRMMeshBuilder object we create is used to add a frame and get the bounding box for the object. The `IDirect3DRMMeshBuilder::AddFrame` method is prototyped as:

```
HRESULT AddFrame(LPDIRECT3DRMFRAME lpD3DRMFrame);
```

This method takes the frame we wish to add as its parameter and attaches it to our MeshBuilder. The call is:

```
// Add the requested frame to our MeshBuilder object
mbuilder->AddFrame(frame);
```

After the frame has been added to our MeshBuilder, we need to get the bounding box for the object. This method just takes a `D3DRMBOX` structure as a parameter. This structure is described as

```
typedef struct _D3DRMBOX {
 D3DVECTOR min, max;
}D3DRMBOX;
```

This structure contains two vectors which hold the minimum and maximum bounds of the box in the *X-, Y-,* and *Z*-axes. After we get these values. we can release the MeshBuilder object.

```
// Get the bounding box for our object
mbuilder->GetBox(&box);
// Free up the space for our builder
mbuilder->Release();
```

To calculate the dimensions of the box, we just need to subtract the minimum value from the maximum in the *X-, Y-,* and *Z*-axes.

```
// Set the max dimension to the box size
maxDim = box.max.x - box.min.x;
if (box.max.y - box.min.y > maxDim)
 maxDim = box.max.y - box.min.y;
```

```
if (box.max.z - box.min.z > maxDim)
  maxDim = box.max.z - box.min.z;
```

We can pass these maximum dimensions, to the `IDirect3DRMMeshBuilder::AddScale` method. This method scales only our frame's local transformation by (rvX, rvY, rvZ) and is prototyped as:

```
HRESULT AddScale(D3DRMCOMBINETYPE rctCombine, D3DVALUE rvX,
                 D3DVALUE rvY, D3DVALUE rvZ);
```

The parameters to this method are:

- `rctCombine`. A member of the D3DRMCOMBINETYPE enumerated type indicating how we want the new scale combined with the current frame transformation.

- `rvX`, `rvY`, and `rvZ`. Specifies the *X*, *Y*, and *Z* scale factors.

The code to actually add the desired scaling is:

```
// Scale it
frame->AddScale(D3DRMCOMBINE_BEFORE,
    D3DDivide(D3DVAL(ScaleFact), maxDim),
    D3DDivide(D3DVAL(ScaleFact), maxDim),
    D3DDivide(D3DVAL(ScaleFact), maxDim));
```

The final task to perform in this routine is to set the position of the frame relative to our main scene. The new position is set to the passed *X*, *Y*, and *Z* values.

```
frame->SetPosition(info->scene, D3DVAL(x), D3DVAL(y), D3DVAL(z));
```

And that's it. We have the object scaled and positioned. We can return happy!

```
return TRUE;
}
```

Well, we've gotten this far. Our next job is to set the animation callback routine for our frame. This routine takes a pointer to the frame to which we are adding an animation and a pointer to an IDirect3DRMAnimationSet object.

```
// Set up the animation callback
setAnimationCallback(lpFrame, lpAnimSet);
```

We need to create an animation callback structure to hold a pointer to our AnimationSet object and a time slot.

```
// Create our callback argument structures
typedef struct {
  LPDIRECT3DRMANIMATIONSET animset;
  D3DVALUE time;
} animationCallbackArgs;
```

With this defined, we can create our `setAnimationCallback` routine. The `setAnimationCallback` routine is defined as:

```
// Set our animation callback
static BOOL setAnimationCallback(LPDIRECT3DRMFRAME frame,
    LPDIRECT3DRMANIMATIONSET animset)
{
```

All we need to do in this routine is to allocate space for one of the `animationCallbackArgs` structures we just defined:

```
animationCallbackArgs *cb;

cb = (animationCallbackArgs*)malloc(sizeof(animationCallbackArgs));
 if (!cb)
   return FALSE;
```

Once it is created, we can fill up the AnimationSet and time slots:

```
cb->animset = animset;
cb->time = D3DVAL(0);
```

Finally, we can call our frame's method to add this move callback function for the handling of special movement processing. The method to do this is prototyped as:

```
HRESULT AddMoveCallback(D3DRMFRAMEMOVECALLBACK d3drmFMC, VOID * lpArg);
```

The arguments to this method are:

- `d3drmFMC`. Our `D3DRMFRAMEMOVECALLBACK` callback function.
- `lpArg`. The data we defined to be passed to the callback function.

The call structure is:

```
if (FAILED(frame->AddMoveCallback(animationCallback, (void *) cb)))
   return FALSE;
```

The actual callback routine we will define is quite simple. All we are going to do is set the time and increment it to the next time `delta`. This will be used to determine how fast we move to the next position during our animation. If you remember, time is *relative* so how you specify your key frame times is critical to achieving the result you want. The routine is:

```
// Define our animation's callback
static void CDECL animationCallback(LPDIRECT3DRMFRAME obj, void* arg,
        D3DVALUE delta)
{
   animationCallbackArgs* cb = (animationCallbackArgs *) arg;
```

```
  obj = obj;
 cb->animset->SetTime(cb->time);
 cb->time += delta;
}
```

After we have everything completed in our SetAnimationCallback routine, we can return and continue on.

```
return TRUE;
}
```

We can also finish up completely with our task and return in great shape to our main calling routine.

```
return TRUE;
}
```

5.3.4 Loading a frame hierarchy

Well, that was by far the most difficult type of object to load. If you feel comfortable with the animation object loading and handling, you will easily be able to deal with loading any of the objects you will need. If you are still a bit confused, don't worry—I'd recommend going back, rereading the section, and trying to write a simple test routine to load (and maybe display) one animation. Animations look difficult, but once you spend a bit of time with them, they really aren't too tough. I have found the *creation* of these to be the difficult part. 3DStudio will make this task a lot easier, since creating animations is really fairly straightforward. At least with this package, the qualities of your animations are driven by your skills as an artist rather than your ability to battle your way through a poorly written 3D graphics package!

The last type object is a reasonably simple one. If the object we want to load is a frame type, we will call our routine LoadFrameHierarchy. This routine takes the object name and the TutorInfo structure holding our scene information.

```
// If we asked to load a frame
else if (strcmp (type, "FRAME") == 0)
{
  if (name)
  {
    // Load the frame hierarchy

    if (LoadFrameHierarchy(name, info) == FALSE) {
      Msg("Loading and placing of %s failed.\n", name);
    }
  }
}
```

The `LoadFrameHierarchy` routine is used to load a frame hierarchy into our world, place it, and scale it. To do this, we create a frame and load the object into it.

```
// Load a .x object which was converted as a frame hierarchy
static BOOL LoadFrameHierarchy(const char *filename, TutorInfo *info)
{
 LPDIRECT3DRMFRAME lpFrame;

 // Create a new frame for our animation object
 if (FAILED(lpD3DRM->CreateFrame(info->scene, &lpFrame)))
  return FALSE;
```

We will call the `IDirect3DRMFrame::Load` method which defaults to loading the first frame hierarchy in the file specified by the `lpvObjSource` parameter. Our frame calling this method will be used as the parent of the new frame hierarchy.

The `IDirect3DRMFrame::Load` method is prototyped as:

```
HRESULT Load(LPVOID lpvObjSource, LPVOID lpvObjID,
  D3DRMLOADOPTIONS d3drmLOFlags,
  D3DRMLOADTEXTURECALLBACK d3drmLoadTextureProc,
  LPVOID lpArgLTP);
```

The parameters to this method are:

- `lpvObjSource`. This parameter specifies the source for the object we want to load. The source can be a file, resource, memory block, or a stream. Its type is based on the *source flags* we give in the `d3drmLOFlags` parameter.

- `lpvObjID`. This parameter specifies an object name or a position we want loaded. The type of this parameter is based upon the identifier flags we specify in the `d3drmLOFlags` parameter.

  If you specify a `D3DRMLOAD_BYPOSITION` flag, this parameter should hold a pointer to a `DWORD` value specifying our object's order in the file. You can set this value to NULL.

- `d3drmLOFlags`. Gives the value of the `D3DRMLOADOPTIONS` type which describes our load options.

- `d3drmLoadTextureProc`. This parameter specifies a `D3DRMLOADTEXTURECALLBACK` callback function which is used to load any textures used by our object requiring special formatting. You can set this parameter to NULL.

- `lpArgLTP`. Gives the address of our application-defined data which is passed to the `D3DRMLOADTEXTURECALLBACK` callback function.

The actual code to make the call is:

```
// Load the animation
if (FAILED(lpFrame->Load((LPVOID)filename, NULL, D3DRMLOAD_FROMFILE,
```

```
        loadTextures, NULL)))
    return FALSE;
```

With this call we are asking to load the file indicated by the variable *filename*, and use the `loadTextures` routine to load the textures for the object. I mentioned above that I have defined this routine to just call the `IDirect3DRM::LoadTexture` method. Direct3D uses this routine whenever you load an animation, but you only need to define your own routine if you are doing something unique with your textures.

The last thing we need to do when we return to our `LoadFrameHierarchy` routine is to scale our frame to a desired size, position it (I showed this routine to you earlier), and return showing success.

```
    // Scale the frame
    ScaleFrame(lpFrame, info,
          D3DVALUE(8.0),D3DVALUE(0.0),D3DVALUE(0.0),D3DVALUE(15.0));

    return TRUE;
}
```

If everything went well, we can return TRUE from here, and go on with the rest of our program! Also, don't forget to specify the error labels.

```
    return TRUE;
generic_error:
    Msg("A failure occurred while loading our object.\n");
ret_with_error:
    return FALSE;
}
```

5.4 Our new CreateScene routine

Wow! As you can see, that is a lot of code to handle object loading. You probably also noticed that we have added a lot of power to the code by enabling the handling of all of the possible object types. This is a set of capabilities that will help you to create some beautiful scenes and game scenarios. At this point, I would recommend that you spend some time modifying the example code for this chapter to load a variety of combinations of object types. Study the effects of your changes carefully—the order you add objects, the types of objects you choose, and the animation parameters you pick will affect your scene greatly!

Our new `CreateScene` routine creates two light types, a point source and a spot light. We then load the land .x object supplied with DirectX, setting the mesh quality to a flat, unlit model (although I would recommend using a better quality light model), and set our eyepoint by positioning the camera.

The final step we add is the loading of a background texture. This is a new concept, but it is something you will do in most programs since it is a very efficient way of filling in the background which we do not wish to fill with true 3D objects. An example of this is where we generate a 3D landscape but also wish to display mountains or a sky in the background. You would not want to actually generate these in 3D since they are out at a distance where such detail would be a waste of processor power. Instead, you can load a prebuilt picture which is fast and yet still looks realistic. If you want even better realism, you can use DirectDraw to *pan* the picture up, down, left, or right (or a combination thereof) as the eyepoint changes. (I will not go into detail on this since it is really a DirectDraw subject and we do not actually need this for an excellent game.)

The code is:

```
//
// Create a scene with the initial lights
//

BOOL CreateScene(TutorInfo *info)
{
  LPDIRECT3DRMTEXTURE tex;
  LPDIRECT3DRMMESHBUILDER builder = NULL;

  // Create our main scene object
  if (FAILED(lpD3DRM->CreateFrame(NULL, &(info->scene))))
    goto generic_error;

  // Create a camera frame for our scene
  if (FAILED(lpD3DRM->CreateFrame(info->scene, &(info->camera))))
    goto generic_error;
  // Create our lights using the CreateLight routine from chapter 4
  CreateLight("LIGHT_POINT", info->camera, info);
  CreateLight("LIGHT_SPOT", info->scene, info);

LoadObject("MESH", "land4.x", info, (float)50.0, D3DVALUE(0.0),
        D3DVALUE(0.0), D3DVALUE(150.0));

  // Position the camera
  if (FAILED(info->camera->SetPosition(info->scene, D3DVALUE(0.0),
        D3DVALUE(0.0), D3DVALUE(-10.0))))
    goto generic_error;
```

At this point we will load our background image. We first need to load our picture, which for our demo will be the lake.ppm file supplied with DirectX.

```
lpD3DRM->LoadTexture("lake.ppm", &tex);
```

The actual call to load the background image is:

```
if (FAILED(info->scene->SetSceneBackgroundImage(tex)))
  goto generic_error;
```

If the image is a different size or color depth than the viewport, it will first be scaled or converted to the correct depth. For best performance when animating the background, the image should be the same size and color depth. This enables the background to be rendered directly from the image memory without incurring any extra overhead.

The parameter to the `IDirect3DRMFrame::SetSceneBackgroundImage` method is

- `lpTexture`. The address of a Direct3DRMTexture object you wish filled with the new background scene.

Finally, we should just clean up after ourselves and return happy.

```
    RELEASE(tex);

    return TRUE;

generic_error:
  Msg("A failure occurred while creating the scene.\n");

    return FALSE;
}
```

That is all there is to loading an object file in our DirectX program. But, although you now know *how* to load a file in the DirectX file format, you still do not know how a .x file is *formatted* or how to *create* one. The next two sections will show you the structure of a .x file, a question that was unanswered in the Direct3D development world for some time, and how to create your own .x files using 3D Studio or 3D Studio MAX.

5.5 The DirectX file object format— a description

The DirectX file format is quite powerful! It is a template-driven file format which allows us to add meshes, textures, user-definable objects, and animations to our object. You can use instancing and hierarchies, allowing for multiple references to a single object while only needing to store the object's data once. Direct3D can even read and write our .x files in real time as we generate them in our programs!

The DirectX file format provides support for animation sets which can hold paths that we compute and store allowing for real-time playback. The file format gives us low-level primitives which we can have our applications build upon to generate higher level primitives using templates. This is the same technique Direct3D uses to create higher level primitives like matrices, meshes, and animations. The files we create are accessed by Direct3D's Retained-Mode programs using the DirectX file format API. All of the DirectX file format templates are shown in Chapter 38.

5.5.1 The DirectX file format

The DirectX file format is composed of a variety of components. These components are described in the following sections.

The header

There are *several parts* to any DirectX file. The first part, which must *always* be included at the *top* of the file is the *header*. The header is made up of the components shown in table 5.1.

All of the data in the table are required, except the compression type, which is only specified if your file uses compression. As an example, if your header, the first line in your file, were specified as

```
xof 0302bin zip 0064
```

it would indicate that your file contained a DirectX object with a major version of 03, and a minor version of 02, that the file is in a binary format, that it is zipped, and that it uses 64 bit floats.

Comments

When you specify text file format, you may also use comments anywhere in your file. The DirectX file format allows the use of both the standard C++ // operator or a hash character, #, to specify a comment. These comments, as with C++, run to the next new line.

Table 5.1 DirectX file header

Type	Sub type	Size	Contents	Description
Magic number		4 bytes	"xof"	
Version number	Major number	2 bytes	03	Major version 3
	Minor number	2 bytes	02	Minor version 2
Format type		4 bytes	"txt"	Text file
			"bin"	Binary file
			"com"	Compressed file
Compression type		4 bytes	"lzw"	
			"zip"	
			etc...	
Float size		4 bytes	0064	64-bit float
			0032	32-bit float

Templates

The DirectX file format uses templates to specify how our data stream is to be interpreted. A template is composed as described below:

```
template <template-name> {
    <UUID>
    <member 1>;
    ...
    <member n>;
    [restrictions]
}
```

These components are defined below in the following sections.

Table 5.2 Primitive data types

Type	Size
WORD	16 bits
DWORD	32 bits
FLOAT	IEEE float
DOUBLE	64 bits
CHAR	8 bits
UCHAR	8 bits
BYTE	8 bits
STRING	NULL terminated string
CSTRING	Formatted C-String
UNICODE	UNICODE string

Template Name   The template name is an alphanumeric value which can include the underscore character _ and cannot begin with a digit.

UUID   This field optionally specifies a universally unique identifier. It is framed by the angle brackets < and >. Each of the template UUIDs are shown in chapter 38.

Members   Template members are composed of a named data type followed by an optional name or an array of a named data type. The primitive data types are listed in table 5.2.

You can also use templates to define other data types, which may then be used by templates later in the file description (since no forward references are allowed). You can use any valid data type as an array in your template definitions using the following syntax:

```
array <data-type> <name>[<dimension-size>];
```

`<dimension-size>` is allowed to be either an integer or a named reference to another template member. The value of this template member is substituted for this reference when it is used.

You can specify variables as any standard C/C++ *n*-dimensional array, such as

```
array INT My2DimArray[5][12];
array DWORD My1DimArray[60];
```

Open, closed, or restricted templates   Your templates can be defined as *open*, *closed*, or *restricted*. These three types are defined as follows:

An *open* template is a template with no restrictions. It is indicated by three periods enclosed by square brackets:

```
[...]
```

An example of an open template is:

```
template myTemplate {
    FLOAT myVar1;
    FLOAT myVar2;
    FLOAT myVar3;
    [...]
}
```

A *closed* template is a template which rejects all data types. A closed template is specified by using no indicator, for example, no [...].

An example of a closed template is:

```
template myTemplate {
    FLOAT myVar1;
    FLOAT myVar2;
    FLOAT myVar3;
}
```

A *restricted* template specifies which of the data types are allowed to appear in the immediate hierarchy of a data object defined by your template. This template uses a named list of data types and is specified by using a comma separated list of named data types *optionally* followed by their UUIDs enclosed in square brackets:

```
[{data-type [UUID] ,}... ]
```

An example of a restricted template is

```
template FileSystem {
    <UUID>
    STRING name;
    [Directory <UUID>, File <UUID>]
}
```

You should define one final type of template for each of your applications, the header template, for use in defining application-specific information (version information, etc.). If this header exists in a file, and a *flags* member (which should be a DWORD) is available, the system will use this to determine how to interpret the data. One bit, bit 0, is defined currently. If it is 0, the data following it in the file is binary. If it is 1, the data following is text. You can use multiple header data objects to switch between binary and text within the file.

5.5.2 Data

You use data objects in your DirectX files to hold actual data, or else a reference to that data. These data objects each have a template specifying the data type.

The data objects take the form of

```
<Identifier>[name]{
    [UUID]
    <member 1];
    ...
    <member n>;
```

5.5.3 Identifier

A *required,* previously defined, data type or primitive.

5.5.4 Name

An optional name for the data object.

5.5.5 UUID

An optional unique identifier.

5.5.6 Data members

- *Data object.* This nested data object provides the manner in which the hierarchical aspect of the file format can be defined. These types can be restricted using a restricted template as you saw above.

- *Data reference.* Specifies a reference to a previously defined data object. It is defined as

```
{ name [, <UUID> ]}
```

- Integer list. A list of integers separated by semicolons such as:

```
4; 8; 3; 33; 6;
```

- *Float list.* A list of floats separated by semicolons such as:

```
4.1; 8.99; 3.2; 33.7; 6.4;
```

- *String list.* A list of strings separated by semicolons such as:

```
"Peter"; "Monica";"Shannon";
```

5.5.7 Commas and semicolons

Commas in this file are used to delineate array members. Semicolons are used after every data item. To help illustrate the above format information in actual use, if you have a template such as:

```
template myTemplate1 {
    FLOAT myFloat1;
}
```

you would specify an instance of it as:

```
myTemplate {
    3.126556;
}
```

If you define a template which contains another template, such as:

```
template myTemplate2 {
    int var1;
    DWORD var2;
}

template myTemplate3 {
    DWORD aVar5;
    myTemplate2 myTemp;
}
```

you would define an instance of it as:

```
myTemplate3 aTemp3Instance{
    2;
    75;
    55;;
}
```

You probably noticed the *two* semicolons after the last element in the description above. The first semicolon specifies the end of the data item, and the second specifies the end of the template.

If you wish to specify an array, you would do it as follows:

```
Template myArray {
    array DWORD var1[5];
}
```

Array data items are separated by commas so you do not have to use the semi colon except as the indicator of the end of the array.

To create an instance of an array, you would code it as:

```
myArray
{
    6,2,8,4,2;
}
```

5.5.8 An example DirectX file

Let's walk through an example file which creates a rectangle, attaches textures, and animates the object.

The header

The header, the first line of our file, for our application is a simple statement. It is

```
xof 0302txt 0064
```

Here, we are just stating that the file is a DirectX file with a Major Version of 3, a Minor Version of 2, the file is in text format, and it uses 64-bit floats.

Materials

The next lines are *comment* lines They use the standard C++ specification.

```
// Create a Blue Material.
```

The first thing we need to create are the materials we will use on our object. To create a material, we need to specify an RGBA Color, the specular exponent, the specular color, and the emissive color of the material.

The Material specification is as follows:

```
Material BlueMaterial {
    0.000000;0.000000;1.000000;1.000000;; // ColorRGBA R = 0.0, G = 0.0.,
                                           // B = 1.0, A = 1.0
    0.000000;  // Power - Specular exponent of the material
    0.000000;0.000;0.000000;; // specularColor - ColorRGB
    0.000000;0.000;0.000000;; // emissiveColor - ColorRGB
    TextureFilename {
      "tex3.ppm";
    }
}
```

You will also notice that the Material template is a nested template. It contains the simple template, TextureFilename, defined as:

Member name	Type
filename	STRING

The filename is stored as a standard string. Thus, the TextureFilename template specifies that we wish to attach the tex3.ppm file as the texture map.

We also want to define a second Material and Texture, so that we can apply a few different appearances to our rectangles faces. It is very similar to those just specified, and looks like:

```
Material PurpleMaterial {
    1.000000;0.000000;1.000000;1.000000;; // R = 0.0, G = 0.0. B = 1.0
    0.000000;                             // Specular exponent of the material
    0.000000;0.000000;0.000000;;          // Specular color - ColorRGB
    0.000000;0.000000;0.000000;;          // Emissive color - ColorRGB
    TextureFilename {
    "tex6.ppm";
    }
}
```

A Mesh

Now that we have our *textures* and *materials* defined, we can add any other objects. For our demonstration, we first wish to define a mesh describing our desired rectangle. The *Mesh* template, which has two other nested templates, is described as:

```
// Specify a rectangle mesh. This has 8 vertices and 12 triangular faces.
// You can use optional data objects in the mesh to specify materials,
// normals, and texture coordinates.

Mesh MyRectMesh {
```

The following several lines specify the vertices, faces, materials, and texture coordinates for our rectangular object. It is fairly straightforward and thus I have just listed it below for your review:

```
    8;                              // Specify the 8 vertices of the rectangle
    1.000000;2.000000;-2.000000;,    // Vertex 1
    -1.000000;2.000000;-2.000000;,   // Vertex 2
    -1.000000;2.000000;2.000000;,    // .
    1.000000;2.000000;2.000000;,     // .
    1.000000;-2.000000;-2.000000;,
    -1.000000;-2.000000;-2.000000;,
    -1.000000;-2.000000;2.000000;,
    1.000000;-2.000000;2.000000;,

    12;                             // It has 12 faces (2 triangles per side)
    3;0,1,2;,                        // Each face has 3 vertices
    3;0,2,3;,
    3;0,4,5;,
    3;0,5,1;,
    3;1,5,6;,
    3;1,6,2;,
    3;2,6,7;,
    3;2,7,3;,
    3;3,7,4;,
    3;3,4,0;,
    3;4,7,6;,
    3;4,6,5;;

// Now we define the optional data
```

```
MeshMaterialList {
2;  // Number of materials we are using
12; // One material for each of the faces (each face is composed of 2
        triangles)
0,  // One material for each face - either material 0 or 1
0,
0,
0,
0,
0,
0,
1,
1,
1,
1,
1;;
{BlueMaterial}// The materials we defined above
{PurpleMaterial}
}

    MeshTextureCoords {
       8;
       0.000000;1.000000;                 // Define the texture coords
       1.000000;1.000000;                 // for each vertex
       0.000000;1.000000;
       1.000000;1.000000;
       0.000000;0.000000;
       1.000000;0.000000;
       0.000000;0.000000;
       1.000000;0.000000;;
    }
  }

Frame MyRectFrame {
 FrameTransformMatrix {
    1.000000, 0.000000, 0.000000, 0.000000,
    0.000000, 1.000000, 0.000000, 0.000000,
    0.000000, 0.000000, 1.000000, 0.000000,
    0.000000, 0.000000, 0.000000, 1.000000;;
 }
 // You can have the mesh inline, but here
 // we will use an object reference
 {MyRectMesh}
}
```

5.5.9 An AnimationSet in your file

The following segment of the DirectX file is the one area which is going to be completely new to you. So, let's break it down into its components:

This first line defines a D3DRMAnimationSet containing a nested animation. I have just specified a set of position keys for now. These are used to position the texture mapped rectangle through a series of animation frames. The one thing you should try to remember, since it is not immediately obvious, is that the position keys are all relative time references. By specifying my first keys close together in time (100, 101, 102) and then specifying the others 100 apart, the speed of the motion is fairly slow, because you have now set up a large number of *relative ticks* (number of time elements for that segment) compared to a very few when there is the same distance between your numbers/keys (0,100,200,300,...). By putting a small difference between some and a big difference between others, we can slow or speed our animation. The easiest way to understand this is to build and run the example project for this chapter. You will see the rectangular object move from left to right across the screen at a slow rate. Change the numbers to be 100 apart and you will see the rectangle fly across the screen very quickly. So, when you set up your position keys, remember that the time specification needs to always be considered thoroughly.

```
AnimationSet MyAnimationSet {
 Animation MyAnimation {
  {MyRectFrame}
  AnimationKey {
   2;          // The position keys
   11;         // keys
   100; 3; -50.000000, 0.000000, 0.000000;;,
   101; 3; -50.000000, 0.000000, 0.000000;;,
   102; 3; -50.000000, 0.000000, 0.000000;;,
   200; 3; -50.000000, 0.000000, 0.0000000;;,
   300; 3; -40.000000, 0.0000000, 0.000000;;,
   400; 3; -25.500000, 0.000000, 0.000000;;,
   500; 3; 0.000000, 0.000000, 0.000000;;,
   600; 3; 25.500000, 0.000000, 0.000000;;,
   700; 3; 50.000000, 0.0000000, 0.0000000;;,
   800; 3; 75.500000, 0.500000, 0.000000;;,
   1200; 3; 100.00000, 0.000000, 0.000000;;;
  }
 }
}
```

When you run the program for this chapter, you will see a screen similar to the one shown in figure 5.2.

And that is it for the DirectX file format! It is a very powerful format as I mentioned before and experimentation is the best way to learn it.

5.6 Using .3ds files and 3D Studio

As you have seen, creating a DirectX file by hand can be a lot of work if we do not have code written to automate the process. Many times we will need some complex objects that

Figure 5.2 Our Direct X file in action

it is just not feasible for us to create algorithmically. To address this, Microsoft has provided us with a tool to convert a 3D Studio (.3ds) file to the DirectX file format (.x).

conv3ds is a standalone program which you can use by just typing the executables name followed by a combination of options and the file you wish to convert. This tool has several options available for converting files. These options and their meaning are

(None)   Creates a binary *X* file containing hierarchy of frames with no templates. Use `Frame::Load` to load the frame:

```
conv3ds myFile.3ds
```

-A   Convert a .3ds file containing key frame data to an *X* file containing an animation set. Use `AnimationSet::Load` to load the animation:

```
conv3ds -A myFile.3ds
```

-c   Requests that the output X file not contain texture coordinates. The output file will contain 0,0 UV texture coordinates if the 3ds object has no texture coordinates:

```
conv3ds -c myFile.3ds
```

-e   Specifies that you wish to use a different extension for texture map files:

```
conv3ds -e"ppm" myFile.3ds
```

As an example, if you used this option and your file contains references to the texture map file stone.gif, the *X* file would change the output to reference the texture map file stone.ppm. Keep in mind that the actual texture file is *not* converted so you must do this using one of the many existing tools. You must also make sure the file is in one of the directories specified in the D3DPATH when the *X* file is loaded.

-f   States that the X file should not contain any FrameTransformMatrix:

```
conv3ds -f myFile.3ds
```

-h   Requests that the converter not try to resolve any hierarchy information which is usually produced by the keyframer. All of the objects are output as top level frames (if not used with the -m option). Please look back at *chapter 5* for a description of the D3DRMLOAD_BYPOSITION flag that allows us to load each of the objects this option will create in the file:

```
conv3ds -h myFile.3ds
```

-m   Create an *X* file containing a single mesh created from all of the objects in the .3ds file. Use MeshBuilder::Load to load the mesh:

```
conv3ds -m myFile.3ds
```

-N   Specifies that the output *X* file will not contain normal information. All of the D3DRM load calls you make will generate the normals for these objects, since there will be none in the created *X* file.

```
conv3ds -N myFile.3ds
```

-o   Allows you to specify the filename for the produced X File:

```
conv3ds -o myNewFile.x myFile.3ds
```

-r   Reverses the winding order of the faces when the .3ds file is converted. This option should be used when you convert an object and find that the object looks inside-out when viewing it in your Direct3D application. All of the objects created by Lightwave and exported as .3ds files will require you to use this option:

```
conv3ds -r myFile.3ds
```

-s   Specifies a scale factor for all of the objects in the file. The following make the object five times bigger:

```
Conv3ds -s5 myFile.3ds
```

The following make the object one-fifth the original size:

```
Conv3ds -s.2 myFile.3ds
```

-t   States that the output *X* file will not contain texture information:

```
conv3ds -t myFile.3ds
```

-T   Wraps all of the objects and frame hierarchies in a single *top level* frame. This option allows you to load all of the frames and objects in the .3ds file with one call to `Frame::Load`. The top level frame containing all of the other frames and meshes is named x3ds_filename. This option has no effect when used with the -m option.

```
conv3ds -T myFile.3ds
```

-v   Turns on the verbose output mode. This option also requires a number with it, as follows:

     v0   Default

     -v1   Prints out general information on what the converter is doing and bad object warnings.

```
conv3ds -v1 myFile.3ds
```

     -v2   Prints out the basic keyframe information, information about the objects while they are being saved, and information about the objects being included in the conversion process.

```
conv3ds -v2 myFile.3ds
```

     -v3   The most verbose mode for debugging purposes.

```
conv3ds -v3 myFile.3ds
```

-x   Forces the output of a *text* *X* file rather than a binary one. The obvious reason for using this option is to allow you to edit a file, which would not be possible in the binary format. Remember, though, that the text format is larger than the binary format.

```
conv3ds -x myFile.3ds
```

-X   Forces the output to include the D3DRM *X* File templates in the file since these are not included in the default mode.

```
conv3ds -X myFile.3ds
```

-Z or -z   Use these two flags together to adjust the alpha face color value of all of the materials referenced by objects in the file. -z is used to set the face color alpha delta between 0 and 1. -Z is used to set the maximum alpha value to be effected by the delta you set with the -z option. The following command requests that 0.1 be added to all alpha values under 0.3:

```
conv3ds -z0.1 -Z0.3 myFile.3ds
```

The next command requests that 0.1 be subtracted from all alpha values:

```
conv3ds -z"-0.1" -z1 myFile.3ds
```

Conv3ds hints

If textures do not get loaded after you convert the object, make sure the object is referencing either .ppm or .bmp files by using the -e option. You must also verify that the textures have width and heights which are a power of 2. Finally, make sure the texture files are in a directory specified in your D3DPATH.

If you are converting objects exported by the trans3d plug-in for Lightwave, you should use the following command since the objects must have their winding order reversed:

```
conv3ds -r -N -f -h -Tm myTrans3dFile.3ds
```

If you cannot see your object after converting it, try scaling it using the -s option with a large scale factor, such as 100.

If you load your object and the object turns dark grey when you switch between flat and Gouraud shading, try using the -N object when converting the object.

3D Studio

The conv3ds tool works very well in converting .3ds files, but of course using this tool requires that you either have a number of prebuilt objects, (which of course means you will be restricted to these objects until you buy or find others), or that you purchase a 3D graphic tool to create your own objects. There are a large number of 3D graphic tools, with a variety of capabilities and prices. Kinetix has developed and is marketing 3D Studio MAX, an excellent, completely redesigned package from its predecessor, 3D Studio R4. 3D Studio now outputs .3ds.max files rather than .3ds files, but luckily they have also allowed us to export files in the older .3ds format. These can then be converted to .x files using the conv3ds tool supplied with Direct3D. The main screen provided by 3D Studio, with the Object Type subwindow displayed, is shown in figure 5.3.

As you can see, there are a lot of features provided with this tool. Although at first it might seem a little daunting, Kinetix has done a wonderful job of making such a powerful tool easy to use. I have used almost every 3D graphic tool on the market today, and for the PC market, I feel that 3D Studio is the best overall tool you can buy. Some of the features provided in 3D Studio are object-oriented design, modeling and editing, materials definition, animation, rendering, and the use of plug-ins.

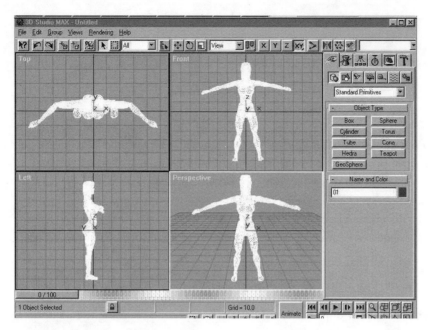

Figure 5.3 The 3D Studio main screen

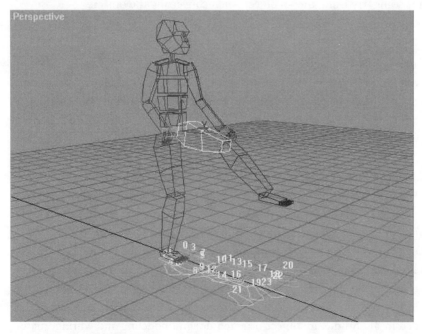

Figure 5.4 The Character Studio screen

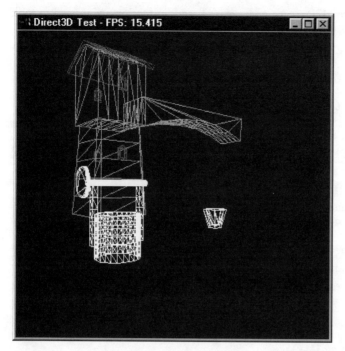

Figure 5.5 A wireframe view of our loaded objects

Plug-ins are one of the most important features provided by 3D Studio. This feature allows third-party developers to create new features which can be plugged into 3D Studio. There are dozens of commercial and public domain plug-ins available.

One of the plug-ins Kinetix has developed is a fantastic 3D character creation tool called Character Studio. This package is composed of two modules—Biped and Physique. The Biped Module allows you to create a biped character and use footstep timing and placement to control the motion of it. The Physique modifier allows you to attach a skinned object to a Biped Skeleton system. Together you can create incredibly realistic biped motion including muscle motion! Currently only the animated biped exports to DirectX format. The Physique mesh will not convert because the mesh modifiers are not handled with the conv3ds tool.

An example screen showing a loaded mesh before attaching the skeleton is shown in figure 5.4.

You will find numerous features in Character Studio which are not found anywhere else in the PC market. Some incredibly useful features include stride length, time to next footstep, and center of mass position. This type of footstep-based animation makes it very simple to create totally realistic animation of human, alien, and even dinosaur characters! If you are interested in creating character based animations, you need to look at this plug-in! Remember though that there is still a lot of work to change a standard biped into a different object (by modifying its parts appearances).

5.7 What does our application look like now?

The screen shown in figure 5.5 shows our view of the world after we have loaded some DirectX objects. You will notice that I have rendered it in wireframe mode. The commands to do this are:

```
D3DRMRENDERQUALITY quality = D3DRMRENDER_WIREFRAME;
builder->SetQuality(quality);
```

You can set the render quality for each object so that if you want one object rendered in wire frame mode and one in Gouraud, all you need to do is set the quality for each object's mesh builder to the desired quality. If you set the render mode using the following commands

```
D3DRMRENDERQUALITY quality = D3DRMRENDER_GOURAUD;
builder->SetQuality(quality);
```

the output of the scene will look as shown in figure 5.6.

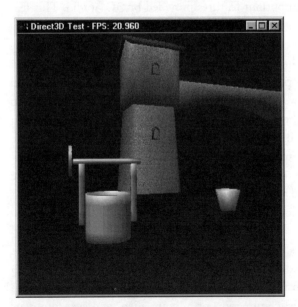

Figure 5.6 A Gouraud shaded view of our loaded objects

5.8 What did we learn?

In this chapter, we covered the creation and use of the Mesh and MeshBuilder objects. These two objects are the basis of all visual objects we will be creating for our virtual worlds. We also covered the design and details of the DirectX file format. We discussed 3D Studio and how we can use it to create objects for our virtual world with numerous attributes including animations. Finally, we briefly looked at Character Studio, a 3D Studio plug-in providing an excellent biped animation facility.

5.9 What's next?

In chapter 6 we will add keyboard and mouse input support for our program. Up until now, we have only been able to look at our objects, without having any ability to move the object or our viewpoint. In this chapter you will learn to create an input handler supporting both keyboard and mouse input—two features required for us to be able to create a useful 3D game!

chapter 6

Adding keyboard and mouse control

6.1 Keyboard input overview

Up until now we have only placed some lights and a few prebuilt objects in our world. Although this would be fine if our application were designed only to produce a static image we wished to screen dump and print, or maybe a demo requiring no user interaction, our goal is to learn how to make great real-time 3D graphics programs! To help you get to that point, we need to add some way for the user to control our world and movement through it.

The most standard, and certainly oldest, method is through the use of keyboard keys assigned various meanings, for example $\Leftarrow$ = left, $\Uparrow$ = up, $\Rightarrow$ = right, and $\Downarrow$ = down, o = open, and so forth. Other input devices and methods include a mouse, joysticks, pedals, rudders, and even head tracking. We will focus on handling keyboard input in the first portion of this chapter.

6.2 What can we do with keyboard input?

If you chose to use keyboard input as your *only* input method, you could make a perfectly enjoyable game! Actually, many of the first person perspective games today are designed to run perfectly with the keyboard as the sole input. There are even many games that allow for two players using a single keyboard, although this often becomes burdensome.

The key thing to consider when planning for keyboard input for your program is that you must make it as easy as possible for the user to switch between the keys. Many people are not touch typists and thus need to either think a bit about, or look at, the keyboard to find the next key. Thus, you should choose logical groupings of keys. This means that motion keys should be next to one another, such as the ⇐, ⇑, ⇒, ⇓, grouping or a *I,J,K,M* grouping.

6.3 Adding the keyboard event handler to our code

The task of writing the code for handling keyboard input is really quite an easy one! One thing we have to make sure of though is that you feel comfortable with the `Window-Proc` routine we wrote in chapter 2. This routine is our *event handler* and so far what we have used it for is to intercept and interpret the system messages and perform the appropriate actions.

This routine is quite extensible and we will use it for handling all of our events. This routine will be familiar to all of you who have programmed in Windows since it is a required routine for any Windows application. For those of you who have come from the UNIX world, you can think of it as the same as what was known as your *event handler* since it serves the same purpose.

For now, let's just add the keyboard event handling. To start with, we want to know any time the user depresses a key. Understand that this means that this event occurs *as soon as* the user depresses the key. It does not wait until the key is released. You need to remember this, because there are several applications out there that wait until the users *releases* the key, some of your users may find this action unexpected.

The code to handle key presses is:

```
case WM_KEYDOWN:
  {
```

As an example of an action you might wish to take when a key is depressed (and I don't mean it's feeling bad!), I have written code that creates the motion vectors and moves the camera whenever you depress the key.

Creating the motion vectors is simple. All you need to remember is that the Direct3D type for a vector is D3DVECTOR. The Direct3D definition is

```
typedef struct _D3DVECTOR {
 union {
  D3DVALUE x;
  D3DVALUE dvX;
 };
 union {
  D3DVALUE y;
  D3DVALUE dvY;
 };
 union {
  D3DVALUE z;
  D3DVALUE dvZ;
 };
} D3DVECTOR, *LPD3DVECTOR;
```

The dvX, dvY, and dvZ slots are D3DVALUE types which hold the *x*, *y*, and *z* values describing the vector. The line to define it in your code is

```
// Define the direction, up, and down vectors for motion information
D3DVECTOR direction, up, right;
```

Whenever a key is pressed, we need to retrieve the orientation of our camera frame relative to the scene's reference frame. This function will return the direction of the frames's *Z*-axis in the direction parameter and the frame's *Y*-axis in the up parameter. These are returned in the *direction* and *up* vectors we have defined, respectively.

The code to acquire the camera's orientation is:

```
// Get the orientation of the camera frame relative to the scene
information->camera->GetOrientation(information->scene, &direction, &up);
```

The IDirectDRMFrame::GetOrientation method of the camera frame is prototyped as:

```
HRESULT GetOrientation(LPDIRECT3DRMFRAME lpRef, LPD3DVECTOR lprvDir,
 LPD3DVECTOR lprvUp);
```

The parameters are:

- lpRef. This parameter holds the address of the Direct3DRMFrame object variable you wish to use as your reference.

- lprvDir, lprvUp. These two parameters contain the addresses of two D3DVECTOR structures we want to be filled with the directions of the frame's *z*- and *y*-axes.

The next thing we want is the camera's position. The IDirectDRMFrame::GetPosition method allows us to get the position of one frame relative to another reference frame. Remember that this distance is then placed in the lprvPos parameter as a vector, not as a linear distance. The parameters to IDirectDRMFrame::GetPosition are:

- lpRef. This parameter holds the address of the Direct3DRMFrame object variable we wish to use as the reference.

- lprvPos. The address of a D3DVECTOR structure we want filled with the frame's position.

Our call is:

```
// Get the position of the camera frame relative to the scene
information->camera->GetPosition (information->scene, &pos);
```

After we have the camera's position, we need to compute the right vector for our frame using the cross product of our up and direction vectors. For this example we will just divide the vector values by 4.5 for when we hit a key later.

The function to calculate the vector cross product is defined as:

```
LPD3DVECTOR D3DRMVectorCrossProduct(    LPD3DVECTOR lpd,
                                        LPD3DVECTOR lps1,
                                        LPD3DVECTOR lps2);
```

The parameters to this routine are:

- lpd. The address of a D3DVECTOR structure to fill with the result of the cross product.

- lps1 and lps2. The addresses of the D3DVECTOR structures whose cross product we wish to calculate.

The call to do this calculation is:

```
// Calculate the vector cross product of the up and direction vectors to
// produce the right vector
D3DRMVectorCrossProduct(&right, &up, &direction);
```

We also need to recalculate the up and right vectors to a lesser value.

```
// Recompute the vectors values
up.x /= D3DVAL(4.5);
up.y /= D3DVAL(4.5);
up.z /= D3DVAL(4.5);
```

```
right.x /= D3DVAL(4.5);
right.y /= D3DVAL(4.5);
right.z /= D3DVAL(4.5);
```

6.3.1 Acting upon the key presses

In the example code, I have used the same keys as Microsoft does for its examples. There is no reason to do this except that the typical Direct3D user is familiar with these keys and thus will not have to relearn the key meanings. Also, the key choices are as logical and organized as most other choices. You are certainly able to use any keys you desire, so feel free to change these.

If the user hit's a *T*, we will want to move forward one step for each key press. To do this, we need to pass the `SetVelocity` message to our camera object.

The `IDirectDRMFrame::SetVelocity` method is defined as:

```
HRESULT SetVelocity(LPDIRECT3DRMFRAME lpRef, D3DVALUE rvX,
                    D3DVALUE rvY, D3DVALUE rvZ, BOOL fRotVel);
```

The parameters to this method are:

- `lpRef`. The address of the Direct3DRMFrame object you want to use as the reference.

- `rvX`, `rvY`, and `rvZ`. The frame's new velocity.

- `fRotVel`. A flag indicating if we wish the rotational velocity of the object to be used when the linear velocity is set. If this flag is set to TRUE, the rotational velocity of the object is included in the calculation.

The code to handle the *T* key press is:

```
// Check for any keyboard key depression
switch (wparam)
{
// If the user hits 'T', sets the velocity of the camera frame relative
// to the scene to the value in the direction vector.
case 'T':
  information->camera->SetVelocity(information->scene, direction.x,
       direction.y, direction.z, FALSE);
  break;
```

If the user hits a *Y*, we want to move backward continuously so we reverse our velocity and start moving backward. We use the `SetVelocity` method you just learned.

```
// If the user hits 'Y', reverse the velocity of the camera relative to
       the scene by a larger
// amount
  case 'Y':
```

```
information->camera->SetVelocity(information->scene, D3DVAL(-100.0) *
    direction.x,
  D3DVAL(-100.0) * direction.y,
  D3DVAL(-100.0) * direction.z, FALSE);
```

If the user hits an *R*, we just want to reverse our velocity and go back one step for each key press.

```
// If the user hits 'R', sets the velocity of the camera frame relative
// to the scene to the reverse value of the direction vector.
case 'R':
 information->camera->SetVelocity(information->scene, -direction.x,
     -direction.y, -direction.z, FALSE);
 break;
```

If the user hits an *E*, we want to start moving forward continuously.

```
// If the user hits 'E', set the velocity of the camera relative to the
// scene to a larger amount
case 'E':
 information->camera->SetVelocity(information->scene, D3DVAL(100.0) *
     direction.x,
   D3DVAL(100.0) * direction.y,
   D3DVAL(100.0) * direction.z, FALSE);
```

If we hit the up arrow, we will move our view forward at the velocity we computed above.

```
// If the up arrow is hit, move forward
case VK_UP:
     MoveForward (direction);
 break;
```

If we hit the down arrow, we will move our view backward at the velocity we computed above.

```
// If the down arrow is hit, move backward
case VK_DOWN:
     MoveBackward (direction);
 break;
```

If we hit the right arrow, we rotate our view to the right.

```
// If the right arrow is hit, rotate to the right
case VK_RIGHT:
     TurnRight (D3DVAL (0.1));
 break;
```

If we hit the left arrow, we will rotate our view to the left.

```
     // If the left arrow is hit, rotate to the left
     case VK_LEFT:
             TurnLeft (D3DVAL (0.1));
      break;
      }
     }
     break;
```

The calls made in our keyboard handler above, MoveForward, MoveBackward, Turn-Right, TurnLeft, StopMove, all do the actual handling of our motion using the SetVelocity and SetRotation methods. We haven't used the SetRotation method before.

The IDirect3DRMFrame::SetRotation method is called when we want to start a frame rotating around a specified vector. The rvTheta parameter specifies the rotation angle in radians we want to move the object each time the IDirect3DRM::Tick or IDirect3DRMFrame::Move method is called. The direction vector we wish to use, [rvX, rvY, rvZ], is defined in the reference frame.

The prototype of this method is:

```
HRESULT SetRotation(LPDIRECT3DRMFRAME lpRef, D3DVALUE rvX, D3DVALUE rvY,
    D3DVALUE rvZ, D3DVALUE rvTheta);
```

The routines we need to define are shown below. Notice that I have defined global variables to hold the camera, scene, and so forth. so we don't have to pass the information structure I have been using up until now. Since *camera* and *information->camera* are equivalent and not many extra keystrokes, it is up to you to decide if you want to use global variables or not.

```
void MoveForward (D3DVECTOR v)
{
 camera->SetVelocity(scene, v.x, v.y, v.z, FALSE);
}

void MoveBackward (D3DVECTOR v)
{
 camera->SetVelocity(scene, -v.x, -v.y, -v.z, FALSE);
}

void TurnRight (D3DVALUE a)
{
 camera->SetRotation (scene, D3DVAL (0.0), D3DVAL (1.0), D3DVAL (0.0), a);
}

void TurnLeft (D3DVALUE a)
{
 camera->SetRotation (scene, D3DVAL (0.0), D3DVAL (1.0), D3DVAL (0.0), -a);
}

void StopMove (void)
```

```
{
camera->SetRotation (scene, D3DVAL (0.0),
    D3DVAL (1.0),
    D3DVAL (0.0),
    D3DVAL (0.0));
camera->SetVelocity (scene, D3DVAL(0.0), D3DVAL(0.0), D3DVAL(0.0), FALSE);
}
```

The next event we need to handle is the Key Up (or key released) event. One of the situations where you will want to handle both key up and down events is where you want to move an object while you hold the key down and have it stop moving when you release it.

In this example, when the user releases a key, we sometimes just want to stop moving so we set our velocity vectors to zero. This happens when we are using the *T* and *R* keys because we only want to move one step. Since the *E* key is used to move forward *continuously* and the *Y* key is used to move backward *continuously*, we do *not* want to check for them since we want to keep moving.

```
// If the user releases a key, see which one it was and do the
// appropriate action
case WM_KEYUP:
  switch (wparam)
  {
  case 'T':
  case 'R':
  case VK_UP:
  case VK_DOWN:
  case VK_LEFT:
  case VK_RIGHT:
    // Set the velocity of the camera to zero to stop our movement
    StopMove();
    break;
  }
  break;
```

Well, that is it for keyboard handling (at least for now). As you can see, it is fairly simple to add keyboard handling and it adds quite a bit of power to your program. You can add any number of additional keys as you need them. Just remember to organize them in a manner that is easy for your user to find and use.

6.4 What about mouse input?

Although the keyboard does a fairly good job of providing us a way of controlling our virtual environment and our interaction with it, many time it is just not enough. I mentioned above that many of the most popular games today, such as the first person perspective games, can be run with just keyboard input. Although these games are designed to allow this type of interaction, they are designed to be played most effectively with a *combination* of both keyboard and mouse input.

A mouse is a fairly common sense pointing device for most people. The natural motion of moving the mouse forward to control forward motion, backward to control backward motion, and so forth, makes it a great device for this type of use.

6.5 Adding the Mouse Handler to our code

Adding mouse control to our application is quite simple. We need to modify our `Win-dowProc` routine so that it checks for mouse button press events. The five events we need to add are: `WM_LBUTTONDOWN`, `WM_LBUTTONUP`, `WM_RBUTTONDOWN`, `WM_RBUTTONUP`, and `WM_MOUSEMOVE`. These events are Windows events which are triggered whenever we press a mouse button or move the mouse.

6.5.1 Implementing mouse selection of visual objects (picking)

The first event we want to handle is the left mouse button press. If the user presses this button, we want to test if the user has selected a *pickable* object. The items which are selectable with the mouse are set by us. For the program we are building, the bucket is an item on which we can click the mouse's left button to *grab* it. When the user picks the bucket, we want to *remove* it from our scene and add it to our *inventory*. This is a standard action in any of the 3D first person perspective adventure games today. Since it is something we will definitely want in our program, let's add this feature.

The event to check for is:

```
case WM_LBUTTONDOWN:
 {
```

We will have to grab the (x, y) point the user selected by pulling it out of the high and low words of the `lparam` argument sent to our `WindowProc` routine.

```
    int size, x = LOWORD(lparam);
    int j, y = HIWORD(lparam);
    D3MinObj *d3mo;
```

We also will want to define several new objects for handling our picked objects. I will explain their purposes as we use them.

```
    LPDIRECT3DRMPICKEDARRAY picked;
    LPDIRECT3DRMFRAMEARRAY frames;
```

```
LPDIRECT3DRMFRAME   lpFrame;
LPDIRECT3DRMVISUALARRAY visuals;
LPDIRECT3DRMVISUAL visual;
D3DRMPICKDESC   PickDesc;
DWORD    dw;
```

Our first task is to get the information on what the user has selected. We will acquire a depth-sorted list of objects, and faces if relevant, which include the path taken in the hierarchy from our root down to the frame containing the selected object. The prototype to this method is:

```
HRESULT Pick(LONG lX, LONG lY,
  LPDIRECT3DRMPICKEDARRAY* lplpVisuals);
```

The arguments to this method are:

- lX and lY. Specify the coordinates we will use for the picking action.

- lplpVisuals. Holds the address of a pointer we want filled with a pointer to the IDirect3DRMPickedArray interface if the call is successful.

The actual call is:

```
view->Pick(x, y, &picked);// We are using our global view variable
```

We will also need to verify that we have picked something. The IDirect3DRMPickedArray::GetPick method can be called to get the Direct3D-RMVisual and Direct3DRMFrame objects which were intersected by our pick. The GetPick method is defined as:

```
HRESULT GetPick(DWORD index, LPDIRECT3DRMVISUAL * lplpVisual,
  LPDIRECT3DRMFRAMEARRAY * lplpFrameArray,
  LPD3DRMPICKDESC lpD3DRMPickDesc);
```

The parameters to this call are:

- index. The index into the pick array which indicates the pick which we wish to retrieve information on.

- lplpVisual. The address we want to fill with a pointer to the Direct3DRMVisual object for the pick we specify.

- lplpFrameArray. The address we want to fill with a pointer to the Direct3DRMFrameArray object for the specified pick.

- lpD3DRMPickDesc. The address of a D3DRMPICKDESC structure containing the pick position plus the face and group identifiers of the objects we are retrieving.

The code to acquire this pick information is:

```
if (picked)
{
 if ((size = picked->GetSize()) > 0)
  {
    picked->GetPick (0, &visual, &frames, &PickDesc);
```

Once we have the frames from our selected object, we want to get the number of elements which were retrieved. With that number in hand, we want to walk through the list of frames.

```
size = frames->GetSize ();
  for (int i=0;i<size;i++)
  {
```

For each element in the array of frames, we want to grab the ith element in the array. The IDIRECT3DRMFRAMEARRAY::GetElement method is prototyped as:

```
HRESULT GetElement(DWORD index, LPDIRECT3DRMFRAME * lplpD3DRMFrame);
```

Our call to get the current frame is:

```
frames->GetElement (i, &lpFrame);
```

The class we will create to handle selection and collision detection in chapter 10 has a method, SetPickable, which we use to set a boolean value indicating whether or not we want the object to be user selectable using the mouse. With this capability, we can keep the user from selecting things like mountains and the ground, but allow them to select things such as switches or things they can pick up or maneuver.

We also need to create a method, GetPickable (this is also shown in detail in chapter 10), for our object which just returns TRUE or FALSE to determine if we wanted the user to be able to select it. Using this, we can determine the pickability of our object, and if we specified it as an object we want the user to be able to select, we continue on to get the details from the object. If it is not an object that we want to be selectable, we just skip it.

```
dw = lpFrame->GetAppData();
  d3mo = (D3MinObj *)dw;
    if (TRUE == d3mo->GetPickable ())
      {
```

If the object is one we want the user to be able to select, we want to remove it from our scene since we are going to represent it as having been *picked up* and placed in our inventory. To do this, we need to get the list of visuals in the frame, get the number of visuals in the list, and walk through the list one at a time. This is done using the following sequence:

```
lpFrame->GetVisuals (&visuals);
```

```
j = visuals->GetSize ();
for (int k=0;k<j;k++)
{
```

The IDirect3DRMVisualArray object class uses the same method as the IDirect3DRMFrameArray type did above. This method, GetElement, grabs the *k*th element from our visual object array. We can then take this and delete each one in the list, using our loop, with a call to the current frame's DeleteVisual method.

```
visuals->GetElement (k, &visual);
lpFrame->DeleteVisual (visual);
}
```

After all of the elements in the selected frame have been deleted, we still need to delete the frame itself. To do this, we just need to call the frame's Release method.

```
j = lpFrame->Release ();
}
}
}
```

Of course, we also need to free up the picked array object.

```
picked->Release();
}
}
break;
```

That's it! We now have the ability to specify *any* object as pickable and define whatever action we wish to have happen once the object is selected. Try experimenting with various ideas for your games using this capability—it is really quite useful and powerful!

6.5.2 Implementing movement using the mouse

A final capability you will want in your programs is the attachment of the mouse movement to the control of the cursor in your window and the acquisition of the mouse button press and release messages. The messages we need to handle for mouse button usage are WM_LBUTTONDOWN, WM_LBUTTONUP, WM_RBUTTONDOWN, and WM_RBUTTONUP.

For our purposes, we will just be using the *right* mouse button, but if you need to use the *left* button, the handling is exactly the same as you will learn about for the right one! So for now, let's just make a blank handling section for the left mouse button messages.

```
int StateOfCur = 1;
double mouse_x = SIGN_EXTEND(LOWORD(lparam));
double mouse_y = SIGN_EXTEND(HIWORD(lparam));
int width = rc.right - rc.left;
```

```
    int height = rc.bottom - rc.top;

  case WM_LBUTTONDOWN:
  break;

  case WM_LBUTTONUP:
  break;
```

For the right mouse button, we want to use the button to control our motion. When the user depresses and holds this button while moving the mouse, it will control their motion through the world. When they release the button, they stop moving.

This code needs to get the camera's orientation, find the window's rectangular coordinates, place them in the rc rect structure, and grab the mouse position. Based upon the position the mouse is at on the screen, we will turn left, turn right, move forward, or move backward through our world. You already saw the routines we built to control motion when we discussed the keyboard handler, so I'll just lay out the code to handle the mouse control using these below. Take a minute to study it and it should be fairly straightforward.

```
  case WM_RBUTTONDOWN:
  {
   // Define the direction, up, and down vectors for motion information
   D3DVECTOR direction, up;

   // Get the orientation of the camera frame relative to the scene
   camera->GetOrientation(scene, &direction, &up);

   GetWindowRect(win, &rc);

   if (mouse_x > 0 && mouse_x <= width/3.0 &&
     mouse_y > 0 && mouse_y <= height/2.0)
   {
    TurnLeft (D3DVAL (0.1));
   } else if (mouse_x > width/3.0 && mouse_x <= 2.0*width/3.0 &&
      mouse_y > 0 && mouse_y <= height/2.0)
   {
    MoveForward (direction);
   } else if (mouse_x > 2.0*width/3.0 && mouse_x < width &&
      mouse_y > 0 && mouse_y <= height/2.0)
   {
    TurnRight (D3DVAL (0.1));
   } else if (mouse_x > 0 && mouse_x <= width/3.0 &&
      mouse_y > height/2.0 && mouse_y < height)
   {
   } else if (mouse_x > width/3.0 && mouse_x <= 2.0*width/3.0 &&
      mouse_y > height/2.0 && mouse_y < height)
   {
   MoveBackward (direction);
   } else if (mouse_x > 2.0*width/3.0 && mouse_x < width &&
      mouse_y > height/2.0 && mouse_y < height)
```

```
    {
    }
  }
  break;
```

When the right key is released, we just want to stop moving.

```
case WM_RBUTTONUP:
  StopMove ();
break;
```

We now will need to handle the mouse movement. If the user is holding down the right mouse button, we will need to check the mouse's (x, y) position and use this to determine which direction we should be moving. Based on this position, we stop the current motion and start moving in the desired direction (forward or backward), turn right or left, or stand still if the mouse is at the center of the window. The code to handle this is:

```
case WM_MOUSEMOVE:
{
  GetWindowRect(win, &rc);

  if (mouse_x > 0 && mouse_x <= width/3.0 &&
    mouse_y > 0 && mouse_y <= height/2.0)
  {
   if (stateOfCur != 1)
   {
    if (wparam & MK_RBUTTON )
    {
     StopMove ();
     TurnLeft (D3DVAL (0.1));
    }
    stateOfCur = 1;
```

The next two commands are new, so let's take a look at them. The first, SetCapture, is called to capture the mouse for our window. The command is a Windows command. After our window has captured the mouse, all of the mouse input is directed to our window, even if the cursor is not within the borders of our window. The prototype of this functions is:

```
HWND SetCapture(
  HWND hWnd        // handle of window to receive mouse capture
  );
```

The parameter is:

- hWnd. This parameter indicates the window in our thread for which we want to capture the mouse.

This function returns the handle of the window which had previously captured the mouse.

```
SetCapture (win);
```

The next command, SetCursor, is called to set the cursor to a particular one we desire. Our first cursor is an arrow which indicates we are turning left. The prototype of this Windows function is:

```
HCURSOR SetCursor(
 HCURSOR hCursor      // handle of cursor
);
```

The parameter is:

- hCursor. Specifies the desired cursor. The cursor specified is required to have been created by the CreateCursor command or loaded using the LoadCursor or LoadImage function. If you pass this parameter as NULL, the cursor will be removed from the screen.

The call is:

```
    SetCursor (hTurnLiCur);
 }
```

The rest of this function is quite easy to understand and uses commands we have already covered. The code to handle the motion and cursor changes is as follows:

```
 } else if (mouse_x > width/3.0 && mouse_x <= 2.0*width/3.0 &&
            mouse_y > 0 && mouse_y <= height/2.0)
{
 if (stateOfCur != 2)
  {
  if (wparam & MK_RBUTTON )
   {
    // Define the direction, up, and down vectors for
    // motion information
    D3DVECTOR direction, up;

    // Get the orientation of the camera frame relative to the scene
    camera->GetOrientation(scene, &direction, &up);

    StopMove ();
   MoveForward (direction);
  }
  stateOfCur = 2;
  SetCapture (win);
 SetCursor (hForwarCur);
 }
```

```
    } else if (mouse_x > 2.0*width/3.0 && mouse_x < width &&
               mouse_y > 0 && mouse_y <= height/2.0)
   {
    if (stateOfCur != 3)
    {
   if (wparam & MK_RBUTTON )
   {
    StopMove ();
    TurnRight (D3DVAL (0.1));
   }
    stateOfCur = 3;
    SetCapture (win);
    SetCursor (hTurnReCur);
  }
} else if (mouse_x > 0 && mouse_x <= width/3.0 &&
           mouse_y > height/2.0 && mouse_y < height)
{
 if (stateOfCur != 4)
 {
  if (wparam & MK_RBUTTON )
  {
   StopMove ();
  }
  stateOfCur = 4;
  SetCapture (win);
  SetCursor (hShiftLiCur);
 }
} else if (mouse_x > width/3.0 && mouse_x <= 2.0*width/3.0 &&
           mouse_y > height/2.0 && mouse_y < height)
{
 if (stateOfCur != 5)
 {
  if (wparam & MK_RBUTTON )
  {
   // Define the direction, up, and down vectors for motion information
   D3DVECTOR direction, up;

   // Get the orientation of the camera frame relative to the scene
   camera->GetOrientation(scene, &direction, &up);

   StopMove ();
   MoveBackward (direction);
  }
  stateOfCur = 5;
  SetCapture (win);
  SetCursor (hBackwarCur);
 }
} else if (mouse_x > 2.0*width/3.0 && mouse_x < width &&
           mouse_y > height/2.0 && mouse_y < height)
{
 if (stateOfCur != 6)
 {
  if (wparam & MK_RBUTTON )
  {
```

```
      StopMove ();
      }
     stateOfCur = 6;
     SetCapture (win);
     SetCursor (hShiftReCur);
     }
    } else {
     StopMove ();
     if (stateOfCur != 0)
     {
      ReleaseCapture();
      SetCursor (arrowCursor);
      stateOfCur = 0;
     }
    }

   }
  break;
```

Well, that is it! We now have full mouse and keyboard control of our world. The interface we have implemented is fairly standard in the industry, so if you build this input style into your games or simulations, it will be easy for most users to understand.

6.6 *What does our application look like now?*

In this chapter, we have added the ability to control our world and our movement through it using the keyboard and mouse. The screen looks just as it did in the last chapter, but now you can move through our world!

6.7 *What did we learn?*

In this chapter, we covered how to implement both a keyboard and a mouse handler. We also found how to set our cursor to various shapes and sizes to represent our current action. These capabilities will help you to design the various user interfaces you will need to develop as you create new Direct3D based programs.

6.8 *What's next?*

In chapter 7 we will learn how to build visual objects from scratch. So far you have only loaded prebuilt objects, and although this gives you a powerful, and easy, way of building a complex, attractive environment, there will be many times where it will be necessary to create objects *on the fly* or algorithmically.

I will show you how to build 3D objects and incorporate them into your scene so that you will have some very versatile environment generation capabilities. Combined with object loading, you will be able to create a game or application with any objects you can imagine (and of course have the artistic or architectural skills to create).

So, on with object creation to help us build our world!

chapter 7

Building an object

7.1 Creating a Direct3D object

So far, we have loaded only prebuilt objects. To create a truly useful application, we will need to be able to create various objects during the execution of our program. This chapter will detail the process of creating landscape objects showing you the steps required to build, add, and display a visual object. You will see how to generate objects face by face so that you will be able to create any shape object you desire. In addition, I will show you how to handle *levels of detail* in your objects to support dynamic level of detail handling (face culling/combining), when objects are far away, to speed rendering.

There are in fact a few other steps you will want to perform when you build your objects—texturing, setting materials, and setting Colors. I will leave these until the next chapter since Mesh and MeshBuilder objects are complicated enough by themselves.

7.1.1 The Mesh object

The first object you will want to understand thoroughly is the IDirect3DRMMesh object. A Mesh object is an object which is used to create the structure of an object. When rendering, oftentimes people think of a *wireframe mesh*. This is one of the ways which a Mesh object can be rendered. You can think of the mesh as the skeleton of your object. It is the defining structure which is the framework upon which you build the object.

There are two ways to create a Mesh object. The first way is to use the `IDirect3DRM::CreateMesh` method. The prototype of this function is:

```
HRESULT CreateMesh(LPDIRECT3DRMMESH* lplpD3DRMMesh);
```

The argument to this method is:

- `lplpD3DRMMesh`. Specifies the address we want filled with a pointer to an IDirect3DRMMesh interface.

The other way you can create a Mesh object is to use the `IDirect3DRMMeshBuilder::CreateMesh` method. The prototype of this function is the same as the IDirect3DRM method:

```
HRESULT CreateMesh(LPDIRECT3DRMMESH* lplpD3DRMMesh);
```

As with the `IDirect3DRM::CreateMesh` method, the argument to this method is:

- `lplpD3DRMMesh`. Specifies the address we want filled with a pointer to an IDirect3DRMMesh interface.

When you make either of these calls, you will create a new Mesh object with no faces. Also, this mesh will not be visible until you add it to a frame!

Since we have now introduced another new object, the `IDirect3DRMMeshBuilder` object, I will show you the basics of it next. From there I will show you how to use these objects together to create the objects in your virtual world.

7.2 The MeshBuilder object

To create a new MeshBuilder object, you need to call the `IDirect3DRM::CreateMesh-Builder` method. This method is prototyped as:

```
HRESULT CreateMeshBuilder(LPDIRECT3DRMMESHBUILDER*
                          lplpD3DRMMeshBuilder);
```

The argument to this method is:

- `lplpD3DRMMeshBuilder`. The address we want filled with a pointer to an IDirect3DRMMeshBuilder interface.

There are a few different ways we can build our objects using the IDirect3DRMMeshBuilder interface. The first one you learned about was using the `load` methods of this object to load prebuilt objects from a file. The second is to use the `IDirect3DRMMeshBuilder ::AddMesh` and `IDirect3DRMMeshBuilder::CreateMesh` methods to add a mesh to our MeshBuilder object. These, as with the load functions, are used most for prebuilt objects (adding them after you load them). Rather than loading the data from a file, this data will typically be held in a data structure within your program and you can load (or remove) objects as needed.

The third, often most useful, and certainly most versatile, way is to use the `IDirect3DRMMeshBuilder::AddFace` and `IDirect3DRMMeshBuilder::AddFaces` methods. These methods allow us to construct our objects one piece at a time. Using these methods, we can add a single face, or multiple faces, to our object.

The `IDirect3DRMMeshBuilder::AddFace` method, which is used to add a single face to a Direct3DRMMeshBuilder object, is prototyped as:

```
HRESULT AddFace(LPDIRECT3DRMFACE lpD3DRMFace);
```

The argument to this is:

• `lpD3DRMFace`. The address of the face to be added.

This face can only be added to *one* mesh at a time.

Our other method, which adds multiple faces to an object, is the `IDirect3DRMMeshBuilder::AddFaces` method which is prototyped as:

```
HRESULT AddFaces(DWORD dwVertexCount, D3DVECTOR * lpD3DVertices,
  DWORD normalCount, D3DVECTOR *lpNormals, DWORD *lpFaceData,
  LPDIRECT3DRMFACEARRAY* lplpD3DRMFaceArray);
```

The arguments to this method are:

• `dwVertexCount`. The number of vertices you wish to add.

• `lpD3DVertices`. The base address of an array of `D3DVECTOR` structures holding the vertices.

• `normalCount`. The number of normals.

• `lpNormals`. The base address of an array of `D3DVECTOR` structures holding the normals.

• `lpFaceData`. For every face, this parameter holds a vertex count followed by the indices into the vertices array. If the `normalCount` parameter is not set to 0, you should set this parameter to contain a vertex count followed by pairs of vertices. The pairs of vertices should have the first index of each pair set to an index into the array of vertices and the second set to an index into the array of normals. You terminate the list of indices with a 0.

- `lplpD3DRMFaceArray`. Passed with the address of a pointer to an IDirect3DRMFaceArray interface you wish filled with a pointer to the new faces.

As you can see, there are several arguments to this method. They consist of the vertex, face, and normal data. The faces are defined by their vertices and the normals for these faces. To help explain how this process works, I have included an example set of routines which show how to build a Terrain object. This object is one which is used to create the visual of the ground which we walk on for the game we are constructing. Since a number of people developing games and simulations want to create this type of object, I felt this would be a good example!

7.3 Using the Mesh and MeshBuilders

The first routine is the main one which defines the data structures and calls the routines to create the points, faces, and normals. Let's walk through this routine:

```
BOOL
BuildPlane (LPDIRECT3DRMMESHBUILDER msh, int x, int y, int step=0)
{
 int vertexCount, normalCount;

 D3DVECTOR *vertices;
 D3DVECTOR *normals;
 unsigned long *faceData;
 HRESULT rval;
```

The first routine we will be constructing is a 3D terrain object named `createPoints`. The routine takes the address of both a vertex and normal list, the number of elements in each list, and the x by y size of the grid, the tile type, and the level of detail desired. It is prototyped as:

```
CreatePoints (&vertices, &normals, vertexCount, normalCount,
              x, y, 0, step);
```

Once the points have been generated, the next task is to create the faces that define our terrain surface. The `step` parameter is used to specify how many tiles make up the face.

```
faceData = CreateFaces (step);
```

The last task in the surface generation process is to add the faces we have created to the terrain mesh. The routine takes the number of vertices along with the vertex list, the number of normals along with the normal list, and the face information. The call is:

```
rval = msh->AddFaces(vertexCount, vertices, normalCount,
        normals, faceData, NULL);
```

The only thing remaining to do is to verify that we have created everything properly, set the mesh rendering quality, and clear up our data structures. The `IDirect3DRMMeshBuilder::SetQuality` method is prototyped as:

```
HRESULT SetQuality(D3DRMRENDERQUALITY quality);
```

The parameters to this method are:

- `quality`. This parameter is set to a member of the `D3DRMRENDERQUALITY` enumerated type which indicates the new rendering quality you wish to use.

I have already shown the list of possible values for the `D3DRMRENDERQUALITY` parameter, but please see the details in chapter 36 to review the structure. You will usually want to use the Gouraud shading value since it provides for good quality rendering while still being quite efficient.

The code to handle these final tasks is:

```
if (FAILED(rval))
{

delete [] vertices;
delete [] normals;
delete [] faceData;
return FALSE;
}

msh->SetQuality (D3DRMSHADE_GOURAUD);

delete [] vertices;
delete [] normals;
delete [] faceData;
return TRUE;
}
```

Now that you understand the calling sequence, let's walk through each of the data structures and routines we called in our build-plane routine. The two new data structures we need to create are the `trans` array used for our normal calculations and the `points` array which holds the points in our terrain. They are:

```
extern float trans[FL][FL];

int points [2][lX][lY] =
{
  {
    {15,0,15,0,15,0,15,0,15,0,15,0,15,0,15,0,15,0,15},
```

```
    {0,0,0,0,0,0,0,0,0,0,0,0,0,0,0,0,0,0,0,0,0},
            .
            .
            .
    {0,0,0,1,1,1,1,1,1,1,1,1,1,1,1,1,1,1,0,0,0},
    {15,0,15,0,3,0,15,0,3,0,15,0,3,0,15,0,3,0,15,0,15},
    {0,0,0,0,0,0,0,0,0,0,0,0,0,0,0,0,0,0,0,0,0},
    {15,0,15,0,15,0,15,0,15,0,15,0,15,0,15,0,15,0,15}
  },{
    {0,0,0,0,0,0,0,0,0,0,0,0,0,0,0,0,0,0,0,0,0},
    {0,0,0,0,0,0,0,0,0,0,0,0,0,0,0,0,0,0,0,0,0},
            .
            .
            .
    {0,0,0,0,0,0,0,0,0,0,0,0,0,0,0,0,0,0,0,0,0},
    {0,0,0,0,0,0,0,0,0,0,0,0,0,0,0,0,0,0,0,0,0},
    {0,0,0,0,0,0,0,0,0,0,0,0,0,0,0,0,0,0,0,0,0}
  }
};
```

The points array is, of course, designed to hold any values you might want to use to define a landscape or other object. Try experimenting with the values to see how it effects the appearance of the landscape. If you want to fill the value with random numbers, just skip the initialization of the array with the preset values.

7.3.1 The createPoints routine

The createPoints routine, the first routine we called in our buildPlane routine, is shown below. This routine does two main things—it generates the point data, and it sets the normal for each point. All we are doing here is creating the lists to hold the vertices and normals, filling them, and then setting the two pointers we passed to them for return of their data.

This routine creates *four* sets of points for us to use in creating the level of detail code I will show you shortly. We will be dynamically checking our distance from our terrain areas and adding or removing polygons based on our distance, to speed our rendering process.

The new global variables and this routine are:

```
const int gTileX = 8;
const int gTileY = 7;
const float m_step = (float)0.5;

void createPoints (D3DVECTOR **v, D3DVECTOR **n,
                   int& vc, int &nc,
                   int x, int y, int typ, int lev)
{
  int i, j, count = 1;
```

```
int step = 1 << lev;

for (i=0;i<lX;i++) for (j=0;j<lY;j++)
{
if (points [0][i][j] & step)
 {
  points [1][i][j] = count++;
 } else points [1][i][j] = 0;
}
D3DVECTOR *vertices = new D3DVECTOR [count-1];
D3DVECTOR *normals = new D3DVECTOR [count-1];
vc = nc = count-1;

for (i=0;i<lX;i++) for (j=0;j<lY;j++)
{
 if (points [1][i][j] > 0)
 {
  switch (typ)
    {
     case 0:
        vertices [points [1][i][j]-1].x = D3DVAL ( ((y-gTi-
        leY/2)*(lY-1)+j)*m_step);
        vertices [points [1][i][j]-1].y =
        D3DVAL(trans[i+x*(lX-1)+1][j+y*(lY-1)+1] - 0.5);
        vertices [points [1][i][j]-1].z = D3DVAL (
        ((x-gTileX/2)*(lX-1)+i)*m_step);
        break;
     case 1:
        vertices [points [1][i][j]-1].x = D3DVAL ( (y*(lY-1)+j)*m_step);
        vertices [points [1][i][j]-1].y = D3DVAL ( (x*(lX-1)+i)*m_step);
        vertices [points [1][i][j]-1].z =
           D3DVAL(trans[i+x*(lX-1)+1][j+y*(lY-1)+1]+
               8*(trans[0][j+y*(lY-1)+1]-0.5)-0.5);
        break;
    }
   getNormal (i+x*(lX-1)+1, j+y*(lY-1)+1, normals [points [1][i][j]-1]);
 }
}
*v = vertices;
*n = normals;
}
```

7.3.2 Normals

This is the first time we have discussed normals, so we will need to go into a bit of detail to help explain them. A *normal vector,* or *normal* for short, is a vector which points in a direction perpendicular to a surface. This direction is determined by whether the coordinate system is right- or left-handed and by the order in which the vertices are defined. The *front* of a face is considered the side where the normal vector of the face is oriented

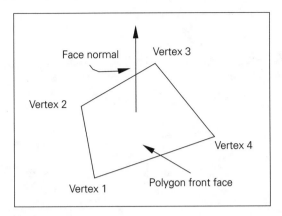

Figure 7.1 Vertex ordering

toward you. Only this side of the face, in which the vertices are defined in clockwise order, is visible. This vertex order and the vector are shown in figure 7.1.

You can specify the normal for the entire surface on a face, but doing this results in a *flat* surface appearance. An object's normal vectors define the orientation of its surface in space. The most important thing this defines is the orientation of the surface relative to the light sources we have defined.

Direct3D will use face normals when you have requested the *flat* mode and vertex normals when you use the *Phong* models. It also uses vertex normals for controlling lighting and texturing effects (see figure 7.2).

There are two ways to define normals: the system can compute them or you can compute them manually. If you wish to have them computed automatically, all you need to do is call the `IDirect3DRMMeshBuilder::GenerateNormals` method. The method is prototyped as:

```
HRESULT GenerateNormals();
```

Allowing the system to compute your normals is sufficient for most applications, but there will also be times where you will wish to compute your own normals. Any time you find that you wish to present *nonstandard* or *unnatural/artistic lighting* effects, you will probably wish to compute your own normals. Two types of objects we might have in our application, Analytic Surfaces and Polygonal Data, will often require your own computation of normals to get accurate lighting.

An analytic surface is a smooth differentiable surface which is defined by one or more mathematical equations. This type of object allows for very accurate modeling of complex objects. Although the computation of the normals for this type of surface is not terribly complex if you have a good mathematical background, these types of surfaces

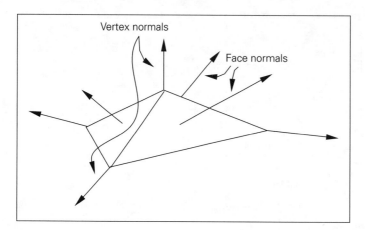

Figure 7.2 Surface and face normals

can be computationally expensive (if you want an accurate, detailed object). There will certainly be times where you will want to build this type of object, but I will not go into the details of computing the normals for the numerous types of surfaces you could define. If you wish to learn how to perform these computations, there are a number of excellent mathematics texts available which cover this area.

The second type of data, polygonal data, is data which define an object using *faces*. If a polygon you wish to use defines the exact shape, such as a cube, you do not need to do any averaging. You just need to use the same normal for each vertex of the facet, or you can define a face normal.

To find the normal for a flat polygon, you can take any three vertices (v1, v2, v3) of the polygon which do not lie in a straight line. The cross product, [v1 - v2] × [v2 - v3], computes the value perpendicular to the polygon. To compute the vector for the normal for a point, you need to average the normals of adjoining facets so no particular one is weighted too heavily.

If you have an object which uses faces to approximate a surface, you need to find the vertex normals for surfaces defined with polygonal data so that the surfaces appear smooth (rather than faceted). You can calculate the normal vectors for each of the polygonal facets. You then average the normals of the neighboring facets to compute the vertex normal for the vertex which the neighboring facets have in common.

The `getNormal` call you saw above passes in a point and returns a normal vector for it. This routine, shown below, uses two routines we have not discussed previously—`D3DRMVectorAdd` and `D3DRMVectorNormalize.`

The `D3DRMVectorAdd` routine is used to add two vectors together and is prototyped as:

```
LPD3DVECTOR D3DRMVectorAdd(LPD3DVECTOR lpd, LPD3DVECTOR lps1,
                           LPD3DVECTOR lps2);
```

The three parameters are:

- lpd. The address of a D3DVECTOR structure where the result is stored.

- lps1 and lps2. The addresses of the two D3DVECTOR structures we want added together.

The D3DRMVectorNormalize routine is used to scale a vector so that its modulus is 1 and is prototyped as:

```
LPD3DVECTOR D3DRMVectorNormalize(LPD3DVECTOR lpv);
```

The parameter to this routine is:

- lpv. The address of a D3DVECTOR structure to be filled with the result of the scaling operation.

Our getNormal routine is called to do the computation for each point of our ground surface. We pass in the point's position and it returns the computed normal vector. If we are at the edge of the world grid, we can just do a simple setting of the normal vector, since it has no neighboring tiles.

```
void getNormal (int i, int j, D3DVECTOR& n)
{
 if (i==0 || j == 0 || i == (FL-1) || j == (FL-1) )
 {
  n.x = D3DVAL (0.0);
  n.y = D3DVAL (1.0);
  n.z = D3DVAL (0.0);
 }
else
 {
```

If we are not at the edge, we need to compute the normal using the vectors we calculate for each of the four points defining the tile surface. The code to set up the values for our computation is:

```
D3DVALUE d1, dza, dzb, dzc, dzd;
D3DVECTOR v1, v2, v3, v4;

d1 = D3DVAL (1.0);
dza = D3DVAL (trans[i][j] - trans[i][j-1]);
dzb = D3DVAL (trans[i+1][j] - trans[i][j]);
dzc = D3DVAL (trans[i][j+1] - trans[i][j]);
dzd = D3DVAL (trans[i-1][j] - trans[i][j]);

v1.x = dza;
```

```
v1.y = -d1;
v1.z = dzb;

v2.x = dzc;
v2.y = -d1;
v2.z = dzb;

v3.x = dzc;
v3.y = d1;
v3.z = -dzd;

v4.x = dza;
v4.y = -d1;
v4.z = -dzd;
```

To add the vectors, we use the D3DRMVectorAdd routine. This function is defined as:

```
LPD3DVECTOR D3DRMVectorAdd(LPD3DVECTOR lpd, LPD3DVECTOR lps1,
  LPD3DVECTOR lps2);
```

The arguments to this routine are:

- lpd. The address of a D3DVECTOR structure we want filled with the result of the addition.

- lps1 and lps2. The addresses of the two D3DVECTOR structures we wish to be added together.

To add our vectors together, we just make three calls to this routine with our four vectors.

```
D3DRMVectorAdd (&n, &v1, &v2);
D3DRMVectorAdd (&n, &n, &v3);
D3DRMVectorAdd (&n, &n, &v4);
```

Once we have added them together, we finally need to normalize the vector. The D3DRMVectorNormalize routine normalizes a vector so that the modulus is 1. The prototype of this function is:

```
LPD3DVECTOR D3DRMVectorNormalize(LPD3DVECTOR lpv);
```

The parameter to this routine is:

- lpv. The address of a D3DVECTOR structure we want to fill with the result of our scaling operation.

The actual call is:

```
  D3DRMVectorNormalize (&n);
 }
}
```

7.3.3 Creating our landscape

We now have the normals calculated for our terrain. The next task is to create the faces for our landscape. The code creating the ground terrain is designed to handle multiple (four) levels of detail. The way this is done is by using fewer of the internal points defining the surface when we wish to use fewer polygons to increase the speed of our rendering. This ability is one which you will probably use in any serious application. After all, more speed is always useful!

The first of the four routines to handle the face creation is shown below. If you wish to look at the other three routines, they are included on the CD accompanying this book in the file *chap7/create.cpp*. This routine, createFaces, just takes the level of detail at which you wish to render and calls the corresponding face generation routine.

```
unsigned long *createFaces1 (void)
{
 int i, j, count = 0;
 // Create an array of values big enough to hold our object
 unsigned long *f = new unsigned long [7*552+1];

 for (i=0,j=0;j<20;j+=2)
 {
  if (j&2)
  {
   f[count++] = 3;
   f[count++] = getP (i+2, j);
   f[count++] = getP (i+2, j);
   f[count++] = getP (i, j);
   f[count++] = getP (i, j);
   f[count++] = getP (i, j+2);
   f[count++] = getP (i, j+2);

        .
        .
        .


  }
  f[count] = 0;

  return f;
 }

 .
 .
 .
```

The last of the main routines handling our terrain creation is the createFaces routine. This function just takes the level of detail at which you wish to render and calls the corresponding face generation routine.

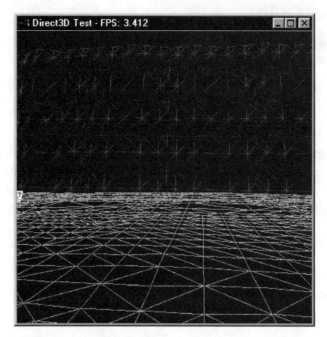

Figure 7.3 The wall at lower polygon detail

```
unsigned long *create_faces (int lev)
{
 switch (lev)
 {
  case 0:
    return createFaces1 ();
  case 1:
    return createFaces2 ();
  case 2:
    return createFaces3 ();
  case 3:
    return createFaces4 ();
 }
 return 0;
}
```

The two screen dumps shown in figures 7.3 and 7.4 illustrate how this level of detail code works. As the eyepoint moves away from an object, the number of polygons representing the surface is lessened. As we move toward it, extra faces are added. The two figures show the transition point where moving one more step forward, we add the extra polygons. This effect is not noticeable to the eye, when we are in Gouraud shading mode, but this removal of unnecessary polygon detail when we are farther away from an object allows us to increase our performance by a few hundred percent!

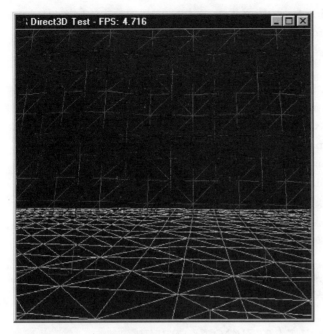

Figure 7.4 The wall at higher polygon detail

I would recommend that you implement a technique something like this for any of your applications where you are using even a medium number of polygons. The savings in processor requirements and the increase in performance is well worth the code design time. Plus, using the code I have provided with the book, this task will not be terribly difficult!

The wall in figure 7.3 is shown at a medium level of detail. The wall in figure 7.4 shows the added faces as we move one more step forward toward it. As you can see, we are removing the need to compute a number of polygon transformations.

That's it. You now know the basics of creating 3D objects algorithmically in Direct3D. The only thing left is to modify our scene creation routine to handle the new mesh-based objects.

7.4 *Putting it all together*

We have two new data objects. The first one holds our ground tile information. For demonstration purposes, the ground tiles are each defined as a *separate* Mesh object. This approach would be useful for scenarios where you have a morphing (changing) landscape. An example of this would be where you have cracks appear in the ground during a earthquake, hills forming from the flat ground, or lakes forming from deserts. By having each portion of the ground represented as a separately animatable object, you will be able to apply new textures or motion attributes to a single tile while not effecting the rest of the landscape.

In most scenarios, I would recommend combining all of your ground tiles into a *single* mesh. This is because the animation of this single object would be the most efficient way of performing the task. After all, you would then only have to apply one transform to the object, or animate it with a single animation, since it would be a single entity. Always remember that the fewer the objects, the quicker your animation will be (assuming the same number of polygons).

The second variable is designed to hold the quality at which we wish to have the object rendered. I have selected Gouraud shading for this example. You can use flat or wireframe if you wish. Remember that you can change this quality for *each* of your objects!

```
// a Container which contains all D3Objects in the scene
LPDIRECT3DRMMESH ground_meshes[gTileX][gTileY][4];
D3DRMRENDERQUALITY quality = D3DRMRENDER_GOURAUD;
```

7.4.1 The additions to our CreateScene routine

You will notice that a large number of commands have been added to the code for our CreateScene routine. For the purposes of our discussion, I have only included the code which creates the ground tiles. I have removed the commands which we covered earlier, such as the scene creation and the camera set up. The first code we will need to add is the definition of the Mesh and MeshBuilder objects we will be using.

```
BOOL
CreateScene()
{

    .
    .

    .
    int i, j, k;

    LPDIRECT3DRMMESHBUILDER plane_builder1, obj_builder = 0;
    LPDIRECT3DRMMESH    plane_mesh1, obj_mesh = 0;
    LPDIRECT3DRMFRAME   plane_frame1;

    HRESULT      rval;

    .
    .

    .
```

As I mentioned previously, you can set the quality (wireframe, flat, etc) of each of your objects separately. Here we just need to specify the highest quality, which is also the default, for our application by setting our device's quality.

```
if (FAILED(dev->SetQuality (quality)))
{
  Msg("Failed to set quality.\n");
 goto generic_error;
}
```

The *field* command below is a new routine which creates the data for the ground terrain. I have only included the function prototype since the code just sets up the face data for the ground. These data are composed of the vertex count, vertices, normal count, and the normals we learned about earlier. The prototype for this function is:

```
void field (int, float[FL][FL]);
```

The call we make to it is:

```
field (8, trans);
```

We also need to create a frame to hold and set the rotation of the object. Remember, a frame inherits its parent's rotation, and other attributes. For example, if the parent is moving with a given velocity, the child frame will also move with that velocity. Furthermore, if the parent is set rotating, the child frame will rotate about the origin of the parent. Here we just need to create a frame to hold the ground frame we will be constructing. Its parent is the main scene since we want the ground handling frame to have the same attributes as the global scene.

```
if (FAILED (lpD3DRM->CreateFrame (scene, &floor_frame)))
{
  Msg("Failed to create frame\n");
 goto generic_error;
}
```

The `IDirect3DRMFrame::AddRotation` method shown below is called to add a rotation of pi radians about the vector [1, 0, 0]. We need to do this to place the object in our scene properly. You will need to orient all of your objects when you load them from files, and oftentimes they may be facing in a different orientation than you might expect. This is tool dependent, so just check your files to see how they appear when you load them. This rotation is combined with the current matrix for our Frame object by multiplying it with the current matrix with the value preceding the current matrix in the equation. It is important that you remember to consider the order of the current matrix and the new one to be multiplied with it since matrix multiplication is *not* commutative.

The D3DRMCOMBINETYPE type is defined as:

```
typedef enum _D3DRMCOMBINETYPE{
  D3DRMCOMBINE_REPLACE,
  D3DRMCOMBINE_BEFORE,
  D3DRMCOMBINE_AFTER
} D3DRMCOMBINETYPE;
```

The value, defining how to combine the two matrices, can be one of the following:

- D3DRMCOMBINE_REPLACE. Replaces the frame's current matrix with the specified one.

- D3DRMCOMBINE_BEFORE. Multiply the specified matrix with the frame's current matrix, having the specified matrix preceding the current matrix in the calculation.

- D3DRMCOMBINE_AFTER. Multiply the specified matrix with the frame's current matrix, having the specified matrix following the current matrix in the calculation.

Our actual call to the AddRotation method is:

```
if (FAILED (floor_frame->AddRotation (  D3DRMCOMBINE_BEFORE , D3DVAL (1.0),
                                         D3DVAL (0.0),
                                         D3DVAL (0.0),
                                         D3DVAL (pi))))
{
  Msg ("Failed to rotate a frame\n");
 goto generic_error;
}
```

At this point, we have added our frame for handling the ground's level of detail to our scene, and we have set its orientation, but we have not yet positioned it within our scene. It wouldn't do us much good to do all the work we've done and then have it show up sitting at the origin (0,0,0), since this is the default position when we create a new child frame! To place our object in its proper place in our virtual world, we just need to call the frame's IDirect3DRMFrame::SetPosition method. This method sets the position of the object (frame) we are adding relative to the specified frame's, in this case our main scene, frame of reference. We are asking for the ground object to be placed a distance of [rvX, rvY, rvZ] from the scene's origin (0,0,0).

```
if (FAILED (floor_frame->SetPosition (scene , D3DVAL (30.0),
        D3DVAL (0.0),
        D3DVAL (30.0))))

{
  Msg ("Failed to position the frame\n");
 goto generic_error;
}
```

With our landscape added and positioned, the last thing we need to do with it is to set up a callback function to handle the adding and removing of tiles as we move along the landscape. Up until now, we have created the frame to handle the landscape viewing and motion and we have positioned it in our world, but we have not put anything in it.

This routine is the guts of the terrain builder you will want to use whenever you have an outdoor scenario, or a complex indoor one, where polygon culling is critical to save computer processor usage. The call that sets up all of our terrain tile addition and subtraction, and could also handle morphing of the tiles if you wanted, is as follows:

```
floor_frame->AddMoveCallback (GroundCheck, 0);
```

I will show you the `GroundCheck` routine in a moment, but let's quickly look at the `IDirect3DRMFrame::AddMoveCallback` method. This method is used to add a callback function to implement any special movement handling we need. In our case, this function handles the tile adding and removing as our position (viewpoint) changes, our most critical task.

It is prototyped as:

```
HRESULT AddMoveCallback(D3DRMFRAMEMOVECALLBACK d3drmFMC,
                        VOID * lpArg);
```

The two arguments it takes are:

- `d3drmFMC`. Our application defined `D3DRMFRAMEMOVECALLBACK` callback function.
- `lpArg`. Our application defined data we want passed to our callback function.

7.4.2 Our motion callback routine for dynamic surface simplification

The `GroundCheck` routine is the motion callback routine which handles adding or subtracting tiles from our terrain as we move through the world.

```
void _cdecl GroundCheck (LPDIRECT3DRMFRAME ground, LPVOID, D3DVALUE delta)
{
D3DVECTOR d3v, d3v1, d3v2;
float fl = (lX-1)*(lY-1)*m_step*m_step;
int i, j;

static int visGField [gTileX][gTileY];

if (FAILED (camera->GetPosition (scene, &d3v))) return;
```

To set up our transformation matrix for the conversion of the position of the camera (relative to our scene) from world coordinates to model coordinates, we call the IDirect3DRMFrame::InverseTransform method. This method is prototyped as:

```
HRESULT InverseTransform(D3DVECTOR *lprvDst, D3DVECTOR *lprvSrc);
```

Its arguments are:

- lprvDst. The address of the D3DVECTOR structure in which we want to place the result of the transformation.

- lprvSrc. The address of the D3DVECTOR structure which is the transformation source.

The call is:

```
ground->InverseTransform (&d3v1, &d3v);
```

With the current camera (eyepoint) position in hand, we can check each of the ground tiles and calculate its position. This (X, Y, Z) position is stored in our d3v2 vector.

```
for (i=0;i<gTileX;i++) for (j=0;j<gTileY;j++)
{
  d3v2.x = D3DVAL ( ((j-gTileY/2)*(lY-1)+lY/2)*m_step);
  d3v2.y = D3DVAL ( trans[lX/2+i*(lX-1)+1][lY/2+j*(lY-1)+1] - 0.5);
  d3v2.z = D3DVAL ( ((i-gTileX/2)*(lX-1)+lX/2)*m_step);
```

Now that we have both the eyepoint position and the position of the current tile we are checking, we just need to subtract the two vectors to determine how far away our eyepoint is from the current tile. To calculate this distance, we subtract the first vector (eyepoint) from the second (tile position) and place the computed value back in the second vector. The D3DRMVectorSubtract routine is prototyped as:

```
LPD3DVECTOR D3DRMVectorSubtract(LPD3DVECTOR lpd, LPD3DVECTOR lps1,
  LPD3DVECTOR lps2);
```

The arguments to this routine are:

- lpd. The address of the D3DVECTOR structure where we will place the result of the vector subtraction.

- lps1. The address of the D3DVECTOR from which we are subtracting lps2.

- lps2. The address of the D3DVECTOR structure to subtract from lps1.

Our call to this routine is:

```
D3DRMVectorSubtract (&d3v2, &d3v2, &d3v1);
```

To get the final distance from the current tile, we use the following equation:

```
float dis = d3v2.x*d3v2.x + d3v2.y*d3v2.y + d3v2.z*d3v2.z;
```

The last thing to do, now that we know the distance to the current tile, is to actually do the check to see how far we are from it. We have broken the world into four range bins for this example. You can certainly decide on more or less range bins, but these seem to work quite well.

The code for each range bin is the same except that we insert the mesh indexed at 0, 1, 2, or 3 in the ground meshes' third dimension. The farthest range bin is stored at position 0 and the closest is at position 3. The closest tiles have the largest number of elements since when we are close to the object, we wish to display the greatest amount of detail.

The check for which range bin of tiles to use is nothing more than a comparison of the distance we are from the object to a multiple of a preset distance. We are using multiples of 4, 3, 2, and 1, but you can vary these and decide on a factor that is optimal for your applications.

Since the code is the same for each range bin, I'll explain the check for the farthest bin and then just show the remaining code for your perusal. The code is:

```
// The Farthest Range Bin
if (dis > 4*fl)
{
  if (visGField[i][j] == 4) continue;
  if (visGField[i][j] > 0)
  {
```

The two new methods we will need to handle the removal and addition of ground tiles (or any other objects) are the IDirect3DRMFrame::DeleteVisual and IDirect-3DRMFrame::AddVisual methods.

DeleteVisual is prototyped as:

```
HRESULT DeleteVisual(LPDIRECT3DRMVISUAL lpD3DRMVisual);
```

This method removes the tile Visual object from our ground frame and destroys it if it is no longer referenced. The argument to this method is:

- lpD3DRMVisual. The address of the Direct3DRMVisual object we want removed.

The code to actually delete the tiles we want to remove from the scene is:

```
if (FAILED(ground->DeleteVisual(
      (LPDIRECT3DRMVISUAL) groundMeshes[i][j][visGFeld[i][j]-1])))
  {
```

```
        Msg("Failed to delete visual.\n");
          return;
        }
    }
```

With the old tiles removed, we need to add the new tiles at the appropriate level of detail. As soon as the tiles are added, they become visible if they are within our view. The `IDirect3DRMFrame::AddVisual` method, which we will use to add the new tiles as a visual object to our frame, is prototyped as:

```
HRESULT AddVisual(LPDIRECT3DRMVISUAL lpD3DRMVisual);
```

The argument to this method is:

- `lpD3DRMVisual`. The address of the Direct3DRMVisual object we wish to add to our frame.

The call to add the new tiles at the desired level of detail is:

```
if (FAILED(ground->AddVisual((LPDIRECT3DRMVISUAL) groundMeshes[i][j][3])))
  {
     Msg("Failed to add visual.\n");
     return;
  }
```

Lastly, we set the level of detail to 4, indicating the lowest level of detail.

```
   visGField[i][j] = 4;
}
```

The remaining code to implement the level of detail handling consists of three more segments which are basically clones of the first segment with only two differences—the distance value is different (to indicate the three closer ranges we wish to check for), and the tile reference changes to 3, 2, or 1 depending on our distance to the tile (indicating which range bin tiles we actually want to use). The code is as follows:

```
else {
  // The Second Farthest Range Bin
  if (dis > 2*fl)
    {
    if (visGField[i][j] == 3) continue;
    if (visGField[i][j] > 0)
      {
      if (FAILED(ground->DeleteVisual(
          (LPDIRECT3DRMVISUAL) groundMeshes[i][j][visGFeld[i][j]-1])))
      {
        Msg("Failed to delete visual.\n");
       return;
      }
```

```
          }
      if (FAILED(ground->AddVisual((LPDIRECT3DRMVISUAL)
                  groundMeshes[i][j][2])))
      {
        Msg("Failed to add visual.\n");
       return;
      }
      visGField[i][j] = 3;
      } else {
       // The Third Farthest Range Bin
       if (dis > 1*fl)
       {
         if (visGField[i][j] == 2) continue;
         if (visGField[i][j] > 0)
         {
           if (FAILED(ground->DeleteVisual(
             (LPDIRECT3DRMVISUAL) groundMeshes[i][j][visGFeld[i][j]-1])))
           {
            Msg("Failed to delete visual.\n");
            return;
                  }
         }
       if (FAILED(ground->AddVisual((LPDIRECT3DRMVISUAL)
                  groundMeshes[i][j][1])))
       {
           Msg("Failed to add visual.\n");
           return;
         }
           visGField[i][j] = 2;
      } else {
        // The Closest Range Bin
        if (visGField[i][j] == 1) continue;
        if (visGField[i][j] > 0)
        {
          if (FAILED(ground->DeleteVisual(
              (LPDIRECT3DRMVISUAL) groundMeshes[i][j][visGFeld[i][j]-1])))
              {
          Msg("Failed to delete visual.\n");
          return;
                  }
        }
       if (FAILED(ground->AddVisual((LPDIRECT3DRMVISUAL)
                  groundMeshes[i][j][0])))
      {
        Msg("Failed to add visual.\n");
       return;
      }
      visGField[i][j] = 1;
      }
    }
   }
  }
 }
}
```

7.5 Some final additions to our CreateScene routine

Back to our `CreateScene` routine. With our callback function defined, we just need to build our landscape. Remember that we actually have a *three*-dimensional array holding the landscape! The first two dimensions define the x × y grid and the data which hold the shape of the landscape tile at that location, while the third dimension is used to hold the four levels of detail for this grid element. The x and y sizes are held in the `gTileX` and `gTileY` variables, respectively.

```
// this is the loop which creates the grass fields ...
 for (i=0;i<gTileX;i++) for (j=0;j<gTileY;j++)
 {
  for (k=0;k<4;k++)
  {
```

In each iteration of the loop, we create a MeshBuilder object to handle the current portion of the landscape we are generating.

```
    plane_builder1 = NULL;

  if (FAILED(lpD3DRM->CreateMeshBuilder (&planeBuilder1)))
  {
    Msg("Failed to create mesh builder.\n");
   goto generic_error;
  }
```

This MeshBuilder object is passed into our `buildPlane` routine which we discussed at the beginning of this chapter. As long as everything returns properly, we set the quality of the tile to the desired level and create the corresponding mesh for our current ground tile. Lastly, we should always remember to release our object so that we don't have a memory leak.

```
  if (!buildPlane (planeBuilder1, i, j, k))
  {
    Msg("Failed to build plane.\n");
   goto generic_error;
  }

  plane_builder1->SetQuality (quality);

  if (FAILED(plane_builder1->CreateMesh (&groundMeshes[i][j][k])))
  {
    Msg("Failed to create mesh.\n");
   goto generic_error;
  }
```

```
          planeBuilder1->Release ();
     }
  }
  .
  .
  .
return TRUE;

generic_error:
 Msg("An error has occured while building the scene.\n");
ret_with_error:
 planeBuilder1->Release ();

 planeMesh1->Release ();

 planeFrame1->Release ();
 return FALSE;
}
```

7.6 What does our application look like now?

After all of that, what does our application look like? The answer is "one heck of a lot better than it did before!" I have included two screen dumps below which show two views of our virtual world now. The first one is shown in figure 7.5.

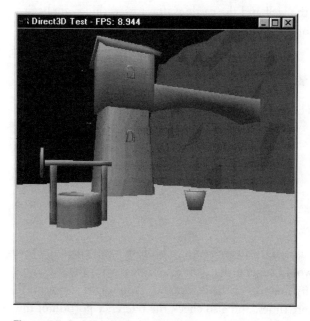

Figure 7.5 A view of our world now

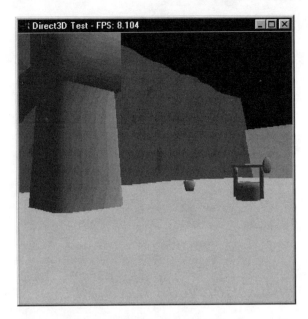

Figure 7.6 Another view of our new world

This certainly looks a lot more like a real world scene! We now have ground tiles representing both the planes and mountains. Combined with the 3D objects we loaded before from prebuilt files, such as the well and the castle watch tower, things are beginning to look good! A second view of our world is below in figure 7.6.

7.7 What did we learn?

In this chapter, we covered a lot! The main things you will want to make sure you have learned are:

- Mesh objects
- MeshBuilder objects
- Movement callbacks
- Vector math functions

These are a set of complex ideas and if you are feeling a bit lost, I can guarantee you that you are in good company. I would suggest that you experiment with the functions for a while until you grasp the many nuances of the commands. You might also want to read through this chapter a few more times, and also check the reference portion of this book of course, to make sure you have grasped these ideas thoroughly.

At this point, I hope you are starting to feel like you could create a real simulation or game! The power of Direct3D is starting to show through as we begin to seriously try to take advantage of it.

7.8 What's next?

In chapter 8, we will cover the other half of object creation—texturing and materials. When you ran the code for this chapter, I am sure you quickly noticed that the world was only grey shaded and tile-like. To make realistic virtual worlds, you will also need to understand the many nuances of texturing, animated textures, and mipmapping.

With these capabilities added to all of the things we have learned about Direct3D so far, you will be at a point where you could implement as good of a game as many of the first-person perspective games available today. But, let's not think that way. By the time you read the remaining chapters, you'll be able to create a better simulation or game! After all, that's what many of us want. And for those in the simulation or advertising fields, you will be surprised at what you can do with a PC and a good 3D software library (and maybe a good 3D graphic accelerator board).

chapter 8

Attaching materials and textures

8.1 Direct3D texture and material overview

As I mentioned at the end of the last chapter, you probably quickly noticed that so far, every object we have created has appeared *smooth*. This is because up until now, we have not added what we need for a true simulation of real world objects—textures and materials. In this chapter, we will cover the creation of a visual object having material attributes and texture-mapped faces. Since textures are the entities which give the greatest amount of realism to our objects, let's cover the basics of texturing first.

8.2 The IDirect3DRMTexture interface

Direct3D implements textures using the IDirect3DRMTexture interface. This interface is defined as an interface to a DirectDraw surface object rather than being a true Direct3D Texture object. A DirectDrawSurface object represents the display memory we are viewing on our monitor.

The following code is an example of acquiring a Direct3D texture surface from a DirectDrawSurface object:

```
LPDIRECTDRAWSURFACE      lpDirectDrawSurface;
LPDIRECT3DTEXTURE    lpD3DTexture;
LPDDSURFACEDESC       lpDDSurfaceDesc,

ddReturnValue = lpDD->CreateSurface(&lpDDSurfaceDesc,
            &lpDirectDrawSurface, NULL);
if (FAILED(ddReturnValue))
{
    // Return an error here
}
.
.
.

ddReturnValue = lpDirectDrawSurface->QueryInterface
(IID_IDirect3Dtexture, &lpD3DTexture);
                if (FAILED(ddReturnValue))
{
    // Return an error here
}
```

8.2.1 Using our DirectDraw surface for textures

Once this surface is acquired, we can use it to add textures (as well as materials) to our 3D objects. Textures are defined as a rectangular array of colored pixels. In Direct3D, this array must be defined in dimensions which are powers of 2. Although the texture does not need to be square, Direct3D is most efficient if you do use a square texture. Thus, if you define a texture, try to keep it in sizes of 1×1, 2×2, 4×4, 8×8, 16×16, 32×32, 64×64, 128×128, or 256×256.

You should try to use a single large texture that is 256×256 whenever you can because this size is the fastest to handle for Direct3D. As an example, if you are using two 128×128 textures and eight 64×64 textures, you should use the same palette for all of the textures and combine them into one 256×256 texture. There are several tools, commercial and public domain/shareware, which allow you to create a common, master palette and associate it with all of your textures. These tools will also let you combine the textures into one large 256×256 image file (either as .ppm or .bmp files, both of which are usable in Direct3D). This common palette and single texture will help reduce the amount of swapping of textures that will be required by the system. Remember though, that since you want to keep the textures as small as possible, do not use this size texture unless you need to.

One thing to keep in mind from the start is that you can optimize your system cache performance for your textures by keeping the textures small. The reason for this is that smaller textures are more likely to be kept in your CPU's secondary memory.

There are three main methods to the IDirect3DRMTexture interface. These are:

- `IDirect3DRM::CreateTexture`. This method allows you to create a texture from a D3DRMImage structure.
- `IDirect3DRM::CreateTextureFromSurface`. This method lets you create a texture from a DirectDraw surface.
- `IDirect3DRM::LoadTexture`. This method lets you load a texture from a file. This file must be in either the .bmp (Windows bitmap) or .ppm (Portable bitmap) format.

Let's take a quick look at the structure and usage of each of these methods for the creation of a texture.

The first, `IDirect3DRM::CreateTexture`, is the method we use to create a new texture from an image stored in memory. The method is prototyped as:

```
HRESULT CreateTexture(LPD3DRMIMAGE lpImage,
    LPDIRECT3DRMTEXTURE* lplpD3DRMTexture);
```

The arguments to this method are:

- `lpImage`. The address of a D3DRMIMAGE structure describing the source for the texture.
- `lplpD3DRMTexture`. The address we want filled with a pointer to an IDirect3DRMTexture interface. The image memory is used each time the texture is rendered rather than copying the memory into Direct3DRM buffers. This was done to let us use the image as both a rendering target and a texture.

The second method for creating a texture is the `IDirect3DRM::CreateTextureFromSurface` method. This method is used to create a texture from a DirectDraw surface. I showed you code to create a DirectDraw surface upon which you can draw earlier in this chapter.

The `IDirect3DRM::CreateTextureFromSurface` method is prototyped as:

```
HRESULT CreateTextureFromSurface(LPDIRECTDRAWSURFACE lpDDS,
    LPDIRECT3DRMTEXTURE * lplpD3DRMTexture);
```

The arguments to this method are:

- `lpDDS`. The address of the DirectDrawSurface object which contains the texture.
- `lplpD3DRMTexture`. The address we want a pointer to an IDirect3DRMTexture interface to be placed in.

The final two methods allow you to load a texture from a file. The first one is the `IDirect3DRM::LoadTexture` method. The texture we wish to load is allowed to have 8,

24, or 32 bits-per-pixel. It is also allowed to be in either the Windows bitmap (.bmp) or the Portable Pixmap (.ppm) P6 format. This method is prototyped as:

```
HRESULT LoadTexture(const char * lpFileName,
    LPDIRECT3DRMTEXTURE* lplpD3DRMTexture);
```

The arguments to this method are:

- `lpFileName`. The name of the .bmp or .ppm file to be loaded.

- `plpD3DRMTexture`. The address of a pointer we want initialized with a valid Direct3DRMTexture pointer.

The second of these two methods, `IDirect3DRM::LoadTextureFromResource`, is similar to the `IDirect3DRM::LoadTexture` method except that rather than loading the texture from a file, it loads the texture from a specified resource. This method is prototyped as:

```
HRESULT LoadTextureFromResource(HRSRC rs,
    LPDIRECT3DRMTEXTURE * lplpD3DRMTexture);
```

The arguments to it are:

- `rs`. The handle of the resource.

- `lplpD3DRMTexture`. The address of a pointer to be initialized with a valid Direct3DRMTexture object.

Now that you have learned the three main techniques to create a texture for your world, you also will need to understand how to create materials in Direct3D. Combined properly with textures, your objects can be given incredibly realistic appearances.

8.3 The IDirect3DRMMaterial interface

The IDirect3DRMMaterial interface in Direct3D is used to apply material properties to our objects. The method you should use to create a new material object, with a given specular property, is the `IDirect3DRM::CreateMaterial` method. The `IDirect3DRM::CreateMaterial` method is used to create a material having a desired *sharpness* for the reflected highlights. The `vPower` parameter allows you to simulate materials ranging all the way from plastic to metallic. By playing with the `vPower` value, you will learn how to simulate most any material type you might desire. At the end of the chapter, I would recommend changing this value for various objects and viewing the effect on these objects.

This method is prototyped as:

```
HRESULT CreateMaterial(D3DVALUE vPower,
    LPDIRECT3DRMMATERIAL * lplpD3DRMMaterial);
```

The parameters to this method are:

- vPower. Indicates the sharpness of the reflected highlights. A value of 5 gives a metallic look and higher values give a more plastic look to the surface when you render it.

- lplpD3DRMMaterial. The address you want filled with a pointer to an IDirect3DRMMaterial interface.

That is all there is to creating materials and textures for application to your objects. The next thing to learn is how to apply them properly to your objects.

8.4 Applying textures and materials to our objects

Once you have a texture defined, you need to decide how you wish to *apply* it to your object. The manner in which we apply a texture is called a *wrap* because it defines how the texture is wrapped around the object. Creating and applying a wrap does not increase the reference count of your objects because wrapping is nothing more than a handy method of calculating texture coordinates. The method to create a texture wrapping function is the IDirect3DRM::CreateWrap method. It is prototyped as:

```
HRESULT CreateWrap(
    D3DRMWRAPTYPE type,                        // Wrap type
    LPDIRECT3DRMFRAME lpRef,                    // Frame we apply the wrap to
    D3DVALUE ox, D3DVALUE oy, D3DVALUE oz,      // Origin of wrap
    D3DVALUE dx, D3DVALUE dy, D3DVALUE dz,      // Z axis
    D3DVALUE ux, D3DVALUE uy, D3DVALUE uz,      // Y axis
    D3DVALUE ou, D3DVALUE ov,                   // Texture origin
    D3DVALUE su, D3DVALUE sv,                   // Texture scale factor
    LPDIRECT3DRMWRAP* lplpD3DRMWrap);
```

This method allows you to generate a wrapping function which you can use to assign texture coordinates to your faces and meshes. The parameters to this method specify the vector [ox, oy, oz] which indicates the origin of the wrap, [dx, dy, dz] which indicates the *Z*-axis, and [ux, uy, uz] which indicates the *Y*-axis of the wrap. The [ou, ov] and [su, sv] vectors specify the origin and scale factor in the texture which is applied to the result of the wrapping function.

The final parameter, lp1pD3DRMWrap, specifies the location where you wish the generated pointer to an IDirect3DRMWrap interface to be stored.

When you have created your wrap using the IDirect3DRM::CreateWrap function, you will need to apply it to your object. This can be done with the IDirect3DRMWrap::Apply method which is used to apply the wrap to the vertices of your object or the IDirect3DRMWrap::ApplyRelative method that transforms the vertices of the wrap as it is applied to your object.

The IDirect3DRMWrap::Apply method is prototyped as:

```
HRESULT Apply (LPDIRECT3DRMOBJECT lpObject);
```

The parameter is:

- lpObject. The address of the object to which we wish to apply a texture.

The IDirect3DRMWrap::ApplyRelative method is prototyped as:

```
HRESULT ApplyRelative (LPDIRECT3DRMFRAME frame, LPDIRECT3DRMOBJECT mesh);
```

The parameters to this method are:

- frame. Specifies a Direct3DRMFrame object indicating the object we wish to wrap
- mesh. The Direct3DRMWrap object we want to apply

You can specify how you want the rasterizer to interpret the texture coordinates when the wrap is applied using the D3DRMMAPPING type's wrapping flags. These flags consist of the D3DRMMAP_WRAPU and D3DRMMAP_WRAPV flags.

8.4.1 Wrapping flags

The rasterizer will always interpolate the shortest distance (a straight line) between texture coordinates. If you use either of the wrapping flags (the D3DRMMAPPING flags), you can effect the way the path of the line is generated and the possible values for the u and v coordinates. The line can wrap around your textures edge in the u or v direction giving the texture a cylindrical or toroidal topology.

If you do not set either wrapping flag, Direct3D will default to flat wrapping mode. In flat wrapping mode, the plane specified by the u and v coordinates is an infinite tiling of the texture. You can use values greater than 1.0 for u and v.

If you set either the D3DRMMAP_WRAPU or D3DRMMAP_WRAPV flags, your texture will be applied as a cylinder having an infinite length and a circumference of 1.0. You can only specify texture coordinates greater than 1.0 in the dimension which is not wrapped.

Finally, if you set both the D3DRMMAP_WRAPU and D3DRMMAP_WRAPV flags, the texture will be a torus. In this mode the system is closed, so texture coordinates greater than 1.0 are invalid.

It is recommended that you set a wrap flag for cylindrical wraps when the intersection of the texture edges does not match the edges of the face. If more than half of a texture is applied to a single face, you should not set the wrap flag.

The four types of wrap flags are:

- Flat (D3DRMWRAP_FLAT)
- Cylindrical (D3DRMWRAP_CYLINDER)
- Spherical (D3DRMWRAP_SPHERE)
- Chrome (D3DRMWRAP_CHROME)

Let's take a look at each of these in detail.

8.4.2 Flat

When you use the flat wrap style, the wrap will fit to the faces of your object acting as if the texture were a piece of rubber which you are stretching over your object.

The [u v] texture coordinates are calculated for a vector [x y z] with the equations:

$u = s_u x - o_u$

$v = s_v y - o_v$

s is the window's scaling factor and o is the window's origin in the above equations. You should use a pair of scaling factors and offsets which map the ranges of x and y to the range from 0 to 1 for u and v.

8.4.3 Cylindrical

When you use the cylindrical wrap style, the wrap will apply the texture like a piece of paper wrapped around a cylinder with the left edge joined to the right edge. This object is then positioned at the middle of the cylinder and the texture is projected inward onto the surface of the object.

The parameters for the cylindrical texture map type are shown in figure 8.1.

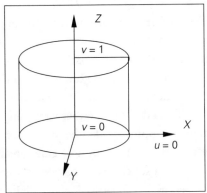

Figure 8.1 Cylindrical wrapping

The up vector indicates the point on the outside of this cylinder at which u equals 0. The direction vector indicates the axis of this cylinder. You will usually leave u unscaled and scale and translate v so that z's range maps to a range from 0 to 1 for v. The $[u\ v]$ texture coordinates are derived for a vector $[x,\ y,\ z]$ using the equations:

$$u = \frac{su}{2\pi}\tan^{-1}\frac{x}{y} - oy$$

$$v = svz - ov$$

8.4.4 Spherical

When you use the spherical wrap, the u-coordinate will be calculated from the angle which the vector $[x,\ y,\ 0]$ forms with the x-axis and the v-coordinate from the angle which the vector $[x,\ y,\ z]$ makes with the z-axis. Note that this mapping will cause distortion of your texture at the z-axis.

You usually will not need the scaling factors and texture origin since the unscaled range of u and v will be 0 through 1. The texture's u- and v-coordinates are calculated using the following equations:

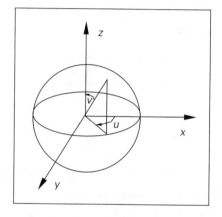

Figure 8.2 Spherical wrapping

$$u = \frac{su}{2\pi}\tan^{-1}\frac{x}{y} - ou$$

$$v = \frac{sv}{\pi}\tan^{-1}\frac{z}{\sqrt{x^2 + y^2 + z^2}} - ov$$

8.4.5 Chrome

The final wrap type, the chrome wrap, sets your texture coordinates in a way that the texture appears to be reflected onto your objects. The chrome wrap method will take your reference frame position and use the mesh's vertex normals to calculate reflected vectors. The texture's u- and v-coordinates are calculated from the intersection of these reflected vectors using an imaginary sphere surrounding your mesh, creating the effect of the mesh reflecting the image wrapped on the sphere.

8.5 Creating a texture and wrapping an object

Let's take a closer look at how we can use these interfaces and their methods to load a texture, create a material, and wrap one of our objects. The first method, `IDirect3DRM::LoadTexture`, allows us to load our textures from either a .bmp or .ppm format image file. If you have files that are in one of the sizes I mentioned earlier (powers of 2), you can load them as a texture for your object using the following command sequence:

```
LPDIRECT3DRMTEXTURE stex = 0, wtex = 0;

rval = lpD3DRM->LoadTexture ("w_stone.bmp", &stex);
 if (rval != D3DRM_OK)
 {
  Msg("Failed to load w_stone.bmp.\n%s", MyErrorToString(rval));
  return FALSE;
 }
```

The file we are loading as the texture is named "w_stone.bmp". If you forget to design your texture file correctly, such as not making it a size which is a factor of 2 or using an incorrect number of colors, you will receive an error and will need to handle it properly. Usually you will want to consider this a critical mistake and drop out of your code.

With the texture loaded, you will want to create your material. In the case of our example, we are specifying a vPower value of 16.0 which gives our object a fairly neutral look in terms of a shiny-to-plastic range of possible values.

```
LPDIRECT3DRMMATERIAL mat = NULL;
if (FAILED (lpD3DRM->CreateMaterial (D3DVAL(16.0), &mat)))
   return FALSE;
```

The `IDirect3DRMMesh::SetGroupTexture` method is used to set the texture you want associated with a group in your Direct3DRMMesh object. This method is prototyped as:

```
HRESULT SetGroupTexture(D3DRMGROUPINDEX id, LPDIRECT3DRMTEXTURE value);
```

It takes two parameters, which are:

- id. The group identifier which must have been produced using the IDirect-3DRMMesh::AddGroup method. You can use the D3DRMGROUP_ALLGROUPS flag to specify that you want the texture applied to every object in the group.
- value. The address of the IDirect3DRMTexture interface for your Direct3DRMMesh object.

The actual call to this method is:

```
if (FAILED(obj_mesh->SetGroupTexture (D3DRMGROUP_ALLGROUPS, stex)))
    return FALSE;
```

We also need to set the material for our group. The method to do this, IDirect-3DRMMesh::SetGroupMaterial, takes two parameters also. The method is prototyped as:

```
HRESULT SetGroupMaterial(D3DRMGROUPINDEX id, LPDIRECT3DRMMATERIAL value);
```

The two parameters are::

- id. The group identifier which must have been produced using the IDirect-3DRMMesh::AddGroup method.
- value. The address of the IDirect3DRMMaterial interface for your Direct3D-RMMesh object.

The code to utilize this method to set the group material for all of the groups in your object is:

```
if (FAILED(obj_mesh->SetGroupMaterial (D3DRMGROUP_ALLGROUPS, mat)))
    return FALSE;
```

The final creation of our texture wrap and the application of the texture was described above. Earlier, when I was discussing setting the color of your object, I showed you some of the potential gotchas that could occur when you attempt to set the color of your objects. Well, there are similar concerns with materials.

Let's consider an example. Say I set the color of my object using the Mesh-builder::SetColor method to blue. I know I assumed that having done this, the color of my object would *be* blue. Silly me. I forgot to pay attention to the emissive and specular properties of my object's materials. The *emissive* color is the color and intensity of the light the object emits. The specular light is the light that comes from a particular direction and bounces off into another, preferred, direction. For example, a shining material object such as metal or plastic will have a high specular component. A material such as carpet would have almost no specular component. Specularity can be thought of as the shininess of an object. If the emissive and specular components of your object are red, even though you set your color to blue, it will look red.

The method to set the emissive property of your material is `IDirect-3DRMMaterial::SetEmissive`. This method is prototyped as:

```
HRESULT SetEmissive(D3DVALUE r, D3DVALUE g, D3DVALUE b)
```

It takes the red, green, and blue components of the emissive color of your object.

You can acquire the emissive property of your material using the `IDirect-3DRMMaterial::GetEmissive` method. It is prototyped as:

```
HRESULT GetEmissive(D3DVALUE *lpr, D3DVALUE *lpg, D3DVALUE *lpb)
```

The color of the specular highlights for your material can be set using the `IDirect-3DRMMaterial::SetSpecular` method. It is prototyped as:

```
HRESULT SetSpecular (D3DVALUE r, D3DVALUE g, D3DVALUE b)
```

The three parameters it takes are the red, green, and blue components of the color of the specular highlights of your object.

You can get the color of the specular highlights of your material using the `IDirect-3DRMMaterial::GetSpecular` method. It is prototyped as:

```
HRESULT GetSpecular (D3DVALUE *lpr, D3DVALUE *lpg, D3DVALUE *lpb)
```

The three parameters to this method are pointers to variables you wish filled with the red, green, and blue components of the color of the specular highlights of your material.

The final thing to remember is a fact that I mentioned back in chapter 4—that color is additive. If you set your color to the same value, say (60,60,60) and then go and set the specular and emissive value to the same values, your object will end up looking quite washed out. This may not necessarily be obvious to you at first, so make sure that you consider the ramifications when you use the emissive and specular methods.

The code for this section uses the following code segment to implement and apply a cylindrical wrap to one of our objects. After you have created your wrap, you apply it (place it on) to your object using the `IDirect3DRMWRAP::Apply` method.

```
if (FAILED(obj_builder->SetColorRGB (D3DVAL(1.0), D3DVAL(1.0), D3DVAL(1.0))))
    return FALSE;

LPDIRECT3DRMWRAP wrap = NULL;

if (FAILED(lpD3DRM->CreateWrap(
    D3DRMWRAP_CYLINDER,              // The wrap type
    NULL,                           // The reference frame for the wrap
    D3DVAL(0.0), D3DVAL(0.0), D3DVAL(0.0), // The origin of the wrap
    D3DVAL(0.0), D3DVAL(1.0), D3DVAL(0.0), // Z axis of the wrap
```

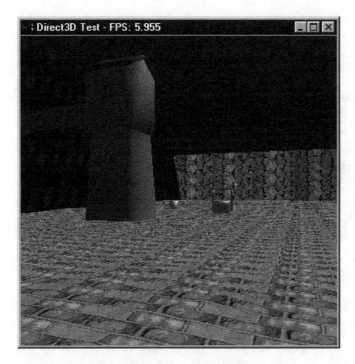

Figure 8.3 Our virtual world with textures applied

```
        D3DVAL(0.0), D3DVAL(0.0), D3DVAL(1.0), // Y axis of the wrap
        D3DVAL(0.0), D3DDivide (miny, height), // Origin of the texture
        D3DVAL(20), D3DDivide (D3DVAL(-20), height), // Scale factor of the texture
        &wrap)))                // Address to be filled with a pointer to an
                                // IDirect3DRMWrap interface
             return FALSE;

    if (FAILED(wrap->Apply ((LPDIRECT3DRMOBJECT)obj_mesh)))
        return FALSE;
```

The texture coordinates for each face in our object define the region of the texture which will be mapped onto it.

At this point, if you want you can compile and run the Chap8 project. The output of the program will look like the scene shown in figure 8.3.

8.6 Advanced texture types

There are several types of textures provided by Direct3D. They are:

• Mipmaps

Figure 8.4 Mipmapping level of detail

- Decals
- Texture transparency

I'll explain the important aspects of these in the paragraphs below. Along with them, I have provided example programs on the CD for each of the main concepts.

8.6.1 Mipmaps

A *mipmap* is a series of textures which are each a prefiltered, progressively lower resolution version of the same image. Figure 8.4 shows the levels of detail contained in a mipmap texture.

Mipmapping is a very efficient way to increase your application's performance and the render quality of your scene. Each level of a mipmap is a power of 2 smaller than the previous one. You can use mipmaps when filtering textures by calling the `IDirect3DRMDevice::SetTextureQuality` method. An example call to perform this is:

```
Device->SetTextureQuality(D3DRMTEXTURE_LINEARMIPLINEAR)
```

This call will set up our DirectDraw device to use mipmapping. This particular mode is the most accurate because it uses an interpolation between the two nearest mipmaps to create the texture. See the `D3DRMTEXTUREQUALITY` description in the reference portion of this book to get full details on the available options if you wish to learn more about mipmapping quality options.

With mipmapping, a high resolution level image is used for objects which are closer to our viewpoint. As we move away from an object, lower resolution level images are used. In DirectDraw these mipmaps are defined as a series (chain) of attached surfaces. The *head* of the chain is the highest resolution texture and attached to it is the next level mipmap. Each of the levels in the chain has an attachment which is the next level resolution image, all the way down to the lowest level of resolution in the mipmap.

The way to create each surface, which represents a single level of mipmap, is to set the `DDSCAPS_MIPMAP` flag in the `DDSURFACEDESC` structure which is passed to the `IDirectDraw2::CreateSurface` method. This method creates a whole mipmap chain in one operation. Since each mipmap is also a texture, you must specify the `DDSCAPS_TEXTURE` flag also.

You can also create each level of a mipmap separately and create a chain by hand using the `IDirecDrawSurface2::AddAttachedSurface` method. This method attaches one surface to another and is defined as:

```
HRESULT AddAttachedSurface(
  LPDIRECTDRAWSURFACE2 lpDDSAttachedSurface);
```

The code to create a chain of five mipmap levels, with sizes of 256×256, 128×128, 64×64, 32×32, and 16×16 is:

```
DDSURFACEDESCdirectDrawSurfaceDesc;
LPDIRECTDRAWSURFACE lpDirectDrawMipMap;

ZeroMemory(&directDrawSurfaceDesc, sizeof(directDrawSurfaceDesc));
directDrawSurfaceDesc.dwSize = sizeof(directDrawSurfaceDesc);
directDrawSurfaceDesc.dwFlags = DDSD_CAPS | DDSD_MIPMAPCOUNT;
directDrawSurfaceDesc.dwMipMapCount = 5;
directDrawSurfaceDescddsCaps.dwCaps = DDSCAPS_TEXTURE | DDSCAPS_MIPMAP |
DDSCAPS_COMPLEX;
directDrawSurfaceDesc.dwWidth = 256UL;
directDrawSurfaceDesc.dwHeight = 256UL;
ddReturnVal = lpDD->CreateSurface(&directDrawSurfaceDesc, lpDirectDrawMipMap);
if (FAILED(ddReturnVal))
{
}
```

If you leave out the specification of the number of mipmap levels, `IDirectDraw2::CreateSurface` will create a chain of surfaces, each being a power of 2 smaller then the previous one, down to the smallest possible size. If you leave out the width and height, `IDirectDraw2::CreateSurface` will generate the number of levels you request. The minimum level size allowed is 1×1.

The code to traverse a chain of mipmap surfaces using the `IDirectDrawSurface2::GetAttachedSurface` method and using the `DDSCAPS_MIPMAP` and `DDSCAPS_TEXTURE` flags in the `DDSCAPS` structure is as follows:

```
LPDIRECTDRAWSURFACE lpDirectDrawLevel,
```

```
                lpDirectDrawNextLevel;
DDSCAPS directDrawSurfaceCaps;

lpDirectDrawLevel = lpDirectDrawMipMap;
lpDirectDrawLevel->AddRef();
directDrawSurfaceCaps.dwCaps = DDSCAPS_TEXTURE | DDSCAPS_MIPMAP;
ddReturnVal = DD_OK;
while (ddReturnVal = DD_OK)
{
    // Process the current level
    .
    .
    .
    ddReturnVal = lpDirectDrawLevel->GetAttachedSurface(
            &directDrawSurfaceCaps, &lpDirectDrawNextLevel);
    lpDirectDrawLevel->Release();
    lpDirectDrawLevel = lpDirectDrawNextLevel;
}
if ((ddReturnVal != DDERR_NOTFOUND))
.
.
.
```

Direct3D also allows us to build flipping mipmap chains. Flipping mipmap chains are used where we want each mipmap level to have an associated chain of back buffer texture surfaces. All surfaces in our flipping chain must be the same size. Each back-buffer texture surface is attached to one level of mipmap. In this scenario, the front buffer in the chain is the only one which has the DDSCAPS_MIPMAP flag set. All of the other buffers are just texture maps created using the DDSCAPS_TEXTURE flag. A mipmap level can have two attached texture maps. The next level in the mipmap chain is the first and it has the DDSCAPS_MIPMAP flag set. The back buffer of the flipping chain is the other and this has the DDSCAPS_BACKBUFFER flag set.

To build a flipping mipmap, you need to either create a mipmap chain and manually attach back buffers using the IDirectDrawSurface2::AddAttachedSurface method or build a sequence of flipping chains and create the mipmap using IDirectDraewurface2::AddAttachedSurface. If you wish to blit to the mipmap chain, you need to blit each level separately.

You should use the IDirectDrawSurface2::Lock or IDirectDrawSurface2::GetSurfaceDesc methods of the top level surface in the chain to acquire the surface description of a mipmap. These will return the DDSURFACEDESC structure, and the dwMipMapCount member will contain the total number of mipmap levels. If you call this method for other levels of the chain, the dwMipMapCount member will be filled with the number of levels from that mipmap to the smallest mipmap in your chain.

Finally, you can use the IDirectDrawSurface2::Flip method to flip all of the levels of a mipmap from the level specified to the lowest level in the mipmap. If you specify a destination surface, all of the levels in the mipmap will flip to the back buffer, the supplied override, in their flipping chain. In the case where the second back buffer in the top-level flipping chain is given as the override, every level in the mipmap will be flipped to this second back buffer.

8.6.2 Decals

There is a unique texture technique supplied by Direct3D that acts very differently then the other ones. This is the *decal*. A decal is a texture that is rendered directly as a visual. This is done by rendering the texture into a viewport-aligned rectangle. You can scale the rectangle by the depth component of your decal's position. The size of your decal is acquired from a rectangle which you define relative to the containing frame using the `IDirect3DRMTexture::SetDecalSize` method. You can get this size using the `IDirect-3DRMTexture::GetDecalSize` method.

Let's quickly walk through the code to implement decals and their animation. I have set up the code to use a move callback function so that we can animate the texture spinning in a circle and change size at timed intervals. We get the decal size using the `IDirect3DRMTexture::GetDecalScale` method and resize it using the `IDirect-3DRMTexture::SetDecalScale` method. The callback function is:

```
// This routine is our Move Callback routine
// As the decal moves, we use a counter to determine whether we
// scale it up or down.
void CDECL
toggleDecalScale(LPDIRECT3DRMFRAME frame, void* arg, D3DVALUE delta)
{
  LPDIRECT3DRMTEXTURE decal = (LPDIRECT3DRMTEXTURE) arg;
  static int i = 0;

  i++;
  if (i == 40)
    {
    int scale;

    i = 0;

    scale = decal->GetDecalScale();
    decal->SetDecalScale(!scale);
  }
}
```

As with all of the examples, I have organized the code to use the `CreateScene` routine to generate the visuals for our 3D environment.

```
// This is our CeateScene routine
// We will create a decal and move it around
```

```
BOOL CreateScene()
{
 LPDIRECT3DRMFRAME frame = NULL;
 LPDIRECT3DRMFRAME axis = NULL;
 LPDIRECT3DRMFRAME circle = NULL;
 LPDIRECT3DRMTEXTURE tex = NULL;
 HRESULT retVal;
 .
 . (Set up our scene and camera)
 .
```

The first thing we will need to do is create and position a frame that we will use as a reference frame about which our decal will rotate.

```
// Create a frame about which our decal will rotate - you could put
// something in it!
retVal = lpD3DRM->CreateFrame(scene, &frame);
if (retVal != D3DRM_OK)
 {
   Msg ("Failed to create the frame.\n%s", MyErrorToString(retVal));
   goto ret_with_error;
 }

// Set the position of our frame
retVal = frame->SetPosition(scene, D3DVAL(0), D3DVAL(0), D3DVAL(15));
if (retVal != D3DRM_OK)
 {
    Msg ("Failed to set the frame position.\n%s", MyErrorToString(retVal));
    goto ret_with_error;
 }
// Set the orientation of the frame
retVal = frame->SetOrientation(scene, D3DVAL(0), D3DVAL(1.0), D3DVAL(0),
                  D3DVAL(0), D3DVAL(0), D3DVAL(1));
if (retVal != D3DRM_OK)
 {
   Msg ("Failed to set the frame orientation.\n%s", MyErrorToString(retVal));
   goto ret_with_error;
 }
```

We also will need to set the frame rotating to demonstrate the animation of decals.

```
// Set the rotation of the frame
retVal = frame->SetRotation(scene, D3DVAL(0), D3DVAL(0.9), D3DVAL(1.0),
              D3DVAL(0.04));
if (retVal != D3DRM_OK)
 {
   Msg ("Failed to set the frame rotation.\n%s", MyErrorToString(retVal));
   goto ret_with_error;
 }
```

The code to load the texture is the same as I showed you at the top of the chapter.

```
// Load in the decal texture
rval = lpD3DRM->LoadTexture("lake.ppm", &tex);
if (rval != D3DRM_OK) {
   Msg("Failed to load lake.ppm.\n");
  goto ret_with_error;
 }
```

With the texture created and loaded, we can set the maximum number of colors we wish to use for rendering the texture. This method, `IDirect3DRMTexture::SetColors`, is prototyped as:

```
HRESULT SetColors(DWORD ulColors);
```

We will set the number of colors to 256.

```
// Set the number of textures to 256
retVal = tex->SetColors(256);
if (retVal != D3DRM_OK)
 {
   Msg ("Failed to set the texture colors.\n%s", MyErrorToString(retVal));
  goto ret_with_error;
 }
```

We will also set the maximum number of shades for each color in the texture. This method, `IDirect3DRMTexture::SetShades`, is prototyped as:

```
HRESULT SetShades(DWORD ulShades);
```

We will just set it to 1.

```
// Set the max number of shades for each color
retVal = tex->SetShades(1);
if (retVal != D3DRM_OK)
 {
   Msg ("Failed to set the shades.\n%s", MyErrorToString(retVal));
  goto ret_with_error;
 }
```

The `IDirect3DRMTexture::SetDecalScale` method, which I introduced in the callback routine, is used to specify that depth should be taken into account when the decal is scaled. If we set the value to FALSE, this depth information will be ignored. This value will default to TRUE.

```
// Sets the scaling property for a decal.
retVal = tex->SetDecalScale(TRUE);
if (retVal != D3DRM_OK)
 {
   Msg ("Failed to set the decal size.\n%s", MyErrorToString(retVal));
  goto ret_with_error;
 }
```

We can set the the origin of our decal as an offset from its top left corner. This method, `IDirect3DRMTexture::SetDecalOrigin`, is prototyped as:

```
HRESULT SetDecalOrigin(LONG lX, LONG lY);
```

The parameters to it are:

- `lX`, `lY`. Your new decal origin, in decal coordinates. The default is [0, 0].

We will set the origin to (128, 128), the center of the texture.

```
// Set the decal origin as an offset of 128, 128 from the left corner
retVal = tex->SetDecalOrigin(128, 128);
if (retVal != D3DRM_OK)
  {
    Msg ("Failed to set the decal origin.\n%s", MyErrorToString(retVal));
   goto ret_with_error;
  }
```

The remainder of our code creates frames to set our decal spinning.

```
// Create the frame for rotating
retVal = lpD3DRM->CreateFrame(frame, &axis);
if (retVal != D3DRM_OK)
  {
    Msg ("Failed to create the frame.\n%s", MyErrorToString(retVal));
   goto ret_with_error;
  }
// Set the rotation of the frame
retVal = FAILED(axis->SetRotation(frame, D3DVAL(0), D3DVAL(1), D3DVAL(0),
        D3DVAL(0.04)));
if (retVal != D3DRM_OK)
  {
    Msg ("Failed to set the rotation.\n%s", MyErrorToString(retVal));
   goto ret_with_error;
  }
// Create the frame for circling around
retVal = lpD3DRM->CreateFrame(axis, &circle);
if (retVal != D3DRM_OK)
  {
    Msg ("Failed to create the frame.\n%s", MyErrorToString(retVal));
   goto ret_with_error;
  }
// Set the position of our circle frame
retVal = circle->SetPosition(axis, D3DVAL(2.6), D3DVAL(0), D3DVAL(0));
if (retVal != D3DRM_OK)
  {
    Msg ("Failed to set the position.\n%s", MyErrorToString(retVal));
   goto ret_with_error;
  }
// Add the texture to our circle frame
retVal = circle->AddVisual((LPDIRECT3DRMVISUAL) tex);
```

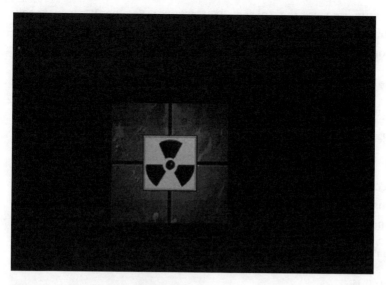

Figure 8.5 Our decal demonstration

```
if (retVal != D3DRM_OK)
  {
    Msg ("Failed to add the visual.\n%s", MyErrorToString(retVal));
    goto ret_with_error;
  }
```

To use the callback routine we defined earlier, we just need to add it to the frame we defined to handle our spinning decal. Remember that this callback will scale the texture up and down in a cyclical manner based on a counter which is incremented/reset in the callback routine.

```
// Set up our callback function for spinning the decal around
circle->AddMoveCallback(toggleDecalScale, (void*) tex);
```

You should run the *Chap8_Decal* code and see how this code works. Try modifying the scale and time parameters (in the callback routine) to see how the application is affected. A screen shot of the moving decal is shown in figure 8.5.

8.6.3 Texture transparency

You can create transparent textures two different ways. Earlier, I discussed using Direct-Draw's color keying which lets you specify colors, or ranges of colors, which are part of either the source or destination of a blit or overlay operation. With these, you can request that your selected colors should either always, or never, be overwritten.

The other technique is to use the `IDirect3DRMTexture::SetDecalTransparency` method to create a transparent texture. This method sets the transparency property of your decal. The prototype of this method is:

```
HRESULT SetDecalTransparency(BOOL bTransp);
```

The one parameter to it is:

- `bTransp`. The decal has a transparent color if you set this value to TRUE. If you set it to FALSE, the default value, you are indicating it has an opaque color.

If you set the decal transparency to TRUE, you also need to set the color you wish to be considered transparent. This is done using the `IDirect3DRMTexture::SetDecal-TransparentColor` method. This method is prototyped as:

```
HRESULT SetDecalTransparentColor(D3DCOLOR rcTransp);
```

The argument to it is:

- `rcTransp`. Your new transparent color, with a default value of black.

8.7 What did we learn?

We covered an incredible amount in this chapter. The number of capabilities provided by Direct3D for texturing enables us to create some very realistic, or some very artistic applications, with relative ease once you understand the nuances of the methods provided. The most important thing you can do is to experiment! Try using the different wrapping techniques on various shaped objects and see the visual effects. Play with transparent textures to see how they can be used. Also, think about how you can apply decals effectively to your scenes.

I will be briefly covering one other concept on textures in chapter 15—animated textures. You have probably seen simple versions of these in various first-person perspective games. Oftentimes people have had virtual rooms with movies playing on them. Well, we are going to do that one, or two, better! We are going to be able to play a video on any complex shaped surface. I'll show you how to play the video on any object including a person's body. Think about how you might be able to use this to create the appearance of skin morphing. You could also use it on various objects to create the appearance of a movie projector aiming at an object in the middle of a room or even the rippling of a lake's surface.

8.8 What's next?

In the next chapter we will be adding joystick control to our application. Up until now, we have been using the keyboard or mouse to handle our movement through the virtual world. Adding a joystick will provide the users of our simulations or games with a much more realistic, and ergonomic, method of control.

chapter 9

Adding joystick control

9.1 A quick joystick input overview

DirectInput API is an application programming interface which I feel is critical for you to learn in conjunction with Direct3D if you are going to develop accurate, enjoyable simulations or games. At this point you should be able to create the visual interface and environment for your users, however, you have only been able to control the world using the mouse or keyboard. Although for many simulations and games these are acceptable input devices, for many others the keyboard and mouse are just not ergonomically acceptable devices for the task at hand.

To address the need for support of analog and digital joystick input, Microsoft has provided DirectInput to allow a simple, consistent access to any of these devices. DirectInput was implemented with device driver models that have greater responsiveness and reliability than the earlier Win32 (SDK). The DirectInput device drivers use the registry to store calibration information for previously configured joysticks and the settings for standard and original equipment manufacturer (OEM) joysticks. These devices can use up to six axes (degrees of freedom), a hat switch, and thirty-two buttons.

DirectInput also provides the ability to utilize tracking devices which use an absolute coordinate system other than joysticks such as light pens, digitizing tablets, and touch screens. Even more exciting is the ability to handle input devices for virtual reality and simulation applications such as rudder pedals and head-mounted displays (HMDs) with head tracking.

Another important advantage DirectInput provides over the past SDKs is the ability to handle up to sixteen digital joysticks. The joystick driver uses *minidrivers,* each of which supports one joystick. DirectInput can also support analog devices, but since they require more system resources than digital devices, fewer devices can be handled.

These analog joysticks can be used in several different configurations. These configurations can range from two analog joysticks tracking four motion axes to four joysticks tracking two motion axes using up to four buttons.

9.1.1 Handling the joystick input

To determine the number of joysticks that are supported by a joystick driver, you can call the joyGetNumDevs function. It is important for you to realize that the value returned by this function is the number of devices supported, not the number actually attached.

This function is prototyped as:

```
UINT joyGetNumDevs(VOID);
```

This routine returns an unsigned integer indicating the number of joysticks which the driver can support. A return value of 0 indicates that no joystick support is provided.

To find if any joysticks are attached to a system, and to get their positions (x, y, and z) and button information, you can call the joyGetPosEx function. This function is prototyped as:

```
MMRESULT joyGetPosEx(UINT uJoyID, LPJOYINFOEX pji);
```

This function also provides you with access to the button state information for up to four buttons, the fourth through sixth axes (r, u, v), rudder information, a hat switch, state information for up to thirty-two buttons, centered scaled data, scaled data for a defined range of values, uncalibrated joystick data (raw), centered scaled data, and scaled data for other values, such as the dead zone surrounding the joystick's neutral position.

Each of the joystick axes has a *range of motion* which is defined as the distance the joystick's handle can be moved from its neutral (centered resting) position to the farthest point from that resting point.

This routine returns a value of JOYERR_NOERROR if the device is attached or a value of JOYERR_UNPLUGGED if it is not.

Each joystick has several capabilities that are available to your application. You can retrieve the capabilities of a joystick, as well as the number of joysticks attached, by using the joyGetDevCaps function. This function fills a JOYCAPS structure with joystick capabilities, such as valid axes of movement for the joystick, minimum and maximum values for its coordinate system, and the number of buttons on the joystick. The function is prototyped as:

```
MMRESULT joyGetDevCaps(UINT uJoyID, LPJOYCAPS pjc,
    UINT cbjc);
```

This routine returns the value JOYERR_NOERROR if it is successful. If a failure occurs, it will either be MMSYSERR_INVALPARAM, indicating that an invalid parameter was passed, or MMSYSERR_NODRIVER, indicating that a driver is not available. The parameters to this function are:

- uJoyID. The identifier of the joystick (JOYSTICKID1 or JOYSTICKID2), you are querying.
- pjc. The address of a JOYCAPS structure to fill with the joystick's capabilities.
- cbjc. The size, in bytes, of the JOYCAPS structure.

The JOYCAPS structure is defined as:

```
typedef struct {
  WORD wMid;
  WORD wPid;
  CHAR szPname[MAXPNAMELEN];
  UINT wXmin;
  UINT wXmax;
  UINT wYmin;
  UINT wYmax;
  UINT wZmin;
  UINT wZmax;
  UINT wNumButtons;
  UINT wPeriodMin;
  UINT wPeriodMax;
\\ The following members are not in previous versions
\\ of Windows.
  UINT wRmin;
  UINT wRmax;
  UINT wUmin;
  UINT wUmax;
  UINT wVmin;
  UINT wVmax;
  UINT wCaps;
  UINT wMaxAxes;
```

```
        UINT wNumAxes;
        UINT wMaxButtons;
        CHAR szRegKey[MAXPNAMELEN];
        CHAR szOEMVxD[MAXOEMVXD];
    } JOYCAPS;
```

9.1.2 The JOYCAPS structure

The members of the JOYCAPS structure are defined as follows:

- wMid. The identifier of the manufacturer.

- wPid. The identifier of the product.

- szPname. The joystick product name stored in a NULL-terminated string.

- wXmin and wXmax. The minimum and maximum values of the x-coordinate.

- wYmin and wYmax. The minimum and maximum values of the y-coordinate.

- wZmin and wZmax. The minimum and maximum values of the z-coordinate.

- wNumButtons. The number of joystick buttons.

- wPeriodMin and wPeriodMax. The minimum and maximum polling frequencies which are supported after a joystick is captured by an application.

- wRmin and wRmax. The minimum and maximum rudder values. The rudder is considered the fourth axis of movement.

- wUmin and wUmax. The minimum and maximum fifth axis, u-coordinate, values.

- wVmin and wVmax. Minimum and maximum sixth axis, v-coordinate, values.

- wCaps. A set of flags indicating the joystick capabilities. The possible flags are:

    JOYCAPS_HASPOV indicates the joystick has point-of-view (POV) information.

    JOYCAPS_HASR indicates the joystick has rudder (fourth axis) data.

    JOYCAPS_HASU indicates the joystick has u-coordinate (fifth axis) data.

    JOYCAPS_HASV indicates the joystick has v-coordinate (sixth axis) data.

    JOYCAPS_HASZ indicates the joystick has z-coordinate (third degrees-of-freedom) data.

    JOYCAPS_ POV4DIR indicates the joystick POV supports discrete values. These values consist of centered, forward, backward, left, and right.

    JOYCAPS_POVCTS indicates the joystick POV supports continuous degree bearings.

- wMaxAxes. The maximum number of axes supported by the joystick.

- wNumAxes. The number of axes in use by the joystick.

- wMaxButtons. The maximum number of buttons the joystick supports.

- szRegKey. The registry key for the joystick which is stored in a NULL-terminated string.

- szOEMVxD. The joystick driver OEM which is stored in a NULL-terminated string.

9.2 Adding joystick input to our world

The code to implement joystick control for our software is fairly simple once you understand the commands I introduced in the last section. The code I have included in the software for this chapter allows you to move around in our virtual world. You will also want to add to your own code the ability to handle the hat switch if you wish to use it to select objects for picking up (remember that we did this using the mouse button previously).

   The first thing we need to define is the range we wish to consider to be the *dead zone,* the percentage of the joystick center range which we wish to consider neutral (e.g., not pushed in any direction).

```
#define JOY_DEADZONE  20    // The percentage of the possible range
                            // defining the dead zone
```

9.2.1 The JOYINFOEX structure

   Next we need to define a structure to hold the information about our joystick such as the joystick position, the point-of-view position, and the button state. The definition is:

```
JOYINFOEX  joystickInfoEx;
```

The actual JOYINFOEX structure is defined as:

```
typedef struct joyinfoex_tag {
  DWORD dwSize;
  DWORD dwFlags;
  DWORD dwXpos;
  DWORD dwYpos;
  DWORD dwZpos;
  DWORD dwRpos;
  DWORD dwUpos;
  DWORD dwVpos;
  DWORD dwButtons;
  DWORD dwButtonNumber;
  DWORD dwPOV;
  DWORD dwReserved1;
  DWORD dwReserved2;
} JOYINFOEX;
```

The members of this structure are:

- `dwSize`. The size of this structure in bytes. The value of this member is also used to identify the version number for the structure when we pass it to the `joyGetPosEx` function.

- `dwFlags`. These flags indicate whether the information returned in this structure is valid. The members which do not contain valid information are set to 0. The following list of flags are supplied by DirectInput:

  JOY_RETURNALL. This value states that we wish to set all of the JOY_RETURN values except JOY_RETURNRAWDATA

  JOY_RETURNBUTTONS. When this flag is set, the `dwButtons` member will contain valid information on the state of each of the joystick buttons.

  JOY_RETURNCENTERED. When this flag is set, the joystick's neutral position is centered to the middle value of each of the axes of movement.

  JOY_RETURNPOV. When this flag is set, the `dwPOV` member will contain valid data, expressed in discrete units, for the POV control

  JOY_RETURNPOVCTS. When this flag is set, the `dwPOV` member will contain valid data, expressed in continuous, one-hundredth of a degree units, for the POV control.

  JOY_RETURNR. When this flag is set, the `dwRpos` member will contain valid rudder pedal information. It also states that we have a fourth axis.

  JOY_RETURNRAWDATA. When this flag is set, the uncalibrated joystick readings will be stored in this structure.

  JOY_RETURNU. When this flag is set, the `dwUpos` member will contain valid data for a fifth axis of the joystick if it is available. If it isn't, 0 will be returned.

  JOY_RETURNV. When this flag is set, the `dwVpos` member will contain valid data for a sixth axis of the joystick if it is available. If it isn't, 0 will be returned.

  JOY_RETURNX. When this flag is set, the `dwXpos` member will contain valid data for the *X*-coordinate of the joystick.

  JOY_RETURNY. When this flag is set, the `dwYpos` member will contain valid data for the *Y*-coordinate of the joystick.

  JOY_RETURNZ. When this flag is set, the `dwZpos` member will contain valid data for the *X*-coordinate of the joystick.

  JOY_USEDEADZONE. When this flag is set, the system will extend the neutral position of the joystick. This region will be considered the dead zone. The joystick driver will return a constant value for any position within the dead zone.

DirectInput also provides flags for us to request data to custom calibrate a joystick. These flags are:

JOY_CAL_READ3. When this flag is set, the *x*-, *y*-, and *z*-coordinates will be read and the raw values will be stored in the dwXpos, dwYpos, and dwZpos members.

JOY_CAL_READ4. The rudder and the *x*-, *y*-, and *z*-coordinate information will be read and DirectInput will store the raw values in the dwRpos, dwXpos, dwYpos, and dwZpos members.

JOY_CAL_READ5. When this flag is set, the *x*-, *y*-, *z*-, *u*-, and rudder coordinates are read and their raw values are stored in the dwRpos, dwXpos, dwYpos, dwZpos, and dwUpos members.

JOY_CAL_READ6. When this flag is set, the *v*-axis raw data is read if a joystick minidriver is present for use to get the information. If it is not, a 0 will be returned.

JOY_CAL_READALWAYS. When this flag is set, the joystick port will be read whether or not a device is detected by the driver.

JOY_CAL_READONLY. When this flag is set, the rudder information will be read if a joystick minidriver is present to give us the data. This raw value will be stored in the dwRpos member. If no driver is present, a 0 will be returned.

JOY_CAL_READUONLY. When this flag is set, the *u*-coordinate information will be read if a joystick minidriver is present to give us the data. This raw value will be stored in the dwUpos member. If no driver is present, a 0 will be returned.

JOY_CAL_READVONLY. When this flag is set, the *v*-coordinate information will be read if a joystick minidriver is present to give us the data. This raw value will be stored in the dwVpos member. If no driver is present, a 0 will be returned.

JOY_CAL_READXONLY. When this flag is set, the *x*-coordinate information will be read and the raw value will be stored in the dwXpos member.

JOY_CAL_READXYONLY. When this flag is set, the *x*- and *y*- coordinate information will be read and the raw values will be stored in the dwXpos and dwYpos members.

JOY_CAL_READYONLY. When this flag is set, the *y*- coordinate information will be read and the raw value will be stored in the dwYpos members.

JOY_CAL_READZONLY. When this flag is set, the *z*- coordinate information will be read and the raw value will be stored in the dwZpos members.

- dwXpos, dwYpos, and dwZpos. The current *x*-coordinate, *y*-coordinate, and *z*-coordinate positions.
- dwRpos. The current position of the rudder or fourth joystick axis.
- dwUpos and dwVpos. The current fifth and sixth axis positions.
- dwButtons. The current state of the thirty-two joystick buttons. This value can be set to any combination of JOY_BUTTONn flags, where n is a value ranging from 1 to 32.
- dwButtonNumber. The number of the current button that is pressed.
- dwPOV. The position of the POV control with values ranging from 0 to 35,900. These values contain the angle, in degrees, multiplied by 100 for each view's angle.
- dwReserved1 and dwReserved2. These are reserved values—do not use them.

If a device has a POV control (a hat switch), and the JOY_RETURNPOV flag is set, the positions are given using the JOY_POV constants below:

- JOY_POVBACKWARD indicates that the POV control is pressed backward. As with some of the other values, the value must be divided by 100 to get the orientation.
- JOY_POVCENTERED indicates that the POV control is at the neutral position. If the value is −1, it indicates that the POV hat does not have any angle to report.
- JOY_POVFORWARD indicates that the POV control is pressed forward. The value must be divided by 100 to get the orientation. The value 0 represents an orientation of 0 degrees.
- JOY_POVLEFT indicates that the POV control is pressed left. The value must be divided by 100 to get the orientation. The value 27,000 represents an orientation of 270 degrees.
- JOY_POVRIGHT indicates that the POV control is pressed right. The value must be divided by 100 to get the orientation. The value 9,000 represents an orientation of 90 degrees.

I would recommend writing your application to accept more than the five discrete directions listed above. The reason they were created this way was to act like the default Windows 95 joystick driver. If you choose to only handle the defined POV values, you need to use the JOY_RETURNPOV flag. If you plan for other degrees of freedom, you will need to use the JOY_RETURNPOVCTS flag to obtain continuous data if it is available. You should plan for these since it will make sure you support more capable joysticks that come out in the future. The JOY_RETURNPOVCTS flag supports the JOY_POV constants used with the JOY_RETURNPOV flag.

The next structure we need to define is our JOYCAPS structure, which I described earlier, to receive the information from our joyGetDevCaps call. This is done as follows:

```
JOYCAPS joystickCaps;
```

Finally, we need to define variables to hold information on whether or not a joystick is present, if that joystick has a throttle, and our flag specifying if we want to use the joystick or the mouse for control. We also need to define the minimum and maximum values for the joystick dead zone.

```
BOOL     joystickPresent;
BOOL     joystickHasThrottle;
BOOL     joystickActive = TRUE;

// The joystick dead zone boundaries
UINT  JoystickDeadXMin, JoystickDeadXMax, JoystickDeadYMin, JoystickDeadYMax;
```

9.2.2 Setting up our joystick

We now get to the actual code. The first addition we need to make to our code is to our WinMain function. The first code you will have to add is the segment to check for the existence of a joystick using the joyGetPosEx routine. If the joystick is not present, we just print a warning in this code, but you might want to do something else. Since we use the mouse when a joystick is not present, there is no problem if the user does not have a joystick (although they probably will have a more difficult time using many simulators or games).

```
// Check for presence of joystick
joystickInfoEx.dwSize = sizeof(joyInfoEx);
joystickPresent = (joyGetPosEx(JOYSTICKID1, &joyInfoEx) == JOYERR_NOERROR);
if (!JoyPresent)
  OutputDebugString("No joystick.\n");
```

As long as a joystick is present, we will need to call the joyGetDevCaps routine to determine the capabilities of the joystick we found. We will check on the first device and place the information in our joystickCaps structure. We can determine if our located joystick has a throttle on it by checking the wCaps flags and seeing if the JOYCAPS_HASZ flag is set, indicating there is a control on the joystick which can be used to control game parameters such as the third dimension (z), or for our purposes, a throttle to control our walking speed.

```
// If present, get joystick capabilities
else
  {
  joyGetDevCaps(JOYSTICKID1, &joystickCaps, sizeof(joystickCaps));
  joystickHasThrottle = (joystickCaps.wCaps & JOYCAPS_HASZ);
```

The last thing we need to do to initialize our joystick information is to calculate the dead zone information. The equations to do this are shown below:

```
// Calculate boundaries of joystick dead zone
int joystickDeadSize = (joystickCaps.wXmax - joystickCaps.wXmin) *
    JOY_DEADZONE / 100;
joystickDeadXMax = (joystickCaps.wXmax - joystickCaps.wXmin) / 2 + (Joy-
    DeadSize / 2);
joystickDeadXMin = joystickDeadXMax - joystickDeadSize;

joystickDeadSize = (joystickCaps.wYmax - joystickCaps.wYmin) *
    JOY_DEADZONE / 100;
joystickDeadYMax = (joystickCaps.wYmax - joystickCaps.wYmin) / 2 + (joy-
    stickDeadSize / 2);
joystickDeadYMin = joystickDeadYMax - joystickDeadSize;
} // end joystick initialization
```

9.2.3 Handling the joystick movement

Now that we have implemented the code to initialize our joystick information, we need to add the code to our WinMain main loop to check the joystick position so we can control our movement through our virtual world. We will add calls to check for whether we are stopped (JoyStop), moving forward (JoyForward), moving backward (JoyBackward), turning left (JoyLeft), or turning right (JoyRight).

The first of these, JoyStop which is the routine we call to determine if we have stopped, calls our GetJoystickCoords routine. This routine fills the JOYINFOEX structure with the joystick's x and y position. The way we do this is to first verify that the joystick is available. If it is, we fill our structure's size slot with the size of the information structure. We also set the flags indicating we want the joystick's x and y values to TRUE. Finally, we call the joyGetPosEx routine, which you learned about before, to collect the values (x and y) we request. This routine is defined as:

```
BOOL GetJoystickCoords(JOYINFOEX *info)
  {
  if (!JoyActive) return FALSE;
  info->dwSize = sizeof(joyInfoEx);
  info->dwFlags = JOY_RETURNX | JOY_RETURNY;
  // returns TRUE if successful
  return (!joyGetPosEx(JOYSTICKID1, info));
  }
```

The actual JoyStop routine is shown below. After we call our GetJoystickCoords routine, all we need to do is return a boolean check verifying that the joystick is positioned in the dead zone. If it is, it indicates that we have stopped moving. We return this value, TRUE or FALSE, as the value of our routine to indicate whether or not we have stopped.

```
BOOL JoyStop(void)
  {
   if (!GetJoystickCoords(&joystickInfoEx)) return FALSE;
   return ((joystickInfoEx.dwYpos > joystickDeadYMin) &&
          (joystickInfoEx.dwYpos < joystickDeadYMax) &&
          (joystickInfoEx.dwXpos > joystickDeadXMin) &&
          (joystickInfoEx.dwXpos < joystickDeadXMax));

  }
```

The JoyForward routine is even simpler than the JoyStop routine. All we do to check for this case is to get the coordinates in the same way as we just did in the JoyStop routine and then see if the *y* position value is less than the minimum *y* dead zone value, which means we have pushed the joystick forward. If we have, the routine returns TRUE, otherwise it returns FALSE.

```
BOOL JoyForward(void)
  {
   if (!GetJoystickCoords(&joystickInfoEx)) return FALSE;
   return (joystickInfoEx.dwYpos < joystickDeadYMin);
  }
```

Our JoyBackward routine acts the same as our JoyForward routine except that we are checking to see if the joystick is pressed downward. As with the JoyForward routine, all we do to check for this case is to get the coordinates in the same way as we just did in the JoyStop routine and then see if the *y* position value is greater than the minimum *y* dead zone value, which means we have pushed the joystick downward. If we have, the routine returns TRUE, otherwise, it returns FALSE.

```
BOOL JoyBackward(void)
  {
   if (!GetJoystickCoords(&joystickInfoEx)) return FALSE;
   return (joystickInfoEx.dwYpos > joystickDeadYMax);
  }
```

Our JoyRight routine again acts the same as our JoyForward routine, except that now we are checking to see if the joystick is pressed to the right. As before, we just get the joystick coordinates, but now we see if the *x* position value is greater than the maximum *x* dead zone value, which means we have pushed the joystick to the right. If we have, the routine returns TRUE; otherwise it returns FALSE.

```
BOOL JoyRight(void)
  {
   if (!GetJoystickCoords(&joystickInfoEx)) return FALSE;
   return (joystickInfoEx.dwXpos > joystickDeadXMax);
  }
```

Our final routine, the JoyLeft routine again acts the same as the JoyForward routine, except that now we are checking to see if the joystick is pressed to the left. As before, we just get the joystick coordinates, but now we see if the *x* position value is less than the minimum *x* dead zone value, which means we have pushed the joystick to the left. If we have, the routine returns TRUE, otherwise it returns FALSE.

```
BOOL JoyLeft(void)
  {
   if (!GetJoystickCoords(&joystickInfoEx)) return FALSE;
   return (joystickInfoEx.dwXpos < joystickDeadXMin);
  }
```

The last code segment we need to create is an addition to our WinMain main loop. In each iteration through the processing loop, we will now need to check the joystick's position using the JoyStop, JoyRight, JoyLeft, JoyForward, and JoyBackward routines we just defined.

To check to see if we have stopped, we just need to remove our cursor, since we do not display one when we are not moving, and call the StopMove routine to stop our motion. StopMove is a very simple routine which just uses the SetRotation and the SetVelocity methods to set our motion and rotation to full stop. The StopMove routine is defined as:

```
void StopMove (void)
{
 camera->SetRotation (scene, D3DVAL (0.0),
             D3DVAL (1.0),
             D3DVAL (0.0),
             D3DVAL (0.0));
 camera->SetVelocity (scene, D3DVAL(0.0), D3DVAL(0.0), D3DVAL(0.0),
       FALSE);
}
```

The actual call sequence to see if we have stopped, and remove the cursor, is as follows:

```
     if (JoyStop())
     {
       SetCursor (NULL);
       StopMove();
     }
```

Our next check is to see if we are turning right. If we are, we set our courser to the right turn cursor, stop our current movement calling the StopMove routine (so we don't accidentally keep moving the way we were heading before), and call the TurnRight routine indicating a parameter of 0.1.

```
else if (JoyRight())
{
  SetCursor (hTurnReCur);
  StopMove();
  TurnRight(D3DVAL (0.1));
}
```

The value of 0.1 we passed indicates we want to set the rotation angle to 0.1 radians rotating about the vector [0.0 1.0 0.0]. Before we set the new rotation though, we want to call our Turn routine to play a sound indicating we are turning.

```
void TurnRight (D3DVALUE a)
{
// calculate the stereo effect (pan). The range is -10000..10000
float pan = (float) 100;
Turn(1);

camera->SetRotation (scene, D3DVAL (0.0), D3DVAL (1.0), D3DVAL (0.0), a);
}
```

We also need to add code for handling the remaining directions we can head. These segments are the same as the JoyRight routine we just discussed, except that they handle our other possible directions—left, forward, or backward.

```
else if (JoyLeft())
{
  SetCursor (hTurnLiCur);
  StopMove();
  TurnLeft(D3DVAL (0.1));
}
else if (JoyForward())
{
  SetCursor (hForwarCur);
  StopMove();
  MoveForward(direction);
}
else if (JoyBackward())
{
  SetCursor (hBackwarCur);
  StopMove();
  MoveBackward(direction);
}
```

To see if the joystick being used has a throttle capability (and we are using a joystick in the first place), we can just check the boolean values we set before.

```
// If the joystick has a throttle, use it to control our speed
if (joystickHasThrottle && joystickActive)
   {
```

Since the joystick has a throttle, we just need to get the position of the hat switch (or other *z*-axis control) and check to see which direction it is pushed. Based on the direction, we set our speed slower, the same, or faster. The code to do this is:

```
// We've already used joystickInfoEx so we don't need to set dwSize
joystickInfoEx.dwFlags = JOY_RETURNZ;
joyGetPosEx(JOYSTICKID1, &joystickInfoEx);

if (joystickInfoEx.dwZpos < (joystickCaps.wZmax - joystickCaps.wZmin)
     * 0.33)
 Speed = normalSpeed - 50;
else if (joystickInfoEx.dwZpos < (joystickCaps.wZmax - joystick-
     Caps.wZmin) * 0.66)
 Speed = normalSpeed;
else
 Speed = normalSpeed + 50;
 }
```

With that, we have now implemented our joystick handling which will allow us to move, and with a few additions interact with, our world.

9.3 What did we learn?

You have now learned how to add joystick handling to your simulation or game. As you have seen, it is actually very simple to add this capability. It enhances your control of your world, and the motion through it, so much that it seems that there is no reason to not supply this support with any simulation or game you develop.

I would recommend that you try adding the hat switch control for your joystick (if your joystick has one). The basics of this code are commented out in the tutorial2.cpp file for this chapter. Try adding the remaining code and write a handler to take advantage of this new controller information.

9.4 What's next?

In the next chapter I will show you how to add collision detection to your world. In any simulation or game, an *accurate* technique of determining whether or not one object collides with another is necessary if we wish to realistically simulate a world. I will show you how to create an advanced collision detection capability to determine if you collide with objects that are of complex shapes. The class is extensible so that as you add new shaped objects to your virtual world, you can quickly add the capability to the collision class!

chapter 10

What about collision detection?

10.1 What is collision detection? An overview

So, now we can create great 3D graphics for our games, add sound, and use a mouse or a joystick. But, when we run the game, and move toward a wall or mountain, we don't bump into it and stop—we walk right through it!

Collision detection is the term used to describe the process where we determine when one object *collides* or *intersects* with another. An example of this that most people are familiar with is in first-person perspective games where the system determines when we collide with a wall and keeps us from walking through it. After all, the computer typically has no concept of *solid*, and thus when your viewpoint (the location of your eye) arrives at the face of another object, it will continue right on through it unless you write code to keep this from happening.

Direct3D does *not* provide any inherent capability for handling the collision detection process. Although this seems to be a feature that every simulation or game development environment should provide (since it is such a necessary feature for developing physically

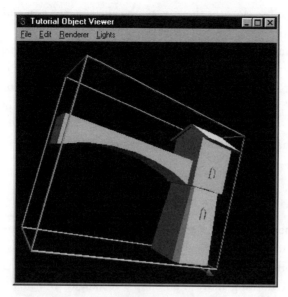

Figure 10.1 A bounding box for our tower

realistic environments), Direct3D is really like most 3D libraries in that it is actually only a *graphic* library and not a *simulation* or *game* library. DirectX as a whole provides us almost all of the features we need for developing state-of-the-art simulations or games, but they have not yet added this feature.

10.2 Using the Mesh object's GetBox method

To have at least a basic collision detection capability, one command provided by Direct3D, GetBox, allows us to acquire the minimum and maximum *x*, *y*, and *z* coordinates of a 3D object. The box representing these bounding values is shown in figure 10.1.

The GetBox method is provided by both the IDirect3DRMMesh and Direct3DRMMeshBuilder interfaces. This method is defined as:

```
HRESULT GetBox(D3DRMBOX * lpD3DRMBox);
```

The coordinates for this bounding box are returned in a D3DRMBOX structure. This structure is described as:

```
typedef struct _D3DRMBOX {
 D3DVECTOR min, max;
}D3DRMBOX;
typedef D3DRMBOX *LPD3DRMBOX;
```

As you will remember, the vector has slots for the *x*, *y*, and *z* values, so the `min` and `max` values will hold the *x*, *y*, and *z* values in their associated slots.

With the minimum and maximum values of the object in hand, we can just make a simple check to see if our eyepoint is *inside* or *outside* of this bounding box. As long as it is outside, it means that we have not hit the object yet. As soon as the point is found to be inside the box, we know that we have hit it. When this happens, we can just stop the motion of the virtual character.

The code to check to see if we have collided with this box is very simple. It is:

```
if ((eye.x >= box.min.x) && (eye.x <= box.max.x) &&
    (eye.y >= box.min.y) && (eye.y <= box.max.y) &&
    (eye.z >= box.min.z) && (eye.z <= box.max.z))
```

As long as this condition evaluates to TRUE, we know we have hit the object's box and thus have collided with it and must stop.

Although this type of check works well for simple objects, and these days most 3D first-person games are composed of nothing more than simple rectangles (for walls, doors, etc.), what happens when the object has a complex shape?

Take a look again and consider the tower in figure 10.1. Although we can easily get the bounding box for this object, how useful is this in determining if we run into it? After all, that bounding box encompasses even the *open* portion of the tower under the arch! I know I would not want my simulation or game to tell me I couldn't walk through an obviously open area just because someone tried to get away with simple collision detection! It is apparent that the bounding box approach is really only applicable for simple rectangular, or approximately rectangular, objects.

10.3 A new collision detection class!

To address the problem of dealing with the collision with complex objects, I will show you how to develop a collision detection class which allows you to define a variety of *object abstractions*. This class allows you to define cylinder, sphere, prism, and box shapes which you can use to determine when another object collides with your object. You can think of them as bounding spheres, bounding prisms, and so forth, like the bounding box we just covered. You can also *easily* add any other shape you wish.

You will want to define a collision object, which is an abstraction of your object, for each of your objects. The reason for this is that it saves a huge amount of computation to use a simple polygon approximation rather than a complex polygon which cannot be defined with a basic mathematical formula. As an example, if you had a virtual sculpture of a person in a room, to determine if you collided with it, you would have to compute whether your eyepoint collided with *every* face in the model of this sculpture or at least with a large number of polygons attempting to approximate the objects volume! This is incredibly computationally expensive and is just not feasible to perform in real time if you have a complex world you also need to animate in real time!

To solve this problem, the collision class I will show you allows you to associate a simple geometric volume, or a combination of these volumes, which is a close approximation of the complex object, to determine whether you collided with it. The shapes we will implement are a rectangle, cylinder, sphere, and a prism. These shapes will work for many of your objects. If you find that you need another shape, such as a hexagon, you can easily add the new shape as a new class inheriting from our base collision class, or combine a few simple shapes to cover your object's volume as a super-class of these classes.

10.4 *The collision detection code*

To implement collision detection code, the first thing we need to do is to create a *callback* function which is called from within our CreateScene routine. The code we need to add to set up this function is:

```
camera->AddMoveCallback (CameraMove, 0);
```

The parameters to this function are the callback function we wish to have called whenever we move and the parameters to that function (in our case there are none so we pass NULL). In this case, we asked the IDirect3DRMFrame::AddMoveCallback method to call our CameraMove function. This function loops through all of the objects in our collision list and determines if we collided with any of them each time we move.

Although I am checking all of the objects, this is only for demonstration purposes. In your games you will want to organize your objects in a 3D grid (or you could use a modified binary space partitioning (BSP) tree). The BSP tree approach is commonly used for hidden surface removal in three dimensions. BSP trees provide a very efficient, and logical, method for sorting polygons using a depth first tree walk. Although, as I mentioned, this information is usually used for processes like hidden surface removal using the painter's algorithm, and so forth, we could modify the concept to sort our *objects* (rather than the *separate polygons*) and group them in *range bins* only drawing the objects that are within a certain distance from our viewpoint.

10.4.1 Our base collision object class

For now, let's work at learning the basic capability of the `CameraMove` callback function understanding that we will check all of the polygons and thus could be more efficient. The routine is defined as:

```
void _cdecl CameraMove (LPDIRECT3DRMFRAME camera, LPVOID, D3DVALUE delta)
{
 D3DVECTOR d3v, d3vv, d3v1, d3v2;
```

Our new base class objects for collision detection are the `D3MinObj` and `ColMinObj` objects. `D3MinObj` is our main object upon which we build our other, differently shaped collision objects. The `D3MinObj` is built on top of the `ColMinObj` object. These objects allow us the ability to set the selectability of the objects (e.g., if you can pick an object with your pointing device) and add the objects to our list of selectable objects. The header file defining these classes is shown below:

```
class ColMinCon;
class D3MinCon;

class ColMinObj
{
 public:
  ColMinObj () {};
  ~ColMinObj () {};
  virtual BOOL collision (D3DVALUE, D3DVALUE, D3DVALUE, D3DVECTOR&) = 0;
};
```

10.4.2 Our other collision classes

The `ColMinLnk` and `ColMinCon` class are two other classes we need to define the linked list structure we will use to keep a list of our collision objects. It uses a standard linked list structure which maintains a link to the element before and after our current one.

```
class ColMinLnk
{
 friend class ColMinCon;

 ColMinLnk *next;
 ColMinLnk *prev;

 ColMinObj *cmo;

 public:
  ColMinLnk () {next = prev = 0; cmo = 0;};
  ColMinLnk (ColMinObj *c) {next = prev = 0; cmo = c; };
  ~ColMinLnk () {};
```

```
    ColMinObj *Insert (ColMinLnk*);
};

class ColMinCon
{
 ColMinLnk *start, *ptr;
 int count;

 public:
  ColMinCon () {start = ptr = 0; count = 0; };
  ~ColMinCon () {};

  ColMinObj *Start (void) { ptr = start;
        if (start != 0) return start->cmo;
        else return 0; };
  ColMinObj *Get (void) { if (ptr != 0) return ptr->cmo; else return 0; }
  ColMinObj *Next (void);
  ColMinObj *Append (ColMinObj *);
};
```

The definition of the D3MinObj, our main collision object, defines methods to add the collision object to our list of objects in our world, determine if we collided with the object, set the pickability of the object so we can allow the user to select some objects with the mouse (for purposes such as allowing some objects to be picked up), and to determine if an object is pickable in the first place.

```
class D3MinObj : public ColMinObj
{
 ColMinCon list;
 int nr;
 BOOL pick;

 public:
  D3MinObj (BOOL b=FALSE) {pick = b;};
  ~D3MinObj () {};
  void AddColObj (ColMinObj *o) { list.Append (o); };
  BOOL collision (D3DVALUE, D3DVALUE, D3DVALUE, D3DVECTOR&);

  void SetPickable (BOOL b) { pick = b; };
  BOOL GetPickable (void) { return pick; };

  int GetNr (void) { return nr; }
  void SetNr (int i) { nr = i; };
};
```

Our D3MinLnk class, which is a friend of our D3MinCon object, holds the links information for an element in our linked list. It maintains the previous and next element in the list for each object.

```
class D3MinLnk
{
```

```
    friend class D3MinCon;

    D3MinLnk *next;
    D3MinLnk *prev;

    D3MinObj *cmo;

    public:
     D3MinLnk () {next = prev = 0; cmo = 0;};
     D3MinLnk (D3MinObj *c) {next = prev = 0; cmo = c; };
     ~D3MinLnk () {};

     D3MinObj *Insert (D3MinLnk*);
    };
```

Our final class, the D3MinCon object, is an object for holding all of the basic information in our object. It holds and handles all of the connectivity information for our linked list.

```
    class D3MinCon
    {
     D3MinLnk *start, *ptr;
     int count;

     public:
      D3MinCon () {start = ptr = 0; count = 0; };
      ~D3MinCon () {};

      D3MinObj *Start (void) { ptr = start;
           if (start != 0) return start->cmo;
           else return 0; };
      D3MinObj *Get (void) { if (ptr != 0) return ptr->cmo; else return 0; }
      D3MinObj *Next (void);
      D3MinObj *Append (D3MinObj *);

      BOOL Collision (D3DVALUE, D3DVALUE, D3DVALUE, D3DVECTOR&);
    };
```

10.4.3 The CameraMove callback function

The actual code for our CameraMove callback is fairly simple, but it is quite powerful. The objects we defined in the routine are used to create an array of the frames (for our objects) in our scene and cycle through them one at a time, determining if we are intersecting any of them.

```
    D3MinObj *d3mo;
    LPDIRECT3DRMFRAMEARRAY lpd3fa;
    LPDIRECT3DRMFRAME lpFrame;
```

The first tasks we need to do are to get the list of objects (children) in our scene, place them in an array (lpd3fa), and make sure we are moving (relative to the scene). If we are not moving, there is no reason to check for collisions, so we can just return.

```
scene->GetChildren (&lpd3fa);
int size = lpd3fa->GetSize ();

if (FAILED (camera->GetVelocity (scene, &d3vv, FALSE))) return;
if (FAILED (camera->GetPosition (scene, &d3v2))) return;
D3DRMVectorScale (&d3v1, &d3vv, delta);
D3DRMVectorAdd (&d3v, &d3v1, &d3v2);

if (d3v1.x + d3v1.y + d3v1.z == 0.0) return;
```

With the list of objects in hand, we can now loop through them grabbing each object, making sure it is not the camera (since we certainly don't need to check to see if it hit itself). If the object is the camera, we can go ahead and check the next object.

```
for (int i=0;i<size;i++)
{
 lpd3fa->GetElement (i, &lpFrame);
 if (lpFrame == camera) continue;
```

Next, we acquire the 32 bits worth of application-specific data we attached to our object. Since the default value is 0, we know that if the value *is* 0, we did not tag this object as one of our objects to detect collision on. This is a handy way to allow us to ignore objects that we know we will never hit, such as things over our heads when we are walking or moving through our world (chandeliers, etc.).

```
if ((d3mo = (D3MinObj *)(lpFrame->GetAppData()) ) == 0) continue;
```

To determine if we hit an object, we just pass our position, and a vector to hold our object transform, into our collision routine. If we have intersected an object, we set our velocity to 0 since we will need to stop and not walk through the wall!

```
lpFrame->InverseTransform (&d3v1, &d3v);
lpFrame->InverseTransform (&d3v2, &d3vv);

if (TRUE == d3mo->collision (d3v1.x, d3v1.y, d3v1.z, d3v2))
{
 if (d3v2.x+d3v2.y+d3v2.z != 0.0)
 {
  lpFrame->Transform (&d3vv, &d3v2);
  camera->SetVelocity (scene, d3vv.x, d3vv.y, d3vv.z, FALSE);
 } else {
  camera->SetVelocity (scene, D3DVAL(0.0), D3DVAL(0.0), D3DVAL(0.0), FALSE);
 }
 }
 }
 }
}
```

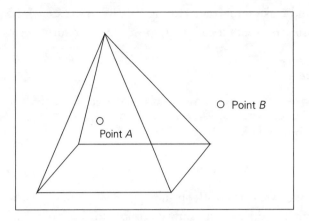

Figure 10.2 Determining if a point is inside a pyramid (prism)

10.4.4 Our overloadable collision member function

The definition of the collision routine we called above is dependent upon the shape of the object with which we are working. Remember that this object is an overloaded C++ object and thus there can be several different functions named *collision*. The member functions I will show below define the collision computation for a pyramid, a sphere, and a cylinder.

The basic collision member function is defined as:

```
BOOL ColMinCon :: collision (D3DVALUE x, D3DVALUE y, D3DVALUE z, D3DVECTOR &v)
{
 if (min.x > x || max.x < x)
 {
  return FALSE;
 } else if (min.y > y || max.y < y)
 {
  return FALSE;
 } else if (min.z > z || max.z < z)
 {
  return FALSE;
 } else {
  return TRUE;
 }
}
```

10.4.5 The prism collision member function

Our first object's overloaded collision member function checks for the collision of a point and a *pyramid* as shown in figure 10.2. Point A would be determined to be inside and Point B to be outside.

```
BOOL ColPrismObj :: collision (D3DVALUE x, D3DVALUE y, D3DVALUE z,
        D3DVECTOR &v)
{
 int s;

 if (sign == 0) return FALSE;

 if (min.x > x || max.x < x)
 {
  return FALSE;
 } else if (min.y > y || max.y < y)
 {
  return FALSE;
 } else if (min.z > z || max.z < z)
 {
  return FALSE;
 } else {
  y = z;

 s = ((points[1][0]-points[0][0])*(points[0][1]-y) -
   (points[1][1]-points[0][1])*(points[0][0]-x)) > 0 ? 1 : -1;
 if (s != sign)
 {
  return FALSE;
 } else {
  s = ((points[2][0]-points[1][0])*(points[1][1]-y) -
   (points[2][1]-points[1][1])*(points[1][0]-x)) > 0 ? 1 : -1;
  if (s != sign)
  {
   return FALSE;
  } else {
   s = ((points[0][0]-points[2][0])*(points[0][1]-y) -
      (points[0][1]-points[2][1])*(points[2][0]-x)) > 0 ? 1 : -1;
   if (s != sign)
   {
    return FALSE;
   } else {
    v.x = D3DVAL (0.0);
    v.y = D3DVAL (0.0);
    v.z = D3DVAL (0.0);
    return TRUE;
   }
  }
 }
}
```

10.4.6 The sphere collision member function

Our second object's collision member function checks for the collision of a point and a *sphere* as shown in figure 10.3. Point *A* would be determined to be inside and Point *B* to be outside.

```
BOOL ColSphereObj::collision (D3DVALUE x, D3DVALUE y, D3DVALUE z,
        D3DVECTOR &v)
{
 if ( (center.x-x)*(center.x-x) +
  (center.y-y)*(center.y-y) +
  (center.z-z)*(center.z-z) > rad*rad)
 {
 return FALSE;
 } else {
 v.x = D3DVAL (0.0);
 v.y = D3DVAL (0.0);
 v.z = D3DVAL (0.0);
 return TRUE;
 }
}
```

10.4.7 The cylinder collision member function

Our final object's collision detection checks for the collision of a point and a *cylinder* as shown in figure 10.4. Point A would be determined to be inside and Point B to be outside.

```
BOOL ColCylObj::collision (D3DVALUE x, D3DVALUE y, D3DVALUE z, D3DVECTOR &v)
{
 if (center.x-rad > x || center.x+rad < x)
 {
 return FALSE;
 } else if (center.y > y || center.y+height < y)
 {
 return FALSE;
 } else if (center.z-rad > z || center.z+rad < z)
 {
 return FALSE;
 } else if ( (center.x-x)*(center.x-x) + (center.z-z)*(center.z-z) >
        rad*rad)
```

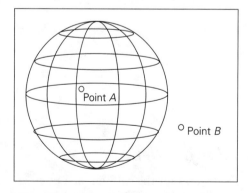

Figure 10.3 Determining if a point is inside a sphere

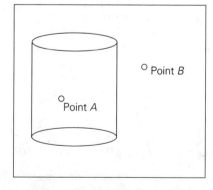

Figure 10.4 Determining if a point is inside a cylinder

```
  {
   return FALSE;
  } else {
   v.x = D3DVAL (0.0);
   v.y = D3DVAL (0.0);
   v.z = D3DVAL (0.0);
   return TRUE;
  }
 }

 BOOL D3MinObj::collision (D3DVALUE x, D3DVALUE y, D3DVALUE z, D3DVECTOR &v)
 {
  if (list.Start () != 0)
  {
   do
   {
    if (TRUE == (list.Get ())->collision (x, y, z, v)) return TRUE;
   } while (list.Next () != 0);
  }
  return FALSE;
 }
```

As you can see, these classes allow us a large amount of diversity in our object shapes. Because of this, with a little imagination you should be able to create a simplified shape which will encompass any of your objects while having a simple mathematical definition so that the intersection can be calculated quickly and easily. I'd suggest you try adding a new object shape, overloading the collision method, and try out this object of your own. You could add a check for collision with a mountain wall fairly easily.

10.5 What does our application look like now?

As in several of our chapters, the code for this one, when executed, at first glance looks like the code for chapter 9. The difference is that when you start to maneuver through the world, you will experience the feel of real walls for the first time. Try to walk through the castle wall or into the well. You will be stopped just as you hit them, the reaction you expect from a *solid* object.

This is the capability we needed to allow us to create rooms which keep us locked in them, castles that keep us out, or rocks we can trip on.

10.6 What did we learn?

In this chapter, we covered how to create a class which handles the difficult task of determining if we collide with an object. You could use a simple *box* approximation for every object and just use the GetBox method to determine the object's bounds. You could then compute the intersection with a simple equation, but the accuracy for any but the simplest of objects is just not good enough for a program worth putting our name on.

The class we created provides collision detection using a reasonable approximation of the surface with which we are trying to detect a collision. We defined the cylinder, sphere, prism, and box shapes. As you find a need for other shapes to more closely match your objects, you should now easily be able to copy one of our shapes and modify the code to handle the new one!

10.7 What's next?

In the next chapter I will cover DirectSound and you will learn how you can add exceptional sound to your applications easily. With this addition, you will have all of the basic knowledge of the DirectX technologies you need to create the games, simulations, or other software you desire.

chapter 11

Adding sound

11.1 A quick DirectSound overview

I know that this book is on Direct3D, but there are a few other aspects of DirectX which I feel you should know if you are going to be able to create great software! You have already learned about using DirectInput for joystick control. Now I want to show you a little about how to handle audio output using another DirectX component, DirectSound.

DirectSound, like all of the DirectX components, is designed to access your sound board from the lowest level to make sure you get the highest quality sound out of your board possible. It will utilize whatever features your hardware has, including additional sound memory add-ons, and sound mixing.

Mixing sounds is where you play multiple sounds simultaneously. In our game we can do this to include sounds for walking, whistling, and background music. To create realistic simulations, an imaginative combination of sounds is critical.

I showed you how Direct3D fit into DirectX and Win32 under Windows 95 earlier. In figure 11.1, I show the structure of sound under Windows 95 and DirectX.

213

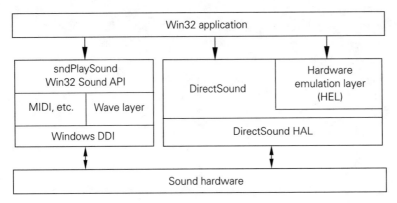

Figure 11.1 DirectSound

Win32 applications use the sndPlaySound API to generate sounds by calling a function within the wave layer which calls the Windows audio device driver interface (DDI). The DDI then communicates with the sound card to produce sounds. These sound drivers only handle playing one sound at a time, so software developers need to do their own mixing of wave files! This wave mixing also is slow, has lower quality since it is 8-bit audio, and has latency problems.

Many developers, prior to DirectX, used WAVEMIX.DLL to mix sounds. This DLL only allows the mixing of up to eight WAV files and can only accurately produce 8-bit waveforms. DirectSound has *no* limit on the number of wave files it can mix and it can use any standard sampling rate. One nice feature is that with soundboards supporting hardware mixing, there is almost no CPU cost for each sound combination. Even on soundboards without hardware mixing, the cost of mixing is very small, with each wave file taking up less than one percent of your CPU time. DirectSound also uses any accelerated sound hardware in your system for things like hardware sound buffer memory and hardware mixing. DirectSound will automatically take advantage on any hardware present, but you can also check the hardware capabilities yourself to optimize hardware resource allocation.

11.2 What is a wave file?

A wave file in DirectSound is composed of a header and the digitized sound data sample. This data, the sound wave, is a scalar value of the average amplitude recorded over an interval on the wave. On an analog sound wave, there are an infinite number of points, each with an amplitude value from 0 to n, where n is the maximum pressure the medium the wave is traveling through (the *wave carrier*) can handle before breaking down.

In the digitized version of the wave, there are a finite number of samples along the wave, with each sample having a duration. Each sample represents what the wave sounds like at that time. The number of samples, and consequently the duration of the sample, is determined by the sampling rate.

As I mentioned before, the wave sample for DirectSound is stored using the WAV format. The wave file header is in the WAVEFORMATEX format which is as follows:

```
typedef struct
{
  WORD wFormatTag;            // The Waveform Format
  WORD nChannels;             // 1 for Mono, 2 for Stereo
  WORD nSamplesPerSec;        // # of samples per second
  WORD nAvgBytesPerSec;       // # bytes per sec for playback
  WORD nBlockAlign;           // The sample's alignment
  WORD wBitsPerSample;        // The sample size
  WORD cbSize;                // The extra bytes for information
}
```

The WAV file is a tagged data file with the header indicating the format and size of the wave file. The reminder of the file can be parsed by searching for four-byte sequences of the characters fmt to locate the header and data to locate the samples.

11.3 Adding a wave file

There are a few different ways to load sound files. Although I often load the files directly within the code, it is sometimes more logical to place the WAV files in your project resources. If you are developing a project such as a game for distribution, *burying* the WAV files in your project allows you to not have to distribute the wave files as separate files. This can be a handy way of keeping your files from being seen when it is not desired.

I use the Microsoft Visual C++ compiler for all of my work since it is the best, most logically assembled, development environment I have found. It also creates quite tight code. Adding the WAV files into your project is very simple with Visual C++. To add the files, you just select the insert menu and then select the resource item from the pull-down menu. This process is shown in figure 11.2.

Once you have selected the resource menu item, a pop-up menu will be displayed requesting what type of resource you wish to add. To add a wave file, you just need to select the *WAVE* menu item. You will then need to select the import button to begin the process of importing a wave file.

To get WAV files for your project, you can either create your own by using one of the many tools for digitizing sound samples, or you can find many public domain samples on the Internet. For generic samples, this is a nice, free way to acquire samples for demonstration software or other projects you may develop. When you get to the point

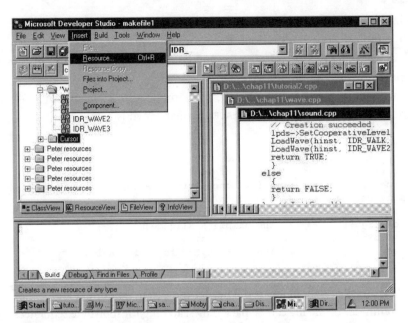

Figure 11.2 Adding a WAV Resource using Microsoft Visual C++ (step 1)

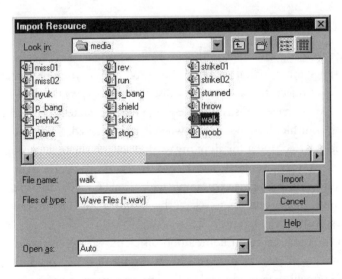

Figure 11.3 Adding a WAV Resource using Microsoft Visual C++ (step 2)

of developing software for distribution as shareware or through standard commercial channels, you will want to create your own samples. I would recommend that you search for the many new packages that are showing up for creating your own WAV and

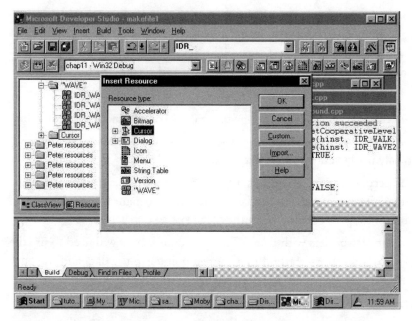

Figure 11.4 Adding a WAV Resource using Microsoft Visual C++ (step 3)

Musical Instrument Digital Interface (MIDI) files and choose the one which best fits your needs. There are also several WAV files on the DirectX distribution CD.

The Import button you use to import a WAV file into your project is shown in figure 11.3.

The final step in importing a WAV file is selecting the file from the import resource menu. You can select the type of file you wish to import, which is the *wave files* entry from the *files of type* drop-down. This window is shown below in figure 11.4.

That is all there is to importing WAV files into your project. Once you have the files you desire, you can get going on the development of the DirectSound to play your new WAV files. Let's see how to do that!

11.4 Adding simple DirectSound capabilities to our world

There is a fair amount of code to add to our program to implement sound. As with the rest of DirectX, DirectSound implement most of the APIs as COM interfaces.

The DirectSoundEnumerate interface is used to determine which DirectSound devices are installed in your system. Although most people have only one sound board on the system, some people will have more than one, or they may have a board with more than one sound component on it. If this is the case, you can choose which device you wish to create your DirectSound object for.

The code we will be creating performs eight basic tasks which are required to utilize DirectSound in our applications. The primary and secondary buffers will be discussed in detail shortly. The tasks are:

1 Create a DirectSound object. This is done using the `DirectSoundCreate` function.

2 Set a cooperative level using the `IDirectSound::SetCooperativeLevel` method. You will usually use `DSSCL_NORMAL`, which is the lowest level.

3 Create your secondary sound buffers using the `IDirectSound::CreateSound-Buffer` method. The creation of secondary buffers is the default for this method so you do not need to specify their type in the `DSBUFFERDESC` structure.

4 Load your secondary buffers with data. When you do this, you will need to use the `IDirectSoundBuffer::Lock` method to acquire a pointer to the data and the `IDirectSoundBuffer::Unlock` method to set the data to the device.

5 Call the `IDirectSoundBuffer::Play` method to play your secondary buffers.

6 Use the `IDirectSoundBuffer::Stop` method of your DirectSoundBuffer object to stop all of your buffers when your application has finished playing sounds.

7 Release your secondary buffers.

8 Release your DirectSound object.

The code to load and play Wave and MIDI files in our program will require the multimedia extensions header file.

```
#include <mmsystem.h>
#include <vfw.h>
#include "sound.h"
```

The new objects we need when adding our sound capabilities are shown below. They are the DirectSound and DirectSound Buffer objects. The DirectSound Buffer objects are the objects we will use to hold the sounds for our program. For the code in this book, I chose to use two sounds—one each time we start walking forward or backward and one for when we turn. You will certainly want to add additional, realistic, sounds for your applications.

```
extern HINSTANCE hTheInstance;   // program instance

LPDIRECTSOUND lpds;
LPDIRECTSOUNDBUFFER lpDSB_Walk, lpDSB_Turn;
```

The `InitSound` routine is our main set-up routine for our DirectSound functionality. The `DirectSoundCreate` call creates a pointer to `IDirectSound` which we can use to access its interfaces. The first parameter is NULL in our example because we want to use the default Windows sound device. If you wish, you can use the GUID which represents the DirectSound driver you get from calling DirectSoundEnumerate. The second parameter will be filled with the pointer to the DirectSound object that is created from this call. The final argument must always be NULL.

```
BOOL InitSound(HWND hwnd, HINSTANCE hinst)
{
if (DirectSoundCreate(NULL, &lpds, NULL) == DS_OK)
{
```

As long as the call is successful, you will need to set the cooperative level of the object before you can use it. I would recommend that you set the cooperative level to DSSCL_NORMAL because it will allow other applications on your system to work with DirectSound. DirectSound allows multiple applications to use DirectSound simultaneously unless it is using the HEL because the system has an old sound board.

```
// If the creation is successful, load the wave files
lpds->SetCooperativeLevel(hwnd, DSSCL_NORMAL);
```

The next thing we need to do is load the wave files. The two files we will load are the sound for when we begin walking forward or backward and the sound for when we turn right or left. The LoadWave routine is discussed in the next section.

```
LoadWave(hinst, IDR_WALK, lpDSB_Walk);
LoadWave(hinst, IDR_WAVE2, lpDSB_Turn);
return TRUE;
}
else
{
return FALSE;
}
} // InitSound()
```

11.5 Loading a wave file

The LoadWave routine loads a sound from a WAV file, creates a secondary sound buffer, and copies the data into that buffer. This secondary buffer is typically used to store common sounds we use throughout our applications. The sound in our secondary buffer can be played as a single event or in a loop with the sound repeating.

This routine takes the hInst of our application, a WAV resource ID, and a pointer to a DirectSound Buffer as its parameters.

```
// LoadWave
// Load the sound data and place it in a DirectSound
// secondary buffer.

void LoadWave(HINSTANCE hinst, int ResourceID,
   LPDIRECTSOUNDBUFFER &lpDSB)
 {
 // Wave file and data information
 LPVOID    lpWaveData;// The return value from our
                     // LoadResource call
 WAVEFILE  WaveFile;// The wave file we will load
 DSBUFFERDESC  dsbd;

 // These variables hold the sound data information for our DirectSound
        buffer
 BYTE     *pbData   = NULL;   // A pointer to the first block of sound data
 BYTE     *pbData2  = NULL;   // A pointer to the second block of sound data
 DWORD    dwLength;           // Length of the first block of data
 DWORD    dwLength2;          // Length of the second block of data
```

The first thing that we need to do in this routine is to call our LoadWaveResource routine to load our wave file from its resource into memory. The call is as follows:

```
lpWaveData = LoadWaveResource (ResourceID, hinst, &WaveFile );
```

The LoadWaveResource routine takes the ID of the resource we wish to load, the application's hInst, and a pointer to the structure we will fill with the wave data. The routine and the required variables are defined as:

```
// Load a wave file into the memory location
// specified by the pWaveFile parameter from a resource.

LPVOID LoadWaveResource
  (int    resID ,        // The resID of the resource
   HANDLE hinst ,        // The hInst of the app
   LPWAVEFILE pWaveFile) // Points to the structure we will fill
{
   HRSRC hResInfo;       // Resource file information returned from the
                         // FindResource call
   HGLOBAL hResData;     // Resource file data from the hResInfo variable
        from
                         // the LoadResource call
   void *pRes;           // The resource we lock
   DWORD dwSize;         // The size of our resource
   LPVOID lpMemory;      // The memory we copy the resource to
```

To load the wave resource into memory, we will first call the Win32 FindResource function to get the location of the resource matching the requested type and name in the specified resource module. The FindResource routine is prototyped as:

```
HRSRC FindResource(
  HMODULE hModule,// The resource-module handle
  LPCTSTR lpName,// A pointer to the resource name
  LPCTSTR lpType // A pointer to the resource type
  );
```

If the resource is located, we also need to make sure we can load it into memory. To do this we call the Win32 LoadResource routine. This routine is prototyped as:

```
HGLOBAL LoadResource(
  HMODULE hModule, // A resource-module handle
  HRSRC hResInfo   // A resource handle
  );
```

Finally, we need to lock our resource in memory. This is achieved using the Win32 LockResource routine. This routine is prototyped as:

```
LPVOID LockResource(
  HGLOBAL hResData // handle to resource to lock
  );
```

The code to do all of this is shown below. If any of the calls are unsuccessful, we just return NULL to indicate that we could not load the wave resource.

```
// Find the resource and load it into memory
if (((hResInfo = FindResource(hinst, MAKEINTRESOURCE(resID), "WAVE")) !=
    NULL) &&
  ((hResData = LoadResource(hinst, hResInfo)) != NULL) &&
  ((pRes = LockResource(hResData)) != NULL)) {
```

As long as the resource could be loaded, we just need to get the size of the resource, allocate some space for the wave data, and copy the resource into our memory. The routine to acquire the size of a resource in bytes is another Win32 routine defined as:

```
DWORD SizeofResource(
  HMODULE hModule,      // The resource-module handle
  HRSRC hResInfo        // The resource handle
  );
```

The code to do this is:

```
// If the resource was found, copy it to the
// memory location we allocate
dwSize = SizeofResource(hinst, hResInfo);
if ((lpMemory = malloc (dwSize)) == NULL)
  return NULL; // If we cannot allocate space
memcpy (lpMemory, pRes, dwSize);
```

The final step in loading our wave resource is to unlock it and free it up. The calls to do this are:

```
UnlockResource(hResData);
FreeResource(hResData);
```

The last portion of this routine, now that we have loaded our wave file into memory and cleaned up after ourselves, is to parse the wave file into its parts. The call to this routine is below:

```
// Parse the wave data into its components
if (ParseWaveMemory(lpMemory,
   &(pWaveFile->pwfxInfo),
   &(pWaveFile->pbData),
   &(pWaveFile->cbSize)))
 {
 return lpMemory; // OK
 }
 }

 return NULL;
}
```

11.6 Parsing a wave file

The actual `ParseWaveMemory` routine is long but really fairly simple. The structure below has three slots to hold the file size, the WAV header, and the WAV data. The variable beneath it, `lpds`, is the pointer to the DirectSound interface which we defined in our main tutorial file.

```
// This structure holds the data for a wave file
typedef struct tagWAVEFILE
 {
 DWORD    cbSize;           // The size of the file
 LPWAVEFORMATEX pwfxInfo;   // The Wave Header
 LPBYTE  pbData;            // The Wave Bits
 }
WAVEFILE, *LPWAVEFILE;

extern LPDIRECTSOUND lpds;
```

The `ParseWaveMemory` routine takes the pointer to the sound memory and returns the WAV header, data, and size. It is defined as:

```
// ParseWaveMemory
// Parses the loaded wave file in memory into its header and samples.
// To do this, search for the "fmt " and "data"
```

CHAPTER 11 ADDING SOUND

```
// fields.

BOOL ParseWaveMemory
  (LPVOID         lpMemory,          // Pointer to ram
   LPWAVEFORMATEX *lplpWaveHeader,   // Pointer to a pointer to the header
   LPBYTE  *lplpWaveSamples,         // Pointer to a pointer to the samples
   LPDWORD  lpWaveSize)              // Pointer to the size
{
   LPDWORD pointMem;
   LPDWORD pdwEnd;
   DWORD dwRiff;
   DWORD dwType;
   DWORD dwLength;
```

The first thing to do is to clear out our variables we will be returning the parsed WAV data in.

```
// Initialize the default values of the parameters passed in
if (lplpWaveHeader)
 *lplpWaveHeader = NULL;
else
 return FALSE;

if (lplpWaveSamples)
 *lplpWaveSamples = NULL;
else
 return FALSE;

if (lpWaveSize)
 *lpWaveSize = 0;
else
 return FALSE;
```

To parse the memory, we need to grab the type and length of our WAV data.

```
// Set up a pointer to indicate the start of the wave
// memory.
pointMem = (DWORD *)lpMemory;

// Get the type and length of the wave memory
dwRiff = *pointMem++;
dwLength = *pointMem++;
dwType = *pointMem++;
```

With that information, we can now make a call to the Win32 multimedia macro, mmioFOURCC, to convert the four characters *R, I, F, F* into a four-character code we can use to compare against the values we parsed out and make sure that the memory contains a RIFF WAVE chunk of data.

```
// Use the mmioFOURCC macro from the Windows SDK to verify
// that this is a RIFF WAVE memory chunk
```

```
if (dwRiff != mmioFOURCC('R', 'I', 'F', 'F'))
  return FALSE; // not even RIFF

if (dwType != mmioFOURCC('W', 'A', 'V', 'E'))
  return FALSE; // not a WAV
```

As long as we have the right type of data, we can continue our parsing efforts. Our first check is to see if we are at the format portion of the data. If we are , we can set our wave header parameter for returning when the function is done. We also want to check to see if we are done parsing the data and if we are, we can return knowing we have all of our data from the WAV information parsed properly.

```
// Get the pointer to the end of our wave memory
pdwEnd = (DWORD *)((BYTE *)pointMem + dwLength-4);

// Walk through the bytes and locate the tags
while (pointMem < pdwEnd)
  {
  dwType = *pointMem++;
  dwLength = *pointMem++;

  switch (dwType)
    {
    // Located the format portion
    case mmioFOURCC('f', 'm', 't', ' '):

      if (lplpWaveHeader && !*lplpWaveHeader)
        {
        if (dwLength < sizeof(WAVEFORMAT))
          return FALSE; // Drop out because this is not a WAV

        // Set the lplpWaveHeader parameter to point to this piece of
        // the memory
        *lplpWaveHeader = (LPWAVEFORMATEX)pointMem;


        // See if we have the bits and the size of the
        // bits filled out yet. If they are, then we have fully parsed
        // the memory and can return happy
        if ((!lplpWaveSamples || *lplpWaveSamples) &&
           (!lpWaveSize || *lpWaveSize))
          {
          return TRUE;
          }
        }
      break;
```

We also need to parse out the data for our WAV sample. If we are at the data portion, we just set our return parameter to this location.

```
    // We are at the samples - fill the values to return
    // for the sample and size
    case mmioFOURCC('d', 'a', 't', 'a'):

     if ((lplpWaveSamples && !*lplpWaveSamples) ||
      (lpWaveSize && !*lpWaveSize))
     {
     // Set the samples pointer to point to this location
     // in the memory.
     if (lplpWaveSamples) *lplpWaveSamples = (LPBYTE)pointMem;
     else
        return FALSE;

     // Set the size of the wave
     if (lpWaveSize) *lpWaveSize = dwLength;
     else
        return FALSE;

     // If the header pointer is filled, we can return happy..
     if (!lplpWaveHeader || *lplpWaveHeader)
      return TRUE;
     }
    break;

 } // End case
```

If we have not parsed the data completely, we set our pointer to the next location in our WAV memory and continue.

```
    // Set the pointer to the next portion of memory
    pointMem = (DWORD *)((BYTE *)pointMem + ((dwLength+1)&~1));
    }

 // If we get to this point, we failed and did not acquire all of the
 // wave data - Return Failure.
 return FALSE;
 } // ParseWaveMemory
```

11.7 Setting up our sound buffers

At this point, we have all of our required information parsed out of the WAV data. We now can clear out our sound buffer and set the DirectSound flags. The DSBCAPS_CTRLDEFAULT flag works the same as using all of the DSBCAPS_CTRLPAN, DSBCAPS_CTRLVOLUME, and DSBCAPS_CTRLFREQUENCY flags. This indicates that we want our buffer to have pan control capability, volume control capability, and frequency control capability. These are capabilities you will usually want, so the DSBCAPS_CTRLDEFAULT flag is fairly handy.

```
// Set up our direct sound buffer.
memset(&dsbd, 0, sizeof(DSBUFFERDESC));
dsbd.dwSize    = sizeof(DSBUFFERDESC);

// Now set up a buffer on the sound card's memory
// (DSBCAPS_STATIC) which can adjust the pan, volume, and
// frequency (DSBCAPS_CTRLDEFAULT)
dsbd.dwFlags   = DSBCAPS_CTRLDEFAULT | DSBCAPS_STATIC ;
```

The final members of the DirectSound buffer structure to fill as the size and format slots.

```
// Set our wave size and format which must be a PCM format
dsbd.dwBufferBytes = WaveFile.cbSize;
dsbd.lpwfxFormat   = WaveFile.pwfxInfo;
```

We now have all of the data filled in, so we can finally create our sound buffer. To create it, we just pass in the sound buffer structure we filled in and as long as everything goes well, the sound buffer will be placed into the lpDSB variable.

```
// Now, create our sound buffer
if (DS_OK != lpds->CreateSoundBuffer(&dsbd, &lpDSB, NULL))
 {
 OutputDebugString("Failed to create sound buffer\n");
 return;
 }
```

I have now brought up both *primary* and *secondary* buffers. I suppose I had better explain them a bit more thoroughly! The primary buffer is the buffer which holds the data that you hear (played through your speakers) and there is only one of these. For our purposes, you will not directly access the primary buffer for playback. Although you could access the primary buffer and directly manipulate it, you would then have to take responsibility for the real-time playback handling of the buffer at all times. Because this would force you to handle all of the time-critical handling yourself, I would recommend you not do this.

The secondary buffers hold the sounds that you are ready to play. If you wish to listen to a sound in a secondary buffer, you can simply play it into the primary buffer. The audio data that is stored in a secondary buffer can be played using the IDirectSound-Buffer::Play method. When you use this method, DirectSound mixes the secondary buffer into the primary buffer. The IDirectSoundBuffer::Play method will default to playing the buffer once and will stop when it hits the end, but you can also tell it to loop continuously using the DSBPLAY_LOOPING flag.

If you wish to play a sound several times, or even simultaneously, you can use the IDirectSound::DuplicateSoundBuffer method to create a second buffer using the same buffer memory as the first sound buffer. Using this method, when you duplicate a sound, you can play both of the buffers independently without using additional buffer memory.

With the buffer created properly, we need to lock it so that we can write to it. The Lock method acquires a valid pointer to our sound buffer's audio data. This pointer is a *write* pointer only! You should never try to read sound data from the pointer since it might not be valid even though the DirectSoundBuffer object contains valid data. One situation where this could occur is where your buffer is in onboard memory and the pointer is an address to a temporary buffer in main system memory. When the memory is unlocked, this temporary buffer would be transferred to onboard memory and our pointer would no longer be valid.

You should write your data to the pointers returned by the IDirectSound-Buffer::Lock method and then call the IDirectSoundBuffer::Unlock method to release the buffer when you are done. Microsoft warns that the sound buffer should not be locked for long periods of time because the play cursor will reach the locked bytes and various audio problems, such as random noise, might occur.

The passed parameters to the Lock method are an offset and a byte count. The returned parameters are two write pointers and their associated sizes. The reason we need two pointers is that sound buffers are circular. If the locked bytes wrap past the end of the buffer, the second buffer will be set to point to the beginning of the buffer. If it does not wrap, it is set to NULL.

If the lplpvAudioPtr2 and lpdwAudioBytes2 parameters are passed as NULL, DirectSound does not lock the wrap-around portion of the buffer.

The DirectSound Lock method is prototyped as:

```
HRESULT Lock(DWORD dwWriteCursor, DWORD dwWriteBytes,
  LPVOID lplpvAudioPtr1, LPDWORD lpdwAudioBytes1,
  LPVOID lplpvAudioPtr2, LPDWORD lpdwAudioBytes2,
 DWORD dwFlags);
```

The parameters to this method are:

- dwWriteCursor. The offset in bytes from the beginning of the buffer to the point the lock begins. This parameter will be ignored if DSBLOCK_FROMWRITECURSOR is specified in the dwFlags parameter.

- dwWriteBytes. The size in bytes of the part of the buffer we wish to lock.

- lplpvAudioPtr1. The address of a pointer which will receive the first block of the sound buffer which will be locked.

- lpdwAudioBytes1. The address of a variable which will receive the number of bytes pointed to by the lplpvAudioPtr1 parameter. If this value is less than the dwWrite-

Bytes parameter, the lplpvAudioPtr2parameter will be set to point to a second block of sound data.

- lplpvAudioPtr2. The address of a pointer which will receive the second block of the sound buffer we want locked. If the value of this parameter is NULL, it means that the lplpvAudioPtr1 parameter points to the whole locked portion of the sound buffer.

- lpdwAudioBytes2. The address of a variable which will receive the number of bytes pointed to by the lplpvAudioPtr2 parameter. If lplpvAudioPtr2 is NULL, this value will be set to 0.

- dwFlags. Only one flag, DSBLOCK_FROMWRITECURSOR, is defined. This flag states that we want the buffer to lock from the current write cursor, making a call to IDirect-SoundBuffer::GetCurrentPosition unnecessary. The dwWriteCursor parameter is ignored if this flag is set.

The call to perform the lock of our buffer is as follows:

```
// We now have a pointer to a DirectSoundBuffer.
// We can copy blocks of sound data into the buffer
// using the Lock and Unlock interfaces on the DirectSoundBuffer:

 // Lock the DirectSound buffer
 if (DS_OK == lpDSB->Lock
   (0 ,            // The offset into the buffer where we will start writing
   WaveFile.cbSize, // The size of the wave file to copy in
   &pbData ,       // The first block of sound data
   &dwLength ,     // The length of the first block of data
   &pbData2 ,      // The second block of sound data
   &dwLength2 ,    // The length of the second block of data
   0L))            // Flags
 {
```

As long as the lock worked as expected, the two blocks of data from the wave file can be copied and we then free up our memory and unlock our buffer.

```
 // Copy the first block of data from the wave file
 memcpy(pbData, WaveFile.pbData, dwLength);

 // Copy the second block of data from the wave file
 if (dwLength2)
  memcpy(pbData2, WaveFile.pbData+dwLength , dwLength2);

 // Free the memory which was allocated in the LoadWaveFile function
 // now that it has been copied to the buffer
 free (lpWaveData);

 // Unlock our buffer
 if (DS_OK != lpDSB->Unlock(pbData, dwLength, pbData2, dwLength2))
```

```
      OutputDebugString("Unlock failed");
   }

   else
   {
   OutputDebugString("Lock failed");
   }
} // LoadWave
```

11.8 Playing our sounds

The last routines we need to define for our WAV file handling are the routines to release our DirectSound object when we are done and the routines which actually make our sounds for us. The CleanUpSound routine is very simple and is as follows:

```
void CleanupSound(void)
   {
    if(lpds!= NULL) lpds->Release(); // Releases the object and buffers
   }
```

Our two routines to play sounds are named Walk and Turn, and their uses should be fairly apparent. The Walk routine just checks to make sure we have a valid pointer to our DirectSound buffer containing the Walk sound and if we do, it plays our walking sound.

The IDirectSoundBuffer::SetPan method is called to specify the relative volume between the left and right channels. The method is prototyped as:

```
HRESULT SetPan(LONG lPan);
```

The lpan parameter indicates the relative volume between the left and right channels. The range of this parameter can be from 10,000 to –10,000 indicating the hundreths of a decibel (dB) for our sound level.

Setting the lpan value to 0 means that we wish both channels to be set at full volume, attenuated by 0 decibels. If you set the lpan value to any other value, you will be indicating that you want one channel at full volume and the other attenuated. As an example, if you were to set the pan to 1000, this would indicate that you want the right channel at full volume and the left channel attenuated by 10.00 dB.

If you set the pan to –10,000, the left channel will be at full volume and the right channel will be silent. Also remember that the pan control is cumulative with the volume control.

Our Walk routine, and its call to the SetPan method, is shown below:

```
void Walk(int pan)
   {
   if (lpDSB_Walk)
    {
     lpDSB_Walk->SetPan(pan);
```

The other method we need to use is the `Play` method. This method is the one which actually plays our sound so we can hear it after all of this set up. This method will mix our secondary buffer into the primary buffer and send it to the sound device. If this is the first buffer to play, a primary buffer will be created and the sound buffer will be played. Primary buffers need to be played with the DSPPLAY_LOOPING flag set.

If the buffer we pass into this method is already playing, the call will be successful and the buffer will keep playing, but the flags will be changed to the ones in our new call.

The `Play` method is prototyped as:

```
HRESULT Play(DWORD dwReserved1, DWORD dwReserved2,
 DWORD dwFlags);
```

The parameters to this method are:

- `dwReserved1`. A reserved parameter which must be set to 0.

- `dwReserved2`. A reserved parameter which must be set to 0.

- `dwFlags`. The flags which indicate how to play the buffer. Only one flag, DSBPLAY_LOOPING, is currently available, and this flag indicates that when the end of our audio buffer is hit, it will begin playing at the head of the buffer again. The play will loop until we stop it. This flag must be set when we are playing primary sound buffers.

The call to play a sound, for one iteration and then stop, each time we begin to walk forward or backward is:

```
    lpDSB_Walk->Play(0, 0, 0);
  }
}
```

I have also created a second routine to play a sound when we turn left or right. This routine illustrates the ability to loop playing our sound continuously until we turn it off, rather than playing it once as we did above. I have the code below checking whether the toggle value is TRUE or FALSE, and turning the sound on or off each time we hit this routine.

```
  void Turn(BOOL ToggleOn)
   {
  if (lpDSB_Turn)
    {
    if (ToggleOn)
     lpDSB_Turn->Play(0, 0, DSBPLAY_LOOPING);
    else
     lpDSB_Turn->Stop();
    ToggleOn = !ToggleOn;
   }
  }
```

The routines which call the Turn and Walk routines are our MoveForward, Move-Backward, TurnRight, and TurnLeft routines. These just set a pan value to 1000, meaning that the right channel is at full volume and the left channel is attenuated by 10.00 dB. These routines are defined as:

```
void MoveForward (D3DVECTOR v)
{
 // Set the stereo effect to 1000
 float pan = (float) 1000;
 Walk(pan);

 camera->SetVelocity(scene, v.x, v.y, v.z, FALSE);
}

void MoveBackward (D3DVECTOR v)
{
 // Set the stereo effect to 1000
 float pan = (float) 1000;
 Walk(pan);

 camera->SetVelocity(scene, -v.x, -v.y, -v.z, FALSE);
}

void TurnRight (D3DVALUE a)
{
 // Set the stereo effect to 1000
 float pan = (float) 1000;
 Turn(pan);

 camera->SetRotation (scene, D3DVAL (0.0), D3DVAL (1.0), D3DVAL (0.0), a);
}

void TurnLeft (D3DVALUE a)
{
 // Set the stereo effect to 1000
 float pan = (float) 1000;
 Turn(pan);

 camera->SetRotation (scene, D3DVAL (0.0), D3DVAL (1.0), D3DVAL (0.0), -a);
}
```

That is all of the code we need to play WAV file sounds. This aspect of Direct-Sound is really quite simple to use. At this point, I'd suggest that you compile the code for this chapter and play with the pan values, setting them from 10,000 to –10,000 and listening for the differences in the sound.

11.9 Playing a MIDI file

The next aspect of sound I would like to show you for implementing sounds into your Direct3D games is the use of MIDI files. DirectSound does not supply functions to handle the playing of MIDI files but we can add this capability to our games using the Windows Multimedia API. This API supplies both high- and low-level support for MIDI playback. The high-level support is through Media Control Interface (MCI) functions, which work with MIDI formats 0 and 1. Imaginative usage of MIDI files, along with good music skills to write them, will add a huge amount of ambiance to your games.

We will need to specify the filename of the MIDI file we will be playing.

```
#define MUSICFILE "peter.mid"
```

Our `PlayMusic` routine takes the name of the MIDI file we wish to play, opens it, and plays it. The routine is defined as:

```
// MCI is used to play a MIDI file.
// When playback is complete done, the window procedure is notified.

DWORD PlayMusic(HWND hwnd, LPSTR lpszMIDIFileName)
 {

// Define the music variables
MCI_OPEN_PARMS mciOpenParms;
MCI_PLAY_PARMS mciPlayParms;
DWORD dwReturnVal;
```

The `mciSendCommand` is used to send a command to our MCI device. In the call below, we open our device by using `MCI_OPEN`, defining the file name and device type, and passing this information in the slots of the `MCI_OPEN_PARMS` structure.

```
// Open the device by specifying the device and filename.
// MCI will then try to choose the MIDI mapper as our output port.
mciOpenParms.lpstrDeviceType = "sequencer";
mciOpenParms.lpstrElementName = lpszMIDIFileName;
if (dwReturnVal = mciSendCommand(NULL, MCI_OPEN,
  MCI_OPEN_TYPE | MCI_OPEN_ELEMENT,
  (DWORD)(LPVOID) &mciOpenParms))
{
  // Failed to open device. Don't close it; just return error.
  return dwReturnVal;
}
```

As long as the device was opened properly, we just need to play the sound by using `MCI_PLAY` and passing the MIDI device information in the slots of the `MCI_PLAY_PARMS` structure.

```
// The device was opened successfully so get the device ID.
wMidiDeviceID = mciOpenParms.wDeviceID;

// Start the playback.
mciPlayParms.dwCallback = (DWORD) hwnd;
if (dwReturnVal = mciSendCommand(wMidiDeviceID, MCI_PLAY, MCI_NOTIFY,
  (DWORD)(LPVOID) &mciPlayParms))
  {
   if (wMidiDeviceID)
    mciSendCommand(wMidiDeviceID, MCI_CLOSE, 0, NULL);
   wMidiDeviceID = 0;

   return dwReturnVal;
  }
 return 0L;
} // PlayMusic()
```

The call in our tutorial2.cpp file to actually start the MIDI music playing just passes the current window and the MIDI file name to the `PlayMusic` routine. This command is:

```
PlayMusic(win, MUSICFILE);
```

The only other thing you need to know how to do is to stop your MIDI music and clean up when you are done. As with the other commands, we use `mciSendCommand` to specify `MCI_CLOSE` to close our MIDI file.

```
if (wMidiDeviceID)
  mciSendCommand(wMidiDeviceID, MCI_CLOSE, 0, NULL);
wMidiDeviceID = 0;
```

That is all there is to the basics of playing MIDI files. You can now easily incorporate introduction, background, or other music easily into your games!

11.10 3D sound

There is one final aspect of DirectSound I feel is very important to learn. I have left it until last because I feel it is the most *fun* area and has some very interesting possibilities if you take full advantage of it. DirectSound provides the capability for us to create sounds with perceived *positions*. The position of a sound is set using the `IDirectSound3Dbuffer` and `IDirectSound3Dlistener` interfaces. Our sound sources can be either a point source, where the sound radiates in every direction, or a cone. If the sound source is defined as a cone, the sounds outside the cone are attenuated. In Direct3D, all sound buffers are sound cones. These sound cones can be created to act like point source sounds by leaving the sound at its default settings (a cone angle of 360

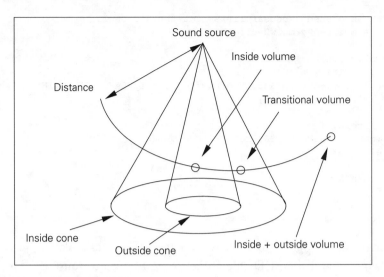

Figure 11.5 A sound cone

degrees) so that the volume will be the same inside and outside the cone. The sound will also have no apparent orientation. By using these defaults, and setting the sound cone to a very wide size, you can make your sound cone act like a sphere.

The listener orientation is very important when attempting to create accurate 3D sound. DirectSound uses two vectors to orient the user—the *top* and the *front* vectors. This *top* vector originates from the center of the listener's head and points straight up through the top of the head. The *front* vector originates from the center of the head and points at a right angle to the top vector forward through the listener's face. The default value for the front vector is (0,0,1.0) and for the top vector is (0,1.0,0).

You can retrieve and set the listener's orientation using the `IDirectSound3DListener::GetOrientatinno` and the `IDirectSound3DListener::SetOrientation` methods.

11.11 Sound cones

The *sound cone* I mentioned above is a sound with a position but an orientation. If a sound has no orientation, it is considered a *point source*. If you define a sound as a sound cone, the cone will have both an inside and an outside cone (see figure 11.5).

The inside cone volume is the maximum volume level of 0 because DirectSound does not support amplification. Because of this, the volume levels are specified as negative numbers, indicating an attenuation of the maximum value. The volume changes gradually from the inside to the outside volume as we move between the them. The outside volume (the volume outside the cone) is the outside volume we specify added to our inside value.

If you use sound cones imaginatively, you can make sounds seem to come from a particular area. If you wanted to make a sound seem to be coming through an open window, you could set the sound source outside the window and orient it toward your window. By setting the sound cone to the width of the window and the outside cone volume to −10,000 (the values are specified in hundredths of a decibel), the inaudible value, you can make it seem as if the sound is coming from outside as you pass by it!

To get and set the cone angles, you use the `IDirectSound3DBuffer::GetConeAngles` and the `IDirectSound3DBuffer::SetConeAngles` methods. To get and set the orientation of the sound cones, you use the `IDirectSound3DBuffer::GetConeOrientation` and the `IDirectSound3DBuffer::SetConeOrientation` methods.

To get and set the outside cone volume, you use the `IDirectSound3DBuffer::GetConeOutsideVolume` and the `IDirectSound3DBuffer::SetConeOutsideVolume` methods.

11.12 Maximum and minimum distances

As a person moves toward a sound source, a sound will get louder and louder. The maximum distance is the distance at which the sound does not get any quieter. The minimum distance for a sound source is the point at which we no longer wish the volume to increase. Usually this is when the maximum value of 0 is reached. You can use the minimum distance to handle the compensation for the difference between the absolute volume levels of different sounds. Sounds need to be recorded at the same volumes, even though in reality they are very different in volume (e.g., a frog is much quieter than a train) due to the limitations in 16-bit audio for handling these large differences. As an example, you could set the minimum distance of the train to 200 meters and that of the frog at 10 centimeters. This way, the train will play at half volume when the listener is 400 meters away and the frog will be at half volume when the listener is 20 meters away.

To get and set the minimum distance values, you use the `IDirectSound3DBuffer::GetMinDistance` and the `IDirectSound3DBuffer::SetMinDistance` methods. To get and set the maximum distance values, you use the `IDirectSound3-DBuffer::GetMaxDistance` and the `IDirectSound3DBuffer::SetMaxDistance` methods.

11.13 Position versus velocity

All 3D sound buffers and 3D listeners have positions and velocities. The position indicates a location in 3D space. The velocity is used to calculate Doppler shift effects. You can change this velocity to minimize or exaggerate the Doppler effect of an object. If you wanted the train sound we discussed above to sound as if it were blasting by you, you could achieve this by increasing its sound buffer's velocity setting. If instead you increased the listener's Doppler shift, *all* sound would be effected. DirectSound will also combine the effects of multiple Doppler shifts when you have listener and sound source velocities.

To get and set your 3D sound buffer's position in 3D space, you use the IDirectSound3DBuffer::GetPosition and the IDirectSound3DBuffer::SetPosition methods. To get and set the velocity value used to calculate Doppler shift effects, you use the IDirectSound3DBuffer::GetVelocity and the IDirectSound3DBuffer::Set-Velocity methods.

Besides setting the velocity, you can also directly affect the Doppler shift by using the IDirectSound3DListener::SetDopplerFactor method (get this value using the IDirectSound3DListener::GetDopplerFactor method). By setting the value from 0 to 10, you can apply a sound up to ten times the Doppler shift you would perceive in the real world. A value of 0 indicates no Doppler shift, 1 indicates a real world Doppler effect, and 2 to 10 will indicate multiples of the real-world Doppler effect.

11.14 The actual code

Now that you have an understanding of the design of DirectSound3D, let's look at what it takes to implement a simple 3D Sound example. The code we will be creating will produce the effect of a sound circling around the listener. I have placed this sound in the 3D world project we have been building upon in all of the previous chapters. In this way, you can easily add other 3D sound effects such as sounds emanating from the tower. The first thing we need to define are the variables controlling the sounds' motion around us and the buffers we will need.

```
#define RADIUS        .5
#define PI            3.1415926535
#define TWOPI         (2*PI)
#define STEP          (TWOPI/180)

BOOL Playing;
LPDIRECTSOUND myDirectSound = NULL;
LPDIRECTSOUNDBUFFER myDirectSoundBuffer = NULL;
```

```
LPDIRECTSOUNDBUFFER myDirectSoundPrimaryBuffer = NULL;
LPDIRECTSOUND3DBUFFER myDirectSound3DBuffer = NULL;
LPDIRECTSOUND3DLISTENER myDirectSound3DListener = NULL;
D3DVALUE      sound3D_x;    // positive X axis points out the right ear
D3DVALUE      sound3D_y;    // positive Y axis points up
D3DVALUE      sound3D_z;    // positive Z axis points away from viewer
static double stepCounter = 0.0;
```

The code we will need to initialize the 3D sound is shown in the next code segment. All we are doing here is setting the initial position for the sound

```
// set the 3D parameters
sound3D_x  = (float)0.0;       // The left/right position set to zero
sound3D_y  = (float)0.0;       // Zero the verticle component
sound3D_z  = (float)RADIUS;    // The radius, in meters, in front of the
           listener
```

To load the 3D sound, we will need to call the routines to load the sound file and set up 3D sound. The calling sequence is as follows:

```
// load the sound file
if(myDirectSound == NULL)
    LoadFile(win);
.
.


void LoadFile(HWND hwnd)
{
 if (myDirectSound == NULL)
  InitDirectSound(hwnd);
.
.

BOOL InitDirectSound(HWND hwnd)
{
 DSBUFFERDESC dsBD = {0};

 if(DS_OK == DirectSoundCreate(NULL, &myDirectSound,NULL))
 {
    myDirectSound->SetCooperativeLevel(hwnd, DSSCL_NORMAL);
```

Once we have DirectSound set up, which you learned about in the last section so I have glossed over it, we need to create our primary 3D sound buffer. This is another task with which you are familiar—the only difference is that we will use the 3D flags DSBCAPS_CNTRL3D for this buffer rather than the 2D flags we used previously.

```
            // create primary 3D buffer
            ZeroMemory( &dsBD, sizeof(DSBUFFERDESC));
            dsBD.dwSize = sizeof(dsBD);
            dsBD.dwFlags = DSBCAPS_CTRL3D | DSBCAPS_PRIMARYBUFFER;
```

```
dsBD.dwBufferBytes = 0; //must be zero for primary buffer..
if (myDirectSound->CreateSoundBuffer(&dsBD,
  &myDirectSoundPrimaryBuffer, NULL) != DS_OK)
{
        Msg("Not able to create DirectSound3D primary buffer");
    ReleaseDirectSound();
    return FALSE;
}
```

If our primary 3D sound buffer is created properly, we have the final critical task of setting up our `IDirectSound3DListener` interface. The 3D listener is used to represent the person listening to the sound generated from the sound buffer. We use the `IDirectSound3DListener` to control the listener's position and velocity in 3D space, as well as other parameters, such as the Doppler shift for sound sources.

To acquire the `IDirectSound3DListener` interface for the primary buffer we just created, we use the `IDirectSound3DListener::QueryInterface` method.

```
// obtain interface pointers to IDirectDound3DListener
if(DS_OK != myDirectSoundPrimaryBuffer->QueryInterface(
  IID_IDirectSound3DListener, (void**)&myDirectSound3DListener))
  {
        Msg("Not able to create Direct 3D Sound Listener object");
    ReleaseDirectSound();
    return FALSE;
  }
}
else
{
  Msg("Not able to create DirectSound object");
  myDirectSound = NULL;
  return FALSE;
}
return TRUE;
}
```

As long as everything goes OK, which it will if you have everything set up as I have shown, we just need to load the wave file we want to play for the 3D sound and set it up for playing.

```
myDirectSoundBuffer =

  DSLoadSoundBuffer(myDirectSound,MAKEINTRESOURCE(IDR_WAVE4));

// Query for the 3D Sound Buffer interface.
myDirectSoundBuffer->QueryInterface(IID_IDirectSound3DBuffer,
    (void**) &myDirectSound3DBuffer);

Playing = TRUE;
}
```

The code to play the sound buffer we just loaded is as simple as initializing the buffer position and telling it to play it, looping continuously.

```
myDirectSoundBuffer->SetCurrentPosition(0);
myDirectSoundBuffer->Play(0, 0, DSBPLAY_LOOPING);
Playing = TRUE;
```

The last code we need to write is an addition to our processing loop (although I'd suggest using a timer instead—I just wrote the code without a timer because it was clearer for purposes of learning how to handle 3D sound). What I am doing is setting the sound to rotate around the listener by resetting (each loop iteration) the position to the next location in a circle around the user's head. The actual positioning of the sound is achieved using the `IDirectSound3DBuffer::SetPosition` method and passing the new desired x, y, z position.

```
stepcounter += STEP;
if(stepcounter>=TWOPI)
  stepcounter = 0.0;
sound3D_x = (float)(RADIUS * cos(stepcounter));
sound3D_z = (float)(RADIUS * sin(stepcounter));

myDirectSound3Dbuffer->SetPosition(sound3D_x,sound3D_y,sound3D_z,
        DS3D_IMMEDIATE);
```

We now have a functioning 3D sound capability added to our 3D world. You can easily add the ability to move the listener's position through the 3D world using the `IDirect3DListener::GetPosition` and `IDirect3DListener::SetPosition` methods. You should remember to do this so that the sounds will be generated relative to your proper position.

11.15 What did we learn?

In this chapter, I covered the loading and playing of WAV files so that you could add sounds to your great simulations and games. You have seen how to create multiple instances of the same sound and to loop sound for continuous replay of your files.

I also covered the loading and playback of MIDI files so that you can now add music to your applications. This will let you add audio excitement to any of your projects which will enhance the feel of your environments.

Finally, I covered 3D sound. Try building and running the Chap11_3D sub-project and listening to the sound. If you have a pair of headphones, I'd suggest using them since you will get a more effective 3D effect. What you will hear is a sound which seems to be circling around you. This effect will continue as you move around.

I'd suggest that as a way to verify that you understand this chapter, you try to produce a project where you attach a sound to the well or tower and make it seem to emanate from inside. Then, try using sound cones to simulate sound emanating from a window. This way you will be able to experiment with the advanced capabilities of DirectSound.

11.16 *What's next?*

In the next chapter, I will cover some final issues to consider when you are developing code in Direct3D. These include my favorite aspects of Direct3D—animation, shadows, and fog.

chapter 12

Some advanced Direct3D features

12.1 Advanced Direct3D features

In this chapter, I am going to cover three features of Direct3D that I feel are very powerful and quite useful. Because of their capabilities, I have left them until last and decided to organize this chapter differently than all of the previous ones. So far, each chapter has built upon the code from the previous one, enhancing the code with new features. I decided to use this approach because it seems that almost all of the books on computer graphics in the past have taken the approach of presenting little code samples showing off one aspect of the SDK in isolation rather than how to use the methods as a whole in conjunction with one another. For the first time, in this chapter I will be presenting standalone programs built upon the set-up code you learned from the previous chapters. (Many of the software code segments are the same as you have seen before.)

In the code for this chapter, we will be using the *tutorial.cpp* file we created previously, *but* the *create.cpp* file will be all new. I will be covering animation, shadows, and fog. Each of these aspects of animation are critical components of a realistic simulation or gaming system. Although you can create a good program without them, the end result of your efforts will be less than realistic and most likely less than the output you expected.

I will cover each of these in a separate section, but keep in mind that you can easily combine them. I would suggest that you try to combine the capabilities implemented in the software examples for this chapter into a single simulation. It would definitely help guarantee that you have learned these subject areas.

12.2 Animations

In my opinion, the feature of Direct3D that lends the greatest potential capability to our applications is the ability to load and play animated 3D objects. This capability is provided through the IDirect3DRMAnimationSet interface. An *Animation* in Direct3D terms is an entity which provides the ability to animate the position, orientation, and scaling of your visuals, lights, and viewports. An *AnimationSet* in Direct3D is an object which provides us an easy method of grouping Direct3DRMAnimation objects together for the simplification of the playback of our complex animation sequences.

The greatest potential I see for these types of objects is for the creation and animation of moving objects in our 3D world. These objects can range from people, to animals, to machines, to simple objects like doors. If you imagine the types of software you might be creating soon, think of what they would be like *without* the ability to have moving parts.

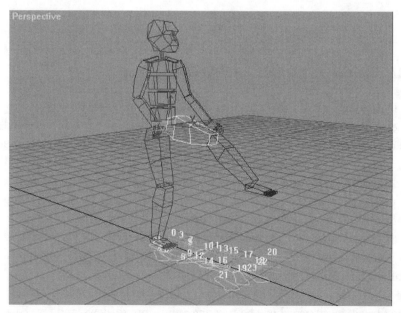

Figure 12.1 The foot step-based animation capabilities of Character Studio in 3D Studio Max

You could add moving objects using the translate and rotate capabilities of Direct3D, but these only give us the ability to move the object as a whole (actually, you could animate each part using the rotate and transform methods but this would be a *lot* of work). With the IDirect3DRMAnimationSet and IDirect3DRMAnimation objects, you can create objects using one of the many excellent 3D tools available today (I use 3D Studio and LightWave myself for the creation of animated people, animals, and creatures). These allow you to create 3D objects with built-in animation capabilities. With a bit of time, and artistic skill, you can create superb moving characters. This motion can consist of anything you might imagine such as running, walking, grasping, jumping, squatting, and so forth.

An example screen showing the foot step-based animation capabilities of Character Studio in 3D Studio is shown in figure 12.1. This is a wonderful feature that allows you to create biped creatures (humans, monsters, or anything else you can imagine).

12.2.1 *Multiple movement animation sequences*

To create an object that truly simulates a character in your virtual world, you will want to build an animation having *multiple* animation sequences, and the *transitions* between them.

I have including some animation objects on the CD. These include objects with walking and running capabilities. You can create an object with multiple states and transitions between them (walking to running to jumping to standing). By playing the separate animation segments contained within the animation, you can create any combination of motions you want. For example, if you just want the character to walk, repeat the walk frames. If you want it to walk and then stop and stand still, repeat the walk frames as long as you want, next play the transition from walk to stand frames, and finally, repeat the stand frames.

To illustrate this, the code below will set the animation to the first frame in the standing sequence since we initialized our time to 0.

```
// Forward to the STAND animation sequence
animationSet->SetTime(time);
.
.
```

The remainder of the code shown below is used to reset the animation to the start of the walking sequence when we get to the end of the desired sequence. This creates the effect of a continuous walking motion. If you use an animation which contains the animations of, and transitions between, several motions (walking, standing, etc.), you can change between the actions by just playing the appropriate segments in the order you desire.

The code to actually check if the animation has reached the end of the walking segment, and to reset it to the beginning, as well as set our current state to *walking*, is shown below.

```
// Reset to the beginning of WALKING if our animation has ended
if (time > WALK_START + NUM_WALKING_FRAMES)
  {
    time       = WALK_START;
    characterState = WALKING;
  }
```

The remainder of this section of the book illustrates an example program showing how to load and play an animation. I have used the *walk.x* file included on the CD. This file was converted from .3ds format to a .x animation using the command

```
conv3ds -A walk.3ds
```

12.2.2 *Setting up our animation callback structure*

The first thing we need to define is the structure to contain our animation callback parameters. This structure holds the AnimationSet itself and the animation time. We also need to define a box structure to acquire our object's dimensions.

```
typedef struct
{
  LPDIRECT3DRMANIMATIONSET animationSet;
  D3DVALUE time;
} animationCallbackArgs;

D3DRMBOX box;
```

Many files you may convert to .x format will use texture formats other than .ppm or .bmp files. By defining your own `loadTextures` routine, you can *wrap* the standard `IDirect3DRM::LoadTexture` method with your own conversion code. For our purposes, we do not need any additional code.

```
//
// The IDirect3DRM::LoadTexture knows how to load PPM and
// BMP files, so it checks to verify that your texture file is of that type.
// To load other formats, you will need to add additional code
// to your callback function. This code will need to load the data into a
// D3DRMIMAGE structure and then call IDirect3DRM::CreateTexture
// to create the texture
HRESULT loadTextures(char *name, void *arg, LPDIRECT3DRMTEXTURE *tex)
{
  return lpD3DRM->LoadTexture(name, tex);
}
```

The next routine is your animation callback routine. This is the *life clock* of your animation. It is used to set and increment the time for your animation to the next time segment. This enables the smooth playback of your animation.

```
//
// This is your animation callback to handle your animation playing
//
static void CDECL animationCallback(LPDIRECT3DRMFRAME obj, void* arg,
        D3DVALUE delta)
{
    animationCallbackArgs* callBack = (animationCallbackArgs *) arg;

    callBack->animationSet->SetTime(callBack->time);
    callBack->time += delta;// The time step you will be using, specified in
        relative ticks
}
```

With your animation callback routine defined, you can specify the routine to set the callback parameters and add the move callback to our frame. All this is really doing is creating a callback structure, filling it with our AnimationSet, and setting the start time to the beginning of the animation. With this done, it adds the callback to our frame.

```
//
// This routine adds the animation callback to your object
//
static BOOL setAnimationCallback(LPDIRECT3DRMFRAME frame,
            LPDIRECT3DRMANIMATIONSET animationSet)
{
    animationCallbackArgs *callBack;

    callBack = (animationCallbackArgs*)malloc(sizeof(animationCallback-
        Args));
    if (!callBack)
      return FALSE;

    callBack->animationSet = animationSet;
    callBack->time = D3DVAL(0);
    if (FAILED(frame->AddMoveCallback(animationCallback, (void *) callBack)))
      return FALSE;
    return TRUE;
}
```

12.2.3 Scaling and positioning our objects

The scaleScene routine is basically the same as the one that Microsoft uses in its examples (take a look at the viewer.cpp file on the Direct3D portion of this book's CD if you wish). I have included the code below, but all you really need to recognize is that it does nothing more than add our objects to the scene (in this case the mannequin mesh), acquire the maximum bounds of the object we are adding to our scene, scale the object to a logical size for our scene, and position it so we can see it.

```
//
// This routine is like the one Microsoft uses in some
// of their example code. It makes sure that no matter
// what the scale of your object is, it will be visible
// when you load it - This is quite handy!
//
static BOOL ScaleScene(LPDIRECT3DRMFRAME frame)
{
 LPDIRECT3DRMMESHBUILDER mbuilder;
 D3DVALUE maxDim;

    // Create a meshBuilder object, add your object frame
    // to it, and get the min-max box for your object
    lpD3DRM->CreateMeshBuilder(&mbuilder);
    mbuilder->AddFrame(frame);
    mbuilder->GetBox(&box);
    mbuilder->Release();

    // Calculate the size of your object
    maxDim = box.max.x - box.min.x;
    if (box.max.y - box.min.y > maxDim)
     maxDim = box.max.y - box.min.y;
    if (box.max.z - box.min.z > maxDim)
     maxDim = box.max.z - box.min.z;

    // Scale the frame according to these dimensions
    frame->AddScale(D3DRMCOMBINE_BEFORE, D3DDivide(D3DVAL(8.0), maxDim),
          D3DDivide(D3DVAL(8.0), maxDim),
          D3DDivide(D3DVAL(8.0), maxDim));

    // Position the frame in your scene
    frame->SetPosition(scene, D3DVAL(0.0), D3DVAL(0.0), D3DVAL(15.0));

    // Return happy
    return TRUE;
}
```

12.2.4 Loading the AnimationSet

The routine we call which actually loads our animation set is called LoadAnimationSet. It creates frame and AnimationSet objects and loads the animation using the IDirect3DRMAnimationSet::Load method. This method will default to loading the first animation set in the file requested in the lpvObjSource parameter. It method is defined as:

```
HRESULT Load(LPVOID lpvObjSource, LPVOID lpvObjID,
    D3DRMLOADOPTIONS d3drmLOFlags,
    D3DRMLOADTEXTURECALLBACK d3drmLoadTextureProc, LPVOID lpArgLTP,
  LPDIRECT3DRMFRAME lpParentFrame);
```

The parameters for it are:

- lpvObjSource. The source of the object we are loading, which can be a file, resource, stream, or a memory block based upon the source flag we specify in the d3drmLOFlags parameter

- lpvObjID. The object name or position you wish to load. If you specify the D3DRMLOAD_BYPOSITION flag for the d3drmLOFlags parameter, this parameter must be a pointer to a DWORD value specifying the objects order in the file. You can set this parameter to NULL.

- d3drmLOFlags. The D3DRMLOADOPTIONS type defining your load options.

- d3drmLoadTextureProc. Your D3DRMLOADTEXTURECALLBACK callback function which is called to load any of your textures which are used by the object that need special formatting. You can set this parameter to NULL.

- lpArgLTP. The address of your application-defined data, which is passed to the D3DRMLOADTEXTURECALLBACK callback function.

- lpParentFrame. The address of your parent Direct3DRMFrame object, so that the frames used by your animation set are not created with a NULL parent.

The code for the LoadAnimationSet routine is shown below. The only feature that should be new to you is the Load method call. In this call, we are requesting to load the file named with the name contained in the filename parameter and also load the textures (if any) associated with the object.

```
//
// This is the routine to load your animation set
//
static BOOL LoadAnimationSet(const char *filename)
{
 LPDIRECT3DRMANIMATIONSET lpAnimationSet;
 LPDIRECT3DRMFRAME lpFrame;

 // Create a new parent frame in the scene for your
 // animation
 if (FAILED(lpD3DRM->CreateFrame(scene, &lpFrame)))
  return FALSE;

 // Now load your animation set object
 if (FAILED(lpD3DRM->CreateAnimationSet(&lpAnimationSet)))
  return FALSE;

 if (FAILED(lpAnimationSet->Load((LPVOID)filename, NULL,
             D3DRMLOAD_FROMFILE, loadTextures,
             NULL, lpFrame)))
  return FALSE;
```

```
    // Scale things so your object show up in the scene
    ScaleScene(lpFrame);

    // Finally, set up the callback function
    setAnimationCallback(lpFrame, lpAnimationSet);

    return TRUE;
}
```

12.2.5 The code to load and view our AnimationSet

For this program, we will be using the CreateScene routine we have been using for all of
our projects, but we will be loading an animation object along with our light objects. To
load this object, we create a MeshBuilder object and call the LoadAnimationSet routine
we just defined. Once the object is loaded, we just need to create a mesh from it, create
a frame to contain it, and add our object to that frame as a visual so we can view it.

```
    //
    // Create and position the main shadow casting light for our scene
    //
  Create our meshbuilder object for loading our x file
    if (FAILED(lpD3DRM->CreateMeshBuilder(&myBuilder)))
       goto generic_error;
    // Load the object - This one is of a digitized woman
    if (!LoadAnimationSet("walk1.x"))
    {
       Msg("Failed to load the animation file.\n");
      goto ret_with_error;
    }
    // Create a mesh
    if (FAILED(myBuilder->CreateMesh(&myMesh)))
      goto generic_error;
    RELEASE(myBuilder);

    // Create a frame in our scene
    if (FAILED(lpD3DRM->CreateFrame(scene, &frame)))
      goto generic_error;

    // Add the mesh we just loaded to the frame
    if (FAILED(frame->AddVisual((LPDIRECT3DRMVISUAL) myMesh)))
      goto generic_error;
```

The end result of our efforts is shown in figures 12.2 and 12.3.

These two screen shots show two images representing phases of our walking
sequence. This scene displays the mannequin walking continuously. Since this program
uses our previous tutorial2.cpp file, you can control your viewpoint using the keyboard the
same way we did before. The object I chose for this animation was a mannequin object
but of course you can use any character you wish for your animations. I have included several human and creature objects which you can use to create your own animations (using

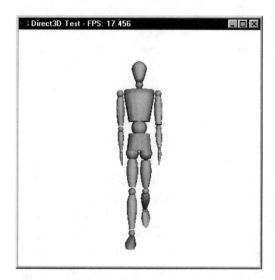

Figure 12.2 A frame of our walking animation object (right foot down)

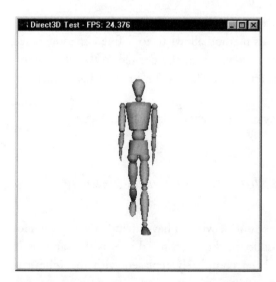

Figure 12.3 A second frame of our walking animation object (left foot down)

3D Studio (or any other program capable of generating 3D animations). Try creating a motion sequence such as swinging a sword or throwing a ball. Also, remember that you can load one of the other animations I have included on the CD!

That is it for animations. As you have seen, they can be quite powerful and provide a great mechanism for animating objects in your virtual worlds.

12.3 Shadows

Shadows are a very important aspect of computer animation that we have not yet addressed. To create a realistic simulation of real world objects and their interaction with other objects, there are key visual queues you need to recreate or simulate. One of the major ones is *shadows*.

If you think about many of the simulations or games you have seen over the years, you might have noticed that at times things seem to be floating over the ground or floor they are supposed to be moving upon. The reason for this is that we have learned from experience that there are certain natural phenomenon which should occur that show one object is touching another—for example, that your foot is touching the ground.

Shadows are the key element to recreate in this type of scenario. When one object is touching another, the shadow will appear to come out of the object and be cast along the ground surface. If instead, the object is above this surface, the shadow will be detached from the object casting it; for example, there will be a gap between the object and the shadow. The greater this gap, the greater the distance the object casting the shadow is from the object receiving the shadow.

Direct3D provides us with a convenient technique for creating shadows—the `IDirect3DRM::CreateShadow` method. This method allows us to define a shadow based upon a light, the plane upon which the shadow is cast, the normal to the plane upon which the shadow is cast, and the object casting the shadow. This method is defined as:

```
HRESULT CreateShadow(LPDIRECT3DRMVISUAL lpVisual,
    LPDIRECT3DRMLIGHT lpLight, D3DVALUE px, D3DVALUE py, D3DVALUE pz,
    D3DVALUE nx, D3DVALUE ny, D3DVALUE nz,
    LPDIRECT3DRMVISUAL * lplpShadow);
```

12.3.1 A CreateScene routine for setting up and viewing our object and its shadow

Below I have listed the entire `CreateScene` routine which I have included in the code for this chapter. The main window set-up code, in the file tutorial.cpp, is the same as in other chapters. The create.cpp file has been completely replaced with the following code, so please read it in detail.

The main components of it are ones you will be familiar with, other than the new shadow casting aspects, so I will not go into detail upon those portions of the code. The environment I am setting up is very simple and consists only of a ground plane, the object casting the shadow, the light casting the shadow, and the shadow itself. The routine is as follows:

```
//
// This routine is used to create the scene to present the
// object casting a shadow
//
BOOL
CreateScene()
{
```

The variables used in our scene generation code should be familiar to you by now. The only difference is that we now have two new variables—`myShadow` and `shadowLight`. The `myShadow` object is a Direct3DRMVisual object, and the `shadowLight` is a Direct3DRMLight object, which is used to place a shadow-casting light in our scene.

```
D3DRMRENDERQUALITY quality = D3DRMRENDER_FLAT;
LPDIRECT3DRMFRAME myLights = NULL;
LPDIRECT3DRMMESHBUILDER myBuilder = NULL;
LPDIRECT3DRMMESH myMesh = NULL;
LPDIRECT3DRMVISUAL myShadow = NULL;
LPDIRECT3DRMFRAME frame = NULL;
LPDIRECT3DRMLIGHT shadowLight = NULL;
LPDIRECT3DRMLIGHT light2 = NULL;
HRESULT returnVal;
```

The majority of the set-up code is quite simple. We just need to

1 Set our rendering quality

2 Create a scene

3 Create a camera

4 Set the desired quality

5 Set our scene's background parameters

6 Create a frame for our lights

7 Set the position of our lights

8 Create our shadow-casting light and add it to our lights

9 Load our 3D object which will cast the shadow

10 Scale the object to our scene

11 Create a frame in which to place our lights and other objects

12 Create a shadow object

13 Add the object and shadow to our frame

14 Set the position, rotation, and orientation of our objects

15 Free everything up since we are done

The first five of these steps are performed as:

```
// We are using flat shading - you could use gouraud
if (FAILED(dev->SetQuality (quality)))
{
  Msg("Failed to set quality.\n");
 goto generic_error;
}

// Create our scene - remember a scene has no parent
if (FAILED(lpD3DRM->CreateFrame(NULL, &scene)))
    goto generic_error;

// Create our camera
if (FAILED(lpD3DRM->CreateFrame(scene, &camera)))
    goto generic_error;
```

To set your scene's background color to a specific RGB color, you make the following call:

```
// Set our scene's background color
if (FAILED(scene->SetSceneBackgroundRGB(D3DVAL(1), D3DVAL(1),
            D3DVAL(1))))
            goto generic_error;
```

Now that we have the general scene and camera configured, we can create the lights for it. There are two lights we will need—the shadow-casting light and the general ambient lighting, so that we have a scene which is lit as if we were in a room or other place with even, nondirectional lighting.

To create our shadow-casting light, all we need to do is create a new frame object for our lights and position it in a way that it will effectively work with our shadow-casting environment.

```
//
// Create and position the main shadow-casting light for our scene
//
if (FAILED(lpD3DRM->CreateFrame(scene, &myLights)))
  goto generic_error;
if (FAILED(myLights->SetPosition(scene, D3DVAL(2), D3DVAL(5),
            -D3DVAL(10))))
            goto generic_error;
```

The actual shadow-casting light is created as any other point source light. You just need to specify the RGB components in the IDirect3DRM::CreateLightRGB call. Once it is created, we add it to our lights.

```
if (FAILED(lpD3DRM->CreateLightRGB(D3DRMLIGHT_POINT, D3DVAL(0.9),
            D3DVAL(0.8), D3DVAL(0.7), &shadowLight)))
            goto generic_error;
if (FAILED(myLights->AddLight(shadowLight)))
    goto generic_error;
```

The general ambient lighting is created and added to our scene using the following call:

```
// Create the ambient light so the overall scene is lit up
if (FAILED(lpD3DRM->CreateLightRGB(D3DRMLIGHT_AMBIENT, D3DVAL(0.1),
                D3DVAL(0.1), D3DVAL(0.1), &light2)))
                goto generic_error;
// Add the light to the scene
if (FAILED(scene->AddLight(light2)))
    goto generic_error;
```

I have placed an excellent mesh of a woman, which was placed in the public domain by Cyberware, into this scene. This mesh was created from a real person using a superb scanning system. I have included this and several other meshes that are of the highest quality I have seen on the CD accompanying this book. There are a few meshes by Cyberware (male and female) and some other excellent ones by different individuals. I have supplied these meshes both in the .x format and the .3ds format. I have included the .3ds files so that you can modify the objects using many of the commonly available tools today. If I had only included them in .x format, it would have been a lot more difficult to modify the objects! Take a look at the meshes, animations, textures, and so forth, that I have included on the CD. I am sure that by combining the objects, textures, animations, you will save a great deal of time in your development efforts.

To load the object, we use the methods you learned about in earlier chapters. The file this woman mesh is included in is called r96012.x. This and many other excellent human meshes, as well as 128 other 3D meshes are on the CD accompanying this book.

```
// Create our meshbuilder object for loading our x file
if (FAILED(lpD3DRM->CreateMeshBuilder(&myBuilder)))
    goto generic_error;
// Load the object - This one is of a digitized woman
returnVal = myBuilder->Load("r96012.x", NULL,
                D3DRMLOAD_FROMFILE, NULL, NULL);
if (returnVal != D3DRM_OK) {
    Msg("Failed to load r96012.x.\n");
    goto ret_with_error;
}
```

The MeshBuilder will need to be scaled to fit in our scene. Careful consideration of scale factors will be critical for your development efforts. Remember that you can scale the .x objects when you create them or after you load them since different applications will probably require different scale factors.

The code to scale the MeshBuilder and create the mesh is:

```
// Since this object is BIG, scale it to ouse scene
if (FAILED(myBuilder->Scale(D3DVALUE(0.01), D3DVALUE(0.01),
        D3DVALUE(0.01))))
    goto generic_error;
```

```
// Create a mesh
if (FAILED(myBuilder->CreateMesh(&myMesh)))
  goto generic_error;
RELEASE(myBuilder);
```

We now get to the actual code to create our shadow object. The first thing we need to do is create a frame which is a child of our scene. This will be used to hold our woman mesh and our shadow.

```
//
// create a frame in our scene
//
if (FAILED(lpD3DRM->CreateFrame(scene, &frame)))
  goto generic_error;
```

The IDirect3DRM::CreateShadow method call is shown below. The method is prototyped as:

```
HRESULT CreateShadow(LPDIRECT3DRMVISUAL lpVisual,
  LPDIRECT3DRMLIGHT lpLight, D3DVALUE px, D3DVALUE py, D3DVALUE pz,
  D3DVALUE nx, D3DVALUE ny, D3DVALUE nz,
  LPDIRECT3DRMVISUAL * lplpShadow);
```

It uses the visual and light we specify to project the shadow onto the plane which is defined by *px*, *py*, and *pz*. This plane has a normal defined by *nx*, *ny*, and *nz*. The shadow which is created is placed in the lplpShadow parameter.

The call is:

```
// Create a shadow object based on the shadow casting light
if (FAILED(lpD3DRM->CreateShadow((LPDIRECT3DRMVISUAL) myMesh,
            shadowLight, D3DVAL(0), D3DVAL(-3), D3DVAL(0), D3DVAL(0),
D3DVAL(1),
            D3DVAL(0), &myShadow)))
            goto generic_error;
```

To add the woman mesh we loaded and the shadow we just created is as simple as:

```
//
// Add the mesh we just loaded to the frame
//
if (FAILED(frame->AddVisual(myMesh)))
  goto generic_error;
// Add the shadow too
if (FAILED(frame->AddVisual(myShadow)))
  goto generic_error;
```

Finally, we just need to set the position and orientation of our camera so we can see our new object and its shadow. In addition, I have set the object rotating, but since we are using the tutorial.cpp code from our previous chapters, moving the mouse will move your viewpoint around in the environment.

```
//
// Position the frame and set its orientation and rotation
//
if (FAILED(camera->SetPosition(scene, D3DVAL(0), D3DVAL(0), -D3DVAL(10))))
  goto generic_error;
if (FAILED(camera->SetOrientation(scene, D3DVAL(0), D3DVAL(0), D3DVAL(1),
                  D3DVAL(0), D3DVAL(1), D3DVAL(0))))
                    goto generic_error;
if (FAILED(frame->SetRotation(scene, D3DVAL(0), D3DVAL(1), D3DVAL(0),
                  D3DVAL(0.02))))
                    goto generic_error;
```

The last thing to do, as always, is to free up all of our objects.

```
// We are done. Free everything up so we don't eat memory
RELEASE(myLights);
RELEASE(myMesh);
RELEASE(myShadow);
RELEASE(frame);
RELEASE(shadowLight);
RELEASE(light2);
return TRUE;
// Hopefully we don't get below here - If we do, we had an error
generic_error:
 Msg("A failure occurred while building our scene.\n");
ret_with_error:
 RELEASE(myLights);
 RELEASE(myBuilder);
 RELEASE(myMesh);
 RELEASE(myShadow);
 RELEASE(frame);
 RELEASE(shadowLight);
 RELEASE(light2);
 return FALSE;
}
```

The view we get using this code is shown in figure 12.4.

Notice that I have placed the object slightly above the ground for illustration purposes. As you can see, the shadow adds realism to our scene. I would suggest you experiment with this code by removing the rotation and placing this, or other objects, directly on the ground plane to see how this adds reality to your world by *attaching* the character to the ground.

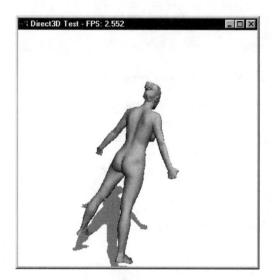

Figure 12.4 The scene generated with the shadow code (Sub-project Chap12 on the CD)

12.4 Fog

Fog is a graphic element which is often used to hide the distant objects in your graphic worlds. This allows the use of an object-culling technique where you do not render objects that are beyond a certain distance from your virtual world viewpoint. If you do not use a method like fog to hide the distant portions of your scenes, there will be a distinct *popping* in and out of objects as they are added or deleted from your scene.

By placing fog slightly closer than the distance at which the object adding/deleting occurs, the objects are occluded by the fog and the user does not notice the objects coming in and out of your scene.

In Direct3D, fog is nothing more than the alpha portion of the color indicated in the specular member of the D3DTLVERTEX structure. You can think of this as if you had an RGBF color where the *R*, *G*, and *B* portions are the standard red, green, and blue components, but the *F* portion defines the *Fog*. It is important to understand also that if you are using the monochromatic lighting mode, fog will only work properly if the fog color is set to black.

There are three fog modes: linear, exponential, and exponential squared. To use linear fog, you need to define a start and end point for the fog effect. The fog will begin at the start point, with a barely visible effect, and increase linearly until it hits its maximum density at the end point.

The code to set these parameters is as follows:

```
D3DCOLOR myColor =
   D3DRMCreateColorRGB(D3DVALUE(255),D3DVALUE(255),D3DVALUE(255));
.
.
.
scene->SetSceneFogMode(D3DRMFOG_LINEAR);
scene->SetSceneFogParams(D3DVALUE(10), D3DVALUE(40), D3DVALUE(0));
scene->SetSceneFogColor(myColor);
scene->SetSceneFogEnable(TRUE);
```

The way fog is implemented, by modifying the colors of your objects, is not realistic in terms of simulating the real world effect of fog. Fog in reality fills a volume of space with a particular density. To accurately simulate this, D3D would have to calculate a dithering density which would be used to fill the scene with a particular number of pixels at each *depth range*. For now, nothing like this has been implemented, so at least we have the ability to simulate fog in a reasonable, if not perfect, manner.

12.5 What did we learn?

In this chapter, I covered animations, shadows, and fog. If you use these features effectively along with the many features you learned in the previous chapters, you should be able to create some awesome applications! As I mentioned above, I would suggest that you combine the features presented in this chapter into a single project to make sure you understand the nuances of these features and you see how together they help create a very realistic simulated world.

12.6 What's next?

In the next chapter, I will be covering the hardware acceleration capabilities of Direct3D. DirectX was implemented in a manner that will automatically take advantage of the hardware in your system and so, if you add a new, or better, graphic board to your system, your software will immediately be aware of these capabilities and take advantage of them. Let's take a quick look at the performance increase you can see.

chapter 13

How to make things run even faster

13.1 Graphics accelerator overview

Direct3D is designed to take advantage of any new graphic hardware we make available on our machines. Because of this, we can easily develop our software to automatically utilize any hardware which is placed on the host machine. All of the code we have written has checked for which capabilities are available on our machine. Because of this, we as code developers can plan for the future by writing code that checks for the performance capabilities of the host machine and upgrades performance (adding better textures, more detailed objects, etc.) as soon as it sees the new hardware.

We no longer have to build to our lowest common denominator. With careful code design, we can create code that runs perfectly on a wide range of machines without requiring the user to manually change parameters.

The graphic hardware industry has become a rapidly changing environment. Within months of the release of a board we consider state-of-the-art, a new board is often introduced that is so far beyond that previous board that it obsoletes the previous one. Although this is certainly a major concern for the hardware developers, it has also been a problem for software developers—until Direct3D. Now we can buy the newest boards and assume that if we did our job, our code will run with no changes as soon as the new drivers are loaded. Plus, not only will it run, but it will run *faster* and *better*.

13.2 What should I look for in an accelerator?

With the huge number of graphic *accelerators* that are being introduced, people are often confused about which features they should look for. This, of course, is dependent upon the type of application you wish to build (or run). There are two main categories of considerations—*full/windowed application* and *hardware capabilities*.

The first of these two considerations, full/windowed applications, is critical in your decision process. Vendors have been introducing 3D graphic accelerators that show excellent performance numbers, but they only run in *Full-Screen* mode! If you are just going to play games, this type of board may be acceptable, but I feel that this critical limitation makes these boards far less desirable than the other boards which allow both Full and Windowed modes.

The 3D accelerators that provide both modes will allow you to not only run full-screen games, but also Windows games and simulations that require other Windows applications to be running at the same time. The performance of these two types of boards tends to be very similar, so make sure you weight your decision criteria appropriately.

The second consideration, *hardware capabilities*, is the key issue to take into account when purchasing hardware, or developing software. It is critical to compare *apples-to-apples* when you do your comparison.

When a vendor specifies performance statistics, such as *polygons-per-second*, make sure that you understand what they mean by this! Since there is no true standard for testing, vendors will skew statistics to their side by picking a few things they do well or by using a simplified version of a test which works well on their device. If they ran the fully detailed test, their boards would not perform nearly as well.

Another feature that I find to be very important is the design of a board to be 3D-*only*. Many of the 3D boards out today perform both 2D and 3D operations on the same board. The problem with this is that when you decide to purchase a new graphic board with better *3D* capabilities, you also have to pay for a new *2D* portion of the board since they are integrated on the same board. Although the 3D-only boards require another slot in your computer, the ability to replace just the 3D, or 2D, portion of your graphic system will save you money in the future. In addition, these boards tend to be faster than the 2D/3D boards since they are the ones being focused upon by many vendors. One of the boards I would suggest looking at are the NEC/Videologic PowerVR line of 3D accelerators. These boards support windowed and full-screen mode and are at a price point almost anyone can afford. With the quality of these boards, the planned continued enhancements of their capabilities, and the power of NEC behind them, I believe these will be the boards for the long hall. Take a look at their web page, http://www.videologic.com, to keep up to date on these boards and to find out where to purchase one.

13.3 A few hints on making your code run faster

1 When you are setting up your lighting, and you are using the Gouraud shading mode (which you will use most of the time to achieve the best realism), Ramp mode Gouraud shading will run about 15–20 percent faster in 8-bit rather than 16-bit color because of the reduced memory bandwidth.

2 Flat shading is 20–30 percent faster than Gouraud shading on large polygons.

3 Both ramp and RGB mode will tend to render faster to system memory than to video memory because of the benefit of CPU cache. Since you will not be able to use page flipping, and will therefore have to blit from your system memory back buffer to a video memory back buffer, you will have to determine which of these techniques runs faster on your hardware. The MMX driver renders far faster to system memory than video memory, but other drivers may not act this way.

4 Keep your number of materials in your textured scenes to a minimum. Modulating materials with the texture color should be done with the RGB drivers (MMX and HW). Only use intensity modulation in ramp mode if you can. In Ramp mode, each material contains a set of color values and a texture handle. Each of these colors in the texture palette will require the ramp driver to build a lookup table of intensities (a ramp). The size of these ramps is defined by the shades field in the material, so a texture with a palette of 64 colors in a material with 16 shades will create 64 ramps with 16 entries. Each ramp will slow down your system because it is using your CPU cache more and more heavily. You will want to try to use one material for all of your texture. In addition, your should try to normalize your palette for all of your textures so that you will only need one texture palette for the whole scene. This is because each texture that uses the same material will share the same ramp for each color that is the same between the two texture palettes.

5 As mentioned earlier in this book, try to keep the number of textures you use down and if you can combine them into one large texture, this will be your best choice.

13.4 What's next?

In the next chapter, I will show you how to create a Terrain Modifier using a pop-up control window to provide editor objects (sliders, etc.) for changing our scene parameters. You will see how to create a terrain which can be modified to simulate a dynamic, or morphing, landscape. With an understanding of these techniques you will be able to add code to perform the processes, such as the simple task of saving the data, necessary to create a full terrain editor!

chapter 14

A Terrain Modifier

Now that we have covered all of the features of Direct3D, I want to show you how to create a program that will illustrate some of the Direct3D features in more detail *and* be useful for both visualizing and changing your data. In addition, this code could be used with minor modifications to add the capability to your code to generate *morphing* landscapes!

Using the concepts I will present here, you can easily create a program to modify landscapes in real time. Imagine simulating earthquakes where the ground undulates and cracks. You can even change the texture attributes to simulate events like mudslides covering grass fields.

The terrain used as the basis of this chapter is a simple 3D array of points to help keep the remainder of the code *uncluttered*. When you have acquired a good understanding of the code, I would suggest you try adding a fractal generator to create the initial points.

For the example code in this chapter, you will be provided a menu with several controls that will allow you to modify parameter including the acceptable range in terrain height, the acceptable height delta, the type of shading used (wireframe, flat, or Gouraud), and whether or not to use textures. The menu provided is presented in figure 14.1.

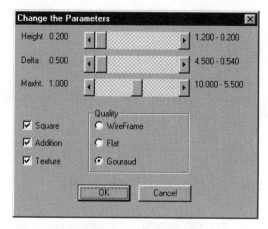

Figure 14.1 The terrain modifier menu

14.1 The program

The menu in figure 14.1 is handled using the SlideProc routine. Let's walk through it. The first segment just defines the parameters that will allow us to control our landscape.

```
int SlideProc (HWND hDlg, UINT iMsg, WPARAM wParam, LPARAM lParam)
{
float dh[] =        {0.2f, 1.2f};
float dd[] =        {0.5f, 4.5f};
float               dmh [] = {1.0f, 10.0f};
static int          tt, iColor[3] ;
char                text[80];
int                 i, j, iCtrlID, iIndex ;
static int          aOrg, sOrg, qOrg, tOrg;
static float        dOrg, hOrg, mhOrg;
HWND                hCtrl;
```

With these defined, we can start checking to see which message we are handling. When we receive the first message, the WM_INITDIALOG message, we will need to set the visual items on the screen to their correct state. Our first step is to save the current values for the parameters so that if the user selects cancel, we can switch the parameters back to the way they were.

```
switch (iMsg)
{
case WM_INITDIALOG :
 aOrg = addition;
 sOrg = square;
 dOrg = sDelta;
```

```
hOrg = h;
mhOrg = maxhoehe;
qOrg = quality;
tOrg = tt;
```

With the old values stored away, we can now set the buttons' visual states. Since the button states are mutually exclusive, we just need to set the proper button indicating whether the render mode is wireframe, flat, or Gouraud.

```
switch (quality)
  {
   case D3DRMRENDER_WIREFRAME:
     CheckRadioButton (hDlg, IDC_RADIO1, IDC_RADIO3, IDC_RADIO1);
     break;
   case D3DRMRENDER_FLAT:
     CheckRadioButton (hDlg, IDC_RADIO1, IDC_RADIO3, IDC_RADIO2);
   break;
   case D3DRMRENDER_GOURAUD:
     CheckRadioButton (hDlg, IDC_RADIO1, IDC_RADIO3, IDC_RADIO3);
   break;
  }
```

The other three check boxes are not mutually exclusive, so we just need to set then to their desired state.

```
CheckDlgButton (hDlg, IDC_CHECK1, square&1);
CheckDlgButton (hDlg, IDC_CHECK2, addition&1);
CheckDlgButton (hDlg, IDC_CHECK3, (~tt)&1);
```

Next, we need to set our scrollbars to their desired positions.

```
for (iCtrlID=IDC_SCROLLBAR1;iCtrlID<IDC_SCROLLBAR1+3;iCtrlID++)
  {
    hCtrl = GetDlgItem (hDlg, iCtrlID) ;
    SetScrollRange (hCtrl, SB_CTL, 0, 100, FALSE) ;
    SetScrollPos (hCtrl, SB_CTL, iColor[iCtrlID-IDC_SCROLLBAR1], FALSE) ;
  }
```

Finally, the code to handle the output of the text indicating what the graphic controllers tasks are, using simple sprintf commands, is as follows.

```
sprintf (text, "Height\t%.3f", dh[0]);
SetDlgItemText (hDlg, IDC_STATIC1, text);
sprintf (text, "Delta\t%.3f", dd[0]);
SetDlgItemText (hDlg, IDC_STATIC2, text);
sprintf (text, "Maxht.\t%.3f", dmh[0]);
SetDlgItemText (hDlg, IDC_STATIC3, text);

sprintf (text, "%.3f - %.3f", dh[1], h);
SetDlgItemText (hDlg, IDC_STATIC4, text);
sprintf (text, "%.3f - %.3f", dd[1], sDelta);
```

```
SetDlgItemText (hDlg, IDC_STATIC5, text);
sprintf (text, "%.3f - %.3f", dmh[1], maxhoehe);
SetDlgItemText (hDlg, IDC_STATIC6, text);

return 1 ;
break;
```

14.2 Manipulating the terrain

The next case statement is used to handle any commands received from the dialog box
window. The first two are the standard checks to see if we have clicked on the OK or
cancel button. If the user selects cancel, we have to set everything back to the way it was
when the user entered. This means that we have to set all of our world parameters back
to the values we saved.

```
case WM_COMMAND:
 switch (LOWORD (wParam))
  {
   case IDOK:
     EndDialog (hDlg, TRUE);
     return TRUE;
     break;
   case IDCANCEL:
     addition = aOrg;
     square = sOrg;
     sDelta = dOrg;
     h = hOrg;
     maxhoehe = mhOrg;
     quality = qOrg;
      tt = tOrg;

      field (8, trans);

      for (i=0;i<gTileX;i++) for (j=0;j<gTileY;j++)
       {
        if (tt)
          changePlane ( planeMeshes [i][j], i, j, 0, 0.0f);
        else
          changePlane ( planeMeshes [i][j], i, j, 0, texRange);
       }
     EndDialog (hDlg, FALSE);
     return TRUE;
     break;
```

If the user selects either square or addition, we need to change our mesh. Also, we
need to check if textures are to be used or not.

```
case IDC_CHECK1:
case IDC_CHECK2:
    square = IsDlgButtonChecked (hDlg, IDC_CHECK1);
```

```
      addition = IsDlgButtonChecked (hDlg, IDC_CHECK2);

      field (8, trans);

      for (i=0;i<gTileX;i++) for (j=0;j<gTileY;j++)
       {
        if (tt)
         changePlane ( planeMeshes [i][j], i, j, 0, 0.0f);
        else
          changePlane ( planeMeshes [i][j], i, j, 0, texRange);
       }

       Render ();
      break;
```

If the user selects the texture check box, we need to rerender the scene with/without textures.

```
  case IDC_CHECK3:
      tt = IsDlgButtonChecked (hDlg, IDC_CHECK3);

      tt = (~tt)&1;
      for (i=0;i<gTileX;i++) for (j=0;j<gTileY;j++)
       {
       if (tt)
         changePlane ( planeMeshes [i][j], i, j, 0, 0.0f);
       else
         changePlane ( planeMeshes [i][j], i, j, 0, texRange);
       }

      Render ();
      break;
```

If the user changes any of the wireframe, flat, or Gouraud radio buttons, we will have to set the quality for the tiles in our scene and rerender it.

```
  case IDC_RADIO1:
  case IDC_RADIO2:
  case IDC_RADIO3:
      for (i=0;i<3;i++)
       {
        if (IsDlgButtonChecked (hDlg, IDC_RADIO1+i)) break;
       }

       switch (i)
       {
        case 0:
           quality = D3DRMRENDER_WIREFRAME;
        break;
        case 1:
           quality = D3DRMRENDER_FLAT;
        break;
```

```
case 2:
    quality = D3DRMRENDER_GOURAUD;
break;
}
for (i=0;i<gTileX;i++) for (j=0;j<gTileY;j++)
{
```

The SetGroupQuality method is used to set the quality for the desired group in the texture. For this program, we set all of the tiles to the same quality, but you could certainly set them differently if you wished.

```
    planeMeshes [i][j]->SetGroupQuality (fkgi[i][j], quality);;
}
```

Finally, we need to redraw the scene so we can see the changes we made.

```
    Render ();
    break;
    }
break;
```

The end result of all of this is shown in figure 14.2. The default scene consists of a fairly flat, texture-mapped terrain (the same as the one we have used for our code throughout the previous chapters).

Figure 14.2 The default terrain before we modify any parameters

Figure 14.3 The default terrain after we have modified it

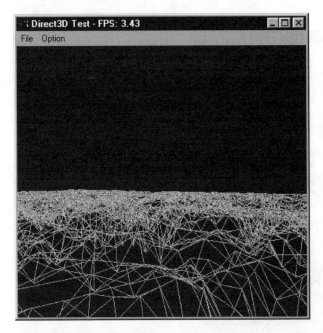

Figure 14.4 The wireframe view of the same terrain as in figure 14.3

By modifying the height, delta, and maximum height parameters, we can change our landscape drastically. What started out as a flat area is suddenly transformed (see figure 14.3) into a mountainous landscape!

Sometimes it is difficult to see the nuances of a landscape when it is textured and shaded. By selecting the wireframe option, you can view your virtual landscape in a manner which may allow you to see some features that would have otherwise been hidden. The type of view you will see when you select the wireframe option is shown in figure 14.4.

14.2.1 The routines to create and organize our landscape

We have two other routines that are worth discussing briefly. The first, `group_plane`, is used to create and organize the landscape vertices into groups when we start up the program. It is defined as:

```
BOOL
groupPlane (LPDIRECT3DRMMESH msh, int x, int y, int step=0, float r=1.0f)
{
  int vertexCount, faceCount;
  unsigned *face_data;
  D3DRMVERTEX *v_objs;

  createVertices (&v_objs, vertexCount, r, x, y, 0, step);
  face_data = createSpecFaces (faceCount);
  rval = msh->AddGroup (vertexCount, faceCount, 0, faceData, &fkgi[x][y]);
```

`IDirect3DRMMesh::SetVertices` enables you to set the vertex positions for a desired group. We are going to set the vertices for the group we just added. This method is prototyped as:

```
HRESULT SetVertices(D3DRMGROUPINDEX id, unsigned index,
  unsigned count, D3DRMVERTEX *values);
```

The parameters are

- `id`. This parameter holds the Identifier of our group which must have been created using the `IDirect3DRMMesh::AddGroup` method.

- `index`. The index at which to begin setting vertex positions in the array you indicated in the `values` parameter

- `count`. The number of vertices you wish to set following the index you specified in the `index` parameter.

- `values`. An array of `D3DRMVERTEX` structures which describe the vertex positions you want set.

Our actual call is:

```
rval = msh->SetVertices (fkgi[x][y], 0, vertexCount, v_objs);
```

Finally we just need to clean everything up.

```
if (FAILED(rval))
 {
  delete [] faceData;
  delete [] v_objs;
  return FALSE;
 }

 delete [] faceData;
 delete [] v_objs;

 return TRUE;
}
```

The second of these two final routines is used to let us change the terrain based upon the user input (or any other program control method you might wish to add, for example, if you wish to create a self-morphing landscape).

```
BOOL
changePlane (LPDIRECT3DRMMESH msh, int x, int y, int step=0, float r=1.0f)
{
 int vertex_count;
 D3DRMVERTEX *v_objs;

 createVertices (&v_objs, vertexCount, r, x, y, 0, step);
 rval = msh->SetVertices (fkgi[x][y], 0, vertexCount, v_objs);
 if (FAILED (rval))
 {
  delete [] v_objs;
  return FALSE;
 }
 delete [] v_objs;
 return TRUE;
}
```

14.2.2 Our new CreateScene routine

The CreateScene routine is again very similar to the ones we have used in the previous chapters. I will just quickly cover the few features that are unique to this program.

```
BOOL
CreateScene()
{
 .
 .
 .
```

```
LPDIRECT3DRMMESHBUILDER plane_builder1;
LPDIRECT3DRMMESH  plane_mesh1, obj_mesh;
LPDIRECT3DRMFRAME  floor_frame = 0;
.
.
.
```

The field routine is the main routine which creates the 3D array that defines our 3D terrain. It does nothing much more than fill this array. If you wish to look at it, please open the field.cpp file in the tutorial's Chap11 subfolders on the CD accompanying this book. Once the array is initialized, we need to create a frame to hold our landscape and position it within our scene.

```
field (8, trans);

if (FAILED (lpD3DRM->CreateFrame (scene, &floor_frame)))
 {
   Msg("Failed to create frame\n");
  goto generic_error;
 }
if (FAILED (floor_frame->SetPosition (scene , D3DVAL (30.0),
         D3DVAL (0.0),
         D3DVAL (20.0))))

 {
   Msg ("Failed to set the position of the frame\n");
  goto generic_error;
 }
```

To actually create our landscapes, we will again use the same code we have used in the past chapters. We just create each tile mesh, set its quality and material, and add it as a visual to our scene so we can view it.

```
// this is the loop which creates the grass fields ...
 for (i=0;i<gTileX;i++) for (j=0;j<gTileY;j++)
 {
 plane_mesh1 = 0;
 lpD3DRM->CreateMesh (&plane_mesh1);

 if (!group_plane (plane_mesh1, i, j, 0, texRange))
 {
   Msg("Failed to build plane.\n");
  goto generic_error;
 }

 if (FAILED(plane_mesh1->SetGroupQuality (fkgi[i][j], quality)))
 {
   Msg("Failed to set group quality.\n");
  goto generic_error;
 }
```

```
    if (FAILED(plane_mesh1->SetGroupMaterial (fkgi[i][j], mat)))
    {
      Msg("Failed to set group material.\n");
     goto generic_error;
    }

    if (texYES == TRUE)
    {
     if (FAILED(plane_mesh1->SetGroupTexture (fkgi[i][j], tex)))
     {
       Msg("Failed to set group texture.\n");
      goto generic_error;
     }
    }

    if (FAILED(floor_frame->AddVisual((LPDIRECT3DRMVISUAL) plane_mesh1)))
    {
      Msg("Failed to add visual.\n");
     goto generic_error;
    }
    plane_meshes [i][j] = plane_mesh1;
    }
    .
    .
    .
```

Our final task is to set our lights to aim at our landscape so it is lit properly.

```
lights->LookAt (floor_frame, scene, D3DRMCONSTRAIN_Z );
    .
    .
    .
}
```

14.3 What did we learn?

In this chapter, I showed you how to create a terrain editor which allows you to dynamically change the attributes of your terrain. By changing the various terrain parameters, you can turn a field into a mountainous region. I would suggest that you take the code for this chapter and modify it to do something even more advanced, such as creating crevices that simulate an earthquake or maybe a mountain or a volcano erupting from the ground.

14.4 What's next?

In the next chapter, I will show you a full screen application. There are several reasons that you might wish to develop a full screen application which I will discuss.

chapter 15

An example full screen application

15.1 Why full screen

Up until this point, all of our efforts have focused upon *windowed* applications. The reason I have spent most of our time on windowed applications is that in this day and age, with Windows 95 as our operating system of choice, the thought of regressing to a single application, full screen, nonwindow environment to run our software seems a bit counter to logic! Many games today are being developed in the Windows 95 environment and work very efficiently.

The reality of the software world is, though, that windowed applications need to work in conjunction with our other applications and our overall desktop. This of course requires our application to live in the screen size we chose for our desktop. There will be times when we wish to have our application run in a larger mode than that provided by the user's desktop (albeit very rarely) or when we wish to avoid the overhead imposed upon us from the Windows system (even though with Windows 95 this has become fairly small).

If you choose to build a full screen application, there are several things to know. The first obvious difference is that a full screen application pays no attention to the Windows environment (as far as it knows or cares, it does not exist). The second is that full screen applications take control of your video card. This gives you the ability to request any of the video modes the cards can support.

15.2 *DirectDraw with Direct3D*

The main difference between full screen and windowed applications is that full screen applications have to perform their own palette handling (and screen update messages are not received from the Windows environment any more). Since the GDI doesn't handle our full screen applications, or at least not easily, we will need to look at how to handle the full screen environment from using DirectDraw and Direct3D.

I'll walk through the code, in the order of our calling sequence, from the main routine on. The WinMain routine, as always, is our main routine.

```
//
// Our main routine
//
int PASCAL WinMain(HANDLE this_inst, HANDLE prev_inst, LPSTR cmdline, int
        cmdshow)
{
  MSGmsg;
  int idle;
  int done = FALSE;
  HWND        hwnd;
```

First is the CreateAndShowWindow routine. This routine is used to create and display our full screen application. The call is as follows:

```
//
// Create and show our window
//
if( !CreateAndShowWindow( this_inst, cmdshow, &hwnd ) )
{
  return FALSE;
}
```

The routine just creates our window and shows it using the ShowWindow and UpdateWindow commands. Since these are the same as in our other windowed applications, I won't show them here again. Please review the code from chapter 12 if you need a refresher.

15.3 The DirectDraw driver COM interface

Since our general environment is set up, we need to create the DirectDraw object to communicate with the Direct3D object we will be creating. A few of the main segments of our code are shown below. The `DirectDrawCreate` function is used to initialize DirectDraw.

```
//
// Create our main DirectDraw object
//
rval = DirectDrawCreate( NULL, &lpDD, NULL );
if( rval != DD_OK )
{
  Msg ("DirectDraw Create Failed.\n%s",
  MyErrorToString(rval));
  return FALSE;
}
```

Once DirectDraw is initialized, we use the `IDirectDraw::SetCooperativeLevel` method to indicate that we will be running in a full screen, exclusive mode. You can use the `DDSCL_ALLOWMODEX` parameter in conjunction with these so that you can use the supported ModeX display modes if you wish.

```
//
// Set us to exclusive mode
//
rval = lpDD->SetCooperativeLevel(hwnd, DDSCL_EXCLUSIVE |
    DDSCL_FULLSCREEN );
if( rval != DD_OK )
{
  Msg ("Set Cooperative Level Failed.\n%s",
  MyErrorToString(rval));
  return FALSE;
}
```

15.4 Setting the display mode

We will now use the `IDirectDraw::SetDisplayMode` method to set the desired display mode to 640×480.

```
//
// Set our video mode to 640x480x8
//
rval = lpDD->SetDisplayMode( 640, 480, 8);
if( rval != DD_OK )
{
  Msg ("Set Display Mode Failed.\n%s",
```

```
            MyErrorToString(rval));
        return FALSE;
    }
```

If you wished to check the hardware and pick a different display mode, you could check which display modes are available on the hardware and pick one based on the capabilities returned. To acquire a list of the supported display modes, and pick one from this list (800×600), you could use the following code segment:

```
CDC* dc;
DWORD currentDisplayDepth;
DWORD getWidth, getDepth, getHeight;

dc = GetDC();
currentDisplayDepth = dc->GetDveiceCaps( BPP);
dc->DeleteDC();
.
.
.
ddraw->EnumDisplayModes(0, 0, 0, AvailableDisplayModes);
.
.
for (i = 0; i < totDisplayModes; i++)
{
    .
    .

    // See if the display mode you want exists
    if (getWidth==800 && getHeight==600 && getDepth==currentDisplayDepth)
    currentDisplayMode = i;
}

    GetDisplayModeDims( currentDisplayMode, width, height, depth);
    ddraw->SetDisplayMode(width, height, depth);
    return totalDisplayModes != 0;
```

Since we are just going to force the mode to 640×480, we do not need to use this code, but, keep it in mind for your future applications.

15.5 Creating a primary surface

Our next task is to create our primary surface. This surface is defined with the DDSUR-FACEDESC structure. The dwSize field of the structure is filled with the size of the structure. The dwFlags field is filled with the flags specifying which fields we are initializing. We use the DDSD_BACKBUFFERCOUNT and DDSD_CAPS flags since we are using the dwBackBufferCount and ddsCaps fields.

```
    //
    // Create the primary surface with 1 back buffer
```

```
//
ddsd.dwSize = sizeof( ddsd );
ddsd.dwFlags = DDSD_CAPS | DDSD_BACKBUFFERCOUNT;
```

We also want a primary surface which can use page flipping, so we use the DDSCAPS_PRIMARYSURFACE, DDSCAPS_FLIP, and the DDSCAPS_COMPLEX flags. We also use the DDSCAPS_3DDEVICE flag to specify that this new surface will be used to create our Direct3D device.

```
ddsd.ddsCaps.dwCaps = DDSCAPS_PRIMARYSURFACE | DDSCAPS_3DDEVICE |
        DDSCAPS_FLIP |
        DDSCAPS_COMPLEX;
```

Setting the dwBackBufferCount field to 1 indicates that we have specified that the primary surface has one back buffer. The back buffer is the buffer which is written to and then exchanged with the primary surface. While your main screen is displaying the lines of your current image in the primary surface, the back buffer surface frame can be composed. This composition is handled using the DirectDrawSurface objects in the display memory to the back buffer.

```
ddsd.dwBackBufferCount = 1;
```

15.6 Creating a DirectDraw surface

With the surface information defined, we can now create it. The IDirectDraw::CreateSurface method is used to create the surface. This method takes the DDSURFACEDESC structure we just defined as the first argument and the address of a pointer to a DirectDrawSurface interface object.

```
//
// Create our surface
//
rval = lpDD->CreateSurface( &ddsd, &lpDDSPrimary, NULL );
if( rval != DD_OK )
{
  Msg ("Create Surface Failed.\n%s",
  MyErrorToString(rval));
  return FALSE;
}
```

We next need to get a pointer to the back buffer so we can use it later to store our visual output data before they are moved, or flipped, to our primary surface. We have to lock down the palette later by setting the peFlags member of the PALETTEENTRY structure for all of the palette entries to D3DPAL_READONLY, to allow Direct3D's Retained

Mode, to use, but not modify, the entries in our palette. I will show you this shortly when I show you the code to create a DirectDraw palette.

```
//
// Get the surface
//
ddscaps.dwCaps = DDSCAPS_BACKBUFFER;
rval = lpDDSPrimary->GetAttachedSurface(&ddscaps, &lpDDSBack);
if( rval != DD_OK )
{
  Msg ("Get Attached Surface Failed.\n%s",
  MyErrorToString(rval));
  return FALSE;
}
```

15.7 Creating a Z-buffer surface

We now can define our Z-buffer surface using the DDSURFACEDESC structure. A Z-buffer, also known as a depth buffer, is used to associate a depth, or distance from the eye (viewpoint) for every pixel on the window (viewport). The distances are used in the hidden-surface removal process where it is decided if a surface is visible or not. We can just use the same ddsd variable we created before for our primary surface for creating this object. To do this, we clear it out using memset.

```
//
// Fill in the info for, and create, the surface
//
memset(&ddsd,0,sizeof(DDSURFACEDESC));
```

The dwSize field is set to the size of the structure. The dwFlags field specifies that we will be providing the surface's width, height, capabilities, and depth of the new Z-buffer.

```
ddsd.dwSize = sizeof(DDSURFACEDESC);
ddsd.dwFlags = DDSD_WIDTH | DDSD_HEIGHT | DDSD_CAPS |
      DDSD_ZBUFFERBITDEPTH;
```

We now need to fill the fields with their values. We must make sure to set the Z-buffer's width and height to the same size as the primary and back buffers.

```
ddsd.dwHeight = 480 ;
ddsd.dwWidth = 640 ;
```

The dwZBufferBitDepth is set to 16 to indicate that we want a 16-bit Z-buffer. This 16-bit Z-buffer provides 65,536 possible z values, so depending upon your application, you might want a greater possible z depth.

```
ddsd.dwZBufferBitDepth = 16 ;
```

CHAPTER 15   FULL SCREEN APPLICATION

The DDSCAPS_SYSTEMMEMORY flag is used to indicate that we want the Z-buffer memory to be allocated from system memory rather than video card memory. Since many people have video cards with small amounts of memory, often a few megabytes, placing the Z-buffer in system memory rather than video card memory will save space on the video card.

```
ddsd.ddsCaps.dwCaps= DDSCAPS_ZBUFFER | DDSCAPS_SYSTEMMEMORY;
```

We can now create our Z-buffer surface and attach it to our back buffer surface. This Z-buffer will now be used automatically by Direct3D.

```
rval = lpDD->CreateSurface(&ddsd, &lpDDZ, NULL);
if (rval != DD_OK)
  {
    Msg ("Create Surface Failed.\n%s",
    MyErrorToString(rval));
    return FALSE;
  }

//
// Add the surface
//
rval = lpDDSBack->AddAttachedSurface(lpDDZ);
if(rval != DD_OK)
  {
    Msg ("Add Attached Surface Surface Failed.\n%s",
    MyErrorToString(rval));
    return FALSE;
  }
```

15.7.1 Using color keying

The IDirectDrawSurface2::SetColorKey method is used to set the destination color key if you want one. Color keys can be used for both blits and overlays. Destination color keying specifies a color or color range that, for blitting, is replaced, or for overlays, is covered up on the destination surface. The destination color key specifies what can, and cannot, be covered up, on our destination surface. Only the pixels matching the color key are changed, or covered up, on the destination surface. The dwColorSpace-LowValue and dwColorSpaceHighValue members of the DDCOLORKEY structure hold the palette entry we wish to use for color keying. For our example, we are using a palette index of 255, which is white. This way, whenever you blit to your back buffer, all of the pixels that are white (255) on your surface will be overwritten by the pixels on the surface you are blitting from. Any pixels that are not white will stay as they are.

```
DDCOLORKEY ddck;
ddck.dwColorSpaceLowValue = 255;
ddck.dwColorSpaceHighValue = 255;
lpDDSBack->SetColorKey(DDCKEY_DESTBLT, &ddck);
```

15.8 Loading a BMP file into a DirectDraw surface and creating a palette

The `IDirectDraw::CreateSurface` method is used to create an off-screen DirectDraw surface using the surface width and height. The `DDSURFACEDESC` structure defines the size of the off-screen surface.

```
ddsd.dwFlags = DDSD_CAPS | DDSD_HEIGHT | DDSD_WIDTH;
 ddsd.ddsCaps.dwCaps = DDSCAPS_OFFSCREENPLAIN;
 ddsd.dwHeight = 480;
 ddsd.dwWidth = 640;
 rval = lpDD->CreateSurface( &ddsd, &lpDDSOne, NULL );
 if( rval != DD_OK )
   {
      Msg ("Create Surface Failed.\n%s",
      MyErrorToString(rval));
      return FALSE;
   }
```

With all of our surfaces created, we still have to create a palette for our application. You can, of course, create your own palette, using the `IDirectDraw::CreatePalette` method and filling it by hand, but for this demo we will acquire the palette from a .bmp file.

The `readBMPIntoSurfaces` routine will load the desired image into our object and grab the palette from it.

```
//
// Get the .bmp loaded into our surface
//
if( !readBMPIntoSurfaces() )
{
  Msg ("Read Bmp Into Surface Failed.\n");
  return FALSE;
}
```

The routine we call to place the .bmp file into our surface is named `readBMPInto-Surfaces`. The `BITMAPFILEHEADER` structure is the first part of the BMP file. This structure is defined in detail in the help facility of the various Microsoft compilers. The structure is:

```
typedef struct tagBITMAPFILEHEADER {
    WORD    bfType;       // The file type
    WORD    bfSize;       // The size of the bitmap in bytes
    WORD    bfReserved1;  // Must be 0
    WORD    bfReserved2;  // Must be 0
    DWORD   bfOffBits;    // The offset in bytes from the BITMAPFILEHEADER
```

```
                           // structure to the bitmap bits
} BITMAPFILEHEADER;
```

If the bfType field contains *BM*, it is a valid BMP file. The BITMAPINFOHEADER structure comes after the BITMAPFILEHEADER in a BMP file. This structure holds the image data and is defined as:

```
typedef struct tagBITMAPINFOHEADER {
    DWORD   biSize;           // Structure size in bytes
    LONG    biWidth;          // Bitmap width in pixels
    LONG    biHeight;         // Bitmap height in pixels
    WORD    biPlanes;         // Number of planes for the target device
    WORD    biBitCount;       // Number of bits per pixel - must be either
                              // 1, 4, 8, 16, 24, OR 32
    DWORD   biCompression;    // The type of compression for a compressed
                              // bottom-up bitmap
    DWORD   biSizeImage;      // Size of the image in bytes
    LONG    biXPelsPerMeter;  // Horizontal resolution in pixels per meter of
                              // the target device for the bitmap
    LONG    biYPelsPerMeter;  // Vertical resolution in pixels per meter of
                              // the target device for the bitmap
    DWORD   biClrUsed;        // The number of color indices in the color
                              // table that are actually used from the bitmap.
                              // If it is 0, the bitmap uses the maximum
                              // number of colors
    DWORD   biClrImportant;   // Number of color indices that are considered `
                              // important for displaying the bitmap. If it
                              // is 0, all colors are important.
} BITMAPFILEHEADER;
```

The biWidth and biHeight fields hold the image dimensions. The biBitCount field contains the image bit depth, such as 8 bit.

```
//
// Reads our bitmap file and stores it in offscreen surface.
// Set the palette for the front and back buffers to the
// the bitmap file's palette.
//
BOOL readBMPIntoSurfaces( void )
{
    LPBYTE              Image;
    HANDLE              hFile;
    BITMAPFILEHEADER    BMPFileHead;
    BITMAPINFOHEADER    BMPFileInfo;
```

The next structure defines the 256 element array of palette entries as RGBQUAD data types:

```
    RGBQUAD             Palette[256];
    DWORD               actualRead;
```

The RGBQUAD type is defined as:

```
typedef struct tagRGBQUAD {
    BYTE rgbBlue;
    BYTE rgbGreen;
    BYTE rgbRed;
    BYTE rgbReserved;
} RGBQUAD;
```

We also need to define a PALETTEENTRY structure array to

```
PALETTEENTRY            pe[256];
```

The PALETTEENTRY type is defined as:

```
typedef struct tagPALETTEENTRY {
    BYTE peRed;
    BYTE peGreen;
    BYTE peBlue;
    BYTE peFlags;
} PALETTEENTRY;
```

Note that the two structures have the red, green, and blue elements in different orders.

```
DDSURFACEDESC       ddsd;
LPSTR               lpBits;
LPSTR               lpSrc;
int                 i;
HRESULT             ddrval;
```

To load our BMP file, we call the openBMP routine.

```
Image = (LPBYTE) LocalAlloc( LPTR, 640*480);
if( Image == NULL )
{
  return FALSE;
}

hFile = openBMP();
```

The actual code to open the .bmp file is in the openBMP routine.

```
//
// Opens our bitmap for DirectDraw.
//
static HANDLE openBMP( void )
{
  HANDLE   hFile;

  hFile = CreateFile("dd.bmp",
          GENERIC_READ,
```

```
                FILE_SHARE_READ,
                (LPSECURITY_ATTRIBUTES) NULL,
                OPEN_EXISTING,
                FILE_ATTRIBUTE_NORMAL,
                (HANDLE) NULL);

    if( hFile != INVALID_HANDLE_VALUE)
       {
       return hFile;
       }
    return INVALID_HANDLE_VALUE;
}
```

As long as the file is OK, we can now read the file header and information.

```
    if( hFile == INVALID_HANDLE_VALUE )
    {
       return FALSE;
    }
    // Read the header and info structures
    if(!ReadFile(hFile, &BMPFileHead, sizeof(BMPFileHead), &actualRead, NULL))
    {
       return FALSE;
    }
    // Read the actual data
    if(!ReadFile(hFile, &BMPFileInfo, sizeof(BMPFileInfo), &actualRead,
          NULL))
    {
       return FALSE;
    }
```

Of course, it had better match our surface size!

```
    // Verify this is a compatible file
    if((BMPFileInfo.biWidth != 640) ||
      (BMPFileInfo.biHeight != 480) ||
      (BMPFileInfo.biBitCount != 8))
    {
       return FALSE;
    }
```

With everything opened, and the general file information acquired, we can load the palette and image from the file.

```
    // Read the palette information
    if(!ReadFile(hFile, Palette, sizeof(Palette), &actualRead, NULL))
    {
       return FALSE;
    }

    // Read the image bits
    if(!ReadFile(hFile, Image, 640*480, &actualRead, NULL))
```

```
   {
     return FALSE;
   }
   CloseHandle(hFile);
```

We are finally at the point where we can copy the palette information into our array of PALETTEENTRY structures. All we need to do is copy the quad array into our palette entry array.

```
// Create a Direct Draw Palette and associate it with our front buffer
if( lpDDPal == NULL )
{
  for(i=0; i<256; i++)
  {
    pe[i].peRed = Palette[i].rgbRed;
    pe[i].peGreen = Palette[i].rgbGreen;
    pe[i].peBlue = Palette[i].rgbBlue;
    pe[i].peFlags = D3DPAL_READONLY; // The rest of the system can only
                                     // READ your palette entries

  }
```

With the data filled up, we are at the point where we can create our actual Direct-Draw palette. This palette is created using the IDirectDraw::CreatePalette method. The DDPCAPS_8BIT constant that we pass tells DirectDraw that the palette we are providing is 8 bit. The palette entry array is the second parameter, and the address of a pointer to the new palette is the third.

```
ddrval = lpDD->CreatePalette( DDPCAPS_8BIT, pe, &lpDDPal, NULL );
if(ddrval != DD_OK)
  return FALSE;
```

Now we attach the new palette to our primary and back buffers.

```
lpDDSPrimary->SetPalette( lpDDPal );
lpDDSBack->SetPalette( lpDDPal );
}
```

The last thing we need to do is to lock the DirectDraw surface and copy the image data to it. This will get our .bmp actually onto our DirectDraw surface.

```
ddsd.dwSize = sizeof( ddsd );
ddrval = lpDDSOne->Lock( NULL, &ddsd, 0, NULL );
if(ddrval != DD_OK)
  {
    return FALSE;
  }

// Copy our bitmap bits from system memory to video memory
lpBits = (LPSTR)ddsd.lpSurface;
```

```
lpSrc = (LPSTR)(&Image[479*640]);
for(i=0; i<480; i++)
  {
    memcpy( lpBits, lpSrc, 640 );
    lpBits += ddsd.lPitch;
    lpSrc -= 640;
  }

int x,y;
lpBits = (LPSTR)ddsd.lpSurface+ddsd.lPitch*430+40;
for (y=0;y<30;y++)
  {
    BYTE byte = 0;
    for (x=0;x<256;x++)
      lpBits[x]=x;
    lpBits += ddsd.lPitch;
  }
```

With everything written, we need to unlock the surface.

```
lpDDSOne->Unlock( NULL );
LocalFree( Image );
return TRUE;
}
```

15.9 Setting up, updating, and viewing our 3D scene

At this point, we can create the device from our DirectDraw surface.

```
//
// Create a device from our surface
//
rval = lpD3DRM->CreateDeviceFromSurface(&DriverGUID[CurrDriver],
                            lpDD, lpDDSBack,
                      &dev);
if (rval != D3DRM_OK)
{
  Msg ("Create Device From Surface Failed.\n%s",
  MyErrorToString(rval));
  return FALSE;
}
```

Setting the render state should be ingrained in your memory by now, so just remember that based upon the bits-per-pixel available, we set the number of shades, texture shades, and dither values.

```
//
// Set up our render info - quality, fill mode,
```

```
// lighting state and color shade info
//
if (!SetRenderState())
  return FALSE;
```

Finally, we can create our scene, viewport, and back clipping plane. This is another segment of code you should understand very well by now, so I'll list it just for review.

```
CreateScene();

width = dev->GetWidth();
height = dev->GetHeight();

// Create our viewport
rval = lpD3DRM->CreateViewport(dev, camera, 0, 0, width,
                height, &view);
if (rval != D3DRM_OK)
{
  dev->Release();
  return FALSE;
}

rval = view->SetBack(D3DVAL(5000.0));

if (rval != D3DRM_OK)
{
  dev->Release();
  view->Release();
  return FALSE;
}

return TRUE;
}
```

Our message-processing loop is also the same as we have used in the past, except for the processing we need to do in our rendering routine. The main loop, up to the Render call, is:

```
//
// Our main processing loop
//
while (!done)
{
  idle = TRUE;
  while (PeekMessage(&msg, NULL, 0, 0, PM_REMOVE))
    {
      idle = FALSE;
      if (msg.message == WM_QUIT)
        {
          done = TRUE;
          break;
        }
```

```
        TranslateMessage(&msg);
         DispatchMessage(&msg);
     }

   if (lpDD)
    Render();
```

In full screen mode, we have to handle our own updating. The new `Render` routine uses the `IDirectDraw::Blt` method to fill each point on a surface to the desired value. We are using it to erase the surface. The `DDBLT_COLORFILL` value is used to indicate that we want the surface to be color filled with color 255 (white).

```
//
// Clear the back buffer, render our scene to the back
// buffer, and blit the scene to the back buffer.
// Finally, call flip() to update our display.
//
void Render()
{
  HRESULT        ddrval;
  RECT          rcRect;
  DDBLTFX ddBltFx;


  rcRect.left= 0;
  rcRect.top= 0;
  rcRect.right= 640;
  rcRect.bottom= 480;

  // Clear the back buffer
  ZeroMemory(&ddBltFx,sizeof(DDBLTFX));
  ddBltFx.dwSize = sizeof(DDBLTFX);
  ddBltFx.dwFillColor = 255;
  lpDDSBack->Blt(NULL,NULL,NULL,DDBLT_COLORFILL | DDBLT_WAIT ,&ddBltFx);
```

With everything cleared out, we can now do our standard `Move`, `Clear`, `Render`, and `Update` like we have done in our other programs.

```
  // Update the 3D Retained-Mode scene
  scene->Move(D3DVALUE(1.0));
  view->Clear();
  view->Render(scene);
  dev->Update();
```

There is a last step to this sequence which we have not done before. This is the actual copying of the source image onto our surface. Since we cleared the surface to white before, we can now color key the bit process to draw it to that surface. Remember that you must set the background color of your scene to white (255) so that anything you blit to your back buffer will overwrite the background of your scene. Using

SetSceneBackground(D3DRGB(1,1,1)) sets your background up correctly if you are using white as your destination color key.

The IDirectDrawSurface::BltFast method is:

```
// Use DDBLTFAST_DESTCOLORKEY to blit the 2D bitmap image onto the
// scene, only updating the white pixels
while( (ddrval = lpDDSBack->BltFast( 0, 0, lpDDSOne, &rcRect,
        DDBLTFAST_DESTCOLORKEY ) ) == DDERR_WASSTILLDRAWING );
// Update the primary surface
while(lpDDSPrimary->Flip( NULL,0 ) == DDERR_WASSTILLDRAWING);
}
```

15.10 The WindowProc routine

We also have to create a new WindowProc routine. This routine is fairly different from the routine of the same name we created for our windowed application. This is due to the fact that we really only need to consider the user's request to quit the application (using the Esc key) and the destruction of the window. The reason for this is that we are now handling the screen updating ourselves since we no longer have the luxury of the Windows environment to do it for us.

```
//
// Handles our main window's messages.
//
//
long FAR PASCAL WindowProc( HWND hWnd, UINT message,
            WPARAM wParam, LPARAM lParam )
{
  static int phase = 0;

  switch( message )
  {
   case WM_KEYDOWN:
    switch( wParam )
    {
     case VK_ESCAPE:
     case VK_F12:
        CleanUpObjects(); // Delete
                    // our objects
          DestroyWindow( hWnd );
        break;
    }
    break;

  case WM_DESTROY:
    ShowCursor( TRUE );
    PostQuitMessage( 0 );
    break;
```

Figure 15.1 The screen from our full screen application

```
default:
  return DefWindowProc(hWnd, message, wParam, lParam);
}

return 0L;

} /* WindowProc */
```

With that, we now have a complete full screen application. Try running the example application for this chapter on the CD and see how this application compares to the windowed applications we created. The output is shown in figure 15.1.

15.11 Animated textures—playing an AVI file on your object!

Now that we have covered the techniques for creating both windowed and full screen Direct3D applications, I want to bring up one more very fun concept—playing an AVI file on a texture! This will let you play videos on surfaces of any shape or size!

I have included a project, *avirm*, on the CD which is available on the Microsoft website that illustrates this process very well. This code is very similar to the code we just created for our full screen application except that rather than blitting an image onto the surface, we copy frames from the avi file onto the surface and update it from the avi stream so that we can actually play the video on any arbitrary surface! I am sure you have seen various first-person games that play *movies* on flat surfaces using simple blitting techniques. Now you can outdo this by playing a moving video on any object, including a person in your virtual world. Try this and experiment with making skin look like it is morphing, water look like it is rippling, or a sky that looks like the clouds are blowing by.

15.12 What did we learn?

Our full screen application is very similar to our windowed applications except for the necessity to handle window updating ourselves. You will have to decide when it is appropriate to develop windowed applications and when you should make full screen applications. I would suggest that you use windowed mode whenever you can since it allows the user to execute other applications at the same time as running your code and it also allows you to use the various Windows 95 features. If you need to keep other applications from interfering with your program, you might want to use the full screen mode.

As a project to make sure you understand this chapter, try adding an object with texture generated by a .bmp file or better yet, an .avi file, to the 3D world we created in the earlier chapters!

15.13 What's next?

In the next three chapters, I will be showing you the basics of the other side of Direct3D—Immediate Mode. Although it will not be an exhaustive coverage like we had for Retained Mode, it should build your foundation of knowledge so that you will be able to write your first Immediate-Mode application comfortably.

chapter 16

Now, after all that, what about Immediate Mode?

16.1 What about the other half—Immediate Mode?

I have spent the last 250 pages or so covering Direct3D Retained-Mode graphics. The reason for putting such an emphasis on Retained Mode was that I have found it to be a very useful environment, and it is also fairly powerful and easy to understand once you play with it for a little while. You can create some very fast, good looking programs using Retained Mode that could effectively be marketed commercially.

With that said, almost every program that has been released commercially has used Immediate Mode rather than Retained Mode for the implementation of the software. There are numerous reasons for this. One of the main reasons is that Immediate Mode was developed with people who were looking for a way to port their software from the DOS environment to the Windows environment in mind. Many of these software packages had their own rendering engines. After all, the DOS environment is fairly limited

291

and thus not many powerful libraries have been developed for 3D applications in the past. Because of this, it was usually up to the developers of the games or other 3D software to create their own 3D libraries and rendering engines. Since they had already spent the large amount of time required to develop these engines, the thought of throwing them away and using the Retained-Mode engine was not very enticing—and often the Retained-Mode engine wasn't as fast in the first place.

Since many people have acquired a fair amount of experience in Immediate Mode porting these old applications, they have tended to continue on with it in the development of their new programs also. For those of you who have had some experience with Immediate Mode in projects like this, and for those who are just learning it, I have set up the next several chapters in a format similar to the Retained-Mode tutorial I presented in chapters 1 through 16. In this chapter, and the next few, I will take you through the step-by-step basics of developing of an Immediate-Mode application.

16.2 Setting up your first Immediate-Mode application

The first thing that I would like to remind you of is that Direct3D works hand-in-hand with DirectDraw, and you will find that a huge amount of our code to set up the foundation of our project is DirectDraw-based rather than Direct3D-based. In this chapter, I will mainly be showing you DirectDraw code, similar to how the set up code for the first few chapters of the Retained-Mode tutorial consisted of Windows-based code.

16.2.1 Debugging your code

The code we will be developing in this and the following chapters will allow you to create either full screen or windowed applications. The main problem I, and most people I know, have had when developing full screen applications is that it is almost impossible to debug the programs! There are a few tools available commercially that allow for remote debugging of full screen applications, but they tend to be fairly expensive and they require you to have two computers. For those of you who are developing applications for fun or for a home business, it may not be too desirable to pay for these tools (and a new computer).

Well, we can solve this problem with an elegant solution that I was shown by Rob Wyatt. In this chapter the DirectDraw code we will be developing, even though it is designed to run in full screen mode, will run in a pop-up window when we run in debug mode if we want it to. This makes debugging a far less daunting task and I would recommend that all of you who decide to develop a full screen game use this approach since it requires very little extra code to implement. An even nicer feature is that all of the debug-specific code is removed by the preprocessor when you perform a release build when you are done debugging. Therefore you end up with a full screen game which you can still debug—rather nice, isn't it?

In the file Example.h there is a set of defines which can be changed for different screen modes—full screen and windowed. We will be adding code which will provide support for automatically detecting a suitable mode but I wouldn't recommend adding these until the last step of your development (when your program has been pretty much debugged and tested) so you can be sure of what you are doing.

When you change the size of your display, it is important to remember to make sure that the size of a real screen mode is picked. Windowed mode will work with any size screen, but obviously full screen won't and this can be the source of a nasty bug that is difficult to find.

16.2.2 The debug files

The *debug.c* and *debug.h* files on the CD in the tutorial\ImmMode1 directory contain the code we need to set up our debugging capabilities. By including debug.c in your project, and debug.h in all of your source files, you will be ready to debug your code. To activate it, add the line

```
DEBUG_MEM_INIT
```

as the beginning of your WinMain routine and

```
DEBUG_MEM_CHECK
```

as the last thing in your WinMain routine before your program quits.

An example of the output of this routine, where it has located a memory leak, is as follows:

```
Detected memory leaks!
Dumping objects ->
test.c(295) : {50} normal block at 0x00825618, 104 bytes long.
 Data: <    L(  ( > 01 00 00 00 01 00 00 00 4C 28 81 00 20 28 81 00
test.c(416) : {35} normal block at 0x008A0FB0, 44 bytes long.
 Data: <  @8  h    > 00 00 E0 40 38 0C 81 00 68 0C 81 00 98 0C 81 00
Object dump complete.
```

As you can see, this will come in *very* handy when you need to catch those nasty bugs!

Using this code, we can insert debug statements throughout our code to catch potential errors. These code segments will compile to nothing when you compile your release version of your code, so there is no reason to remove them from your code—ever. I do not see an easier way to debug. Combining the nice windowed mode of running your full-screen application during debug, and these informative debug statements, you should have a much easier time locating bugs than you have had in the past.

The debug code is shown below. Note that I have removed most of the DirectDraw and Direct3D error strings for sake of brevity here. If you want to see them in totality, please open the debug.c file on the CD.

```c
#include "windows.h"
#include "stdio.h"
#include "stdarg.h"
#include "ddraw.h"
#include "d3d.h"
#include "d3drm.h"
#include "debug.h"


#ifdef _DEBUG

// A printf style function to the output console window....
void __cdecl dprintf(char* str,...)
{
    charbuf[256];

    va_list argptr;
    va_start (argptr,str);
    vsprintf (buf,str,argptr);
    va_end (argptr);

    OutputDebugString(buf);
}


// Convert DirectDraw/direct3D Error codes into text
// This needs to be extended to DirectSound and DirectInput.
char* DirectDrawErrorToString(HRESULT ddrval)
{
    switch(ddrval)
    {
    caseDD_OK:
        return("No error");
    caseDDERR_ALREADYINITIALIZED:
        return("Object already initialised");
    caseDDERR_CANNOTATTACHSURFACE:
        return("Cannot attack surface");
    caseDDERR_CANNOTDETACHSURFACE:
        return("Cannot detach surface");
    caseDDERR_SURFACENOTATTACHED:
        return("Surface Not Attached");
    caseDDERR_TOOBIGHEIGHT:
        return("Height Too Big");
```

```
        caseDDERR_TOOBIGSIZE:
            return("Size Too Big - Height and Width are individually OK");
        caseDDERR_TOOBIGWIDTH:
            return("Width Too Big");
            .
            .
            .
        }
    }


    #else
    // If not a debug build then these functions are empty so the optimized
            build will remove them
    // and any calls to them.
    void __cdecl dprintf(char* str,...)
    {
    }


    #endif
```

16.2.3 · The DirectDraw setup code

Now that we have covered ourselves for error checking code, we need to add the handling of it to our main project. In the *DDSupport.h* file, the main DirectDraw routines are prototyped *and* we also set the DD_WINDOWED variable to TRUE if we are in debug mode or FALSE if we are in full-screen mode. (I am assuming that you want to run in full screen mode for your final application. If you choose to run in windowed mode, you can set the value accordingly.

```
    #ifndef _h_ddsupport
    #define _h_ddsupport

    #include "Windows.h"
    #include "DDraw.h"

    #define DD_FULLSCREEN0

    // DD_WINDOWED is only defined in the debug build
    // Release code only runs in full screen mode.
    #ifdef _DEBUG
    #define DD_WINDOWED1
    #else
    #define DD_WINDOWED0
    #endif


    // Init functions
    BOOL DirectDraw_Init(int width,int height,int bpp,DWORD flags);
    void DirectDraw_Close(void);
```

```
// Service functions
BOOL DirectDraw_SetPalette(PALETTEENTRY *cols,DWORD start,DWORD count);
void DirectDraw_ClearBackBuffer(void);
void DirectDraw_SwapBuffers(void);

// Internal functions
LPDIRECTDRAW     __GetDDObject(void);
LPDIRECTDRAWSURFACE__GetDDBackSurface(void);

#endif
```

We will also need to define the main routines that perform the rendering and displaying of our 3D world. This code is contained in the *Example.h* file in the Immediate-Mode projects on the CD accompanying this book.

Besides declaring our routines, we will declare here the default values of whether we wish to run in windowed or full screen mode and the default size of our screen. Remember that for your final code, you will be checking to verify that the hardware you are running on supports your desired mode (e.g., the screen size and bits-per-pixel), but for debugging purposes we will initially assume that this mode is supported (I hope that you know the capabilities of your graphic card—if not, please look it up now).

```
#ifndef _h_examplemain
#define _h_examplemain

#include "DDSupport.h"

#define SCREEN_WIDTH         640
#define SCREEN_HEIGHT        480
#define SCREEN_BPP           16

// SCREEN_FLAGS can be either DD_FULLSCREEN or DD_WINDOWED, this is
// ignored in a release build.
#define SCREEN_FLAGS         DD_WINDOWED


static long WINAPI WindowProc(HWND hWnd,UINT message,WPARAM wParam,LPARAM
lParam);
static BOOL InitApp(void);
static void CloseApp(void);
static int DoMainLoop(void);
static BOOL InitServices(void);
static void CloseServices(void);


#endif
```

Our last file, *global.c,* includes the globals that we wish to use throughout our program. For our debug setup process, we only need two. These initially are pretty basic:

```
#include "global.h"

// Add application width global variables here
// Most should be the windows bits required to get
// the thing to work

HINSTANCE          hInst;
HWND               hWnd;
```

The final code we will need to add for our basic DirectDraw/Direct3D handling are a few routines that handle getting the DirectDraw and Surface objects we will be using. They are simple one liners as follows:

```
// internal function called by the D3D library
LPDIRECTDRAW __GetDDObject(void)
{
    return(lpDD);
}


// internal function called by the D3D library
LPDIRECTDRAWSURFACE__GetDDBackSurface(void)
{
    return(lpDDSBack);
}
```

16.2.4 The main loop

The code to handle our processing loop is defined in the `mainloop.c` routine. Our first lines just define the include files, set a few globals, and call the application `init` routine.

```
#include "windows.h"
#include "Example.h"
#include "debug.h"
#include "global.h"
#include "DDSupport.h"


static BOOL       AppActive=FALSE;
static BOOL       Quit=FALSE;

int WINAPI WinMain
(
    HINSTANCE hInstance,
    HINSTANCE hPrevInstance,
    LPSTR lpCmdLine,
    int nCmdShow
)
```

```
{
    int     rval;

    DEBUG_MEM_INIT;

    hInst=hInstance;

    if (InitApp()==FALSE)
        return(FALSE);
```

16.2.5 The InitApp routine

The InitApp routine itself sets up the window parameters, including the screen size we decided to use. It then displays the window for us. This is standard Windows code and thus I will just show it below for your review.

```
static BOOL InitApp(void)
{
  WNDCLASSwc;

  wc.style = 0;
  wc.lpfnWndProc = WindowProc;
  wc.cbClsExtra = 0;
  wc.cbWndExtra = 0;
  wc.hInstance = hInst;
  wc.hIcon = NULL;
  wc.hCursor = NULL;
  wc.hbrBackground = NULL;
  wc.lpszMenuName = NULL;
  wc.lpszClassName = "IMExample";
  if (RegisterClass( &wc )==0)
        return(FALSE);

  hWnd = CreateWindowEx(
    0,
    "IMExample",
        "D3D IM Example",
    WS_POPUP,          // window is not visible
    0,0,
    SCREEN_WIDTH,
    SCREEN_HEIGHT,
    NULL,
    NULL,
    hInst,
    NULL );

  if( !hWnd )
    return(FALSE);

  ShowWindow(hWnd,SW_NORMAL);

    return(TRUE);
}
```

After our window is created, we will need to expend a fair amount of effort initializing DirectDraw. The call to the routine that passes the set-up parameters to DirectDraw is:

```
if (InitServices()==FALSE)
   return(FALSE);
```

16.2.6 The InitServices routine

The routine we define to do this passing is defined below. Notice we pass in the screen size, bits per pixel, and the necessary flags.

```
static BOOL InitServices(void)
{
  if (DirectDraw_Init(  SCREEN_WIDTH,SCREEN_HEIGHT,
                        SCREEN_BPP,SCREEN_FLAGS)==FALSE)
    {
        return(FALSE);
    }
    return(TRUE);
}
```

The actual DirectDraw set up code we are calling to do all this work is contained in the *ddsupport.c* file. The include files and globals we will be using are:

```
#include "Windows.h"
#include "ddraw.h"
#include "DDSupport.h"
#include "global.h"
#include "debug.h"

static void RestorePrimarySurfaces(void);

static LPDIRECTDRAW          lpDD=NULL;        // The main DirectDraw object
static LPDIRECTDRAWSURFACE   lpDDSPrimary=NULL;// The Primary Surface object
static LPDIRECTDRAWSURFACE   lpDDSBack=NULL;   // The Back Buffer object
static LPDIRECTDRAWPALETTE   lpDDPal=NULL;     // Our Palette
static BYTE                  bDDbpp=0;     // The bits per pixel we will have
static DWORD                 dwDDInitFlags=0; // Our initialization flags
```

16.2.7 Initializing DirectDraw

With all of our global variables defined, we can now deal with the code for the actual initialization process. The first thing we always must do is to create a DirectDraw object to use for rendering. It is important to remember that there can be more than one DirectDraw device on any machine. Although a lot of people have tried to set up their code to determine the *most capable* device, these heuristics oftentimes are not accurate and you end up getting the less capable device. Because of this, I'd suggest adding a pop-up dialog box to ask the user (or some other requester of your choice) which device he wishes to use.

We use the `DirectDrawCreate` routine to create an interface to the DirectDraw driver which is linked to a device. The first parameter takes a GUID representing the display device wanted. Since we want to use the *default* display device, we can call this routine with *NULL* for the first parameter. We pass the address of a pointer which will identify the location of the DirectDraw object, as long as it gets created successfully, as the second parameter. The third parameter is *always* set to NULL since it is reserved for future expansion.

```
BOOL DirectDraw_Init
(
    int width,
    int height,
    int bpp,
    DWORD flags
)
{
    HRESULT ddrval;
    DDSURFACEDESCddsd;
    DDSCAPS ddscaps;

#ifdef _DEBUG
    HDC         hdc;
#endif

    ASSERTMSG(lpDD==NULL,"DirectDraw is already initialised");

    if ((ddrval = DirectDrawCreate(NULL,&lpDD,NULL))!=DD_OK)
        return(FALSE);
```

Once we have created our DirectDraw object successfully, we need to consider if we will always be running in full screen mode, or if we will be running in windowed mode. Since I think that the debug capabilities provided in the windowing mode I presented above are hugely valuable, I'd suggest at least adding windowed mode capability for this. Some of the 3D graphic boards available do not allow windowed mode—they only work in full screen. Personally I stay away from those boards, but if you have one or intend to buy one, you will have to set up your code to handle full screen mode. By writing code that allows you to run in both modes as I am suggesting, you will be able to run your code on the greatest possible number of platforms.

To allow the user to run in windowed mode while they are debugging, we want to indicate that we wish our application to run as a *normal* Windows application. To do this, we pass the `DDSCL_NORMAL` flag to `IDirectDraw::SetCooperativeLevel` method. If you wish to have your program run only in full screen mode, thus disabling the debugging capabilities I have shown you, you would pass the DDSCL_EXCLUSIVE and DDSCL_FULLSCREEN flags instead (DDSCL_EXCLUSIVE | DDSCL_FULLSCREEN).

You will also notice that we pass a window, our hWnd parameter, which Windows uses to determine if an application terminates properly or abnormally. If a critical error occurs, normally the user would not be able to get the Windows screen back. Direct-Draw avoids this by using a background process that traps messages which are sent to that window. These messages can then be used by DirectDraw to determine when our application terminates.

If you do attempt to set your mode to exclusive mode, and the call to IDirect-Draw::SetCoorperativeLevel does not succeed (it does not return DD_OK), you will still be able to run your application, but since it cannot run in exclusive mode, it probably will not run very efficiently. I would suggest you warn the users of your code that this has occurred and let them decide if they wish to continue.

```
    dwDDInitFlags=flags;

#ifdef _DEBUG
    // we only run in windowed mode if we are debug build..
    if (flags & DD_WINDOWED)
    {
        // we can only run in a window while we are debugging
        ddrval=lpDD->lpVtbl->SetCoopera-
        tiveLevel(lpDD,hWnd,DDSCL_NORMAL);
        if(ddrval != DD_OK )
        {
            dprintf("SetCooperativeLevel failed
                [%s]...\n",DirectDrawErrorToString(ddrval));
            return(FALSE);
        }
    }
```

As long as we can successfully set the cooperative mode properly, we will want to set the window position and set the flags which define our surface requirements in a DDSUR-FACEDESC structure. The DDSD_CAPS flag we are using indicates that we want to use the DDSCAPS structure.

```
        SetWindowPos(hWnd,NULL,0,0,width,height,SWP_NOMOVE);
        ddsd.dwFlags = DDSD_CAPS;
```

The dwCaps member we are using specifies the flags that we want used in the DDSCAPS structure. Below we are telling the system that we want a primary surface.

```
        ddsd.ddsCaps.dwCaps = DDSCAPS_PRIMARYSURFACE;
        ddsd.dwSize = sizeof(ddsd);
```

16.2.8 Creating our surfaces

Once our `DDSURFACEDESC` structure has been filled, we can use it along with the Direct-Draw instance we created a little while ago, to call the `IDirectDraw::CreateSurface` method to create our first surface. As long as it returns successfully, the `lpDDSPrimary` parameter will point to the primary surface we wanted (and the system created for us).

```
ddrval = lpDD->lpVtbl->CreateSurface(lpDD,&ddsd,&lpDDSPri-
mary,NULL);
if (ddrval!=DD_OK)
    return(FALSE);

memset(&ddsd,0,sizeof(ddsd));
ddsd.dwSize = sizeof(ddsd);
ddsd.dwFlags = DDSD_CAPS | DDSD_HEIGHT |DDSD_WIDTH;
ddsd.ddsCaps.dwCaps = DDSCAPS_OFFSCREENPLAIN|DDSCAPS_3DDEVICE;
ddsd.dwWidth = width;
ddsd.dwHeight = height;

ddrval=lpDD->lpVtbl->CreateSurface(lpDD,&ddsd, &lpDDSBack, NULL);
if (ddrval!=DD_OK)
{
    dprintf("CreateSurface failed
        [%s]...\n",DirectDrawErrorToString(ddrval));
    lpDDSPrimary->lpVtbl->Release(lpDDSPrimary);
    return(FALSE);
}
DirectDraw_ClearBackBuffer();
}
else
#endif
```

If we are going to run in full screen mode, because we are not debugging, we will make a series of calls that are very similar to the ones we made for windowed mode. The key difference is that when we set the `IDirectDraw::SetCooperativeLevel` to `DDSCL_NORMAL`, you can only create surfaces that blit between other surfaces!

Now that we are going to set up a full screen, exclusive mode instead, we will be able to create surfaces that flip between other surfaces. The flags we are specifying indicate that we want exclusive mode, full screen mode, and that we want to allow the use of ModeX display modes.

```
{
ddrval = lpDD->lpVtbl>SetCooperativeLevel(
        lpDD,hWnd,DDSCL_EXCLUSIVE|DDSCL_FULLSCREEN|DDSCL_ALLOWMODEX);
if(ddrval != DD_OK )
{
    dprintf("SetCooperativeLevel failed [%s]...\n",
        DirectDrawErrorToString(ddrval));
    return(FALSE);
```

```
    }
```

We will also need to set our display mode, where we define the screen size and bits-per-pixel, to one of the sizes the user's hardware supports.

```
ddrval = lpDD->lpVtbl->SetDisplayMode(lpDD,width,height,bpp);
if( ddrval != DD_OK )
{
    lpDD->lpVtbl->SetCooperativeLevel(lpDD,hWnd,DDSCL_NORMAL);
    dprintf("SetDisplayMode failed [%s]...\n",DirectDrawError-
    ToString(ddrval));
    return(FALSE);
}
```

In this mode, the exclusive mode, I mentioned we can create surfaces that flip between other surfaces (rather than just letting you blit between them). We will be filling the structures as we did before, but this time we will be creating a primary surface and a secondary surface we can flip between rather than just blit between. We will then check to make sure we were able to create this surface. If we can't, we will fall back to windowed mode. Our lpDDSPrimary variable will be filled with a pointer to the primary surface when we make the call to IDirectDraw::CreateSurface.

```
// Create the primary surface with the required back buffers
ddsd.dwSize = sizeof(ddsd);
ddsd.dwFlags = DDSD_CAPS | DDSD_BACKBUFFERCOUNT;
ddsd.ddsCaps.dwCaps =
    DDSCAPS_PRIMARYSURFACE|DDSCAPS_FLIP|DDSCAPS_COMPLEX|DDSCAPS_3
    DDEVICE|DDSCAPS_MODEX;
ddsd.dwBackBufferCount=1;
ddrval=lpDD->lpVtbl->CreateSurface(lpDD,&ddsd,&lpDDSPrimary,NULL);
if (ddrval!=DD_OK)
{
    lpDD->lpVtbl->SetCooperativeLevel(lpDD,hWnd,DDSCL_NORMAL);
    lpDD->lpVtbl->RestoreDisplayMode(lpDD);
    dprintf("CreateSurface failed [%s]...\n",DirectDrawError-
    ToString(ddrval));
    return(FALSE);
}
```

Next we will want to create our back buffer and attach it to the primary surface we just created. To acquire a pointer to the back buffer, we call the IDirectDrawSurface::GetAttachedSurface method. If the call does not succeed, we will want to switch back to the mode we were just in before we tried to switch.

```
// Get a pointer to the back buffer interface
ddscaps.dwCaps=DDSCAPS_BACKBUFFER;
ddrval=lpDDSPrimary->lpVtbl->GetAttachedSurface(
    lpDDSPrimary,&ddscaps,&lpDDSBack);
if (ddrval!=DD_OK)
{
```

```
    lpDD->lpVtbl->SetCooperativeLevel(lpDD,hWnd,DDSCL_NORMAL);
    lpDD->lpVtbl->RestoreDisplayMode(lpDD);
    dprintf("GetAttachedSurface failed [%s]...\n",DirectDrawError-
    ToString(ddrval));
    return(FALSE);
    }
```

With our buffers prepared, we just need to make the calls to clear them.

```
    // Ensure that both of the buffers are clear
    DirectDraw_ClearBackBuffer();
    DirectDraw_SwapBuffers();
    DirectDraw_ClearBackBuffer();
    bDDbpp=bpp;
}
```

16.2.9 Clearing the back buffer

The _ClearBackBuffer routine we now will declare uses the IDirectDrawSurface2::Blt method to fill the screen with the requested color to clear it.

```
void DirectDraw_ClearBackBuffer(void)
{
    DDBLTFX     ddbltfx;
    HRESULT     res;

    ddbltfx.dwSize=sizeof(ddbltfx);
    ddbltfx.dwFillColor=0;
    while(1)
    {
        if ((res=lpDDSBack->lpVtbl->Blt(lpDDSBack,
                NULL,NULL,NULL,DDBLT_COLORFILL,&ddbltfx))==DD_OK)
            break;
        if (res==DDERR_SURFACELOST)
        {
            RestorePrimarySurfaces();
            break;
        }
    }
}
```

While we are at it, we might as well also define the routine we will use to restore the surfaces we will be using in our flipping chain. We also need to handle the case where we are in windowed mode and we want to restore the surfaces.

```
static void RestorePrimarySurfaces(void)
{
    HRESULTres;

    // This will restores any surfaces that are in the flipping chain
    while (1)
    {
```

```
            res=lpDDSPrimary->lpVtbl->Restore(lpDDSPrimary);
            if (res==DD_OK)
                break;                    // fall through and free the next
            if (res==DDERR_WASSTILLDRAWING)
                continue;
            break;
        }


#ifdef _DEBUG
        // This loop will fail if the back surface is attached to the
        // primary surface; such is the case when in full screen and
        // we are page flipping.
        // This is required because in Windows the back surface is just a
        // normal surface that can be lost
        while (1)
        {
            res=lpDDSBack->lpVtbl->Restore(lpDDSBack);
            if (res==DD_OK)
                return;
            if (res==DDERR_WASSTILLDRAWING)
                continue;
            break;
        }
#endif
}
```

16.2.10 Swapping buffers

We will also need to define our routine to swap buffers when we wish. The reason for
making this a separate routine is that it lets us wrap the call with the error handling that
we need to perform if the call is unsuccessful.

```
void DirectDraw_SwapBuffers(void)
{
    HRESULTddrval;
#ifdef _DEBUG
    if (dwDDInitFlags & DD_WINDOWED)
    {
        ddrval=lpDDSPrimary->lpVtbl->BltFast(lpDDSPrimary,0,0,
            lpDDSBack,NULL,DDBLTFAST_WAIT|DDBLTFAST_NOCOLORKEY);
        if (ddrval==DDERR_SURFACELOST)
            RestorePrimarySurfaces();
    }
    else
    {
#endif
        while(1)
        {
            ddrval=lpDDSPrimary->lpVtbl->Flip(lpDDSPrimary,NULL,0);
            if (ddrval==DD_OK )
            {
```

```
                break;
        }

        if (ddrval==DDERR_SURFACELOST )
        {
            RestorePrimarySurfaces();
            break;
        }

        if (ddrval!=DDERR_WASSTILLDRAWING)
        {
            DEBUGSTR("FlipSurfaces: \n");
            break;
        }
    }
#ifdef _DEBUG
    }
#endif
}
```

16.2.11 Create our color map

With our surfaces all defined, we can now set up our color map. The method that you will need to know to understand this routine is IDirectDraw2::CreatePalette.

You will also need to understand the basics of palette objects to make the following code clear. A DirectDrawPalette object allows the direct manipulation of 16- and 256-color palettes, and it is usually attached to a DirectDrawSurface object. The object allows the direct manipulation of the color table as an array of color values, usually RGB triplets. It can contain 16- or 24-bit RGB entries which define the colors associated with each index.

Once the palette has been defined, you can create the DirectDraw palette. In our case shown below, we are creating an 8-bit palette and initializing it by passing a zeroed array.

DirectDraw allows us to create 2 entry (1-bit), 4 entry (2-bit), 16 entry (4-bit), and 256 entry (8-bit) palettes. You need to keep in mind that you can only attach a palette to a surface with a matching pixel format. As an example, if you create a 256 entry palette using the DDPCAPS_8BIT flag, you can only attach it to an 8-bit surface.

```
// Set the palette in 256 color mode
if (bpp==8)
{
    PALETTEENTRYcols[256];
    int i;

    for( i=0; i<10; i++ )
        cols[i].peFlags = D3DPAL_READONLY;
    for (i = 10; i < 246; i++)
        cols[i].peFlags = D3DPAL_FREE | PC_RESERVED;
```

```
        for (I = 246; I < 256; I++)
            cols[I].peFlags = D3DPAL_READONLY;

        // Create and set the palette
        ddrval=lpDD->lpVtbl->CreatePalette(
            lpDD,DDPCAPS_8BIT,cols,&lpDDPal,NULL);
        if (ddrval!=DD_OK)
        {
            dprintf("CreatePalette failed
                [%s]...\n",DirectDrawErrorToString(ddrval));
            return(FALSE);
        }

        // Set it anyway just to ensure it is attached to all screen surfaces
        DirectDraw_SetPalette(cols,0,256);
    }
    return(TRUE);
}
```

16.2.12 Setting our palette

Once the palette has been created, we will want to set its entries and then set the primary and secondary surface's palettes to the palette we just created. The routine to do this is fairly self explanatory:

```
BOOL DirectDraw_SetPalette
(
    PALETTEENTRY        *cols,
    DWORD               start,
    DWORD               count
)
{
    HRESULT             ddrval;

    _ASSERTE(cols!=NULL);
    _ASSERTE(count<=256);
    _ASSERTE(start<=256);
    _ASSERTE(count+start<=256);
```

We will want to set the primary and secondary surfaces palettes to the palette we just created. Palettes can be attached to any palletized surface. These can be primary, back buffer, off screen, plain, or texture map surfaces.

Two things you should remember are that DirectDraw blits will never perform color conversion, so any palettes you have attached to the source or destination surface of a blit will be ignored. Second, only the palettes that are attached to primary surfaces will have any effect on the system palette.

The IDirectDrawPalette::SetEntries method allows us to modify the entries in our palette whenever we want. We will be using it here to initialize our table, and we will use it later to set our table's values.

You should not set any of the Windows static entries, the first 10 (indices 0–9) and the last 10 (246–255), unless you are resetting *all* of the entries. In our code below, we are setting all 256 entries because we called this routine with *start* set to 0 and *count* set to 256.

```
if (bDDbpp==8)
{
    ddrval=lpDDPal->lpVtbl->SetEntries(lpDDPal,0,start,count,cols);
    if (ddrval!=DD_OK)
    {
        return(FALSE);
    }

    // We have to set the palette on the primary and back surfaces
    // because DirectDraw allows them to be different
    ddrval=lpDDSPrimary->lpVtbl->SetPalette(lpDDSPrimary,lpDDPal);
    if (ddrval!=DD_OK)
    {
        return(FALSE);
    }
    ddrval=lpDDSBack->lpVtbl->SetPalette(lpDDSBack,lpDDPal);
    if (ddrval!=DD_OK)
    {
        return(FALSE);
    }
}
return(TRUE);
}
```

16.2.13 Sharing palettes

You probably noticed that I had set the same palette for both the primary and back surfaces. DirectDraw allows us to share palettes between multiple surfaces. Each time we attach a palette to one of our surfaces, using the IDirectDrawSurface2::SetPalette method, our surface will increment the reference count of the palette. When the reference count hits 0, the surface decrements the reference count of its associated palette. You can also detach a palette from a surface by using IDIrcetDrawSurface2::SetPalette with a NULL palette interface pointer. In this case, the reference count of your surface's palette will be decremented. We now need to hide our cursor and start the main loop as follows:

```
ShowCursor(FALSE);

rval=DoMainLoop();
```

Once we have all of our surfaces defined, we can define our main message dispatch loop. This loop is very similar to any other Windows application, so I just list it below.

```
static int DoMainLoop(void)
{
    MSG          msg;

    while (!Quit)
    {
        if( PeekMessage( &msg, NULL, 0, 0, PM_NOREMOVE ) )
        {
            if(GetMessage( &msg, NULL, 0, 0 ) )
            {
                TranslateMessage(&msg);
                DispatchMessage(&msg);
            }
            else
            {
                Quit=TRUE;
            }
        }

        // Even if we process a message we still do a frame
        if (AppActive)
        {
            ProcessFrame();
        }
        else
        {
            // If our app is not active then suspend it to avoid wasting
            // processor time
            if (!Quit)
                WaitMessage();// Only call WaitMessage if we have not quit,
                              // because the quit message is the last
                              // message that we receive. We
                              // will get stuck within the VMM.
        }
    }

    return(0);
}
```

Our `ProcessFrame` routine, which we called in the message loop we just defined, will be the one which we use for each iteration of our rendering loop. For now, I am just defining it as an empty place holder routine.

```
void ProcessFrame(void)
{
    //DirectDraw_ClearBackBuffer();
    //DirectDraw_SwapBuffers();
}
```

The last routines we need to define before we get to the `WindowProc` definition are the `CloseApp`, `CloseServices`, and `DirectDraw_Close` routines. These are used together to free up all of the objects we created for our application, such as the palettes and surfaces we generated.

```c
static void CloseApp(void)
{
    CloseServices();
    DestroyWindow(hWnd);
}

static void CloseServices(void)
{
    DirectDraw_Close();
}

void DirectDraw_Close(void)
{
    if (bDDbpp==8)
    {
        // free the palette
        if (lpDDPal)
        {
            lpDDPal->lpVtbl->Release(lpDDPal);
            lpDDPal=NULL;
        }
    }


#ifdef _DEBUG
    if (dwDDInitFlags & DD_WINDOWED)
    {
        // If we are windowed then the back surface is a normal surface
        // that is not attached to the primary so it needs to be freed
        if (lpDDSBack)
        {
            lpDDSBack->lpVtbl->Release(lpDDSBack);
            lpDDSBack=NULL;
        }
    }
#endif

    if (lpDDSPrimary)
    {
        lpDDSPrimary->lpVtbl->Release(lpDDSPrimary);
        lpDDSPrimary=NULL;
    }
    if (lpDD)
    {
        lpDD->lpVtbl->Release(lpDD);
        lpDD=NULL;
    }
}
```

16.2.14 Message handling

We finally get to the last segment of our code! This is the `WindowProc` routine which checks to see which message we have received and acts upon it. For now, all we will be checking is for `WM_ACTIVATEAPP` and `WM_DESTROY` messages. We will be adding a number of messages in the next chapter when we add our actual 3D rendering code.

```
static long WINAPI WindowProc
(
    HWND hWnd,
    UINT message,
    WPARAM wParam,
    LPARAM lParam
)
{
  switch( message )
  {
    case WM_ACTIVATEAPP:
      AppActive = wParam;
      break;

    case WM_DESTROY:
      PostQuitMessage(0);
      break;
  }
  return DefWindowProc(hWnd, message, wParam, lParam);
}
```

16.3 What did we learn?

Just like Retained Mode, there is an incredible amount of code necessary just to set up our application so that we can even *start* writing code using Immediate Mode. But, again, just like Retained Mode, this code is completely reusable, so you will only have to write it once (or copy it from the CD) and learn it thoroughly.

At this point, I would suggest you experiment with this code. Try setting the window to various sizes using windowed mode and full screen mode. If you have not determined what modes your particular video card supports, you might want to do that now also.

16.4 What's next?

Now that we have defined all of our base code for setting up the DirectDraw and standard Windows aspects of the code, let's look at the more fun part and begin defining a basic 3D application you can continue to expand upon.

chapter 17

Setting up Immediate Mode for 3D

17.1 Getting ready for 3D

In the last chapter, I showed you the basics of setting up DirectDraw to support Immediate-Mode applications. One thing I glossed over was the enumeration of the DirectDraw devices. I showed you how to get a device if you knew your system's capabilities, but in reality you will need to have your software check for the devices that are available on the system.

The code to handle this is as follows:

```
BOOL FAR PASCAL DirectDrawEnumCallback (  GUID FAR* lpGUID;
                                          LPSTR lpDriverDesc,
                                          LPSTR lpDriverName,
                                          LPVOID lpContext)
{
    DDCAPS DDcaps;
    DDCAPS HELcaps;
    LPDIRECTDRAW lpDD;
```

```
// Create the DirectDraw device using the GUID we passed in
if (DirectDrawCreate(lpGUID, &lpDD, NULL) != DD_OK)
    // Forget this one
    return 1;

// Acquire the caps for this DirectDraw driver
memset(&DDcaps, 0, sizeof(DDcaps));
DDcaps.dwsize = sizeof(DDcaps);
memset(&HELcaps, 0, sizeof(HELcaps));
HELcaps.dwSizw = sizeof(HELcaps);
if (lpDD->GetCaps(&DDcaps, &HELcaps) != DD_OK)
{
    // Failed - go to next driver
    lpDD->Release();
    lpDD = 0;
    return 1;
}

// The device is valid so add it to our list of good ones

//Your code goes here to add the device to a list

}
```

You will need to remember that the lpGUID is NULL only for the primary device. Any other device should have a non-NULL lpGUID.

17.2 Choosing your DirectDraw device

After you have the list of devices, you will need to choose which one you want to use. I mentioned before that it is probably best to let the user choose which one they wish. After you, or your users, have chosen the device to be used, you will have to create an interface to the DirectDraw driver that is linked to that device. This is done using the DirectDrawCreate function and passing a pointer to the GUID of the device you want to use. This routine will return a pointer to an IDirectDraw object.

17.3 Enumerating the display modes

Whenever you write code to support full screen modes, it will be necessary for you to enumerate all of the available display modes for any code you intend to distribute. You can do this using the IDirectDraw::EnumDisplayModes method.

This method will enumerate all of the display modes available and execute the callback you handed it. You should write your callback so that it stores away the display mode information so you can use it later (preferably by having the user choose the display mode he or she wants).

17.4 Creating your IDirect3D object

We have now gotten to the point where I left you in the last chapter, but we have now asked the system to describe the available devices rather than always assuming we know what they are.

We can now see if the IDirectDraw object we created earlier with our call to `DirectDrawCreate` can support Direct3D. If it does, the pointer we pass this routine will be set to a pointer to a D3D object. The code to perform this is:

```
LPDIRECTDRAW lpDD;
if (lpDD->QueryInterface(IID_DIRECT3D, (LPVOID *) &lpD3D) != DD_OK)
    goto generic_error;
```

17.5 Enumerating the D3D Drivers

Now that we have pointers to our IDirectDraw and IDirect3D objects, we will need to enumerate the D3D drivers which are associated with our DirectDraw device. This is done by calling the `IDirect3D::EnumDevices` method. This method takes a callback to a function which is called for each of the installed D3D drivers. This routine also takes a pointer to a data structure which is application-specific—you can place the driver information into it and whatever else you might want. You should check to see that the driver meets some minimum criteria before you store it since you will need to define the point at what a particular platform is not powerful enough to run your application. You can check the `dwFlags` parameter of the `LPD3DDEVICEDESC` to see if it is a hardware or a software driver.

The code to perform the enumeration callback can be as follows:

```
static HRESULT WINAPI enumDeviceFunc
(
  LPGUID lpGuid,
  LPSTR lpDeviceDescription,
  LPSTR lpDeviceName,
  LPD3DDEVICEDESC lpHWDesc,
  LPD3DDEVICEDESC lpHELDesc,
  LPVOID lpContext
)
{
  FINDRENDER*fblock=(FINDRENDER*)lpContext;

  dprintf("%s\n",lpDeviceDescription);

  if (fblock->Found)
  {
    return (D3DENUMRET_OK);
```

```
        }
        if (lpHWDesc->dcmColorModel)
        {
          // We have found an hardware card!!
          if (fblock->Type==D3D_HARDWARE)
          {
              memcpy(fblock->lpGuid,lpGuid,sizeof(GUID));
              memcpy(&DeviceDesc,lpHWDesc,sizeof(D3DDEVICEDESC));
              fblock->Found=TRUE;
              IsHardware=TRUE;
              if (!(lpHWDesc->dwDevCaps &
                  D3DDEVCAPS_TEXTURESYSTEMMEMORY))
              {
                  // We cannot use system ram so our chaching system
                  // needs to be used
                  SystemTexture=FALSE;
              }
              else
              {
                  SystemTexture=TRUE;
              }
          }
        }
      else
      {
        // Software renderers can always use system ram, so the manual says
        if (fblock->Type==D3D_SOFTWARE_RAMP)
        {
            if (lpHELDesc->dcmColorModel==D3DCOLOR_MONO)
            {
                memcpy(fblock->lpGuid,lpGuid,sizeof(GUID));
                memcpy(&DeviceDesc,lpHELDesc,sizeof(D3DDEVICEDESC));
                fblock->Found=TRUE;
                IsHardware=FALSE;
                SystemTexture=TRUE;
            }
        }
        else if (fblock->Type==D3D_SOFTWARE_RGB)
        {
            if (lpHELDesc->dcmColorModel==D3DCOLOR_RGB)
            {
                memcpy(fblock->lpGuid,lpGuid,sizeof(GUID));
                memcpy(&DeviceDesc,lpHELDesc,sizeof(D3DDEVICEDESC));
                fblock->Found=TRUE;
                IsHardware=FALSE;
                SystemTexture=TRUE;
            }
        }
      }
      return (D3DENUMRET_OK);
}
```

17.6 Choosing your D3D driver

Now that you have a LPDIRECTDRAW object, an LPDIRECT3D object, and a list of Direct3D drivers, you can ask the user to choose a driver (or choose one yourself). You can ask the user by popping up a dialog box or whatever other approach you like. We'll store it in the `D3Ddriver`.

17.7 Setting the cooperative level

I showed you how to set this in the previous chapter. I just wanted to point out that this is where you would perform this task, using the `DirectDraw_Init` routine we defined there. Although this is a DirectDraw command, we will need it to use it to decide if we are running in full screen or windows mode.

17.8 Creating your front buffer, back buffers, and clipper

This is another process I showed you in the previous chapter, but this time we also need to specify the `DDSCAPS_3DDEVICE` flag for the `dwCaps` structure. Here we will be creating our primary surface, our back buffer, and a clipper to attach to our application's window so we do not overdraw its boundaries.

The code to create these for either a windowed or a full screen applications is shown again, but here we are adding the code to generate our clipper when we are in windowed mode.

```
lpClipper;

BOOL DirectDraw_Init
(
    int width,
    int height,
    int bpp,
    DWORD flags
)
{
    HRESULT             ddrval;
    DDSURFACEDESC       ddsd;
    DDSCAPS             ddscaps;

#ifdef _DEBUG
    HDC                 hdc;
```

```
#endif

    ASSERTMSG(lpDD==NULL,"DirectDraw is already initialized");

    if ((ddrval = DirectDrawCreate(NULL,&lpDD,NULL))!=DD_OK)
        return(FALSE);

    dwDDInitFlags=flags;

#ifdef _DEBUG
    // We only run in windowed mode if we are doing a debug build.
    if (flags & DD_WINDOWED)
    {
        // we can only run in a window while we are debugging
        ddrval=lpDD->lpVtbl->SetCoopera-
        tiveLevel(lpDD,hWnd,DDSCL_NORMAL);
        if(ddrval != DD_OK )
        {
            dprintf("SetCooperativeLevel failed
                    [%s]...\n",DirectDrawErrorToString(ddrval));
            return(FALSE);
        }

        SetWindowPos(hWnd,NULL,0,0,width,height,SWP_NOMOVE);

        ddsd.dwFlags = DDSD_CAPS;
        ddsd.ddsCaps.dwCaps = DDSCAPS_PRIMARYSURFACE;
        ddsd.dwSize = sizeof(ddsd);

        ddrval = lpDD->lpVtbl->CreateSurface(lpDD,&ddsd,&lpDDSPri-
        mary,NULL);
        if (ddrval!=DD_OK)
            return(FALSE);

        memset(&ddsd,0,sizeof(ddsd));
        ddsd.dwSize = sizeof(ddsd);
        ddsd.dwFlags = DDSD_CAPS | DDSD_HEIGHT |DDSD_WIDTH;
        ddsd.ddsCaps.dwCaps = DDSCAPS_OFFSCREENPLAIN|DDSCAPS_3DDEVICE;
        ddsd.dwWidth = width;
        ddsd.dwHeight = height;

        ddrval=lpDD->lpVtbl->CreateSurface(lpDD,&ddsd, &lpDDSBack, NULL);
        if (ddrval!=DD_OK)
        {
            dprintf("CreateSurface failed
                    [%s]...\n",DirectDrawErrorToString(ddrval));
            lpDDSPrimary->lpVtbl->Release(lpDDSPrimary);
            return(FALSE);
        }
        DirectDraw_ClearBackBuffer();

        // Create our clipper
        if (lpDD->CreateClipper(o, &lpClipper, NULL) != DD_OK)
            return(FALSE);
```

```
            if (lpDDSPrimary->SetClipper(lpClipper) != DD_OK)
                return(FALSE);

            // Get the actual bit depth of the GDI screen
            hdc = GetDC(NULL);
            bDDbpp=GetDeviceCaps(hdc, PLANES) * GetDeviceCaps(hdc, BITSPIXEL);
            ReleaseDC(NULL, hdc);
        }
        else
#endif
        {
        ddrval = lpDD->lpVtbl>SetCooperativeLevel(
            lpDD,hWnd,DDSCL_EXCLUSIVE|DDSCL_FULLSCREEN|DDSCL_ALLOWMODEX);
        if(ddrval != DD_OK )
        {
            dprintf("SetCooperativeLevel failed
                [%s]...\n",DirectDrawErrorToString(ddrval));
            return(FALSE);
        }

        ddrval = lpDD->lpVtbl->SetDisplayMode(lpDD,width,height,bpp);
        if( ddrval != DD_OK )
        {
            lpDD->lpVtbl->SetCooperativeLevel(lpDD,hWnd,DDSCL_NORMAL);
            dprintf("SetDisplayMode failed
                [%s]...\n",DirectDrawErrorToString(ddrval));
            return(FALSE);
        }

// Create the primary surface with the required back buffers
ddsd.dwSize = sizeof(ddsd);
ddsd.dwFlags = DDSD_CAPS | DDSD_BACKBUFFERCOUNT;
ddsd.ddsCaps.dwCaps =
        DDSCAPS_PRIMARYSURFACE|DDSCAPS_FLIP|DDSCAPS_COMPLEX|DDSCAPS_3DDE
        VICE|DDSCAPS_MODEX;
ddsd.dwBackBufferCount=1;
ddrval=lpDD->lpVtbl->CreateSurface(lpDD,&ddsd,&lpDDSPrimary,NULL);
        if (ddrval!=DD_OK)
        {
            lpDD->lpVtbl->SetCooperativeLevel(lpDD,hWnd,DDSCL_NORMAL);
            lpDD->lpVtbl->RestoreDisplayMode(lpDD);
        dprintf("CreateSurface failed
                [%s]...\n",DirectDrawErrorToString(ddrval));
            return(FALSE);
        }

// Get a pointer to the back buffer interface
ddscaps.dwCaps=DDSCAPS_BACKBUFFER;
ddrval=lpDDSPrimary->lpVtbl->GetAttachedSurface
            (lpDDSPrimary,&ddscaps,&lpDDSBack);
        if (ddrval!=DD_OK)
        {
            lpDD->lpVtbl->SetCooperativeLevel(lpDD,hWnd,DDSCL_NORMAL);
            lpDD->lpVtbl->RestoreDisplayMode(lpDD);
```

```
          dprintf("GetAttachedSurface failed
              [%s]...\n",DirectDrawErrorToString(ddrval));
          return(FALSE);
      }

      // Ensure that both of the buffers are clear
      DirectDraw_ClearBackBuffer();
      DirectDraw_SwapBuffers();
      DirectDraw_ClearBackBuffer();
      bDDbpp=bpp;
  }
```

17.9 Creating your Z-buffer

We now have a front and a back buffer, but since we are using Direct3D, we will also need a Z-buffer if we want to do depth-buffered hidden surface removal. You do not *have* to do this, but if you want one, you have to create it before your IDirect3DDevice, which we will create next.

```
// Create a Z buffer and attach it to the back buffer so that D3D will
// find it.
// Can the width and height be different from the surface that they
// are attached to? (It will match the viewport)
static BOOL D3DCreateZBuffer(DWORD w,DWORD h)
{
  DDSURFACEDESC ddsd;
  DWORD         devdepth;
  HRESULT       ddrval;
  BYTE          *zbits;
  DWORD         y;

  // We don't support Z buffering on this renderer so we cannot create one.
  if (!CanZBuffer)
    return FALSE;

  memset(&zblddsd,0,sizeof(DDSURFACEDESC));
  zblddsd.dwSize=sizeof(DDSURFACEDESC);

  memset(&ddsd, 0 ,sizeof(DDSURFACEDESC));
  ddsd.dwSize = sizeof( ddsd );
  ddsd.dwFlags = DDSD_WIDTH | DDSD_HEIGHT | DDSD_CAPS |
      DDSD_ZBUFFERBITDEPTH;
  ddsd.ddsCaps.dwCaps = DDSCAPS_ZBUFFER;
  ddsd.dwHeight = h;
  ddsd.dwWidth = w;

  // If this is a hardware D3D driver, the Z-Buffer MUST end up in video
  // memory. Otherwise, it MUST end up in system memory.
  if (IsHardware)
    ddsd.ddsCaps.dwCaps |= DDSCAPS_VIDEOMEMORY;
```

```
else
  ddsd.ddsCaps.dwCaps |= DDSCAPS_SYSTEMMEMORY;
/*
 * Get the Z buffer bit depth from this driver's D3D device description
 */
devdepth = DeviceDesc.dwDeviceZBufferBitDepth;
if ((devdepth & DDBD_16)==0)
  {
      // we must be able to do 16 bits otherwise the voxels cannot be drawn
      // this should not be a problem
      return(FALSE);
  }
ddsd.dwZBufferBitDepth = 16;
ddrval = GetDDObject()->lpVtbl->CreateSurface(GetDDObject(),
        &ddsd,&lpZBuffer,NULL);
if(ddrval != DD_OK)
{
      return(FALSE);
}

//Attach the Z-buffer to the back buffer so D3D will find it
ddrval=lpDDSurface->lpVtbl->AddAttachedSurface(lpDDSurface,lpZBuffer);
if (ddrval!=DD_OK)
{
  // If this fails it is most likely the size of the Z-buffer is incorrect
  goto exit_with_error;
}

// Lets us clear out the Z-buffer to far back
memset(&ddsd,0,sizeof(DDSURFACEDESC));
ddsd.dwSize=sizeof(DDSURFACEDESC);
ddrval=lpZBuffer->lpVtbl->Lock(lpZBuffer,NULL,&ddsd,
  DDLOCK_SURFACEMEMORYPTR|DDLOCK_WAIT,NULL);
if (ddrval != DD_OK)
{
  lpZBuffer->lpVtbl->Release(lpZBuffer);
  return (FALSE);
}
zbits=(char*)ddsd.lpSurface;

for (y=0;y<SurfaceHeight;y++)
{
  if (y<h)
      memset(zbits,0xff,w*2);          // 16 bit-scan line
  else
      memset(zbits,0x00,w*2);          // 16-bit scan line
                                       // (panel is front to help clipping)
  zbits+=ddsd.lPitch;
}

lpZBuffer->lpVtbl->Unlock(lpZBuffer,ddsd.lpSurface);
return TRUE;

exit_with_error:
```

```
        lpZBuffer->lpVtbl->Release(lpZBuffer);
        lpZBuffer=NULL;
    return FALSE;
}
```

17.10 Creating the IDirect3DDevice

Now that we have our buffers created, and we have chosen a device from the list of possibilities, we can finally create the IDirect3DDevice.

```
LPDIRECTDRAWSURFACE lpSurface;

ddrval=lpSurface->lpVtbl->QueryInterface(lpSurface,lpGuid,
        (LPVOID*)&lpD3DDevice);
if (ddrval!=DD_OK)
{
    DXERROR(ddrval);
    D3DClose();
    return(FALSE);
}
```

Phew! With all of that complete, we finally have a D3D device and all of the necessary buffers we can use.

17.11 Creating your IDirect3DViewport and attaching it to your D3DDevice

The last thing you will need to do to complete the D3D initialization process, is create an IDirect3DViewport and attach it to the IDirect3DDevice we created. The code to do this is:

```
HRESULT         ddrval;
D3DVIEWPORT     viewdata;
.
.
ddrval=lpD3D->lpVtbl->CreateViewport(lpD3D,&lpD3DViewport,NULL);
if (ddrval!=D3D_OK)
{
    D3DClose();
    return(FALSE);
}

ddrval=lpD3DDevice->lpVtbl->AddViewport(lpD3DDevice,lpD3DViewport);
if (ddrval!=D3D_OK)
{
    DXERROR(ddrval);
```

```
        D3DClose();
        return(FALSE);
    }


    memset(&viewdata, 0, sizeof(D3DVIEWPORT));
    viewdata.dwSize = sizeof(D3DVIEWPORT);
    viewdata.dwX = xo;
    viewdata.dwY = yo;
    viewdata.dwWidth = w;
    viewdata.dwHeight = h;
    viewdata.dvScaleX = viewdata.dwWidth / (float)2.0;
    viewdata.dvScaleY = viewdata.dwHeight / (float)2.0;
    viewdata.dvMaxX = (float)D3DDivide(D3DVAL(viewdata.dwWidth),D3DVAL(2
        *
    viewdata.dvScaleX));
    viewdata.dvMaxY = (float)D3DDivide(D3DVAL(viewdata.dwHeight),D3DVAL(2
        *
    viewdata.dvScaleY));
    drval=lpD3DViewport->lpVtbl->SetViewport(lpD3DViewport,&viewdata);
    if (ddrval!=D3D_OK)
    {
        DXERROR(ddrval);
        D3DClose();
        return(FALSE);
    }
```

17.12 Drawing to your screen

We now have all of the necessary objects for rendering a 3D scene to our screen. You can either flip or blit to them as I mentioned in the last chapter. In full screen mode, you *page flip* from back to front. In windowed mode, you *blit* from back to front.

```
    void DirectDraw_SwapBuffers(void)
    {
        HRESULTddrval;
#ifdef _DEBUG
        if (dwDDInitFlags & DD_WINDOWED)
        {
            ddrval=lpDDSPrimary->lpVtbl->BltFast(lpDDSPrimary,0,0,
                    lpDDSBack,NULL,
                DDBLTFAST_WAIT|DDBLTFAST_NOCOLORKEY);
            if (ddrval==DDERR_SURFACELOST)
                    RestorePrimarySurfaces();
        }
        else
        {
#endif
            while(1)
            {
                    ddrval=lpDDSPrimary->lpVtbl->Flip(lpDDSPrimary,NULL,0);
```

```
                        if (ddrval==DD_OK )
                        {
                            break;
                        }

                        if (ddrval==DDERR_SURFACELOST )
                {
                        RestorePrimarySurfaces();
                        break;
                        }

                        if (ddrval!=DDERR_WASSTILLDRAWING)
                        {
                            DEBUGSTR("FlipSurfaces: \n");
                            break;
                        }
                    }
#ifdef _DEBUG
        }
#endif
}
```

You will also need to know how to clear your surfaces. If you want to set the color to something other than black, you can pass in a parameter that holds the desired color. The code to handle this is:

```
void DirectDraw_ClearBackBuffer(void)
{
    DDBLTFX        ddbltfx;
    HRESULT        res;


    ddbltfx.dwSize=sizeof(ddbltfx);
    ddbltfx.dwFillColor=0;
    while(1)
    {
        if ((res=lpDDSBack->lpVtbl->Blt(lpDDSBack,
                NULL,NULL,NULL,DDBLT_COLORFILL,&ddbltfx))==DD_OK)
            break;
        if (res==DDERR_SURFACELOST)
        {
            RestorePrimarySurfaces();
            break;
        }
        if (res!=DDERR_WASSTILLDRAWING)
        {
            DEBUGSTR("EraseRect: \n");
            break;
        }
    }
}
```

17.13 What did we learn?

At this point, you should understand how to set up an Immediate-Mode Direct3D application, including creating primary buffers, back buffers, Z-buffers, and clearing or filling the screen. Although that may not sound like a lot, as you can see from the quantity of code, it is a lot of work to get to this point. Please review the code I have shown you and try creating a program to flip between two buffers.

17.14 What's next?

The next chapter is the last one on Immediate-Mode programming. I will show you some final pieces you will need to create your 3D applications. Several of them are not exactly user friendly, but I will try to make some sense out of them for you.

chapter 18

Creating and displaying 3D objects in Immediate Mode

18.1 How do I make a 3D object?

It has taken us two chapters, and we have still not gotten to the core of what you probably want to know—how to create 3D objects we can view.

Well, it isn't really easy, but once you learn it, it isn't terrible either. Unlike Retained Mode, where we can easily create objects on the fly or load them into our applications with a fairly simple call, by using Immediate Mode we have stripped ourselves of this ability. In Immediate Mode, Direct3D is controlled with the use of execute buffers. We add commands and data to these execute buffers and then pass the filled buffer to our Direct3D driver. This data is then parsed and executed by the driver.

18.2 So, what does an execute buffer look like?

An execute buffer is a chunk of memory composed of a stream of vertices followed by commands. All of these are DWORD aligned. This buffer is passed to our Direct3D driver and it parses it.

The basic structure of an execute buffer to define a 3D object is as follows:

Data	Length
Vertex data	variable
OP_CODE	fixed
OP_CODE_PARAMS	variable

.

.

Any number of op-codes

.

.

QWORD UNALIGNER	fixed (if desired)
OP_TRIANGLE_LIST	fixed
Triangle Data	variable
OP_EXIT	

Let's take a quick look at each of these components.

18.2.1 Vertex data

These data define the position, normal, and color information for a vertex. There are three types of vertices:

1   D3DVERTEX stores position, normal, and texture coordinate information.

2   D3DLVERTEX stores position, diffuse color, specular color, and texture coordinate information for an untransformed and lit vertex.

3   D3DTLVERTEX stores position, diffuse color, specular color, and texture coordinate information for a textured and lit vertex.

18.2.2 Process vertices

The next instructions are usually OP_PROCESS_VERTICES and PROCESSVERTICES_DATA. These instructions, like all OP_xxx instructions, insert instructions into our execute buffer.

PROCESSVERTICES_DATA macro inserts op-code parameters. If you are using D3DVERTEX vertices, the processing type will be D3DPROCESSVERTICES_TRANSFORMLIGHT. If you are using D3DLVERTEX vertices, the processing type will be D3DPROCESSVERTICES_TRANSFORM. Finally, if you are using D3DTLVERTEX vertices, the processing type will be D3DPROCESSVERTICES_COPY.

18.2.3 Triangle data

The triangle data, defining our objects, are placed in the list using the OP_TRIANGLE_LIST followed by a list of triangles. These triangles are defined by three indices into the vertex data which is at the beginning of the execute buffer.

A key issue to remember is that your triangle data needs to be QWORD aligned (8-byte boundaries). To deal with this, the instruction, for triangle data needs to be unaligned. The command to do this is:

```
if (QWORD_ALIGNED (lpPointer))
{
    OP_NOP(lpPointer);
}
OP_TRIANGLE_LIST(1, lpPointer);
```

18.2.4 OP_EXIT

The last instruction is the OP_EXIT instruction, which notifies D3D that it has hit the end of the execute buffer and can stop processing the data.

18.3 Creating the execute buffer

Before we start dealing with the actual filling of the execute buffer, we will need to create the elements that compose our 3D scene and the execute buffer we want to fill. In the example I show you below, we are setting up a scene that consists of a single light, a viewport, the background and surface material, three transformation matrices, and the execute buffer which will hold the state changes and drawing primitives.

The first segment of our routine, CreateScene, just defines our local variables and verifies that the other necessary variables have been initialized properly.

```
static HRESULT
CreateScene(void)
{
  HRESULT              hRes;
  D3DMATERIAL          d3dMaterial;
  D3DLIGHT             d3dLight;
  DWORD                dwVertexSize;
```

```
DWORD                     dwInstructionSize;
DWORD                     dwExecuteBufferSize;
D3DEXECUTEBUFFERDESC      d3dExecuteBufferDesc;
D3DEXECUTEDATA            d3dExecuteData;

ASSERT(NULL != lpd3d);
ASSERT(NULL != lpd3dDevice);
ASSERT(NULL == lpd3dViewport);
ASSERT(NULL == lpd3dMaterial);
ASSERT(NULL == lpd3dBackgroundMaterial);
ASSERT(NULL == lpd3dExecuteBuffer);
ASSERT(NULL == lpd3dLight);
ASSERT(0UL == hd3dWorldMatrix);
ASSERT(0UL == hd3dViewMatrix);
ASSERT(0UL == hd3dProjMatrix);
```

After we have our variables ready, we will want to define our light. We create it using the `IDirect3D::CreateLight` method:

```
HRESULT CreateLight(LPDIRECT3DLIGHT* lplpDirect3DLight,
  IUnknown* pUnkOuter);
```

The first parameter holds the address we wish filled with a pointer to an `IDirect3DLight` interface as long as our call succeeds.

```
//
// Create our light.
//
hRes = lpd3d->CreateLight( &lpd3dLight, NULL);
if (FAILED(hRes))
   return hRes;
```

Once we have our light, we will want to fill up all of its attributes. These include the size of the structure, the type of light we want, the color of the light, the position, and the attenuation. In Retained Mode this would consist of a sequence of calls to methods such as `IDirect3DRMLight::SetColorRGB`. In Immediate Mode, we instead fill the light attributes with these desired values. Once we have the values set, we use the `IDirect3Dlight::SetLight` method to set the light information for our Direct3DLight object. This method is prototyped as:

```
HRESULT SetLight(LPD3DLIGHT lpLight);
```

The sequence of commands to fill a light is as follows:

```
ZeroMemory(&d3dLight, sizeof(d3dLight));
d3dLight.dwSize = sizeof(d3dLight);
d3dLight.dltType = D3DLIGHT_POINT;
d3dLight.dcvColor.dvR = D3DVAL( 1.0);
d3dLight.dcvColor.dvG = D3DVAL( 1.0);
```

```
d3dLight.dcvColor.dvB   = D3DVAL( 1.0);
d3dLight.dcvColor.dvA   = D3DVAL( 1.0);
d3dLight.dvPosition.dvX = D3DVAL( 1.0);
d3dLight.dvPosition.dvY = D3DVAL(-1.0);
d3dLight.dvPosition.dvZ = D3DVAL(-1.0);
d3dLight.dvAttenuation0 = D3DVAL( 1.0);
d3dLight.dvAttenuation1 = D3DVAL( 0.1);
d3dLight.dvAttenuation2 = D3DVAL( 0.0);
hRes = lpd3dLight->SetLight(&d3dLight);
if (FAILED(hRes))
  return hRes;
```

To create a material, we perform a similar set of tasks. First we call the IDirect3D::CreateMaterial method to allocate a Direct3DMaterial object. This method is prototyped as:

```
HRESULT CreateMaterial(LPDIRECT3DMATERIAL* lplpDirect3DMaterial,
    IUnknown* pUnkOuter);
```

As long as our material is created properly, we set the diffuse, ambient, and specular characteristics. This is similar to using the various IDirect3DRMMaterial methods, such as IDirect3DMaterial::SetSpecular, but rather than using a method we are directly filling the attribute values, one at a time.

```
//
// Create our background material.
//
hRes = lpd3d ->CreateMaterial(&lpd3dBackgroundMaterial, NULL);
if (FAILED(hRes))
  return hRes;

ZeroMemory(&d3dMaterial, sizeof(d3dMaterial));
d3dMaterial.dwSize = sizeof(d3dMaterial);
d3dMaterial.dcvDiffuse.r = D3DVAL(0.0);
d3dMaterial.dcvDiffuse.g = D3DVAL(0.0);
d3dMaterial.dcvDiffuse.b = D3DVAL(0.0);
d3dMaterial.dcvAmbient.r = D3DVAL(0.0);
d3dMaterial.dcvAmbient.g = D3DVAL(0.0);
d3dMaterial.dcvAmbient.b = D3DVAL(0.0);
d3dMaterial.dcvSpecular.r = D3DVAL(0.0);
d3dMaterial.dcvSpecular.g = D3DVAL(0.0);
d3dMaterial.dcvSpecular.b = D3DVAL(0.0);
d3dMaterial.dvPower     = D3DVAL(0.0);
```

Once we have our material defined, we can set the material for our background object using the IDirect3DMaterial::SetMaterial method:

```
HRESULT SetMaterial(LPD3DMATERIAL lpMat);
```

The code to perform this is:

```
//
// This is the background material, so we don't want a ramp allocated -
// after all, we
// are not going to be smooth shading the background).
//
d3dMaterial.dwRampSize  = 1UL;

hRes = lpd3dBackgroundMaterial->SetMaterial(&d3dMaterial);
if (FAILED(hRes))
  return hRes;
hRes = lpd3dBackgroundMaterial->GetHandle(
                      lpd3dDevice,
                      &hd3dBackgroundMaterial);
if (FAILED(hRes))
  return hRes;
```

Next we need to define our viewport so we will be able to see the fruits of our efforts. The `IDirect3D::CreateViewport` method creates a `Direct3DViewport` for us. We can associate this viewport with a `Direct3DDevice` object using the `IDirect3DDevice::AddViewport` method.

```
//
// Create our viewport.
//
// The actual viewport parameters are set in the function UpdateViewport
// which is called in response to WM_SIZE.
//
hRes = lpd3d->CreateViewport(&lpd3dViewport, NULL);
if (FAILED(hRes))
  return hRes;

hRes = lpd3dDevice->AddViewport(lpd3dViewport);
if (FAILED(hRes))
  return hRes;
```

We can now use the `IDirect3Dviewport::SetBackground` method to set our background associated with the viewport we have defined. We will also add our light to the viewport so we will be able to see our objects using the `IDirect3DViewport::AddLight` method. These two methods are prototyped as follows:

```
HRESULT SetBackground(D3DMATERIALHANDLE hMat);

HRESULT AddLight(LPDIRECT3DLIGHT lpDirect3DLight);
```

The code to perform this is:

```
hRes = lpd3dViewport->SetBackground(hd3dBackgroundMaterial);
if (FAILED(hRes))
  return hRes;
hRes = lpd3dViewport->AddLight(lpd3dLight);
```

```
    if (FAILED(hRes))
      return hRes;
```

Now that the lighting and other environment information is set up, we should define the world, view, and projection matrices. The method to create a matrix is defined as:

```
HRESULT CreateMatrix(LPD3DMATRIXHANDLE lpD3DMatHandle);
```

The method to apply this matrix to a matrix handle once we have created it is:

```
HRESULT SetMatrix(D3DMATRIXHANDLE d3dMatHandle,
  LPD3DMATRIX lpD3DMatrix);
```

The code sequence to create and set our three matrices is:

```
//
// Create the matrices we need.
//
hRes = lpd3dDevice->CreateMatrix(&hd3dWorldMatrix);
if (FAILED(hRes))
  return hRes;
hRes = lpd3dDevice->SetMatrix(hd3dWorldMatrix, &d3dWorldMatrix);
if (FAILED(hRes))
  return hRes;
hRes = lpd3dDevice->CreateMatrix(&hd3dViewMatrix);
if (FAILED(hRes))
  return hRes;
hRes = lpd3dDevice->SetMatrix(hd3dViewMatrix, &d3dViewMatrix);
if (FAILED(hRes))
  return hRes;
hRes = lpd3dDevice->CreateMatrix(&hd3dProjMatrix);
if (FAILED(hRes))
  return hRes;
SetPerspectiveProjection(&d3dProjMatrix, HALF_HEIGHT, FRONT_CLIP,
      BACK_CLIP);
hRes = lpd3dDevice ->SetMatrix(hd3dProjMatrix, &d3dProjMatrix);
if (FAILED(hRes))
  return hRes;
```

We will now want to create a material for our object. I showed you how to create the background material, so I will just list the code below since it is basically the same:

```
//
// Create our surface material.
//
hRes = lpd3d ->CreateMaterial(&lpd3dMaterial, NULL);
if (FAILED(hRes))
  return hRes;
ZeroMemory(&d3dMaterial, sizeof(d3dMaterial));
d3dMaterial.dwSize = sizeof(d3dMaterial);
```

```
//
// Set up a base red material with white specular.
//
d3dMaterial.dcvDiffuse.r  = D3DVAL(1.0);
d3dMaterial.dcvDiffuse.g  = D3DVAL(0.0);
d3dMaterial.dcvDiffuse.b  = D3DVAL(0.0);
d3dMaterial.dcvAmbient.r  = D3DVAL(0.0);
d3dMaterial.dcvAmbient.g  = D3DVAL(0.4);
d3dMaterial.dcvAmbient.b  = D3DVAL(0.0);
d3dMaterial.dcvSpecular.r = D3DVAL(1.0);
d3dMaterial.dcvSpecular.g = D3DVAL(1.0);
d3dMaterial.dcvSpecular.b = D3DVAL(1.0);
d3dMaterial.dvPower       = D3DVAL(20.0);
d3dMaterial.dwRampSize    = 16UL;

hRes = lpd3dMaterial->SetMaterial(&d3dMaterial);
if (FAILED(hRes))
   return hRes;

hRes = lpd3dMaterial->GetHandle(lpd3dDevice, &hd3dSurfaceMaterial);
if (FAILED(hRes))
   return hRes;
```

We now have everything we need to render our world, so we can fill our execute
buffer. The code below allocates an execute buffer of the size we request for our display
list. The `IDirect3DDevice::CreateExecuteBuffer` method is prototyped as:

```
HRESULT CreateExecuteBuffer(LPDIRECT3DEXECUTEBUFFERDESC lpDesc,
   LPDIRECT3DEXECUTEBUFFER* lplpDirect3DExecuteBuffer,
   IUnknown* pUnkOuter);
```

The code to do it is:

```
//
// Build our execute buffer.
//
dwVertexSize      = (NUM_VERTICES     * sizeof(D3DVERTEX));
dwInstructionSize = (NUM_INSTRUCTIONS * sizeof(D3DINSTRUCTION))   +
          (NUM_STATES      * sizeof(D3DSTATE))         +
          (NUM_PROCESSVERTICES * sizeof(D3DPROCESSVERTICES)) +
          (NUM_TRIANGLES    * sizeof(D3DTRIANGLE));
dwExecuteBufferSize = dwVertexSize + dwInstructionSize;
ZeroMemory(&d3dExecuteBufferDesc, sizeof(d3dExecuteBufferDesc));
d3dExecuteBufferDesc.dwSize      = sizeof(d3dExecuteBufferDesc);
d3dExecuteBufferDesc.dwFlags     = D3DDEB_BUFSIZE;
d3dExecuteBufferDesc.dwBufferSize = dwExecuteBufferSize;
hRes = lpd3dDevice->CreateExecuteBuffer(
                    &d3dExecuteBufferDesc,
                    &lpd3dExecuteBuffer,
                    NULL);
if (FAILED(hRes))
```

```
      return hRes;
```

With the buffer created, we can now fill it. I have listed the `FillExecuteBuffer` routine below this routine and we will walk through it in a second. Just to complete this routine, let's look at the call at the last step of setting our execute buffer:

```
//
// Fill our execute buffer with the vertices, state
// instructions and drawing primitives.
//
hRes = FillExecuteBuffer();
if (FAILED(hRes))
  return hRes;
```

After the execute buffer has been filled, we call the `IDirect3DExecuteBuffer::SetExecuteData` method to set the execute data state of the Direct3DExecuteBuffer object. This execute data is used to define the contents of our Direct3DExecuteBuffer object. This method is prototyped as:

```
HRESULT SetExecuteData(LPD3DEXECUTEDATA lpData);
```

The call will fail if the execute buffer is locked. The code to fill this data and set it is as follows:

```
//
// Set the execute data so Direct3D knows how many vertices are in the
// buffer and where the instructions start.
//
ZeroMemory(&d3dExecuteData, sizeof(d3dExecuteData));
d3dExecuteData.dwSize = sizeof(d3dExecuteData);
d3dExecuteData.dwVertexCount    = NUM_VERTICES;
d3dExecuteData.dwInstructionOffset = dwVertexSize;
d3dExecuteData.dwInstructionLength = dwInstructionSize;
hRes = lpd3dExecuteBuffer->SetExecuteData(&d3dExecuteData);
if (FAILED(hRes))
  return hRes;

return DD_OK;
}
```

18.4 *Filling the execute buffer*

The task of filling our execute buffer is as monotonous and long as these other set-up tasks, but also like them it is fairly easy to understand the process just by looking at it for a few minutes. The routine below shows you how to fill a basic buffer that only contains one triangle.

```
static HRESULT
FillExecuteBuffer(void)
{
  HRESULT            hRes;
  D3DEXECUTEBUFFERDESC d3dExeBufDesc;
  LPD3DVERTEX         lpVertex;
  LPD3DINSTRUCTION    lpInstruction;
  LPD3DPROCESSVERTICES lpProcessVertices;
  LPD3DTRIANGLE       lpTriangle;
  LPD3DSTATE          lpState;

  ASSERT(NULL != lpd3dExecuteBuffer);
  ASSERT(0UL != hd3dSurfaceMaterial);
  ASSERT(0UL != hd3dWorldMatrix);
  ASSERT(0UL != hd3dViewMatrix);
  ASSERT(0UL != hd3dProjMatrix);
```

It is critical to remember to lock your buffer when you are going to change it and to unlock it when you are done setting it up. The process of locking it is:

```
//
// Lock our execute buffer.
//
ZeroMemory(&d3dExeBufDesc, sizeof(d3dExeBufDesc));
d3dExeBufDesc.dwSize = sizeof(d3dExeBufDesc);
hRes = lpd3dExecuteBuffer->Lock(&d3dExeBufDesc);
if (FAILED(hRes))
  return hRes;
```

18.4.1 The vertex data

Once we have it locked, we can fill up the vertex data first. We only have one triangle, but the large number of lines is due to the fact that we have to set each of the X, Y, and Z values separately. Notice we are setting the vertex position, normal, and texture coordinates here. We are not applying a texture though, so we will not be specifying a texture for this buffer.

```
//
// We fill the execute buffer by casting a pointer to the execute
// buffer to the appropriate data structures.
//
// !!! REMEMBER: alignment.
//
lpVertex = (LPD3DVERTEX)d3dExeBufDesc.lpData;

//
// First vertex.
//
lpVertex->dvX = D3DVAL( 0.0); / The position in model coordinates
lpVertex->dvY = D3DVAL( 2.0);
```

```
lpVertex->dvZ = D3DVAL( 0.0);
lpVertex->dvNX = D3DVAL( 0.0);  // The normalized illumination normal
lpVertex->dvNY = D3DVAL( 0.0);
lpVertex->dvNZ = D3DVAL(-2.0);
lpVertex->dvTU = D3DVAL( 0.0);  // The texture coordinates - not used
                                // in this case
lpVertex->dvTV = D3DVAL( 2.0);
lpVertex++;

//
// Second vertex.
//
lpVertex->dvX = D3DVAL( 2.0);  // The position in model coordinates
lpVertex->dvY = D3DVAL(-2.0);
lpVertex->dvZ = D3DVAL( 0.0);
lpVertex->dvNX = D3DVAL( 0.0);  // The normalized illumination normal
lpVertex->dvNY = D3DVAL( 0.0);
lpVertex->dvNZ = D3DVAL(-2.0);
lpVertex->dvTU = D3DVAL( 2.0);  // Texture coordinates - not used
                                // in this case
lpVertex->dvTV = D3DVAL( 2.0);
lpVertex++;

//
// Third vertex.
//
lpVertex->dvX = D3DVAL(-2.0);  // The position in model coordinates
lpVertex->dvY = D3DVAL(-2.0);
lpVertex->dvZ = D3DVAL( 0.0);
lpVertex->dvNX = D3DVAL( 0.0);  // The normalized illumination normal
lpVertex->dvNY = D3DVAL( 0.0);
lpVertex->dvNZ = D3DVAL(-2.0);
lpVertex->dvTU = D3DVAL( 2.0);  // Texture coordinates - not used
                                // in this case
lpVertex->dvTV = D3DVAL( 0.0);
lpVertex++;
```

18.4.2 The state information

All that just to indicate three vertices, their normals, and their texture coordinates. Worse yet, we are not close to done. We will now need to set up the transform matrices to be used. We defined these in the code we discussed in the last section, so all we need to do now is to set up the local state changes. *Local state changes* are usually inserted directly into our triangle/vertex execute buffer as part of our command stream. There are also *global state changes* which are usually placed in an execute buffer of their own for managing *states,* such as the Z-buffer state.

The code to specify the transforms to be used is as follows:

```
//
// The transform state - world, view and projection.
```

```
//
lpInstruction = (LPD3DINSTRUCTION)lpVertex;
lpInstruction->bOpcode = D3DOP_STATETRANSFORM;
lpInstruction->bSize  = sizeof(D3DSTATE);
lpInstruction->wCount = 3U;
lpInstruction++;
lpState = (LPD3DSTATE)lpInstruction;
lpState->dtstTransformStateType = D3DTRANSFORMSTATE_WORLD;
lpState->dwArg[0] = hd3dWorldMatrix;
lpState++;
lpState->dtstTransformStateType = D3DTRANSFORMSTATE_VIEW;
lpState->dwArg[0] = hd3dViewMatrix;
lpState++;
lpState->dtstTransformStateType = D3DTRANSFORMSTATE_PROJECTION;
lpState->dwArg[0] = hd3dProjMatrix;
lpState++;
```

We will also want to specify the lighting state. The light state for the D3DOP_STATELIGHT opcode is shown below. The D3DLIGHTSTATE_MATERIAL value describes the material that is lit and will be used to compute the color and intensity values during rasterization. The D3DLIGHTSTATE_AMBIENT value is used to set the color and intensity of the current ambient light.

```
//
// The lighting state.
//
lpInstruction = (LPD3DINSTRUCTION)lpState;
lpInstruction->bOpcode = D3DOP_STATELIGHT;
lpInstruction->bSize  = sizeof(D3DSTATE);
lpInstruction->wCount = 2U;
lpInstruction++;
lpState = (LPD3DSTATE)lpInstruction;
lpState->dlstLightStateType = D3DLIGHTSTATE_MATERIAL;
lpState->dwArg[0] = hd3dSurfaceMaterial;
lpState++;
lpState->dlstLightStateType = D3DLIGHTSTATE_AMBIENT;
lpState->dwArg[0] = RGBA_MAKE(128, 128, 128, 128);
lpState++;
```

The other state information we need to describe is the render state. We are specifying D3DRENDERSTATE_FILLMODE as D3DFILL_SOLID, D3DRENDERSTATE_SHADEMODE as D3DSHADE_GOURAUD, and D3DRENDERSTATE_DITHERENABLE as TRUE. This means we wish to fill solids, use Gouraud shading, and enable dithering.

```
//
// The render state.
//
lpInstruction = (LPD3DINSTRUCTION)lpState;
lpInstruction->bOpcode = D3DOP_STATERENDER;
lpInstruction->bSize  = sizeof(D3DSTATE);
```

```
lpInstruction->wCount = 3U;
lpInstruction++;
lpState = (LPD3DSTATE)lpInstruction;
lpState->drstRenderStateType = D3DRENDERSTATE_FILLMODE;
lpState->dwArg[0] = D3DFILL_SOLID;
lpState++;
lpState->drstRenderStateType = D3DRENDERSTATE_SHADEMODE;
lpState->dwArg[0] = D3DSHADE_GOURAUD;
lpState++;
lpState->drstRenderStateType = D3DRENDERSTATE_DITHERENABLE;
lpState->dwArg[0] = TRUE;
lpState++;
```

18.4.3 Vertex handling

Next, we will need to indicate how we wish the vertices to be handled. Since we want Direct3D to handle the complete pipeline, we use the D3DPROCESSVERTICES_TRANSFORMLIGHT instruction. This indicates that the driver should light and transform our vertices.

```
//
// The process vertices instruction tells the driver what we want
// done with the vertices in the buffer. For our simple example, we want
// Direct3D to perform the entire pipeline for us so
// the instruction is D3DPROCESSVERTICES_TRANSFORMLIGHT.
//
lpInstruction = (LPD3DINSTRUCTION)lpState;
lpInstruction->bOpcode = D3DOP_PROCESSVERTICES;
lpInstruction->bSize  = sizeof(D3DPROCESSVERTICES);
lpInstruction->wCount = 1U;
lpInstruction++;
lpProcessVertices = (LPD3DPROCESSVERTICES)lpInstruction;
lpProcessVertices->dwFlags  = D3DPROCESSVERTICES_TRANSFORMLIGHT;
lpProcessVertices->wStart   = 0U;       /* First source vertex */
lpProcessVertices->wDest    = 0U;
lpProcessVertices->dwCount  = NUM_VERTICES; /* Number of vertices */
lpProcessVertices->dwReserved = 0UL;
lpProcessVertices++;
```

18.4.4 Drawing our object

At this point, we use the D3DOP_TRIANGLE opcode to send our triangle to the renderer. This opcode requires that the operand data be described using the D3DTRIANGLE structure, which they were.

```
//
// Draw the triangle.
//
lpInstruction = (LPD3DINSTRUCTION)lpProcessVertices;
lpInstruction->bOpcode = D3DOP_TRIANGLE;
lpInstruction->bSize  = sizeof(D3DTRIANGLE);
```

```
lpInstruction->wCount = 1U;
lpInstruction++;
lpTriangle = (LPD3DTRIANGLE)lpInstruction;
lpTriangle->wV1   = 0U;
lpTriangle->wV2   = 1U;
lpTriangle->wV3   = 2U;
lpTriangle->wFlags = D3DTRIFLAG_EDGEENABLETRIANGLE;
lpTriangle++;
```

The last thing we need to specify in our execute buffer is the D3DOP_EXIT opcode. This indicates we have hit the end of our buffer.

```
//
// Stop the execution of the buffer.
//
lpInstruction = (LPD3DINSTRUCTION)lpTriangle;
lpInstruction->bOpcode = D3DOP_EXIT;
lpInstruction->bSize  = 0UL;
lpInstruction->wCount = 0U;
```

The very last thing we need to do is to unlock our buffer so it can be used later.

```
//
// Unlock the execute buffer.
//
lpd3dExecuteBuffer->Unlock();

return DD_OK;
}
```

18.5 Rendering the scene

You should now have a basic understanding of how to create and fill an execute buffer. The only other thing that you *must* know how to do to at least be able to generate a basic Direct3D Immediate-Mode scene is how to execute your execute buffer.

This process is probably the easiest thing of all the things I have shown you up until now. First we will want to clear our back-buffer and our Z-buffer before we attempt to render. There are times where you will not necessarily want to do this, but for all basic situations you will want to clear these. The code to perform this is:

```
static HRESULT
RenderScene(void)
{
  HRESULT hRes;
  D3DRECT d3dRect;

  ASSERT(NULL != lpd3dViewport);
  ASSERT(NULL != lpd3dDevice);
```

```
    ASSERT(NULL != lpd3dExecuteBuffer);

    //
    // Clear both back and Z-buffer.
    //
    // NOTE: It's safe to specify the Z-buffer clear flag even if we
    // don't have an attached Z-buffer. Direct3D will simply discard
    // the flag if no Z-buffer is being used.
    //
    // NOTE: For maximum efficiency we only want to clear those
    // regions of the device surface and Z-buffer which we actually
    // rendered to in the last frame. This is the purpose of the
    // array of rectangles and count passed to this function. It is
    // possible to query Direct3D for the regions of the device
    // surface that were rendered to by that execute. The application
    // can then accumulate those rectangles and clear only those
    // regions. However this is a very simple example and so, for
    // simplicity, we will just clear the entire device surface and
    // Z-buffer. Probably not something you want to do in a real
    // application.
    //
    d3dRect.lX1 = rSrcRect.left;
    d3dRect.lX2 = rSrcRect.right;
    d3dRect.lY1 = rSrcRect.top;
    d3dRect.lY2 = rSrcRect.bottom;
    hRes = lpd3dViewport->Clear(
                    1UL,
                    &d3dRect,
                    D3DCLEAR_TARGET | D3DCLEAR_ZBUFFER);
    if (FAILED(hRes))
        return hRes;
```

Note that we used the D3DCLEAR_TARGET flag to clear the rendering target to the background material we specified earlier, and the D3DCLEAR_ZBUFFER flag to clear the Z-buffer.

18.6 BeginScene / EndScene

The final things we will need to do to get our scene rendered and visible are to call IDirect3DDevice::BeginScene, execute the buffer using IDirect3DDevice::Execute, and then call IDirect3DDevice::EndScene.

I want to stress as strongly as I can that you need to use the IDirect3DDevice::BeginScene and IDirect3DDevice::EndScene methods *properly*! Remember that a scene in Immediate Mode consists of a collection of all of the vertices and drawing primitives to be used to draw a *single* frame. These primitives consist of triangles, lines, and points.

`IDirect3DDevice::BeginScene` is used to mark the beginning of your scene, and thus the start of your frame. `IDirect3DDevice::EndScene` is used to mark the end of your scene, and thus the end of your frame. It is critical that all of your execute buffer executions used to draw a *single* frame be bracketed by a *single* `IDirect3D-Device::BeginScene`/ `IDirect3DDevice::EndScene` pair.

The reason for this is that a large number of 3D hardware accelerators being introduced do *not* use a conventional Z-buffer to handle hidden surface removal. These boards instead use varying techniques, such as polygon sorting and internal tiling, to perform hidden surface removal and need to process the *entire* geometry database *each frame*. Boards such as the PowerVR board do this and thus require that you write your software correctly using `IDirect3DDevice::BeginScene` / `IDirect3DDevice::EndScene` pairs or they will not work properly. The cost reduction to the manufacturer, and to you, of removing the Z-buffer from the board is fairly substantial. I would assume we will be seeing methods such as these more and more, and thus we will need to be even more certain that we follow these rules.

Accelerators such as these use a process called *scene capture*. This means that they store the geometric information from the execute buffer for processing later. It is thus critical to have a single `IDirect3DDevice::BeginScene` / `IDirect3DDevice::EndScene` pair bracketing all of the drawing instructions that make up a single frame. If you goof up and make multiple `IDirect3DDevice::BeginScene` / `IDirect3DDevice::EndScene` calls during the composition of a single frame, the accelerator board will end up not being able to resolve the hidden surface interactions between triangles executed in different scene contexts correctly.

You also need to make sure that you do not attempt to use multiple `IDirect3DD-evice::BeginScene` / `IDirect3DDevice::EndScene` calls per frame just because you do not have any hidden surface interactions between the triangles in different scene contexts. This is due to the fact that several accelerator boards use scene capture to handle special effects such as semitransparent objects and shadows and thus need the complete geometric database for a frame in order to accelerate them. If you broke it up with several `IDirect3DDevice::BeginScene` / `IDirect3DDevice::EndScene` pairs, this would not be possible.

One other thing to watch for is that some of these accelerators which use scene capture will not be able to intermix 2D operations, such as blits, and 3D operations in single scene context. The boards that have this restriction export the DirectDraw capability bit `DDCAPS2_NO2DDURING3DSCENE`. You should check this bit and if you find it set, you should not perform DirectDraw `Blt`, `GetDC`, or `Lock` methods of the rendering surface between calls to `IDirect3DDevice::BeginScene` and `IDirect3DDevice::EndScene`.

Remember that the rendering primitives in your execute buffer may not be rendered to your target surface until the scene is complete (IDirect3DDevice::EndScene has been called) so don't assume they are, just because the IDirect3DDevice::Execute method returned!

Let me restate them so you remember these rules:

- Precede the execution of any execute buffers holding triangles or other rendering primitives instructions with a single call to IDirect3DDevice::BeginScene and follow it with a single call to IDirect3DDevice::EndScene.

- Make sure that you do not assume that your rendering primitives in the execute buffer have been rendered to a target surface just because IDirect3DDevice::Execute returned. Many cards will hold off rendering until the IDirect3DDevice::EndScene method has been called.

- If the DirectDraw capability bit DDCAPS2_NO2DDURING3DSCENE is set, do *not* call the DirectDraw Blt(), GetDC(), or Lock() methods on your rendering surface between the calls to IDirect3DDevice::BeginScene and IDirect3DDevice::EndScene. Instead, use these methods after the IDirect3DDevice::EndScene call.

The code to perform the IDirect3DDevice::BeginScene and IDirect3DDevice::EndScene handling, and execute our execute buffer is:

```
//
// Start the scene.
//
// This function must be called once and once only for every frame
// of animation. If you have multiple execute buffers comprising a
// single frame you must have one call to BeginScene() before
// submitting those execute buffers.
//
// NOTE: If you have more than one device being rendered in a
// single frame, say a rear view mirror in a racing game, call
// BeginScene() and EndScene() once for each device.
//
hRes = lpd3dDevice->BeginScene();
if (FAILED(hRes))
  return hRes;

//
// Submit the execute buffer.
//
// We want Direct3D to clip the data on our behalf so we specify
// D3DEXECUTE_CLIPPED.
//
hRes = lpd3dDevice->Execute(
                   lpd3dExecuteBuffer,
```

```
                   lpd3dViewport,
                   D3DEXECUTE_CLIPPED);
    if (FAILED(hRes))
    {
      lpd3dDevice->EndScene();
      return hRes;
    }

    //
    // End the scene.
    //
    hRes = lpd3dDevice->EndScene();
    if (FAILED(hRes))
      return hRes;

    //
    // At this point the scene will have been rendered and the device
    // surface will hold the contents of the rendering.
    //

    return DD_OK;
}
```

18.7 *What did we learn?*

Well, that is it for Direct3D Immediate Mode. We have just scratched the surface of Immediate Mode, but I hope you can now at least create a basic Immediate-Mode application. You should also now have the foundation to be able to interpret the Immediate-Mode examples that come with Direct3D a little easier. I would suggest that you open one of the Immediate-Mode example projects on the CD and try modifying one of the execute buffers. You could do this by adding in a new face or performing some other experiment such as modifying points and seeing the impact. The best way to learn is through experimentation, and Immediate Mode really is not that difficult, even though its structure may seem a bit daunting.

18.8 *What's next?*

Now that we have covered the techniques for creating both windowed and full-screen Direct3D applications, including using animated textures, and the basics of Immediate Mode, let's consider a few last thoughts about the applications we can create using Direct3D.

chapter 19

Some final ideas

19.1 Where can we go from here?

You have now made it through the entire set of tutorials! I hope that your comfort level with Direct3D has gone up a great deal. Even more importantly, I hope that at this point you have the knowledge to develop the simulations or games you hoped to gain when you picked up this book.

I have shown you all of the major abilities of Direct3D Retained Mode, and we have covered many of the advanced 3D techniques that previously would have taken you many thousands of lines of code, and many weeks (or months) to implement. We have covered:

- Texture-mapping, which allows us to create almost photo-realistic worlds
- Mipmapping, allowing us to use level-of-detail textures to save processor loading
- Video-mapping, enabling us to play animated textures (videos) on objects (in the avirm project on the CD accompanying this book)
- Collision detection, one of the most critical capabilities since it provides for accurate control of objects moving through our virtual world
- Lighting effects, to create realistic effects in our environments

343

- Loading prebuilt 3D objects from files
- Creating 3D objects algorithmically
- Controlling our world and our movement through it using the keyboard, a mouse, or a joystick
- Picking of objects to manipulate them
- Shadows, allowing for more realistic scenes
- Using animations to create very realistic motion

We combined all of these features into a functional simulation of a virtual world, through which we can walk and with which we can interact.

With this core knowledge, the main task at hand is to decide *what* you want to build using Direct3D and how you can best implement it in Direct3D.

19.2 DirectX 5—DrawPrimitive

I have supplied the entire DirectX 5 release on the CD of this book including some great new Immediate Mode-examples from Microsoft. DirectX 5 has added a new capability called DrawPrimitive. These examples use DrawPrimitive to show how much simpler it is to create an application using DrawPrimitive as opposed to the standard Immediate-Mode execute buffer approach we discussed earlier. This interface is designed to provide us a much easier to use manner of drawing 3D triangles, lines, and points into Direct-Draw surfaces. See Appendix A for an example of how to create a DrawPrimitive based application. This API is composed of 17 methods.

1 `Begin`. Use this to start drawing primitives—triangles, lines, or points.

2 `BeginIndexed`. Use this to start drawing indexed primitives—triangles, lines, or points.

3 `DrawIndexedPrimitive`. Use this to draw a primitive from an indexed list.

4 `DrawPrimitive`. Use this to draw a primitive.

5 `End`. Use this to complete the drawing primitives.

6 `GetStatus`. Use this to get the current value of a state variable.

7 `GetTransform`. Use this to get the transform from world space (3D) to screen coordinates (2D).

8 `Index`. Use this to add an entry to an index.

9 `Lvertex`. Use this to add a vertex.

10 `MultiplyTransform`. Use this to effect your transformation formula.

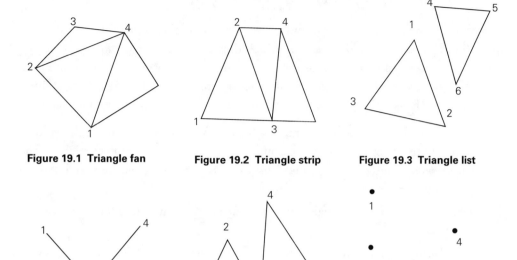

Figure 19.1 Triangle fan   **Figure 19.2 Triangle strip**   **Figure 19.3 Triangle list**

Figure 19.4 Line list   **Figure 19.5 Line strip**   **Figure 19.6 Point list**

11 `SetCurrentViewport`. Use this to define the area of 3D space you want to be viewed on the 2D screen.

12 `SetLightState`. Use this to set a state variable for a light.

13 `SetRenderState`. Use this to set a state variable in the drawing engine.

14 `SetRenderTarget`. Use this to select a DirectDraw surface to which you want to draw.

15 `SetTransform`. Use this to set the transformation formula from world to screen coordinates.

16 `TLVertex`. Use this to add an indexed list of vertices.

17 `Vertex`. Use this to add a vertex.

19.2.1 The core draw primitives of DrawPrimitive

DrawPrimitive supports three types of primitives—triangle lists, triangle strips, and triangle fans, lines, and points. See figures 19.1 through 19.6 for representations of these primitives.

Primitives can be in two formats. These are either a list of vertices or a list of vertices with an index into the list of vertices. For the former, the draw engine will process the vertices in the order they appear in the list. For the latter, the draw engine will process the list of vertices in the order specified in the index.

19.2.2 The architecture of DrawPrimitive

`DrawPrimitive` uses the core set of functions I listed at the beginning of this section to pass 3D primitives to the draw engine which draws these primitives to a DirectDraw surface. The transform formula is used by the engine to transform the values from 3D to 2D space. State variables are used to define the end appearance of the draw operation.

The three Direct3D device components are transform, draw engine, and state variables.

1 *Transform.* This is a set of formulas which define how to transform the vertices from 3D to 2D space. Transform consists of three matrix formulas which are the world, view, and projection matrices. You use the `SetTransform` and `MultiplyTransform` methods to set up define matrices.

2 *Draw Engine.* The draw engine performs the tasks of transformation, lighting, and rasterization.

3 *State Variables.* The state variables define the current style settings for the drawing operations.

The `DrawPrimitive` architecture is shown in figure 19.7.

I think that this new API has a lot of potential since it removes much of the grunt work we have to go through now in Immediate Mode. Using DrawPrimitive, there are three steps to drawing your 3D objects.

The first step is to create and initialize your DirectDraw and Direct3D devices.

The second step is to set the transform state and define any state variables you wish to use.

The third step is to draw your primitives. You draw each of your groups of primitives in blocks of commands. If you wished to draw a triangle, you could either create it using a list of vertices as follows:

```
lpD3DDevice->DrawIndexedPrimitive(0, TriangleStrip, Vertex, lpVertexList,
    dwVertexCount, lpIndex, dwIndexCount);
```

or, you could specify each vertex separately, like so:

```
lpD3DDevice->Begin(0, Vertex, TriangleList)  // Pass the type of vertex
                                             // and triangle list
lpD3DDevice->Vertex(lpVertex1);              // The first vertex
lpD3DDevice->Vertex(lpVertex2);              // The second vertex
lpD3DDevice->Vertex(lpVertex3);              // The third vertex
lpD3DDevice->End(0);                         // End of our drawing
```

Either way, this is a lot simpler than the standard Immediate-Mode approach. If you need a reminder of the difference, please look back at the Immediate-Mode example in chapters 16 through 18, where we created a similar triangle.

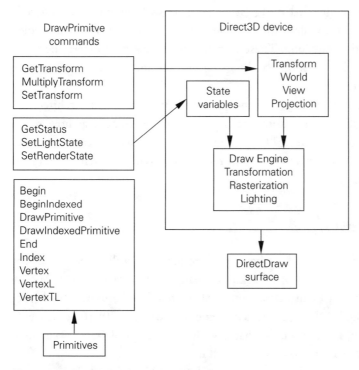

Figure 19.7 DrawPrimitive architecture

The diagram shows boxes labeled:

DrawPrimitve commands

GetTransform
MultiplyTransform
SetTransform

GetStatus
SetLightState
SetRenderState

Begin
BeginIndexed
DrawPrimitive
DrawIndexedPrimitive
End
Index
Vertex
VertexL
VertexTL

Primitives

Direct3D device

State variables

Transform
World
View
Projection

Draw Engine
Transformation
Rasterization
Lighting

DirectDraw surface

19.3 Simulation and game applications

One of the areas I've mentioned several times is simulation. Direct3D is a great environment for our development of simulations because of its real-time capabilities. I have worked in numerous areas of simulation including the development of F-15 and F-16 aircraft, the Apache helicopter, land vehicles, and submarine simulators.

One important thing about simulation is that you cannot simulate just the main object you are trying to imitate; you also have to simulate the world it exists in. After all, when you intend to simulate a car, if you ignore the road it drives upon you will not be able to create a very realistic simulation! Using Direct3D, you can easily build virtual landscapes, roads, signs, buildings, and so forth.

By intelligently incorporating collision detection with your objects, and adding callback functions, you can have an object *react* as it would in the real world. As an example, imagine creating a virtual car and driving it down a virtual road using a steering wheel connected using DirectInput. Each of the road signs, trees, and, perhaps, moving animals, can be controlled using either animations built into their DirectX object description or by using algorithms implemented in callback functions called each iteration through the code loop. These moving objects can each determine when they come into contact with other object's by using the collision detection routines we have already implemented.

If you sit back and imagine all of the possible applications (an architectural walk-through, a car collision simulation, etc.) you might be amazed at how much power is available to you in Direct3D. We can also just as easily create computer games such as first-person perspective adventure games, driving or racing games, or even sports simulations.

19.4 Virtual reality

I mentioned in the beginning that I have been involved in virtual reality since before the term was coined. A company I was with back in the early 1980s created one of the very first HMD. It consisted of a flight helmet and a fiber optic bundle tether which projected a stereo image. The HMD used dual lenses and provided a 1280×1024 display to each eye. Ever since then, I have been fascinated with the concept of *immersive simulation* as we called it then, or *virtual reality*, as we call it now.

Since then I have also developed remotely piloted vehicles which incorporated graphic displays in the remote cockpit as well as virtual gauge displays on the surround image. In these automobile piloting cockpits, we supplied the visual to the driver through everything from one display, to wrap around displays, all the way to an HMD with head tracking.

Today the prices on equipment capable of producing a fully immersive VR environment have begun to get to the point where they are affordable to the consumer rather than just to the government or a lucky few. You can set up a home system with a dual 640×480 LCD HMD, head-tracking, stereo 3D sound, and a joystick or other input device with a minor version of force feedback.

With a setup as I just described, you can develop some incredibly enjoyable virtual worlds. If you are interested in VR, I would suggest that you start by learning how to accurately, and innovatively, read a user's inputs such as the head, eye, hand, finger, and other limb motions. There are some new devices coming out that even make acquiring this type of information affordable. If you come up with a better device that does this in a more effective manner, I guarantee you will be well known very rapidly!

19.5 Advertising

A final area that has huge potential is the marketing arena. The amount of interest in, as well as money spent on, advertising is growing all the time and has already hit incredible proportions. The type of advertising that comes to mind when we hear the term is usually what we see on television. Although there is possibility for using Direct3D there, I am actually referring to many of the other areas of advertising.

One place that has great potential is the huge convention market that has grown up in the last ten years. Today there are conventions with enough people to fill every hotel even in cities having the greatest amount of hotel space (Las Vegas, etc.). With such an incredible influx of people, having a unique marketing concept has become far more critical in order to attract people to your display. Many companies have used 3D animation and even virtual reality to market their products and attract new customers.

Direct3D is a tool which you can use to develop numerous advertising concepts which could be displayed in booths, on TV, or on a distribution CD (to name just a few possibilities).

19.6 Have fun!

I have to say that I had a great amount of fun learning Direct3D and implementing different software ideas using it. I have been developing software for the home since the very first personal computers came out, and the recent developments in 3D rendering hardware has, for the first time, excited me about the fact that we are getting to the point of rendering truly realistic simulations and games for the home.

It will definitely require a lot of ingenuity from you to create complex environments that will run in real time (e.g., approximately 30 frames per second). Even with the capabilities provided by Direct3D, without skillful software design and coding, you will not achieve a goal of real time if your virtual world is complex. I hope that with the examples I have shown you, and the 3D models I have included, you will have a great head start over many others interested in Direct3D.

The remainder of this book consists of a reference on Direct3D Retained Mode. Each of the interfaces and their methods are shown along with examples of using the commands in context.

Good luck with Direct3D!

PART II

A Direct3D Retained-Mode reference

chapter 20

Direct3D Retained Mode overview

20.1 The Direct3D Retained-Mode interfaces

The Direct3D Retained-Mode interfaces will each be shown in the following chapters. In addition, the Functions and Callback Functions will also be shown.

The name of each of these interface and functions is listed below.

> IDirect3DRM
> IDirect3DRMAnimation
> IDirect3DRMAnimationSet
> IDirect3DRMArray
> IDirect3DRMDeviceArray
> IDirect3DRMFaceArray
> IDirect3DRMFrameArray
> IDirect3DRMLightArray

IDirect3DRMPickedArray
IDirect3DRMViewportArray
IDirect3DRMVisualArray
IDirect3DRMDevice
IDirect3DRMFace
IDirect3DRMFrame
IDirect3DRMLight
IDirect3DRMMaterial
IDirect3DRMMesh
IDirect3DRMMeshBuilder
IDirect3DRMObject
IDirect3DRMShadow
IDirect3DRMTexture
IDirect3DRMUserVisual
IDirect3DRMViewport
IDirect3DRMWinDevice
IDirect3DRMWrap

Functions
Callback functions
Structures
Enumerated types
Other types

20.2 The format for the D3D Retained Mode commands

Each of the following chapters will use the following paragraphs to describe all of the objects and their associated method:

20.2.1 Description

This section details the object interface methods for the current object. The basic functionality and object usage is defined.

20.2.2 C++ specification

This section shows the methods C++ specification syntax. The appropriate calling structure is explained.

20.2.3 Parameters

Each of the object's parameters and details on the possible values thereof are defined.

20.2.4 Returns

The return value of the function, as well as the effects upon the calling parameters, are explained.

20.2.5 Include file

The include file within which this class is specified is given.

20.2.6 See also (related objects/messages)

Each of the related member functions are listed along with a reference to the page upon which the function's definition can be found.

20.2.7 Example

A detailed example, showing how the object's member function should be used, is given. The member function is shown in conjunction with the necessary support functions in context in order to show the reader how to properly construct usable code.

chapter 21

The IDirect3DRM interface

The IDirect3DRM interface and methods

The IDirect3DRM methods are used to create Direct3DRM objects and use system level variables. Like all COM interfaces, this interface inherits the IUnknown interface methods. These consist of `AddRef`, `QueryInterface`, and `Release`.

You create the IDirect3DRM COM interface using the `Direct3DRMCreate` function.

The methods of the IDirect3DRM interface are categorized into the groups shown in table 21.1.

Table 21.1 IDirect3DRM methods

Group	Methods
Animation	CreateAnimation
	CreateAnimationSet
Devices	CreateDevice
	CreateDeviceFromClipper
	CreateDeviceFromD3D
	CreateDeviceFromSurface
	GetDevices
Enumeration	EnumerateObjects
Faces	CreateFace
Frames	CreateFrame
Lights	CreateLight
	CreateLightRGB
Materials	CreateMaterial
Meshes	CreateMesh
	CreateMeshBuilder
Miscellaneous	CreateObject
	CreateUserVisual
	GetNamedObject
	Load
	Tick
Search paths	AddSearchPath
	GetSearchPath
	SetSearchPath
Shadows	CreateShadow
Textures	CreateTexture
	CreateTextureFromSurface
	LoadTexture
	LoadTextureFromResource
	SetDefaultTextureColors
	SetDefaultTextureShades
Viewports	CreateViewport
Wraps	CreateWrap

IDirect3DRM::AddSearchPath

Description
This method is used to add a list of directories to the end of the current file search path.

C++ specification
```
HRESULT AddSearchPath(LPCSTR lpPath);
```

Parameters
lpPath. The address of a NULL-terminated string containing the path we wish to add to our current search path. The path is a list of directories separated by semicolons.

Returns
Successful: D3DRM_OK

Error: One of the Direct3D Retained-Mode return values.

See also
IDirect3DRM::SetSearchPath

Example
```
MyD3DRM->AddSearchPath("c:\dxsdk\sdk\myProgs\;c:\dxsdk\sdk");
```

IDirect3DRM::CreateAnimation

Description
This method is used to create an empty Direct3DRMAnimation object.

C++ specification
```
HRESULT CreateAnimation(LPDIRECT3DRMANIMATION * lplpD3DRMAnimation);
```

Parameters
lplpD3DRMAnimation. An address which we wish to be filled with a pointer to an IDirect3DRMAnimation interface.

Returns
Successful: D3DRM_OK

Error: One of the Direct3D Retained-Mode return values.

See also
IDirect3DRMAnimation::SetOptions

IDirect3DRMAnimation::AddPositionKey
IDirect3DRMAnimation::SetFrame

Example

```
LPDIRECT3DRMANIMATION          lpAnim = NULL;
// Create our animation
lpD3DRM->CreateAnimation(&lpAnim);
// Set up our animation options
lpAnim->SetOptions(D3DRMANIMATION_OPEN |
            D3DRMANIMATION_LINEARPOSITION |
            D3DRMANIMATION_POSITION);

// Add our starting position as a keyframe
lpAnim->AddPositionKey(D3DVAL(0), D3DVAL(200), D3DVAL(2000),
        D3DVAL(0));

// Add our ending position as a keyframe
lpAnim->AddPositionKey(D3DVAL(1), D3DVAL(700), D3DVAL(100),
        D3DVAL(0));

// Make the camera follow our animation
lpAnim->SetFrame(Camera);
```

IDirect3DRM::CreateAnimationSet

Description
This method is called to create an empty Direct3DRMAnimationSet object.

C++ specification
```
HRESULT CreateAnimationSet (LPDIRECT3DRMANIMATIONSET *
        lplpD3DRMAnimationSet);
```

Parameters
lplpD3DRMAnimationSet. An address you wish to be filled with a pointer to an
    IDirect3DRMAnimationSet interface.

Returns
Successful: D3DRM_OK
Error: One of the Direct3D Retained-Mode return values.

See also
IDirect3DRMAnimationSet::Load

Example
```
const char *myFilename
```

```
TutorInfo *myInfo
LPDIRECT3DRMANIMATIONSET lpAnimSet;
LPDIRECT3DRMFRAME lpFrame;

// Create a new parent frame for the animation, load it, and set up the
// callback
if (FAILED(lpD3DRM->CreateFrame(myInfo->scene, &lpFrame)))
 return FALSE;

if (FAILED(lpD3DRM->CreateAnimationSet(&lpAnimSet)))
 return FALSE;

if (FAILED(lpAnimSet->Load((LPVOID)myFilename, NULL,
            D3DRMLOAD_FROMFILE, loadTextures,
            NULL, lpFrame)))
 return FALSE;
```

IDirect3DRM::CreateDeviceFromClipper

Description

This method is used to create a Direct3DRM Windows device using a passed DirectDrawClipper object. If the system does not find a hardware device, it will load the ramp (monochromatic) driver. You should enumerate the devices rather than passing lpGUID as NULL if you desire settings other than those supplied by the defaults.

C++ specification

```
HRESULT CreateDeviceFromClipper(LPDIRECTDRAWCLIPPER lpDDClipper,
  LPGUID lpGUID, int width, int height,
  LPDIRECT3DRMDEVICE * lplpD3DRMDevice);
```

Parameters

lpDDClipper. The address of a DirectDrawClipper object.

lpGUID. The address of a GUID. You can pass this parameter as NULL. If this parameter is set to NULL, the system will search for a device with a default set of device capabilities. Microsoft suggests you create a Retained-Mode device this way since it will always work, even if you install new hardware.

Direct3D uses the following flags from the D3DPRIMCAPS structure in internal device enumeration calls to set the default settings:

```
D3DPCMPCAPS_LESSEQUAL, D3DPMISCCAPS_CULLCCW,
D3DPRASTERCAPS_FOGVERTEX, D3DPSHADECAPS_ALPHAFLATSTIPPLED,
D3DPTADDRESSCAPS_WRAP, D3DPTBLENDCAPS_COPY |
```

```
D3DPTBLENDCAPS_MODULATE, D3DPTEXTURECAPS_PERSPECTIVE |
D3DPTEXTURECAPS_TRANSPARENCY, D3DPTFILTERCAPS_NEAREST
```

width and height. The width and height of the device we are creating.

lplpD3DRMDevice. The address we wish to be filled with a pointer to an IDirect-
3DRMDevice interface.

Returns

Successful: D3DRM_OK

Error: One of the Direct3D Retained-Mode return values.

See also

IDirect3DRM::CreateDeviceFromD3D

IDirect3DRM::CreateDeviceFromSurface

Example

```
HWND window;
D3DRMCOLORMODEL model;
// Define a rect structure variable
RECT rect;

// Get the rectangle for the client space of our window
GetClientRect(window, &rect);

// Try to create a Direct3DRM windows device by using a specified
// DirectDrawClipper object
if (FAILED(lpD3DRM->CreateDeviceFromClipper(lpDDClipper,
        FindDevice(model), rect.right, rect.bottom, &dev)))
 goto generic_error;
```

IDirect3DRM::CreateDeviceFromD3D

Description

This method is used to create a Direct3DRM Windows device using the passed
Direct3D objects.

C++ specification

```
HRESULT CreateDeviceFromD3D(LPDIRECT3D lpD3D,
  LPDIRECT3DDEVICE lpD3DDev, LPDIRECT3DRMDEVICE * lplpD3DRMDevice);
```

Parameters

lpD3D. The address of a Direct3D instance.

lpD3DDev. The address of a Direct3D device object.

lp1pD3DRMDevice. The address you wish filled with a pointer to an IDirect3DRMDevice interface.

Returns

Successful: D3DRM_OK

Error: One of the Direct3D Retained-Mode return values.

See also

IDirect3DRM::CreateDeviceFromClipper

IDirect3DRM::CreateDeviceFromSurface

Example

```
LPDIRECT3D D3D;
LPDIRECT3DDEVICE D3Ddevice;
LPDIRECT3DRMDEVICE myD3DRMDevice;
HRESULT d3drval;
  .

  .
// Create the D3DRM device
d3drval=D3DRM->CreateDeviceFromD3D(D3D, D3DDevice, &D3DRMDevice);
```

IDirect3DRM::CreateDeviceFromSurface

Description

This method is used to create a Windows device for rendering from our specified DirectDraw surface.

C++ specification

```
HRESULT CreateDeviceFromSurface(LPGUID lpGUID, LPDIRECTDRAW lpDD,
  LPDIRECTDRAWSURFACE lpDDSBack,
  LPDIRECT3DRMDEVICE * lp1pD3DRMDevice);
```

Parameters

lpGUID. The address of the GUID we wish to be used as the device driver. If we pass this parameter as NULL, Direct3D will use the default device driver.

lpDD. The address of the DirectDraw object which is the source of our DirectDraw surface.

lpDDSBack. The address of the DirectDrawSurface object for our back buffer.

lp1pD3DRMDevice. The address we wish filled with a pointer to an IDirect-3DRMDevice interface.

Returns

Successful: D3DRM_OK

Error: One of the Direct3D Retained-Mode return values.

See also

IDirect3DRM::CreateDeviceFromD3D

IDirect3DRM::CreateDeviceFromClipper

Example

```
GUID DriverGUID[MAX_DRIVERS];  // The GUIDs of the available D3D
LPDIRECTDRAW      lpDD = NULL;      // drivers. DirectDraw object
LPDIRECTDRAWSURFACE   lpDDSBack = NULL;  //DirectDrawbacksurface
LPDIRECT3DRMDEVICE rmdev = NULL;  // Direct3DRM device
HRESULT ddrval;
.
.
ddrval = lpD3DRM->CreateDeviceFromSurface( &DriverGUID[CurrDriver],
                    lpDD,
                    lpDDSBack,
                    &rmdev);
```

IDirect3DRM::CreateFace

Description

Creates an instance of the IDirect3DRMFace interface.

C++ specification

```
HRESULT CreateFace(LPDIRECT3DRMFACE * lplpd3drmFace);
```

Parameters

lplpd3drmFace. The address you wish filled with a pointer to an IDirect-3DRMFace interface.

Returns

Successful: D3DRM_OK

Error: One of the Direct3D Retained-Mode return values.

See also

All IDirect3DRMFace Methods

Example

```
LPDIRECT3DRMFACE * lplpd3drmFace;
LPDIRECT3DRM * MY3DRM;
MY3DRM->CreateFace(lplpd3drmFace);
```

IDirect3DRM::CreateFrame

Description

You can use this method to create a new child frame for your passed parent frame. If a frame does not have a parent, which is achieved by passing NULL as the parent, it will be created as a *scene*. This child frame will inherit the motion attributes of its parent (e.g. if the parent is rotating, the child will rotate about the origin of the parent).

C++ specification

```
HRESULT CreateFrame(LPDIRECT3DRMFRAME lpD3DRMFrame,
  LPDIRECT3DRMFRAME* lplpD3DRMFrame);
```

Parameters

lpD3DRMFrame. The address of a frame you wish to use as the parent of the new frame.

lplpD3DRMFrame. The address you wish filled with a pointer to an IDirect3DRMFrame interface.

Returns

Successful: D3DRM_OK

Error: One of the Direct3D Retained-Mode return values.

See also

All IDirect3DRMFrame methods

Example

```
TutorInfo *myInfo
LPDIRECT3DRMFRAME frame = NULL;
  .
  .
if (FAILED(lpD3DRM->CreateFrame(myInfo->scene, &frame)))
  goto generic_error;
```

IDirect3DRM::CreateLight

Description

This method is used to create a new light source with the passed type and color.

C++ specification

```
HRESULT CreateLight(D3DRMLIGHTTYPE d3drmltLightType,
  D3DCOLOR cColor, LPDIRECT3DRMLIGHT* lplpD3DRMLight);
```

Parameters

d3drmltLightType. The light type we desire. It must be one of the values from the D3DRMLIGHTTYPE enumerated type.

cColor. The desired color for the light.

lplpD3DRMLight. The address we wish to be filled with a pointer to an IDirect-3DRMLight.

Returns

Successful: D3DRM_OK

Error: One of the Direct3D Retained-Mode return values.

See also

All IDirect3DRMLight methods

Example

```
LPDIRECT3DRMLIGHT light = NULL;
LPDIRECT3DRMFRAME frame = NULL;
HRESULT rval;
// Create a meshbuilder to hold our object representing the light
if (FAILED(lpD3DRM->CreateMeshBuilder(&builder)))
  goto generic_error;
// See if we are creating a directional light
if (strcmp(wparam, "LIGHT_DIRECTIONAL") == 0) {
  // If so, load the .x object
  rval = builder->Load("camera.x", NULL, D3DRMLOAD_FROMFILE,
              NULL, NULL);
  if (rval != D3DRM_OK) {
    Msg("Failed to load camera.x.\n%s", MyErrorToString(rval));
    goto ret_with_error;
  }
  // Set the rendering quality
  if (FAILED(builder->SetQuality(D3DRMRENDER_UNLITFLAT)))
    goto generic_error;
// Set up a color
D3DCOLOR myColor;
int r = 255, g = 0, b = 255; // r, g, b range from 0-255

myColor = ((D3DCOLOR) (((r) << 16) | ((g) << 8) | (b)));

if (FAILED(lpD3DRM->CreateLight
  (D3DRMLIGHT_DIRECTIONAL, myColor, &light)))
  goto generic_error;
```

IDirect3DRM::CreateLightRGB

Description

This method is used to create a new light source with the passed type and color.

C++ specification

```
HRESULT CreateLightRGB(D3DRMLIGHTTYPE ltLightType, D3DVALUE vRed,
   D3DVALUE vGreen, D3DVALUE vBlue, LPDIRECT3DRMLIGHT* lplpD3DRMLight);
```

Parameters

ltLightType. The light type we desire. It must be one of the values from the
D3DRMLIGHTTYPE enumerated type.

vRed, vGreen, and vBlue. The desired RGB color for the light.

lplpD3DRMLight. The address we wish to be filled with a pointer to an IDirect-
3DRMLight.

Returns

Successful: D3DRM_OK

Error: One of the Direct3D Retained-Mode return values.

See also

All IDirect3DRMLight methods

Example

```
LPDIRECT3DRMLIGHT light = NULL;
LPDIRECT3DRMFRAME frame = NULL;
HRESULT rval;

if (FAILED(lpD3DRM->CreateMeshBuilder(&builder)))
  goto generic_error;

if (strcmp(wparam, "LIGHT_DIRECTIONAL") == 0) {
  rval = builder->Load("camera.x", NULL, D3DRMLOAD_FROMFILE,
             NULL, NULL);
  if (rval != D3DRM_OK) {
    Msg("Failed to load camera.x.\n%s", MyErrorToString(rval));
    goto ret_with_error;
  }
  if (FAILED(builder->SetQuality(D3DRMRENDER_UNLITFLAT)))
    goto generic_error;
  if (FAILED(lpD3DRM->CreateLightRGB
    (D3DRMLIGHT_DIRECTIONAL, D3DVAL(1.0), D3DVAL(1.0), D3DVAL(1.0),
       &light)))
    goto generic_error;
```

IDirect3DRM::CreateMaterial

Description

This method is used to create a material with the specified specular property.

C++ specification

```
HRESULT CreateMaterial(D3DVALUE vPower,
  LPDIRECT3DRMMATERIAL * lplpD3DRMMaterial);
```

Parameters

vPower. The sharpness of the reflected highlights. A value of 5 will give a metallic look and a higher value will give a more plastic-like look to our surface.

lplpD3DRMMaterial. The address we wish filled with a pointer to an IDirect-3DRMMaterial interface.

Returns

Successful: D3DRM_OK

Error: One of the Direct3D Retained-Mode return values.

See also

All IDirect3DRMMaterial methods

Example

```
LPDIRECT3DRMMATERIAL mat = NULL;
if (FAILED (lpD3DRM->CreateMaterial (D3DVAL(16.0), &mat)))
  goto generic_error;
```

IDirect3DRM::CreateMesh

Description

This method is used to create a new mesh object with no faces. This new mesh will not be visible until you add it to a frame.

C++ specification

```
HRESULT CreateMesh(LPDIRECT3DRMMESH* lplpD3DRMMesh);
```

Parameters

lplpD3DRMMesh. The address you wish to be filled with a pointer to an IDirect-3DRMMesh interface.

Returns

Successful: D3DRM_OK

Error: One of the Direct3D Retained-Mode return values.

See also

IDirect3DRMMeshBuilder::CreateMesh

All IDirect3DRMMesh methods

Example

```
LPDIRECT3DRMMESHBUILDER obj_builder = 0;
LPDIRECT3DRMMESH    obj_mesh = 0;
// load mesh file
if (FAILED(lpD3DRM->CreateMeshBuilder(&obj_builder)))
 goto generic_error;
if (FAILED (lpD3DRM->CreateMesh(&obj_mesh)))
 goto generic_error;
```

IDirect3DRM::CreateMeshBuilder

Description

This method is used to creates a new mesh builder object.

C++ specification

```
HRESULT CreateMeshBuilder(LPDIRECT3DRMMESHBUILDER*
      lplpD3DRMMeshBuilder);
```

Parameters

lplpD3DRMMeshBuilder. The address you wish filled with a pointer to an IDirect-3DRMMeshBuilder interface.

Returns

Successful: D3DRM_OK

Error: One of the Direct3D Retained-Mode return values.

See also

IDirect3DRMMeshBuilder::CreateMesh

All IDirect3DRMMeshBuilder methods

Example

```
LPDIRECT3DRMMESHBUILDER obj_builder = 0;
LPDIRECT3DRMMESH    obj_mesh = 0;
// load mesh file
if (FAILED(lpD3DRM->CreateMeshBuilder(&obj_builder)))
  goto generic_error;
if (FAILED (obj_builder->CreateMesh(&obj_mesh)))
  goto generic_error;
```

IDirect3DRM::CreateObject

Description

This method is used to create a new object. You can use this method to implement aggregation in Direct3DRM objects. The object is *not* initialized. Unlike the other creation methods which initialize the created objects automatically, you must initialize the object that is created. To do this, you can use the `Init` method for the object. You should call the `Init` method only once to initialize an object.

C++ specification

```
HRESULT CreateObject(REFCLSID rclsid, LPUNKNOWN pUnkOuter,
  REFIID riid, LPVOID FAR* ppv);
```

Parameters

`rclsid`. The class identifier for our new object.

`pUnkOuter`. Used to allow COM aggregation features.

`riid`. The interface identifier for the object we are creating.

`ppv`. The address of a returned pointer to the object.

Returns

Successful: D3DRM_OK

Error: One of the Direct3D Retained-Mode return values.

Example

```
LPDIRECT3DRM myD3DRM;
REFCLSID classId;
LPUNKNOWN pUnkOuter;
REFIID riid;
LPVOID FAR* objPtr;
HRESULT rval;
   .
   .
   .
rval = myD3DRM->CreateObject(classId, pUnkOuter, riid, objPtr);
```

IDirect3DRM::CreateShadow

Description

This method is used to create a shadow using the passed visual and light. The shadow is projected onto the specified plane. You should add the shadow visual to the frame containing the visual.

C++ specification

```
HRESULT CreateShadow(LPDIRECT3DRMVISUAL lpVisual,
```

```
            LPDIRECT3DRMLIGHT lpLight, D3DVALUE px, D3DVALUE py, D3DVALUE pz,
            D3DVALUE nx, D3DVALUE ny, D3DVALUE nz,
            LPDIRECT3DRMVISUAL * lplpShadow);
```

Parameters

lpVisual. The address of the Direct3DRMVisual object casting the shadow.

lpLight. The address of the IDirect3DRMLight interface which is our light source.

px, py, and pz. The plane we wish the shadow to be projected upon.

nx, ny, and nz. The normal to the plane that we wish the shadow to be projected upon.

lplpShadow. The address of a pointer we wish initialized with a pointer to the shadow visual.

Returns

Successful: D3DRM_OK

Error: One of the Direct3D Retained-Mode return values.

See also

IDirect3DRMShadow::Init

Example

```
LPD3DRM  myD3DRM;
LPDIRECT3DRMVISUAL lpVisual;
LPDIRECT3DRMLIGHT lpLight;
D3DVALUE px; // Plane the shadow is projected on
D3DVALUE py;
D3DVALUE pz;
D3DVALUE nx; // Normal to the plane the shadow is projected upon
D3DVALUE ny;
D3DVALUE nz;
LPDIRECT3DRMVISUAL * lplpShadow;
.
.
if (FAILED(myD3DRM->CreateShadow(lpVisual, lpLight, px, py, pz,
        nx, ny, nz, lplpShadow)))
    goto generic_error;
```

IDirect3DRM::CreateTexture

Description

This method is used to creates a texture from an image in memory. The image memory is used every time the texture is rendered instead of copying the memory into Direct3DRM's buffers. This approach enables us to use the image as both a rendering target and a texture.

C++ specification

```
HRESULT CreateTexture(LPD3DRMIMAGE lpImage,
  LPDIRECT3DRMTEXTURE* lplpD3DRMTexture);
```

Parameters

lpImage. The address of a D3DRMIMAGE structure which describes the texture source.

lplpD3DRMTexture. The address you wish filled with a pointer to an IDirect-3DRMTexture interface.

Returns

Successful: D3DRM_OK

Error: One of the Direct3D Retained-Mode return values.

See also

All IDirect3DRMTexture methods

Example

```
LPD3DRMIMAGE TextureImage;
LPDIRECT3DRMTEXTURE tex;
.
.
if (FAILED(lpD3DRM->CreateTexture(&TextureImage, &tex)))
    goto generic_error;
```

IDirect3DRM::CreateTextureFromSurface

Description

This method is used to create a texture from a desired DirectDraw surface.

C++ specification

```
HRESULT CreateTextureFromSurface(LPDIRECTDRAWSURFACE lpDDS,
  LPDIRECT3DRMTEXTURE * lplpD3DRMTexture);
```

Parameters

lpDDS. The address of the DirectDrawSurface object which contains our texture.

lplpD3DRMTexture. The address you wish filled with a pointer to an IDirect-3DRMTexture.

Successful: D3DRM_OK

Error: One of the Direct3D Retained-Mode return values.

See also

All IDirect3DRMTexture methods

Example

```
LPDIRECTDRAWSURFACE lpDDS;
LPDIRECT3DRMTEXTURE * lplpD3DRMTexture;
..
if (FAILED(lpD3DRM->CreateTextureFromSurface(lpDDS,
        lplpD3DRMTexture)))
    goto generic_error;
```

IDirect3DRM::CreateUserVisual

Description

This method is used to create a visual object that can then be added to our scene and rendered with an application-defined handler.

C++ specification

```
HRESULT CreateUserVisual(D3DRMUSERVISUALCALLBACK fn,
    LPVOID lpArg, LPDIRECT3DRMUSERVISUAL * lplpD3DRMUV);
```

Parameters

fn. Our application-defined D3DRMUSERVISUALCALLBACK callback function.

lpArg. The address of our application-defined data which we wish passed to our callback function.

lplpD3DRMUV. The address we wish filled with a pointer to an IDirect-3DRMUserVisual interface.

Returns

Successful: D3DRM_OK

Error: One of the Direct3D Retained-Mode return values.

See also

All IDirect3DRMUserVisual methods

Example

```
myObjType* myObj;
LPDIRECT3DRMUSERVISUAL myvisual = NULL;
```

```
myObj = (myObjType*)malloc(sizeof(myObjType));
if (!myObj)
  goto ret_with_error;
memset(myObj, 0, sizeof(myObjType));

if (FAILED(lpD3DRM->CreateUserVisual(myCallback, (void*) myObj,
    myvisual)))
  goto ret_with_error;
```

IDirect3DRM::CreateViewport

Description

This method is used to create a viewport on a device with the device coordinates (dwXPos, dwYPos) to (dwXPos + dwWidth, dwYPos + dwHeight). This viewport will display the objects within our scene containing our camera. The view direction and up vector are taken from the camera.

C++ specification

```
HRESULT CreateViewport(LPDIRECT3DRMDEVICE lpDev,
  LPDIRECT3DRMFRAME lpCamera, DWORD dwXPos,
  DWORD dwYPos, DWORD dwWidth, DWORD dwHeight,
  LPDIRECT3DRMVIEWPORT* lplpD3DRMViewport);
```

Parameters

lpDev. The device which the viewport is to be created upon.

lpCamera. The frame defining the position and direction of our view.

dwXPos, dwYPos, dwWidth, and dwHeight. The position and size of your viewport in device coordinates.

lplpD3DRMViewport. The address you wish filled with a pointer to an IDirect-3DRMViewport interface.

Returns

Successful: D3DRM_OK

Error: One of the Direct3D Retained-Mode return values.

See also

All IDirect3DRMViewport methods

Example

```
LPDIRECT3DRMFRAME  camera;
LPDIRECT3DRMDEVICE  dev;
LPDIRECT3DRMVIEWPORT view;
if (FAILED(lpD3DRM->CreateViewport(
```

```
        dev,      // The device on which the viewport will be created
        camera,   // The frame describing the views position
                  // and direction
        0, 0,     // X, Y position of the viewport
        dev->GetWidth(),  // Width of the viewport
        dev->GetHeight(), // Height of the viewport
        &view)))  // Address which will be filled with a
                  // pointer to a Direct3DRMViewport interface
    goto generic_error;
```

IDirect3DRM::CreateWrap

Description

This method is used to create a wrapping function which can be used to assign texture coordinates to your faces and meshes. The vector [ox oy oz] specifies the origin of your wrap, [dx dy dz] specifies its z-axis, and [ux uy uz] gives the y-axis. The 2D vectors [ou ov] and [su sv] are used to indicate an origin and scale factor in the texture applied to the result of the wrapping function.

C++ specification

```
HRESULT CreateWrap(D3DRMWRAPTYPE type, LPDIRECT3DRMFRAME lpRef,
    D3DVALUE ox, D3DVALUE oy, D3DVALUE oz, D3DVALUE dx, D3DVALUE dy,
    D3DVALUE dz, D3DVALUE ux, D3DVALUE uy, D3DVALUE uz, D3DVALUE ou,
    D3DVALUE ov, D3DVALUE su, D3DVALUE sv,
    LPDIRECT3DRMWRAP* lplpD3DRMWrap);
```

Parameters

type. Indicates one of the members of the D3DRMWRAPTYPE enumerated type.

lpRef. The reference frame for your wrap.

ox, oy, and oz. The origin of your wrap.

dx, dy, and dz. The z-axis of your wrap.

ux, uy, and uz. The y-axis of your wrap.

ou and ov. The origin in the texture.

su and sv . The scale factor in the texture.

lplpD3DRMWrap. The address you wish filled with a pointer to an IDirect3DRMWrap interface.

Returns

Successful: D3DRM_OK

Error: One of the Direct3D Retained-Mode return values.

See also

All IDirect3DRMWrap methods

Example

```
LPDIRECT3DRMWRAP wrap = NULL;
D3DVALUE miny, maxy;
D3DVALUE height;

if (FAILED(lpD3DRM->CreateWrap(D3DRMWRAP_SPHERE, NULL,
              D3DVAL(0.0), D3DVAL(0.0), D3DVAL(0.0),
              D3DVAL(0.0), D3DVAL(1.0), D3DVAL(0.0),
              D3DVAL(0.0), D3DVAL(0.0), D3DVAL(1.0),
              D3DVAL(0.0), D3DDivide (miny, height),
              D3DVAL(50), D3DDivide (D3DVAL(-50), height),
              &wrap)))
goto generic_error;
```

IDirect3DRM::EnumerateObjects

Description

This method is used to call the callback function you specified with the `func` parameter on each of your active Direct3DRM objects.

C++ specification

```
HRESULT EnumerateObjects(D3DRMOBJECTCALLBACK func, LPVOID lpArg);
```

Parameters

func. Your application-defined `D3DRMOBJECTCALLBACK` callback function you wish called with each Direct3DRMObject object and your application-defined argument.

lpArg. The address of the application-defined data passed to your callback function.

Returns

Successful: D3DRM_OK

Error: One of the Direct3D Retained-Mode return values.

Example

```
LPDIRECT3DRM myD3DRM;
D3DRMOBJECTCALLBACK func;
LPVOID lpArg;

    .
    .
```

```
if (myD3DRM->EnumerateObjects( func, lpArg) != D3DRM_OK)
  goto generic_error;
```

IDirect3DRM::GetDevices

Description

This method returns all of the Direct3DRM devices which have been created.

C++ specification

```
HRESULT GetDevices(LPDIRECT3DRMDEVICEARRAY* lplpDevArray);
```

Parameters

lplpDevArray. The address of a pointer you wish filled with the acquired array of
    Direct3DRM devices.

Returns

Successful: D3DRM_OK
Error: One of the Direct3D Retained-Mode return values.

See also

All IDirect3DRMDeviceArray interface methods.

Example

```
LPDIRECT3DRM myD3DRM;
LPDIRECT3DRMDEVICEARRAY* lplpDevArray;
.
.
if (D3DRM->GetDevices(lplpDevArray) != D3DRM_OK)
  goto generic_error;
```

IDirect3DRM::GetNamedObject

Description

This method is used to find a Direct3DRMObject with the requested name.

C++ specification

```
HRESULT GetNamedObject(const char * lpName,
  LPDIRECT3DRMOBJECT* lplpD3DRMObject);
```

Parameters

lpName. The name of the object you wish to search for.

lplpD3DRMObject. The address of a pointer you wish initialized with a valid Direct3DRMObject pointer.

Returns

Successful: D3DRM_OK

Error: One of the Direct3D Retained-Mode return values.

Example

```
// Retrieve the frames
LPDIRECT3DRMmyD3DRM;
LPDIRECT3DRMOBJECT tmp;
LPDIRECT3DRMFRAME lpFrame = NULL;

if (FAILED(myD3DRM->GetNamedObject("x3ds_part", &tmp)))
    goto generic_error;
lpFrame = (LPDIRECT3DRMFRAME)tmp;
```

IDirect3DRM::GetSearchPath

Description

This method is used to acquire the current file search path.

C++ specification

```
HRESULT GetSearchPath(DWORD * lpdwSize, LPSTR lpszPath);
```

Parameters

lpdwSize. The address of the number of returned path elements which cannot be NULL.

lpszPath. The address of a null-terminated string indicating the search path. If you pass this parameter as NULL, the method will return the size of your required string in the location you specify in the lpdwSize parameter.

Returns

Successful: D3DRM_OK

Error: One of the Direct3D Retained-Mode return values.

See also

IDirect3DRM::SetSearchPath

Example

```
LPDIRECT3DRM myD3DRM;
DWORD * lpdwSize;
```

```
LPSTR     lpszPath = NULL;
          HRESULT err;
   .

   .

if (FAILED(myD3DRM->GetSearchPath(lpdwSize, lpszPath))
{
   Msg("Failed to get search path.\n");
   return;
}
```

IDirect3DRM::Load

Description

This method is used to load an object.

C++ specification

```
HRESULT Load(LPVOID lpvObjSource, LPVOID lpvObjID,
   LPIID * lplpGUIDs, DWORD dwcGUIDs, D3DRMLOADOPTIONS d3drmLOFlags,
   D3DRMLOADCALLBACK d3drmLoadProc, LPVOID lpArgLP,
   D3DRMLOADTEXTURECALLBACK d3drmLoadTextureProc, LPVOID lpArgLTP,
   LPDIRECT3DRMFRAME lpParentFrame);
```

Parameters

lpvObjSource. The source for the object you wish loaded. The source can be a file, resource, memory block, or stream, based upon the source flags you specify in the d3drmLOFlags parameter.

lpvObjID. The object name or position you wish loaded. The way this parameter is used is dependent upon the identifier flags you specify in the d3drmLOFlags parameter. If you specify the D3DRMLOAD_BYPOSITION flag, this parameter will be a pointer to a DWORD value indicating the order of the object in the file. This parameter can be NULL.

lplpGUIDs. The address of an array of interface identifiers you wish loaded. As an example, if you pass a two-element array containing IID_IDirect3DRMMesh and IID_IDirect3DRMLight, this method will load all of the mesh and light objects.

dwcGUIDs. The number of elements given in the lplpGUIDs parameter.

d3drmLOFlags. The value of the D3DRMLOADOPTIONS type defining the load options.

d3drmLoadProc. A D3DRMLOADCALLBACK callback function called when the specified object is read by the system.

lpArgLP. The address of the application-defined data passed to the D3DRMLOADCALLBACK callback function.

d3drmLoadTextureProc. A D3DRMLOADTEXTURECALLBACK callback function which is called to load any textures used by an object which need special formatting. You may specify this parameter as NULL.

lpArgLTP. The address of the application-defined data passed to the D3DRMLOADTEXTURECALLBACK callback function.

lpParentFrame. The address of your parent frame. Although this parameter can be NULL, this information can be helpful when you load a Direct3DRM-AnimationSet or a Direct3DRMFrame object since otherwise they would be created with a NULL parent.

Returns

Successful: D3DRM_OK

Error: One of the Direct3D Retained-Mode return values.

Example

```
HRESULT err;
LPVOID lpvObjSource;
LPVOID lpvObjID,
LPIID * lplpGUIDs;
DWORD dwcGUIDs;
D3DRMLOADOPTIONS d3drmLOFlags;
D3DRMLOADCALLBACK d3drmLoadProc;
LPVOID lpArgLP,
D3DRMLOADTEXTURECALLBACK d3drmLoadTextureProc;
LPVOID lpArgLTP;
LPDIRECT3DRMFRAME lpParentFrame;
LPDIRECT3DRM myD3DRM;
   .
   .
if (FAILED(myD3DRM->Load(lpvObjSource, lpvObjID, lplpGUIDs, dwcGUIDs,
        d3drmLOFlags, d3drmLoadProc, lpArgLP, d3drmLoadTextureProc,
        lpArgLTP, lpParentFrame))
{
   Msg("Failed to load the object.\n");
   return;
}
```

IDirect3DRM::LoadTexture

Description

This method is used to load a texture from the passed file. Your texture can have 8, 24, or 32 bits-per-pixel and should be in either the Windows bitmap (.bmp) or Portable Pixmap (.ppm) P6 format.

C++ specification

```
HRESULT LoadTexture(const char * lpFileName,
    LPDIRECT3DRMTEXTURE* lplpD3DRMTexture);
```

Parameters

`lpFileName`. The name of the requested .bmp or .ppm file.

`lplpD3DRMTexture`. The address of a pointer you wish to be initialized with a valid
Direct3DRMTexture pointer.

Returns

Successful: D3DRM_OK

Error: One of the Direct3D Retained-Mode return values.

See also

IDirect3DRM::LoadTextureFromResource

IDirect3DRM::SetDefaultTextureColors

IDirect3DRM::SetDefaultTextureShades

All IDirect3DRMTexture methods

Example

```
LPDIRECT3DRM myD3DRM;
HRESULT rval;
LPDIRECT3DRMTEXTURE stex = 0;
  .
  .
  .
rval = myD3DRM->LoadTexture ("w_stone.bmp", &stex);
if (rval != D3DRM_OK)
  {
   Msg("Failed to load w_stone.bmp.\n%s", MyErrorToString(rval));
   return FALSE;
  }
```

IDirect3DRM::LoadTextureFromResource

Description

This method loads a texture from a requested resource.

C++ specification

```
HRESULT LoadTextureFromResource(HRSRC rs,
    LPDIRECT3DRMTEXTURE * lplpD3DRMTexture);
```

Parameters

`rs`. The resource handle.

lplpD3DRMTexture. The address of a pointer you wish initialized with a valid Direct3DRMTexture object.

Returns

Successful: D3DRM_OK

Error: One of the Direct3D Retained-Mode return values.

See also

IDirect3DRM::LoadTexture

IDirect3DRM::SetDefaultTextureColors

IDirect3DRM::SetDefaultTextureShades

Example

```
HRSRC rs;
LPDIRECT3DRMTEXTURE * lplpD3DRMTexture;
LPDIRECT3DRM myD3DRM;
  .

  .
rval = myD3DRM->LoadTextureFromResource (rs, lplpD3DRMTexture);
if (rval != D3DRM_OK)
 {
  Msg("Failed to load texture from resource .\n%s", MyError-
      ToString(rval));
  return FALSE;
 }
```

IDirect3DRM::SetDefaultTextureColors

Description

This method is used to set the default colors you wish used for a Direct3DRMTexture object. It will only affect the texture colors when it is called before the IDirect3DRM::CreateTexture method. It will have no effect on your textures that have already been created.

C++ specification

```
HRESULT SetDefaultTextureColors(DWORD dwColors);
```

Parameters

dwColors. The number of colors.

Returns

Successful: D3DRM_OK

Error: One of the Direct3D Retained-Mode return values.

See also

> IDirect3DRM::LoadTexture
> IDirect3DRM::LoadTextureFromResource
> IDirect3DRM::SetDefaultTextureShades

Example

```
LPDIRECT3DRM myD3DRM;
  .
  .
case 16:
 // Set the number of shades in the ramp of colors for shading to 32
 if (FAILED(dev->SetShades(32)))
    goto generic_error;
 // Set the default colors for a Direct3DRMTexture object to 64
 if (FAILED(myD3DRM->SetDefaultTextureColors(64)))
    goto generic_error;
 // Set the default shades to be used for a Direct3DRMTexture object to
      32
 if (FAILED(myD3DRM->SetDefaultTextureShades(32)))
    goto generic_error;
 // Sets the dither flag for the device to FALSE
 if (FAILED(dev->SetDither(FALSE)))
    goto generic_error;
 break;
```

IDirect3DRM::SetDefaultTextureShades

Description

> This method is used to set the default shades you wish used for your Direct3DRMTexture object. It will only affect the texture shades when it is called before the `IDirect3DRM::CreateTexture` method. It will have no effect on your textures that have already been created.

C++ specification

```
HRESULT SetDefaultTextureShades(DWORD dwShades);
```

Parameters

> `dwShades`. The number of shades.

Returns

> Successful: D3DRM_OK
> Error: One of the Direct3D Retained-Mode return values.

IDirect3DRM::LoadTexture

IDirect3DRM::LoadTextureFromResource

IDirect3DRM::SetDefaultTextureColors

Example

```
LPDIRECT3DRM myD3DRM;
   .
   .
switch (bpp)
{
   .
   .
case 16:
   // Set the number of shades in the ramp of colors for shading to 32
   if (FAILED(dev->SetShades(32)))
      goto generic_error;
   // Set the default colors for a Direct3DRMTexture object to 64
   if (FAILED(myD3DRM->SetDefaultTextureColors(64)))
      goto generic_error;
   // Set the default shades to be used for a Direct3DRMTexture object to
         32
   if (FAILED(myD3DRM->SetDefaultTextureShades(32)))
      goto generic_error;
   // Sets the dither flag for the device to FALSE
   if (FAILED(dev->SetDither(FALSE)))
      goto generic_error;
   break;
```

IDirect3DRM::SetSearchPath

Description

This method is used to set the current file search path. The default search path is taken from the value of the D3DPATH environment variable. If this variable is not set, the search path will be empty. When your code requires opening a file, the system will first look for that file in the current working directory and then check each of the directories in the search path.

C++ specification

```
HRESULT SetSearchPath(LPCSTR lpPath);
```

Parameters

lpPath. The address of a null-terminated string specifying the path you wish to set as the current search path.

Returns

>Successful: D3DRM_OK
>Error: One of the Direct3D Retained-Mode return values.

See also

>IDirect3DRM::GetSearchPath

Example

```
LPDIRECT3DRM myD3DRM;
HRESULT rval;
     .
     .
rval = MyD3DRM->SetSearchPath("c:\dxsdk\sdk\myProgs\;c:\dxsdk\sdk");
```

IDirect3DRM::Tick

Description

>This method handles the Direct3DRM system heartbeat. Whenever this method is called, 1) all of the moving frames positions will be updated based upon their motion attributes, 2) the scene will be rendered to your current device, and 3) the callback functions will be called at their appropriate time. The control is returned when the rendering cycle has completed.

C++ specification

```
HRESULT Tick(D3DVALUE d3dvalTick);
```

Parameters

>d3dvalTick. The velocity and rotation step for the IDirect3DRMFrame::SetRotation and IDirect3DRMFrame::SetVelocity methods.

Returns

>Successful: D3DRM_OK
>Error: One of the Direct3D Retained-Mode return values.

Example

```
LPDIRECT3DRM myD3DRM;
     .
     .
// Trigger doing everything - renders scene and updates everyting
myD3DRM->Tick(D3DVALUE(1.0));
```

chapter 22

The IDirect3DRMAnimation interface

The IDirect3DRMAnimation interface and methods

The IDirect3DRMAnimation methods are used to animate the orientation, position, and scale of viewports, visuals, and lights. The Direct3DRMAnimation object is created by calling the `IDirect3DRM::CreateAnimation` method.

Like all COM interfaces, this interface inherits the IUnknown interface methods. These consist of `AddRef`, `QueryInterface`, and `Release`.

The IDirect3DRMAnimation interface methods can be organized into the groups shown in table 22.1.

Table 22.1 IDirect3DRMAnimation methods

Group	Methods
Keys	AddPositionKey
	AddRotateKey
	AddScaleKey
	DeleteKey
Miscellaneous	SetFrame
	SetTime
Options	GetOptions
	SetOptions

The IDirect3DRMAnimation interface also inherits the methods in table 22.2 from the IDirect3DRMObject interface:

Table 22.2 Methods inherited from IDirect3DRMObject

Methods
Clone
DeleteDestroyCallback
GetAppData
GetClassName
GetName
SetAppData
SetName

IDirect3DRMAnimation::AddPositionKey

Description

This method is used to add a position key to the animation. The transformation that is applied by this method is a translation.

C++ specification

```
HRESULT AddPositionKey(D3DVALUE rvTime, D3DVALUE rvX,
  D3DVALUE rvY, D3DVALUE rvZ);
```

Parameters

rvTime. The time in the animation to store the position key. It is critical to remember that these time units are arbitrary and zero-based. As an example, a key with an rvTime value of 34 will occur at exactly the middle of your animation if the last key has an rvTime value of 67.

rvX, rvY, and rvZ. The position to add.

Returns

Successful: D3DRM_OK

Error: One of the Direct3D Retained-Mode return values.

See also

IDirect3DRMAnimation::DeleteKey

IDirect3DRMAnimation::AddRotateKey

IDirect3DRMAnimation::AddScaleKey

Example

```
LPDIRECT3DRMANIMATION lpAnim;
// Calculate the vector to keep your object in view
D3DVECTOR cameraPosition;
    .
    .
    .
D3DVECTOR Camera;
Camera.x = (float)abs((int)yourPos.z - (int)hisPos.z) +
        D3DVAL(200);
Camera.y = cameraPosition.y;
Camera.z = cameraPosition.z;

// Add the keyframes to your animation
if (lpAnim->AddPositionKey(D3DVAL(1), Camera.x, Camera.y, Camera.z) !=
        D3DRM_OK)
    goto generic_error;
```

IDirect3DRMAnimation::AddRotateKey

Description

This method is used to add a rotate key to your animation. It applies a rotation transform to perform this action.

C++ specification

```
HRESULT AddRotateKey(D3DVALUE rvTime, D3DRMQUATERNION *rqQuat);
```

Parameters

rvTime. Indicates the time in the animation to store the rotate key. These time units are arbitrary and zero-based. As an example, a key with an rvTime value of 34 will occur at exactly the middle of your animation if the last key has an rvTime value of 67.

rqQuat. A quaternion representing the rotation.

Returns

Successful: D3DRM_OK

Error: One of the Direct3D Retained-Mode return values.

See also

IDirect3DRMAnimation::AddPositionKey

IDirect3DRMAnimation::AddScaleKey

IDirect3DRMAnimation::DeleteKey

Example

```
LPDIRECT3DRMANIMATION myAnim;
D3DVALUE rvTime;
LPD3DRMQUATERNION myQuat;
LPD3DVECTOR lpv;
D3DVALUE theta;
lpv = [0 1 0];
theta = .08;
myQuat = D3DRMQuaternionFromRotation(myQuat, lpv, theta);
    .
    .
rvTime = 67;
if (myAnim->AddRotateKey( rvTime, myQuat) != D3DRM_OK)
    goto generic_error;
```

IDirect3DRMAnimation::AddScaleKey

Description

This method is used to add a scale key to your animation. It applies a scale transform to perform this action.

C++ specification

```
HRESULT AddScaleKey(D3DVALUE rvTime, D3DVALUE rvX, D3DVALUE rvY,
    D3DVALUE rvZ);
```

Parameters

rvTime. The time in the animation to store the scale key. These time units are arbitrary and zero-based. As an example, a key with an rvTime value of 34 will occur at exactly the middle of your animation if the last key has an `rvTime` value of 67.

rvX, rvY, and rvZ. The scale factor.

Returns

Successful: D3DRM_OK

Error: One of the Direct3D Retained-Mode return values.

See also

IDirect3DRMAnimation::DeleteKey

IDirect3DRMAnimation::AddPositionKey

IDirect3DRMAnimation::AddRotateKey

Example

```
D3DVALUE rvTime;
D3DVALUE rvX;
D3DVALUE rvY;
D3DVALUE rvZ;
LPDIRECT3DRMANIMATION myAnim;
 .
 .
rvTime = 67;
rvX = rvY = rvZ = .7;
if (myAnim->AddScaleKey( rvTime, rvX, rvY, rvZ) != D3DRM_OK)
 goto generic_error;
```

IDirect3DRMAnimation::DeleteKey

Description

This method is used to remove a key from your animation.

C++ specification

```
HRESULT DeleteKey(D3DVALUE rvTime);
```

Parameters

rvTime. The time which identifies the key which will be removed from your animation.

Returns

Successful: D3DRM_OK

Error: One of the Direct3D Retained-Mode return values.

See also

IDirect3DRMAnimation::AddPositionKey

IDirect3DRMAnimation::AddRotateKey

IDirect3DRMAnimation::AddScaleKey

Example

```
LPDIRECT3DRMANIMATION myAnim;
D3DVALUE rvTime;

rvTime = 67;
if (myAnim->DeleteKey( rvTime) != D3DRM_OK)
 goto generic_error;
```

IDirect3DRMAnimation::GetOptions

Description

This method is used to retrieve the animation options from your animations.

C++ specification

```
D3DRMANIMATIONOPTIONS GetOptions();
```

Returns

Returns the value of the D3DRMANIMATIONOPTIONS type which define your animation options.

See also

IDirect3DRMAnimation::SetOptions

Example

```
LPDIRECT3DRMANIMATION   myAnimation;
D3DRMANIMATIONOPTIONS   myOptions;
.
.
myOptions = myAnimation->GetOptions();
switch (myOptions)
{
  // The animation plays continuously
  case D3DRMANIMATION_CLOSED:

    ...
  // The animation's position is set linearly
  case D3DRMANIMATION_LINEARPOSITION:

    ...
  // The animation will play once and stop
  case D3DRMANIMATION_OPEN:

    ...
```

```
  // The animation's position matrix will overwrite any transformation
        matrices
  case D3DRMANIMATION_POSITION:
    …
  // The animation's scale and rotation matrix will overwrite any
        transformation matrices
  case D3DRMANIMATION_SCALEANDROTATION:
    …
  // The animation's position will be set using splines
  case D3DRMANIMATION_SPLINEPOSITION:
    …
  break;
}
```

IDirect3DRMAnimation::SetFrame

Description

This method is used to set the frame for your animation.

C++ specification

```
HRESULT SetFrame(LPDIRECT3DRMFRAME lpD3DRMFrame);
```

Parameters

lpD3DRMFrame. The address of a variable which represents the frame to set for your animation.

Returns

Successful: D3DRM_OK

Error: One of the Direct3D Retained-Mode return values.

Example

```
// And attach the camera to the animation
LPDIRECT3DRMFRAME  Camera;
LPDIRECT3DRMANIMATION   myAnim;
HRESULT myResult;
.

.
myResult = myAnim->SetFrame(Camera);
if (myResult != D3DRM_OK)
 goto generic_error;
```

IDirect3DRMAnimation::SetOptions

Description

This method is used to set your animation options.

C++ specification

```
HRESULT SetOptions(D3DRMANIMATIONOPTIONS d3drmanimFlags);
```

Parameters

d3drmanimFlags. The D3DRMANIMATIONOPTIONS type value which describes your animation options.

Returns

Successfu: D3DRM_OK

Error: One of the Direct3D Retained-Mode return values.

See also

IDirect3DRMAnimation::GetOptions

Example

```
LPDIRECT3DRMANIMATION  anim;

// Set your animation options
if (anim->SetOptions(D3DRMANIMATION_OPEN |
            D3DRMANIMATION_LINEARPOSITION |
              D3DRMANIMATION_POSITION) != D3DRM_OK)
  goto generic_error;
```

IDirect3DRMAnimation::SetTime

Description

This method is used to set the current time for your animation.

C++ specification

```
HRESULT SetTime(D3DVALUE rvTime);
```

Parameters

rvTime. The new current time for your animation. These time units are arbitrary and zero-based. As an example, a key with an rvTime value of 34 will occur at exactly the middle of your animation if the last key has an rvTime value of 67.

Returns

Successful: D3DRM_OK

Error: One of the Direct3D Retained-Mode return values.

Example

```
LPDIRECT3DRMANIMATION  myAnim;
static D3DVALUE time = D3DVAL(0.0f);
  .
  .
// Step forward the animation
time += D3DVAL(0.03);

// Set the animation time
if (myAnim->SetTime(time) != D3DRM_OK)
 goto generic_error;
```

chapter 23

The IDirect3DRMAnimationSet interface

The IDirect3DRMAnimationSet interface and methods

The IDirect3DRMAnimationSet methods are used to group Direct3DRMAnimation objects together in order to simplify the playback of your complex animation sequences. The Direct3DRMAnimationSet object is created by calling the `IDirect3DRM::Create-AnimationSet` method.

Like all COM interfaces, this interface inherits the IUnknown interface methods. This consist of `AddRef`, `QueryInterface`, and `Release`.

The IDirect3DRMAnimationSet interface methods can be organized into the groups in table 23.1.

Table 23.1 IDirect3DRMAnimationSet methods

Group	Methods
Adding, loading, and removing	AddAnimation
	DeleteAnimation
	Load
Time	SetTime

The IDirect3DRMAnimationSet interface also inherits the following methods from the IDirect3DRMObject interface:

Table 23.2   Methods inherited from IDirect3DRMObject

Methods
AddDestroyCallback
Clone
DeleteDestroyCallback
GetAppData
GetClassName
GetName
SetAppData
SetName

IDirect3DRMAnimationSet::AddAnimation

Description

This method is used to add an animation to your animation set.

C++ specification

```
HRESULT AddAnimation(LPDIRECT3DRMANIMATION lpD3DRMAnimation);
```

Parameters

lpD3DRMAnimation. The address of the Direct3DRMAnimation object you wish to add to your animation set.

Returns

Successful: D3DRM_OK

Error: One of the Direct3D Retained-Mode return values.

IDirect3DRM::CreateAnimation
IDirect3DRMAnimationSet::DeleteAnimation

Example

```
LPDIRECT3DRMANIMATION    myAnimation;
LPDIRECT3DRMANIMATIONSET    myAnimationSet;
 .
 .
 .
if (myAnimationSet->AddAnimation(myAnimation) != D3DRM_OK)
 goto generic_error;
```

IDirect3DRMAnimationSet::DeleteAnimation

Description

This method is used to remove an animation from the animation set.

C++ specification

```
HRESULT DeleteAnimation(LPDIRECT3DRMANIMATION lpD3DRMAnimation);
```

Parameters

lpD3DRMAnimation. The address of the Direct3DRMAnimation object you wish to remove from your animation set.

Returns

Successful: D3DRM_OK
Error: One of the Direct3D Retained-Mode return values.

See also

IDirect3DRM::CreateAnimation
IDirect3DRMAnimationSet::AddAnimation

Example

```
LPDIRECT3DRMANIMATION    myAnimation;
LPDIRECT3DRMANIMATIONSET    myAnimationSet;
 .
 .
 .
if (myAnimationSet->DeleteAnimation(myAnimation) != D3DRM_OK)
 goto generic_error;
```

IDirect3DRMAnimationSet::Load

Description

This method is used to load an animation set. This method defaults to loading the first animation set in the file you specify in the `lpvObjSource` parameter.

C++ specification

```
HRESULT Load(LPVOID lpvObjSource, LPVOID lpvObjID,
    D3DRMLOADOPTIONS d3drmLOFlags,
    D3DRMLOADTEXTURECALLBACK d3drmLoadTextureProc, LPVOID lpArgLTP,
    LPDIRECT3DRMFRAME lpParentFrame);
```

Parameters

lpvObjSource. This parameter specifies the source for the object to be loaded. The source can be a file, resource, memory block, or stream, based upon the source flags you specify in the `d3drmLOFlags` parameter.

lpvObjID. The name or position you wish to load. The use of this parameter is based upon the identifier flags you specify in the `d3drmLOFlags` parameter. If you specify the `D3DRMLOAD_BYPOSITION` flag, this parameter will be a pointer to a `DWORD` value which holds the order of the object in the file. You can set this parameter to NULL.

d3drmLOFlags. The value of the `D3DRMLOADOPTIONS` type which defines the load options.

d3drmLoadTextureProc. A `D3DRMLOADTEXTURECALLBACK` callback function which will be called to load any textures that are used by the object which require special formatting. You can set this parameter to NULL.

lpArgLTP The address of your application-defined data passed to the `D3DRMLOADTEXTURECALLBACK` callback function.

lpParentFrame. The address of your parent Direct3DRMFrame object. This is used to prevent the frames referred to by your animation set from being created with a NULL parent.

Returns

Successful: D3DRM_OK

Error: One of the Direct3D Retained-Mode return values.

See also

IDirect3DRM::CreateAnimationSet

Example

```
LPDIRECT3DRMFRAME          myFrame = NULL;
LPDIRECT3DRMANIMATIONSET    myAnimSet = NULL;
```

```
LPDIRECT3DRMmyD3DRM;
.
.
.

// Load our model
if (myD3DRM->CreateAnimationSet(&myAnimSet) != D3DRM_OK)
 goto generic_error;

// Load our model and animation
if (myAnimSet->Load("myModel.X", NULL, D3DRMLOAD_FROMFILE, LoadTex-
        tures, NULL, myFrame) != D3DRM_OK)
 goto generic_error;
```

IDirect3DRMAnimationSet::SetTime

Description

This method is used to set the time for this animation set.

C++ specification

```
HRESULT SetTime(D3DVALUE rvTime);
```

Parameters

rvTime. The new time.

Returns

Successful: D3DRM_OK

Error: One of the Direct3D Retained-Mode return values.

See also

IDirect3DRM::CreateAnimationSet

Example

```
#define WALK_START          D3DVAL(54)
LPDIRECT3DRMANIMATIONSET   myAnimSet = NULL;
.
.
.
if (myD3DRM->CreateAnimationSet(&myAnimSet) != D3DRM_OK)
goto generic_error;
// Load our model and animation
if (myAnimSet->Load("myModel.X", NULL, D3DRMLOAD_FROMFILE, LoadTex-
        tures, NULL, myFrame) != D3DRM_OK)
 goto generic_error;
if (myAnimSet->SetTime(WALK_START) != D3DRM_OK)
 goto generic_error;
```

chapter 24

The IDirect3DRMDevice interface

The IDirect3DRMDevice interface and methods

The IDirect3DRMDevice methods are used to interact with the output device. The Direct3DRMDevice object is created by calling the `IDirect3DRM::CreateDevice` method.

   Like all COM interfaces, this interface inherits the IUnknown interface methods. These consist of `AddRef`, `QueryInterface`, and `Release`.

   The IDirect3DRMDevice interface methods can be organized into the groups in table 24.1.

Table 24.1 IDirect3DRMDevice methods

Group	Methods
Buffer counts	GetBufferCount
	SetBufferCount
Color models	GetColorModel
Dithering	GetDither
	SetDither
Initialization	Init
	InitFromClipper
	InitFromD3D
Miscellaneous	GetDirect3DDevice
	GetHeight
	GetTrianglesDrawn
	GetViewports
	GetWidth
	GetWireframeOptions
	Update
Notifications	AddUpdateCallback
	DeleteUpdateCallback
Rendering quality	GetQuality
	SetQuality
Shading	GetShades
	SetShades
Texture quality	GetTextureQuality
	SetTextureQuality

In addition, the IDirect3DRMDevice interface inherits the following methods from the IDirect3DRMObject interface:

Table 24.2 Methods inherited from IDirect3DRMObject

Methods
AddDestroyCallback
Clone
DeleteDestroyCallback
GetAppData
GetClassName
GetName
SetAppData
SetName

IDirect3DRMDevice::AddUpdateCallback

Description

This method is used to add a callback function which notifies your application when a change occurs to the device. This callback function is called whenever your application calls the `IDirect3DRMDevice::Update` method.

C++ specification

```
HRESULT AddUpdateCallback(D3DRMUPDATECALLBACK d3drmUpdateProc, LPVOID
    arg);
```

Parameters

`d3drmUpdateProc`. The address of your application-defined callback function, `D3DRMUPDATECALLBACK`.

`arg`. The private data you wish to pass to the update callback function.

Returns

Successful: D3DRM_OK

Error: One of the Direct3D Retained-Mode return values.

See also

IDirect3DRMDevice::DeleteUpdateCallback
IDirect3DRMDevice::Update
D3DRMUPDATECALLBACK

Example

```
LPDIRECT3DRMDEVICE myDevice;
.
.
// We are passing NULL, but any arg list is acceptable
// MyCheck is the callback routine name
if (myDev->AddUpdateCallback (MyCheck, NULL) != D3DRM_OK)
 goto generic_error;
```

IDirect3DRMDevice::DeleteUpdateCallback

Description

This method is called to remove an update callback function which you added previously by calling the `IDirect3DRMDevice::AddUpdateCallback` method.

C++ specification

```
HRESULT DeleteUpdateCallback(D3DRMUPDATECALLBACK d3drmUpdateProc,
  LPVOID arg);
```

Parameters

d3drmUpdateProc. The address of an application-defined callback function, D3DRMUPDATECALLBACK.

arg. The private data which was passed to your update callback function.

Returns

Successful: D3DRM_OK

Error: One of the Direct3D Retained-Mode return values.

See also

IDirect3DRMDevice::AddUpdateCallback
IDirect3DRMDevice::Update
D3DRMUPDATECALLBACK

Example

```
LPDIRECT3DRMDEVICE myDev;
  .
  .
// We are passing NULL, but any arg list is acceptable
// MyCheck is the callback routine name
if (myDev->DeleteUpdateCallback(MyCheck, NULL) != D3DRM_OK)
 goto generic_error;
```

IDirect3DRMDevice::GetBufferCount

Description

This method is used to acquire the value set in a call to the IDirect3DRMDevice::SetBufferCount method.

C++ specification

```
DWORD GetBufferCount();
```

Parameters

None

Returns

This method returns the number of buffers. One indicates single-buffering, two indicates double-buffering, and so forth.

See also

IDirect3DRMDevice::SetBufferCount

```
LPDIRECT3DRMDEVICE dev;
DWORD          numBufs;
.

.

numBufs = dev->GetBufferCount();
```

IDirect3DRMDevice::GetColorModel

Description

This method is used to acquire the color model of your device.

C++ specification

```
D3DCOLORMODEL GetColorModel();
```

Parameters

None

Returns

This method returns one of the values from the D3DCOLORMODEL enumerated type defining the Direct3D color model which can be either RGB or monochrome.

See also

D3DRMCOLORMODEL

Example

```
LPDIRECT3DRMDEVICE dev;
D3DCOLORMODEL myColorModel;
.

.

myColorModel = dev->GetColorModel();
```

IDirect3DRMDevice::GetDirect3DDevice

Description

This method is used to acquire a pointer to an Immediate-Mode device.

C++ specification

```
HRESULT GetDirect3DDevice(LPDIRECT3DDEVICE * lplpD3DDevice);
```

Parameters

lplpD3DDevice. The address of a pointer which will be initialized with a pointer to an Immediate-Mode device object.

Returns

    Successful: D3DRM_OK

    Error: One of the Direct3D Retained-Mode return values.

See also

    IDirect3DRM::CreateDeviceFromClipper

    IDirect3DRM::CreateDeviceFromD3D

    IDirect3DRM::CreateDeviceFromSurface

Example

```
LPDIRECT3DDEVICE lpD3DDev = NULL;
LPDIRECT3DRMDEVICE dev;
   .

   .
if (dev->GetDirect3DDevice(&lpD3DDev) != D3DRM_OK)
    // Handle Error
    goto generic_error;
```

IDirect3DRMDevice::GetDither

Description

    This method is used to acquire the dither flag for your device.

C++ specification

```
BOOL GetDither();
```

Parameters

    None

Returns

    This method returns TRUE if the dither flag is set; otherwise it returns FALSE.

See also

    IDirect3DRMDevice::SetDither

Example

```
LPDIRECT3DRMDEVICE  dev;
   .

   .
// Get the current dither flag for the device
BOOL oldDither = dev->GetDither();
```

IDirect3DRMDevice::GetHeight

Description

This method acquires the height of a device in pixels.

C++ specification

```
DWORD GetHeight();
```

Parameters

None

Returns

The height is returned.

See also

IDirect3DRM::CreateDeviceFromClipper
IDirect3DRM::CreateDeviceFromD3D
IDirect3DRM::CreateDeviceFromSurface

Example

```
LPDIRECT3DRMDEVICE   dev;
.
.
// Get the height for the device
DWORD oldHeight = dev->GetHeight();
```

IDirect3DRMDevice::GetTrianglesDrawn

Description

This method is used to retrieve the number of triangles that have been drawn to a device since its creation. This number includes the triangles which were passed but not rendered since they were backfaced. The number does not include the triangles which were skipped because they were outside of your viewing frustum.

C++ specification

```
DWORD GetTrianglesDrawn();
```

Parameters

None

Returns

Returns the number of triangles.

See also

    IDirect3DRM::CreateDeviceFromClipper

    IDirect3DRM::CreateDeviceFromD3D

    IDirect3DRM::CreateDeviceFromSurface

Example

```
LPDIRECT3DRMDEVICE  dev;
.
.
int numTriangles = dev->GetTrianglesDrawn();
```

IDirect3DRMDevice::GetQuality

Description

    This method acquires the rendering quality for your device.

C++ specification

```
D3DRMRENDERQUALITY GetQuality();
```

Parameters

    None

Returns

    This method returns one or more of the members of the enumerated types indicated by the D3DRMRENDERQUALITY type.

See also

    IDirect3DRMDevice::SetQuality

Example

```
LPDIRECT3DRMDEVICE  dev;
.
.
// Get the current dither flag for the device
int old_dither = dev->GetDither();
// Get the rendering quality for the device.
D3DRMRENDERQUALITY old_quality = dev->GetQuality();
// Get the number of shades available on the device
int old_shades = dev->GetShades();
```

IDirect3DRMDevice::GetShades

Description

This method is used to get the number of shades in your ramp of colors used for shading.

C++ specification

```
DWORD GetShades();
```

Returns

This method returns the number of shades.

See also

IDirect3DRMDevice::SetShades

Example

```
LPDIRECT3DRMDEVICE  dev;.
.
// Get the current dither flag for the device
int old_dither = dev->GetDither();
// Get the rendering quality for the device.
D3DRMRENDERQUALITY old_quality = dev->GetQuality();
// Get the number of shades available on the device
int old_shades = dev->GetShades();
```

IDirect3DRMDevice::GetTextureQuality

Description

This method is used to acquire the current texture quality for an RGB device.

C++ specification

```
D3DRMTEXTUREQUALITY GetTextureQuality();
```

Returns

This method returns one of the members of the D3DRMTEXTUREQUALITY enumerated type.

See also

IDirect3DRMDevice::SetTextureQuality

Example

```
LPDIRECT3DRMDEVICE  dev;
.
.
D3DRMTEXTUREQUALITY texQual = dev->GetTextureQuality();
```

IDirect3DRMDevice::GetViewports

Description

This method is used to construct a Direct3DRMViewportArray object representing the viewports which we constructed from the device.

C++ specification

```
HRESULT GetViewports(LPDIRECT3DRMVIEWPORTARRAY* lplpViewports);
```

Parameters

lplpViewports. The address of a pointer you wish initialized with a Direct-3DRMViewportArray object.

Returns

Successful: D3DRM_OK

Error: One of the Direct3D Retained-Mode return values.

See also

IDirect3DRM::CreateDeviceFromClipper

IDirect3DRM::CreateDeviceFromD3D

IDirect3DRM::CreateDeviceFromSurface

Example

```
LPDIRECT3DRMDEVICE dev;
 .
 .
 .
LPDIRECT3DRMVIEWPORTARRAY* lplpViewports;
if (dev->GetViewports(lplpViewports) != d3drm_ok)
 goto generic_error;
```

IDirect3DRMDevice::GetWidth

Description

This method is used to acquire the width of a device in pixels.

C++ specification

```
DWORD GetWidth();
```

Returns

Returns the width.

See also

IDirect3DRM::CreateDeviceFromClipper

IDirect3DRM::CreateDeviceFromD3D
IDirect3DRM::CreateDeviceFromSurface

Example
```
LPDIRECT3DRMDEVICE dev;
   .
   .
if (FAILED(lpD3DRM->CreateViewport(dev, camera, 0, 0,
   dev->GetWidth(),
   dev->GetHeight(),
   &iview)))
   goto generic_error;
```

IDirect3DRMDevice::GetWireframeOptions

Description

This method is called to acquire the wireframe options of a device.

C++ specification
```
DWORD GetWireframeOptions();
```

Parameters

None

Returns

This method returns a bitwise OR of D3DRMWIREFRAME_CULL (indicating the faces are not drawn) and D3DRMWIREFRAME_HIDDENLINE (indicating that wireframe-rendered lines are obscured by nearer objects)

See also

IDirect3DRM::CreateDeviceFromClipper
IDirect3DRM::CreateDeviceFromD3D
IDirect3DRM::CreateDeviceFromSurface

Example
```
LPDIRECT3DRMDEVICE dev;
   .
   .
DWORD retVal = dev->GetWireframeOptions();
```

IDirect3DRMDevice::InitFromClipper

Description

This method is used to initialize a device from your specified DirectDrawClipper object.

C++ specification

```
HRESULT InitFromClipper(LPDIRECTDRAWCLIPPER lpDDClipper,
    LPGUID lpGUID, int width, int height);
```

Parameters

lpDDClipper. The address of your DirectDrawClipper object you wish to use as an initializer.

lpGUID. The address of your GUID used as the interface identifier.

width and height. The width and height of your device.

Returns

Successful: D3DRM_OK

Error: One of the Direct3D Retained-Mode return values.

See also

IDirect3DRM::CreateDeviceFromClipper

IDirect3DRM::CreateDeviceFromD3D

IDirect3DRM::CreateDeviceFromSurface

Example

```
LPDIRECT3DRMDEVICE dev;
HRESULT result;
LPDIRECTDRAWCLIPPER lpDDClipper;
LPGUID lpGUID;
int width;
int height;
    .
    .
    .
result = dev->InitFromClipper(lpDDClipper, lpGUID, width,
        height);
if (result != D3DRM_OK)
    goto generic_error;
```

IDirect3DRMDevice::InitFromD3D

Description

This method is used to initialize your Retained-Mode device from a passed Direct3D Immediate-Mode object and Immediate-Mode device.

C++ specification

```
HRESULT InitFromD3D(LPDIRECT3D lpD3D, LPDIRECT3DDEVICE lpD3DIMDev);
```

Parameters

lpD3D. The address of your Direct3D Immediate-Mode object you wish to use to initialize your Retained-Mode device.

lpD3DIMDev. The address of the Immediate-Mode device to use to initialize the Retained-Mode device.

Returns

Successful: D3DRM_OK

Error: One of the Direct3D Retained-Mode return values.

See also

```
IDirect3DRM::CreateDeviceFromClipper
IDirect3DRM::CreateDeviceFromD3D
IDirect3DRM::CreateDeviceFromSurface
Example
LPDIRECT3DRMDEVICE dev;
LPDIRECT3D lpD3D;
LPDIRECT3DDEVICE lpD3DIMDev;
 .
 .

if (dev->InitFromD3D(lpD3D, lpD3DIMDev) != D3DRM_OK)
 goto generic_error;
```

IDirect3DRMDevice::SetBufferCount

Description

This method is used to set the number of buffers to be used by the application. You must use this method if you choose to use double, triple, and so forth, buffering in order to tell the system how many buffers your application is using.

C++ specification

```
HRESULT SetBufferCount(DWORD dwCount);
```

Parameters

dwCount. This parameter dictates the number of buffers. One indicates single-buffering, two indicates double-buffering, and so forth. The default value is 1 (indicating single-buffered window operation) which is only correct if you are in that mode. Otherwise you need to explicitly state the correct value.

Returns

Successful: D3DRM_OK

Error: One of the Direct3D Retained-Mode return values.

See also

IDirect3DRMDevice::GetBufferCount

Example

```
LPDIRECT3DRM myD3DRM = 0;// D3DRM Object
LPGUID  myDriverGUID=0;// guid of the Direct3D Driver used
LPDIRECT3DDEVICE  myD3DDevice = NULL; // The Direct3D device
LPDIRECTDRAWSURFACE  myBackBuffer = NULL;    // The BackBuffer surface
LPDIRECT3DRMDEVICE   myD3DRMDevice = NULL; // The Direct3D RM Device
LPDIRECT3DDEVICE    myD3DDevice = NULL;   // TheDirect3D device
LPDIRECT3D  myD3D  = 0;  // D3D Object
   .
   .
// Create Direct3D device
if (myBackBuffer->QueryInterface(*myDriverGUID,(LPVOID
      *)&myD3DDevice)…)
   .
   .
// Create the D3DRM device
if (myD3DRM->CreateDeviceFromD3D(myD3D,myD3DDevice,&myD3DRMDevice)…)
   .
   .
// Tell the system we are going to do double buffering
if (myD3DRMDevice->SetBufferCount(2) != D3DRM_OK)
 goto generic_error;
```

IDirect3DRMDevice::SetDither

Description

This method is used to set the dither flag for your device. Dithering is used to increase the number of displayable colors (at the expense of spatial resolution). Dithering uses a combination of some colors to create the effect of other colors.

C++ specification

```
HRESULT SetDither(BOOL bDither);
```

Parameters

bDither. The new dithering mode for your device. The default value is TRUE.

Returns

Successful: D3DRM_OK

Error: One of the Direct3D Retained-Mode return values.

See also

IDirect3DRMDevice::GetDither

Example

```
// Set the number of shades in the ramp of colors for shading to 32
if (FAILED(dev->SetShades(32)))
    goto generic_error;
// Set the default colors for a Direct3DRMTexture object to 64
if (FAILED(lpD3DRM->SetDefaultTextureColors(64)))
    goto generic_error;
// Set the default shades to be used for a Direct3DRMTexture object to 32
if (FAILED(lpD3DRM->SetDefaultTextureShades(32)))
    goto generic_error;
// Sets the dither flag for the device to FALSE
if (dev->SetDither(FALSE) != D3DRM_OK)
 goto generic_error;
```

IDirect3DRMDevice::SetQuality

Description

This method is used to set the rendering quality of your device Remember that this value is the *maximum* quality at which rendering will be performed on the rendering surface of your device. You can set the rendering quality for each mesh differently, but none can have a value higher than the value indicated in this call. You can also give different devices different qualities.

C++ specification

```
HRESULT SetQuality (D3DRMRENDERQUALITY rqQuality);
```

Parameters

rqQuality. Consists of one or more of the members of the enumerated types from the D3DRMRENDERQUALITY type. The default value is D3DRMRENDER_FLAT.

Successful: D3DRM_OK

Error: One of the Direct3D Retained-Mode return values.

See also

IDirect3DRMDevice::GetQuality

Example

```
D3DRMRENDERQUALITY quality = D3DRMRENDER_GOURAUD;
LPDIRECT3DRMDEVICE dev;
    .

    .
if (dev->SetQuality (quality) != D3DRM_OK)
 {
     Msg("Failed to set quality.\n");
     goto generic_error;
 }
```

IDirect3DRMDevice::SetShades

Description

This method is used to set the number of shades in a ramp of colors to be used for shading.

C++ specification

```
HRESULT SetShades(DWORD ulShades);
```

Parameters

ulShades. The new number of shades. This parameter must have a value that is a power of 2. The default value is 32.

Returns

Successful: D3DRM_OK

Error: One of the Direct3D Retained-Mode return values.

See also

IDirect3DRMDevice::GetShades

Example

```
LPDIRECT3DRMDEVICE dev;
    .

    .
// Set the number of shades in the ramp of colors for shading to 32
if (dev->SetShades(32) != D3DRM_OK)
```

```
  goto generic_error;
// Set the default colors for a Direct3DRMTexture object to 64
if (FAILED(lpD3DRM->SetDefaultTextureColors(64)))
  goto generic_error;
// Set the default shades to be used for a Direct3DRMTexture object to 32
if (FAILED(lpD3DRM->SetDefaultTextureShades(32)))
  goto generic_error;
// Sets the dither flag for the device to FALSE
if (FAILED(dev->SetDither(FALSE)))
  goto generic_error;
```

IDirect3DRMDevice::SetTextureQuality

Description

This method is used to set the texture quality for your device.

C++ specification

```
HRESULT SetTextureQuality(D3DRMTEXTUREQUALITY tqTextureQuality);
```

Parameters

tqTextureQuality. This parameter indicates one of the members of the D3DRM-TEXTUREQUALITY enumerated type. The default value is D3DRMTEXTURE_-NEAREST.

Returns

Successful: D3DRM_OK

Error: One of the Direct3D Retained-Mode return values.

See also

IDirect3DRMDevice::GetTextureQuality

Example

```
LPDIRECT3DRMDEVICE dev;
 .
 .
BOOLFiltering=FALSE;// Set texture filtering to off
if (Filtering)
if (dev->SetTextureQuality(D3DRMTEXTURE_NEAREST) != D3DRM_OK)
  goto generic_error;
else
    if (dev->SetTextureQuality(D3DRMTEXTURE_LINEAR) != D3DRM_OK)
  goto generic_error;
```

IDirect3DRMDevice::Update

Description

This method is used to copy the image which has been rendered to your display. It also provides a heartbeat function to your device driver. Every time this method is called, the system will call your application-defined callback function, D3DRMUPDATECALLBACK. To add a callback function, you use the IDirect3D-RMDevice::AddUpdateCallback method.

C++ specification

```
HRESULT Update();
```

Returns

Successful: D3DRM_OK
Error: One of the Direct3D Retained-Mode return values.

See also

IDirect3DRMDevice::AddUpdateCallback, D3DRMUPDATECALLBACK

Example

```
LPDIRECT3DRMDEVICE dev;
  .
  .
// Copy our rendered image to the display
if (dev->Update() != D3DRM_OK)
  goto generic_error;
```

chapter 25

The IDirect3DRMFace interface

The IDirect3DRMFace interface and methods

The IDirect3DRMFace methods are used to interact with a single polygon in a mesh. The Direct3DRMFace object is created by calling the `IDirect3DRM::CreateFace` method.

Like all COM interfaces, this interface inherits the IUnknown interface methods. These consist of `AddRef`, `QueryInterface`, and `Release`.

The IDirect3DRMDevice interface methods can be organized into the groups in table 25.1.

Table 25.1 IDirect3DRMDevice methods

Group	Methods
Buffer counts	GetBufferCount
	SetBufferCount
Color models	GetColorModel
Dithering	GetDither
	SetDither
Initialization	Init
	InitFromClipper
	InitFromD3D
Miscellaneous	GetDirect3DDevice
	GetHeight
	GetTrianglesDrawn
	GetViewports
	GetWidth
	GetWireframeOptions
	Update
Notifications	AddUpdateCallback
	DeleteUpdateCallback
Rendering quality	GetQuality
	SetQuality
Shading	GetShades
	SetShades
Texture quality	GetTextureQuality
	SetTextureQuality

In addition, the IDirect3DRMFace interface inherits the following methods from the IDirect3DRMObject interface:

Table 25.2 Methods inherited from IDirect3DRMFace

Methods
AddDestroyCallback
Clone
DeleteDestroyCallback
GetAppData
GetClassName
GetName
SetAppData
SetName

IDirect3DRMFace::AddVertex

Description

Adds a vertex to a Direct3DRMFace object.

C++ specification

```
HRESULT AddVertex(D3DVALUE x, D3DVALUE y, D3DVALUE z);
```

Parameters

x, y, and z. The x, y, and z components of your new vertex's position.

Returns

Successful: D3DRM_OK

Error: One of the Direct3D Retained-Mode return values.

See also

IDirect3DRMFace::GetVertex

Example

```
LPDIRECT3DRMFACE myFace;
if (myFace->AddVertex(D3DVALUE(x),D3DVALUE(z),D3DVALUE(y)) !=
        D3DRM_OK)
    goto generic_error;
```

IDirect3DRMFace::AddVertexAndNormalIndexed

Description

This method is used to add a vertex and a normal to your Direct3DRMFace object. The method takes two parameters holding an index for the vertex and an index for the normal in the MeshBuilder containing the vertex. The face, vertex, and normal are required to already be part of a Direct3DRMMeshBuilder object.

C++ specification

```
HRESULT AddVertexAndNormalIndexed(DWORD vertex, DWORD normal);
```

Parameters

vertex. Index of the vertex you wish to add.

normal. Index of the normal you wish to add.

Returns

Successful: D3DRM_OK

Error: One of the Direct3D Retained-Mode return values.

See also

IDirect3DRMFace::GetVertex

Example

```
LPDIRECT3DRMFACE face;
DWORD vertex;
DWORD normal;
   .
   .
if (face->AddVertexAndNormalIndexed(vertex, normal) != D3DRM_OK)
   goto generic_error;
```

IDirect3DRMFace::GetColor

Description

This method is used to retrieve the color of your Direct3DRMFace object.

C++ specification

```
D3DCOLOR GetColor();
```

Returns

The color of your object.

See also

IDirect3DRMFace::SetColor

Example

```
D3DCOLOR c;

if (mesh->GetFaceCount()) {
  LPDIRECT3DRMFACEARRAY faces;
  LPDIRECT3DRMFACE face;
  mesh->GetFaces(&faces);
  faces->GetElement(0, &face);
  c = face->GetColor();
  RELEASE(face);
  RELEASE(faces);
}
```

IDirect3DRMFace::GetMaterial

Description

This method is used to acquire the material of your Direct3DRMFace object.

C++ specification

```
HRESULT GetMaterial(LPDIRECT3DRMMATERIAL* lplpMaterial);
```

Parameters

lplpMaterial. This parameter holds the address of a variable you wish filled with a pointer to the Direct3DRMMaterial object applied to this face.

Returns

Successful: D3DRM_OK

Error: One of the Direct3D Retained-Mode return values.

See also

IDirect3DRMFace::SetMaterial

Example

```
HRESULT hRes;
IDirect3DRMFace* pFace;
IDirect3DRMMaterial* pD3DRMMat;
  .

  .
hRes = pFace->GetMaterial(&pD3DRMMat);
if (hRes != D3DRM_OK)
  goto generic_error;
```

IDirect3DRMFace::GetNormal

Description

This method is used to acquire the normal vector of the Direct3DRMFace object.

C++ specification

```
HRESULT GetNormal(D3DVECTOR *lpNormal);
```

Parameters

lpNormal. The address of a D3DVECTOR structure you wish filled with the normal vector of this face.

Returns

Successful: D3DRM_OK

Error: One of the Direct3D Retained-Mode return values.

See also

IDirect3DRMFace::AddVertexAndNormalIndexed

```
HRESULT hRes;
IDirect3DRMFace* pFace;
D3DVECTOR *lpNormal;
  .

  .
hRes = pFace->GetNormal(lpNormal);
if (hRes != D3DRM_OK)
  goto generic_error;
```

IDirect3DRMFace::GetTexture

Description

This method is used to acquire the Direct3DRMTexture object which is applied to the Direct3DRMFace object.

C++ specification

```
HRESULT GetTexture(LPDIRECT3DRMTEXTURE* lplpTexture);
```

Parameters

lplpTexture. The address of a variable you wish filled with a pointer to the texture which is applied to the face.

Returns

Successful: D3DRM_OK

Error: One of the Direct3D Retained-Mode return values.

See also

IDirect3DRMFace::SetTexture

Example

```
IDirect3DRMTexture* myTex;
IDirect3DRMFaceArray* myFaceArray;
IDirect3DRMFace* myFace;
IDirect3DRMMeshBuilder* myMeshBuilder;
  .

  .
myMeshBuilder->GetFaces(&myFaceArray);
myFaceArray->GetElement(0, &myFace);
HRESULT result = myFace->GetTexture(&myTex);
if (result != D3DRM_OK)
  goto generic_error;
```

IDirect3DRMFace::GetTextureCoordinateIndex

Description

This method is used to acquire the index of the vertex, corresponding to the index you pass in the `dwIndex` parameter, for texture coordinates in your face's mesh.

C++ specification

```
int GetTextureCoordinateIndex(DWORD dwIndex);
```

Parameters

`dwIndex`. The index within the face of the vertex.

Returns

The requested index.

See also

IDirect3DRMFace::GetTextureCoordinates
IDirect3DRMFace::GetTextureTopology

Example

```
DWORD dwIndex;
LPDIRECT3DRMFACE myFace;
  .
  .
index = myFace->GetTextureCoordinateIndex(dwIndex);
```


IDirect3DRMFace::GetTextureCoordinates

Description

This method is used to acquire the texture coordinates of a vertex in your Direct3DRMFace object.

C++ specification

```
HRESULT GetTextureCoordinates(DWORD index, D3DVALUE *lpU,
  D3DVALUE *lpV);
```

Parameters

`index`. The index of the vertex.

`lpU` and `lpV`. The addresses of variables you wish filled with the texture coordinates of the vertex.

Successful: D3DRM_OK

Error: One of the Direct3D Retained-Mode return values.

See also

IDirect3DRMFace::GetTextureCoordinateIndex

IDirect3DRMFace::GetTextureTopology

Example

```
DWORD index;
D3DVALUE *lpU = NULL;
D3DVALUE *lpV = NULL;
LPDIRECT3DRMFACE myFace;
     .
     .
HRESULT result = myFace->GetTextureCoordinates(index, lpU, lpV);
if (RESULT != d3drm_ok)
    goto generic_error;
```

IDirect3DRMFace::GetTextureTopology

Description

This method is used to acquire the texture topology of your Direct3DRMFace object.

C++ specification

```
HRESULT GetTextureTopology(BOOL *lpU, BOOL *lpV);
```

Parameters

lpU and lpV. These parameters hold the addresses of variables which are set or cleared based upon how the cylindrical wrapping flags are set for this face.

Returns

Successful: D3DRM_OK

Error: One of the Direct3D Retained-Mode return values.

See also

IDirect3DRMFace::GetTextureCoordinates

IDirect3DRMFace::SetTextureTopology

Example

```
BOOL * lpbWrap_u;
BOOL * lpbWrap_v;
```

```
LPDIRECT3DRMFRAME myFrame;
  .
  .
if (myFrame->GetTextureTopology(lpbWrap_u, lpbWrap_v) != D3DRM_OK)
    goto generic_error;
```

IDirect3DRMFace::GetVertex

Description

This method is used to acquire the position and normal of a vertex in your Direct3DRMFace object.

C++ specification

```
HRESULT GetVertex(DWORD index, D3DVECTOR *lpPosition,
  D3DVECTOR *lpNormal);
```

Parameters

index. The index of the vertex.

lpPosition and lpNormal. The addresses of two D3DVECTOR structures you wish filled with the position and normal of the vertex

Returns

Successful: D3DRM_OK

Error: One of the Direct3D Retained-Mode return values.

See also

IDirect3DRMFace::GetVertexCount

IDirect3DRMFace::GetVertexIndex

IDirect3DRMFace::GetVertices

Example

```
LPDIRECT3DRMFACE myFace;
D3DVECTOR vecFace, vecNormalFace;
if (myFace->GetVertex(0,&vecFace, &vecNormalFace) != D3DRM_OK)
    goto generic_error;
```

IDirect3DRMFace::GetVertexCount

Description

This method is used to acquire the number of vertices in your Direct3DRMFace object.

C++ specification

```
int GetVertexCount();
```

Returns

This method is used to return the number of vertices for the face.

See also

IDirect3DRMFace::GetVertex
IDirect3DRMFace::GetVertexIndex
IDirect3DRMFace::GetVertices

Example

```
LPDIRECT3DRMFACE myFace;
int myVertexCount = myFace->GetVertexCount();
```

IDirect3DRMFace::GetVertexIndex

Description

This method is used to acquire the index of the vertex, which corresponds to the index in the dwIndex parameter, in your face's mesh.

C++ specification

```
int GetVertexIndex (DWORD dwIndex);
```

Parameters

dwIndex. The index of your vertex in this face.

Returns

This method returns the index of the vertex.

See also

IDirect3DRMFace::GetVertex
IDirect3DRMFace::GetVertexCount
IDirect3DRMFace::GetVertices

Example

```
LPDIRECT3DRMFACE myFace;
DWORD dwIndex;
.

.
int myVertexIndex = myFace->GetVertexIndex(dwIndex);
```

IDirect3DRMFace::GetVertices

Description

This method acquires the position and normal vector of each vertex in your Direct3DRMFace object.

C++ specification

```
HRESULT GetVertices(DWORD *lpdwVertexCount, D3DVECTOR *lpPosition,
  D3DVECTOR *lpNormal);
```

Parameters

lpdwVertexCount. The address of a variable you wish to be filled with the number of vertices. You cannot set this parameter to NULL.

lpPosition and lpNormal. Two arrays of D3DVECTOR structures you wish to be filled with the positions and normal vectors of the vertices. If you set both of these parameters to NULL, the method will fill the lpdwVertexCount parameter with the number of vertices which are acquired.

Returns

Successful: D3DRM_OK

Error: One of the Direct3D Retained-Mode return values.

See also

IDirect3DRMFace::GetVertex

IDirect3DRMFace::GetVertexCount

IDirect3DRMFace::GetVertexIndex

Example

```
LPDIRECT3DRMFACE myFace;
D3DVECTOR lpPosition[100], lpNormal[100];
DWORD numVert;
    .
    .
if (myFace->GetVertices(&numVert, lpPosition, lpNormal ) != D3DRM_OK)
    goto generic_error;
```

IDirect3DRMFace::SetColor

Description

This method is used to set a Direct3DRMFace object to a specified color. Setting the color of your object's faces will also cause your textures to acquire this color also.

C++ specification
```
HRESULT SetColor(D3DCOLOR color);
```

Parameters

color. The color you wish to set.

Returns

Successful: D3DRM_OK

Error: One of the Direct3D Retained-Mode return values.

See also

IDirect3DRMFace::GetColor

IDirect3DRMFace::SetColorRGB

Example
```
LPDIRECT3DRMFACE myFace;
D3DCOLOR myColor;
if (myFace->SetColor( myColor ) != D3DRM_OK)
    goto generic_error;
```

IDirect3DRMFace::SetColorRGB

Description

This method is used to set your Direct3DRMFace object to a requested color. Like IDirect3DRMFace::SetColor, setting your object's color will also cause the texture applied to take on this color.

C++ specification
```
HRESULT SetColorRGB(D3DVALUE red, D3DVALUE green, D3DVALUE blue);
```

Parameters

red, green, and blue. The red, green, and blue components of your color.

Returns

Successful: D3DRM_OK

Error: One of the Direct3D Retained-Mode return values.

See also

IDirect3DRMFace::GetColor

IDirect3DRMFace::SetColor

Example
```
LPDIRECT3DRMFACE myFace;
```

Plate 1 abomsnow.jpg

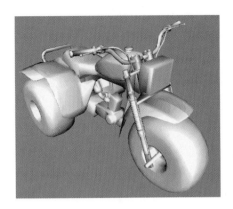

Plate 2 83atc110.jpg

Plate 3 b17.jpg

Plate 4 bridget.jpg

Plate 5 lady2.jpg

Plate 6 dartbord.jpg

Plate 7 chrflwbr.jpg

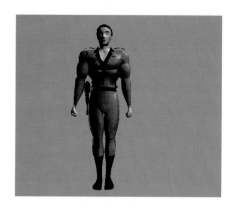

Plate 8 mark.jpg

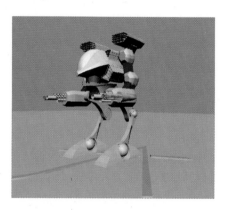

Plate 9 robot.jpg

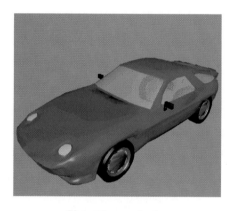

Plate 10 porsche.jpg

Plate 11 female2.jpg

Plate 12 r96033.jpg

Plate 13 indycar1.jpg

Plate 14 gidget.jpg

Plate 15 roller.jpg

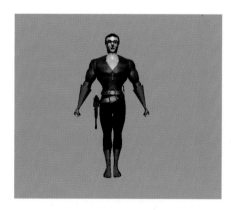

Plate 16 frank.jpg

Plate 17 r96005a.jpg

Plate 18 mallet.jpg

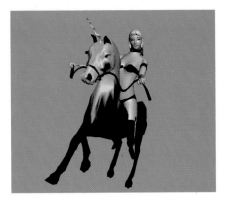

Plate 19 dominique.jpg

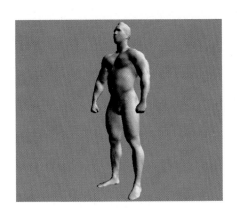

Plate 20 theo16.jpg

Plate 21 pcc11.jpg

Plate 22 bull.jpg

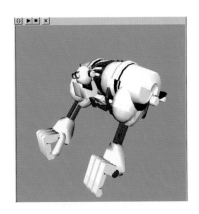

Plate 23 ape1.jpg

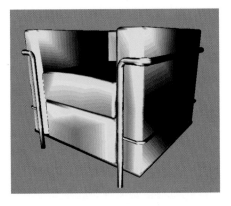

Plate 24 corbu.jpg

```
if (myFace->SetColorRGB( D3DVALUE(.69), D3DVALUE(.72),
    D3DVALUE(.96)) != D3DRM_OK)
    goto generic_error;
```

IDirect3DRMFace::SetMaterial

Description

This method is used to set the material of your Direct3DRMFace object.

C++ specification

```
HRESULT SetMaterial(LPDIRECT3DRMMATERIAL lpD3DRMMaterial);
```

Parameters

lpD3DRMMaterial. The address of your material.

Returns

Successful: D3DRM_OK

Error: One of the Direct3D Retained-Mode return values.

See also

IDirect3DRMFace::GetMaterial

Example

```
LPDIRECT3DRMMATERIAL myMaterial;
LPDIRECT3DRMFACE myFace;
    .
    .
if (myMaterial==0)
    d3drm->CreateMaterial( D3DVALUE(5), &myMaterial );
if (myFace->SetMaterial( myMaterial ) != D3DRM_OK)
    goto generic_error;
```

IDirect3DRMFace::SetTexture

Description

This method is used to set the texture of your Direct3DRMFace object.

C++ specification

```
HRESULT SetTexture(LPDIRECT3DRMTEXTURE lpD3DRMTexture);
```

Parameters

lpD3DRMTexture. The address of your texture.

Successful: D3DRM_OK

Error: One of the Direct3D Retained-Mode return values.

See also

IDirect3DRMFace::GetTexture

Example

```
IDirect3DRMFace* myFace;
IDirect3DRMTexture* myTex;
if(myTex)
{
 myTex->SetDecalScale(TRUE);
 myTex->SetDecalOrigin(128,128);
 myTex->SetShades(1);
 myTex->SetColors(256);
 if (myFace->SetTexture(myTex) != D3DRM_OK)
    goto generic_error;
 myTex->Release();
}
```

IDirect3DRMFace::SetTextureCoordinates

Description

This method is used to set the texture coordinates of a requested vertex in your Direct3DRMFace object.

C++ specification

```
HRESULT SetTextureCoordinates(DWORD vertex, D3DVALUE u, D3DVALUE v);
```

Parameters

vertex. The index of the vertex you wish set.

u and v. The texture coordinates you wish to assign to the requested vertex.

Returns

Successful: D3DRM_OK

Error: One of the Direct3D Retained-Mode return values.

See also

IDirect3DRMFace::GetTextureCoordinateIndex

IDirect3DRMFace::GetTextureTopology

Example

```
LPDIRECT3DRMTEXTURE texture;
```

```
LPDIRECT3DRMFACE CurrFace;
int myLeftTop;
int myRightTop;
int myRightBottom;
int myLeftBottom;
.
.
.
if (texture)
 {
   CurrFace->SetTexture(texture);
   if (CurrFace->SetTextureCoordinates(myLeftTop,
       D3DVAL(0.0),D3DVAL(0.0)) != D3DRM_OK)
    goto generic_error;
   if (CurrFace->SetTextureCoordinates(myRightTop,
       D3DVAL(1.0),D3DVAL(0.0)) != D3DRM_OK)
    goto generic_error;
  if (CurrFace->SetTextureCoordinates(myRightBottom,
       D3DVAL(1.0),D3DVAL(1.0)) != D3DRM_OK)
    goto generic_error;
   if (CurrFace->SetTextureCoordinates(myLeftBottom,
       D3DVAL(0.0),D3DVAL(1.0)) != D3DRM_OK)
    goto generic_error;
 }
```

IDirect3DRMFace::SetTextureTopology

Description

This method is used to set the texture topology of your Direct3DRMFace object.

C++ specification

```
HRESULT SetTextureTopology(BOOL cylU, BOOL cylV);
```

Parameters

cylU and cylV. These parameters are used to indicate if the texture has a cylindrical topology in the u and v dimensions.

Returns

Successful: D3DRM_OK

Error: One of the Direct3D Retained-Mode return values.

See also

IDirect3DRMFace::GetTextureTopology

IDirect3DRMFace::GetTextureCoordinateIndex

Example

```
LPDIRECT3DRMTEXTURE texture;
LPDIRECT3DRMFACE CurrFace;
BOOL cylU = TRUE;
BOOL cylV = FALSE;
 .
 .
if (texture)
 {
   if (CurrFace->SetTextureTopology(cylU, cylV) != D3DRM_OK)
    goto generic_error;
```

chapter 26

The IDirect3DRMFrame interface

The IDirect3DRMFrame interface and methods

The methods of the IDirect3DRMFrame interface are used to interact with an object's frame of reference (frames).

You obtain the Direct3DRMFrame object by calling the `IDirect3DRM::Create-Frame` method.

Like all COM interfaces, this interface inherits the IUnknown interface methods. These consist of `AddRef`, `QueryInterface`, and `Release`.

The IDirect3DRMFrame interface methods can be organized into the groups shown in table 26.1.

Table 26.1 IDirect3DRMFrame methods

Group	Methods
Background	GetSceneBackground
	GetSceneBackgroundDepth
	SetSceneBackground
	SetSceneBackgroundDepth
	SetSceneBackgroundImage
	SetSceneBackgroundRGB
Color	GetColor
	SetColor
	SetColorRGB
Fog	GetSceneFogColor
	GetSceneFogEnable
	GetSceneFogMode
	GetSceneFogParams
	SetSceneFogColor
	SetSceneFogEnable
	SetSceneFogMode
	SetSceneFogParams
Hierarchies	AddChild
	DeleteChild
	GetChildren
	GetParent
	GetScene
Lighting	AddLight
	DeleteLight
	GetLights
Loading	Load
Material modes	GetMaterialMode
	SetMaterialMode
Positioning and Movement	AddMoveCallback
	AddRotation
	AddScale
	AddTranslation
	DeleteMoveCallback
	GetOrientation
	GetPosition
	GetRotation

Table 26.1 IDirect3DRMFrame methods

	GetVelocity
	LookAt
	Move
	SetOrientation
	SetPosition
	SetRotation
	SetVelocity
Sorting	GetSortMode
	GetZbufferMode
	SetSortMode
	SetZbufferMode
Textures	GetTexture
	GetTextureTopology
	SetTexture
	SetTextureTopology
Transformations	AddTransform
	GetTransform
	InverseTransform
	Transform
Visual objects	AddVisual
	DeleteVisual
	GetVisuals

In addition, the IDirect3DRMFrame interface inherits the following methods from the IDirect3DRMObject interface:

Table 26.2 Methods inherited from IDirect3DRMObject

Methods
AddDestroyCallback
Clone
DeleteDestroyCallback
GetAppData
GetClassName
GetName
SetAppData
SetName

IDirect3DRMFrame::AddChild

Description

This method is used to add a child frame to your frame hierarchy. If you add a frame as a child which already has a parent, this method will remove it from its previous parent before it is added to the new parent.

If you wish to preserve your object's transformation information, you need to use the IDirect3DRMFrame::GetTransform method. This will retrieve your object's transformation, which you need to do before using the AddChild method. You then can reapply the transformation after your frame has been added.

C++ specification

```
HRESULT AddChild(LPDIRECT3DRMFRAME lpD3DRMFrameChild);
```

Parameters

lpD3DRMFrameChild. The address of your Direct3DRMFrame object you wish to be added as a child.

Returns

Successful: D3DRM_OK

Error: One of the Direct3D Retained-Mode return values.

See also

IDirect3DRM::GetTextureCreateFace

Example

```
LPDIRECT3DRMFRAME RotationFrame;
LPDIRECT3DRMFRAME myFrame;
.
.
if (RotationFrame->AddChild(myFrame) != D3DRM_OK)
    goto generic_error;
```

IDirect3DRMFrame::AddLight

Description

This method is used to add a light to your frame.

C++ specification

```
HRESULT AddLight(LPDIRECT3DRMLIGHT lpD3DRMLight);
```

Parameters

    lpD3DRMLight. The address of a variable containing the Direct3DRMLight object you wish to add to your frame.

Returns

    Successful: D3DRM_OK

    Error: One of the Direct3D Retained-Mode return values.

See also

    IDirect3DRM::CreateLight

Example

```
LPDIRECT3DRMMESHBUILDER builder = NULL;
LPDIRECT3DRMLIGHT light = NULL;
LPDIRECT3DRMFRAME frame = NULL;
HRESULT rval;
 .

 .
if (FAILED(lpD3DRM->CreateLightRGB (D3DRMLIGHT_POINT, D3DVAL(1.0),
                            D3DVAL(1.0),
                            D3DVAL(1.0),
                            &light)))
   goto generic_error;
 } else if (strcmp(wparam, "LIGHT_SPOT") == 0)
 {
  rval = builder->Load("camera.x", NULL, D3DRMLOAD_FROMFILE, NULL,
       NULL);
  if (rval != D3DRM_OK)
  {
   Msg("Failed to load camera.x.\n%s", MyErrorToString(rval));
   goto ret_with_error;
  }
  if (FAILED(builder->SetQuality(D3DRMRENDER_UNLITFLAT)))
   goto generic_error;
  if (FAILED(lpD3DRM->CreateLightRGB(D3DRMLIGHT_SPOT, D3DVAL(1.0),
                            D3DVAL(1.0),
                            D3DVAL(1.0),
                            &light)))
   goto generic_error;
 }
 if (FAILED(lpD3DRM->CreateFrame(scene, &frame)))
  goto generic_error;
 if (FAILED(frame->SetPosition (camera, D3DVAL(0.0), D3DVAL(0.0),
       D3DVAL(10.0))))
  goto generic_error;
 if (FAILED(frame->AddVisual (builder)))
  goto generic_error;
```

```
if (frame->AddLight (light) != D3DRM_OK)
    goto generic_error;
```

IDirect3DRMFrame::AddMoveCallback

Description

This method is used to add a callback function for your special movement processing.

C++ specification

```
HRESULT AddMoveCallback(D3DRMFRAMEMOVECALLBACK d3drmFMC, VOID * lpArg);
```

Parameters

d3drmFMC. Your application-defined D3DRMFRAMEMOVECALLBACK callback function.

lpArg. Your application-defined data, which can be NULL, you wish passed to the callback function.

Returns

Successful: D3DRM_OK

Error: One of the Direct3D Retained-Mode return values.

See also

IDirect3DRMFrame::Move

IDirect3DRMFrame::DeleteMoveCallback

Example

```
LPDIRECT3DRMFRAME      floor_frame;
 .
 .
if (FAILED (lpD3DRM->CreateFrame (scene, &floor_frame)))
 {
  Msg("Failed to create frame\n");
  goto generic_error;
 }
if (FAILED (floor_frame->AddRotation (D3DRMCOMBINE_BEFORE , D3DVAL
      (1.0),
                            D3DVAL (0.0),
                            D3DVAL (0.0),
                            D3DVAL (pi))))
 {
  Msg ("Failed to rotate a frame\n");
  goto generic_error;
 }

if (FAILED (floor_frame->SetPosition (scene , D3DVAL (30.0),
                        D3DVAL (0.0),
```

```
                D3DVAL (30.0))))
    {
     Msg ("Failed to rotate a frame\n");
     goto generic_error;
    }

    if (floor_frame->AddMoveCallback (GroundCheck, 0) != D3DRM_OK)
        goto generic_error;
```

IDirect3DRMFrame::AddRotation

Description

This method is used to add a rotation about (rvX, rvY, rvZ) by the number of radians passed in rvTheta for this frame. The objects in this frame are effected only once as opposed to the IDirect3DRMFrame::SetRotation, which changes the matrix every render tick.

C++ specification

```
HRESULT AddRotation(D3DRMCOMBINETYPE rctCombine, D3DVALUE rvX,
  D3DVALUE rvY, D3DVALUE rvZ, D3DVALUE rvTheta);
```

Parameters

rctCombine. This parameter holds a member of the D3DRMCOMBINETYPE enumerated type which specifies how you wish to combine the new rotation with any current frame transformation.

rvX, rvY, and rvZ. The axis about which to rotate.

rvTheta. The angle of rotation in radians.

Returns

Successful: D3DRM_OK

Error: One of the Direct3D Retained-Mode return values.

See also

IDirect3DRMFrame::SetRotation

Example

```
LPDIRECT3DRMFRAME      floor_frame;
    .
    .
    if (FAILED (lpD3DRM->CreateFrame (scene, &floor_frame)))
    {
      Msg("Failed to create frame\n");
      goto generic_error;
```

```
    }
    if (floor_frame->AddRotation (D3DRMCOMBINE_BEFORE , D3DVAL (1.0),
                                  D3DVAL (0.0),
                                  D3DVAL (0.0),
                                  D3DVAL (pi)) != D3DRM_OK)
      goto generic_error;
{
  Msg ("Failed to rotate a frame\n");
  goto generic_error;
}
```

IDirect3DRMFrame::AddScale

Description

This method is used to scale the frame's local transformation by (rvX, rvY, rvz).

C++ specification

```
HRESULT AddScale(D3DRMCOMBINETYPE rctCombine, D3DVALUE rvX,
  D3DVALUE rvY, D3DVALUE rvZ );
```

Parameters

rctCombine. A member of the D3DRMCOMBINETYPE enumerated type which indicates how to combine your new scale with the current frame transformation.

rvX, rvY, and rvz. The x, y, and z scale factors.

Returns

Successful: D3DRM_OK

Error: One of the Direct3D Retained-Mode return values.

See also

IDirect3DRMFrame::AddTransform

IDirect3DRMFrame::AddTranslation

Example

```
// Scale our scene
LPDIRECT3DRMMESHBUILDER mbuilder;
D3DRMBOX box;
D3DVALUE maxDim;

lpD3DRM->CreateMeshBuilder(&mbuilder);
mbuilder->AddFrame(frame);
mbuilder->GetBox(&box);
mbuilder->Release();maxDim = box.max.x - box.min.x;
if (box.max.y - box.min.y > maxDim)
  maxDim = box.max.y - box.min.y;
```

```
if (box.max.z - box.min.z > maxDim)
  maxDim = box.max.z - box.min.z;

if (frame->AddScale(D3DRMCOMBINE_BEFORE, D3DDivide(D3DVAL(8.0),
      maxDim),
        D3DDivide(D3DVAL(8.0), maxDim),
        D3DDivide(D3DVAL(8.0), maxDim)) != D3DRM_OK)
    goto generic_error;
```

IDirect3DRMFrame::AddTransform

Description

This method is used to transform the local coordinates of the frame by the specified affine transformation using the value of the rctCombine parameter. A 4-by-4 matrix is specified but the last column must be set to the transpose of [0 0 0 1] for the transformation to be affine.

C++ specification

```
HRESULT AddTransform(D3DRMCOMBINETYPE rctCombine,
  D3DRMMATRIX4D rmMatrix);
```

Parameters

rctCombine. The member of the D3DRMCOMBINETYPE enumerated type indicating how you wish to combine the new transformation with the current transformation.

rmMatrix. A member of the D3DRMMATRIX4D array describing the transformation matrix you wish to combine.

Returns

Successful: D3DRM_OK

Error: One of the Direct3D Retained-Mode return values.

See also

IDirect3DRMFrame::AddScale
IDirect3DRMFrame::AddTranslation

Example

```
LPDIRECT3DRMFRAME     camera = NULL;
D3DRMMATRIX4D myMatrix;
   .

   .
if (camera>AddTransform(D3DRMCOMBINE_AFTER, myMatrix) != D3DRM_OK)
    goto generic_error;
```

IDirect3DRMFrame::AddTranslation

Description

This method is used to add a translation of (rvX, rvY, rvZ) to your frame's local coordinate system.

C++ specification

```
HRESULT AddTranslation(D3DRMCOMBINETYPE rctCombine, D3DVALUE rvX,
    D3DVALUE rvY, D3DVALUE rvZ);
```

Parameters

rctCombine. A member of the D3DRMCOMBINETYPE enumerated type indicating how you wish to combine the new translation with the current translation.

rvX, rvY, and rvZ. Describes the amount to move in the x, y, and z directions.

Returns

Successful: D3DRM_OK

Error: One of the Direct3D Retained-Mode return values.

See also

IDirect3DRMFrame::AddScale

IDirect3DRMFrame::AddTranslation

Example

```
LPDIRECT3DRMFRAME     camera = NULL;
.
.
D3DVALUE Step = (wParam == VK_UP) ? 0.3f : -0.3f;
if (camera>AddTranslation(D3DRMCOMBINE_AFTER, 0.0f, D3DVAL(Step),
        0.0f) != D3DRM_OK)
    goto generic_error;
```

IDirect3DRMFrame::AddVisual

Description

This method is used to add a visual object (mesh, texture, etc.) to your frame. When you add an object to your frame, it will become visible when the frame is in view. This visual object is referenced by the frame.

C++ specification

```
HRESULT AddVisual(LPDIRECT3DRMVISUAL lpD3DRMVisual);
```

Parameters

lpD3DRMVisual. The address of a the Direct3DRMVisual object you wish to add to your frame.

Returns

Successful: D3DRM_OK

Error: One of the Direct3D Retained-Mode return values.

See also

IDirect3DRMFrame::DeleteVisual

Example

```
LPDIRECT3DRMMESH ground_meshes[gTileX][gTileY][4];
LPDIRECT3DRMFRAME ground;
    .
    .

if (ground->AddVisual(LPDIRECT3DRMVISUAL) ground_meshes[i][j][3]) !=
        D3DRM_OK)
    {
     Msg("Failed to add visual.\n");
     goto generic_error;
    }
```

IDirect3DRMFrame::DeleteChild

Description

This method is used to remove a frame from the hierarchy. If this frame is no longer referenced by anything (reference count = 0), it will be destroyed along with any child frames, lights, and meshes.

C++ specification

HRESULT DeleteChild(LPDIRECT3DRMFRAME lpChild);

Parameters

lpChild. The address of the Direct3DRMFrame object you wish to use as the child.

Returns

Successful: D3DRM_OK

Error: One of the Direct3D Retained-Mode return values.

See also

IDirect3DRMFrame::AddChild

```
static LPDIRECT3DRMFRAME selFrame = NULL, clipboardFrame;
 .
 .
void CutVisual()
{
  LPDIRECT3DRMFRAME frame;

  if (clipboardFrame)
    clipboardFrame->Release();

  if (selFrame)
   {
    clipboardFrame = selFrame;
    clipboardVisual = selVisual;

    DeselectVisual();

    clipboardFrame->AddRef();
    clipboardFrame->GetParent(&frame);
    if (frame) {
      if (frame->DeleteChild(clipboardFrame) != D3DRM_OK)
            goto generic_error;
      frame->Release();
    }
  }
}
```

IDirect3DRMFrame::DeleteLight

Description

This method is used to remove a light from your frame. It will be destroyed if it is no longer referenced.

C++ specification

```
HRESULT DeleteLight(LPDIRECT3DRMLIGHT lpD3DRMLight);
```

Parameters

lpD3DRMLight. This parameter contains the address the Direct3DRMLight object you wish to remove.

Returns

Successful: D3DRM_OK
Error: One of the Direct3D Retained-Mode return values.

See also

>   IDirect3DRMFrame::AddLight

Example

```
HRESULT hRes;
IDirect3DRMFrame* pFrame;
IDirect3DRMObject* pObject;
   .
   .
if ( pFrame->DeleteLight((LPDIRECT3DRMLIGHT)pObject) != D3DRM_OK)
    goto generic_error;
```

IDirect3DRMFrame::DeleteMoveCallback

Description

>   This method is used to remove a callback function.

C++ specification

```
HRESULT DeleteMoveCallback(D3DRMFRAMEMOVECALLBACK d3drmFMC,
    VOID * lpArg);
```

Parameters

>   d3drmFMC. Your application-defined D3DRMFRAMEMOVECALLBACK callback function.
>   lpArg. Your application-defined data which was passed to the callback function.

Returns

>   Successful: D3DRM_OK
>   Error: One of the Direct3D Retained-Mode return values.

See also

>   IDirect3DRMFrame::AddMoveCallback
>   IDirect3DRMFrame::Move

Example

```
LPDIRECT3DRMOBJECT pObj;
LPAPPLYWRAPCB myAW; // A pointer to the structure which holds the move
        callback information
HRESULT myResult;
   .
   .
ASSERT(pObj);

myAW = (LPAPPLYWRAPCB)pObj->GetAppData();
```

```
if(myAW && myAW->pFrame)
 {
  // previous callback installed -> delete
  hRes = myAW->pFrame->DeleteMoveCallback(cbApplyRelativeWrap,
       (LPVOID)myAW);
  if (hRes != D3DRM_OK)
    goto generic_error;
```

IDirect3DRMFrame::DeleteVisual

Description

This method is used to remove a visual object from your frame. It will be destroyed if it is no longer referenced.

C++ specification

```
HRESULT DeleteVisual(LPDIRECT3DRMVISUAL lpD3DRMVisual);
```

Parameters

lpD3DRMVisual. The address of the Direct3DRMVisual object to be removed.

Returns

Successful: D3DRM_OK

Error: One of the Direct3D Retained-Mode return values.

See also

IDirect3DRMFrame::AddVisual

Example

```
static int visGFeld [gTileX][gTileY];

if (visGFeld[i][j] > 0)
 {
  if (ground->DeleteVisual(
      (LPDIRECT3DRMVISUAL) ground_meshes[i][j][visGFeld[i][j]-1]))) !=
       D3DRM_OK)
   {
     Msg("Failed to delete visual.\n");
     goto generic_error;
   }
 }
```

IDirect3DRMFrame::GetChildren

Description

This method is used to acquire a list of child frames returned in a Direct3DRMFrameArray object.

C++ specification

```
HRESULT GetChildren(LPDIRECT3DRMFRAMEARRAY* lplpChildren);
```

Parameters

lplpChildren. The address of a pointer you wish to have initialized with a Direct3DRMFrameArray pointer.

Returns

Successful: D3DRM_OK

Error: One of the Direct3D Retained-Mode return values.

See also

Direct3DRMFrameArray

Example

```
LPDIRECT3DRMFRAME scene;
LPDIRECT3DRMFRAMEARRAY lpd3fa;
   .
   .
if (scene->GetChildren (&lpd3fa) != D3DRM_OK)
    goto generic_error;
// Get the number of elements in the array
DWORD NumEle = lpd3fa->GetSize();
```

IDirect3DRMFrame::GetColor

Description

This method is used to acquire the color of your frame.

C++ specification

```
D3DCOLOR GetColor();
```

Parameters

None

Returns

The color of the Direct3DRMFrame object.

        IDirect3DRMFrame::SetColor

Example
```
LPDIRECT3DRMFRAME lpFrame;
D3DCOLOR color;
.
.
color = lpFrame->GetColor();
```

IDirect3DRMFrame::GetLights

Description

This method is used to acquire a list of lights in the frame. The are returned as a Direct3DRMLightArray object.

C++ specification
```
HRESULT GetLights(LPDIRECT3DRMLIGHTARRAY* lplpLights);
```

Parameters

lplpLights. The address of a pointer you wish to be initialized with a Direct3DRMLightArray pointer.

Returns

Successful: D3DRM_OK

Error: One of the Direct3D Retained-Mode return values.

See also

    IDirect3DRMLightArray

Example
```
LPDIRECT3DRMFRAME lpFrame;
IDirect3DRMLightArray* pLightArray;
.
.
if(lpFrame->GetLights(&pLightArray) != D3DRM_OK)
 {
    // Couldn't get lights properly - Handle Error
    goto generic_error;
}

// Get the number of lights in the returned array
DWORD numLights = pLightArray->GetSize();
```

IDirect3DRMFrame::GetMaterialMode

Description
This method is used to acquire the material mode of your frame.

C++ specification
```
D3DRMMATERIALMODE GetMaterialMode();
```

Parameters
None

Returns
A member of the D3DRMMATERIALMODE enumerated type defining the current material mode.

See also
IDirect3DRMFrame::SetMaterialMode

Example
```
LPDIRECT3DRMFRAME lpFrame;
D3DRMMATERIALMODE mode;
  .

  .
mode = lpFrame->GetMaterialMode();
```

IDirect3DRMFrame::GetOrientation

Description
This method is used to acquire the orientation of a frame relative to the specified reference frame.

C++ specification
```
HRESULT GetOrientation(LPDIRECT3DRMFRAME lpRef, LPD3DVECTOR
      lprvDir,
  LPD3DVECTOR lprvUp);
```

Parameters
lpRef. The address of the Direct3DRMFrame object you wish to use as the reference.

lprvDir and lprvUp. The addresses of two D3DVECTOR structures you wish filled with the directions of the frame's z-axis and y-axis.

Returns
Successful: D3DRM_OK

Error: One of the Direct3D Retained-Mode return values.

See also

IDirect3DRMFrame::SetOrientation

Example

```
LPDIRECT3DRMFRAME scene;
LPDIRECT3DRMFRAME camera;
D3DVECTOR direction, up;
   .
   .
// Get the orientation of the camera frame relative to the scene
if (camera->GetOrientation(scene, &direction, &up) != D3DRM_OK)
    goto generic_error;
```

IDirect3DRMFrame::GetParent

Description

This method is used to retrieve the parent frame of the current frame.

C++ specification

```
HRESULT GetParent(LPDIRECT3DRMFRAME* lplpParent);
```

Parameters

lplpParent. The address of a pointer you wish filled with the pointer to the Direct3DRMFrame object representing the frame's parent. This pointer will be NULL when the method returns if the this frame is the root.

Returns

Successful: D3DRM_OK
Error: One of the Direct3D Retained-Mode return values.

See also

IDirect3DRMFrame::DeleteChild
IDirect3DRMFrame::Release

Example

```
static LPDIRECT3DRMFRAME selFrame = NULL;
   .
   .
void CutVisual()
{
  LPDIRECT3DRMFRAME frame;
```

```
      if (clipboardFrame)
        clipboardFrame->Release();

      if (selFrame)
       {
        clipboardFrame = selFrame;
        clipboardVisual = selVisual;

        DeselectVisual();

        clipboardFrame->AddRef();
        if ( clipboardFrame->GetParent(&frame) != D3DRM_OK)
          goto generic_error;
        if (frame) {
          frame->DeleteChild(clipboardFrame);
          frame->Release();
        }
       }
}
```

IDirect3DRMFrame::GetPosition

Description

This method is used to acquire the position of your frame relative to the passed reference frame. This distance will be stored in the lprvPos parameter as a vector rather than as a linear measure.

C++ specification

```
HRESULT GetPosition(LPDIRECT3DRMFRAME lpRef, LPD3DVECTOR lprv-
    Pos);
```

Parameters

lpRef. The address of the Direct3DRMFrame object you wish to use as the reference.

lprvPos. The address of a D3DVECTOR structure you wish filled with the frame's position.

Returns

Successful: D3DRM_OK

Error: One of the Direct3D Retained-Mode return values.

See also

IDirect3DRMFrame::SetPosition

Example

```
LPDIRECT3DRMFRAME scene;
LPDIRECT3DRMFRAME camera;
// Define the direction, up, and down vectors for motion information
D3DVECTOR pos, direction, up, right;
    .
    .
// Get the position of the camera frame relative to the scene
if (camera->GetPosition (scene, &pos) != D3DRM_OK)
    goto generic_error;
```

IDirect3DRMFrame::GetRotation

Description

This method is used to acquire the rotation of the frame relative to the specified frame of reference.

C++ specification

```
HRESULT GetRotation(LPDIRECT3DRMFRAME lpRef, LPD3DVECTOR lprvAxis,
    LPD3DVALUE lprvTheta);
```

Parameters

lpRef. The address of the Direct3DRMFrame object you wish to use as the reference.

lprvAxis. The address of a D3DVECTOR structure you wish to be filled with your frame's axis of rotation.

lprvTheta. The address of a variable which will hold the frame's rotation, in radians.

Returns

Successful: D3DRM_OK

Error: One of the Direct3D Retained-Mode return values.

See also

IDirect3DRMFrame::SetRotation

Example

```
IDirect3DRMFrame* pRefFrame;
D3DVECTOR dVector;
D3DVALUE dTheta;
IDirect3DRMFrame* pFrame;
HRESULT hRes;
    .
    .
```

```
hRes = pFrame->GetRotation(pRefFrame, &dVector, &dTheta);
if (hRes != D3DRM_OK)
    goto generic_error;
```

IDirect3DRMFrame::GetScene

Description

This method is used to acquire the root frame of the hierarchy which contains the passed frame.

C++ specification

```
HRESULT GetScene(LPDIRECT3DRMFRAME* lplpRoot);
```

Parameters

lplpRoot. The address of the pointer you wish filled with the pointer to the scene's root frame.

Returns

Successful: D3DRM_OK

Error: One of the Direct3D Retained-Mode return values.

See also

IDirect3DRMFrame::GetSceneBackground
IDirect3DRMFrame::GetSceneBackgroundDepth

Example

```
IDirect3DRMFrame* pRootFrame;
HRESULT hRes;
    .
    .
hRes = pFrame->GetScene(pRootFrame);
if (hRes != D3DRM_OK)
    goto generic_error;
```

IDirect3DRMFrame::GetSceneBackground

Description

This method is used to acquire the background color of a scene.

C++ specification

```
D3DCOLOR GetSceneBackground();
```

Returns

The requested color.

See also

IDirect3DRMFrame::GetScene
IDirect3DRMFrame::GetSceneBackgroundDepth

Example

```
LPDIRECT3DRMFRAME scene;
.
.
COLORREF bgcolor;
if (scene)
{
  D3DCOLOR scenecolor=scene->GetSceneBackground();
  bgcolor=D3DCOLOR_2_COLORREF(scenecolor);
}
```

IDirect3DRMFrame::GetSceneBackgroundDepth

Description

This method is used to acquire the current background-depth buffer for the scene.

C++ specification

```
HRESULT GetSceneBackgroundDepth(
  LPDIRECTDRAWSURFACE * lplpDDSurface);
```

Parameters

lplpDDSurface. The address of a pointer which is initialized with the address of a DirectDraw surface representing the current background-depth buffer.

Returns

Successful: D3DRM_OK
Error: One of the Direct3D Retained-Mode return values.

See also

IDirect3DRMFrame::SetScene
IDirect3DRMFrame::SetSceneBackgroundDepth

Example

```
HRESULT hRes;
LPDIRECT3DRMFRAME scene;
LPDIRECTDRAWSURFACE * lplpDDSurface;
```

```
   .
   if (scene)
   {
     hRes = scene->GetSceneBackgroundDepth(lplpDDSurface);
     if (hRes != D3DRM_OK)
     {
       goto generic_error;
     }
   }
```

IDirect3DRMFrame::GetSceneFogColor

Description

This method is used to retrieve the fog color of your scene.

C++ specification

```
D3DCOLOR GetSceneFogColor();
```

Returns

The fog color.

See also

IDirect3DRMFrame::GetSceneFogEnable
IDirect3DRMFrame::GetSceneFogMode
IDirect3DRMFrame::GetSceneFogParams

Example

```
LPDIRECT3DRMFRAME scene;
D3DCOLOR color = scene->GetSceneFogColor();
```

IDirect3DRMFrame::GetSceneFogEnable

Description

This method returns a boolean indicating whether fog is enabled for this scene.

C++ specification

```
BOOL GetSceneFogEnable();
```

Returns

Returns TRUE if fog is enabled, and FALSE otherwise.

See also

IDirect3DRMFrame::GetSceneFogColor

IDirect3DRMFrame::GetSceneFogMode
IDirect3DRMFrame::GetSceneFogParams

Example

```
LPDIRECT3DRMFRAME scene;
BOOL enabled = scene->GetSceneFogEnable();
```

IDirect3DRMFrame::GetSceneFogMode

Description

This method is called to acquire the current fog mode for this scene.

C++ specification

```
D3DRMFOGMODE GetSceneFogMode();
```

Returns

A member of the D3DRMFOGMODE enumerated type indicating the current fog mode.

See also

IDirect3DRMFrame::GetSceneFogColor
IDirect3DRMFrame::GetSceneFogEnable
IDirect3DRMFrame::GetSceneFogParams

Example

```
LPDIRECT3DRMFRAME scene;
D3DRMFOGMODE fogMode = scene->GetSceneFogMode();
```

IDirect3DRMFrame::GetSceneFogParams

Description

This method is used to acquire the fog parameters for your scene.

C++ specification

```
HRESULT GetSceneFogParams(D3DVALUE * lprvStart, D3DVALUE * lprvEnd,
    D3DVALUE * lprvDensity);
```

Parameters

lprvStart, lprvEnd, and lprvDensity. Pointers to variables you wish filled with
the fog start, end, and density values.

Returns

Successful: D3DRM_OK

Error: One of the Direct3D Retained-Mode return values.

See also

IDirect3DRMFrame::GetSceneFogColor

IDirect3DRMFrame::GetSceneFogEnable

IDirect3DRMFrame::GetSceneFogMode

Example

```
LPDIRECT3DRMFRAME scene;
HRESULT hRes;
D3DVALUE * lprvStart;
D3DVALUE * lprvEnd;
D3DVALUE * lprvDensity;
.
.

if ( scene->GetSceneFogParams(lprvStart, lprvEnd, lprvDensity) !=
        D3DRM_OK)
    goto generic_error;
```

IDirect3DRMFrame::GetSortMode

Description

This method is used to acquire the sorting mode used to process child frames.

C++ specification

```
D3DRMSORTMODE GetSortMode();
```

Returns

Returns a member of the D3DRMSORTMODE enumerated type indicating the sorting mode.

See also

IDirect3DRMFrame::SetSortMode

Example

```
LPDIRECT3DRMFRAME myFrame;
.
.

D3DRMSORTMODE sortMode = myFrame->GetSortMode();
```

IDirect3DRMFrame::GetTexture

Description
This method is used to acquire the texture of the frame.

C++ specification
```
HRESULT GetTexture(LPDIRECT3DRMTEXTURE* lplpTexture);
```

Parameters
lplpTexture. The address of the pointer you wish filled with the address of the frame's texture.

Returns
Successful: D3DRM_OK
Error: One of the Direct3D Retained-Mode return values.

See also
IDirect3DRMFrame::SetTexture

Example
```
LPDIRECT3DRMFRAME lpFrame;
LPDIRECT3DRMTEXTURE* lplpTexture;
HRESULT hRes;
    .
    .
hres = lpFrame->GetTexture(lplpTexture);
if (hRes != D3DRM_OK)
    goto generic_error;
```

IDirect3DRMFrame::GetTextureTopology

Description
This method is used to acquire the topological properties of a texture when mapped onto objects in the frame.

C++ specification
```
HRESULT GetTextureTopology(BOOL * lpbWrap_u, BOOL * lpbWrap_v);
```

Parameters
lpbWrap_u and lpbWrap_v. The addresses of variables which are set to TRUE if your texture is mapped in the u and v directions.

Returns

Successful: D3DRM_OK

Error: One of the Direct3D Retained-Mode return values.

See also

IDirect3DRMFrame::SetTextureTopology

Example

```
BOOL * lpbWrap_u;
BOOL * lpbWrap_v;
LPDIRECT3DRMFRAME lpFrame;
HRESULT hRes;
.
.
hres = lpFrame->GetTextureTopology(lpbWrap_u, lpbWrap_y);
if (hres != D3DRM_OK)
    goto generic_error;
```

IDirect3DRMFrame::GetTransform

Description

This method is used to acquire the local transformation of the frame as a 4-by-4 affine matrix.

C++ specification

```
HRESULT GetTransform(D3DRMMATRIX4D rmMatrix);
```

Parameters

rmMatrix. A D3DRMMATRIX4D array you wish filled with the address of your frame's transformation.

Returns

Successful: D3DRM_OK

Error: One of the Direct3D Retained-Mode return values.

See also

IDirect3DRMFrame::AddTransform

Example

```
LPDIRECT3DRMFRAME lpFrame;
D3DRMMATRIX4D rmMatrix
.
.
if (lpFrame->GetTextureTopology(rmMatrix) != D3DRM_OK)
    goto generic_error;
```

IDirect3DRMFrame::GetVelocity

Description

This method is used to acquire the velocity of your frame relative to the passed reference frame.

C++ specification

```
HRESULT GetVelocity(LPDIRECT3DRMFRAME lpRef, LPD3DVECTOR lprvVel,
    BOOL fRotVel);
```

Parameters

lpRef. The address of the Direct3DRMFrame object you wish to use as the reference.

lprvVel. The address of a D3DVECTOR structure you wish filled with the frame's velocity.

fRotVel. A flag indicating whether the rotational velocity of the object should be used when the linear velocity is retrieved. If you set this to TRUE, the object's rotational velocity will be included in the calculation.

Returns

Successful: D3DRM_OK

Error: One of the Direct3D Retained-Mode return values.

See also

IDirect3DRMFrame::SetVelocity

Example

```
LPDIRECT3DRMFRAME scene;
LPDIRECT3DRMFRAME camera;
D3DVECTOR d3vv;
.
.
if (camera->GetVelocity (scene, &d3vv, FALSE) != D3DRM_OK)
    goto generic_error;
```

IDirect3DRMFrame::GetVisuals

Description

This method is used to acquire a list of visuals in your frame.

C++ specification

```
HRESULT GetVisuals(LPDIRECT3DRMVISUALARRAY* lplpVisuals);
```

Parameters

lplpVisuals. The address of a pointer you wish to be initialized with a Direct3D-RMVisualArray pointer.

Returns

Successful: D3DRM_OK

Error: One of the Direct3D Retained-Mode return values.

See also

IDirect3DRMFrame::DeleteVisual

IDirect3DRMVisualArray::GetSize

Example

```
D3MinObj *d3mo;
LPDIRECT3DRMFRAME      lpFrame;
LPDIRECT3DRMVISUALARRAY visuals;
LPDIRECT3DRMVISUAL     visual;
DWORD                  dw;
   .
   .
d3mo = (D3MinObj *)dw;
if (TRUE == d3mo->GetPickable ())
  {
    if (lpFrame->GetVisuals (&visuals) != D3DRM_OK)
       goto generic_error;
    int j = visuals->GetSize ();
    for (int k=0;k<j;k++)
     {
       visuals->GetElement (k, &visual);
       lpFrame->DeleteVisual (visual);
     }
    j = lpFrame->Release ();
  }
```

IDirect3DRMFrame::GetZbufferMode

Description

This method is used to acquire the z-buffer mode which indicates whether z-buffering is enabled or disabled.

C++ specification

```
D3DRMZBUFFERMODE GetZbufferMode();
```

Returns

One of the members of the D3DRMZBUFFERMODE enumerated type.

See also

IDirect3DRMFrame::SetZbufferMode

Example

```
LPDIRECT3DRMFRAME myFrame;
D3DRMZBUFFERMODE mode;
  .

  .
mode = myFrame->GetZbufferMode();
```

IDirect3DRMFrame::InverseTransform

Description

This method is used to transform the vector in the lprvSrc parameter which is in world coordinates to model coordinates. The result is returned in the lprvDst parameter.

C++ specification

```
HRESULT InverseTransform(D3DVECTOR *lprvDst, D3DVECTOR *lprvSrc);
```

Parameters

lprvDst. The address of a D3DVECTOR structure you wish filled with the result of the transformation.

lprvSrc. The address of a D3DVECTOR structure which is the source of the transformation.

Returns

Successful: D3DRM_OK

Error: One of the Direct3D Retained-Mode return values.

See also

IDirect3DRMFrame::Transform

Example

```
D3DVECTOR d3v, d3v1;
LPDIRECT3DRMFRAME lpFrame;
HRESULT hRes;
  .

  .
hRes = lpFrame->InverseTransform (&d3v1, &d3v);
```

```
if (hRes != D3DRM_OK)
    goto generic_error;
```

IDirect3DRMFrame::Load

Description

This method is used to load a Direct3DRMFrame object. This method will load a frame hierarchy in the file specified by the `lpvObjSource` parameter and defaults to loading the first frame hierarchy parameter. The frame which used this method is used as the parent of the new frame hierarchy. The frame can be loaded from several sources—a file, memory block, resource, or stream.

C++ specification

```
HRESULT Load(LPVOID lpvObjSource, LPVOID lpvObjID,
    D3DRMLOADOPTIONS d3drmLOFlags,
    D3DRMLOADTEXTURECALLBACK d3drmLoadTextureProc, LPVOID lpArgLTP);
```

Parameters

lpvObjSource. The source for the object you wish loaded. The source can be a file, resource, memory block, or stream, based upon the source flags you specify in the d3drmLOFlags parameter.

lpvObjID. The object name or position you wish to load. The use of this parameter is dependent upon the identifier flags you specify in the d3drmLOFlags parameter. If you specify the D3DRMLOAD_BYPOSITION flag, this parameter will be a pointer to a DWORD value specifying the object's order in the file. You can pass this parameter as NULL.

d3drmLOFlags. The value of the D3DRMLOADOPTIONS type defining the load options.

d3drmLoadTextureProc. A D3DRMLOADTEXTURECALLBACK callback function which is called to load any textures that are used by the object requiring special formatting. You can set this parameter to NULL.

lpArgLTP. The address of your application-defined data passed to the D3DRMLOADTEXTURECALLBACK callback function.

Returns

Successful: D3DRM_OK

Error: One of the Direct3D Retained-Mode return values.

See also

IDirect3DRM::CreateFrame

```
LPDIRECT3DRMFRAME scene;
:
:
static BOOL LoadFrameHierarchy(const char *filename, AppInfo *info)
{
 LPDIRECT3DRMFRAME lpFrame;

 if (FAILED(lpD3DRM->CreateFrame(info->scene, &lpFrame)))
  return FALSE;

 if (lpFrame->Load((LPVOID)filename, NULL, D3DRMLOAD_FROMFILE,
             loadTextures, NULL) != D3DRM_OK)
   goto generic_error;

 ScaleScene(lpFrame, info);

 return TRUE;
}
```

IDirect3DRMFrame::LookAt

Description

This method is used to face your frame toward the target frame, relative to the given reference frame. The rotation is locked by the given constraints.

C++ specification

```
HRESULT LookAt(LPDIRECT3DRMFRAME lpTarget, LPDIRECT3DRMFRAME lpRef,
  D3DRMFRAMECONSTRAINT rfcConstraint);
```

Parameters

lpTarget and lpRef. The addresses of the Direct3DRMFrame objects you wish to use as the target and reference, respectively.

rfcConstraint. The member of the D3DRMFRAMECONSTRAINT enumerated type which indicates the axis of rotation to constrain.

Returns

Successful: D3DRM_OK

Error: One of the Direct3D Retained-Mode return values.

See also

IDirect3DRMFrame::SetPosition

Example

```
LPDIRECT3DRMFRAME        lights;
LPDIRECT3DRMFRAME        floor_frame;
LPDIRECT3DRMFRAME        scene;
    .
    .
if (FAILED(lights->SetPosition (scene, D3DVAL(40.0), D3DVAL(40.0),
        D3DVAL(40.0))))
  {
   Msg("Failed to SetPosition - lights & scene.\n");
   goto generic_error;
  }
lights->SetRotation (scene, D3DVAL (0.0), D3DVAL (1.0), D3DVAL (0.0),
        D3DVAL (0.02));
if (lights->LookAt (floor_frame, scene, D3DRMCONSTRAIN_Z ) != D3DRM_OK)
    goto generic_error;
```

IDirect3DRMFrame::Move

Description

This method applies the rotations and velocities to all of the frames in the given hierarchy.

C++ specification

```
HRESULT Move(D3DVALUE delta);
```

Parameters

delta: The amount you wish to change the velocity and rotation.

Returns

Successful: D3DRM_OK

Error: One of the Direct3D Retained-Mode return values.

See also

IDirect3DRMFrame::SetPosition

IDirect3DRMFrame::SetRotation

Example

```
LPDIRECT3DRMFRAME        scene;
    .
    .
// Applies the rotations and velocities for all frames in the given
// hierarchy. Change the velocity and rotation by 1.0
if (scene->Move(D3DVAL(SPEED)) != D3DRM_OK)
    goto generic_error;
```

IDirect3DRMFrame::SetColor

Description

This method is used to set the color of your frame. This color will be used for meshes in your frame when the D3DRMMATERIALMODE enumerated type is D3DRMMATERIAL_FROMFRAME.

C++ specification

```
HRESULT SetColor(D3DCOLOR rcColor);
```

Parameters

rcColor. The new color for your frame.

Returns

Successful: D3DRM_OK

Error: One of the Direct3D Retained-Mode return values.

See also

IDirect3DRMFrame::GetColor

IDirect3DRMFrame::SetMaterialMode

Example

```
LPDIRECT3DRMFRAME      myFrame;
     .
     .
D3DCOLOR frameColor=scene->GetSceneBackground();
if (myFrame->SetColor( frameColor ) != D3DRM_OK)
    goto generic_error;
```

IDirect3DRMFrame::SetColorRGB

Description

This method is used to sets the color of your frame. This color is then used for meshes in your frame when the D3DRMMATERIALMODE enumerated type is set to D3DRMMATERIAL_FROMFRAME.

C++ specification

```
HRESULT SetColorRGB(D3DVALUE rvRed, D3DVALUE rvGreen,
  D3DVALUE rvBlue);
```

Parameters

rvRed, rvGreen, and rvBlue. The new color for your frame. Each component of your color should range from 0 to 1.

Returns

    Successful: D3DRM_OK

    Error: One of the Direct3D Retained-Mode return values.

See also

    IDirect3DRMFrame::SetMaterialMode

Example

```
LPDIRECT3DRMFRAME     myFrame;
.
.
.
if (myFrame->SetColorRGB( D3DVALUE(.67), D3DVALUE(.82),
        D3DVALUE(.94) != D3DRM_OK))
    goto generic_error;
```

IDirect3DRMFrame::SetMaterialMode

Description

    This method is used to set the material mode for your frame. This material mode is used to determine the source of material information for your objects (visuals) which are rendered with the frame—if it is from the visual (mesh) object itself, from its parent, or from the frame.

C++ specification

```
HRESULT SetMaterialMode(D3DRMMATERIALMODE rmmMode);
```

Parameters

    rmmMode. Set to one of the members of the D3DRMMATERIALMODE enumerated type.

Returns

    Successful: D3DRM_OK

    Error: One of the Direct3D Retained-Mode return values.

See also

    IDirect3DRMFrame::GetMaterialMode

    D3DRMMATERIALMODE

Example

```
LPDIRECT3DRMFRAME     myFrame;
.
.
.
if (myFrame->SetMaterialMode(D3DRMMATERIAL_FROMFRAME) !=
        D3DRM_OK)
    goto generic_error;
```

IDirect3DRMFrame::SetOrientation

Description

This method is used to align a frame so that its z-direction points along the direction vector [rvDx, rvDy, rvDz] and its y-direction points along the vector [rvUx, rvUy, rvUz]. The default orientation of a frame has a direction vector of [0, 0, 1] and an up vector of [0, 1, 0].

If [rvUx, rvUy, rvUz] is parallel to [rvDx, rvDy, rvDz], the D3DRMERR_BADVALUE error value will be returned; otherwise, the [rvUx, rvUy, rvUz] vector passed to the method will be projected onto the plane which is perpendicular to [rvDx, rvDy, rvDz].

C++ specification

```
HRESULT SetOrientation(LPDIRECT3DRMFRAME lpRef, D3DVALUE rvDx,
    D3DVALUE rvDy, D3DVALUE rvDz, D3DVALUE rvUx, D3DVALUE rvUy,
    D3DVALUE rvUz);
```

Parameters

lpRef. The address of the Direct3DRMFrame object you wish to use as the reference.

rvDx, rvDy, and rvDz. The new z-axis for the frame.

rvUx, rvUy, and rvUz. The new y-axis for the frame.

Returns

Successful: D3DRM_OK

Error: One of the Direct3D Retained-Mode return values.

See also

IDirect3DRMFrame::GetOrientation

Example

```
LPDIRECT3DRMFRAME  scene, camera;

if (FAILED(camera->SetOrientation (scene, -D3DVAL(0.0), -D3DVAL(0.0),
        D3DVAL(1.0), D3DVAL(0.0), D3DVAL(1), D3DVAL(0.0))))
 {
  Msg("Failed to SetOrientation - camera/scene.\n");
  goto generic_error;
 }

if (camera->AddMoveCallback (CameraMove, 0) != D3DRM_OK)
    goto generic_error;
```

IDirect3DRMFrame::SetPosition

Description

This method is used to set the position of a frame relative to the frame of reference. The frame will be placed a distance of [rvX, rvY, rvZ] from the reference. When you create a child frame within your parent, it will be placed at [0, 0, 0] in your parent frame.

C++ specification

```
HRESULT SetPosition(LPDIRECT3DRMFRAME lpRef, D3DVALUE rvX, D3DVALUE
    rvY,
  D3DVALUE rvZ);
```

Parameters

lpRef. The address of the Direct3DRMFrame object you wish to use as the reference.

rvX, rvY, and rvZ. The new position for your frame.

Returns

Successful: D3DRM_OK

Error: One of the Direct3D Retained-Mode return values.

See also

IDirect3DRMFrame::GetPosition

Example

```
// distance between 2 nodes of the field
const double m_step = 0.5;
int i, j;

LPDIRECT3DRMFRAME      plane_frame1;
LPDIRECT3DRMFRAME      floor_frame;
.
:
if (plane_frame1->SetPosition (floor_frame, D3DVAL(j*m_step*(FELD-
      LAENGE-1)), D3DVAL(0.0), D3DVAL(i*m_step*(FELDLAENGE-1)) !=
      D3DRM_OK)
    goto generic_error;
```

IDirect3DRMFrame::SetRotation

Description

This method is used to set a frame rotating around the given vector by the given angle at each call to the `IDirect3DRM::Tick` or `IDirect3DRMFrame::Move` method. This direction vector [rvX, rvY, rvZ] is defined in the reference frame.

C++ specification

```
HRESULT SetRotation(LPDIRECT3DRMFRAME lpRef, D3DVALUE rvX, D3DVALUE
        rvY, D3DVALUE rvZ, D3DVALUE rvTheta);
```

Parameters

lpRef. The address of the Direct3DRMFrame object you wish to use as the reference.

rvX, rvY, and rvZ. The vector about which rotation will occur.

rvTheta. The rotation angle in radians.

Returns

Successful: D3DRM_OK

Error· One of the Direct3D Retained-Mode return values.

See also

IDirect3DRMFrame::AddRotation

IDirect3DRMFrame::GetRotation

Example

```
LPDIRECT3DRMFRAME  lights;
LPDIRECT3DRMFRAME  scene;
.
.
.
if (lights->SetRotation (scene, D3DVAL (0.0), D3DVAL (1.0), D3DVAL
        (0.0), D3DVAL (0.02)) != D3DRM_OK)
    goto generic_error;
```

IDirect3DRMFrame::SetSceneBackground

Description

This method is used to set the background color of your scene.

C++ specification

```
HRESULT SetSceneBackground(D3DCOLOR rcColor);
```

Parameters

> rcColor. The new color for your background.

Returns

> Successful: D3DRM_OK
>
> Error: One of the Direct3D Retained-Mode return values.

See also

> IDirect3DRMFrame::SetSceneBackgroundDepth
>
> IDirect3DRMFrame::SetSceneBackgroundImage
>
> IDirect3DRMFrame::SetSceneBackgroundRGB

Example

```
D3DCOLOR myColor
LPDIRECT3DRMFRAME  scene;
.
.
if (scene->SetSceneBackground(D3DRGB(1,1,1)) != D3DRM_OK)
    goto generic_error;
```

IDirect3DRMFrame::SetSceneBackgroundDepth

Description

> This method is used to indicate a background-depth buffer for your scene. This image must have a depth of 16. The image will be scaled first if your image and viewport sizes are different. You should set your image the same size as your viewport for the best performance when animating the background-depth buffer. This allows the depth buffer to be updated from the image memory with no added overhead.

C++ specification

```
HRESULT SetSceneBackgroundDepth(LPDIRECTDRAWSURFACE lpImage);
```

Parameters

> lpImage. The address of a DirectDraw surface you wish to store the new background depth for your scene.

Returns

> Successful: D3DRM_OK
>
> Error: One of the Direct3D Retained-Mode return values.

See also

> IDirect3DRMFrame::GetSceneBackground

IDirect3DRMFrame::SetSceneBackgroundImage
IDirect3DRMFrame::SetSceneBackgroundRGB

Example

```
HRESULT res;
LPDIRECTDRAWSURFACE myImage

res = myFrame->SetSceneBackgroundDepth(myImage);
if (res != D3DRM_)K(
    goto generic_error;
```

IDirect3DRMFrame::SetSceneBackgroundImage

Description

This method is used to specify a background image for your scene. If your image is not the same size or color depth as the viewport, your image will be scaled or converted to the correct color depth first. Because of this, you should set the image to the same size and color depth as the backgound to get the best performance for animating the background. The reason this is more efficient is that the background will be rendered directly from the image memory without the extra overhead required to manipulate the image.

C++ specification

```
HRESULT SetSceneBackgroundImage(LPDIRECT3DRMTEXTURE lpTexture);
```

Parameters

lpTexture. The address of a Direct3DRMTexture object which will contain the new background scene.

Returns

Successful: D3DRM_OK
Error: One of the Direct3D Retained-Mode return values.

See also

IDirect3DRMFrame::SetSceneBackground
IDirect3DRMFrame::SetSceneBackgroundDepth
IDirect3DRMFrame::SetSceneBackgroundRGB

Example

```
LPDIRECT3DRMTEXTURE tex;
    .

    .
lpD3DRM->LoadTexture("lake.ppm", &tex);
```

```
if (FAILED(tex->SetColors(256)))
  goto generic_error;
if (FAILED(tex->SetShades(1)))
  goto generic_error;
if (info->scene->SetSceneBackgroundImage(tex) != D3DRM_OK)
    goto generic_error;
```

IDirect3DRMFrame::SetSceneBackgroundRGB

Description

This method is used to set the background color of your scene.

C++ specification

```
HRESULT SetSceneBackgroundRGB(D3DVALUE rvRed, D3DVALUE rvGreen,
  D3DVALUE rvBlue);
```

Parameters

rvRed, rvGreen, and rvBlue. The new RGB color for your background.

Returns

Successful: D3DRM_OK

Error: One of the Direct3D Retained-Mode return values.

See also

IDirect3DRMFrame::SetSceneBackground
IDirect3DRMFrame::SetSceneBackgroundDepth
IDirect3DRMFrame::SetSceneBackgroundImage

Example

```
LPDIRECT3DRMFRAME  scene;
  .
  .
if (scene->SetSceneBackgroundRGB (D3DVAL (0.0), D3DVAL (0.0),
        D3DVAL (1.0)) != D3DRM_OK)
    goto generic_error;
```

IDirect3DRMFrame::SetSceneFogColor

Description

This method is used to set the fog color of your scene.

C++ specification

```
HRESULT SetSceneFogColor(D3DCOLOR rcColor);
```

Parameters

rcColor. The new color for your fog.

Returns

Successful: D3DRM_OK

Error: One of the Direct3D Retained-Mode return values.

See also

IDirect3DRMFrame::SetSceneFogEnable

IDirect3DRMFrame::SetSceneFogMode

IDirect3DRMFrame::SetSceneFogParams

Example

```
D3DCOLOR myColor;
if (scene->SetSceneFogColor(myColor) != D3DRM_OK)
    goto generic_error;
```

IDirect3DRMFrame::SetSceneFogEnable

Description

This method is used to set the fog enable state.

C++ specification

```
HRESULT SetSceneFogEnable(BOOL bEnable);
```

Parameters

bEnable. The new fog enable state.

Returns

Successful: D3DRM_OK

Error: One of the Direct3D Retained-Mode return values.

See also

IDirect3DRMFrame::SetSceneFogColor

IDirect3DRMFrame::SetSceneFogMode

IDirect3DRMFrame::SetSceneFogParams

Example

```
BOOL bFog = (bFog==TRUE)? FALSE:TRUE; // toggle
if (scene->SetSceneFogEnable(bFog) != D3DRM_OK)
    goto generic_error;
```

IDirect3DRMFrame::SetSceneFogMode

Description
This method is used to set the fog mode.

C++ specification
```
HRESULT SetSceneFogMode(D3DRMFOGMODE rfMode);
```

Parameters
rfMode. This parameter, used to specify your new fog mode, holds one of the members of the D3DRMFOGMODE enumerated type.

Returns
Successful: D3DRM_OK

Error: One of the Direct3D Retained-Mode return values.

See also
IDirect3DRMFrame::SetSceneFogColor

IDirect3DRMFrame::SetSceneFogEnable

IDirect3DRMFrame::SetSceneFogParams

Example
```
if (scene->SetSceneFogMode(D3DRMFOG_LINEAR) != D3DRM_OK)
    goto generic_error;
```

IDirect3DRMFrame::SetSceneFogParams

Description
This method is used to set the current fog parameters for your scene.

C++ specification
```
HRESULT SetSceneFogParams(D3DVALUE rvStart, D3DVALUE rvEnd,
    D3DVALUE rvDensity);
```

Parameters
rvStart and rvEnd. These parameters set the fog start and end points for linear fog mode. You use these settings to indicate the distance from the camera at which you wish fog effects to first become visible and the distance at which you wish fog to reach its maximum density.

rvDensity. The fog density for the exponential fog modes with a range from 0 through 1.

Successful: D3DRM_OK

Error: One of the Direct3D Retained-Mode return values.

See also

IDirect3DRMFrame::SetSceneFogColor

IDirect3DRMFrame::SetSceneFogEnable

IDirect3DRMFrame::SetSceneFogMode

Example

```
HRESULT result;
D3DVALUE rvStart, rvEnd, rvDensity;
:
:
:
rvStart = 100;
rvEnd = 500;
rvDensity = .5;
result = SetSceneFogParams(rvStart, rvEnd, rvDensity);
if (result != D3DRM_OK)
    goto generic_error;
```

IDirect3DRMFrame::SetSortMode

Description

This method is used to set the sorting mode you wish to use to process child frames. You can use this method to change the properties of the hidden-surface-removal algorithms.

C++ specification

```
HRESULT SetSortMode(D3DRMSORTMODE d3drmSM);
```

Parameters

d3drmSM. This parameter is to be set to one of the members of the D3DRMSORTMODE enumerated type which specifies the sorting mode. The default value is D3DRMSORT_FROMPARENT.

Returns

Successful : D3DRM_OK

Error: One of the Direct3D Retained-Mode return values.

See also

IDirect3DRMFrame::GetSortMode

```
LPDIRECT3DRMFRAME myFrame;
.
.
D3DRMSORTMODE sortMode = D3DRMSORT_FROMPARENT;
if (myFrame->SetSortMode(sortMode) != D3DRM_OK)
    goto generic_error;
```

IDirect3DRMFrame::SetTexture

Description

This method is used to set the texture of your frame. This texture is used for meshes in your frame when the D3DRMMATERIALMODE enumerated type is D3DRMMAT-ERIAL_FROMFRAME. You can disable your frame's texture using a NULL texture.

C++ specification

```
HRESULT SetTexture(LPDIRECT3DRMTEXTURE lpD3DRMTexture);
```

Parameters

lpD3DRMTexture. The address the Direct3DRMTexture object which will be used.

Returns

Successful: D3DRM_OK
Error: One of the Direct3D Retained-Mode return values.

See also

IDirect3DRMFrame::GetTexture
IDirect3DRMFrame::SetMaterialMode

Example

```
LPDIRECT3DRMFRAME myFrame;
D3DRMIMAGE TextureImage;
LPDIRECT3DRMTEXTURE tex;
.
.
TextureImage.buffer1 = ddsd.lpSurface;
lpD3DRM->CreateTexture(&TextureImage, &tex);

tex->SetColors(256);
```

IDirect3DRMFrame::SetTextureTopology

Description

This method is used to specify the topological properties to be used for the texture coordinates for objects in your frame.

C++ specification

```
HRESULT SetTextureTopology(BOOL bWrap_u, BOOL bWrap_v);
```

Parameters

bWrap_u and bWrap_v . These parameters are set to TRUE if you wish to map the texture in the u- and v-directions.

Returns

Successful: D3DRM_OK

Error: One of the Direct3D Retained-Mode return values.

See also

IDirect3DRMFrame::GetTextureTopology

Example

```
HRESULT res;
BOOL cylU = TRUE;
BOOL cylV = TRUE;
LPDIRECT3DRMFACE myFace;.
   .
if (myFace->SetTextureTopology( cylU, cylV) != D3DRM_OK)
    goto generic_error;
```

IDirect3DRMFrame::SetVelocity

Description

This method is used to set the velocity of your frame relative to the reference frame. Your frame will be moved by the vector [rvX, rvY, rvZ] relative to your reference frame each time the IDirect3DRM::Tick or IDirect3DRMFrame::Move method are called.

C++ specification

```
HRESULT SetVelocity(LPDIRECT3DRMFRAME 
    D3DVALUE rvY, D3DVALUE
```

Parameters

lpRef. The address of the Direct3DRMFrame object you wish to use as the reference.

rvX, rvY, and rvZ. The new velocity for your frame.

fRotVel. The flag indicating if the rotational velocity of your object should be used when setting the linear velocity. If the value of this is TRUE, the rotational velocity of your object will be included in the calculation.

Returns

Successful: D3DRM_OK

Error: One of the Direct3D Retained-Mode return values.

See also

IDirect3DRMFrame::GetVelocity

Example

```
void _cdecl CameraMove (LPDIRECT3DRMFRAME camera, LPVOID, D3DVALUE
        delta)
{
 D3DVECTOR d3v, d3vv, d3v1, d3v2;
 D3MinObj *d3mo;
 LPDIRECT3DRMFRAMEARRAY lpd3fa;
 LPDIRECT3DRMFRAME lpFrame;

 scene->GetChildren (&lpd3fa);
 int size = lpd3fa->GetSize ();

 if (FAILED (camera->GetVelocity (scene, &d3vv, FALSE))) return;
 if (FAILED (camera->GetPosition (scene, &d3v2))) return;
 D3DRMVectorScale (&d3v1, &d3vv, delta);
 D3DRMVectorAdd (&d3v, &d3v1, &d3v2);

 if (d3v1.x + d3v1.y + d3v1.z == 0.0) return;

 for (int i=0;i<size;i++)
 {
  lpd3fa->GetElement (i, &lpFrame);
  if (lpFrame == camera) continue;
  if ((d3mo = (D3MinObj *)(lpFrame->GetAppData()) ) == 0) continue;

  lpFrame->InverseTransform (&d3v1, &d3v);
  lpFrame->InverseTransform (&d3v2, &d3vv);

  if (TRUE == d3mo->collision (d3v1.x, d3v1.y, d3v1.z, d3v2))
  {
   if (d3v2.x+d3v2.y+d3v2.z != 0.0)
```

```
      {
        lpFrame->Transform (&d3vv, &d3v2);
        if (camera->SetVelocity (scene, d3vv.x, d3vv.y, d3vv.z, FALSE); !=
            D3DRM_OK)
        goto generic_error;
      } else {
        camera->SetVelocity (scene, D3DVAL(0.0), D3DVAL(0.0), D3DVAL(0.0),
            FALSE);
      }
    }
  }
}
```

IDirect3DRMFrame::SetZbufferMode

Description

This method is used to set whether Z-buffering is enabled or disabled (the Z-buffer mode).

C++ specification

```
HRESULT SetZbufferMode(D3DRMZBUFFERMODE d3drmZBM);
```

Parameters

d3drmZBM. This parameter specifies one of the members of the D3DRMZBUFFERMODE enumerated type. This value defines the Z-buffer mode with a default value of D3DRMZBUFFER_FROMPARENT.

Returns

Successful: D3DRM_OK

Error: One of the Direct3D Retained-Mode return values.

See also

IDirect3DRMFrame::GetZbufferMode

Example

```
LPDIRECT3DRMFRAME  myFrame = NULL;     // Arena frame
  :
  :
if (myFrame->SetZbufferMode(D3DRMZBUFFER_DISABLE) != D3DRM_OK)
    goto generic_error;
```

IDirect3DRMFrame::Transform

Description

This method is used to transform the vector in the lpd3dVSrc parameter in model coordinates to world coordinates. The result is returned in the lpd3dVDst parameter.

C++ specification

```
HRESULT Transform(D3DVECTOR *lpd3dVDst, D3DVECTOR *lpd3dVSrc);
```

Parameters

lpd3dVDst. The address of a D3DVECTOR structure you wish filled with the result of the transformation operation.

lpd3dVSrc. The address of a D3DVECTOR structure which is the source of the transformation operation.

Returns

Successful: D3DRM_OK

Error: One of the Direct3D Retained-Mode return values.

See also

IDirect3DRMFrame::InverseTransform,

Example

```
void _cdecl CameraMove (LPDIRECT3DRMFRAME camera, LPVOID, D3DVALUE
     delta)
{
 D3DVECTOR d3v, d3vv, d3v1, d3v2;
 D3MinObj *d3mo;
 LPDIRECT3DRMFRAMEARRAY lpd3fa;
 LPDIRECT3DRMFRAME lpFrame;

 scene->GetChildren (&lpd3fa);
 int size = lpd3fa->GetSize ();

 if (FAILED (camera->GetVelocity (scene, &d3vv, FALSE))) return;
 if (FAILED (camera->GetPosition (scene, &d3v2))) return;
 D3DRMVectorScale (&d3v1, &d3vv, delta);
 D3DRMVectorAdd (&d3v, &d3v1, &d3v2);

 if (d3v1.x + d3v1.y + d3v1.z == 0.0) return;

 for (int i=0;i<size;i++)
 {
  lpd3fa->GetElement (i, &lpFrame);
  if (lpFrame == camera) continue;
  if ((d3mo = (D3MinObj *)(lpFrame->GetAppData()) ) == 0) continue;
```

```
lpFrame->InverseTransform (&d3v1, &d3v);
lpFrame->InverseTransform (&d3v2, &d3vv);

if (TRUE == d3mo->collision (d3v1.x, d3v1.y, d3v1.z, d3v2))
{
  if (d3v2.x+d3v2.y+d3v2.z != 0.0)
  {
   if ( lpFrame->Transform (&d3vv, &d3v2) != D3DRM_OK)
     goto generic_error;
   camera->SetVelocity (scene, d3vv.x, d3vv.y, d3vv.z, FALSE);
  } else {
     camera->SetVelocity (scene, D3DVAL(0.0), D3DVAL(0.0),
       D3DVAL(0.0), FALSE);
  }
 }
}
}
```

chapter 27

The IDirect3DRMLight interface

The IDirect3DRMLight interface and methods

The methods of the IDirect3DRMLight interface are used to create and interact with the lights in your scene.

You obtain the Direct3DRMLight object by calling the `IDirect3DRM::Create-Light` or the `IDirect3DRM::CreateLightRGB` methods.

Like all COM interfaces, this interface inherits the IUnknown interface methods. These consist of `AddRef`, `QueryInterface`, and `Release`.

The IDirect3DRMLight interface methods can be organized into the groups in table 27.1.

483

Table 27.1 IDirect3DRMLight methods

Group	Methods
Attenuation	GetConstantAttenuation
	GetLinearAttenuation
	GetQuadraticAttenuation
	SetConstantAttenuation
	SetLinearAttenuation
	SetQuadraticAttenuation
Color	GetColor
	SetColor
	SetColorRGB
Enable frames	GetEnableFrame
	SetEnableFrame
Light types	GetType
	SetType
Range	GetRange
	SetRange
Spotlight options	GetPenumbra
	GetUmbra
	SetPenumbra
	SetUmbra

In addition, the IDirect3DRMLight interface inherits the following methods from the IDirect3DRMObject interface:

Table 27.2 Methods inherited from IDirect3DRMObject

Methods
AddDestroyCallback
Clone
DeleteDestroyCallback
GetAppData
GetClassName
GetName
SetAppData
SetName

IDirect3DRMLight::GetColor

Description
This method is used to acquire the color of your current Direct3DRMLight object.

C++ specification
```
D3DCOLOR GetColor();
```

Parameters
None

Returns
Returns the requested color.

See also
IDirect3DRMLight::SetColor

Example
```
LPDIRECT3DRMLIGHT light1 = NULL;
   .
   .
D3DCOLOR color = light1->GetColor();
```

IDirect3DRMLight::GetConstantAttenuation

Description
This method is used to acquire the constant attenuation factor for your Direct3DRMLight object. The constant attenuation value will affect your light intensity inversely. This means that a constant attenuation value of 2 will reduce the intensity of your light by half.

C++ specification
```
D3DVALUE GetConstantAttenuation();
```

Returns
Returns the constant attenuation value.

See also
IDirect3DRMLight::SetConstantAttenuation

Example
```
LPDIRECT3DRMLIGHT myLight = NULL;
   .
```

```
D3DVALUE myFAttConst = (float)myLight->GetConstantAttenuation();
D3DVALUE myFAttLinear= (float)myLight->GetLinearAttenuation();
D3DVALUE myFAttQuad = (float)myLight->GetQuadraticAttenuation();

D3DVALUE myFRange = (float)myLight->GetRange();
```

IDirect3DRMLight::GetEnableFrame

Description

This method is used to acquire the enable frame for your light.

C++ specification

```
HRESULT GetEnableFrame(LPDIRECT3DRMFRAME * lplpEnableFrame);
```

Parameters

lplpEnableFrame. The address of a pointer you wish to fill with the enable frame
for the current Direct3DRMFrame object.

Returns

Successful: D3DRM_OK

Error: One of the Direct3D Retained-Mode return values.

See also

IDirect3DRMLight::SetEnableFrame

Example

```
HRESULT result;
LPDIRECT3DRMFRAME lpEnableFrame;
LPDIRECT3DRMLIGHT myLight;
    .
    .
if (myLight->GetEnableFrame(lpEnableFrame) != D3DRM_OK)
    goto generic_error;
```

IDirect3DRMLight::GetLinearAttenuation

Description

This method is used to acquire the linear attenuation factor for your light.

C++ specification

```
D3DVALUE GetLinearAttenuation();
```

Returns

Returns the linear attenuation value.

See also

IDirect3DRMLight::SetLinearAttenuation

Example

```
LPDIRECT3DRMLIGHT myLight = NULL;
       .

       .
D3DVALUE myFAttConst = (float)myLight->GetConstantAttenuation();
D3DVALUE myFAttLinear= (float)myLight->GetLinearAttenuation();
D3DVALUE myFAttQuad = (float)myLight->GetQuadraticAttenuation();

D3DVALUE myFRange = (float)myLight->GetRange();
```

IDirect3DRMLight::GetPenumbra

Description

This method is used to acquire the penumbra angle of your spotlight.

C++ specification

```
D3DVALUE GetPenumbra();
```

Parameters

None

Returns

Returns the penumbra value.

See also

IDirect3DRMLight::SetPenumbra

Example

```
LPDIRECT3DRMLIGHT myLight;
D3DVALUE myPenumbra;
       .

       .
myPenumbra = myLight->GetPenumbra();
```

IDirect3DRMLight::GetQuadraticAttenuation

Description
This method is used to acquire the quadratic attenuation factor for your light.

C++ specification
```
D3DVALUE GetQuadraticAttenuation();
```

Parameters
None

Returns
This method returns the quadratic attenuation value.

See also
IDirect3DRMLight::SetQuadraticAttenuation

Example
```
LPDIRECT3DRMLIGHT myLight = NULL;
    :
    :
D3DVALUE myFAttConst = (float)myLight->GetConstantAttenuation();
D3DVALUE myFAttLinear= (float)myLight->GetLinearAttenuation();
D3DVALUE myFAttQuad = (float)myLight->GetQuadraticAttenuation();

D3DVALUE myFRange = (float)myLight->GetRange();
```

IDirect3DRMLight::GetRange

Description
This method is used to acquire the range of your current Direct3DRMLight object.

C++ specification
```
D3DVALUE GetRange();
```

Returns
Returns the range.

See also
IDirect3DRMLight::SetRange

Example
```
LPDIRECT3DRMLIGHT myLight = NULL;
```

```
     :
     :
     D3DVALUE myFAttConst = (float)myLight->GetConstantAttenuation();
     D3DVALUE myFAttLinear= (float)myLight->GetLinearAttenuation();
     D3DVALUE myFAttQuad = (float)myLight->GetQuadraticAttenuation();

     D3DVALUE myFRange = (float)myLight->GetRange();
```

IDirect3DRMLight::GetType

Description
This method is used to acquire the type of your light.

C++ specification
```
D3DRMLIGHTTYPE GetType();
```

Parameters
None

Returns
Returns one of the members of the D3DRMLIGHTTYPE enumerated type.

See also
IDirect3DRMLight::SetType

Example
```
D3DRMLIGHTTYPE myLightType;
LPDIRECT3DRMLIGHT myLight;
     :
     :
myLightType = myLight->GetType();
```

IDirect3DRMLight::GetUmbra

Description
This method is used to acquire the umbra angle of your Direct3DRMLight object.

C++ specification
```
D3DVALUE GetUmbra();
```

Parameters
None

Returns the umbra angle.

See also

IDirect3DRMLight::SetUmbra

Example

```
LPDIRECT3DRMLIGHT myLight;
.
.
D3DVALUE umbraVal = myLight->GetUmbra();
```

IDirect3DRMLight::SetColor

Description

This method is used to set the color of your light.

C++ specification

```
HRESULT SetColor(D3DCOLOR rcColor);
```

Parameters

rcColor. The new color for your light.

Returns

Successful: D3DRM_OK

Error: One of the Direct3D Retained-Mode return values.

See also

IDirect3DRMLight::GetColor

Example

```
D3DCOLOR color;
LPDIRECT3DRMLIGHT myLight;
.
.
color =
      D3DRMCreateColorRGB
      ( D3DVAL(200.0),
        D3DVAL(100.0),
        D3DVAL(255.0)
      );
if (myLight->SetColor(color) != D3DRM_OK)
    goto generic_error;
```

IDirect3DRMLight::SetColorRGB

Description

This method is used to set the RGB color of your light.

C++ specification

```
HRESULT SetColorRGB(D3DVALUE rvRed, D3DVALUE rvGreen,
                    D3DVALUE rvBlue);
```

Parameters

rvRed, rvGreen, and rvBlue. The new color components (RGB) for your light.

Returns

Successful: D3DRM_OK

Error: One of the Direct3D Retained-Mode return values.

Example

```
LPDIRECT3DRMLIGHT myLight;
  .

  .
if (FAILED(myLight->SetColorRGB(D3DVAL(1.0), D3DVAL(1.0), D3DVAL(1.0))))
   goto generic_error;
```

IDirect3DRMLight::SetConstantAttenuation

Description

This method is used to set the constant attenuation factor for your light. The constant attenuation value will affect the light intensity inversely. As an example, a constant attenuation value of 2 will reduce the intensity of your light by half.

C++ specification

```
HRESULT SetConstantAttenuation(D3DVALUE rvAtt);
```

Parameters

rvAtt. Your new attenuation factor.

Returns

Successful: D3DRM_OK

Error: One of the Direct3D Retained-Mode return values.

See also

IDirect3DRMLight::GetConstantAttenuation

```
LPDIRECT3DRMLIGHT     myLight;


:
if(myLight)
 {
  if (myLight->SetConstantAttenuation((D3DVALUE)myfAttConst) != D3DRM_OK)
    goto generic_error;
  myLight->SetLinearAttenuation((D3DVALUE)myfAttLinear);
  myLight->SetQuadraticAttenuation((D3DVALUE)myfAttQuad);
 }
```

IDirect3DRMLight::SetEnableFrame

Description

This method is used to set the enable frame for your light.

C++ specification

```
HRESULT SetEnableFrame(LPDIRECT3DRMFRAME lpEnableFrame);
```

Parameters

lpEnableFrame. The address of your light's enable frame. The child frames of your
frame will also be enabled for this light source.

Returns

Successful: D3DRM_OK

Error: One of the Direct3D Retained-Mode return values.

See also

IDirect3DRMLight::GetEnableFrame

Example

```
LPDIRECT3DRMFRAMEmyFrame;
LPDIRECT3DRMLIGHT myLight;


:
:
// Enable the directional light only to hit the players, not the arena
if (myLight ->SetEnableFrame(myFrame) != D3DRM_OK)
    goto generic_error;
```

IDirect3DRMLight::SetLinearAttenuation

Description
This method is used to set the linear attenuation factor for your light.

C++ specification
```
HRESULT SetLinearAttenuation(D3DVALUE rvAtt);
```

Parameters
rvAtt. Your new attenuation factor.

Returns
Successful: D3DRM_OK

Error: One of the Direct3D Retained-Mode return values.

See also
IDirect3DRMLight::GetLinearAttenuation

Example
```
LPDIRECT3DRMLIGHT     myLight;

    .

if(myLight)
 {
  myLight->SetConstantAttenuation((D3DVALUE)myfAttConst);
  if (myLight->SetLinearAttenuation((D3DVALUE)myfAttLinear) != D3DRM_OK)
    goto generic_error;
  myLight->SetQuadraticAttenuation((D3DVALUE)myfAttQuad);
 }
```

IDirect3DRMLight::SetPenumbra

Description
This method is used to set the angle of your penumbra cone.

C++ specification
```
HRESULT SetPenumbra(D3DVALUE rvAngle);
```

Parameters
rvAngle. The new penumbra angle which must be greater than or equal to the angle of the umbra. If you accidentally set the penumbra angle to less than the umbra angle, the umbra angle will be set equal to the penumbra angle. The default value for this parameter is 0.5 radians.

Successful: D3DRM_OK

Error: One of the Direct3D Retained-Mode return values.

See also

IDirect3DRMLight::GetPenumbra

Example

```
LPDIRECT3DRMLIGHT spotlight;
.
.
.
spotlight->SetUmbra( D3DVALUE(0.2) );
if (spotlight->SetPenumbra( D3DVALUE(0.5) ) != D3DRM_OK)
    goto generic_error;
```

IDirect3DRMLight::SetQuadraticAttenuation

Description

This method is used to set the quadratic attenuation factor for your light.

C++ specification

```
HRESULT SetQuadraticAttenuation(D3DVALUE rvAtt);
```

Parameters

rvAtt. Your new attenuation factor.

Returns

Successful: D3DRM_OK

Error: One of the Direct3D Retained-Mode return values.

See also

IDirect3DRMLight::GetQuadraticAttenuation

Example

```
LPDIRECT3DRMLIGHT     myLight;
.
.
.
if(myLight)
 {
  myLight->SetConstantAttenuation((D3DVALUE)myfAttConst);
  myLight->SetLinearAttenuation((D3DVALUE)myfAttLinear);
  if (myLight->SetQuadraticAttenuation((D3DVALUE)myfAttQuad) != D3DRM_OK)
    goto generic_error;
 }
```

IDirect3DRMLight::SetRange

Description

This method is used to set the range of your light. The light only affects objects which are within this range.

C++ specification

```
HRESULT SetRange(D3DVALUE rvRange);
```

Parameters

rvRange. The new range with a default value of 256.

Returns

Successful: D3DRM_OK

Error: One of the Direct3D Retained-Mode return values.

See also

IDirect3DRMLight::GetRange

Example

```
LPDIRECT3DRMFRAME lights;
LPDIRECT3DRMLIGHT light1;
  .

  .
if (FAILED(lpD3DRM->CreateLightRGB (D3DRMLIGHT_PARALLELPOINT,
               D3DVAL(0.8), D3DVAL(0.6), D3DVAL(0.7),
               &light1)))
    goto generic_error;
if (light1->SetRange (500.0) != D3DRM_OK)
    goto generic_error;
if (lights->AddLight(light1) != D3DRM_OK)
    goto generic_error;
```

IDirect3DRMLight::SetType

Description

This method is used to changes your light's type.

C++ specification

```
HRESULT SetType(D3DRMLIGHTTYPE d3drmtType);
```

Parameters

d3drmtType. Your new light type which must be one of the members of the D3DRMLIGHTTYPE enumerated type.

Returns

Successful: D3DRM_OK

Error: One of the Direct3D Retained-Mode return values.

See also

IDirect3DRMLight::GetType

Example

```
LPDIRECT3DRMLIGHT light1;
 .
 .
if (light1->SetType (D3DRMLIGHT_PARALLELPOINT) != D3DRM_OK)
    goto generic_error;
```

IDirect3DRMLight::SetUmbra

Description

This method is used to set the angle of your umbra cone.

C++ specification

```
HRESULT SetUmbra(D3DVALUE rvAngle);
```

Parameters

rvAngle. Your new umbra angle which must be less than or equal to the angle of the penumbra. If you set the umbra angle to a value greater than your penumbra angle, the penumbra angle will be set equal to the umbra angle. The default value for this parameter is 0.4 radians.

Returns

Successful: D3DRM_OK

Error: One of the Direct3D Retained-Mode return values.

See also

IDirect3DRMLight::GetUmbra

IDirect3DRMLight::SetPenumbra

Example

```
LPDIRECT3DRMLIGHT spotlight;
 .
 .
if (spotlight->SetUmbra( D3DVALUE(0.2) ) != D3DRM_OK)
    goto generic_error;
if (spotlight->SetPenumbra( D3DVALUE(0.5) ) != D3DRM_OK)
    goto generic_error;
```

chapter 28

The IDirect3DRMMaterial interface

The IDirect3DRMMaterial interface and methods

The methods of the IDirect3DRMMaterial interface are used to interact with your material objects.

You obtain the Direct3DRMMaterial object by calling the `IDirect3DRM::CreateMaterial` method.

Like all COM interfaces, this interface inherits the IUnknown interface methods. These consist of `AddRef`, `QueryInterface`, and `Release`.

The IDirect3DRMMaterial interface methods can be organized into the groups in table 28.1.

Table 28.1 IDirect3DRMMaterial methods

Group	Methods
Emission	GetEmissive
	SetEmissive
Power for	GetPower
specular exponent	SetPower
Specular	GetSpecular
	SetSpecular

In addition, the IDirect3DRMMaterial interface inherits the following methods from the IDirect3DRMObject interface:

Table 28.2 Methods inherited from IDirect3DRMObject

Methods
AddDestroyCallback
Clone
DeleteDestroyCallback
GetAppData
GetClassName
GetName
SetAppData
SetName

IDirect3DRMMaterial::GetEmissive

Description

This method is used to acquire the setting for the emissive property of your material. The setting of this property specifies the color and intensity of your object's emissive light.

C++ specification

```
HRESULT GetEmissive(D3DVALUE *lpr, D3DVALUE *lpg, D3DVALUE *lpb);
```

Parameters

lpr, lpg, and lpb. Returns the addresses of variables holding the red, green, and blue components of the emissive color.

Returns

    Successful: D3DRM_OK

    Error: One of the Direct3D Retained-Mode return values.

See also

    IDirect3DRMMaterial::SetEmissive

Example

```
D3DVALUE er, eg, eb;
D3DVALUE power;
LPDIRECT3DRMMATERIAL material;
   .
   .
if (material==0)
    D3DRM->CreateMaterial( D3DVALUE(5), &material );

if (material->GetEmissive( &er, &eg, &eb ) != D3DRM_OK)
    goto generic_error;
```

IDirect3DRMMaterial::GetPower

Description

    This method is used to acquire the power used for the specular exponent in your material.

C++ specification

```
D3DVALUE GetPower();
```

Parameters

    None

Returns

    The value indicating the power of your specular exponent.

See also

    IDirect3DRMMaterial::SetPower

Example

```
D3DVALUE power;
LPDIRECT3DRMMATERIAL material;
   .
   .
if (material==0)
    D3DRM->CreateMaterial( D3DVALUE(5), &material );
power=material->GetPower();
```

IDirect3DRMMaterial::GetSpecular

Description

This method is used to acquire the color of the specular highlights of your material.

C++ specification

```
HRESULT GetSpecular(D3DVALUE *lpr, D3DVALUE *lpg, D3DVALUE *lpb);
```

Parameters

lpr, lpg, and lpb. Returns the addresses of variables holding the red, green, and blue components of the specular highlights of you material.

Returns

Successful: D3DRM_OK

Error: One of the Direct3D Retained-Mode return values.

See also

IDirect3DRMMaterial::SetSpecular

Example

```
D3DVALUE sr, sg, sb;.
LPDIRECT3DRMMATERIAL material;
.
.
.
if (material==0)
    D3DRM->CreateMaterial( D3DVALUE(5), &material );
if (material->GetSpecular( &sr, &sg, &sb ) != D3DRM_OK)
    goto generic_error;
```

IDirect3DRMMaterial::SetEmissive

Description

This method is used to set the emissive property of your material.

C++ specification

```
HRESULT SetEmissive(D3DVALUE r, D3DVALUE g, D3DVALUE b);
```

Parameters

r, g, and b. The red, green, and blue components of the emissive color.

Returns

Successful: D3DRM_OK

Error: One of the Direct3D Retained-Mode return values.

See also

IDirect3DRMMaterial::GetEmissive

Example
```
D3DVALUE er, eg, eb;
D3DVALUE power;
LPDIRECT3DRMMATERIAL material;
    .
    .
if (material==0)
    D3DRM->CreateMaterial( D3DVALUE(5), &material );
    .
    .
if (material->SetEmissive( er, eg, eb ) != D3DRM_OK)
    goto generic_error;
```

IDirect3DRMMaterial::SetPower

Description

This method is used to set the power used for the specular exponent in your material.

C++ specification
```
HRESULT SetPower(D3DVALUE rvPower);
```

Parameters

rvPower. The new specular exponent.

Returns

Successful: D3DRM_OK

Error: One of the Direct3D Retained-Mode return values.

See also

IDirect3DRMMaterial::GetPower

Example
```
D3DVALUE power;
LPDIRECT3DRMMATERIAL material;
    .
    .
if (material==0)
    D3DRM->CreateMaterial( D3DVALUE(5), &material );
    .
    .
if (material->SetPower(power) != D3DRM_OK)
    goto generic_error;
```

IDirect3DRMMaterial::SetSpecular

Description

This method is used to set the specular highlights for your material.

C++ specification

```
HRESULT SetSpecular(D3DVALUE r, D3DVALUE g, D3DVALUE b);
```

Parameters

r. Red component of your color for the specular highlights.

g. Green component of your color for the specular highlights.

b. Blue component of your color for the specular highlights.

Returns

Successful: D3DRM_OK

Error: One of the Direct3D Retained-Mode return values.

See also

IDirect3DRMMaterial::GetSpecular

Example

```
D3DVALUE r = 10, g = 10, b = 10;
LPDIRECT3DRMMATERIAL material;
  .
  .
if (material==0)
    D3DRM->CreateMaterial( D3DVALUE(5), &material );
  .
  .
if (material->SetSpecular(r, g, b) != D3DRM_OK)
    goto generic_error;
```

chapter 29

The IDirect3DRMMesh interface

The IDirect3DRMMesh interface and methods

The methods of the IDirect3DRMMesh interface are used to interact with groups of mesh objects.

You obtain the Direct3DRMMesh object by calling the `IDirect3DRM::CreateMesh` method.

Like all COM interfaces, this interface inherits the IUnknown interface methods. These consist of `AddRef`, `QueryInterface`, and `Release`.

The `IDirect3DRMMesh` interface methods can be organized into the groups in table 29.1.

Table 29.1 IDirect3DRMMesh methods

Group	Methods
Color	GetGroupColor
	SetGroupColor
	SetGroupColorRGB
Creation and information	AddGroup
	GetBox
	GetGroup
	GetGroupCount
Materials	GetGroupMaterial
	SetGroupMaterial
Miscellaneous	Scale
	Translate
Rendering quality	GetGroupQuality
	SetGroupQuality
Texture mapping	GetGroupMapping
	SetGroupMapping
Textures	GetGroupTexture
	SetGroupTexture
Vertex positions	GetVertices
	SetVertices

In addition, the IDirect3DRMMesh interface inherits the following methods from the IDirect3DRMObject interface:

Table 29.2 Methods inherited from IDirect3DRMObject

Methods
AddDestroyCallback
Clone
DeleteDestroyCallback
GetAppData
GetClassName
GetName
SetAppData
SetName

IDirect3DRMMesh::AddGroup

Description

This method is used to group a collection of faces and acquire an identifier for the group.

This new group will have the following default properties when it is added:

1 White

2 No texture

3 No specular reflection

4 The position, normal, and color of each vertex in the vertex array will be zero

C++ specification

```
HRESULT AddGroup(unsigned vCount, unsigned fCount,
    unsigned vPerFace, unsigned *fData, D3DRMGROUPINDEX *returnId);
```

Parameters

vCount and fCount. The number of vertices and faces in your group.

vPerFace. The number of vertices per face in your group as long as all of the faces have the same vertex count. If the group contains faces with differing vertex counts, this parameter should be zero.

fData. The address of your face data.

If the vPerFace parameter has a non-zero value, this data consists of a list of indices into the group's vertex array.

If the vPerFace parameter is zero, the vertex indices should be preceded by an integer giving the number of vertices in that face. As an example, if the vPerFace parameter has a value of zero and the group is made up of triangular and quadrilateral faces, the data could be as follows: 4 index index index index 3 index index index 3 index index index ...

returnId. The address of a variable identifying the group when this method returns.

Returns

Successful: D3DRM_OK

Error: One of the Direct3D Retained-Mode return values.

See also

IDirect3DRMMesh::SetVertices

Example

```
unsigned vertexOrder[] = { 0,1,2,3,4,5,6,7,8,9,10,11,
        12,13,14,15,16,17,18,19,20,21,22,23 };

// The vertex list is as follows - lets make a VERTEX definition for
       it.
// Remember that the vertex looks like this -
// typedef struct _D3DRMVERTEX{
//   D3DVECTOR position;
//   D3DVECTOR normal;
//   D3DVALUE tu, tv;
//   D3DCOLOR color;
// } D3DRMVERTEX;

#define VERTEX(px,py,pz,nx,ny,nz,tu,tv) \
    { { D3DVALUE(px),D3DVALUE(py),D3DVALUE(pz) }, \
     { D3DVALUE(nx),D3DVALUE(ny),D3DVALUE(nz), }, \
     D3DVALUE(tu),D3DVALUE(tv),D3DCOLOR(0) }

static D3DRMVERTEX myVertexList[]=
{
    // The left face of our cube
    VERTEX( 0,0,0, -1,0,0, 0,1 ),
    VERTEX( 0,0,2, -1,0,0, 0,0 ),
    VERTEX( 0,2,2, -1,0,0, 1,0 ),
    VERTEX( 0,2,0, -1,0,0, 1,1 ),
    // The right face of our cube
    VERTEX( 2,0,0, 1,0,0, 0,0 ),
    VERTEX( 2,2,0, 1,0,0, 1,0 ),
    VERTEX( 2,2,2, 1,0,0, 1,1 ),
    VERTEX( 2,0,2, 1,0,0, 0,1 ),
    // The front face of our cube
    VERTEX( 0,0,0, 0,0,-1, 0,0 ),
    VERTEX( 0,2,0, 0,0,-1, 1,0 ),
    VERTEX( 2,2,0, 0,0,-1, 1,1 ),
    VERTEX( 2,0,0, 0,0,-1, 0,1 ),
    // The back face of our cube
    VERTEX( 0,0,2, 0,0,1, 0,1 ),
    VERTEX( 2,0,2, 0,0,1, 0,0 ),
    VERTEX( 2,2,2, 0,0,1, 1,0 ),
    VERTEX( 0,2,2, 0,0,1, 1,1 ),
    // The top face of our cube
    VERTEX( 0,2,0, 0,1,0, 0,0 ),
    VERTEX( 0,2,2, 0,1,0, 1,0 ),
    VERTEX( 2,2,2, 0,1,0, 1,1 ),
    VERTEX( 2,2,0, 0,1,0, 0,1 ),
    // The bottom face of our cube
    VERTEX( 0,0,0, 0,-1,0, 0,0 ),
```

```
        VERTEX( 2,0,0, 0,-1,0, 1,0 ),
        VERTEX( 2,0,2, 0,-1,0, 1,1 ),
        VERTEX( 0,0,2, 0,-1,0, 0,1 ),
    };

    LPDIRECT3DRMMESH myMesh;
    D3DRMGROUPINDEX myGroup;

    // ------- MESH --------
    D3DRM->CreateMesh( &myMesh );
    if (myMesh->AddGroup( 24, 6, 4, vertexOrder, &myGroup ) != D3DRM_OK)
        goto generic_error;
    myMesh->SetVertices( myGroup, 0, 24, myVertexList );
    myMesh->Translate( D3DVALUE(-0.5), D3DVALUE(-0.5), D3DVALUE(-0.5) );
    myMesh->Scale( D3DVALUE(15), D3DVALUE(15), D3DVALUE(15) );
```

IDirect3DRMMesh::GetBox

Description

This method is used to acquire the bounding box of a Direct3DRMMesh object.
The bounding box holds the minimum and maximum coordinates of the mesh in
each dimension.

C++ specification

```
HRESULT GetBox(D3DRMBOX * lpD3DRMBox);
```

Parameters

lpD3DRMBox. The address of a D3DRMBOX structure you wish to be filled with
the bounding box coordinates.

Returns

Successful: D3DRM_OK
Error: One of the Direct3D Retained-Mode return values.

See also

D3DRMBOX

Example

```
LPDIRECT3DRMMESH myMesh = NULL;
D3DRMBOX box;

    .
    .
if (myMesh->GetBox(&box) != D3DRM_OK)
    goto generic_error;
```

IDirect3DRMMesh::GetGroup

Description

This method is used to acquire the data associated with this group.

C++ specification

```
HRESULT GetGroup(D3DRMGROUPINDEX id, unsigned *vCount,
  unsigned *fCount, unsigned *vPerFace, DWORD *fDataSize,
  unsigned *fData);
```

Parameters

id. The identifier for the group which must have been produced by using the IDirect3DRMMesh::AddGroup method.

vCount and fCount. The addresses of two variables you wish to have filled with the number of vertices and the number of faces for the group when the method returns. These parameters can be NULL.

vPerFace. The address of a variable you wish to have filled with the number of vertices per face for the group when the method returns. This parameter can be NULL.

fDataSize. The address of a variable indicating the number of unsigned elements in the buffer pointed to by the fData parameter. This parameter cannot be NULL.

fData. The address of a buffer you wish to have filled with the face data for the group when the method returns. The format of this data is the same as we specified in the call to the IDirect3DRMMesh::AddGroup method.

If this parameter is NULL, the method will return the buffer's required size in the fDataSize parameter.

Returns

Successful: D3DRM_OK

Error: One of the Direct3D Retained-Mode return values.

See also

IDirect3DRMMesh::GetGroupColor
IDirect3DRMMesh::GetGroupColorRGB
IDirect3DRMMesh::GetGroupCount
IDirect3DRMMesh::GetGroupMapping

Example

```
LPDIRECT3DRMMESH myMesh;
LPDIRECT3DRMMESHBUILDER myMeshBuilder;
D3DRMGROUPINDEX groupId;
```

```
     .
     .
     .
myMeshBuilder->CreateMesh( &myMesh );
     .
     .

myMesh->AddGroup(VertCount, faceCount, vertPerFace, &FaceData,
        &GroupId);
     .
     .

unsigned vertCount, faceCount;
DWORD ds;
if (myMesh->GetGroup( 0, &vertCount, &faceCount, 0, &ds, 0) != D3DRM_OK)
    goto generic_error;
```

IDirect3DRMMesh::GetGroupColor

Description

This message is used to acquire the color for your group.

C++ specification

```
D3DCOLOR GetGroupColor(D3DRMGROUPINDEX id);
```

Parameters

id. The identifier of your group which must have been created using the
IDirect3DRMMesh::AddGroup method.

Returns

Returns a D3DCOLOR variable indicating the color if the call is successful;
zero is returned otherwise.

See also

IDirect3DRMMesh::SetGroupColor
IDirect3DRMMesh::SetGroupColorRGB

Example

```
D3DRMGROUPINDEX id = 0;
LPDIRECT3DRMMESH myMesh;
LPDIRECT3DRMMESHBUILDER myMeshBuilder;
D3DRMGROUPINDEX groupId;


     .

myMeshBuilder->CreateMesh( &myMesh );
     .
     .
```

```
myMesh->AddGroup(VertCount, faceCount, vertPerFace, &FaceData,
        &GroupId);
    .
    .
D3DCOLOR color=myMesh->GetGroupColor( id );
```

IDirect3DRMMesh::GetGroupCount

Description
This method is used to acquire the number of groups for your Direct3DRMMesh object.

C++ specification
```
unsigned GetGroupCount();
```

Parameters
None

Returns
Successful: The number of groups
Error: Zero

See also
IDirect3DRMMesh::GetGroup
IDirect3DRMMesh::GetGroupColor
IDirect3DRMMesh::GetGroupMapping
IDirect3DRMMesh::GetGroupMaterial

Example
```
LPDIRECT3DRMMESH myMesh;
LPDIRECT3DRMMESHBUILDER myMeshBuilder;
    .
    .
myMeshBuilder->CreateMesh( &myMesh );
    .
    .
myMesh->AddGroup(VertCount, faceCount, vertPerFace, &FaceData,
        &GroupId);
    .
    .
unsigned count=myMesh->GetGroupCount();
```

IDirect3DRMMesh::GetGroupMapping

Description

This method returns a description of how textures are mapped to a group in your Direct3DRMMesh object.

C++ specification

```
D3DRMMAPPING GetGroupMapping(D3DRMGROUPINDEX id);
```

Parameters

id. The identifier of your group which must have been produced using the `IDirect3DRMMesh::AddGroup` method.

Returns

Successful: One of the `D3DRMMAPPING` values defining how the textures are mapped to a group
Error: Zero

See also

IDirect3DRMMesh::GetGroup
IDirect3DRMMesh::GetGroupColor
IDirect3DRMMesh::GetGroupMaterial
IDirect3DRMMesh::SetGroupMapping

Example

```
LPDIRECT3DRMMESH myMesh;
D3DRMGROUPINDEX myGroup;
D3DRMGROUPINDEX id = 0;

// ------- MESH --------
D3DRM->CreateMesh( &myMesh );
myMesh->AddGroup( 24, 6, 4, vertexOrder, &myGroup );
myMesh->SetVertices( myGroup, 0, 24, myVertexList );
myMesh->Translate( D3DVALUE(-0.5), D3DVALUE(-0.5), D3DVALUE(-0.5) );
myMesh->Scale( D3DVALUE(15), D3DVALUE(15), D3DVALUE(15) );

D3DRMMAPPING mapping = myMesh->GetGroupMapping( id );
```

IDirect3DRMMesh::GetGroupMaterial

Description

This method is used to acquire a pointer to the material associated with a group in your Direct3DRMMesh object.

C++ specification

```
HRESULT GetGroupMaterial(D3DRMGROUPINDEX id,
    LPDIRECT3DRMMATERIAL *returnPtr);
```

Parameters

> id. The identifier of the group which must have been produced using the
> `IDirect3DRMMesh::AddGroup` method.

> returnPtr. The address of a pointer to a variable you wish to have filled with the
> IDirect3DRMMaterial interface for the group when the method returns.

Returns

> Successful: D3DRM_OK
> Error: One of the Direct3D Retained-Mode return values.

See also

> IDirect3DRMMesh::GetGroup
> IDirect3DRMMesh::GetGroupColor
> IDirect3DRMMesh::SetGroupMapping
> IDirect3DRMMesh::SetGroupMaterial

Example

```
// ------- MESH --------
D3DRM->CreateMesh( &myMesh );
myMesh->AddGroup( 24, 6, 4, vertexOrder, &myGroup );
myMesh->SetVertices( myGroup, 0, 24, myVertexList );
myMesh->Translate( D3DVALUE(-0.5), D3DVALUE(-0.5), D3DVALUE(-0.5) );
myMesh->Scale( D3DVALUE(15), D3DVALUE(15), D3DVALUE(15) );
.
.
LPDIRECT3DRMMATERIAL *material;
if (myMesh->GetGroupMaterial( id, material ) != D3DRM_OK)
  goto generic_error;
```

IDirect3DRMMesh::GetGroupQuality

Description

> This method is used to acquire the rendering quality for a specified group in your
> Direct3DRMMesh object.

C++ specification

```
D3DRMRENDERQUALITY GetGroupQuality(D3DRMGROUPINDEX id);
```

Parameters

id. The identifier of the group which must have been created by using the `IDirect3DRMMesh::AddGroup` method.

Returns

Successful: The values from the enumerated types represented by `D3DRMRENDERQUALITY`. These values include the shading, lighting, and fill modes for the object.
Error: Zero

See also

IDirect3DRMMesh::GetGroup
IDirect3DRMMesh::GetGroupColor
IDirect3DRMMesh::SetGroupQuality
IDirect3DRMMesh::SetGroupMapping
IDirect3DRMMesh::SetGroupMaterial

Example

```
D3DRMGROUPINDEX id = 0;
LPDIRECT3DRMMESH myMesh;
LPDIRECT3DRMMESHBUILDER myMeshBuilder;
    .
    .
myMeshBuilder->CreateMesh( &myMesh );
    .
    .
myMesh->AddGroup(VertCount, faceCount, vertPerFace, &FaceData,
        &GroupId);
    .
    .
D3DRMRENDERQUALITY quality=myMesh->GetGroupQuality( id );
```

IDirect3DRMMesh::GetGroupTexture

Description

This method is used to acquire an address of the texture associated with a group in your Direct3DRMMesh object.

C++ specification

```
HRESULT GetGroupTexture(D3DRMGROUPINDEX id,
    LPDIRECT3DRMTEXTURE *returnPtr);
```

Parameters

id. The identifier of the group which must have been produced using the `IDirect3DRMMesh::AddGroup` method.

returnPtr. The address of a pointer to a variable you wish filled with the IDirect3DRMTexture interface for the group when the method returns.

Returns

Successful: D3DRM_OK

Error: One of the Direct3D Retained-Mode return values.

See Also

IDirect3DRMMesh::SetGroupTexture
IDirect3DRMMesh::GetGroup
IDirect3DRMMesh::GetGroupColor
IDirect3DRMMesh::SetGroupQuality
IDirect3DRMMesh::SetGroupMapping
IDirect3DRMMesh::SetGroupMaterial
IDirect3DRMMesh::SetGroupTexture

Example

```
HRESULT returnVal;
D3DRMGROUPINDEX id = 0;
LPDIRECT3DRMMESH myMesh;
LPDIRECT3DRMMESHBUILDER myMeshBuilder;
.
.
myMeshBuilder->CreateMesh( &myMesh );
.
.
myMesh->AddGroup(VertCount, faceCount, vertPerFace, &FaceData,
        &GroupId);
.
.
LPDIRECT3DRMTEXTURE groupTex;
returnVal = myMesh->GetGroupTexture( id, groupTex );
if (returnVal != D3DRM_OK)
  goto generic_error;
```

IDirect3DRMMesh::GetVertices

Description

This method is used to acquire the vertex positions for a specified group in your Direct3DRMMesh object.

C++ specification

```
HRESULT GetVertices(D3DRMGROUPINDEX id, DWORD index,
   DWORD count, D3DRMVERTEX *returnPtr);
```

Parameters

>   id. The identifier of the group which must have been produced using the
>   `IDirect3DRMMesh::AddGroup` method.

>   index. The index into the array of D3DRMVERTEX structures at which to begin
>   returning vertex positions.

>   count. The number of D3DRMVERTEX structures (vertices) to acquire following the
>   index given in the index parameter. This parameter cannot be NULL.

>   returnPtr. The array of D3DRMVERTEX structures you wish filed with the vertex
>   positions when the method returns. If this parameter is NULL, the method
>   will return the required number of D3DRMVERTEX structures in the count
>   parameter.

Returns

>   Successful: D3DRM_OK

>   Error: One of the Direct3D Retained-Mode return values.

See also

>   IDirect3DRMMesh::SetVertices

Example

```
DWORD index, count;
D3DRMGROUPINDEX groupId
static D3DRMVERTEX vertices[30];
LPDIRECT3DRMMESH myMesh;
LPDIRECT3DRMMESHBUILDER myMeshBuilder;
   .
   .
if (myMeshBuilder->CreateMesh( &myMesh ) != D3DRM_OK)
   goto generic_error;

index = 0;
count = 30;
if (myMesh->GetVertices( groupId, index, count, vertices ) != D3DRM_OK)
   goto generic_error;
```

IDirect3DRMMesh::Scale

Description
This method is used to scale a Direct3DRMMesh object by the specified scaling factors parallel to the x-, y-, and z-axes in model coordinates.

C++ specification
```
HRESULT Scale(D3DVALUE sx, D3DVALUE sy, D3DVALUE sz);
```

Parameters
sx, sy, and sz. The scaling factors which are applied along the x-, y-, and z-axes.

Returns
Successful: D3DRM_OK
Error: One of the Direct3D Retained-Mode return values.

See also
D3DVALUE

Example
```
LPDIRECT3DRMMESH myMesh;
D3DRMGROUPINDEX myGroup;

// ------- MESH --------
D3DRM->CreateMesh( &myMesh );
myMesh->AddGroup( 24, 6, 4, vertexOrder, &myGroup );
myMesh->SetVertices( myGroup, 0, 24, myVertexList );
myMesh->Translate( D3DVALUE(-0.5), D3DVALUE(-0.5), D3DVALUE(-0.5) );
if (myMesh->Scale( D3DVALUE(15), D3DVALUE(15), D3DVALUE(15) ) !=
        D3DRM_OK)
    goto generic_error;
```

IDirect3DRMMesh::SetGroupColor

Description
This method is used to set the color of a group in your Direct3DRMMesh object.

C++ specification
```
HRESULT SetGroupColor(D3DRMGROUPINDEX id, D3DCOLOR value);
```

Parameters
id. The identifier of the group which must have been produced by using the IDirect3DRMMesh::AddGroup method.
value. The color of your group.

Returns

> Successful: D3DRM_OK
>
> Error: One of the Direct3D Retained-Mode return values.

See also

> IDirect3DRMMesh::GetGroup
>
> IDirect3DRMMesh::GetGroupColor
>
> IDirect3DRMMesh::SetGroupColorRGB
>
> IDirect3DRMMesh::SetGroupMapping
>
> IDirect3DRMMesh::SetGroupMaterial
>
> IDirect3DRMMesh::SetGroupQuality
>
> IDirect3DRMMesh::SetGroupTexture

Example

```
LPDIRECT3DRMMESH myMesh;
D3DRMGROUPINDEX myGroup;

// ------- MESH --------
D3DRM->CreateMesh( &myMesh );
myMesh->AddGroup( 24, 6, 4, vertexOrder, &myGroup );
myMesh->SetVertices( myGroup, 0, 24, myVertexList );
myMesh->Translate( D3DVALUE(-0.5), D3DVALUE(-0.5), D3DVALUE(-0.5) );
myMesh->Scale( D3DVALUE(15), D3DVALUE(15), D3DVALUE(15) );
D3DCOLOR myColor = 100;
if (myMesh->SetGroupColor( 0, myColor ) != D3DRM_OK)
    goto generic_error;
```

IDirect3DRMMesh::SetGroupColorRGB

Description

> This method is used to set the color of a group in your Direct3DRMMesh object using individual RGB values.

C++ specification

```
HRESULT SetGroupColorRGB(D3DRMGROUPINDEX id, D3DVALUE red,
  D3DVALUE green, D3DVALUE blue);
```

Parameters

> id. The identifier of your group which must have been produced by using the `IDirect3DRMMesh::AddGroup` method.
>
> red, green, and blue. The red, green, and blue components of your group color.

Returns

Successful: D3DRM_OK

Error: One of the Direct3D Retained-Mode return values.

See also

IDirect3DRMMesh::GetGroup

IDirect3DRMMesh::GetGroupColor

IDirect3DRMMesh::SetGroupColor

IDirect3DRMMesh::SetGroupMapping

IDirect3DRMMesh::SetGroupMaterial

IDirect3DRMMesh::SetGroupQuality

IDirect3DRMMesh::SetGroupTexture

Example

```
if (FAILED(lpD3DRM->CreateMeshBuilder(lpD3DRM, &builder)))
  goto generic_error;
rval = builder->Load(builder, "myObject.x", NULL,
        D3DRMLOAD_FROMFILE, NULL, NULL);
if (rval != D3DRM_OK) {
  Msg("Failed to load myObject.x.\n");
  goto ret_with_error;
}
if (FAILED(builder->SetTexture(builder, tex)))
  goto generic_error;
if (FAILED(builder->SetQuality(builder, D3DRMRENDER_GOURAUD)))
  goto generic_error;
if (FAILED(builder->CreateMesh(builder, &mesh)))
  goto generic_error;
RELEASE(builder);


if (FAILED(mesh->SetGroupColorRGB(mesh, 0, D3DVAL(0.6), D3DVAL(0.6),
    D3DVAL(0.2))))
  goto generic_error;
if (FAILED(mesh->SetGroupColorRGB(mesh, 1, D3DVAL(1.0), D3DVAL(1.0),
    D3DVAL(1.0))))
  goto generic_error;

if (FAILED(frame->lpVtbl->AddVisual(frame, (LPDIRECT3DRMVISUAL)
    mesh)))
  goto generic_error;
```

IDirect3DRMMesh::SetGroupMapping

Description

This method is used to set the mapping for your group in a Direct3DRMMesh object. This mapping is used to control how textures are mapped to our surface.

C++ specification

```
HRESULT SetGroupMapping(D3DRMGROUPINDEX id, D3DRMMAPPING value);
```

Parameters

id. The identifier of the group which must have been produced by using the `IDirect3DRMMesh::AddGroup` method.

value. The value of the `D3DRMMAPPING` type which defines the mapping for the group.

Returns

Successful: D3DRM_OK

Error: One of the Direct3D Retained-Mode return values.

See also

IDirect3DRMMesh::GetGroupMapping

Example

```
LPDIRECT3DRMMESH myMesh;
D3DRMGROUPINDEX myGroup;
LPDIRECT3DRMTEXTURE myTexture;

D3DRM->CreateMesh( &myMesh );
myMesh->AddGroup( 24, 6, 4, vertexOrder, &myGroup );
HRSRC textureId = FindResource( NULL,
        MAKEINTRESOURCE(IDR_TEXTURE), "TEXTURE" );
d3drm->LoadTextureFromResource( textureId, &myTexture );
myMesh->SetGroupTexture( myGroup, myTexture );
if (myMesh->SetGroupMapping( myGroup, D3DRMMAP_PERSPCORRECT ) !=
    D3DRM_OK)
    goto generic_error;
myTexture->Release();
myTexture=0;
```

IDirect3DRMMesh::SetGroupMaterial

Description

This method is used to set the material associated with a group in your Direct3DRMMesh object.

C++ specification

```
HRESULT SetGroupMaterial(D3DRMGROUPINDEX id, LPDIRECT3DRMMATERIAL
    value);
```

Parameters

id. The identifier of the group. which must have been produced using the `IDirect3DRMMesh::AddGroup` method.

value. The address of the `IDirect3DRMMaterial` interface for your Direct3DRMMesh object.

Returns

Successful: D3DRM_OK

Error: One of the Direct3D Retained-Mode return values.

See also

IDirect3DRMMesh::GetGroup
IDirect3DRMMesh::GetGroupColor
IDirect3DRMMesh::GetGroupMaterial
IDirect3DRMMesh::SetGroupColorRGB
IDirect3DRMMesh::SetGroupMapping
IDirect3DRMMesh::SetGroupQuality
IDirect3DRMMesh::SetGroupTexture

Example

```
DWORD w;
HRESULT rval;
LPDIRECT3DRMMESHBUILDER obj_builder = 0;
LPDIRECT3DRMMESH    obj_mesh = 0;
D3DRMRENDERQUALITY quality = D3DRMRENDER_GOURAUD;
LPDIRECT3DRMMATERIAL mat = NULL;
rval = lpD3DRM->LoadTexture ("roof.bmp", &wtex);
if (rval != D3DRM_OK)
 {
  Msg("Failed to load roof.bmp.\n%s", MyErrorToString(rval));
  return FALSE;
 }

if (FAILED (lpD3DRM->CreateMaterial (D3DVAL(16.0), &mat)))
```

```
    return FALSE;


  // load mesh file
  if (FAILED(lpD3DRM->CreateMeshBuilder(&obj_builder)))
    return FALSE;

  // create a frame within the scene
  w = 0;
  rval = obj_builder->Load ("out2.x", (void *)&w,
        D3DRMLOAD_BYPOSITION, NULL, NULL);
  if (rval != D3DRM_OK)
   {
    Msg("Failed to load op_bot.x\n%s", MyErrorToString(rval));
    return FALSE;
   }

  obj_builder->SetQuality (quality);

  if (FAILED (obj_builder->CreateMesh(&obj_mesh)))
    return FALSE;

  if (FAILED(obj_mesh->SetGroupTexture (D3DRMGROUP_ALLGROUPS, stex)))
    return FALSE;

  if (obj_mesh->SetGroupMaterial (D3DRMGROUP_ALLGROUPS, mat) !=
        D3DRM_OK)
    goto generic_error;

  if (FAILED(obj_mesh->SetGroupQuality (D3DRMGROUP_ALLGROUPS, quality)))
    return FALSE;
```

IDirect3DRMMesh::SetGroupQuality

Description

This method is used to set the rendering quality for a requested group in your
Direct3DRMMesh object.

C++ *specification*

```
HRESULT SetGroupQuality(D3DRMGROUPINDEX id, D3DRMRENDERQUALITY
        value);
```

Parameters

id. The identifier of the group which must have been produced by using the
IDirect3DRMMesh::AddGroup method.

value. The values from the enumerated types represented by the D3DRMREN-DERQUALITY type. These values can include the shading, lighting, and fill modes for your object.

Returns
Successful: D3DRM_OK
Error: One of the Direct3D Retained-Mode return values.

See also
IDirect3DRMMesh::GetGroup
IDirect3DRMMesh::GetGroupColor
IDirect3DRMMesh::GetGroupMaterial
IDirect3DRMMesh::GetGroupQuality
IDirect3DRMMesh::SetGroupColorRGB
IDirect3DRMMesh::SetGroupMapping
IDirect3DRMMesh::SetGroupTexture

Example
```
DWORD w;
HRESULT rval;
LPDIRECT3DRMMESHBUILDER obj_builder = 0;
LPDIRECT3DRMMESH    obj_mesh = 0;
D3DRMRENDERQUALITY quality = D3DRMRENDER_GOURAUD;
LPDIRECT3DRMMATERIAL mat = NULL;

rval = lpD3DRM->LoadTexture ("roof.bmp", &wtex);
if (rval != D3DRM_OK)
  {
   Msg("Failed to load roof.bmp.\n%s", MyErrorToString(rval));
   return FALSE;
  }

if (FAILED (lpD3DRM->CreateMaterial (D3DVAL(16.0), &mat)))
   return FALSE;


// load mesh file
if (FAILED(lpD3DRM->CreateMeshBuilder(&obj_builder)))
   return FALSE;

// create a frame within the scene
w = 0;
rval = obj_builder->Load ("out2.x", (void *)&w, D3DRMLOAD_BYPOSITION,
        NULL, NULL);
if (rval != D3DRM_OK)
  {
```

```
    Msg("Failed to load op_bot.x\n%s", MyErrorToString(rval));
    return FALSE;
  }

obj_builder->SetQuality (quality);

if (FAILED (obj_builder->CreateMesh(&obj_mesh)))
  return FALSE;

if (FAILED(obj_mesh->SetGroupTexture (D3DRMGROUP_ALLGROUPS, stex)))
  return FALSE;

 if (FAILED(obj_mesh->SetGroupMaterial (D3DRMGROUP_ALLGROUPS, mat)))
  return FALSE;

if (obj_mesh->SetGroupQuality (D3DRMGROUP_ALLGROUPS, quality) !=
    D3DRM_OK)
  goto generic_error;
```

IDirect3DRMMesh::SetGroupTexture

Description

This method is used to set the texture associated with a group in your Direct-3DRMMesh object.

C++ specification
```
HRESULT SetGroupTexture(D3DRMGROUPINDEX id, LPDIRECT3DRMTEXTURE
    value);
```

Parameters

id. The identifier of your group which must have been produced by using the `IDirect3DRMMesh::AddGroup` method.

value. The address of the IDirect3DRMTexture interface for your Direct3D-RMMesh object.

Returns

Successful: D3DRM_OK

Error: One of the Direct3D Retained-Mode return values.

See also

IDirect3DRMMesh::GetGroup
IDirect3DRMMesh::GetGroupColor
IDirect3DRMMesh::GetGroupMaterial
IDirect3DRMMesh::GetGroupQuality

IDirect3DRMMesh::GetGroupTexture
IDirect3DRMMesh::SetGroupColorRGB
IDirect3DRMMesh::SetGroupMapping

Example

```
DWORD w;
HRESULT rval;
LPDIRECT3DRMMESHBUILDER obj_builder = 0;
LPDIRECT3DRMMESH     obj_mesh = 0;
D3DRMRENDERQUALITY quality = D3DRMRENDER_GOURAUD;
LPDIRECT3DRMMATERIAL mat = NULL;

rval = lpD3DRM->LoadTexture ("roof.bmp", &wtex);
if (rval != D3DRM_OK)
 {
  Msg("Failed to load roof.bmp.\n%s", MyErrorToString(rval));
  return FALSE;
 }

if (FAILED (lpD3DRM->CreateMaterial (D3DVAL(16.0), &mat)))
  return FALSE;


// load mesh file
if (FAILED(lpD3DRM->CreateMeshBuilder(&obj_builder)))
  return FALSE;

// create a frame within the scene
w = 0;
rval = obj_builder->Load ("out2.x", (void *)&w, D3DRMLOAD_BYPOSITION,
        NULL, NULL);
if (rval != D3DRM_OK)
 {
  Msg("Failed to load op_bot.x\n%s", MyErrorToString(rval));
  return FALSE;
 }

obj_builder->SetQuality (quality);

if (FAILED (obj_builder->CreateMesh(&obj_mesh)))
  return FALSE;

if (obj_mesh->SetGroupTexture (D3DRMGROUP_ALLGROUPS, stex) != D3DRM_OK)
goto generic_error;

  if (FAILED(obj_mesh->SetGroupMaterial (D3DRMGROUP_ALLGROUPS, mat)))
   return FALSE;
```

```
if (FAILED(obj_mesh->SetGroupQuality (D3DRMGROUP_ALLGROUPS, quality)))
   return FALSE;
```

IDirect3DRMMesh::SetVertices

Description

This method is used to set the vertex positions for an indicated group in your
Direct3DRMMesh object. The vertices are local to the group, so if your application
needs to share vertices between two different groups, the vertices will have to be
duplicated in both of your groups.

C++ specification

```
HRESULT SetVertices(D3DRMGROUPINDEX id, unsigned index,
   unsigned count, D3DRMVERTEX *values);
```

Parameters

id. The identifier of the group which must have been produced by using the
IDirect3DRMMesh::AddGroup method.

index. The index into the array, passed in the values parameter, at which to begin
setting vertex positions.

count. The number of vertices to set following the index specified in the index
parameter.

values. The array of D3DRMVERTEX structures indicating the vertex positions to be
set.

Returns

Successful: D3DRM_OK

Error: One of the Direct3D Retained-Mode return values.

See also

IDirect3DRMMesh::GetVertices

Example

```
LPDIRECT3DRMMESH myMesh;
D3DRMGROUPINDEX myGroup;

// ------- MESH --------
D3DRM->CreateMesh( &myMesh );
myMesh->AddGroup( 24, 6, 4, vertexOrder, &myGroup );
if (myMesh->SetVertices( myGroup, 0, 24, myVertexList ) != D3DRM_OK)
   goto generic_error;
myMesh->Translate( D3DVALUE(-0.5), D3DVALUE(-0.5), D3DVALUE(-0.5) );
myMesh->Scale( D3DVALUE(15), D3DVALUE(15), D3DVALUE(15) );
```

IDirect3DRMMesh::Translate

Description

This method is used to add the indicated offsets to the vertex positions of your Direct3DRMMesh object.

C++ specification

```
HRESULT Translate(D3DVALUE tx, D3DVALUE ty, D3DVALUE tz);
```

Parameters

tx, ty, and tz. The offsets which are added to the x-, y-, and z-coordinates of each vertex position.

Returns

Successful: D3DRM_OK

Error: One of the Direct3D Retained-Mode return values.

See also

IDirect3DRMMesh::Scale

Example

```
LPDIRECT3DRMMESH myMesh;
D3DRMGROUPINDEX myGroup;

// ------- MESH --------
D3DRM->CreateMesh( &myMesh );
myMesh->AddGroup( 24, 6, 4, vertexOrder, &myGroup );
myMesh->SetVertices( myGroup, 0, 24, myVertexList );
if (myMesh->Translate( D3DVALUE(-0.5), D3DVALUE(-0.5), D3DVALUE(-0.5)
        ) != D3DRM_OK)
    goto generic_error;
myMesh->Scale( D3DVALUE(15), D3DVALUE(15), D3DVALUE(15) );
```

chapter 30

The IDirect3DRMMeshBuilder interface

The IDirect3DRMMeshBuilder interface and methods

The methods of the IDirect3DRMMeshBuilder interface are used to interact with mesh objects.

You obtain the Direct3DRMMeshBuilder object by calling the `IDirect-3DRM::CreateMeshBuilder` method.

Like all COM interfaces, this interface inherits the IUnknown interface methods. These consist of `AddRef`, `QueryInterface`, and `Release`.

The IDirect3DRMMeshBuilder interface methods can be organized into the groups in table 30.1.

Table 30.1 IDirect3DRMMeshBuilder methods

Group	Methods
Color	GetColorSource
	SetColor
	SetColorRGB
	SetColorSource
Creation and information	GetBox
Faces	AddFace
	AddFaces
	CreateFace
	GetFaceCount
	GetFaces
Loading	Load
Meshes	AddMesh
	CreateMesh
Miscellaneous	AddFrame
	AddMeshBuilder
	ReserveSpace
	Save
	Scale
	SetMaterial
	Translate
Normals	AddNormal
	GenerateNormals
	SetNormal
Perspective	GetPerspective
	SetPerspective
Rendering quality	GetQuality
	SetQuality
Textures	GetTextureCoordinates
	SetTexture
	SetTextureCoordinates
	SetTextureTopology
Vertices	AddVertex
	GetVertexColor
	GetVertexCount

Table 30.1 IDirect3DRMMeshBuilder methods

GetVertices

SetVertex

SetVertexColor

SetVertexColorRGB

In addition, the IDirect3DRMMeshBuilder interface inherits the following methods from the IDirect3DRMObject interface:

Table 30.2 Methods inherited from IDirect3DRMObject

Methods

AddDestroyCallback

Clone

DeleteDestroyCallback

GetAppData

GetClassName

GetName

SetAppData

SetName

IDirect3DRMMeshBuilder::AddFace

Description

This method is used to add a face to a Direct3DRMMeshBuilder object. Each face can exist in only one mesh at a time.

C++ specification

```
HRESULT AddFace(LPDIRECT3DRMFACE lpD3DRMFace);
```

Parameters

lpD3DRMFace. The address of the face you are adding.

Returns

Successful: D3DRM_OK

Error: One of the Direct3D Retained-Mode return values.

See also

IDirect3DRMMeshBuilder::AddFaces

Example

```
HRESULT res;
LPDIRECT3DRMFACE myFace;
LPDIRECT3DRMMESHBUILDER myMeshBuilder;
    .
    .
if (myMeshBuilder->AddFace(myFace) != D3DRM_OK)
    goto generic_error;
```

IDirect3DRMMeshBuilder::AddFaces

Description

This method is used to add faces to your Direct3DRMMeshBuilder object.

C++ specification

```
HRESULT AddFaces(DWORD dwVertexCount, D3DVECTOR * lpD3DVertices,
    DWORD normalCount, D3DVECTOR *lpNormals, DWORD *lpFaceData,
    LPDIRECT3DRMFACEARRAY* lplpD3DRMFaceArray);
```

Parameters

dwVertexCount. The number of vertices.

lpD3DVertices. The base address of an array of D3DVECTOR structures storing your vertex positions.

normalCount. The number of normals.

lpNormals. The base address of an array of D3DVECTOR structures containing your normal positions.

lpFaceData. Holds, for each face, a vertex count followed by the indices into your vertices array. If you do not set normal count to zero, you should set this parameter to a vertex count followed by pairs of indices. The first index of each pair should index into your array of vertices. The second index indexes into your array of normals. You must terminate this list of indices with a zero.

lplpD3DRMFaceArray. The address of a pointer to an IDirect3DRMFaceArray interface you want filled with a pointer to the new faces.

Returns

Successful : D3DRM_OK

Error: One of the Direct3D Retained-Mode return values.

See also

IDirect3DRMMeshBuilder::AddFace

Example

```
// Define the face data
static unsigned long faces[] =
{

// Face data goes here

};

D3DVECTOR vertex[16];
D3DVECTOR normal[8];
.
.
// Calculate or fill vertices
.
.
// Calculate or fill normals
.
.
// Add the faces
if (mesh->AddFaces(16, vertex, 8, normal, faces, NULL) !=
        D3DRM_OK)
  goto generic_error;
```

IDirect3DRMMeshBuilder::AddFrame

Description

This method is used to add the contents of a frame to your Direct3DRMMeshBuilder object.

C++ specification

```
HRESULT AddFrame(LPDIRECT3DRMFRAME lpD3DRMFrame);
```

Parameters

lpD3DRMFrame. The address of the frame you are adding the contents of.

Returns

Successful: D3DRM_OK

Error: One of the Direct3D Retained-Mode return values.

See also

IDirect3DRM::CreateMeshBuilder

Example

```
LPDIRECT3DRMMESHBUILDER mbuilder;
LPDIRECT3DRMFRAME frame;

lpD3DRM->CreateMeshBuilder(&mbuilder);
if (mbuilder->AddFrame(frame) != D3DRM_OK)
    goto generic_error;
```

IDirect3DRMMeshBuilder::AddMesh

Description

This method is used to add a mesh to your Direct3DRMMeshBuilder object.

C++ specification

```
HRESULT AddMesh(LPDIRECT3DRMMESH lpD3DRMMesh);
```

Parameters

lpD3DRMMesh. The address of the mesh you are adding.

Returns

Successful: D3DRM_OK

Error: One of the Direct3D Retained-Mode return values.

See also

IDirect3DRM::CreateMesh

Example

```
LPDIRECT3DRMMESHBUILDER myMeshBuilder;
LPDIRECT3DRMMESH myMesh;
.
.
if (myMeshBuilder.AddMesh(myMesh) != D3DRM_OK)
    goto generic_error;
```

IDirect3DRMMeshBuilder::AddMeshBuilder

Description

This method is used to add the contents of a Direct3DRMMeshBuilder object to another one of your Direct3DRMMeshBuilder objects.

C++ specification

```
HRESULT AddMeshBuilder(LPDIRECT3DRMMESHBUILDER lpD3DRMMeshBuild);
```

Parameters

lpD3DRMMeshBuild. The address of the Direct3DRMMeshBuilder object whose contents you are adding.

Returns

Successful : D3DRM_OK

Error: One of the Direct3D Retained-Mode return values.

See also

IDirect3DRM::CreateMeshBuilder

Example

```
LPDIRECT3DRMMESHBUILDER myMeshBuilder, myMeshBuilder2;

if (myMeshBuilder->AddMeshBuilder(myMeshBuilder2) != D3DRM_OK)
    goto generic_error;
```

IDirect3DRMMeshBuilder::AddNormal

Description

This method is used to add a normal to your Direct3DRMMeshBuilder object. You can use this when you are building an object from scratch and you wish to generate the normals.

C++ specification

```
int AddNormal(D3DVALUE x, D3DVALUE y, D3DVALUE z);
```

Parameters

x. The x component of the direction of your new normal.

y. The y component of the direction of your new normal.

z. The z component of the direction of your new normal.

Returns

The index of your normal.

See also

IDirect3DRMMeshBuilder::GenerateNormals

Example

```
LPDIRECT3DRMMESHBUILDER myMeshBuilder;
D3DVALUE x;
D3DVALUE y;
D3DVALUE z;
```

```
        .
        .
        int index = myMeshBuilder->AddNormal(x, y, z);
```

IDirect3DRMMeshBuilder::AddVertex

Description

This method is used to add a vertex to your Direct3DRMMeshBuilder object.

C++ specification

```
int AddVertex(D3DVALUE x, D3DVALUE y, D3DVALUE z);
```

Parameters

x. The x component of the position of your new vertex.

y. The y component of the position of your new vertex.

z. The z component of the position of your new vertex.

Returns

The index of your vertex.

See also

IDirect3DRMMeshBuilder::GetVertexColor

IDirect3DRMMeshBuilder::GetVertexCount

IDirect3DRMMeshBuilder::GetVertices

Example

```
D3DVALUE x = 100.0;
D3DVALUE y = 81.3;
D3DVALUE z = 13.6;
LPDIRECT3DRMMESHBUILDER myMeshBuilder;
int index;
        .
        .
index = myMeshBuilder->AddVertex(x, y, z);
```

IDirect3DRMMeshBuilder::CreateFace

Description

This method is used to create a new face with no vertices and add it to your Direct3DRMMeshBuilder object.

C++ specification

```
HRESULT CreateFace(LPDIRECT3DRMFACE* lp1pD3DRMFace);
```

Parameters

lp1pD3RMFace. The address of a pointer to an IDirect3DRMFace interface you wish filled with a pointer to the face which was created.

Returns

Successful: D3DRM_OK

Error: One of the Direct3D Retained-Mode return values.

See also

IDirect3DRMMeshBuilder::GetFaceCount

IDirect3DRMMeshBuilder::GetFaces

Example

```
HRESULT result;
LPDIRECT3DRMMESHBUILDER myMeshBuilder;
LPDIRECT3DRMFACE * myFace;
 .
 .
result = myMeshBuilder->CreateFace(myFace);
if (result != D3DRM_OK)
    goto generic_error;
```

IDirect3DRMMeshBuilder::CreateMesh

Description

This method is used to create a new mesh from your Direct3DRMMeshBuilder object.

C++ specification

```
HRESULT CreateMesh(LPDIRECT3DRMMESH* lp1pD3RMMesh);
```

Parameters

lp1pD3RMMesh. The address you wish filled with a pointer to an IDirect-3DRMMesh interface.

Returns

Successful: D3DRM_OK

Error: One of the Direct3D Retained-Mode return values.

IDirect3DRM::CreateMeshBuilder

Example

```
HRESULT result;
LPDIRECT3DRMMESHBUILDER myMeshBuilder;
LPDIRECT3DRMMESH myMesh;
LPDIRECT3DRMFACE * myFace;
.
.
result = myMeshBuilder-> CreateMesh( &myMesh );
if (result != D3DRM_OK)
   goto generic_error;
.
.
//
// You now would add the face to your object
//

myMeshBuilder->Release();
myMeshBuilder=0;
```

IDirect3DRMMeshBuilder::GenerateNormals

Description

This method is used to process your Direct3DRMMeshBuilder object and generate
vertex normals which are the average of each vertex's adjoining face normals. The
averaging of normals of back-to-back faces produces a zero normal. By using this
method, you will not need to create the normals yourself.

C++ specification

```
HRESULT GenerateNormals();
```

Parameters

None

Returns

Successful: D3DRM_OK
Error: One of the Direct3D Retained-Mode return values.

See also

IDirect3DRMMeshBuilder::AddNormal

Example

```
HRESULT result;
```

```
LPDIRECT3DRMMESHBUILDER myMeshBuilder;
.
.
result = myMeshBuilder->GenerateNormals();
if (result != D3DRM_OK)
   goto generic_error;
```

IDirect3DRMMeshBuilder::GetBox

Description

This method is used to acquire the bounding box containing your Direct3DRMMeshBuilder object. The bounding box specifies the minimum and maximum model coordinates for each dimension.

C++ specification

```
HRESULT GetBox(D3DRMBOX *lpD3DRMBox);
```

Parameters

lpD3DRMBox. The address of a D3DRMBOX structure you wish filled with the bounding box coordinates.

Returns

Successful: D3DRM_OK

Error: One of the Direct3D Retained-Mode return values.

See also

IDirect3DRM::CreateMeshBuilder

Example

```
LPDIRECT3DRMMESHBUILDER obj_builder = 0;
LPDIRECT3DRMMESH     obj_mesh = 0;

D3DRMBOX box;
D3DVALUE miny, maxy;
D3DVALUE height;

HRESULT rval;

// load mesh file
if (FAILED(lpD3DRM->CreateMeshBuilder(&obj_builder)))
   return FALSE;

// create a frame within the scene
w = 0;
```

```
rval = obj_builder->Load ("out2.x", (void *)&w, D3DRMLOAD_BYPOSITION,
      NULL, NULL);
if (rval != D3DRM_OK)
{
 Msg("Failed to load op_bot.x\n%s", MyErrorToString(rval));
 return FALSE;
}

obj_builder->SetQuality (quality);

if (obj_builder->GetBox (&box) != D3DRM_OK)
    goto generic_error;
```

IDirect3DRMMeshBuilder::GetColorSource

Description

This method is used to acquire the color source of your Direct3DRMMeshBuilder object. This color source can be either a face or a vertex.

C++ specification

```
D3DRMCOLORSOURCE GetColorSource();
```

Parameters

None

Returns

A member of the D3DRMCOLORSOURCE enumerated type.

See also

IDirect3DRMMeshBuilder::SetColorSource

Example

```
LPDIRECT3DRMMESHBUILDER myMeshbuilder = 0;
.
.
int myColorSource;
switch(myMeshbuilder->GetColorSource())
 {
  case D3DRMCOLOR_FROMFACE:   myColorSource = 0; break;
  case D3DRMCOLOR_FROMVERTEX: myColorSource = 1; break;
  default: ASSERT(0); break;
 }
```

IDirect3DRMMeshBuilder::GetFaceCount

Description

This method is used to acquire the number of faces in your Direct3DRMMeshBuilder object.

C++ specification

```
int GetFaceCount();
```

Parameters

None

Returns

The number of faces.

See also

IDirect3DRMMeshBuilder::GetFaces

Example

```
LPDIRECT3DRMMESHBUILDER myMeshbuilder = 0;
    .
    .
if (myMeshbuilder->GetFaceCount())
 {
   LPDIRECT3DRMFACEARRAY faces;
   LPDIRECT3DRMFACE face;
   myMeshbuilder->GetFaces(&faces);
   faces->GetElement(0, &face);
   c = face->GetColor();
   RELEASE(face);
   RELEASE(faces);
 }
```

IDirect3DRMMeshBuilder::GetFaces

Description

This method is used to acquire the faces of your Direct3DRMMeshBuilder object.

C++ specification

```
HRESULT GetFaces(LPDIRECT3DRMFACEARRAY* lplpD3DRMFaceArray);
```

Parameters

lplpD3DRMFaceArray. The address of a pointer to an IDirect3DRMFaceArray interface you wish filled with the address of the faces.

Returns

Successful: D3DRM_OK

Error: One of the Direct3D Retained-Mode return values.

See also

IDirect3DRMMeshBuilder::GetFaceCount

Example

```
LPDIRECT3DRMMESHBUILDER myMeshbuilder = 0;
 .
 .
if (myMeshbuilder->GetFaceCount())
 {
   LPDIRECT3DRMFACEARRAY faces;
   LPDIRECT3DRMFACE face;
   if (myMeshbuilder->GetFaces(&faces) != D3DRM_OK)
      goto generic_error;
   faces->GetElement(0, &face);
   c = face->GetColor();
   RELEASE(face);
   RELEASE(faces);
 }
```

IDirect3DRMMeshBuilder::GetPerspective

Description

This method is used to determine whether perspective correction is on for your Direct3DRMMeshBuilder object.

C++ specification

```
BOOL GetPerspective();
```

Parameters

None

Returns

TRUE if perspective correction is on; otherwise FALSE.

See also

IDirect3DRMMeshBuilder::SetPerspective

Example

```
BOOL perspective;
LPDIRECT3DRMMESHBUILDER myMeshbuilder;
.
.
perspective = myMeshbuilder->GetPerspective();
```

IDirect3DRMMeshBuilder::GetQuality

Description

This method is used to acquire the rendering quality of your Direct3D-RMMeshBuilder object.

C++ specification

```
D3DRMRENDERQUALITY GetQuality();
```

Parameters

None

Returns

Returns a member of the D3DRMRENDERQUALITY enumerated type indicating the rendering quality of your mesh.

See also

IDirect3DRMMeshBuilder::SetQuality

Example

```
D3DRMRENDERQUALITY meshQuality;
LPDIRECT3DRMMESHBUILDER myMeshbuilder;
.
.
if (myMeshbuilder)
{
    meshQuality=myMeshbuilder->GetQuality();
    if ( meshQuality==D3DRMRENDER_WIREFRAME )
    .
    .
}
```

IDirect3DRMMeshBuilder::GetTextureCoordinates

Description

This method is used to acquire the texture coordinates of the indicated vertex in your Direct3DRMMeshBuilder object.

C++ specification

```
HRESULT GetTextureCoordinates(DWORD index, D3DVALUE *lpU,
    D3DVALUE *lpV);
```

Parameters

index. The index of the vertex.

lpU and lpV. The addresses of two variables you wish filled with the texture coordinates of the vertex when the method returns.

Returns

Successful: D3DRM_OK

Error: One of the Direct3D Retained-Mode return values.

See also

IDirect3DRMMeshBuilder::SetTextureCoordinates

Example

```
HRESULT myResult;
DWORD index;
D3DVALUE *lpU;
D3DVALUE *lpV;
LPDIRECT3DRMMESHBUILDER myMeshbuilder;
 .
 .
index = 5;
if (myMeshbuilder->GetTextureCoordinates(index, lpU, lpV) != D3DRM_OK)
    goto generic_error;
```

IDirect3DRMMeshBuilder::GetVertexColor

Description

This method is used to acquire the color of the requested vertex in your Direct3DRMMeshBuilder object.

C++ specification

```
D3DCOLOR GetVertexColor(DWORD index);
```

Parameters

    `index`. The index of the vertex.

Returns

    The requested color.

See also

    IDirect3DRMMeshBuilder::SetVertexColor

Example

```
D3DCOLOR myColor;
DWORD index;
LPDIRECT3DRMMESHBUILDER myMeshbuilder;
.
.
myColor = myMeshbuilder ->GetVertexColor(index);
```

IDirect3DRMMeshBuilder::GetVertexCount

Description

    This method is used to acquire the number of vertices in your Direct3D-RMMeshBuilder object.

C++ specification

    `int GetVertexCount();`

Parameters

    None

Returns

    The number of vertices.

See also

    IDirect3DRMMeshBuilder::AddVertex
    IDirect3DRMMeshBuilder::GetVertexColor
    IDirect3DRMMeshBuilder::GetVertices

Example

```
int numVert;
LPDIRECT3DRMMESHBUILDER myMeshbuilder;
.
.
numVert = myMeshbuilder->GetVertexCount();
```

IDirect3DRMMeshBuilder::GetVertices

Description

This method acquires the vertices, normals, and face data for your Direct3DRMMeshBuilder object.

C++ specification

```
HRESULT GetVertices(DWORD *vcount, D3DVECTOR *vertices,
  DWORD *ncount, D3DVECTOR *normals, DWORD *face_data_size,
  DWORD *face_data);
```

Parameters

vcount. The address of a variable you wish to fill with the number of vertices.

vertices. The address of an array of D3DVECTOR structures to fill with the vertices for your Direct3DRMMeshBuilder object.

ncount. The address of a variable you wish filled with the number of normals.

normals. An array of D3DVECTOR structures you wish filled with the normals for your Direct3DRMMeshBuilder object.

face_data_size. The address of a variable indicating the size of the buffer pointed to by the face_data parameter. The size is specified in units of DWORD values and cannot be NULL.

face_data. The address of the face data for your Direct3DRMMeshBuilder object. This data is in the same format as specified in the IDirect3D-RMMeshBuilder::AddFaces method except that it is null-terminated. If this parameter is NULL, the method will return the required size of the face-data buffer in the face_data_size parameter.

Returns

Successful: D3DRM_OK

Error: One of the Direct3D Retained-Mode return values.

See also

IDirect3DRMMeshBuilder::AddVertex
IDirect3DRMMeshBuilder::GetVertexColor
IDirect3DRMMeshBuilder::GetVertexCount

Example

```
HRESULT myResult;
LPDIRECT3DRMMESHBUILDER myMeshbuilder;
DWORD *vcount;
D3DVECTOR *vertices;
DWORD *ncount;
```

```
D3DVECTOR *normals;
DWORD *faceDataSize;
DWORD *faceData;
.
.
myResult = myMeshbuilder->GetVertices(vcount, vertices,
   ncount, normals, faceDataSize, faceData);
if (myResult != D3DRM)
goto generic_error;
```

IDirect3DRMMeshBuilder::Load

Description

This method is called to load a `Direct3DRMMeshBuilder` object and defaults to loading the first mesh from the source you specify in the `lpvObjSource` parameter.

C++ specification

```
HRESULT Load(LPVOID lpvObjSource, LPVOID lpvObjID,
   D3DRMLOADOPTIONS d3drmLOFlags,
   D3DRMLOADTEXTURECALLBACK d3drmLoadTextureProc, LPVOID lpvArg);
```

Parameters

lpvObjSource. The source for the object you wish loaded. This source can be a file, resource, memory block, or stream, based upon the source flags you pass in the d3drmLOFlags parameter.

lpvObjID. The object name or position you wish to be loaded. The use of this parameter depends upon the identifier flags specified in the d3drmLOFlags parameter. If you specify the D3DRMLOAD_BYPOSITION flag, this parameter will be a pointer to a DWORD value indicating the object's order in the file. You can pass his parameter as NULL.

d3drmLOFlags. The value of the D3DRMLOADOPTIONS type defining the load options.

d3drmLoadTextureProc. A D3DRMLOADTEXTURECALLBACK callback function you wish called to load any textures used by an object requiring special formatting. You can set this parameter as NULL.

lpvArg. The address of your application-defined data passed to the D3DRMLOADTEXTURECALLBACK callback function.

Returns

Successful: D3DRM_OK

Error: One of the Direct3D Retained-Mode return values.

See also

IDirect3DRMMeshBuilder::SetQuality

Example

```
LPDIRECT3DRMMESHBUILDER builder = NULL;
LPDIRECT3DRMLIGHT light = NULL;
LPDIRECT3DRMFRAME frame = NULL;
HRESULT rval;
.
.
if (strcmp(wparam, "LIGHT_DIRECTIONAL") == 0)
 {
  rval = builder->Load("camera.x", NULL, D3DRMLOAD_FROMFILE, NULL, NULL);
  if (rval != D3DRM_OK)
  {
   Msg("Failed to load camera.x.\n%s", MyErrorToString(rval));
   goto ret_with_error;
  }
  if (FAILED(builder->SetQuality(D3DRMRENDER_UNLITFLAT)))
   goto generic_error;
  if (FAILED(lpD3DRM->CreateLightRGB (D3DRMLIGHT_DIRECTIONAL,
       D3DVAL(1.0),
                               D3DVAL(1.0),
                               D3DVAL(1.0),
                               &light)))
   goto generic_error;
} else if (strcmp(wparam, "LIGHT_PARALLEL_POINT") == 0)
{
  rval = builder->Load ("sphere2.x", NULL, D3DRMLOAD_FROMFILE, NULL,
       NULL);
  if (rval != D3DRM_OK)
  {
   Msg ("Failed to load sphere2.x.\n%s", MyErrorToString(rval));
   goto ret_with_error;
  }
  if (FAILED(builder->SetQuality(D3DRMRENDER_UNLITFLAT)))
   goto generic_error;
  if (FAILED(builder->Scale(D3DVAL(0.2), D3DVAL(0.2), D3DVAL(0.2))))
   goto generic_error;
```

IDirect3DRMMeshBuilder::ReserveSpace

Description

This method is used to reserve space within your Direct3DRMMeshBuilder object for the requested number of vertices, normals, and faces so the system can use memory more efficiently.

C++ specification
```
HRESULT ReserveSpace(DWORD vertexCount, DWORD normalCount,
  DWORD faceCount);
```

Parameters

vertexCount. The number of vertices to allocate space for.

normalCount. The number of normals to allocate space for.

faceCount. The number of faces to allocate space for.

Returns

Successful: D3DRM_OK

Error: One of the Direct3D Retained-Mode return values.

See also

IDirect3DRMMeshBuilder::AddNormal

IDirect3DRMMeshBuilder::AddVertex

IDirect3DRMMeshBuilder::CreateFace

Example
```
HRESULT myResult;
DWORD vertexCount;
DWORD normalCount;
DWORD faceCount;
LPDIRECT3DRMMESHBUILDER myMeshbuilder;
   .
   .
vertexCount = 120;
normalCount = 120;
if (myMeshbuilder->ReserveSpace(vertexCount, normalCount,faceCount)
       != D3DRM_OK)
   goto generic_error;
```

IDirect3DRMMeshBuilder::Save

Description

This method is used to save a Direct3DRMMeshBuilder object.

C++ specification
```
HRESULT Save(const char * lpFilename,
   D3DRMXOFFORMAT d3drmXOFFormat, D3DRMSAVEOPTIONS d3drmSOContents);
```

Parameters

lpFilename. The address indicating the name of the file that is created. This file
must have a .x file name extension.

d3drmXOFFormat. The format to save the MeshBuilder data in one of the D3DRMXOFFORMAT enumerated type values.

d3drmSOContents. A value from the D3DRMSAVEOPTIONS type defining the save options.

Returns

Successful: D3DRM_OK

Error: One of the Direct3D Retained-Mode return values.

See also

IDirect3DRM::CreateMeshBuilder

IDirect3DRMMeshBuilder::Save

Example

```
LPDIRECT3DRMMESHBUILDER myMeshbuilder;
D3DVALUE meshScale;
D3DVALUE restoreScale;
HRESULT retVal;
.
.
CString filename;
.
.
D3DVALUE restoreScale=D3DVALUE(1)/meshScale;
retVal = myMeshbuilder->Scale( restoreScale, restoreScale, restoreS-
      cale );
if (retVal != D3DRM_OK)
  {
   Msg ("Failed to scale the meshbuilder.\n%s", MyError-
      ToString(retVal));
   goto ret_with_error;
  }
retVal = myMeshbuilder->Save( filename, D3DRMXOF_BINARY,
      D3DRMXOFSAVE_ALL );
if (retVal != D3DRM_OK)
  {
   Msg ("Failed to Save.\n%s", MyErrorToString(retVal));
   goto ret_with_error;
  }
retVal = myMeshbuilder->Scale( meshScale, meshScale, meshScale );
if (retVal != D3DRM_OK)
  {
   Msg ("Failed to scale the meshbuilder.\n%s", MyError-
      ToString(retVal));
   goto ret_with_error;
  }
```

IDirect3DRMMeshBuilder::Scale

Description

This method is used to scale your Direct3DRMMeshBuilder object by the requested scaling factors, parallel to the x-, y-, and z-axes in model coordinates.

C++ specification

```
HRESULT Scale(D3DVALUE sx, D3DVALUE sy, D3DVALUE sz);
```

Parameters

sx, sy, and sz. The scaling factors you wish applied along the x-, y-, and z-axes.

Returns

Successful: D3DRM_OK

Error: One of the Direct3D Retained-Mode return values.

See also

IDirect3DRMMesh::Scale

IDirect3DRMMeshBuilder::Translate

Example

```
HRESULT retVal;
LPDIRECT3DRMMESHBUILDER myMeshbuilder;
CString filename;
   .
   .
// If we want to save the file in a different scale than it is in cur-
        rently, scale it, save it, then scale it back
D3DVALUE restoreScale=D3DVALUE(1)/meshScale;
retVal = myMeshbuilder->Scale( restoreScale, restoreScale, restoreScale );
if (retVal != D3DRM_OK)
   {
    Msg ("Failed to scale the meshbuilder.\n%s", MyError-
        ToString(retVal));
    goto ret_with_error;
   }
retVal = myMeshbuilder->Save( filename, D3DRMXOF_BINARY,
        D3DRMXOFSAVE_ALL );
if (retVal != D3DRM_OK)
   {
    Msg ("Failed to load save the meshbuilder.\n%s", MyError-
        ToString(retVal));
    goto ret_with_error;
   }
retVal = myMeshbuilder->Scale( meshScale, meshScale, meshScale );
if (retVal != D3DRM_OK)
```

```
      {
       Msg ("Failed to scale the meshbuilder.\n%s", MyError-
            ToString(retVal));
       goto ret_with_error;
      }
```

IDirect3DRMMeshBuilder::SetColor

Description

This method is used to set all the faces of your Direct3DRMMeshBuilder object to the requested color.

C++ specification

```
HRESULT SetColor(D3DCOLOR color);
```

Parameters

`color`. The color to apply to the faces.

Returns

Successful: D3DRM_OK

Error: One of the Direct3D Retained-Mode return values.

See also

IDirect3DRMMeshBuilder::SetColorRGB

Example

```
HRESULT retVal;
LPDIRECT3DRMMESHBUILDER myMeshbuilder;
 .
 .
D3DCOLOR myMeshColor = D3DRMCreateColorRGB( 100,100,200 );
retVal = myMeshbuilder->SetColor( myMeshColor );
if (retVal != D3DRM_OK)
   {
    Msg ("Failed to set the color.\n%s", MyErrorToString(retVal));
    goto ret_with_error;
   }
```

IDirect3DRMMeshBuilder::SetColorRGB

Description

This method is used to set all of the faces in your Direct3DRMMeshBuilder object to a specified color.

C++ specification

```
HRESULT SetColorRGB(D3DVALUE red, D3DVALUE green, D3DVALUE blue);
```

Parameters

red, green, and blue. The red, green, and blue components of your color.

Returns

Successful: D3DRM_OK

Error: One of the Direct3D Retained-Mode return values.

See also

IDirect3DRMMeshBuilder::SetColor

Example

```
HRESULT retVal;
LPDIRECT3DRMMESHBUILDER myMeshbuilder;
.
.
retVal = myMeshBuilder->SetColorRGB( D3DVALUE(.93), D3DVALUE(.73),
        D3DVALUE(.2) );
if (retVal != D3DRM_OK)
  {
   Msg ("Failed to set the RGB color.\n%s", MyErrorToString(retVal));
   goto ret_with_error;
  }
```

IDirect3DRMMeshBuilder::SetColorSource

Description

This method is used to set the color source of your Direct3DRMMeshBuilder object.

C++ specification

```
HRESULT SetColorSource(D3DRMCOLORSOURCE source);
```

Parameters

source. A member of the D3DRMCOLORSOURCE enumerated type which indicates the new color source to you wish to use.

Returns

Successful: D3DRM_OK

Error: One of the Direct3D Retained-Mode return values.

Example

```
HRESULT retVal;
LPDIRECT3DRMMESHBUILDER myMeshbuilder;
   .
   .
   .
D3DRMCOLORSOURCE dSrc = D3DRMCOLOR_FROMVERTEX;
retVal = myMeshbuilder->SetColorSource(dSrc);
if (retVal != D3DRM_OK)
   {
    Msg ("Failed to set the color source.\n%s", MyErrorToString(rval));
    goto ret_with_error;
   }
```

IDirect3DRMMeshBuilder::SetMaterial

Description

This method is used to set the material of all the faces of your Direct3DRMMeshBuilder object.

C++ specification

```
HRESULT SetMaterial(LPDIRECT3DRMMATERIAL lpIDirect3DRMmaterial);
```

Parameters

lpIDirect3DRMmaterial. The address of the IDirect3DRMMaterial interface for your Direct3DRMMeshBuilder object.

Returns

Successful: D3DRM_OK

Error: One of the Direct3D Retained-Mode return values.

See also

IDirect3DRM::CreateMaterial

IDirect3DRMMeshBuilder::SetTexture

Example

```
HRESULT retVal;
LPDIRECT3DRMMATERIAL mat = NULL;
LPDIRECT3DRMTEXTURE tex = NULL;
LPDIRECT3DRMMESHBUILDER builder = NULL;
   .
   .
```

```
retVal = lpD3DRM->LoadTexture("tex4.ppm", &tex);
if (FAILED(lpD3DRM->CreateMaterial(D3DVAL(10.0), &mat)))
    goto generic_error;

if (FAILED(builder->SetTexture(tex)))
    goto generic_error;
if (builder->SetMaterial(mat) != D3DRM_OK)
    goto generic_error;
```

IDirect3DRMMeshBuilder::SetNormal

Description

This method is used to set the normal vector of the requested vertex in your Direct3DRMMeshBuilder object.

C++ specification

```
HRESULT SetNormal(DWORD index, D3DVALUE x, D3DVALUE y, D3DVALUE z);
```

Parameters

index. The index of the normal you wish to set.

x, y, and z. The x, y, and z components of the vector you wish to assign to the indicated normal.

Returns

Successful: D3DRM_OK

Error: One of the Direct3D Retained-Mode return values.

See also

IDirect3DRMMeshBuilder::GenerateNormals

Example

```
HRESULT myResult;
DWORD index;
D3DVALUE x;
D3DVALUE y;
D3DVALUE z;
LPDIRECT3DRMMESHBUILDER myMeshbuilder;
    .
    .
if (myMeshbuilder->SetNormal( index, x, y, z) != D3DRM_OK)
    goto generic_error;
```

IDirect3DRMMeshBuilder::SetPerspective

Description

This method is used to enable or disable perspective-correct texture-mapping for your Direct3DRMMeshBuilder object.

C++ specification

```
HRESULT SetPerspective(BOOL perspective);
```

Parameters

perspective. This parameter should be set to TRUE if you wish the mesh to be texture-mapped with perspective correction; otherwise this parameter should be set to FALSE.

Returns

Successful: D3DRM_OK

Error: One of the Direct3D Retained-Mode return values.

See also

IDirect3DRMMeshBuilder::GetPerspective

Example

```
LPDIRECT3DRMMESHBUILDER myMeshbuilder;
   .
   .
if (myMeshbuilder->SetPerspective(TRUE) != D3DRM_OK)
    goto generic_error;
```

IDirect3DRMMeshBuilder::SetQuality

Description

This method is used to set the rendering quality of your Direct3DRMMeshBuilder object.

C++ specification

```
HRESULT SetQuality(D3DRMRENDERQUALITY quality);
```

Parameters

quality. A member of the D3DRMRENDERQUALITY enumerated type indicating the new rendering quality you wish to use.

Returns

Successful: D3DRM_OK

Error: One of the Direct3D Retained-Mode return values.

See also

IDirect3DRMMeshBuilder::GetQuality

Example

```
LPDIRECT3DRMMESHBUILDER builder = NULL;
HRESULT rval;
 .
 .
rval = builder->Load("camera.x", NULL, D3DRMLOAD_FROMFILE, NULL,
      NULL);
if (rval != D3DRM_OK)
  {
   Msg("Failed to load camera.x.\n%s", MyErrorToString(rval));
   goto ret_with_error;
  }
if (builder->SetQuality(D3DRMRENDER_UNLITFLAT) != D3DRM_OK)
   goto generic_error;
```

IDirect3DRMMeshBuilder::SetTexture

Description

This method is used to set the texture of all of the faces of your Direct3D-RMMeshBuilder object.

C++ specification

```
HRESULT SetTexture(LPDIRECT3DRMTEXTURE lpD3DRMTexture);
```

Parameters

lpD3DRMTexture. The address of the Direct3DRMTexture object to use.

Returns

Successful: D3DRM_OK

Error: One of the Direct3D Retained-Mode return values.

See also

IDirect3DRM::CreateTexture

IDirect3DRMMeshBuilder::SetTextureTopology

Example

```
LPDIRECT3DRMMESHBUILDER builder = NULL;
D3DRMIMAGE TextureImage;
HRESULT rval;
```

```
LPDIRECT3DRMTEXTURE tex = 0;

D3DRMPALETTEENTRY TexturePal[256];
D3DRMIMAGE TextureImage = {
  256, 256,
  1, 1,
  8, FALSE,
  256,
  NULL, NULL,
  0xfc, 0xfc, 0xfc, 0xfc,
  256, TexturePal,
};
.

.
TextureImage.buffer1 = ddsd.lpSurface;
D3DRM->CreateTexture(&TextureImage, &tex);

tex->SetColors(256);
rval = builder->SetTexture(tex);
if (rval != D3DRM_OK)
  {
   Msg("Failed to set texture.\n%s", MyErrorToString(rval));
   goto ret_with_error;
  }
```

IDirect3DRMMeshBuilder::SetTextureCoordinates

Description

This method is used to set the texture coordinates of a desired vertex in your Direct3DRMMeshBuilder object.

C++ specification

```
HRESULT SetTextureCoordinates(DWORD index, D3DVALUE u, D3DVALUE v);
```

Parameters

index. The index of the vertex you wish to set.

u and v. The texture coordinates you want to assign to the indicated mesh vertex.

Returns

Successful: D3DRM_OK

Error: One of the Direct3D Retained-Mode return values.

See also

IDirect3DRMMeshBuilder::GetTextureCoordinates

```
LPDIRECT3DRMMESHBUILDER builder = NULL;
.
.
if (builder->SetTextureCoordinates(iLeftTop,D3DVAL(0.0),D3DVAL(0.0))
        != D3DRM_OK)
goto generic_error;
if (builder ->SetTextureCoordinates(iRight-
        Top,D3DVAL(1.0),D3DVAL(0.0)) != D3DRM_OK)
    goto generic_error;
if (builder ->SetTextureCoordinates(iRightBot-
        tom,D3DVAL(1.0),D3DVAL(1.0)) != D3DRM_OK)
    goto generic_error;
if (builder ->SetTextureCoordinates(iLeftBot-
        tom,D3DVAL(0.0),D3DVAL(1.0)) != D3DRM_OK)
    goto generic_error;
```

IDirect3DRMMeshBuilder::SetTextureTopology

Description

This method is used to set the texture topology of your Direct3DRMMeshBuilder object.

C++ specification

```
HRESULT SetTextureTopology(BOOL cylU, BOOL cylV);
```

Parameters

cylU and cylV. These parameters should be set to TRUE if you want the texture to have a cylindrical topology in the u and v dimensions respectively. If not, you should set the value to FALSE.

Returns

Successful: D3DRM_OK
Error: One of the Direct3D Retained-Mode return values.

See also

IDirect3DRMMeshBuilder::SetTexture

Example

```
HRESULT hRes;
LPDIRECT3DRMMESHBUILDER builder = NULL;
BOOL myTexWrapU = TRUE, myTexWrapV = TRUE.
.
.
```

```
  hRes = builder->SetTextureTopology(myTexWrapU, myTexWrapV);
  if (hRes != D3DRM_OK)
    {
     Msg("Failed to set texture topology.\n%s", MyErrorToString(hRes));
     goto ret_with_error;
    }
```

IDirect3DRMMeshBuilder::SetVertex

Description

This method is used to set the position of a requested vertex in your
Direct3DRMMeshBuilder object.

C++ specification

```
HRESULT SetVertex(DWORD index, D3DVALUE x, D3DVALUE y, D3DVALUE z);
```

Parameters

index. The index of the vertex you wish to set.

x, y, and z. The x, y, and z components of the position you wish to assign to the
    requested vertex.

Returns

Successful: D3DRM_OK

Error: One of the Direct3D Retained-Mode return values.

See also

IDirect3DRM::CreateMeshBuilder

Example

```
HRESULT hRes;
LPDIRECT3DRMMESHBUILDER builder = NULL;
DWORD index;
D3DVALUE x;
D3DVALUE y;
D3DVALUE z;
    .
    .
index = 22;
x = 100.0;
y = 200.0
z = 33.0;
hRes = builder->SetVertex(index, x, y, z);
if (hRes != D3DRM_OK)
  {
    Msg("Failed to set the vertex.\n%s", MyErrorToString(hRes));
```

```
      goto ret_with_error;
   }
```

IDirect3DRMMeshBuilder::SetVertexColor

Description

This method is used to set the color of a requested vertex in your Direct3D-RMMeshBuilder object.

C++ specification

```
HRESULT SetVertexColor(DWORD index, D3DCOLOR color);
```

Parameters

index. The index of the vertex you wish to set.

color. The color you wish to assign to the requested vertex.

Returns

Successful: D3DRM_OK

Error: One of the Direct3D Retained-Mode return values.

See also

IDirect3DRMMeshBuilder::GetVertexColor

IDirect3DRMMeshBuilder::SetVertexColorRGB

Example

```
HRESULT hRes;
LPDIRECT3DRMMESHBUILDER builder = NULL;
DWORD index = 22;
D3DCOLOR color;
   .

   .
hRes = builder->SetVertexColor(index, color);
if (hRes != D3DRM_OK)
   {
    Msg("Failed to set vertex color.\n%s", MyErrorToString(hRes));
    goto ret_with_error;
   }
```

IDirect3DRMMeshBuilder::SetVertexColorRGB

Description

This method is used to set the color of a desired vertex in your Direct3D-RMMeshBuilder object.

C++ specification

```
HRESULT SetVertexColorRGB(DWORD index, D3DVALUE red,
  D3DVALUE green, D3DVALUE blue);
```

Parameters

`index`. The index of the vertex you wish set.

`red`, `green`, and `blue`. The red, green, and blue components of the color you wish to assign to the requested vertex.

Returns

Successful: D3DRM_OK

Error: One of the Direct3D Retained-Mode return values.

See also

IDirect3DRMMeshBuilder::GetVertexColor

IDirect3DRMMeshBuilder::SetVertexColor

Example

```
HRESULT hRes;
LPDIRECT3DRMMESHBUILDER builder = NULL;
DWORD index = 22;
D3DVALUE red;
D3DVALUE green;
D3DVALUE blue;
    .

    .
red = 100;
green = 50;
blue = 200;
hRes = builder->SetVertexColorRGB(index, red, green, blue);
if (hRes != D3DRM_OK)
  {
   Msg("Failed to set RGB vertex color.\n%s", MyErrorToString(hRes));
   goto ret_with_error;
  }
```

IDirect3DRMMeshBuilder::Translate

Description

This method is used to add the passed offsets to the vertex positions of your Direct3DRMMeshBuilder object.

C++ specification

```
HRESULT Translate(D3DVALUE tx, D3DVALUE ty, D3DVALUE tz);
```

Parameters

tx, ty, and tz. The offsets which are added to the x-, y-, and z-coordinates of each vertex position.

Returns

Successful: D3DRM_OK

Error: One of the Direct3D Retained-Mode return values.

See also

IDirect3DRMMeshBuilder::Scale

Example

```
HRESULT hRes;
LPDIRECT3DRMMESHBUILDER myBuilder = NULL;
D3DVALUE tx;
D3DVALUE ty;
D3DVALUE tz;
    .
    .
tx = 100.0;
ty = 50.0;
tz = 50.0;
hRes = myBuider->Translate(tx, ty, tz);
if (hRes != D3DRM_OK)
   {
    Msg("Failed to translate this object.\n%s", MyErrorToString(hRes));
    goto ret_with_error;
   }
```

chapter 31

The IDirect3DRMObject interface

The IDirect3DRMObject interface and methods

The methods of the IDirect3DRMObject interface are used to work with the object superclass of Direct3DRM objects.

The Direct3DRMObject object can be acquired through the appropriate call to the QueryInterface method from your Direct3DRM objects. All Direct3DRM objects inherit the IDirect3DRMObject interface methods.

Like all COM interfaces, this interface inherits the IUnknown interface methods. These consist of AddRef, QueryInterface, and Release.

The IDirect3DRMObject interface methods can be organized into the groups in table 31.1.

Table 31.1 IDirect3DRMObject methods

Group	Methods
Application-specific	GetAppData
data	SetAppData
Cloning	Clone
Naming	GetClassName
	GetName
	SetName
Notifications	AddDestroyCallback
	DeleteDestroyCallback

IDirect3DRMObject::AddDestroyCallback

Description

This method is used to register a function to be called when an object is destroyed.

C++ specification

```
HRESULT AddDestroyCallback(D3DRMOBJECTCALLBACK lpCallback,
  LPVOID lpArg);
```

Parameters

lpCallback. The user-defined callback function you wish to be called when your object is destroyed.

lpArg. The address of application-defined data to be passed to your callback function. Due to the fact that this function is called after your object has been destroyed, you should not call this function with the object as an argument.

Returns

Successful: D3DRM_OK

Error: One of the Direct3D Retained-Mode return values.

See also

IDirect3DRMObject::DeleteDestroyCallback

Example

```
HRESULT myResult;
  .
  .
  .
myResult = myObject->AddDestroyCallback(cleanupObjects, &info);
if (myResult!= D3DRM_OK)
  {
```

```
    Msg("Failed to add destoy callback\n%s", MyErrorToString(myResult));
    return FALSE;
}
```

IDirect3DRMObject::Clone

Description

This method is used to create a copy of one of your objects.

C++ specification

```
HRESULT Clone(LPUNKNOWN pUnkOuter, REFIID riid, LPVOID *ppvObj);
```

Parameters

pUnkOuter. This parameter allows COM aggregation features.

riid. The identifier of the object you are copying.

ppvObj. The address to place the copy of the object when this method returns.

Returns

Successful: D3DRM_OK

Error: One of the Direct3D Retained-Mode return values.

See also

IDirect3DRMObject::GetAppData

IDirect3DRMObject::SetAppData

Example

```
LPDIRECT3DRMOBJECT myObject = NULL;
.
.
.
if (myObject)
    myObject->Release();
HRESULT myResult = object->Clone(0, IID_IDirect3DRMObject, (void **)
        &myObject);
if (myResult!= D3DRM_OK)
 {
  Msg("Failed to add clone the object\n%s", MyErrorToString(myResult));
  return FALSE;
 }
```

IDirect3DRMObject::DeleteDestroyCallback

Description

This method is used to remove a function which you previously registered with the `IDirect3DRMObject::AddDestroyCallback` method.

C++ specification

```
HRESULT DeleteDestroyCallback(D3DRMOBJECTCALLBACK d3drmObjProc,
  LPVOID lpArg);
```

Parameters

d3drmObjProc. The user-defined `D3DRMOBJECTCALLBACK` callback function you wish to be called when the object is destroyed.

lpArg. The address of your application-defined data passed to the callback function.

Returns

Successful: D3DRM_OK

Error: One of the Direct3D Retained-Mode return values.

See also

IDirect3DRMObject::AddDestroyCallback

Example

```
typedef struct _myData {
  .
  .
  LPDIRECT3DEXECUTEBUFFER eb;
  LPDIRECT3DMATERIAL material;
  LPDIRECT3DRMDEVICE device;
} myData;
.
.
void CDECL CleanupMyObjects(LPDIRECT3DRMOBJECT dev, void* arg)
{
  myData* data = (myData*) arg;

  if (data->eb) {
    data->eb->Release();
    data->material->Release();
    data->eb = NULL;
    data->device = NULL;
  }
}

void CDECL DestroyMyObject(LPDIRECT3DRMOBJECT obj, void* arg)
{
```

```
      .
   myResult = data->device->DeleteDestroyCallback(CleanupMyObjects, arg);
   if (myResult!= D3DRM_OK)
   {
     Msg("Failed to delete destoy callback\n%s", MyError-
        ToString(myResult));
     return FALSE;
   }
   CleanupMyObjects((LPDIRECT3DRMOBJECT)myData->device, (void*)
        myData);
   free(myData);
}
```

IDirect3DRMObject::GetAppData

Description

This method is used to acquire the 32 bits of application-specific data from your object. The default value is 0.

C++ specification

```
DWORD GetAppData();
```

Parameters

None

Returns

The data value which is defined by your application.

See also

IDirect3DRMObject::GetClassName
IDirect3DRMObject::SetAppData

Example

```
LPDIRECT3DRMFRAME f;
   .
   .
D3MinObj *d3mo = new D3MinObj;
if ((d3mo = (D3MinObj *)(lpFrame->GetAppData()) ) == 0) continue;

if (FAILED(f->AddVisual ((LPDIRECT3DRMVISUAL)obj_mesh)))
  return FALSE;

f->SetAppData ((DWORD)d3mo);
d3mo->SetNr (frameNr++);
```

IDirect3DRMObject::GetClassName

Description

This method is used to acquire the name of your object's class.

C++ specification

```
HRESULT GetClassName(LPDWORD lpdwSize, LPSTR lpName);
```

Parameters

lpdwSize. The address of a variable which holds the size, in bytes, of the buffer pointed to by the lpName parameter.

lpName. The address of a variable you wish filled with a null-terminated string identifying the class name when the method returns. If this parameter is set to NULL, the lpdwSize parameter will be filled with the required size for the string when the method returns.

Returns

Successful: D3DRM_OK

Error: One of the Direct3D Retained-Mode return values.

See also

IDirect3DRMObject::GetAppData

Example

```
HRESULT myResult;
LPDWORD buffSize;
LPSTR className;
LPDIRECT3DRMOBJECT myObject;
  .
  .
HRESULT myResult = myObject->GetClassName(buffSize, className);
if (myResult!= D3DRM_OK)
  {
    Msg("Failed to get the class name\n%s", MyErrorToString(myResult));
    return FALSE;
  }
```

IDirect3DRMObject::GetName

Description

This method is used to acquire the object's name.

C++ specification

```
HRESULT GetName(LPDWORD lpdwSize, LPSTR lpName);
```

Parameters

lpdwSize. The address of a variable which contains the size, in bytes, of the buffer pointed to by the lpName parameter.

lpName. The address of a variable you wish filled with a null-terminated string specifying the object's name when the method returns. If this parameter is set to NULL, the lpdwSize parameter will be filled with the required size for the string when this method returns.

Returns

Successful: D3DRM_OK

Error: One of the Direct3D Retained-Mode return values.

See also

IDirect3DRMObject::SetName

Example

```
LPDIRECT3DRMOBJECT myObject;
HRESULT myResult;
DWORD dwSize;
char szName[256];

if(!pObject)
  return FALSE;
.
.
.
dwSize = (DWORD)(sizeof(szName)/sizeof(char)) - 1;
myResult = myObject->GetName(&dwSize, szName);
if (myResult!= D3DRM_OK)
  {
    Msg("Failed to get the object's name\n%s", MyErrorToString(myRe-
        sult));
    return FALSE;
  }
```

IDirect3DRMObject::SetAppData

Description

This method is used to set the 32 bits of your application-specific data in your object.

C++ specification

```
HRESULT SetAppData(DWORD ulData);
```

Parameters

ulData. The user-defined data you wish to be stored with the object.

Returns

Successful: D3DRM_OK

Error: One of the Direct3D Retained-ModeRetained-Mode return values.

See also

IDirect3DRMObject::GetAppData

Example

```
LPDIRECT3DRMOBJECT f;
.
.
D3MinObj *d3mo = new D3MinObj;
if ((d3mo = (D3MinObj *)(lpFrame->GetAppData()) ) == 0) continue;

if (FAILED(f->AddVisual ((LPDIRECT3DRMVISUAL)obj_mesh)))
  return FALSE;

HRESULT myResult = f->SetAppData ((DWORD)d3mo);
if (myResult!= D3DRM_OK)
  {
    Msg("Failed to set the application data\n%s", MyErrorToString(myRe-
        sult));
    return FALSE;
  }
```

IDirect3DRMObject::SetName

Description

This method is used to set your object's name.

C++ specification

```
HRESULT SetName(const char * lpName);
```

Parameters

lpName. Your user-defined data you wish to be the name for your object.

Returns

Successful: D3DRM_OK

Error: One of the Direct3D Retained-Mode return values.

See also

IDirect3DRMObject::GetName

Example

```
char name[30] = "myName";
LPDIRECT3DRMOBJECT myObject;
HRESULT myResult;
  .
  .
myResult = myObject->SetName(name);
if (myResult!= D3DRM_OK)
  {
    Msg("Failed to set the object's name\n%s", MyErrorToString(myRe-
        sult));
    return FALSE;
  }
```

chapter 32

The IDirect3DRMPickedArray interface

The IDirect3DRMPickedArray interface and methods

The methods of the IDirect3DRMPickedArray interface are used to organize pick objects.

The Direct3DRMObject object can be acquired through the `IDirect3D-RMViewport::Pick` method.

Like all COM interfaces, this interface inherits the IUnknown interface methods. These consist of `AddRef`, `QueryInterface`, and `Release`.

571

The IDirect3DRMPickedArray interface inherits the following methods from the IDirect3DRMObject interface:

Table 32.1 Methods inherited from IDirect3DRMObject

Methods

AddDestroyCallback

Clone

DeleteDestroyCallback

GetAppData

GetClassName

GetName

SetAppData

SetName

IDirect3DRMPickedArray::GetPick

Description

This method is used to acquire the Direct3DRMVisual and Direct3DRMFrame objects intersected by the indicated pick.

C++ specification

```
HRESULT GetPick(DWORD index, LPDIRECT3DRMVISUAL * lplpVisual,
    LPDIRECT3DRMFRAMEARRAY * lplpFrameArray,
    LPD3DRMPICKDESC lpD3DRMPickDesc);
```

Parameters

index. The index into your pick array which indicates the pick you want to acquire information for.

lplpVisual. The address you want filled with a pointer to the Direct3DRMVisual object associated with your indicated pick.

lplpFrameArray. The address you want filled with a pointer to the Direct3D-RMFrameArray object associated with your indicated pick.

lpD3DRMPickDesc. The address of a D3DRMPICKDESC structure which defines the pick position and face and group identifiers for the objects it will get.

Returns

Successful: D3DRM_OK

Error: One of the Direct3D Retained-Mode return values.

See also

IDirect3DRMViewport::Pick

IDirect3DRMPickedArray::GetSize

Example

```
void Locateand ChooseVisual(LPDIRECT3DRMVIEWPORT view, int x, int y)
{
  LPDIRECT3DRMVISUAL visual;
  LPDIRECT3DRMFRAME frame;
  LPDIRECT3DRMPICKEDARRAY picked;
  LPDIRECT3DRMFRAMEARRAY frames;
  LPDIRECT3DRMMESHBUILDER mesh;

  DeselectVisual();

  // Get a depth-sorted list of objects (and faces, if they exist).
       These will include the path which was
  // taken in the hierarchy going from the root down to the frame con-
       taining the object
  view->Pick(x, y, &picked);
  // As long as there are items, let's deal with them
  if (picked)
  {
    // Get the number of elements in the picked array
    if (picked->GetSize())
    {
      // Get the visual and frame objects that were intersected
      // by the pick
      picked->GetPick(0, &visual, &frames, 0);
      // Get the closest frame
      frames->GetElement(frames->GetSize() - 1, &frame);
      if (SUCCEEDED(visual->QueryInterface(IID_IDirect3DRMMeshBuilder,
        (void **) &mesh)))
      {
        // Select the object
        SelectVisual(mesh, frame);
        mesh->Release();
      }
      // Free everything up
      frame->Release();
      frames->Release();
      visual->Release();
    }
    picked->Release();
  }
}
```

IDirect3DRMPickedArray::GetSize

Description

This method is used to acquire the number of elements contained in a Direct3D-RMPickedArray object.

C++ specification

```
DWORD GetSize();
```

Parameters

None

Returns

The number of elements in the IDirect3DRMPickedArray object.

See also

IDirect3DRMPickedArray::GetPick

Example

```
void LocateandChooseVisual(LPDIRECT3DRMVIEWPORT view, int x, int y)
{
  LPDIRECT3DRMVISUAL visual;
  LPDIRECT3DRMFRAME frame;
  LPDIRECT3DRMPICKEDARRAY picked;
  LPDIRECT3DRMFRAMEARRAY frames;
  LPDIRECT3DRMMESHBUILDER mesh;

  DeselectVisual();

  // Get a depth-sorted list of objects (and faces, if they exist).
       These will include the path which was
  // taken in the hierarchy going from the root down to the frame con-
       taining the object
  view->Pick(x, y, &picked);
  // As long as there are items, let's deal with them
  if (picked)
  {
    // Get the number of elements in the picked array
    if (picked->GetSize())
    {
      // Get the visual and frame objects that were intersected by the pick
      picked->GetPick(0, &visual, &frames, 0);
      // Get the closest frame
      frames->GetElement(frames->GetSize() - 1, &frame);
      if (SUCCEEDED(visual->QueryInterface(IID_IDirect3DRMMeshBuilder,
        (void **) &mesh)))
      {
```

```
        // Select the object
        SelectVisual(mesh, frame);
        mesh->Release();
    }
    // Free everything up
    frame->Release();
    frames->Release();
    visual->Release();
  }
  picked->Release();
 }
}
```

chapter 33

The IDirect3DRMShadow interface

The IDirect3DRMShadow interface and methods

The methods of the IDirect3DRMShadow interface are used to initialize Direct3DRMShadow objects. You do not need to initialize these objects if you call the `IDirect3DRM::CreateShadow` method; but you do need to initialize them if your application calls the `IDirect3DRM::CreateObject` method to create the shadow.

The IDirect3DRMShadow interface supports the `Init` method. And like all COM interfaces, this interface inherits the IUnknown interface methods. These consist of `AddRef`, `QueryInterface`, and `Release`.

The IDirect3DRMShadow interface also inherits the methods shown in table 33.1 from the IDirect3DRMObject interface:

Methods
AddDestroyCallback
Clone
DeleteDestroyCallback
GetAppData
GetClassName
GetName
SetAppData
SetName

IDirect3DRMShadow::Init

Description

This method is used to initialize a Direct3DRMShadow object.

C++ specification

```
HRESULT Init(LPDIRECT3DRMVISUAL lpD3DRMVisual,
    LPDIRECT3DRMLIGHT lpD3DRMLight, D3DVALUE px, D3DVALUE py,
    D3DVALUE pz, D3DVALUE nx, D3DVALUE ny, D3DVALUE nz);
```

Parameters

lpD3DRMVisual. The address of your Direct3DRMVisual object which is casting the shadow.

lpD3DRMLight. The address of the Direct3DRMLight object providing the light which defines the shadow.

px, py, and pz. The coordinates of a point on the plane upon which the shadow is cast.

nx, ny, and nz. The coordinates of the normal vector of the plane upon which the shadow is cast.

Returns

Successful: D3DRM_OK

Error: One of the Direct3D Retained-Mode return values.

See also

IDirect3DRM::CreateShadow

Example

```
LPDIRECT3DRMSHADOW shadow;
LPDIRECT3DRMLIGHT pointLight
```

```
     .
     .
if (shadow->Init((LPDIRECT3DRMVISUAL*)&well , pointlight,
        D3DVALUE(0), box.max.y+D3DVALUE(0.1), D3DVALUE(0),
        D3DVALUE(0), box.max.y+D3DVALUE(1.0), D3DVALUE(0)) !=
        D3DRM_OK)
    goto generic_error;
```

chapter 34

The IDirect3DRM Texture interface

The IDirect3DRM Texture interface and methods

The methods of the IDirect3DRMTexture interface are used to work with textures.

And like all COM interfaces, this interface inherits the IUnknown interface methods. These consist of `AddRef`, `QueryInterface`, and `Release`.

The methods of the IDirect3DRMTexture interface can be organized into the groups in table 34.1.

Table 34.1 IDirect3DRMTexture methods

Group	Methods
Color	GetColors
	SetColors
Decals	GetDecalOrigin
	GetDecalScale
	GetDecalSize
	GetDecalTransparency
	GetDecalTransparentColor
	SetDecalOrigin
	SetDecalScale
	SetDecalSize
	SetDecalTransparency
	SetDecalTransparentColor
Images	GetImage
Initialization	InitFromFile
	InitFromResource
	InitFromSurface
Renderer notification	Changed
Shading	GetShades
	SetShades

The IDirect3DRMTexture interface also inherits the following methods from the IDirect3DRMObject interface:

Table 34.2 Methods inherited from IDirect3DRMObject

Methods
AddDestroyCallback
Clone
DeleteDestroyCallback
GetAppData
GetClassName
GetName
SetAppData
SetName

IDirect3DRMTexture::Changed

Description

This method is used to inform the renderer that your application has changed the pixels or the palette of a texture.

C++ specification

```
HRESULT Changed(BOOL bPixels, BOOL bPalette);
```

Parameters

bPixels. If this parameter is set to TRUE, it indicates the pixels have changed.
bPalette. If this parameter is set to TRUE, it indicates the palette has changed.

Returns

Successful: D3DRM_OK
Error: One of the Direct3D Retained-Mode return values.

See also

You might wish to pick up some DirectDraw reference information to learn more about DirectDraw

Example

```
LPDIRECT3DRMTEXTURE myTex = NULL;
LPDIRECTDRAWSURFACE   lpDDSTexture = NULL; // Z-buffer
RECT rc;
RECT rcSrc;
HRESULT rVal;
SetRect(&rc,0,0,256,256);
SetRect(&rcSrc,0,0,dwWidth,dwHeight);
    .
    .
lpDDSTexture->Unlock(NULL);
lpDDSTexture->Blt(&rc, lpDDSSource, &rcSrc, DDBLT_WAIT, NULL);
lpDDSTexture->Lock(NULL, &ddsd, DDLOCK_WAIT, NULL);
rVal = myTex->Changed(TRUE, FALSE);
if (rval != D3DRM_OK)
  {
   Msg("Failed to get changed status for this texture.\n%s", MyError-
       ToString(rval));
   goto ret_with_error;
  }
Render();
```

IDirect3DRMTexture::GetColors

Description

This method is used to retrieve the maximum number of colors used for rendering a texture. This method returns the number of colors which the texture was quantized to, *not* the number of colors in the image from which your texture was created. Because of this, the number of colors which is returned will usually match the colors you set by calling the `IDirect3DRM::SetDefaultTextureColors` method, unless you used the `IDirect3DRMTexture::SetColors` method explicitly to change the colors for your texture.

C++ specification

```
DWORD GetColors();
```

Parameters

None

Returns

Returns the number of colors.

See also

IDirect3DRMTexture::SetColors

Example

```
LPDIRECT3DRMTEXTURE tex = NULL;
DWORD numColors;
    .
    .
    .
numColors = tex->GetColors();
```

IDirect3DRMTexture::GetDecalOrigin

Description

This method is used to acquire the current origin of your decal.

C++ specification

```
HRESULT GetDecalOrigin(LONG * lplX, LONG * lplY);
```

Parameters

lplX and lplY. The addresses of variables you wish to be filled with the origin of your decal when the method returns.

Returns

Successful: D3DRM_OK

Error: One of the Direct3D Retained-Mode return values.

See also

IDirect3DRMTexture::SetDecalOrigin

Example

```
LPDIRECT3DRMTEXTURE tex = NULL;
HRESULT myResult;
LONG * lplX;
LONG * lplY;
   .

   .
myResult = tex->GetDecalOrigin(lplX, lplY);
if (myResult != D3DRM_OK)
  {
   Msg("Failed to get changed status for this decal.\n%s", MyError-
       ToString(rval));
   goto ret_with_error;
  }
```

IDirect3DRMTexture::GetDecalScale

Description

The method is used to acquire the scaling property of your decal.

C++ specification

```
DWORD GetDecalScale();
```

Parameters

None

Returns

Successful: The scaling property

Error: -1

See also

IDirect3DRMTexture::SetDecalScale

Example

```
LPDIRECT3DRMTEXTURE tex = NULL;
DWORD scale;
   .
```

```
    .
scale = tex->GetDecalScale();
if (scale == -1)
  {
   Msg("Failed to get scaling property for this decal.\n%s", MyError-
        ToString(rval));
   goto ret_with_error;
  }
```

IDirect3DRMTexture::GetDecalSize

Description

This method is used to acquire the size of your decal.

C++ specification

```
HRESULT GetDecalSize(D3DVALUE *lprvWidth, D3DVALUE *lprvHeight);
```

Parameters

lprvWidth. The address of a variable you wish filled with the width of your decal
when the method returns.

lprvHeight. The addresses of a variable you wish filled with the height of your
decal when the method returns.

Returns

Successful: D3DRM_OK

Error: One of the Direct3D Retained-Mode return values.

See also

IDirect3DRMTexture::SetDecalSize

Example

```
LPDIRECT3DRMTEXTURE tex = NULL;
D3DVALUE *lprvWidth = NULL;
D3DVALUE *lprvHeight = NULL;
    .
    .
scale = tex->GetDecalSize(lprvWidth, lprvHeight);
if (myResult == -1)
  {
   Msg("Failed to get the size for this decal.\n%s", MyError-
        ToString(rval));
   goto ret_with_error;
  }
```

IDirect3DRMTexture::GetDecalTransparency

Description

This method is used to acquire the transparency property of your decal.

C++ specification

```
BOOL GetDecalTransparency();
```

Parameters

None

Returns

Returns TRUE if the decal has a transparent color, FALSE otherwise.

See also

IDirect3DRMTexture::SetDecalTransparency

Example

```
LPDIRECT3DRMTEXTURE tex = NULL;
BOOL transparency;
   .
   .
transparency = tex->GetDecalTransparency();
```


IDirect3DRMTexture::GetDecalTransparentColor

Description

This method is used to acquire the transparent color of your decal.

C++ specification

```
D3DCOLOR GetDecalTransparentColor();
```

Parameters

None

Returns

The value of your transparent color.

See also

IDirect3DRMTexture::SetDecalTransparentColor

Example

```
LPDIRECT3DRMTEXTURE tex = NULL;
D3DCOLOR transparentColor;
```

```
                .
                .
        transparentColor = tex->GetDecalTransparenctColor();
```

IDirect3DRMTexture::GetImage

Description

This method is used to acquire an address of the image which your texture was created with.

C++ specification

```
D3DRMIMAGE * GetImage();
```

Parameters

None

Returns

The address of the D3DRMIMAGE structure that your current texture was created with.

See also

IDirect3DRM::LoadTexture

Example

```
HRESULT loadTextures(char *name, void *arg, LPDIRECT3DRMTEXTURE *tex-
        ture)
{
    HRESULT returnVal = g_D3DRM->LoadTexture(name, texture);
    LPDIRECT3DRMTEXTURE myTexture = *texture;
    if (!myTexture) return -1;

    D3DRMIMAGE *image;

    // if the texture is a bmp then flip it
    if (strstr(name, ".bmp") == NULL)
    {
        image = myTexture->GetImage();
        void *line = malloc(image->bytes_per_line);
        if(!line)
          return -1;
        for(int i=0;i<image->height/2;i++)
        {
            memcpy(line,(char *)image->buffer1+i*
                    image->bytes_per_line, image->bytes_per_line);
            memcpy((char *)image->buffer1+i*image->bytes_per_line,
                    (char *)image->buffer1+(image->height - 1 - i)*
                        image->bytes_per_line,
```

```
                    image->bytes_per_line);
            memcpy((char *)image->buffer1+(image->height - 1 - i)*
                image->bytes_per_line, line,image->bytes_per_line);
        }
        myTexture->Changed(TRUE,FALSE);
        free(line);
    }
  return returnVal;
}
```

IDirect3DRMTexture::GetShades

Description

This method is used to acquire the number of shades used for each color in your texture when it is rendered.

C++ specification

```
DWORD GetShades();
```

Parameters

None

Returns

The number of shades.

See also

IDirect3DRMTexture::SetShades

Example

```
LPDIRECT3DRMTEXTURE tex = NULL;
DWORD numShades;
.
.
numShades = tex->GetShades();
```

IDirect3DRMTexture::InitFromFile

Description

This method is used to initialize your texture using the information in a specified file. The texture to be initialized must have been created using the `IDirect-3DRM::CreateObject` method.

C++ specification

```
HRESULT InitFromFile(const char *filename);
```

Parameters

filename. The address of a string indicating the file where your initialization information is stored.

Returns

Successful: D3DRM_OK

Error: One of the Direct3D Retained-Mode return values.

See also

IDirect3DRMTexture::InitFromResource

IDirect3DRMTexture::InitFromSurface

Example

```
HRESULT myResult;
char *filename;
LPDIRECT3DRMTEXTURE tex = NULL;
 .
 .
 .
// Create texture using IDirect3DRM::CreateObject
 .
 .
 .
myResult = tex->InitFromFile(filename);
if (myResult != D3DRM_OK)
  {
   Msg("Failed to initialize this texture.\n%s", MyError-
       ToString(rval));
   goto ret_with_error;
  }
```

IDirect3DRMTexture::InitFromResource

Description

This method is used to initialize your Direct3DRMTexture object from a specified resource.

C++ specification

```
HRESULT InitFromResource(HRSRC rs);
```

Parameters

rs. The handle of the specified resource.

Returns

Successful: D3DRM_OK

Error: One of the Direct3D Retained-Mode return values.

See also

IDirect3DRMTexture::InitFromFile

IDirect3DRMTexture::InitFromSurface

Example

```
HRESULT myResult;
HRSRC resource;
LPDIRECT3DRMTEXTURE tex = NULL;
 .
 .
myResult = tex->InitFromResource(resource);
if (myResult != D3DRM_OK)
  {
   Msg("Failed to initialize this texture.\n%s", MyError-
       ToString(rval));
   goto ret_with_error;
  }
```

IDirect3DRMTexture::InitFromSurface

Description

This method is used to initialize your texture using the data from your passed DirectDraw surface.

C++ specification

```
HRESULT InitFromSurface(LPDIRECTDRAWSURFACE lpDDS);
```

Parameters

lpDDS. The address of your DirectDraw surface where your initialization information will be drawn.

Returns

Successful: D3DRM_OK

Error: One of the Direct3D Retained-Mode return values.

See also

IDirect3DRMTexture::InitFromFile

IDirect3DRMTexture::InitFromResource

```
HRESULT myResult;
LPDIRECTDRAWSURFACE mySurface;
LPDIRECT3DRMTEXTURE myTexture;
  .
  .
myResult = myTexture->InitFromSurface(mySurface);
if (myResult != D3DRM_OK)
  {
   Msg("Failed to initialize this texture.\n%s", MyError-
       ToString(rval));
   goto ret_with_error;
  }
```

IDirect3DRMTexture::SetColors

Description

This method is used to set the maximum number of colors you wish to use for rendering a texture. This method is only required for the ramp color model.

C++ specification

```
HRESULT SetColors(DWORD ulColors);
```

Parameters

`ulColors`. The number of colors with a default value of 8.

Returns

Successful: D3DRM_OK

Error: One of the Direct3D Retained-Mode return values.

See also

IDirect3DRMTexture::GetColors

Example

```
LPDIRECT3DRMTEXTURE myTexture;
  .
  .
lpD3DRM->LoadTexture("testurePict.ppm", &myTexture);
if (myTexture->SetColors(256) != D3DRM_OK)
   goto generic_error;
if (myTexture->SetShades(1) != D3DRM_OK)
   goto generic_error;
```

IDirect3DRMTexture::SetDecalOrigin

Description

This method is used to set the origin of your decal as an offset from the top left of the decal. The decal's origin is mapped to its frame's position when it is rendered.

C++ specification

```
HRESULT SetDecalOrigin(LONG lX, LONG lY);
```

Parameters

lX and lY. The new origin for the decal in decal coordinates. The default origin is [0, 0].

Returns

Successful: D3DRM_OK

Error: One of the Direct3D Retained-Mode return values.

See also

IDirect3DRMTexture::GetDecalOrigin

Example

```
LPDIRECT3DRMTEXTURE myTexture;
HRESULT returnVal;
.
.
returnVal = lpD3DRM ->LoadTexture(lpD3DRM, "myPicture.ppm", &tex);
if (returnVal != D3DRM_OK)
  {
    Msg("Failed to load ppm file.\n");
    goto ret_with_error;
  }
returnVal = myTexture->SetColors(tex, 32);
if (returnVal != D3DRM_OK)
{
    Msg("Failed to set the texture colors.\n");
    goto ret_with_error;
}
returnVal = myTexture->SetDecalScale(tex, TRUE);
if (returnVal != D3DRM_OK)
{
    Msg("Failed to set the decal scale.\n");
    goto ret_with_error;
}
returnVal = myTexture->SetDecalOrigin(tex, 128, 128)))
if (returnVal != D3DRM_OK)
{
```

```
        Msg("Failed to set the decal origin.\n");
        goto ret_with_error;
    }
```

IDirect3DRMTexture::SetDecalScale

Description
This method is used to set the scaling property for your decal.

C++ specification
```
HRESULT SetDecalScale(DWORD dwScale);
```

Parameters
dwScale. The depth is taken into account when the decal is scaled if this parameter is set to TRUE. The depth information is ignored if this parameter is set to FALSE. The default value of this parameter is TRUE.

Returns
Successful: D3DRM_OK

Error: One of the Direct3D Retained-Mode return values.

See also
IDirect3DRMTexture::GetDecalScale

Example
```
LPDIRECT3DRMTEXTURE myTexture;
HRESULT returnVal;
    .
    .
returnVal = lpD3DRM ->LoadTexture(lpD3DRM, "myPicture.ppm", &tex);
if (returnVal != D3DRM_OK)
  {
    Msg("Failed to load ppm file.\n");
    goto ret_with_error;
  }
returnVal = myTexture->SetColors(tex, 32);
if (returnVal != D3DRM_OK)
{
    Msg("Failed to set the texture colors.\n");
    goto ret_with_error;
}
returnVal = myTexture->SetDecalScale(tex, TRUE);
if (returnVal != D3DRM_OK)
{
    Msg("Failed to set the decal scale.\n");
```

```
        goto ret_with_error;
    }
returnVal = myTexture->SetDecalOrigin(tex, 128, 128)))
if (returnVal != D3DRM_OK)
{
    Msg("Failed to set the decal origin.\n");
    goto ret_with_error;
```

IDirect3DRMTexture::SetDecalSize

Description

This method is used to set the size of your decal if it is being scaled according to its depth in your scene.

C++ specification

```
HRESULT SetDecalSize(D3DVALUE rvWidth, D3DVALUE rvHeight);
```

Parameters

rvWidth . The new width in model coordinates of your decal. Default size = 1.0.

rvHeight. The new height in model coordinates of the decal. Default size = 1.0.

Returns

Successful: D3DRM_OK

Error: One of the Direct3D Retained-Mode return values.

See also

IDirect3DRMTexture::GetDecalSize

Example

```
LPDIRECT3DRMTEXTURE myTexture;
HRESULT rval;
    .
    .
rval = lpD3DRM ->LoadTexture(lpD3DRM, "myPicture.ppm", &tex);
if (rval != D3DRM_OK)
  {
    Msg("Failed to load ppm file.\n");
    goto ret_with_error;
  }
rval = (myTexture->SetColors(tex, 32);
if (rval != D3DRM_OK)
  {
    Msg("Failed to set the texture colors.\n");
    goto ret_with_error;
  }
```

```
rval = myTexture->SetDecalScale(tex, TRUE);
if (rval != D3DRM_OK)
  {
    Msg("Failed to set the decal scale.\n");
    goto ret_with_error;
  }
rval = myTexture->SetDecalSize(decalTex, D3DVAL(2.0), D3DVAL(2.0)));
if (rval != D3DRM_OK)
  {
    Msg("Failed to set decal size.\n");
    goto ret_with_error;
  }
rval = myTexture->SetDecalOrigin(tex, 128, 128);
if (rval != D3DRM_OK)
  {
    Msg("Failed to set the decal origin.\n");
    goto ret_with_error;
  }
```

IDirect3DRMTexture::SetDecalTransparency

Description

This method is used to set the transparency property of your decal.

C++ specification

```
HRESULT SetDecalTransparency(BOOL bTransp);
```

Parameters

bTransp. If this parameter is TRUE it indicates the decal has a transparent color. If
it is FALSE it indicates it has an opaque color. The default value of this parameter is FALSE.

Returns

Successful: D3DRM_OK
Error: One of the Direct3D Retained-Mode return values.

See also

IDirect3DRMTexture::GetDecalTransparency

Example

```
returnVal = lpD3DRM->LoadTexture(lpD3DRM, "checker.ppm", &tex);
if (returnVal != D3DRM_OK) {
    Msg("Failed to load checker.ppm.\n");
    goto ret_with_error;
}
```

```
rval = tex->SetDecalTransparency(tex, TRUE);
if (rval != D3DRM_OK)
  {
    Msg("Failed to set the decal transparency.\n");
    goto ret_with_error;
  }

if (FAILED(obj->SetGroupTexture(obj, D3DRMGROUP_ALLGROUPS, tex)))
    goto generic_error;

if (FAILED(obj->SetGroupMapping(obj, D3DRMGROUP_ALLGROUPS,
   D3DRMMAP_PERSPCORRECT)))
    goto generic_error;
```

IDirect3DRMTexture::SetDecalTransparentColor

Description

This method is used to set the transparent color of your decal.

C++ specification

```
HRESULT SetDecalTransparentColor(D3DCOLOR rcTransp);
```

Parameters

rcTransp. The new transparent color for your decal with a default of black.

Returns

Successful: D3DRM_OK

Error: One of the Direct3D Retained-Mode return values.

See also

IDirect3DRMTexture::GetDecalTransparentColor

Example

```
LPDIRECT3DRMTEXTURE myTexture;
HRESULT rval;
 .
 .
rval = lpD3DRM ->LoadTexture(lpD3DRM, "myPicture.ppm", &tex);
if (rval != D3DRM_OK)
  {
    Msg("Failed to load ppm file.\n");
    goto ret_with_error;
  }
rval = (myTexture->SetColors(tex, 32);
if (rval != D3DRM_OK)
  {
```

```
        Msg("Failed to set the texture colors.\n");
        goto ret_with_error;
      }
    rval = myTexture->SetDecalScale(tex, TRUE);
    if (rval != D3DRM_OK)
      {
        Msg("Failed to set the decal scale.\n");
        goto ret_with_error;
      }
    rval = myTexture->SetDecalSize(decalTex, D3DVAL(2.0), D3DVAL(2.0)));
    if (rval != D3DRM_OK)
      {
        Msg("Failed to set decal size.\n");
        goto ret_with_error;
      }
    rval = myTexture->SetDecalOrigin(tex, 128, 128);
    if (rval != D3DRM_OK)
      {
        Msg("Failed to set the decal origin.\n");
        goto ret_with_error;
      }
    rval = myTexture->SetDecalTransparentColor(D3DVAL(0));
    if (rval != D3DRM_OK)
      {
        Msg("Failed to set the decal transparent color.\n");
        goto ret_with_error;
      }
```

IDirect3DRMTexture::SetShades

Description

This method is used to set the maximum number of shades to use for each color of your texture when rendering. This method is only required for the ramp color model.

C++ specification

```
HRESULT SetShades(DWORD ulShades);
```

Parameters

ulShades. The new number of shades for your texture. This value must be a power of 2 and the default value is 16.

Returns

Successful: D3DRM_OK

Error: One of the Direct3D Retained-Mode return values.

See also

　　IDirect3DRMTexture::GetShades

Example

```
LPDIRECT3DRMTEXTURE myTexture;
HRESULT rval;
.
.
.
lpD3DRM->LoadTexture("lake.ppm", &myTexture);
rval = myTexture->SetColors(256);
if (rval != D3DRM_OK)
  {
    Msg("Failed to set the texture colors.\n");
    goto ret_with_error;
  }
rval = myTexture->SetShades(1);
if (rval != D3DRM_OK)
  {
    Msg("Failed to set the texture shades.\n");
    goto ret_with_error;
  }
```

chapter 35

The IDirect3DRMUserVisual interface

The IDirect3DRMUserVisual interface and methods

The IDirect3DRMUserVisual interface is used to initialize Direct3DRMUserVisual objects. The `init` method is required only if your application calls the `IDirect3DRM::CreateObject` method to create your user-visual object. It is not necessary to use this initialization if your application calls the `IDirect3DRM::CreateUserVisual` method.

Like all COM interfaces, this interface inherits the IUnknown interface methods. These consist of `AddRef`, `QueryInterface`, and `Release`.

The IDirect3DRMUserVisual interface only supports the `Init` method.

The IDirect3DRMUserVisual interface also inherits the methods shown in table 35.1 from the IDirect3DRMObject interface.

IDirect3DRMUserVisual::Init

Description

This method is used to initialize a Direct3DRMUserVisual object. The `IDirect3DRM::CreateUserVisual` method can be used to create and initialize a user-visual object all at once. You will only need to call the `IDirect3DRMUserVisual::Init` method when you create a user visual object by calling the `IDirect3DRM::CreateObject` method.

C++ specification

```
HRESULT Init(D3DRMUSERVISUALCALLBACK d3drmUVProc, void * lpArg);
```

Parameters

`d3drmUVProc`. Your application-defined D3DRMUSERVISUALCALLBACK callback function.

`lpArg`. Your application-defined data you wish passed to your callback function.

Returns

Successful: D3DRM_OK

Error: One of the Direct3D Retained-Mode return values.

See also

IDirect3DRM::CreateObject

Example

```
typedef struct _stuff {
  D3DVECTOR parts[MAX_PARTS];
  LPDIRECT3DRMDEVICE dev;
  LPDIRECT3DEXECUTEBUFFER eb;
  LPDIRECT3DMATERIAL mat;
```

```
} MyStuff;

void CDECL DestroyStuff(LPDIRECT3DRMOBJECT obj, void* arg)
{
  MyStuff* stuff = (MyStuff*) arg;

  if (stuff->dev)
    stuff->DeleteDestroyCallback(CleanupMyObjects, arg);
  CleanupMyObjects((LPDIRECT3DRMOBJECT)stuff->dev, (void*) stuff);
  delete stuff;
}

int CDECL MyCallback(LPDIRECT3DRMUSERVISUAL uvis,
        void* arg,
        D3DRMUSERVISUALREASON reason,
        LPDIRECT3DRMDEVICE dev,
        LPDIRECT3DRMVIEWPORT view)
{
  MyStuff* stuff = (MyStuff*) arg;

  if (reason == D3DRMUSERVISUAL_CANSEE)
    return TRUE;

  if (reason == D3DRMUSERVISUAL_RENDER) {
    if (!RenderMyStuff(stuff, dev, view))
      return DDERR_GENERIC;
    else
      return D3D_OK;
  }

  return 0;
}
.
.
LPDIRECT3DRMUSERVISUAL uvis = NULL;

MyStuff hold;
hold = (MyStuff*)malloc(sizeof(MyStuff));
if (!hold)
  goto ret_with_error;
memset(hold, 0, sizeof(MyStuff));

D3DRM->CreateObject(uvis);
if (uvis->Init(MyCallback, (void*) hold) != D3DRM_OK)
  goto generic_error;
// Or you could do the following
//if (FAILED(lpD3DRM->CreateUserVisual(MyCallback, (void*) hold,
        &uvis)))
//  goto ret_with_error;
if (FAILED(uvis->AddDestroyCallback(DestroyStuff, (void*) hold)))
  goto ret_with_error;
```

chapter 36

The IDirect3DRMViewport interface

The IDirect3DRMViewport interface and methods

This IDirect3DRMViewport interface methods are used to work with viewport objects Like all COM interfaces, this interface inherits the IUnknown interface methods. These consist of AddRef, QueryInterface, and Release.

The methods of the IDirect3DRMViewport interface are arranged in the groups shown table 36.1.

Table 36.1 IDirect3DRMViewport methods

Group	Methods
Camera	GetCamera
	SetCamera
Clipping planes	GetBack
	GetFront
	GetPlane
	SetBack
	SetFront
	SetPlane
Dimensions	GetHeight
	GetWidth
Field of view	GetField
	SetField
Initialization	Init
Miscellaneous	Clear
	Configure
	ForceUpdate
	GetDevice
	GetDirect3Dviewport
	Pick
	Render
Offsets	GetX
	GetY
Projection types	GetProjection
	SetProjection
Scaling	GetUniformScaling
	SetUniformScaling
Transformations	InverseTransform
	Transform

The IDirect3DRMViewport interface also inherits the following methods from the IDirect3DRMObject interface:

Table 36.2 Methods inherited from IDirect3DRMObject

Methods

AddDestroyCallback

Clone

DeleteDestroyCallback

GetAppData

GetClassName

GetName

SetAppData

SetName

IDirect3DRMViewport::Clear

Description

This method is used to clear your viewport to the current background color.

C++ specification

```
HRESULT Clear();
```

Parameters

None

Returns

Successful: D3DRM_OK

Error: One of the Direct3D Retained-Mode return values.

See also

IDirect3DRM::CreateViewport

Example

```
LPDIRECT3DRMVIEWPORT view;
.
.
// Clears the viewport to the current background color.
HRESULT rval = view->Clear();
if (rval != D3DRM_OK)
  {
   Msg("Failed to clear the viewport.\n%s", MyErrorToString(rval));
   goto ret_with_error;
  }
```

IDirect3DRMViewport::Configure

Description

This method is used to reconfigure the origin and dimensions of your viewport.

C++ specification

```
HRESULT Configure(LONG lX, LONG lY, DWORD dwWidth, DWORD dwHeight);
```

Parameters

lX and lY. The new position of your viewport.

dwWidth. The new width of your viewport.

dwHeight. The new height of your viewport.

Returns

D3DRMERR_BADVALUE if lX + dwWidth or lY + dwHeight is greater than the width or height of your device, or if lX, lY, dwWidth, or dwHeight have a value less than zero.

See also

IDirect3DRM::CreateViewport

Example

```
int myWidth;
int myHeight;.
HRESULT myResult;
LPDIRECT3DRMVIEWPORT viewport;
 .
 .
myResult = myD3DRM->CreateViewport(dev, camera, 0, 0,
                   devWidth,
                   devHeight,
               &viewport);
// If we failed to create it, return an error.
if (rval != D3DRM_OK)
 {
  Msg("Failed to create the viewport.\n%s", MyErrorToString(rval));
  return 1;
 }

rval = viewport->Configure(0,0,myWidth, myHeight);
if (rval != D3DRM_OK)
  {
   Msg("Failed to configure the viewport.\n%s", MyErrorToString(rval));
   goto ret_with_error;
  }
viewport->SetBack(D3DVAL(5000.0));
int viewWidth = viewport->GetWidth();
```

```
int viewHeight = viewport->GetHeight();
int devWidth  = dev->GetWidth();
int devHeight = dev->GetHeight();
```

IDirect3DRMViewport::ForceUpdate

Description

This method is used to force an area of your viewport to be updated. This area will be copied to the screen on the next call to the `IDirect3DRMDevice::Update` method. The system may actually update a region that is larger than the rectangle you specify which may be as large as your entire window.

C++ specification

```
HRESULT ForceUpdate(DWORD dwX1, DWORD dwY1, DWORD dwX2,
  DWORD dwY2);
```

Parameters

dwX1 and dwY1. The upper-left corner of the area you want updated.

dwX2 and dwY2. The lower-right corner of the area you want updated.

Returns

Successful: D3DRM_OK

Error: One of the Direct3D Retained-Mode return values.

See also

IDirect3DRM::CreateViewport

Example

```
DWORD ScreenW, ScreenH;
HRESULT myResult;
  .
  .
myResult = view->ForceUpdate(0, 0, ScreenW, ScreenH))
if (myResult != D3DRM_OK)
  {
   Msg("Failed to force the update.\n%s", MyErrorToString(myResult));
   goto ret_with_error;
  }
```

IDirect3DRMViewport::GetBack

Description

This method is used to acquire the position of the back clipping plane for your viewport.

C++ specification

```
D3DVALUE GetBack();
```

Parameters

None

Returns

A value defining the position.

See also

IDirect3DRMViewport::SetBack

Example

```
IDirect3DRMViewport* myViewport = GetViewport();

if(!myViewport)
  return FALSE;

D3DVALUE myfFront = (float)myViewport->GetFront();
D3DVALUE myfBack = (float)myViewport->GetBack();
D3DVALUE myfFOV  = (float)myViewport->GetField();

D3DRMPROJECTIONTYPE myProj;
myProj      = myViewport->GetProjection();
BOOL myUniScale = myViewport->GetUniformScaling();

switch(myProj)
  {
  case D3DRMPROJECT_ORTHOGRAPHIIC: myProjection = 0; break;
  case D3DRMPROJECT_PERSPECTIVE: myProjection = 1; break;
  default: ASSERT(0); break;
  }
```

IDirect3DRMViewport::GetCamera

Description

This method is used to acquire the camera for your viewport.

```
HRESULT GetCamera(LPDIRECT3DRMFRAME *lpCamera);
```

Parameters

lpCamera. The address of a variable holding your Direct3DRMFrame Camera object.

Returns

Successful: D3DRM_OK

Error: One of the Direct3D Retained-Mode return values.

See also

IDirect3DRMViewport::SetCamera

Example

```
IDirect3DRMViewport* myViewport;
IDirect3DRMFrame* myScene, *myCamera;
HRESULT myResult;
.
.
if(myViewport)
  {
    myResult = myViewport->GetCamera(&myCamera);

    if (myResult != D3DRM_OK)
     {
       Msg("Failed to get the camera.\n%s", MyErrorToString(myResult));
       goto ret_with_error;
     }
```

IDirect3DRMViewport::GetDevice

Description

This method is used to acquire the device associated with your viewport.

C++ specification

```
HRESULT GetDevice(LPDIRECT3DRMDEVICE *lpD3DRMDevice);
```

Parameters

lpD3DRMDevice. The address of a variable holding your Direct3DRMDevice object.

Returns

Successful: D3DRM_OK

Error: One of the Direct3D Retained-Mode return values.

See also

IDirect3DRM::CreateDeviceFromSurface
IDirect3DRM::CreateDeviceFromD3D
IDirect3DRM::CreateDeviceFromClipper

Example

```
IDirect3DRMViewport* myViewport;
IDirect3DRMFrame* myScene;
IDirect3DRMDevice* myDevice;
HRESULT myResult;
.
.
if (myViewport)
  {
    myResult = myViewport->GetDevice(&myDevice);

    if (myResult != D3DRM_OK)
     {
       Msg("Failed to get the device.\n%s", MyErrorToString(myResult));
       goto ret_with_error;
     }
```

IDirect3DRMViewport::GetDirect3DViewport

Description

This method is used to acquire the current Direct3DRMViewport.

C++ specification

```
HRESULT GetDirect3DViewport(LPDIRECT3DVIEWPORT * lplpD3DViewport);
```

Parameters

lplpD3DViewport. The address of a pointer which is initialized with a pointer to your Direct3DViewport object.

Returns

Successful: D3DRM_OK
Error: One of the Direct3D Retained-Mode return values.

See also

IDirect3DRMDevice::GetDirectD3DDevice

Example

```
LPDIRECT3DDEVICE lpD3DDev = NULL;
LPDIRECT3DVIEWPORT lpD3DView = NULL;
```

```
     .
     .
dev->GetDirect3DDevice(&lpD3DDev);
HRESULT myResult = view->GetDirect3DViewport(&lpD3DView);
if (myResult != D3DRM_OK)
    {
        Msg("Failed to get the viewport.\n%s", MyErrorToString(myRe-
            sult));
        goto ret_with_error;
    }
```

IDirect3DRMViewport::GetField

Description
This method is used to acquire the field of view for your viewport.

C++ specification
```
D3DVALUE GetField();
```

Parameters
None

Returns
Your field of view.

See also
IDirect3DRMViewport::SetField

Example
```
IDirect3DRMViewport::SetField
IDirect3DRMViewport* myViewport = GetViewport();

if(!myViewport)
  return FALSE;

D3DVALUE myfFront = (float)myViewport->GetFront();
D3DVALUE myfBack  = (float)myViewport->GetBack();
D3DVALUE myfFOV   = (float)myViewport->GetField();

D3DRMPROJECTIONTYPE myProj;
myProj     = myViewport->GetProjection();
BOOL myUniScale = myViewport->GetUniformScaling();

switch(myProj)
  {
    case D3DRMPROJECT_ORTHOGRAPHIC: myProjection = 0; break;
```

```
  case D3DRMPROJECT_PERSPECTIVE: myProjection = 1; break;
  default: ASSERT(0); break;
  }
```

IDirect3DRMViewport::GetFront

Description

This method is used to acquire the position of the front clipping plane for your viewport.

C++ specification

```
D3DVALUE GetFront();
```

Parameters

None

Returns

The requested position.

See also

IDirect3DRMViewport::SetFront

Example

```
IDirect3DRMViewport* myViewport;

if(!myViewport)
  return FALSE;

D3DVALUE myfFront = (float)myViewport->GetFront();
D3DVALUE myfBack = (float)myViewport->GetBack();
D3DVALUE myfFOV  = (float)myViewport->GetField();

D3DRMPROJECTIONTYPE myProj;
myProj     = myViewport->GetProjection();
BOOL myUniScale = myViewport->GetUniformScaling();

switch(myProj)
 {
  case D3DRMPROJECT_ORTHOGRAPHIC: myProjection = 0; break;
  case D3DRMPROJECT_PERSPECTIVE: myProjection = 1; break;
  default: ASSERT(0); break;
 }
```

IDirect3DRMViewport::GetHeight

Description
This method is used to acquire the height of your viewport in pixels.

C++ specification
```
DWORD GetHeight();
```

Parameters
None

Returns
The pixel height of your viewport.

See also
IDirect3DRMViewport::Configure

Example
```
IDirect3DRMViewport* myViewport;
int myWidth;
int myHeight;
HRESULT myResult;
  .
  .
myResult = myD3DRM->CreateViewport(dev, camera, 0, 0,
                    devWidth,
                    devHeight,
                &viewport);
// If we failed to create it, return an error.
if (rval != D3DRM_OK)
  {
   Msg("Failed to create the viewport.\n%s", MyErrorToString(rval));
   return 1;
  }

viewport->Configure(0,0,myWidth, myHeight);
rval = viewport->SetBack(D3DVAL(5000.0));
if (rval != D3DRM_OK)
  {
   Msg("Failed to create the back clipping plane.\n%s", MyError-
        ToString(rval));
   return 1;
  }

int viewWidth = viewport->GetWidth();
int viewHeight = viewport->GetHeight();
int devWidth  = dev->GetWidth();
int devHeight = dev->GetHeight();
```

IDirect3DRMViewport::GetPlane

Description

This method is used to acquire the dimensions of your viewport on the front clipping plane.

C++ specification

```
HRESULT GetPlane(D3DVALUE *lpd3dvLeft, D3DVALUE *lpd3dvRight,
    D3DVALUE *lpd3dvBottom, D3DVALUE *lpd3dvTop);
```

Parameters

lpd3dvLeft. Addresses of a variable you wish filled with the left (x) value of your viewport on the front clipping plane.

lpd3dvRight. Addresses of a variable you wish filled with the right (x) value of your viewport on the front clipping plane.

lpd3dvBottom. Addresses of a variable you wish filled with the bottom (y) value of your viewport on the front clipping plane.

lpd3dvTop. Addresses of a variable you wish filled with the top (y) value of your viewport on the front clipping plane.

Returns

Successful: D3DRM_OK

Error: One of the Direct3D Retained-Mode return values.

See also

IDirect3DRMViewport::SetPlane

Example

```
HRESULT myResult;
IDirect3DRMViewport* myViewport;
D3DVALUE *lpd3dvLeft;
D3DVALUE *lpd3dvRight;
D3DVALUE *lpd3dvBottom;
D3DVALUE *lpd3dvTop;
   .
   .
myResult = myViewport->GetPlane(lpd3dvLeft, lpd3dvRight, lpd3dvBottom,
        lpd3dvTop);
```

IDirect3DRMViewport::GetProjection

Description

This method is used to acquire the projection type for your viewport which can be either orthographic or perspective projection.

C++ specification

```
D3DRMPROJECTIONTYPE GetProjection();
```

Parameters

None

Returns

One of the members of the D3DRMPROJECTIONTYPE enumerated type.

See also

IDirect3DRMViewport::SetProjection

Example

```
IDirect3DRMViewport* myViewport = GetViewport();

if(!myViewport)
  return FALSE;

D3DVALUE myfFront = (float)myViewport->GetFront();
D3DVALUE myfBack  = (float)myViewport->GetBack();
D3DVALUE myfFOV   = (float)myViewport->GetField();

D3DRMPROJECTIONTYPE myProj;
myProj       = myViewport->GetProjection();
BOOL myUniScale = myViewport->GetUniformScaling();

switch(myProj)
  {
  case D3DRMPROJECT_ORTHOGRAPHIC: myProjection = 0; break;
  case D3DRMPROJECT_PERSPECTIVE: myProjection = 1; break;
  default: ASSERT(0); break;
  }
```

IDirect3DRMViewport::GetUniformScaling

Description

This method is used to acquire the scaling property used to scale your viewing volume.

C++ specification
```
BOOL GetUniformScaling();
```

Parameters
None

Returns
TRUE if your viewport scales uniformly; otherwise FALSE is returned.

See also
IDirect3DRMViewport::SetUniformScaling

Example
```
IDirect3DRMViewport* myViewport;
.
.
if(!myViewport)
  return FALSE;

D3DVALUE myfFront = (float)myViewport->GetFront();
D3DVALUE myfBack  = (float)myViewport->GetBack();
D3DVALUE myfFOV   = (float)myViewport->GetField();

D3DRMPROJECTIONTYPE myProj;
myProj      = myViewport->GetProjection();
BOOL myUniScale = myViewport->GetUniformScaling();

switch(myProj)
 {
  case D3DRMPROJECT_ORTHOGRAPHIC: myProjection = 0; break;
  case D3DRMPROJECT_PERSPECTIVE: myProjection = 1; break;
  default: ASSERT(0); break;
 }
```

IDirect3DRMViewport::GetWidth

Description
This method is used to acquire the width of your viewport in pixels.

C++ specification
```
DWORD GetWidth();
```

Parameters
None

Returns

The pixel width of your viewport.

See also

IDirect3DRMViewport::Configure

Example

```
int myWidth;
int myHeight;
HRESULT myResult;
IDirect3DRMViewport* viewport;

  .
  .

myResult = myD3DRM->CreateViewport(dev, camera, 0, 0,
                  devWidth,
                  devHeight,
              &viewport);
// If we failed to create it, return an error.
if (rval != D3DRM_OK)
 {
  Msg("Failed to create the viewport.\n%s", MyErrorToString(rval));
  return 1;
 }

viewport->Configure(0,0,myWidth, myHeight);
rval = viewport->SetBack(D3DVAL(5000.0));
if (rval != D3DRM_OK)
 {
  Msg("Failed to create the back clipping plane.\n%s", MyError-
      ToString(rval));
  return 1;
 }
  .
  .

int viewWidth = viewport->GetWidth();
int viewHeight = viewport->GetHeight();
int devWidth  = dev->GetWidth();
int devHeight = dev->GetHeight();
```

IDirect3DRMViewport::GetX

Description

This method is used to acquire the x-offset of the start of your viewport on a device.

C++ specification
```
LONG GetX();
```

Parameters

None

Returns

The requested x-offset.

See also

IDirect3DRMViewport::GetY

Example
```
IDirect3DRMViewport* viewport;
HRESULT myResult;

myResult = myD3DRM->CreateViewport(dev, camera, 0, 0,
                    devWidth,
                    devHeight,
              &viewport);
// If we failed to create it, return an error.
if (myResult != D3DRM_OK)
  {
   Msg("Failed to create the viewport.\n%s", MyErrorToString(myResult));
   return 1;
  }

viewport->Configure(0,0,myWidth, myHeight);
myResult = viewport->SetBack(D3DVAL(5000.0));
if (myResult != D3DRM_OK)
  {
   Msg("Failed to create the back clipping plane.\n%s", MyError-
        ToString(myResult));
   return 1;
  }
 .
 .
int viewWidth = viewport->GetWidth();
int viewHeight = viewport->GetHeight();
int devWidth  = dev->GetWidth();
int devHeight = dev->GetHeight();
LONG viewX = viewport->GetX();
LONG viewY = viewport->GetY();
```

IDirect3DRMViewport::GetY

Description

This method is used to acquire the y-offset of the start of your viewport on a device.

C++ specification

```
LONG GetY();
```

Parameters

None

Returns

The requested y-offset.

See Also

IDirect3DRMViewport::GetX

Example

```
HRESULT myResult;
IDirect3DRMViewport* viewport;

myResult = myD3DRM->CreateViewport(dev, camera, 0, 0,
                    devWidth,
                    devHeight,
                    &viewport);
// If we failed to create it, return an error.
if (myResult!= D3DRM_OK)
  {
   Msg("Failed to create the viewport.\n%s", MyErrorToString(myResult));
   return 1;
  }

viewport->Configure(0,0,myWidth, myHeight);
rval = viewport->SetBack(D3DVAL(5000.0));
if (myResult != D3DRM_OK)
  {
   Msg("Failed to create the back clipping plane.\n%s", MyError-
        ToString(myResult));
   return 1;
  }
 .
 .
int viewWidth = viewport->GetWidth();
int viewHeight = viewport->GetHeight();
int devWidth  = dev->GetWidth();
int devHeight = dev->GetHeight();
```

```
int viewX = viewport->GetX();
int viewY = viewport->GetY();
```

IDirect3DRMViewport::Init

Description

This method is used to initialize your Direct3DRMViewport object.

C++ specification

```
HRESULT Init(LPDIRECT3DRMDEVICE lpD3DRMDevice,
    LPDIRECT3DRMFRAME lpD3DRMFrameCamera, DWORD xpos, DWORD ypos,
    DWORD width, DWORD height);
```

Parameters

lpD3DRMDevice. The address of the DirectD3DRMDevice object associated with your viewport.

lpD3DRMFrameCamera. The address of the camera frame associated with your viewport.

xpos. The x-coordinate of the upper-left corner of your viewport.

ypos. The y-coordinate of the upper-left corner of your viewport.

width. The width of your viewport.

height. The height of your viewport.

Returns

Successful: D3DRM_OK

Error: One of the Direct3D Retained-Mode return values.

See also

IDirect3DRMViewport::GetX

IDirect3DRMViewport::GetY

Example

```
HRESULT myResult;
LPDIRECT3DRMDEVICE dev;
LPDIRECT3DRMFRAME frameCamera;
DWORD xpos = 0;
DWORD ypos = 0;
DWORD width = 500;
DWORD height = 500;
  .
  .
myResult = view->Init( dev, frameCamera, xpos, ypos, width, height);
```

IDirect3DRMViewport::InverseTransform

Description

This method is used to transform the lprvSrc vector, which is in screen coordinates, to world coordinates. The result is returned in the lprvDst parameter.

C++ specification

```
HRESULT InverseTransform(D3DVECTOR * lprvDst, D3DRMVECTOR4D * lprvSrc);
```

Parameters

lprvDst. The address of a D3DVECTOR structure you wish filled with the result of the transform.

lprvSrc. The address of a D3DRMVECTOR4D structure containing the source of the transform to be returned.

Returns

Successful: D3DRM_OK

Error: One of the Direct3D Retained-Mode return values.

See also

IDirect3DRM::CreateViewport

Example

```
HRESULT myResult;
IDirect3DRMViewport* viewport;

myResult = myD3DRM->CreateViewport(dev, camera, 0, 0,
                    devWidth,
                    devHeight,
              &viewport);
// If we failed to create it, return an error.
if (myResult!= D3DRM_OK)
  {
  Msg("Failed to create the viewport.\n%s", MyErrorToString(myResult));
  return 1;
  }

D3DVECTOR d3v, d3vv, d3v1, d3v2;

D3DRMVectorScale (&d3v1, &d3vv, delta);
D3DRMVectorAdd (&d3v, &d3v1, &d3v2);

myResult = viewport->InverseTransform (&d3v1, &d3v);
if (myResult!= D3DRM_OK)
  {
```

```
Msg("Failed to get inverse transform.\n%s", MyErrorToString(myRe-
    sult));
return 1;
}
```

IDirect3DRMViewport::Pick

Description

This method is used to find a depth-sorted list of objects and faces (if required) including the path taken in the hierarchy from the root down to the frame containing the object.

C++ specification

```
HRESULT Pick(LONG lX, LONG lY,
    LPDIRECT3DRMPICKEDARRAY* lplpVisuals);
```

Parameters

lX. The x coordinate to be used for picking.

lY. The y coordinate to be used for picking.

lplpVisuals. The address of a pointer you wish initialized with a valid pointer to the IDirect3DRMPickedArray interface.

Returns

Successful: D3DRM_OK

Error: One of the Direct3D Retained-Mode return values.

See also

IDirect3DRM::CreateViewport

Example

```
LPDIRECT3DRMVIEWPORT view;
int x;
int y;
LPDIRECT3DRMVISUAL visual;
LPDIRECT3DRMFRAME frame;
LPDIRECT3DRMPICKEDARRAY picked;
LPDIRECT3DRMFRAMEARRAY frames;
LPDIRECT3DRMMESHBUILDER mesh;

myResult = view->Pick(x, y, &picked);
if (myResult!= D3DRM_OK)
  {
   Msg("Failed to handle the pick.\n%s", MyErrorToString(myResult));
   return 1;
```

```
      }
    if (picked)
      {
        if (picked->GetSize())
          {
            picked->GetPick(0, &visual, &frames, 0);
            frames->GetElement(frames->GetSize() - 1, &frame);
              .
              .
              .
            frame->Release();
            frames->Release();
            visual->Release();
          }
        picked->Release();
      }
    }
```

IDirect3DRMViewport::Render

Description

This method is used to render a frame hierarchy to your viewport. Only those visuals for the requested frame and its children are rendered.

C++ specification

```
HRESULT Render(LPDIRECT3DRMFRAME lpD3DRMFrame);
```

Parameters

lpD3DRMFrame. The address of a variable containing the Direct3DRMFrame object representing the frame hierarchy you wish rendered.

Returns

Successful: D3DRM_OK

Error: One of the Direct3D Retained-Mode return values.

See also

IDirect3DRMViewport::Clear

Example

```
LPDIRECT3DRMFRAME scene;
LPDIRECT3DRMVIEWPORT view;
  .
  .
// Clears the viewport to the current background color.
if (FAILED(view->Clear()))
  return FALSE;
```

```
// Renders the frame hierarchy to the given viewport.
// Only the visuals on the given frame (and any frames below
// it in the hierarchy) are rendered.
 if (FAILED(view->Render(scene)))
   return FALSE;
```

IDirect3DRMViewport::SetBack

Description

This method is used to set the position of the back clipping plane for your viewport.

C++ specification

```
HRESULT SetBack(D3DVALUE rvBack);
```

Parameters

rvBack. The new position of your back clipping plane.

Returns

Successful : D3DRM_OK

Error: One of the Direct3D Retained-Mode return values.

See also

IDirect3DRMViewport::GetBack
IDirect3DRMViewport::SetFront

Example

```
int myWidth;
int myHeight;
LPDIRECT3DRMVIEWPORT viewport;
HRESULT myResult;
 .

 .
myResult = myD3DRM->CreateViewport(dev, camera, 0, 0,
                devWidth,
                devHeight,
                &viewport);
// If we failed to create it, return an error.
if (myResultl != D3DRM_OK)
 {
  Msg("Failed to create the viewport.\n%s", MyErrorToString(myResult));
  return 1;
 }

int viewWidth = viewport->GetWidth();
```

```
int viewHeight = viewport->GetHeight();
int devWidth  = dev->GetWidth();
int devHeight = dev->GetHeight();

viewport->Configure(0,0,myWidth, myHeight);
myResult = viewport->SetBack(D3DVAL(5000.0));
if (myResult != D3DRM_OK)
 {
  Msg("Failed to create the back clipping plane.\n%s", MyError-
      ToString(myResult));
  return 1;
 }
```

IDirect3DRMViewport::SetCamera

Description

This method is used to set a camera for your viewport by setting the viewport's position, direction, and orientation to the given camera frame's. This view is oriented along the positive z-axis of the camera frame where the up direction is in the direction of the positive y-axis.

C++ specification

```
HRESULT SetCamera(LPDIRECT3DRMFRAME lpCamera);
```

Parameters

lpCamera. The address of a variable pointing to the Direct3DRMFrame camera object.

Returns

Successful: D3DRM_OK

Error: One of the Direct3D Retained-Mode return values.

See also

IDirect3DRMViewport::GetCamera

Example

```
LPDIRECT3DRMFRAME camera;
LPDIRECT3DRMVIEWPORT view;
HRESULT rval;
 .

 .
if (camera)
   rval = view->SetCamera(Camera);
```

```
if (rval != D3DRM_OK)
 {
  Msg("Could not set camera.\n%s", MyErrorToString(rval));
  return 1;
 }
```

IDirect3DRMViewport::SetField

Description

This method is used to set the field of view for your viewport.

C++ specification

```
HRESULT SetField(D3DVALUE rvField);
```

Parameters

rvField. Your new field of view with a default value of 0.5. If this value is specified as less than or equal to zero, this method will return the D3DRMERR_BADVALUE error.

Returns

Successful: D3DRM_OK

Error: One of the Direct3D Retained-Mode return values.

See also

IDirect3DRMViewport::GetField

Example

```
LPDIRECT3DRMVIEWPORT view;
HRESULT rval;
 .
 .
rval = view->SetField(D3DVAL(0.8));
if (rval != D3DRM_OK)
 {
  Msg("Could not set the field of view.\n%s", MyErrorToString(rval));
  return 1;
 }
```

IDirect3DRMViewport::SetFront

Description

This method is used to set the position of the front clipping plane for your viewport. The default position is 1.0. If you attempt to set this value to less than or equal to zero, this method will return the D3DRMERR_BADVALUE error.

C++ specification

```
HRESULT SetFront(D3DVALUE rvFront);
```

Parameters

rvFront. The new position for your front clipping plane.

Returns

Successful: D3DRM_OK

Error: One of the Direct3D Retained-Mode return values.

See also

IDirect3DRMViewport::GetFront

Example

```
floatback;
floatFOV;
floatFront;
LPDIRECT3DRMVIEWPORT viewport;
HRESULT rval;


  .
  .
rval = viewport->SetFront((D3DVALUE)Front);
if (rval != D3DRM_OK)
 {
  Msg("Could not set the front clipping plane.\n%s", MyError-
      ToString(rval));
  return 1;
 }
rval = viewport->SetBack((D3DVALUE)Back);
rval = viewport->SetField((D3DVALUE)FOV);
```

IDirect3DRMViewport::SetPlane

Description

This method is used to set the dimensions of your viewport on the front clipping plane relative to your camera's z-axis. This method will allow you to specify a viewport of arbitrary proportion and position. The `IDirect3DRMViewport::SetField` method, which specifies a centered proportional viewport, does not allow this. This method could be used to create a sheared viewing frustum in order to create a right- or left-eye stereo view.

C++ specification

```
HRESULT SetPlane(D3DVALUE rvLeft, D3DVALUE rvRight, D3DVALUE rvBottom,
    D3DVALUE rvTop);
```

Parameters

rvLeft. Minimum x coordinate of your viewport.

rvRight. Maximum x coordinate of your viewport.

rvBottom. Minimum y coordinate of your viewport.

rvTop. Maximum y coordinate of your viewport.

Returns

Successful: D3DRM_OK

Error: One of the Direct3D Retained-Mode return values.

See also

IDirect3DRMViewport::GetPlane

IDirect3DRMViewport::SetField

Example

```
HRESULT rval;
D3DVALUE rvLeft;
D3DVALUE rvRight;
D3DVALUE rvBottom;
D3DVALUE rvTop;
LPDIRECT3DRMVIEWPORT view;
 .
 .
rval = viewport->SetPlane(rvLeft, rvRight, rvBottom, rvTop);
if (rval != D3DRM OK)
  {
  Msg("Could not set the dimensions.\n%s", MyErrorToString(rval));
  return 1;
  }
```

IDirect3DRMViewport::SetProjection

Description

This method is used to set the projection type for your viewport.

C++ specification
```
HRESULT SetProjection(D3DRMPROJECTIONTYPE rptType);
```

Parameters

rptType. This parameter contains one of the members of the D3DRMPROJECT-IONTYPE enumerated type.

Returns

Successful: D3DRM_OK

Error: One of the Direct3D Retained-Mode return values.

See also

IDirect3DRMViewport::GetProjection

Example
```
HRESULT myResult;
D3DRMPROJECTIONTYPE projType;
    .
    .
projType = D3DRMPROJECT_PERSPECTIVE;
myResult = SetProjection(projType);
if (myResult != D3DRM_OK)
  {
  Msg("Could not set the projection type for your viewport.\n%s", MyEr-
      rorToString(myResult));
  return 1;
  }
```

IDirect3DRMViewport::SetUniformScaling

Description

This method is used to set the scaling property used to scale the viewing volume into the larger dimension of your window. This method is often used with the IDirect3DRMViewport::SetPlane method in order to support banding.

C++ specification
```
HRESULT SetUniformScaling(BOOL bScale);
```

Parameters

bScale. Your new scaling property, which if set to TRUE, will use the same horizontal and vertical scaling factor to scale the viewing volume. If it is FALSE, a different scaling factors will used to scale the viewing volume into your window exactly. The default setting for this is TRUE.

Returns

> Successful: D3DRM_OK
>
> Error: One of the Direct3D Retained-Mode return values.

See also

> IDirect3DRMViewport::GetUniformScaling

Example

```
HRESULT myResult;
  .
  .
myResult = SetUniformScaling(TRUE);
if (myResult != D3DRM_OK)
 {
  Msg("Could not set the new scale.\n%s", MyErrorToString(myResult));
  return 1;
 }
```

IDirect3DRMViewport::Transform

Description

> This method is used to transform your vector in the lprvSrc parameter, which you specify in world coordinates, into screen coordinates. The result is returned in the lprvDst parameter..This result is a four-element homogeneous vector.

C++ specification

```
HRESULT Transform(D3DRMVECTOR4D * lprvDst, D3DVECTOR * lprvSrc);
```

Parameters

> lprvDst. The address of a D3DRMVECTOR4D structure which is the destination for your transformation operation.
>
> lprvSrc. The address of a D3DVECTOR structure which is the source for your transformation operation.

Returns

> Successful: D3DRM_OK
>
> Error: One of the Direct3D Retained-Mode return values.

See also

> D3DRMVECTOR4D

Example

```
D3DVECTOR p1;
```

```
D3DRMVECTOR4D p2;
LPDIRECT3DRMFRAME frame;
LPDIRECT3DRMVIEWPORT view;
.
.
frame->GetPosition(scene, &p1);
if(view->Transform(&p2, &p1)!=D3DRM_OK)
  goto generic_error;
```

chapter 37

The IDirect3DRMWinDevice interface

The IDirect3DRMWinDevice interface and methods

This IDirect3DRMWinDevice interface methods are used to respond to window messages in your window procedure.

The Direct3DRMWinDevice object can be acquired using the `IDirect-3DRMObject::QueryInterface` method and specifying `IID_IDirect3DRMWinDevice`. You can also acquire it using a method like `IDirect3DRM::CreateDeviceFromD3D`. The methods are inherited from the IDirect3DRMDevice interface.

Like all COM interfaces, this interface inherits the IUnknown interface methods. These consist of `AddRef`, `QueryInterface`, and `Release`.

The methods of the IDirect3DRMWinDevice interface are HandleActivate and HandlePaint.

IDirect3DRMWinDevice::HandleActivate

Description

This method is used to respond to a Windows WM_ACTIVATE message which guarentees that the colors are correct in your active rendering window.

C++ specification

```
HRESULT HandleActivate(WORD wParam);
```

Parameters

wParam. This holds the WPARAM parameter which is passed to the message-processing procedure with the WM_ACTIVATE message.

Returns

Successful: D3DRM_OK

Error: One of the Direct3D Retained-Mode return values.

See also

IDirect3DRMWinDevice::HandlePaint

Example

```
LPDIRECT3DRMDEVICE dev;
.
.
case WM_ACTIVATE:
  {
    LPDIRECT3DRMWINDEVICE windev;

    if (SUCCEEDED(dev->QueryInterface(IID_IDirect3DRMWinDevice, (void
        **) &windev)))
    {
      if (windev->HandleActivate(wparam) != D3DRM_OK)
        Msg("Failed to handle WM_ACTIVATE.\n");
      windev->Release();
    }
    else
    {
      Msg("Failed to create Windows device to handle WM_ACTIVATE.\n");
    }
  }
  break;
```

IDirect3DRMWinDevice::HandlePaint

Description

This method responds to a Windows WM_PAINT message. You should take the hDC parameter from the PAINTSTRUCT structure which is given to the Windows Begin-Paint function. You should call this method before repainting any application areas in your window since it may repaint areas which are outside the viewports which have been created on your device.

C++ specification

```
HRESULT HandlePaint(HDC hDC);
```

Parameters

hDC. The handle of the device context.

Returns

Successful: D3DRM_OK

Error: One of the Direct3D Retained-Mode return values.

See also

IDirect3DRMWinDevice::HandleActivate

Example

```
// Handle the window paint message and update the window
case WM_PAINT:
  {
  RECT r;
  PAINTSTRUCT ps;
  LPDIRECT3DRMWINDEVICE windev;

  // Retrieve the coordinates of the smallest rectangle that
  // completely encloses the
  // update region of the specified window (win)
  if (GetUpdateRect(win, &r, FALSE))
  {
    // The BeginPaint function prepares the window for painting and
    // fills a PAINTSTRUCT structure (ps) with information about
    // the painting.
    BeginPaint(win, &ps);
    // The Direct3DRMWinDevice object is obtained by calling
    // the IDirect3DRMObject::QueryInterface method and specifying
    // IID_IDirect3DRMWinDevice, or by calling a method such as
    // IDirect3DRM::CreateDeviceFromD3D. Its methods are inherited
    // from the IDirect3DRMDevice interface.
    if (SUCCEEDED(dev->QueryInterface(IID_IDirect3DRMWinDevice, (void
        **) &windev)))
```

```
{
    if (FAILED(windev->HandlePaint(ps.hdc)))
     Msg("Failed to handle WM_PAINT.\n");
    windev->Release();
   } else {
    Msg("Failed to create Windows device to handle WM_PAINT.\n");
   }
   // The EndPaint function denotes the end of painting in the
   // specified window (window).
   // It is required to call the function for each call to the
   // BeginPaint function, after all painting is complete.
   EndPaint(win, &ps);
  }
 }
```

chapter 38

The IDirect3DRMWrap interface

The IDirect3DRMWrap interface and methods

This IDirect3DRMWrap interface methods are used to work with Wrap objects. The Direct3DRMWrap object can be acquired using the `IDirect3DRMObject::CreateWrap` method.

Like all COM interfaces, this interface inherits the IUnknown interface methods. These consist of `AddRef`, `QueryInterface`, and `Release`.

The methods of the IDirect3DRMWinDevice interface are shown in table 38.1.

634

Table 38.1 IDirect3DRMWinDevice methods

Group	Methods
Initialization	Init
Wrap	Apply
	ApplyRelative

The IDirect3DRMWrap interface also inherits the following methods from the IDirect3DRMObject interface:

Table 38.2 Methods inherited from IDirect3DRMObject

Methods
AddDestroyCallback
Clone
DeleteDestroyCallback
GetAppData
GetClassName
GetName
SetAppData
SetName

IDirect3DRMWrap::Apply

Description

This method is used to apply a Direct3DRMWrap object to your destination object which is usually a mesh or a face object.

C++ specification

```
HRESULT Apply(LPDIRECT3DRMOBJECT lpObject);
```

Parameters

lpObject. The address of your destination object.

Returns

Successful: D3DRM_OK

Error: One of the Direct3D Retained-Mode return values.

See also

IDirect3DRM::CreateWrap

Example

```
HRESULT rval;
DWORD w;
LPDIRECT3DRMMESHBUILDER obj_builder = 0;
LPDIRECT3DRMMESH    obj_mesh = 0;
D3DRMRENDERQUALITY quality = D3DRMRENDER_GOURAUD;
LPDIRECT3DRMWRAP wrap = NULL;
D3DRMBOX box;
D3DVALUE miny, maxy;
D3DVALUE height;
.
.
// load mesh file
if (FAILED(lpD3DRM->CreateMeshBuilder(&obj_builder)))
  return FALSE;

// create a frame within the scene
w = 0;
rval = obj_builder->Load ("out2.x", (void *)&w, D3DRMLOAD_BYPOSITION,
        NULL, NULL);
if (rval != D3DRM_OK)
 {
  Msg("Failed to load op_bot.x\n%s", MyErrorToString(rval));
  return FALSE;
 }

obj_builder->SetQuality (quality);

if (FAILED (obj_builder->GetBox (&box)))
  return FALSE;

maxy = box.max.y;
miny = box.min.y;
height = maxy - miny;

if (FAILED (obj_builder->CreateMesh(&obj_mesh)))
  return FALSE;

d3mo->AddColObj (new ColBoxObj (*D3DRMVectorSubtract (&d3v1, &box.min,
        &sbD3V),
                *D3DRMVectorAdd (&d3v2, &box.max, &sbD3V)));

if (FAILED(obj_mesh->SetGroupTexture (D3DRMGROUP_ALLGROUPS, stex)))
  return FALSE;
```

```
if (FAILED(obj_mesh->SetGroupMaterial (D3DRMGROUP_ALLGROUPS, mat)))
  return FALSE;

if (FAILED(obj_builder->SetColorRGB (D3DVAL(1.0), D3DVAL(1.0),
      D3DVAL(1.0))))
  return FALSE;

if (FAILED(lpD3DRM->CreateWrap(D3DRMWRAP_SPHERE, NULL,
            D3DVAL(0.0), D3DVAL(0.0), D3DVAL(0.0),
            D3DVAL(0.0), D3DVAL(1.0), D3DVAL(0.0),
            D3DVAL(0.0), D3DVAL(0.0), D3DVAL(1.0),
            D3DVAL(0.0), D3DDivide (miny, height),
            D3DVAL(50), D3DDivide (D3DVAL(-50), height),
            &wrap)))
            return FALSE;

  if (wrap->Apply ((LPDIRECT3DRMOBJECT)obj_mesh) != D3DRM_OK)
      goto generic_error;
```

IDirect3DRMWrap::ApplyRelative

Description

This method is used to apply the wrap to the vertices of your object. The vertex is first transformed by the frame's world transformation and the inverse world transformation of the wrap's reference frame.

C++ specification

```
HRESULT ApplyRelative(LPDIRECT3DRMFRAME frame,
  LPDIRECT3DRMOBJECT mesh);
```

Parameters

frame. The Direct3DRMFrame object which contains your object to wrap.

mesh. The Direct3DRMWrap object you wish to apply.

Returns

Successful: D3DRM_OK

Error: One of the Direct3D Retained-Mode return values.

See also

IDirect3DRM::CreateWrap

Example

```
void CDECL applyMyWrap(LPDIRECT3DRMFRAME frame, void* arg, D3DVALUE
      delta)
{
```

```
LPDIRECT3DRMWRAP wrap = (LPDIRECT3DRMWRAP) arg;
LPDIRECT3DRMVISUALARRAY visualArray;
LPDIRECT3DRMVISUAL visual;
int count, i;

frame->GetVisuals(&visualArray);
if (visualArray)
{
  count = visualArray->GetSize();

  for (i = 0; i < count; i++)
  {
    visualArray->GetElement(i, &visual);
    if (wrap-> ApplyRelative(frame, (LPDIRECT3DRMOBJECT) visual) !=
      D3DRM_OK)
        goto generic_error;
    visual->Release();
  }
  visualArray->Release();
}
}


void CDECL cleanupMyWrap(LPDIRECT3DRMOBJECT obj, void* arg)
{
  LPDIRECT3DRMWRAP myWrap = (LPDIRECT3DRMWRAP) arg;
  myWrap->Release();
}
```

IDirect3DRMWrap::Init

Description

This method is used to initialize a Direct3DRMWrap object.

C++ specification

```
HRESULT Init(D3DRMWRAPTYPE d3drmwt, LPDIRECT3DRMFRAME lpd3drmfRef,
    D3DVALUE ox, D3DVALUE oy, D3DVALUE oz,
    D3DVALUE dx, D3DVALUE dy, D3DVALUE dz,
    D3DVALUE ux, D3DVALUE uy, D3DVALUE uz,
    D3DVALUE ou, D3DVALUE ov, D3DVALUE su, D3DVALUE sv);
```

Parameters

d3drmwt. Specifies one of the members of the D3DRMWRAPTYPE enumerated type.

lpd3drmfRef. The address of the reference frame for this Direct3DRMWrap object.

ox, oy, and oz. The origin of the wrap.

dx, dy, and dz. The z-axis of the wrap.

ux, uy, and uz. The y-axis of the wrap.

ou and ov. The origin in the texture.

su and sv. The scale factor in the texture.

Returns

Successful: D3DRM_OK

Error: One of the Direct3D Retained-Mode return values.

See also

IDirect3DRM::CreateWrap

Example

```
LPDIRECT3DRMWRAP wrap;
D3DRMWRAPTYPE wrapType;
LPDIRECT3DRMFRAME refFrame;
D3DVALUE ox, oy, oz;
D3DVALUE dx, dy, dz,
D3DVALUE ux, uy, uz,
D3DVALUE ou, ov;
D3DVALUE su, sv;
HRESULT result;
  .
  .
result = wrap->Init(wrapType, refFrame, ox, oy, oz, dx, dy, dz, ux, uy,
        uz, ou, ov, su, sv);
if (result != D3DRM_OK)
  goto generic_error;
```

chapter 39

The Direct3D Retained Mode structures

This chapter lists the Direct3D Retained-Mode structures. Each structure is defined in terms of its use and parameters.

D3DRMBOX

Definition

This structure defines the bounding box which is acquired using the `IDirect3D-RMMesh::GetBox` and `IDirect3DRMMeshBuilder::GetBox` methods.

C++ specification

```
typedef struct _D3DRMBOX {
  D3DVECTOR min, max;
}D3DRMBOX;
typedef D3DRMBOX *LPD3DRMBOX;
```

Members

min. The minimum bounding values of the box.

max. The maximum bounding values of the box.

See also

D3DVECTOR,

IDirect3DRMMesh::GetBox

IDirect3DRMMeshBuilder::GetBox

D3DRMIMAGE

Definition

This structure describes an image which is attached to a texture using the IDirect-3DRM::CreateTexture method. The IDirect3DRMTexture::GetImage method is used to return the address of this image.

C++ specification

```
typedef struct _D3DRMIMAGE {
    int         width, height;
    int         aspectx, aspecty;
    int         depth;
    int         rgb;
    int         bytes_per_line;
    void*       buffer1;
    void*       buffer2;
    unsigned long   red_mask;
    unsigned long   green_mask;
    unsigned long   blue_mask;
    unsigned long   alpha_mask;
    int         palette_size;
    D3DRMPALETTEENTRY* palette;
}D3DRMIMAGE;
typedef D3DRMIMAGE, *LPD3DRMIMAGE;
```

Members

width . The width of the image in pixels.

height. The height of the image in pixels.

aspectx. The x value for the aspect ratio for nonsquare pixels.

aspecty. The y value for the aspect ratio for nonsquare pixels.

depth. The bits per pixel.

rgb. The pixels encode RGB values if this is TRUE. The pixels are indices into a palette if this value is FALSE.

bytes_per_line. The number of bytes of memory for a scanline which must have a value which is a multiple of four.

buffer1. The first buffer memory to render into.

buffer2. The second rendering buffer for double buffering. This member should be set to NULL for single buffering.

red_mask, green_mask, blue_mask, and alpha_mask. If RGB is set to TRUE, these members specify masks for the red, green, and blue portions of a pixel. If we are not in RGB mode, these values hold masks for the significant bits of the red, green, and blue elements in the palette.

palette_size. The number of entries in the palette.

palette. If rgb is set to FALSE, this member holds the address of a D3DRMPALETTEENTRY structure which holds the palette entry.

See also

IDirect3DRM::CreateTexture

IDirect3DRMTexture::GetImage

D3DRMLOADMEMORY

Definition

This structure describes a resource which will be loaded when your application calls the IDirect3DRM::Load method, or any of the other Load methods, and specifies D3DRMLOAD_FROMMEMORY.

C++ specification

```
typedef struct _D3DRMLOADMEMORY {
  LPVOID lpMemory;
  DWORD dSize;
} D3DRMLOADMEMORY, *LPD3DRMLOADMEMORY;
```

Members

lpMemory. The address of a block of memory you wish loaded.

dSize. The size in bytes of the block of memory you wish loaded.

See also

IDirect3DRM::Load

IDirect3DRMAnimationSet::Load

IDirect3DRMFrame::Load

IDirect3DRMMeshBuilder::Load

D3DRMLOADOPTIONS

D3DRMLOADRESOURCE

D3DRMLOADRESOURCE

Definition

This structure describes a resource you wish loaded when your application calls the IDirect3DRM::Load method, or any of the other Load methods, and you specify D3DRMLOAD_FROMRESOURCE.

If you set the high-order word of the lpName or lpType member to zero, then the low-order word will define the integer identifier of the name or type of the resource.

If they are not set to zero, these parameters are long pointers to null-terminated strings.

If you set the first character of the string to a pound sign (#), the remaining characters will hold a decimal number defining the integer identifier of your resource's name or type. As an example, the string "#324" represents the integer identifier 324. You can reduce the amount of memory required by your application for your resources by referring to them by integer identifiers rather than by name.

If your program calls a Load method and passes D3DRMLOAD_FROMRESOURCE, it will not be required to find, or unlock, any of your resources since the system will handle it automatically.

C++ specification

```
typedef struct _D3DRMLOADRESOURCE {
    HMODULE hModule;
    LPCTSTR lpName;
    LPCTSTR lpType;
} D3DRMLOADRESOURCE, *LPD3DRMLOADRESOURCE;
```

Members

hModule. The handle of the module which contains the resource you wish to load. If you set this member to NULL, your resource must be attached to your calling executable file.

lpName. The name of the resource you wish loaded.

lpType. Your user-defined type which identifies the resource.

See also

IDirect3DRM::Load
IDirect3DRMAnimationSet::Load
IDirect3DRMFrame::Load
IDirect3DRMMeshBuilder::Load
D3DRMLOADMEMORY
D3DRMLOADOPTIONS

D3DRMPALETTEENTRY

Definition

This structure defines the color palette used in a D3DRMIMAGE structure. This structure will only be used if the rgb member of the D3DRMIMAGE structure is set to FALSE.

C++ specification

```
typedef struct _D3DRMPALETTEENTRY {
  unsigned char red;
  unsigned char green;
  unsigned char blue;
  unsigned char flags;
}D3DRMPALETTEENTRY;
typedef D3DRMPALETTEENTRY, *LPD3DRMPALETTEENTRY;
```

Members

red, green, and blue. Values defining the primary color components which define your palette. These values can range from 0 through 255.

flags. Value defining how you want the palette used by the renderer. This value is one of the members of the D3DRMPALETTEFLAGS enumerated type.

See also

D3DRMIMAGE

D3DRMPALETTEFLAGS

D3DRMPICKDESC

Definition

This structure holds the pick position plus the face and group identifiers of your objects which are acquired using the IDirect3DRMPickedArray::GetPick method.

C++ specification

```
typedef struct _D3DRMPICKDESC {
  ULONG     ulFaceIdx;
  LONG      lGroupIdx;
  D3DVECTOR vPosition;
} D3DRMPICKDESC, *LPD3DRMPICKDESC;
```

Members

ulFaceIdx. The face index of your retrieved object.

lGroupIdx. The group index of your retrieved object.

vPosition. The value specifying the position of your retrieved object.

See also

D3DVECTOR

IDirect3DRMPickedArray::GetPick

D3DRMVECTOR4D

Definition

This structure is used to define the screen coordinates which are used as the destination of a transformation by the `IDirect3DRMViewport::Transform` method and as the source of a transformation by the `IDirect3DRMViewport::InverseTransform` method.

C++ specification

```
typedef struct _D3DRMVECTOR4D {
  D3DVALUE x;
  D3DVALUE y;
  D3DVALUE z;
  D3DVALUE w;
}D3DRMVECTOR4D;
typedef D3DRMVECTOR4D, *LPD3DRMVECTOR4D;
```

Members

x, y, z, and w. These parameters describe homogeneous values defining the result of your transformation.

See also

IDirect3DRMViewport::Transform

IDirect3DRMViewport::InverseTransform

D3DRMVERTEX

Definition

This structure defines a vertex in your Direct3DRMMesh object.

C++ specification

```
typedef struct _D3DRMVERTEX{
  D3DVECTOR position;
  D3DVECTOR normal;
  D3DVALUE tu, tv;
  D3DCOLOR color;
} D3DRMVERTEX;
```

Members

position. The position of your vertex.

normal. The normal vector for your vertex.

tu. The horizontal texture coordinates for your vertex.

tv. The vertical texture coordinates for your vertex.

color. The vertex color.

See also

IDirect3DRMMesh::GetVertices

IDirect3DRMMesh::SetVertices

chapter 40

The Direct3D Enumerated and other types

This chapter lists the Direct3D Enumerated and other types. Each of these types is defined in terms of its use and parameters.

D3DRMCOLORSOURCE

Definition

This type is used to define the color source of your Direct3DRMMeshBuilder object. The color source can be set using the `IDirect3DRMMeshBuilder::SetColorSource` method. To acquire the value, you use the `IDirect3DRMMeshBuilder::GetColorSource` method.

C++ specification

```
typedef enum _D3DRMCOLORSOURCE{
  D3DRMCOLOR_FROMFACE,
  D3DRMCOLOR_FROMVERTEX
} D3DRMCOLORSOURCE;
```

Members

D3DRMCOLOR_FROMFACE. The color source for the object is a face.

D3DRMCOLOR_FROMVERTEX. The color source for the object is a vertex.

See also

IDirect3DRMMeshBuilder::SetColorSource

IDirect3DRMMeshBuilder::GetColorSource

D3DRMCOMBINETYPE

Definition

This type is used to define how to combine two matrices. You need to remember that the order of the supplied and current matrices is important when they are multiplied together since matrix multiplication is not commutative.

C++ specification

```
typedef enum _D3DRMCOMBINETYPE{
  D3DRMCOMBINE_REPLACE,
  D3DRMCOMBINE_BEFORE,
  D3DRMCOMBINE_AFTER
} D3DRMCOMBINETYPE;
```

Members

D3DRMCOMBINE_REPLACE. The matrix you provide replaces your frame's current matrix.

D3DRMCOMBINE_BEFORE. The matrix you provide is multiplied with your frame's current matrix. It will precede your current matrix in the calculation.

D3DRMCOMBINE_AFTER. The matrix you provide is multiplied with the frame's current matrix. It will follow your current matrix in the calculation.

See also

IDirect3DRMFrame::AddRotation

IDirect3DRMFrame::AddScale

IDirect3DRMFrame::AddTransform

IDirect3DRMFrame::AddTranslation

D3DRMFILLMODE

Definition

This type is one of the enumerated types which is used in the definition of the D3DRMRENDERQUALITY type.

C++ specification

```
typedef enum _D3DRMFILLMODE {
  D3DRMFILL_POINTS    = 0 * D3DRMLIGHT_MAX,
  D3DRMFILL_WIREFRAME = 1 * D3DRMLIGHT_MAX,
  D3DRMFILL_SOLID     = 2 * D3DRMLIGHT_MAX,
  D3DRMFILL_MASK      = 7 * D3DRMLIGHT_MAX,
  D3DRMFILL_MAX       = 8 * D3DRMLIGHT_MAX
} D3DRMFILLMODE;
```

Members

D3DRMFILL_POINTS. You wish to only fill points. This is the minimum fill mode.

D3DRMFILL_WIREFRAME. You wish to fill wireframes.

D3DRMFILL_SOLID. You wish to fill solid objects.

D3DRMFILL_MASK. You wish to fill using a mask.

D3DRMFILL_MAX. The maximum value for the fill mode.

See also

D3DRMLIGHTMODE
D3DRMSHADEMODE
D3DRMRENDERQUALITY

D3DRMFOGMODE

Definition

This enumerated type contains values which specify the manner, and how rapidly, the fog effect intensifies with increasing distance from the camera. The fog mode can be thought of as a visibility measure.

The fog's density, as well as its start and end points, can be set with the IDirect3DRMFrame::SetSceneFogParams method.

In the formulas for the exponential fog modes shown below, *e* is the base of the natural logarithms. The value for this parameter is approximately 2.71828.

C++ specification

```
typedef enum _D3DRMFOGMODE{
  D3DRMFOG_LINEAR,
  D3DRMFOG_EXPONENTIAL,
```

```
    D3DRMFOG_EXPONENTIALSQUARED
} D3DRMFOGMODE;
```

Members

    `D3DRMFOG_LINEAR`. With this mode, the fog effect will intensify linearly between the start and end points, based on the following formula:

$$f = \frac{\text{end} - z}{\text{end} - \text{start}}$$

    `D3DRMFOG_EXPONENTIAL`. With this mode, the fog effect will intensify exponentially, based on the following formula:

$$f = e^{-(\text{density} \times z)}$$

    `D3DRMFOG_EXPONENTIALSQUARED`. With this mode, the fog effect will intensify exponentially with the square of the distance, based on the following formula:

$$f = e^{-(\text{density} \times z)^2}$$

See also

    IDirect3DRMFrame::SetSceneFogMode
    IDirect3DRMFrame::SetSceneFogParams

D3DRMFRAMECONSTRAINT

Definition

    This enumerated type is used to define the axes of rotation you wish constrained when viewing a Direct3DRMFrame object. This enumerated type is used by the `IDirect3DRMFrame::LookAt` method.

C++ specification

```
typedef enum _D3DRMFRAMECONSTRAINT {
    D3DRMCONSTRAIN_Z,
    D3DRMCONSTRAIN_Y,
    D3DRMCONSTRAIN_X
} D3DRMFRAMECONSTRAINT;
```

Members

    `D3DRMCONSTRAIN_Z`. You wish to only use x and y rotations.
    `D3DRMCONSTRAIN_Y`. You wish to only use x and z rotations.
    `D3DRMCONSTRAIN_X`. You wish to only use y and z rotations.

See also

    IDirect3DRMFrame::LookAt

D3DRMLIGHTMODE

Definition

This is one of the enumerated types which is used in the definition of the D3DRM-RENDERQUALITY type.

C++ specification

```
typedef enum _D3DRMLIGHTMODE {
  D3DRMLIGHT_OFF   = 0 * D3DRMSHADE_MAX,
  D3DRMLIGHT_ON    = 1 * D3DRMSHADE_MAX,
  D3DRMLIGHT_MASK  = 7 * D3DRMSHADE_MAX,
  D3DRMLIGHT_MAX   = 8 * D3DRMSHADE_MAX
} D3DRMLIGHTMODE;
```

Members

D3DRMLIGHT_OFF. Lighting is turned off.

D3DRMLIGHT_ON. Lighting is turned on.

D3DRMLIGHT_MASK. Lighting will use a mask.

D3DRMLIGHT_MAX. The maximum lighting mode.

See also

D3DRMFILLMODE
D3DRMSHADEMODE
D3DRMRENDERQUALITY

D3DRMLIGHTTYPE

Definition

This enumerated type is used to define the light type in calls to the IDirect-3DRM::CreateLight method.

C++ specification

```
typedef enum _D3DRMLIGHTTYPE{
  D3DRMLIGHT_AMBIENT,
  D3DRMLIGHT_POINT,
  D3DRMLIGHT_SPOT,
  D3DRMLIGHT_DIRECTIONAL,
  D3DRMLIGHT_PARALLELPOINT
} D3DRMLIGHTTYPE;
```

Members

D3DRMLIGHT_AMBIENT. The light is an ambient source.

D3DRMLIGHT_POINT. The light is a point source.

D3DRMLIGHT_SPOT. The light is a spotlight source.

D3DRMLIGHT_DIRECTIONAL . The light is a directional source.

D3DRMLIGHT_PARALLELPOINT. The light is a parallel point source.

D3DRMMATERIALMODE

Definition

This enumerated type is used to define the type which is acquired using the IDirect3DRMFrame::GetMaterialMode method. Is is also used to define the type when you use the IDirect3DRMFrame::SetMaterialMode method.

C++ specification

```
typedef enum _D3DRMMATERIALMODE{
  D3DRMMATERIAL_FROMMESH,
  D3DRMMATERIAL_FROMPARENT,
  D3DRMMATERIAL_FROMFRAME
} D3DRMMATERIALMODE;
```

Members

D3DRMMATERIAL_FROMMESH. When you use this value, the default setting, the material information will be retrieved from the mesh (visual object) itself.

D3DRMMATERIAL_FROMPARENT. When you use this value, the material color, and texture information, will be inherited from the parent frame.

D3DRMMATERIAL_FROMFRAME. When you use this value, the material information will be acquired from the frame. This will take precedence over any previous material information your visual object may have contained.

See also

IDirect3DRMFrame::GetMaterialMode

IDirect3DRMFrame::SetMaterialMode

D3DRMPALETTEFLAGS

Definition

This enumerated type is used to describe how a color can be used in the D3DRMPALETTEENTRY structure.

C++ specification

```
typedef enum _D3DRMPALETTEFLAGS {
  D3DRMPALETTE_FREE,
```

```
        D3DRMPALETTE_READONLY,
        D3DRMPALETTE_RESERVED
    } D3DRMPALETTEFLAGS;
```

Members

D3DRMPALETTE_FREE. The renderer can use this entry freely.

D3DRMPALETTE_READONLY. This entry is fixed but can be used by the renderer.

D3DRMPALETTE_RESERVED. This entry cannot be used by the renderer.

See also

D3DRMPALETTEENTRY

D3DRMPROJECTIONTYPE

Definition

This enumerated type is used to describe the type of projection you wish to use in a Direct3DRMViewport object. This enumerated type is used by the `IDirect3DRMViewport::GetProjection` and `IDirect3DRMViewport::SetProjection` methods.

C++ specification

```
typedef enum _D3DRMPROJECTIONTYPE{
    D3DRMPROJECT_PERSPECTIVE,
    D3DRMPROJECT_ORTHOGRAPHIC
} D3DRMPROJECTIONTYPE;
```

Members

D3DRMPROJECT_PERSPECTIVE. The projection type you wish to use is perspective.

D3DRMPROJECT_ORTHOGRAPHIC. The projection type you wish to use is orthographic.

See also

IDirect3DRMViewport::GetProjection
IDirect3DRMViewport::SetProjection

D3DRMRENDERQUALITY

Definition

This enumerated type is used to combine descriptions of the shading mode, lighting mode, and filling mode for your Direct3DRMMesh object.

C++ specification

```
typedef enum _D3DRMSHADEMODE {
```

```
        D3DRMSHADE_FLAT      = 0,
        D3DRMSHADE_GOURAUD    = 1,
        D3DRMSHADE_PHONG     = 2,
        D3DRMSHADE_MASK      = 7,
        D3DRMSHADE_MAX       = 8
    } D3DRMSHADEMODE;

    typedef enum _D3DRMLIGHTMODE {
        D3DRMLIGHT_OFF     = 0 * D3DRMSHADE_MAX,
        D3DRMLIGHT_ON      = 1 * D3DRMSHADE_MAX,
        D3DRMLIGHT_MASK     = 7 * D3DRMSHADE_MAX,
        D3DRMLIGHT_MAX     = 8 * D3DRMSHADE_MAX
    } D3DRMLIGHTMODE;

    typedef enum _D3DRMFILLMODE {
        D3DRMFILL_POINTS    = 0 * D3DRMLIGHT_MAX,
        D3DRMFILL_WIREFRAME  = 1 * D3DRMLIGHT_MAX,
        D3DRMFILL_SOLID     = 2 * D3DRMLIGHT_MAX,
        D3DRMFILL_MASK      = 7 * D3DRMLIGHT_MAX,
        D3DRMFILL_MAX       = 8 * D3DRMLIGHT_MAX
    } D3DRMFILLMODE;

    typedef DWORD D3DRMRENDERQUALITY;

    #define D3DRMRENDER_WIREFRAME
            (D3DRMSHADE_FLAT+D3DRMLIGHT_OFF+D3DRMFILL_WIREFRAME)

    #define D3DRMRENDER_UNLITFLAT
            (D3DRMSHADE_FLAT+D3DRMLIGHT_OFF+D3DRMFILL_SOLID)

    #define D3DRMRENDER_FLAT
            (D3DRMSHADE_FLAT+D3DRMLIGHT_ON+D3DRMFILL_SOLID)

    #define D3DRMRENDER_GOURAUD
            (D3DRMSHADE_GOURAUD+D3DRMLIGHT_ON+D3DRMFILL_SOLID)

    #define D3DRMRENDER_PHONG
            (D3DRMSHADE_PHONG+D3DRMLIGHT_ON+D3DRMFILL_SOLID)
```

Members

D3DRMSHADEMODE, D3DRMLIGHTMODE, and D3DRMFILLMODE. These enumerated types are used to define the shade, light, and fill modes for your Direct3DRMMesh objects.

D3DRMRENDER_WIREFRAME. Indicates you wish to display only the edges.

D3DRMRENDER_UNLITFLAT. Indicates you want flat shading without lighting.

D3DRMRENDER_FLAT. Indicates you want flat shading.

D3DRMRENDER_GOURAUD. Indicates you want Gouraud shading.

D3DRMRENDER_PHONG. Indicates you want Phong shading.

See also

IDirect3DRMMesh::GetGroupQuality

IDirect3DRMMesh::SetGroupQuality

D3DRMSHADEMODE

Definition

This type defines the enumerated types that are used in the definition of the D3DRMRENDERQUALITY type.

C++ specification

```
typedef enum _D3DRMSHADEMODE {
   D3DRMSHADE_FLAT    = 0,
   D3DRMSHADE_GOURAUD = 1,
   D3DRMSHADE_PHONG   = 2,
   D3DRMSHADE_MASK    = 7,
   D3DRMSHADE_MAX     = 8
} D3DRMSHADEMODE;
```

See also

D3DRMFILLMODE

D3DRMLIGHTMODE

D3DRMRENDERQUALITY

D3DRMSORTMODE

Definition

This enumerated type is used to define how child frames are sorted in your scene.

C++ specification

```
typedef enum _D3DRMSORTMODE {
   D3DRMSORT_FROMPARENT,
   D3DRMSORT_NONE,
   D3DRMSORT_FRONTTOBACK,
   D3DRMSORT_BACKTOFRONT
} D3DRMSORTMODE;
```

Members

D3DRMSORT_FROMPARENT. The default setting indicating your child frames will inherit the sorting order of their parents.

D3DRMSORT_NONE. The child frames will not be sorted.

D3DRMSORT_FRONTTOBACK. The child frames will be sorted front-to-back.

D3DRMSORT_BACKTOFRONT. The child frames will be sorted back-to-front.

See also

IDirect3DRMFrame::GetSortMode

IDirect3DRMFrame::SetSortMode

D3DRMTEXTUREQUALITY

Definition

This enumerated type defines the texture quality for the IDirect3D-RMDevice::SetTextureQuality and IDirect3DRMDevice::GetTextureQuality methods.

C++ specification

```
typedef enum _D3DRMTEXTUREQUALITY{
   D3DRMTEXTURE_NEAREST,
   D3DRMTEXTURE_LINEAR,
   D3DRMTEXTURE_MIPNEAREST,
   D3DRMTEXTURE_MIPLINEAR,
   D3DRMTEXTURE_LINEARMIPNEAREST,
   D3DRMTEXTURE_LINEARMIPLINEAR
} D3DRMTEXTUREQUALITY;
```

Members

D3DRMTEXTURE_NEAREST. Indicates you wish the system to choose the nearest pixel in the texture.

D3DRMTEXTURE_LINEAR. Indicates you wish the system to linearly interpolate the four nearest pixels.

D3DRMTEXTURE_MIPNEAREST. This value is similar to D3DRMTEXTURE_NEAREST, but indicates you wish to use the appropriate mipmap rather than the texture.

D3DRMTEXTURE_MIPLINEAR. This value is similar to D3DRMTEXTURE_LINEAR, but indicates you wish to use the appropriate mipmap instead of the texture.

D3DRMTEXTURE_LINEARMIPNEAREST. This value is similar to D3DRMTEXTURE_MIPNEAREST, but indicates you wish the system to interpolate between the two nearest mipmaps.

D3DRMTEXTURE_LINEARMIPLINEAR. This value is similar to D3DRMTEXTURE_MIPLINEAR, but indicates you wish the system to interpolate between the two nearest mipmaps.

D3DRMUSERVISUALREASON

Definition

This enumerated type is used to describe the reason the system has called the D3DRMUSERVISUALCALLBACK callback function.

C++ specification

```
typedef enum _D3DRMUSERVISUALREASON {
  D3DRMUSERVISUAL_CANSEE,
  D3DRMUSERVISUAL_RENDER
} D3DRMUSERVISUALREASON;
```

Members

D3DRMUSERVISUAL_CANSEE. Indicates that the callback function should return TRUE if your user-visual object is visible in your viewport.

D3DRMUSERVISUAL_RENDER. Indicates that your callback function should render your user-visual object.

See also

D3DRMUSERVISUALCALLBACK

D3DRMWRAPTYPE

Definition

This enumerated type is used to define the type of Direct3DRMWrap object created by the IDirect3DRM::CreateWrap method. You may also use this enumerated type to initialize a Direct3DRMWrap object when you make a call to the IDirect3DRMWrap::Init method.

C++ specification

```
typedef enum _D3DRMWRAPTYPE{
  D3DRMWRAP_FLAT,
  D3DRMWRAP_CYLINDER,
  D3DRMWRAP_SPHERE,
  D3DRMWRAP_CHROME
} D3DRMWRAPTYPE;
```

Members

D3DRMWRAP_FLAT. Your wrap is flat.

D3DRMWRAP_CYLINDER. Your wrap is cylindrical.

D3DRMWRAP_SPHERE. Your wrap is spherical.

D3DRMWRAP_CHROME. Your wrap will allocate texture coordinates in a manner that makes the texture appear to be reflected onto your objects.

See also

IDirect3DRM::CreateWrap

IDirect3DRMWrap::Init

D3DRMXOFFORMAT

Definition

This enumerated type is used to define the file type to be used by the IDirect-3DRMMeshBuilder::Save method. The D3DRMXOF_BINARY and D3DRMXOF_TEXT settings are mutually exclusive.

C++ specification

```
typedef enum _D3DRMXOFFORMAT{
    D3DRMXOF_BINARY,
    D3DRMXOF_COMPRESSED,
    D3DRMXOF_TEXT
} D3DRMXOFFORMAT;
```

Members

D3DRMXOF_BINARY. The default setting indicating that the file is in binary format.

D3DRMXOF_COMPRESSED. Indicates the file is compressed.

D3DRMXOF_TEXT. Indicates that the file is in text format.

See also

IDirect3DRMMeshBuilder::Save

D3DRMZBUFFERMODE

Definition

This enumerated type is used to define if z-buffering is enabled.

C++ specification

```
typedef enum _D3DRMZBUFFERMODE {
    D3DRMZBUFFER_FROMPARENT,
    D3DRMZBUFFER_ENABLE,
    D3DRMZBUFFER_DISABLE
} D3DRMZBUFFERMODE;
```

Members

D3DRMZBUFFER_FROMPARENT. The default setting which indicates you wish the frame to inherit the z-buffer setting from its parent frame.

D3DRMZBUFFER_ENABLE. Indicates that Z-buffering is enabled.

D3DRMZBUFFER_DISABLE. Indicates that Z-buffering is disabled.

See also

IDirect3DRMFrame::GetZbufferMode
IDirect3DRMFrame::SetZbufferMode

Other types

D3DRMANIMATIONOPTIONS

Definition

This type is used to indicate values which are used by the `IDirect3DRM-Animation::GetOptions` and `IDirect3DRMAnimation::SetOptions` methods in order to define how your animations are played.

C++ specification

```
typedef DWORD D3DRMANIMATIONOPTIONS;
#define D3DRMANIMATION_CLOSED                0x02L
#define D3DRMANIMATION_LINEARPOSITION        0x04L
#define D3DRMANIMATION_OPEN                  0x01L
#define D3DRMANIMATION_POSITION              0x00000020L
#define D3DRMANIMATION_SCALEANDROTATION      0x00000010L
#define D3DRMANIMATION_SPLINEPOSITION        0x08L
```

Members

D3DRMANIMATION_CLOSED. Indicates that you wish the animation to play continually. This means that it will loop back to the beginning whenever it reaches the end. The last key in the animation should be a repeat of the first. This will create a repeated key which is used to specify the time difference between the last and first keys in your looping animation.

D3DRMANIMATION_LINEARPOSITION. The position of your animation is set linearly.

D3DRMANIMATION_OPEN. Your animation will play once and stop.

D3DRMANIMATION_POSITION. The position matrix for your animation will overwrite any transformation matrices which might be set by other methods.

D3DRMANIMATION_SCALEANDROTATION. The scale and rotation matrix for your animation should overwrite any transformation matrices which might be set by other methods.

D3DRMANIMATION_SPLINEPOSITION. The position of your animation is set using splines.

D3DRMCOLORMODEL

Definition

This type is used to define the color model implemented by the device.

C++ specification

```
typedef D3DCOLORMODEL D3DRMCOLORMODEL;
```

D3DRMLOADOPTIONS

Definition

This type is used to describe the options, which modify how your object is loaded, for the `IDirect3DRM::Load`, `IDirect3DRMAnimationSet::Load`, `IDirect3DRMFrame::Load`, and `IDirect3DRMMeshBuilder::Load` methods.

The load methods all use an `lpvObjSource` parameter to indicate the source of the object and a `lpvObjID` parameter to identify that object. The system will interpret the contents of the `lpvObjSource` parameter depending upon your source flags, and the contents of the `lpvObjID` parameter based upon your identifier flags

The instance flags do not change the interpretation of any of the parameters.

If you use the `D3DRMLOAD_INSTANCEBYREFERENCE` flag, your application can load the same file twice without creating any new objects.

If one of your objects does not have a name, and you set the `D3DRM-LOAD_INSTANCEBYREFERENCE` flag, it will have the same end effect as setting the `D3DRMLOAD_INSTANCEBYCOPYING` flag, where the loader will create each unnamed object as a new one, whether or not some of your objects are identical.

C++ specification

```
typedef DWORD D3DRMLOADOPTIONS;
#define D3DRMLOAD_FROMFILE          0x00L
#define D3DRMLOAD_FROMRESOURCE      0x01L
#define D3DRMLOAD_FROMMEMORY        0x02L
#define D3DRMLOAD_FROMSTREAM        0x03L
#define D3DRMLOAD_BYNAME            0x10L
#define D3DRMLOAD_BYPOSITION        0x20L
#define D3DRMLOAD_BYGUID            0x30L
#define D3DRMLOAD_FIRST             0x40L
#define D3DRMLOAD_INSTANCEBYREFERENCE 0x100L
#define D3DRMLOAD_INSTANCEBYCOPYING   0x200L
```

Members

Source flags

D3DRMLOAD_FROMFILE. The default setting indicating you want to load from a file.
D3DRMLOAD_FROMMEMORY. Indicates you wish to load from memory. The `lpvObjSource` parameter of your calling Load method has to point to a `D3DRMLOADMEMORY` structure.

D3DRMLOAD_FROMRESOURCE. Indicates you wish to load from a resource. The `lpvObjSource` parameter of your calling Load method has to point to a `D3DRM-LOADRESOURCE` structure.

D3DRMLOAD_FROMSTREAM. Indicates you wish to load from a stream.

Identifier flags

D3DRMLOAD_BYGUID. You wish to load any object using a requested GUID.

D3DRMLOAD_FIRST. The default setting indicating you wish to load the first stand-alone object of the given type. This means that the first stand-alone mesh object will be loaded if you call IDirect3DRMMeshBuilder::Load.

D3DRMLOAD_BYNAME. Indicates you wish to load any object by using a specified name.

D3DRMLOAD_BYPOSITION. Indicates you wish to load a stand-alone object based upon a specified zero-based. This means you wish to load the nth object in a file. Remember that stand-alone objects may contain other objects but they are not contained by any other objects.

Instance flags

D3DRMLOAD_INSTANCEBYCOPYING. Indicates you wish to check whether an object already exists with the same name you specified. If it does, it will copy that object.

D3DRMLOAD_INSTANCEBYREFERENCE. Indicates you wish to check whether an object already exists with the same name you specified. If it does, the system will use an instance of that object rather than create a new one.

D3DRMMAPPING

Definition

This type is used to indicate values which are used by the IDirect3DRMMesh::GetGroupMapping and IDirect3DRMMesh::SetGroupMapping methods to define how your textures are mapped to a group.

You use the D3DRMMAP_WRAPU and D3DRMMAP_WRAPV flags to specify how the rasterizer will interpret texture coordinates. The rasterizer will always interpolate the shortest distance, a line, between texture coordinates. The path taken which this line takes, as well as the valid u- and v-coordinates values, will vary based upon the use of the wrapping flags.

If you set either or both of these flags, the line can wrap around the texture edge in the u or v direction. This acts as if your texture has a cylindrical or toroidal topology. For more information, see *IDirect3DRMWrap interface*.

C++ specification

```
typedef DWORD D3DRMMAPPING, D3DRMMAPPINGFLAG;
static const D3DRMMAPPINGFLAG D3DRMMAP_WRAPU = 1;
static const D3DRMMAPPINGFLAG D3DRMMAP_WRAPV = 2;
```

```
                static const D3DRMMAPPINGFLAG D3DRMMAP_PERSPCORRECT = 4;
```

Members

    D3DRMMAPPINGFLAG. This type is the same as D3DRMMAPPING.

    D3DRMMAP_WRAPU. Your texture wraps in the u direction.

    D3DRMMAP_WRAPV. Your texture wraps in the v direction.

    D3DRMMAP_PERSPCORRECT. Your texture wrapping is perspective-corrected.

See also

    IDirect3DRMWrap interface
    IDirect3DRMMesh::GetGroupMapping
    IDirect3DRMMesh::SetGroupMapping

D3DRMMATRIX4D

Definition

    This type is used to represent a transformation as an array. The matrix entries are structured as D3DRMMATRIX4D[row][column].

C++ specification

```
                typedef D3DVALUE D3DRMMATRIX4D[4][4];
```

Members

    None

See also

    IDirect3DRMFrame::AddTransform
    IDirect3DRMFrame::GetTransform

D3DRMSAVEOPTIONS

Definition

    This type specifies options for the IDirect3DRMMeshBuilder::Save method.

C++ specification

```
                typedef DWORD D3DRMSAVEOPTIONS;
                #define D3DRMXOFSAVE_NORMALS 1
                #define D3DRMXOFSAVE_TEXTURECOORDINATES 2
                #define D3DRMXOFSAVE_MATERIALS 4
                #define D3DRMXOFSAVE_TEXTURENAMES 8
                #define D3DRMXOFSAVE_ALL 15
                #define D3DRMXOFSAVE_TEMPLATES 16
```

Members

D3DRMXOFSAVE_ALL. This member is used to indicate you wish to save normal vectors, texture coordinates, materials, and texture names in addition to the basic geometry.

D3DRMXOFSAVE_MATERIALS. This member is used to indicate you wish to save materials in addition to the basic geometry.

D3DRMXOFSAVE_NORMALS. This member is used to indicate you wish to save the normal vectors in addition to the basic geometry.

D3DRMXOFSAVE_TEMPLATES. This member is used to indicate you wish to save templates with the file. Templates are not saved by default.

D3DRMXOFSAVE_TEXTURECOORDINATES. This member is used to indicate you wish to save texture coordinates in addition to the basic geometry.

D3DRMXOFSAVE_TEXTURENAMES. This member is used to indicate you wish to save texture names in addition to the basic geometry.

chapter 41

The Direct3D Retained Mode file format templates

Direct3D Retained Mode templates

In chapter 5 I showed you the DirectX File Format and how to create a DirectX object file by hand. In this chapter I show you each of the templates available to you in Retained Mode. If you need a quick reminder of the file structure, you can open the house.x object on the CD accompanying this book.

   Although you can use the conv3ds tool, or the PolyTrans software demo I have included on the CD, to convert .3ds objects to .x objects, knowing the File Format will come in very useful if you decide to write your own converters or you want to create a file algorithmically (e.g., you want to have a program write a .x file for you).

665

Animation template

Description

This template holds the animations referencing a previous frame and should consist of one reference to a frame and *at least* one set of AnimationKeys. It may also hold an AnimationOptions data object. You can use any of the optional data objects with this template

UUID

```
<3D82AB4F-62DA-11cf-AB39-0020AF71E433>
```

Members

None

AnimationKey template

Description

You use this template to describe a set of animation keys. The `keyType` parameter is used to define the key type (rotation (0), scale(1), or position(2)).

UUID

```
<10DD46A8-775B-11cf-8F52-0040333594A3>
```

Members

Name	Type	Optional Array Size
keyType	DWORD	
nKeys	DWORD	
keys	array TimedFloatKeys	nKeys

AnimationOptions template

Description

You use this template to set the D3DRM Animation options. You set the `openclosed` parameter to `0` for a closed animation and `1` for an open (the default) animation. You set the position quality parameter to describe the position quality for any position keys you define. This parameter is set to `0` to indicate *spline positions* or `1` to indicate *linear positions* (the default).

UUID

```
<E2BF56C0-840F-11cf-8F52-0040333594A3>
```

Members

Name	Type
openclosed	*DWORD*
positionquality	*DWORD*

AnimationSet template

Description

This template holds one or more Animation objects. Each animation within the animation set has the same time at any particular point. If you increase the animation set's time, it will increase the time for all of the animations it contains. This is the same as the Retained Mode AnimationSet. You have the option to use the Animation data object with his template

UUID

<3D82AB50-62DA-11cf-AB39-0020AF71E433>

Members

None

Boolean template

Description

You use this template, with the WORD member set to 0 or 1, to define a boolean type.

UUID

<4885AE61-78E8-11cf-8F52-0040333594A3>

Members

Name	Type
WORD	truefalse

Boolean2d template

Description

You use this template to describe a set of two boolean values which are used in the MeshFaceWraps template to define the texture topology of an individual face.

UUID

    <4885AE63-78E8-11cf-8F52-0040333594A3>

Members

Name	Type
u	Boolean
v	Boolean

ColorRGB template

Description

You use this template to describe the RGB color object.

UUID

    <D3E16E81-7835-11cf-8F52-0040333594A3>

Members

Name	Type
red	FLOAT
green	FLOAT
blue	FLOAT

ColorRGBA template

Description

You use this template to define a color object with an alpha component. You use this for the face color for defining your material template.

UUID

    <35FF44E0-6C7C-11cf-8F52-0040333594A3>

Members

Name	Type
red	FLOAT
green	FLOAT
blue	FLOAT
alpha	FLOAT

Coords2d template

Description

You use this template to create a two dimensional vector defining your mesh's texture coordinates.

UUID

<F6F23F44-7686-11cf-8F52-0040333594A3>

Members

Name	Type
u	FLOAT
v	FLOAT

FloatKeys template

Description

You use this template to describe an array of floats and the number of elements in that array for defining sets of animation keys.

UUID

<10DD46A9-775B-11cf-8F52-0040333594A3>

Members

Name	Type	Optional Array Size
nValues	DWORD	
values	array FLOAT	nValues

Frame template

Description

You use this template to define a frame which can contain Mesh and FrameTransformMatrix objects. You can use any of the optional data objects

UUID

<3D82AB46-62DA-11cf-AB39-0020AF71E433>

Members

FrameTransformMatrix template

Description

You use this template to describe a local transform for a frame and its child objects.

UUID

    <F6F23F41-7686-11cf-8F52-0040333594A3>

Members

Name	Type
frameMatrix	Matrix4×4

Header template

Description

You can use this template to describe your application specific header. Remember that this is for use with the DirectX File Format in Retained Mode. Retained Mode uses the major and minor flags to indicate the current major and minor versions for the retained mode file format. These are 1 (major) and 0 (minor).

UUID

    <3D82AB43-62DA-11cf-AB39-0020AF71E433>

Members

Name	Type
major	WORD
minor	WORD
flags	DWORD

Indexed Color template

Description

You use this template to define mesh vertex colors using an index, defining the vertex to which you are applying the color, and an RGBA color.

UUID

    <1630B820-7842-11cf-8F52-0040333594A3>

Members

Name	Type
index	DWORD
ColorRGBA	indexColor

Material template

Description

You use this template to describe a basic material color that you can apply to either individual faces or a whole mesh. The ambient color requires an alpha component and the power is the specular component of the color. You can use any optional data objects with this template. If the TextureFilename optional data object is not present, the face is untextured.

UUID

<3D82AB4D-62DA-11cf-AB39-0020AF71E433>

Members

Name	Type
faceColor	ColorRGBA
power	FLOAT
specularColor	ColorRGB
emissiveColor	ColorRGB

Matrix4x4 template

Description

You can use this template to define a 4×4 matrix for use as your frame transformation matrix.

UUID

<F6F23F45-7686-11cf-8F52-0040333594A3>

Members

Name	Type	Optional Array Size
matrix	array FLOAT	16

Mesh template

Description

You use this template to define a simple mesh. The vertices array defines the list of vertices and the faces array defines the list of faces in the mesh using an index into the vertex array.

UUID

```
<3D82AB44-62DA-11cf-AB39-0020AF71E433>
```

Members

Name	Type	Optional Array Size	Optional Data Objects
nVertices	DWORD		Any
vertices	array Vector	nVertices	
nFaces	DWORD		
faces	array MeshFace	nFaces	

MeshFace template

Description

This template is used by the Mesh template to describe a mesh's faces. The elements of the `nFaceVertexIndices` array each reference a mesh vertex which is used to hold the face.

UUID

```
<3D82AB5F-62DA-11cf-AB39-0020AF71E433>
```

Members

Name	Type	Optional Array Size
nFaceVertexIndices	DWORD	
faceVertexIndices	array DWORD	nFaceVertexIndicies

MeshFaceWraps template

Description

You can use this template to describe the texture topology for each of the faces in a wrap. The `nFaceWrapValues` parameter is set to the number of faces in your mesh.

    <4885AE62-78E8-11cf-8F52-0040333594A3>

Members

Name	Type
nFaceWrapValues	DWORD
faceWrapValues	Boolean2d

MeshMaterialList template

Description

You use this template in a mesh object to define what material is applied to which face. The nMaterials parameter indicates how many materials. The optional Material object defines the material to be applied.

UUID

    <F6F23F42-7686-11cf-8F52-0040333594A3>

Members

Name	Type	Optional Array Size	Optional Data Objects
nMaterials	DWORD		Material
nFaceIndexes	DWORD		
FaceIndexes	array DWORD	nFaceIndexes	

MeshNormals template

Description

You use this template to define the normals for your mesh. The first array of vectors contain the normal vectors for your object. The second array holds the indices that specify which normals are applied to each face. The nFaceNormals parameter indicates the number of faces in the mesh.

UUID

    <F6F23F43-7686-11cf-8F52-0040333594A3>

Members

Name	Type	Optional Array Size
nNormals	DWORD	
normals	array Vector	nNormals
nFaceNormals	DWORD	
faceNormals	array MeshFace	nFaceNormals

MeshTextureCoords template

Description

You use this template to describe your mesh's texture coordinates.

UUID

```
<F6F23F40-7686-11cf-8F52-0040333594A3>
```

Members

Name	Type	Optional Array Size
nTextureCoords	DWORD	
textureCoords	array Coords2d	nTextureCoords

MeshVertexColors template

Description

You use this template to define the vertex colors for a mesh.

UUID

```
<1630B821-7842-11cf-8F52-0040333594A3>
```

Members

Name	Type	Optional Array Size
nVertexColors	DWORD	
vertexColors	array IndexedColor	nVertexColors

Quaternion template

Description

This template is not used in Version 3.

UUID

```
<10DD46A3-775B-11cf-8F52-0040333594A3>
```

Members

Name	Type
s	FLOAT
v	Vector

TextureFilename template

Description

You can use this template within a Material object to define the filename of the texture you wish to apply to a face or mesh.

UUID

```
<A42790E1-7810-11cf-8F52-0040333594A3>
```

Members

Name	Type
filename	STRING

TimedFloatKeys template

Description

You use this template to describe a set of floating point values and a time to be used in your animation (this time value must be positive).

UUID

```
<F406B180-7B3B-11cf-8F52-0040333594A3>
```

Members

Name	Type
time	DWORD
tfkeys	FloatKeys

Vector template

Description

You use this template to define a vector.

UUID

```
<3D82AB5E-62DA-11cf-AB39-0020AF71E433>
```

Members

Name	Type
x	FLOAT
y	FLOAT
z	FLOAT

A Direct3D DrawPrimitive tutorial

One of the capabilities added to DirectX 5 is DrawPrimitive. This is Microsoft's new approach to allow rendering without the use of execute buffers in Immediate Mode. Rather than being a wrapper to aid in the creation of Immediate Mode execute buffers, DrawPrimitive is a new method to access 3D hardware accelerators (or emulating them if none exist) without the use of execute buffers. This provides a method that is faster than Immediate Mode and conceptually easier.

Please refer to the section in chapter 19 where I discussed DrawPrimitive's capabilities which let you create triangles, lines, and points on a DirectDraw surface. As with any D3D application, you create a device and viewport and then render these new primitives by setting up an array of vertex structures and passing them, with the information of how to render them, to the DrawPrimitive() or DrawIndexedPrimitive() method.

The first step in using DrawPrimitive is to set up a DirectDraw surface. We will be creating a DirectDraw surface and a standard top-level window and setting its cooperative level. Let's create a 640x480 full-screen application with 16bpp.

```
#define SCREEN_WIDTH 640
#define SCREEN_HEIGHT 480
#define SCREEN_BITS 16
LPDIRECTDRAW myDD;

CreateDD()
{
    // Create the main DirectDraw object
    if (DirectDrawCreate(NULL, &myDD, NULL) != DD_OK)
        return FALSE;
    // Now set the cooperative level
```

```
    if (myDD->SetCooperativeLevel(GetSafeHwnd(), DDSCL_FULLSCREEN |
            DDSCL_EXCLUSIVE | DDSCL_ALLOWMODEX) != DD_OK)
        return FALSE;
    // and finally set the display mode
    if (myDD->SetDisplayMode(SCREEN_WIDTH, SCREEN_HEIGHT, SCREEN_BITS))
        return FALSE;
} // End of CreateDD
```

With that set up, we need to create the primary display surface and the back buffer, just as we did for the full-screen application. The DirectDraw surface will be created using the DDSCAPS_3DDEVICE caps flag. We will be creating our back buffer with this flag and attach it to our primary surface using the AddAttachedSurface() method. This back buffer can be displayed using the primary surface's Flip() method.

We will be flipping the buffers, but there are a lot of reasons to just Blt the back-buffer to your primary surface, speed being the principal one. Below is the code to create our primary and secondary (back) buffers.

```
CreateObjects()
{
    LPDIRECTDRAWSURFACE myPrimary;
    LPDIRECTDRAWSURFACE myBackBuffer;

    // Get your primary display surface
    ZeroMemory(&ddsd, sizeof(ddsd));
    ddsd.dwSize = sizeof(ddsd);
    ddsd.dwFlags = DDSD_CAPS;
    if (hardware)
        ddsd.ddsCaps.dwCaps = DDSCAPS_PRIMARYSURFACE;
    else
        ddsd.ddsCaps.dwCaps = DDSCAPS_PRIMARYSURFACE |
        DDSCAPS_SYSTEMMEMORY;
    if (myDD->CreateSurface(&ddsd, &myPrimary, NULL) != DD_OK)
        return FALSE;

    // Create your back buffer and attach it to your primary display
    // create. This gives you a flippable surface
    ZeroMemory(&ddsd, sizeof(ddsd));
    ddsd.dwSize = sizeof(ddsd);
    ddsd.dwFlags = DDSD_CAPS | DDSD_WIDTH | DDSD_HEIGHT;
    ddsd.dwWidth = SCREEN_WIDTH;
    ddsd.dwHeight = SCREEN_HEIGHT;
    if (hardware)
        ddsd.ddsCaps.dwCaps = DDSCAPS_OFFSCREENPLAIN | DDSCAPS_3DDEVICE |
        DDSCAPS_VIDEOMEMORY;
    else
        ddsd.ddsCaps.dwCaps = DDSCAPS_OFFSCREENPLAIN | DDSCAPS_3DDEVICE |
        DDSCAPS_SYSTEMMEMORY;
    if (myDD->CreateSurface(&ddsd, &myBackBuffer, NULL) != DD_OK)
        return FALSE;
    if (myPrimary->AddAttachedSurface(myBackBuffer) != DD_OK)
        return FALSE;
```

You can flip to the primary surface with the `Flip()` method. This is done as:

```
// Flip the back buffer to the primary surface
m_yPrimary->Flip(NULL,DDFLIP_WAIT);
```

The next step is to create our Direct3D object. This also is done as you have seen earlier using the DirectDraw object's `QueryInterface()` method.

```
LPDIRECT3D2 myD3D;
if (myDD->QueryInterface(IID_IDirect3D2, (LPVOID *)&myD3D) != DD_OK)
    return FALSE;
```

With our Direct3D interface ready to go, we need to get a compatible device to use for rendering to our back buffer.

```
// Get our device
D3DFINDDEVICESEARCH search;
D3DFINDDEVICERESULT result;
ZeroMemory(&search, sizeof(search));
search.dwSize = sizeof(search);
search.dwFlags = D3DFDS_HARDWARE;
search.bHardware = hardware;
ZeroMemory(&result, sizeof(result));
result.dwSize = sizeof(result);
if (myD3D->FindDevice(&search, &result) != D3D_OK)
    return FALSE;

// Create the D3D device
if (myD3D->CreateDevice(result.guid, myBackBuffer, &myDevice) !=
    D3D_OK)
    return FALSE;
} // End CreateObjects
```

The viewport

With our D3D device ready, we now have to create the viewport so we can see our world. This is also the same as we have done in our earlier projects.

```
CreateViewPort()
{
    // Create a viewport
    D3DVIEWPORT view;
    ZeroMemory(&view, sizeof(view));
    view.dwSize = sizeof(view);
    view.dwWidth = SCREEN_WIDTH;
    view.dwHeight = SCREEN_HEIGHT;
    view.dvScaleX = SCREEN_WIDTH / 2.0;
    view.dvScaleY = SCREEN_HEIGHT / 2.0;
    view.dvMaxX = D3DVAL(1.0);
```

```
        view.dvMaxY = D3DVAL(1.0);
        if (myD3D->CreateViewport(&myViewport, NULL) != D3D_OK)
            return FALSE;
        if (myDevice->AddViewport(myViewport) != D3D_OK)
            return FALSE;
        if (myViewport->SetViewport(&view) != D3D_OK)
            return FALSE;
        if (myDevice->SetCurrentViewport(myViewport) != D3D_OK)
            return FALSE;
    } // End of CreateViewPort
```

To render, use Begin/EndScene as we saw earlier in the Immediate Mode tutorial.

```
Render()
{
    myDevice->BeginScene();
    .
    .
    myDevice->EndScene();
} // Render
```

Using DrawPrimitive

You can create primitives using either `DrawPrimitive()` or `DrawIndexedPrimitive()`. The `DrawPrimitive()` method is used if you wish to create the primitive using an array of vertices. If you wish to create a set of triangles that share vertices, this would be inefficient, as for five triangles you would need fifteen entries. If you instead use the `DrawIndexedPrimitive()` method, the system will use a pointer to a vertex array. Each of your triangles is defined as three words which contain indices into this vertex array.

DrawPrimitive takes the type of primitive you will be drawing as the first parameter. These can be points, lines, polylines, triangles, triangle strips, and triangle fans (See page 345 for a picture of these types). Point lists are specified with the `D3DPT_POINTLIST` identifier; line lists are specified with the `D3DPT_LINELIST` identifier; polylines are specified with the `D3DPT_LINESTRIP` identifier; triangle lists are specified with the `D3DPT_TRIANGLELIST` identifier; strips are specified with the `D3DPT_TRIANGLESTRIP` identifier; and triangle fans are specified with the `D3DPT_TRIANGLEFAN` identifier.

The second parameter to DrawPrimitive defines the vertex type which describes the type of structures in the vertex array. The three types are:

- `D3DVT_TLVERTEX`. Indicates you want to use vertices that are of the type D3DTLVERTEX. Used to pass vertex coordinates in screen space relative to (0,0) in the upper left corner, lighting information, and texture coordinates.

- `D3DVT_LVERTEX`. Indicates that the vertices are of the type D3DLVERTEX. Used to pass vertex coordinates in world space. This allows DrawPrimitive to transform your points by the world, view, and projection matrices automatically which removes a number of manual steps you would otherwise have to take.

- D3DVT_VERTEX. This value indicates that the vertices are of the type D3DTLVERTEX. This type tells the system to transform and light the vertices, based on your specification for world coordinates, the normal vector for lighting, and the texture coordinates.

Drawing the most simple object

As an example of the most simple thing we can do with DrawPrimitive, let's look at how we would draw a single colored triangle

```
#include d3d.h    // Include the standard D3D header
.
.
```

We will be creating three D3DTLVERTEX vertices. These take a D3DVECTOR as the first argument and the rhw field as the second. In this example, we are drawing a flat triangle, with the default Gouraud shading, so we will set this second value to 1.

The next three values represent the diffuse color with three color components. If you set each of these to a different value, DrawPrimitive will use Gouraud shading to shade the in-between pixels.

The next three values represent the specular color component which is used for Phong shading. We will use (0,0,0) since we are using Gouraud.

The final two values represent the UV coordinates for texture mapping, and since we are not interested in using that at this point, we will set them to 0 also.

```
// Create a single triangle
D3DTLVERTEX vertex[3];
vertex[0] = D3DTLVERTEX(D3DVECTOR(D3DVAL(40), D3DVAL(20),
        D3DVAL(0)),1,D3DRGB(D3DVAL(0), D3DVAL(0),
        D3DVAL(1)),D3DRGB(D3DVAL(0), D3DVAL(0), D3DVAL(0)),0,0);
vertex[1] = D3DTLVERTEX(D3DVECTOR(D3DVAL(80), D3DVAL(40),
        D3DVAL(0)),1,D3DRGB(D3DVAL(1), D3DVAL(0),
        D3DVAL(0)),D3DRGB(D3DVAL(0), D3DVAL(0), D3DVAL(0)),0,0);
vertex[2] = D3DTLVERTEX(D3DVECTOR(D3DVAL(8), D3DVAL(40),
        D3DVAL(0)),1,D3DRGB(D3DVAL(0), D3DVAL(1),
        D3DVAL(1)),D3DRGB(D3DVAL(0), D3DVAL(0), D3DVAL(0)),0,0);
```

Finally, we will be using D3DTLVERTEX structures to allow us to use prelit and transformed vertices in screen space.

```
myDevice-
>DrawPrimitive(D3DPT_TRIANGLELIST,D3DVT_TLVERTEX,(LPVOID)vertex,3,NULL);
```

Creating a more complex 3D object

At this point you have a flat triangle presented on your screen. Since we are interested in useful 3D visuals, I suppose you find this fairly useless, but I felt we should look at the key aspects of DrawPrimitive before learning the other critical details.

Now, let's look at the additional code needed to create a 3D view that we can control. The following code contains the main steps to present a 3D view of a cube to the user. We will also add lighting to illuminate our scene. First we will need to clear the back buffer to black.

```
DoBox()
{
    // Clear the back buffer
    DDBLTFX bltfx;
    ZeroMemory(&bltfx, sizeof(bltfx)); // Sets dwFillColor to 0
    bltfx.dwSize = sizeof(bltfx);
    myBackBuffer->Blt(NULL,NULL,NULL,DDBLT_WAIT|DDBLT_COLORFILL,&bltfx);
```

Next, we use `BeginScene()` to indicate we are at the start of our execute buffer's commands and we wish to use textures. If the device does not handle texturing, we will drop to using no textures.

```
    // Start our DrawPrimitive scene
    myDevice->BeginScene();

    // Set our current texture
    if (myDevice->SetRenderState(D3DRENDERSTATE_TEXTUREHANDLE,
            myTextureHandle) != D3D_OK)
        myDevice->SetRenderState(D3DRENDERSTATE_TEXTUREHANDLE, NULL);
```

With the system ready to go, we can set up the vertices for our 3D cube. This is very straightforward and shown below. The five values passed to the D3DLVERTEX variable are:

- The coordinate in 3D world space
- The diffuse color component
- The specular color component
- The UV texture coordinates (two values)

```
    // Set up and render each face of a texture mapped cube
    D3DLVERTEX vertex[4];
    // Face 1
    vertex[0] = D3DLVERTEX(D3DVECTOR(-2, 2, 9),D3DRGB(0.9, 0.9,0.9),
        D3DRGB(0,0,0),0,0);
```

```
vertex[1] = D3DLVERTEX(D3DVECTOR( 2, 2, 9),D3DRGB(0.9, 0.9, 0.9),
    D3DRGB(0,0,0),1,0);
vertex[2] = D3DLVERTEX(D3DVECTOR(-2, 2, 9),D3DRGB(0.9, 0.9, 0.9),
    D3DRGB(0,0,0),0,1);
vertex[3] = D3DLVERTEX(D3DVECTOR( 2,-2, 9),D3DRGB(0.9, 0.9, 0.9),
    D3DRGB(0,0,0),1,1);
myDevice->DrawPrimitive(D3DPT_TRIANGLESTRIP,
                    D3DVT_LVERTEX,(LPVOID)vetex,4,NULL);
// Face 2
vertex[0] = D3DLVERTEX(D3DVECTOR( 2, 2,9),D3DRGB(0.5,0.5,0.5),
    D3DRGB(0,0,0),0,0);
vertex[1] = D3DLVERTEX(D3DVECTOR( 2, 2,18),D3DRGB(0.5,0.5,0.5),
    D3DRGB(0,0,0),1,0);
vertex[2] = D3DLVERTEX(D3DVECTOR( 2,-2,9),D3DRGB(0.5,0.5,0.5),
    D3DRGB(0,0,0),0,1);
vertex[3] = D3DLVERTEX(D3DVECTOR( 2,-2,18),D3DRGB(0.5,0.5,0.5),
    D3DRGB(0,0,0),1,1);
myDevice->DrawPrimitive(D3DPT_TRIANGLESTRIP,
                    D3DVT_LVERTEX,(LPVOID)vertex,4,NULL);
// Face 3
vertex[0] = D3DLVERTEX(D3DVECTOR( 2, 2,18),D3DRGB(0.9, 0.9,0.9),
    D3DRGB(0,0,0),0,0);
vertex[1] = D3DLVERTEX(D3DVECTOR(-2, 2,18),D3DRGB(0.9, 0.9, 0.9),
    D3DRGB(0,0,0),1,0);
vertex[2] = D3DLVERTEX(D3DVECTOR( 2,-2,18),D3DRGB(0.9, 0.9, 0.9),
    D3DRGB(0,0,0),0,1);
vertex[3] = D3DLVERTEX(D3DVECTOR(-2,-2,18),D3DRGB(0.9, 0.9, 0.9),
    D3DRGB(0,0,0),1,1);
myDevice->DrawPrimitive(D3DPT_TRIANGLESTRIP,
                    D3DVT_LVERTEX,(LPVOID)vertex,4,NULL);
// Face 4
vertex[0] = D3DLVERTEX(D3DVECTOR(-2, 2,18),D3DRGB(0.5,0.5,0.5),
    D3DRGB(0,0,0),0,0);
vertex[1] = D3DLVERTEX(D3DVECTOR(-2, 2,9),D3DRGB(0.5,0.5,0.5),
    D3DRGB(0,0,0),1,0);
vertex[2] = D3DLVERTEX(D3DVECTOR(-2,-2,18),D3DRGB(0.5,0.5,0.5),
    D3DRGB(0,0,0),0,1);
vertex[3] = D3DLVERTEX(D3DVECTOR(-2,-2,9),D3DRGB(0.5,0.5,0.5),
    D3DRGB(0,0,0),1,1);
myDevice->DrawPrimitive(D3DPT_TRIANGLESTRIP,
                    D3DVT_LVERTEX,(LPVOID)vertex,4,NULL);
// Face 5
vertex[0] = D3DLVERTEX(D3DVECTOR(-2, 2,18),D3DRGB(0.1,0.1,0.1),
    D3DRGB(0,0,0),0,0);
vertex[1] = D3DLVERTEX(D3DVECTOR( 2, 2,18),D3DRGB(0.1,0.1,0.1),
    D3DRGB(0,0,0),1,0);
vertex[2] = D3DLVERTEX(D3DVECTOR(-2, 2,9),D3DRGB(0.1,0.1,0.1),
    D3DRGB(0,0,0),0,1);
vertex[3] = D3DLVERTEX(D3DVECTOR( 2, 2,9),D3DRGB(0.1,0.1,0.1),
    D3DRGB(0,0,0),1,1);
myDevice->DrawPrimitive(D3DPT_TRIANGLESTRIP,
                    D3DVT_LVERTEX,(LPVOID)vertex,4,NULL);
// Face 6
vertex[0] = D3DLVERTEX(D3DVECTOR(-2,-2,9),D3DRGB(0.3,0.3,0.3),
    D3DRGB(0,0,0),0,0);
```

```
    vertex[1] = D3DLVERTEX(D3DVECTOR( 2,-2,9),D3DRGB(0.3,0.3,0.3),
        D3DRGB(0,0,0),1,0);
    vertex[2] = D3DLVERTEX(D3DVECTOR(-2,-2,18),D3DRGB(0.3,0.3,0.3),
        D3DRGB(0,0,0),0,1);
    vertex[3] = D3DLVERTEX(D3DVECTOR( 2,-2,18),D3DRGB(0.3,0.3,0.3),
        D3DRGB(0,0,0),1,1);
    myDevice->DrawPrimitive(D3DPT_TRIANGLESTRIP,
                    D3DVT_LVERTEX,(LPVOID)vertex,4,NULL);

    // Rendering is complete
    myDevice->EndScene();
} // End DoBox
```

Handling the world, view, and projection matrices

At this point, what you have created is still not terribly useful because you cannot move it around. Even though it is a 3D cube, it looks like it is 2D. To allow us to create a 3D view of our world, we need to define two DrawPrimitive functions to create the camera and view matrices.

ViewMatrix() takes a camera position, the target, and the roll value to create a matrix for our camera. Using this, you can move your viewpoint by calling the rotate or translate methods to create a matrix that you can apply to your camera's matrix.

ProjectionMatrix() is used to create a matrix to define how your object is perspectively projected onto the screen. This method takes the distance to the near clipping plane, the distance to the far clipping plane, and the field of view in radians.

Remember also that the world matrix is the matrix you use to position each object in 3D space.

DirectX did not provide a good set of routines to build and manipulate our matrices, but we can easily create our own. The ones everyone seems to find most useful are:

1 IdentityMatrix(). Returns a D3DMATRIX which is set to the identity matrix.

2 MatrixMultiply(). Multiplies two matrices.

3 ZeroMatrix(). Returns a D3DMATRIX with all of its elements set to 0.

4 RotateX(). Returns a matrix which will rotate your data about the X axis by the angle you indicate.

5 RotateY(). Returns a matrix which will rotate your data about the Y axis by the angle you indicate.

6 RotateZ(). Returns a matrix which will rotate your data about the Z axis by the angle you indicate.

7 `Scale()`. Returns a matrix which scales your data by the requested scale factor.

8 `Translate()`. Returns a matrix which will translate your data by the requested vector.

The code for each of these is:

```
// This routine is used to set up the Identity matrix
D3DMATRIX IdentityMatrix()
{
    return D3DMATRIX(1,0,0,0, 0,1,0,0, 0,0,1,0, 0,0,0,1);
} // End of IdentityMatrix

// This routine is used to multiply two matrices together.
D3DMATRIX MatrixMultiply(const D3DMATRIX a, const D3DMATRIX b)
{
    D3DMATRIX myMatrix = ZeroMatrix();
    for (int i=0; i<4; i++)
        for (int j=0; j<4; j++)
            for (int k=0; k<4; k++)
                myMatrix(i, j) += a(k, j) * b(i, k);
    return myMatrix;
} // End of MatrixMultiply()

// This routine is used to set up the Projection matrix
D3DMATRIX ProjectionMatrix(
    const float nearPlane,    // The distance to the near clipping plan
    const float farPlane,     // The distance to the far clipping plane
    const float fov)          // The Field of View
{
    float cosine, sine, val;

    cosine = (float)cos(fov*0.5);
    sine = (float)sin(fov*0.5);
    val = sin/(1.0 - nearPlane/farPlane);
    D3DMATRIX newMatrix = ZeroMatrix();
    newMatrix(0, 0) = cosine;
    newMatrix(1, 1) = cosine;
    newMatrix(2, 2) = val;
    newMatrix(3, 2) = -val*nearPlane;
    newMatrix(2, 3) = sine;
    return newMatrix;
} // End of ProjectionMatrix()

// This routine is used to set up a matrix to rotate about the X axis
D3DMATRIX RotateX(const float radians)
{
    float cosine, sine;
    cosine = (float)cos(radians);
    sine = (float)sin(radians);
    D3DMATRIX newMatrix = IdentityMatrix();
    newMatrix(1,1) = cosine;
    newMatrix(2,2) = cosine;
```

```
    newMatrix(1,2) = -sine;
    newMatrix(2,1) = sine;
    return newMatrix;
} // End of RotateX()


// This routine is used to set up a matrix to rotate about the Y axis
D3DMATRIX RotateY(const float radians)
{
    float cosine, sine;

    cosine = (float)cos(radians);
    sine = (float)sin(radians);
    D3DMATRIX newMatrix = IdentityMatrix();
    newMatrix(0,0) = cosine;
    newMatrix(2,2) = cosine;
    newMatrix(0,2) = sine;
    newMatrix(2,0) = -sine;
    return newMatrix;
} // End of RotateY()


// This routine is used to set up a matrix to rotate about the Z axis
D3DMATRIX RotateZ(const float radians)
{
    float cosine, sine;

    cosine = (float)cos(radians);
    sine = (float)sin(radians);
    D3DMATRIX newMatrix = IdentityMatrix();
    newMatrix(0,0) = cosine;
    newMatrix(1,1) = cosine;
    newMatrix(0,1) = -sine;
    newMatrix(1,0) = sine;
    return newMatrix;
} // End of RotateZ()


// This routine is used to set up a scale matrix
D3DMATRIX Scale(const float scale)
{
    D3DMATRIX newMatrix = IdentityMatrix();
    newMatrix(0, 0) = scale;
    newMatrix(1, 1) = scale;
    newMatrix(2, 2) = scale;
    return newMatrix;
} // End of Scale()


// This method is used to set up a translation matrix
D3DMATRIX Translate(const float dx, const float dy, const float dz)
{
    D3DMATRIX newMatrix = IdentityMatrix();
    newMatrix(3, 0) = dx;
    newMatrix(3, 1) = dy;
    newMatrix(3, 2) = dz;
    return newMatrix;
```

```
} // End of Translate()

// This method is used to create our view matrix
D3DMATRIX ViewMatrix(const D3DVECTOR Camera,      // Our camera's location
                     const D3DVECTOR cameraLookAt, // The look-at value for our
                                                   // camera
                     const D3DVECTOR worldUp,      // Our world's up vector
                     const float roll)             // The roll in radians
{
    D3DMATRIX view = IdentityMatrix();
    D3DVECTOR up, right, viewDirection;

    viewDirection = Normalize(cameraLookAt - Camera);
    right = CrossProduct(worldUp, viewDirection);
    up = CrossProduct(viewDirection, right);
    right = Normalize(right);
    up = Normalize(up);

    view(0, 0) = right.x;
    view(1, 0) = right.y;
    view(2, 0) = right.z;
    view(0, 1) = up.x;
    view(1, 1) = up.y;
    view(2, 1) = up.z;
    view(0, 2) = viewDirection.x;
    view(1, 2) = viewDirection.y;
    view(2, 2) = viewDirection.z;
    view(3, 0) = -DotProduct(right, Camera);
    view(3, 1) = -DotProduct(up, Camera);
    view(3, 2) = -DotProduct(viewDirection, Camera);

    if (roll != 0.0)
    {
        view = MatrixMultiply(RotateZ(-roll), view);
    }

    return view;
} // End of ViewMatrix()

D3DMATRIX ZeroMatrix(void) // initializes our matrix to zero
{
    D3DMATRIX newMatrix;
    for (int i=0; i<4; i++)
        for (int j=0; j<4; j++)
            newMatrix(i, j) = 0.0;
    return newMatrix;
} // End of ZeroMatrix()
```

Now that we have all of our matrix handling routines done, we are ready to set up the world, view, and projection matrices. The code below creates the matrices, requesting that the world matrix is 0, the camera is at the origin looking in the positive *Z* direction, and the projection matrix has a 70-degree field of view. When they have been created, we can set them using the `SetTransform()` routine.

```
// Create our matrices
myWorld = IdentityMatrix();
myView = ViewMatrix(D3DVECTOR(0,0,0), D3DVECTOR(0,0,1), D3DVECTOR(0,1,0),
        0);
myProjection = ProjectionMatrix(1.0, 1000.0, (float)(70*PI/180));

// Initialize them
myDevice->SetTransform(D3DTRANSFORMSTATE_WORLD, &myWorld);
myDevice->SetTransform(D3DTRANSFORMSTATE_VIEW, &myView);
myDevice->SetTransform(D3DTRANSFORMSTATE_PROJECTION, &myProjection);
```

It is important to remember that in world space, the origin is centered on the screen, *x* is positive to the right, *y* is positive up, and *z* is positive into the screen. Also remember that the winding order of your polygon points is critical for backface removal.

With that, all that is left to do is to let you move around in your world so you can view your objects from various positions. To do this, we just control our view matrix. As you have seen before, you can make sure you control the "steps" in your movement by using the `timeGetTime()` function from the mutimedia extensions. For our purposes we will be controlling movement with the keyboard. You could, of course, use Direct-Input if you wish.

The code below is a lot like the key-based motion code we created for our main Retained Mode tutorial (and all of the other smaller ones). The difference is that we need to apply our transforms differently, using the new routines above since we are no longer in Retained Mode.

Assuming we use a function called `update()` (this seems to be the standard name everyone uses) to check the keypresses and transform the camera matrix accordingly, we can use this to check the time since the last frame to keep our frame rate steady. Let's define speed increases using the SHIFT key, rotate left using the left arrow key, rotate right using the right arrow key, and "slide left" or "slide right" using a combination of the <ALT> and the left or right arrow keys. Finally, the up and down arrow keys move you forward and backward. The body of the routine would be as follows:

```
#define KeyPressed(key) (GetAsyncKeyState(key) & 0x8000)

// Get the current time, calculate the time that has passed, and update
// the previous time for the next frame
DWORD now = timeGetTime();
DWORD timePassed = now - previous;
previous = now;

// If the user is holding down the shift key, multiply the timePassed by
// 1.5 so we get a visual speed up
```

```
      if (KeyPressed(VK_SHIFT)) timePassed *= 1.5;

    // Check for keypresses and update the camera matrix
    #define MOVEMENT_SPEED 0.02
    #define TURN_SPEED    0.002

    // Move forward
    if (KeyPressed(VK_UP))
        myView = MatrixMult(Translate(0,0,-MOVEMENT_SPEED*timePassed),
            myView);

    // Move backward
    if (KeyPressed(VK_DOWN))
        myView = MatrixMult(Translate(0,0, MOVEMENT_SPEED*timePassed),
            myView);

    if (GetAsyncKeyState(VK_MENU) & 0x8000)
    {
        // Slide left or right
         if (KeyPressed(VK_LEFT))  myView = MatrixMult(Translate(
            MOVEMENT_SPEED*timePassed,0,0), myView);
        if (KeyPressed(VK_RIGHT)) myView = MatrixMult(Translate(-
            MOVEMENT_SPEED*timePassed,0,0), myView);
    }
    else
    {
        // Rotate left or right
        if (KeyPressed(VK_LEFT))
            myView = MatrixMult(RotateY(-TURN_SPEED*timePassed), myView);
        if (KeyPressed(VK_RIGHT))
            myView = MatrixMult(RotateY( TURN_SPEED*timePassed), myView);
    }

    // Finally,  set the new view matrix to our changed values based on the
    // user input
    myDevice->SetTransform(D3DTRANSFORMSTATE_VIEW, &myView);
```

Conclusion

As you can see, DrawPrimitive is conceptually simple, but very powerful. I suggest you sit down and start experimenting. The first thing I recommend is applying a texture to your object. After that, try something more complex. Everyone demos triangles or squares (and I fell into this also) when explaining the basics, but when you start rendering "real" scenes, like rooms, etc., you will begin to see the full capabilities of DrawPrimitive! To see some of the excellent capabilities of DrawPrimitive, run some of the new Microsoft demos I have included on the CD.

appendix B

The new Direct3D Retained Mode interfaces for DirectX 5.0

Microsoft has added several interfaces to DirectX 5.0 which support some very powerful new capabilities like morphing through mesh interpolation (wonderful for character animation, landscape animation, etc.) and progressive meshes which allow you to use objects with levels of detail, similar in capability to the technique in chapter 7. Please look back to chapter 20 if you wish to review the list of interfaces that were provided with DirectX 3.

The new interfaces added to DirectX 5.0 are:

- `IDirect3DRM2`
- `IDirect3DRMDevice2`
- `IDirect3DRMFrame2`
- `IDirect3DRMInterpolator`
- `IDirect3DRMMeshBuilder2`
- `IDirect3DRMPicked2Array`
- `IDirect3DRMProgressiveMesh`
- `IDirect3DRMTexture2`

Each of these interfaces and its associated methods are defined below.

690

The IDirect3DRM2 interface

As you will remember, the `IDirect3DRM` interface's methods were used to create the various Direct3DRM interfaces you work with.

The IDirect3DRM2 interface was designed to support all of the methods in the `IDirect3DRM` interface. The methods that are defined for the `IDirect3DRM` interface to create a DIRECT3DRMDEVICE2 object are `IDirect3DRM2::CreateDeviceFromSurface`, `IDirect3DRM2::CreateDeviceFromD3D`, and `IDirect3DRM2::CreateDeviceFromClipper`.

To allow your application access to the IDirect3DRM's COM interface, you must first create an IDirect3DRM object using the `Direct3DRMCreate` method and then request the `IDirect3DRM2` interface from the `IDirect3DRM` interface.

Also, a completely new method was added, namely :`IDirect3DRM2::CreateProgressiveMesh`. This method is used to create the new Progressive Mesh.

Like all COM interfaces, this one inherits the `AddRef`, `QueryInterface`, and the `Release` methods from the `IUnknown` interface.

The methods of the `IDirect3DRM2` interface can be organized into the groups in table B.1:

Table B.1 IDirect3DRM2 methods

Animation	CreateAnimation
	CreateAnimationSet
Devices	CreateDevice
	CreateDeviceFromClipper
	CreateDeviceFromD3D
	CreateDeviceFromSurface
	GetDevices
Enumeration	EnumerateObjects
Faces	CreateFace
Frames	CreateFrame
Lights	CreateLight
	CreateLightRGB
Materials	CreateMaterial
Meshes	CreateMesh
	CreateMeshBuilder
Miscellaneous	CreateObject
	CreateUserVisual
	GetNamedObject
	Load

Table B.1 IDirect3DRM2 methods (continued)

Miscellaneous (continued)	Tick
Progressive Meshes	CreateProgressiveMesh
Search paths	AddSearchPath
	GetSearchPath
	SetSearchPath
Shadows	CreateShadow
Textures	CreateTexture
	CreateTextureFromSurface
	LoadTexture
	LoadTextureFromResource
	SetDefaultTextureColors
	SetDefaultTextureShades
Viewports	CreateViewport
Wraps	CreateWrap

IDirect3DRM2::AddSearchPath

This method has the same definition as `IDirect3DRM::AddSearchPath`. Please see page 358 for details.

IDirect3DRM2::CreateAnimation

This method has the same definition as `IDirect3DRM::CreateAnimation`. Please see page 358 for details.

IDirect3DRM2::CreateAnimationSet

This method has the same definition as `IDirect3DRM::CreateAnimationSet`. Please see page 359 for details.

IDirect3DRM2::CreateDeviceFromClipper

Description

This method is used to create a Direct3DRMDevice2 Windows device using the passed DirectDrawClipper object. The `IDirect3DRMDevice2` interface is used with an `IDirect3DDevice2` Immediate Mode device and supports the `DrawPrimitive` interface as well as execute buffers. You need to use this for progressive meshes and for alpha blending and sorting of transparent objects.

The system describes the default settings by using the following flags from the D3DPRIMCAPS structure in internal device-enumeration calls:

- D3DPSHADECAPS_ALPHAFLATSTIPPLED

- D3DPTBLENDCAPS_COPY | D3DPTBLENDCAPS_MODULATE

- D3DPMISCCAPS_CULLCCW

- D3DPRASTERCAPS_FOGVERTEX

- D3DPCMPCAPS_LESSEQUAL

- D3DPTFILTERCAPS_NEAREST

- D3DPTEXTURECAPS_PERSPECTIVE

- D3DPTEXTURECAPS_TRANSPARENCY

- D3DPTADDRESSCAPS_WRAP

If a hardware device is not found, the monochromatic (ramp) software driver is loaded. An application should enumerate devices instead of specifying NULL in the lpGUID parameter if it has special needs that are not met by this list of default settings.

C++ specification

```
HRESULT CreateDeviceFromClipper(
    LPDIRECTDRAWCLIPPER lpDDClipper,
    LPGUID lpGUID,
    int width,
    int height,
    LPDIRECT3DRMDEVICE2 * lplpD3DRMDevice
    );
```

Parameters

lpDDClipper. The address of a DirectDrawClipper object.

lpGUID. The address of a globally unique identifier (GUID). If this is set to NULL, the system will search for a device with a set of default device capabilities. Microsoft recommends you create a Retained Mode device this way since this method will always work whenever new hardware is installed.

width. The width of the device to be created.

height. The height of the device to be created.

lplpD3DRMDevice. The address you wish filled with a pointer to an IDirect3-DRMDevice2 interface.

Successful: D3DRM_OK

Error: One of the Direct3DRM Retained Mode return values.

See also

IDirect3DRM2::CreateDeviceFromD3D

Example

```
HWND window;
D3DRMCOLORMODEL model;
// Define a rect structure variable
RECT rect;
// Get the rectangle for the client space of our window
GetClientRect(window, &rect);
// Try to create a Direct3DRM2 windows device using the specified
// clipper object
if (FAILED(lpD3DRM2->CreateDeviceFromClipper(lpDDClipper,
        FindDevice(model), rect.right, rect.bottom, &dev)))
    goto generic_error;
```

IDirect3DRM2::CreateDeviceFromD3D

Description

This method is used to create a Direct3DRMDevice2 Windows device using the passed Direct3D objects. You can use an IDirect3DRMDevice2 interface with an IDirect3DDevice2 Immediate Mode device. It is required for progressive meshes and for alpha blending and sorting of transparent objects. This device also supports the DrawPrimitive interface and execute buffers.

C++ specification

```
HRESULT CreateDeviceFromD3D(
    LPDIRECT3D2 lpD3D,
    LPDIRECT3DDEVICE2 lpD3DDev,
    LPDIRECT3DRMDEVICE2 * lplpD3DRMDevice
    );
```

Parameters

lpD3D. The address of a Direct3D2 instance.

lpD3DDev. The address of a Direct3D2 device object.

lplpD3DRMDevice. The address you wish filled with a pointer to an IDirect3DRMDevice2 interface.

Successful: D3DRM_OK

Error: One of the Direct3DRM Retained Mode return values.

See also

IDirect3DRM::CreateDeviceFromD3D

IDirect3DRM2::CreateDeviceFromClipper

Example

```
LPDIRECT3D2 D3D2;
LPDIRECT3DDEVICE2 D3DDevice2;
LPDIRECT3DRMDEVICE2 myD3DRMDevice2;
.
.
.
// Create the D3DRMDevice
lpD3DRM2->CreateDeviceFromD3D(D3D2, D3DDevice2, &D3DRMDevice2);
```

IDirect3DRM2::CreateDeviceFromSurface

Description

The IDirect3DRMDevice2 interface is used with an IDirect3DDevice2 Immediate Mode device. This method is used to create a Direct3DRMDevice2 Windows device which you can use for rendering from the specified DirectDraw surfaces. The IDirect3DDevice2 device is required for progressive meshes and for alpha blending and sorting of transparent objects. It also supports the DrawPrimitive interface as well as execute buffers.

C++ specification

```
HRESULT CreateDeviceFromSurface(
    LPGUID lpGUID,
    LPDIRECTDRAW lpDD,
    LPDIRECTDRAWSURFACE lpDDSBack,
    LPDIRECT3DRMDEVICE2 * lplpD3DRMDevice
    );
```

Parameters

lpGUID. The address of the GUID which is used as the required device driver. When this parameter is set to NULL, the default device driver will be used.

lpDD. The address of the DirectDraw object which is the source of the Direct-Draw surface.

lpDDSBack. The address of the DirectDrawSurface object representing the back buffer.

lplpD3DRMDevice. The address you wish to be filled with a pointer to an IDirect3DRMDevice2 interface.

Returns

Successful: D3DRM_OK

Error: One of the Direct3DRM Retained Mode return values.

See also

IDirect3DRM::CreateDeviceFromSurface

IDirect3DRM2::CreateDeviceFromClipper

Example

```
HRESULT hRes;
GUID DriverGUID[MAX_DRIVERS];            // The GUIDs of the
                                         // available D3D drivers
LPDIRECTDRAW lpDD = NULL; // DirectDraw object
LPDIRECTDRAWSURFACE lpDDSBack = NULL;// DirectDraw back surface
LPDIRECT3DRMDEVICE2 rmdev2  = NULL;  // Direct3DRM2 device
.
.
.
// Create the D3DRMDevice
hRes = CreateDeviceFromSurface(&DriverGUID[CurrDriver],
       lpDD,  lpDDSBack, &rmdev2);
    );
```

IDirect3DRM2::CreateFace

This method has the same definition as IDirect3DRM::CreateFace. Please see page 363 for details.

IDirect3DRM2::CreateFrame

Description

This method is used to create a new child frame, which is a Direct3DRMFrame2 object, of the passed parent frame. Remember that the child frame will inherit its parent's motion attributes. Also, you can create a scene (a frame without a parent) by passing NULL as the value for the parent. If you later choose to associate a frame with no parent to a parent frame you can do this using the IDirect3-DRMFrame2::AddChild method.

C++ specification

```
HRESULT CreateFrame(
```

```
          LPDIRECT3DRMFRAME lpD3DRMFrame,
          LPDIRECT3DRMFRAME2* lplpD3DRMFrame2
          );
```

Parameters

lpD3DRMFrame. The address of a DIRECT3DRMFRAME object you wish to use as the parent of the new frame.

lplpD3DRMFrame. The address that you wish to be filled with a pointer to an IDirect3DRMFrame2 interface.

Returns

Successful: D3DRM_OK

Error: One of the Direct3DRM Retained Mode return values.

See also

IDirect3DRMFrame2::AddChild
IDirect3DRM::CreateFrame

Example

```
HRESULT hRes;
LPDIRECT3DRMFRAME scene;
LPDIRECT3DRMFRAME2 frame;
LPDIRECT3DRM2 lpD3DRM2;
.
.
if (FAILED(lpD3DRM2->CreateFrame(scene, &frame))
    goto generic_error;
```

IDirect3DRM2::CreateLight

This method has the same definition as IDirect3DRM::CreateLight. Please see page 364 for details.

IDirect3DRM2::CreateLightRGB

This method has the same definition as IDirect3DRM::CreateLightRGB. Please see page 366 for details.

IDirect3DRM2::CreateMaterial

This method has the same definition as IDirect3DRM::CreateMaterial. Please see page 367 for details.

IDirect3DRM2::CreateMesh

This method has the same definition as `IDirect3DRM::CreateMesh`. Please see page 367 for details.

IDirect3DRM2::CreateMeshBuilder

Description
This member function is used to create a new mesh builder object.

C++ specification
```
HRESULT CreateMeshBuilder(
    LPDIRECT3DRMMESHBUILDER2* lplpD3DRMMeshBuilder2
    );
```

Parameters
`lplpD3DRMMeshBuilder`. The address you wish filled with a pointer to an `IDirect3DRMMeshBuilder2` interface.

Returns
Successful: D3DRM_OK

Error: One of the Direct3DRM Retained Mode return values.

See also
IDirect3DRM::CreateMeshBuilder

Example
```
LPDIRECT3DRMMESHBUILDER2 obj_builder2;
if (FAILED(lpD3DRM2->CreateMeshBuilder(&obj_builder2)))
    goto generic_error;
```

IDirect3DRM2::CreateObject

This method has the same definition as `IDirect3DRM::CreateObject` except that we are creating a Direct3DRM2 object rather than a Direct3DRM object. Please see page 369 for details.

IDirect3DRM2::CreateProgressiveMesh

Description
This method is used to create a new progressive mesh object with no faces. This mesh will not be visible until it is added to a frame.

C++ specification
```
HRESULT CreateProgressiveMesh(
    LPDIRECT3DRMPROGRESSIVEMESH* lplpD3DRMProgressiveMesh
    );
```

Parameters
lplpD3DRMProgressiveMesh. The address to be filled with a pointer to an IDirect3DRMProgressiveMesh interface.

Returns
Successful: D3DRM_OK
Error: One of the Direct3DRM Retained Mode return values.

Example
```
HRESULT result;
LPDIRECT3DRMPROGRESSIVEMESH ProgressiveMesh

result = CreateProgressiveMesh(&ProgressiveMesh);
```

IDirect3DRM2::CreateShadow

This method has the same definition as IDirect3DRM::CreateShadow. Please see page 369 for details.

IDirect3DRM2::CreateTexture

Description
This method is used to create a texture from an image in memory. Instead of copying the memory into the Direct3DRM's buffer, the image's memory is used each time the texture is rendered. In this way, the image can be used as both a rendering target and a texture.

C++ specification
```
HRESULT CreateTexture(
    LPD3DRMIMAGE lpImage,
```

```
      LPDIRECT3DRMTEXTURE2* lplpD3DRMTexture2
      );
```

Parameters

lpImage. The address of a D3DRMIMAGE structure which defines the texture source.

lplpD3DRMTexture2. The address you wish filled with a pointer to an IDirect-3DRMTexture2 interface.

Returns

Successful: D3DRM_OK

Error: One of the Direct3DRM Retained Mode return values.

See also

IDirect3DRM::CreateTexture

Example

```
HRESULT result;
LPD3DRMIMAGE TextureImage,
LPDIRECT3DRMTEXTURE2 tex.
.
.
if (FAILED(lpD3DRM2->CreateTexture(&TextureImage, &tex)))
    goto generic_error;
```

IDirect3DRM2::CreateTextureFromSurface

Description

This method is used to create a texture from a specified DirectDraw surface.

C++ specification

```
HRESULT CreateTextureFromSurface(
    LPDIRECTDRAWSURFACE lpDDS,
    LPDIRECT3DRMTEXTURE2 * lplpD3DRMTexture2
    );
```

Parameters

lpDDS. The address of the DirectDrawSurface object which contains the texture.

lplpD3DRMTexture. The address you wish filled with a pointer to an IDirect-3DRMTexture2 interface.

Returns

Successful: D3DRM_OK

Error: One of the Direct3DRM Retained Mode return values.

See also

    IDirect3DRM::CreateTextureFromSurface

Example

```
HRESULT result;
LPDIRECTDRAWSURFACE lpDDS,
LPDIRECTRMTEXTURE2 tex;
    .
    .
if (FAILED(lpD3DRM2->CreateTextureFromSurface(lpDDS, &tex)))
    goto generic_error;
```

IDirect3DRM2::CreateUserVisual

This method has the same definition as `IDirect3DRM::CreateUserVisual`. Please see page 372 for details.

IDirect3DRM2::CreateViewport

Description

This method is used to create a viewport on a Direct3DRMDevice2 device with device coordinates (`dwXPos`, `dwYPos`) to (`dwXPos + dwWidth`, `dwYPos + dwHeight`). The `IDirect3DRMDevice2` interface is designed to work with an IDirect3D-Device2 Immediate Mode device. The IDirect3DDevice2 device is required for progressive meshes, alpha blending and sorting of transparent objects, the `DrawPrimitive` interface, and execute buffers.

C++ specification

```
HRESULT CreateViewport(
    LPDIRECT3DRMDEVICE2 lpDev,
    LPDIRECT3DRMFRAME lpCamera,
    DWORD dwXPos,
    DWORD dwYPos,
    DWORD dwWidth,
    DWORD dwHeight,
    LPDIRECT3DRMVIEWPORT* lplpD3DRMViewport
    );
```

Parameters

    `lpDev`. The address of a Direct3DRMDevice2 device on which you wish the viewport to be created.

    `lpCamera`. The address of a frame defining the position and direction of your view.

dwXPos, dwYPos, dwWidth, and dwHeight. The position and size, in device coordinates, of your vewport. If you attempt to set the viewport size larger than the physical device, this method will fail.

lplpD3DRMViewport. The address that you wish filled with a pointer to an IDirect3DRMViewport interface.

Returns

Successful: D3DRM_OK

Error: One of the Direct3DRM Retained Mode return values. If your viewport is larger than your physical device, a value of D3DRMERR_BADVALUE will be returned.

See also

IDirect3DRM::CreateViewport

Example

```
LPDIRECT3DRMDEVICE2 lpDev;
LPDIRECT3DRMFRAME lpCamera;
LPDIRECT3DVIEWPORT2 lpView;
DWORD dwXPos,  dwYPos,  dwWidth,  dwHeight;
    .
    .
CreateViewport( lpDev,  lpCamera,  dwXPos,  dwYPos,  dwWidth,
      dwHeight, &lpView);
```

IDirect3DRM2::CreateWrap

This method has the same definition as IDirect3DRM::CreateWrap. Please see page 374 for details.

IDirect3DRM2::EnumerateObjects

This method has the same definition as IDirect3DRM::EnumerateObjects. Please see page 375 for details.

IDirect3DRM2::GetDevices

This method has the same definition as IDirect3DRM::GetDevices. Please see page 376 for details.

IDirect3DRM2::GetNamedObject

This method has the same definition as `IDirect3DRM::GetNamedObject`. Please see page 376 for details.

IDirect3DRM2::GetSearchPath

This method has the same definition as `IDirect3DRM::GetSearchPath`. Please see page 377 for details.

IDirect3DRM2::Load

This method has the same definition as `IDirect3DRM::Load`. Please see page 378 for details.

IDirect3DRM2::LoadTexture

Description

This method is used to load a Direct3DRMTexture2 texture from a file. This texture can be in either the Windows bitmap (.bmp) or Portable Pixmap (.ppm) P6 format. It can have 8, 24, or 32 bits-per-pixel.

C++ specification

```
HRESULT LoadTexture(
    const char * lpFileName,
    LPDIRECT3DRMTEXTURE2* lplpD3DRMTexture
    );
```

Parameters

`lpFileName`. The address of the name of the .bmp or .ppm file.

`lplpD3DRMTexture`. The address of a pointer you wish initialized with an `IDirect3DRMTexture2` pointer.

Returns

Successful: D3DRM_OK

Error: One of the Direct3DRM Retained Mode return values.

See also

IDirect3DRM::LoadTexture

Example

```
LPDIRECT3DRMTEXTURE2 *texarray;

HRESULT loadTextures(char *name, void *arg,
                     LPDIRECT3DRMTEXTURE2 *tex)
{
    if (FAILED(lpD3DRM2->LoadTexture(name, tex)) {
    {
        return NULL;
    }

    texArray[current++] = tex;

    // Use AddRef to keep a reference to each texture loaded by
    // your texture callback
    tex->AddRef();

    return tex;
}
```

IDirect3DRM2::LoadTextureFromResource

Description

This method is used to load a Direct3DRMTexture2 texture from a resource.

C++ specification

```
HRESULT LoadTextureFromResource(
    HMODULE hModule,
    LPCTSTR strName,
    LPCTSTR strType,
    LPDIRECT3DRMTEXTURE2 * lplpD3DRMTexture
    );
```

Parameters

hModule. The handle of the module whose executable file contains the resource.

strName. A null-terminated string containing the name of the resource you wish to use as the texture.

strType. A null-terminated string which indicates the type name of the resource which can be one of the following:

Value	Meaning
RT_BITMAP	Bitmap resource
RT_RCDATA	Application-defined resource (raw data)

lplpD3DRMTexture. The address of a pointer you wish initialized with a valid IDirect3DRMTexture2 object.

Returns

Successful: D3DRM_OK

Error: One of the Direct3DRM Retained Mode return values.

See also

IDirect3DRM::LoadTextureFromResource

Example

```
HRESULT result;
LPDIRECT3DRMTEXTURE2 tex;
HMODULE module,
LPCTSTR name,
LPCTSTR type,
    .
    .
result =  LoadTextureFromResource( module, name, type, &tex);
```

IDirect3DRM2::SetDefaultTextureColors

Description

This method is used to set the default colors to use for a Direct3DRMTexture2 object. It affects only the texture colors if it is called before you call the IDirect3DRM2::CreateTexture method. Once the textures have been created, it has no effect.

C++ specification

```
HRESULT SetDefaultTextureColors(
    DWORD dwColors
    );
```

Parameters

dwColors. The number of colors.

Returns

Successful: D3DRM_OK

Error: One of the Direct3DRM Retained Mode return values.

See also

IDirect3DRM::SetDefaultTextureColors

```
LPDIRECT3DRM2 myD3DRM2;
.
.
.
switch (bpp)
{
.
.
.
case 16:
    .
    .
    .
    // Set the default number of colors to 64
    if (FAILED(myD3DRM2->SetDefaultTextureColors(64))
        goto generic_error;
    // Set the default shades to 32
    if (FAILED(myD3DRM2->SetDefaultTextureShades(32))
        goto generic_error;
```

IDirect3DRM2::SetDefaultTextureShades

Description

This method is used to set the default shades you wish to use for a `Direct3DRMTexture2` object. It affects only the texture shades if it is called before you call the `IDirect3DRM2::CreateTexture` method. Once the textures have been created, it has no effect.

C++ specification

```
HRESULT SetDefaultTextureShades(
    DWORD dwShades
    );
```

Parameters

`dwShades`. The number of shades.

Returns

Successful: D3DRM_OK

Error: One of the Direct3DRM Retained Mode return values.

See also

IDirect3DRM::SetDefaultTextureShades

Example

```
LPDIRECT3DRM2 myD3DRM2;
.
.
```

```
switch (bpp)
{
.
.
.
case 16:
    .
    .
    // Set the default number of colors to 64
    if (FAILED(myD3DRM2->SetDefaultTextureColors(64))
        goto generic_error;
    // Set the default shades to 32
    if (FAILED(myD3DRM2->SetDefaultTextureShades(32))
        goto generic_error;
```

IDirect3DRM2::SetSearchPath

This method has the same definition as `IDirect3DRM::SetSearchPath`. Please see page 383 for details.

IDirect3DRM2::Tick

This method has the same definition as `IDirect3DRM::Tick`. Please see page 384 for details.

The IDirect3DRMDevice2 interface

As with the `IDirect3DRMDevice` interface, the `IDirect3DRMDevice2` interface is used to handle our output device. This device supports the new `DrawPrimitive` interface, execute buffers, alpha blending, sorting of transparent objects, and progressive meshes. We create the IDirect3DRMDevice2 object with the call to the `IDirect3DRM2::CreateDevice` method. You can create an IDirect3DRMDevice2 device with the `IDirect3DRM2` interface and you can initialize it with the `IDirect3DRMDevice2::InitFromClipper`, `IDirect3DRMDevice::InitFromD3D`, or the `IDirect3DRMDevice2::InitFromSurface` methods. This object can work with an Immediate Mode IDirect3DDevice2 device.

As with the old `Direct3DRMDevice::SetQuality` method, you can set the quality of the new devices using the `IDirect3DRMDevice2::SetQuality` method. As in the past, the default device quality is `D3DRMRENDER_FLAT`. This means that objects are flat shaded, the lights are on, and solid fill is used.

Also as in the past, other objects can have their quality set to anything equal or less than this top level (the device's) quality. You can use the methods associated with the other new objects which are: `IDirect3DRMProgressiveMesh::SetQuality`, `IDirect3DRMMeshBuilder::SetQuality`, and `IDirect3DRMMeshBuilder2::SetQuality`. Finally, remember that the only exception to these rules is any Direct3DRMMesh object which ignores your device's settings and instead uses the group quality setting which defaults to `D3DRMRENDER_GOURAUD`.

The Direct3DRMDevice2 object can be acquired by calling the `IDirect3DRM2::CreateDevice` method.

Like all COM interfaces, this interface inherits the IUnknown interface methods. They consist of `AddRef`, `QueryInterface`, and `Release`.

The following are IDirect3DRMDevice2 methods can be organized into the groups in table B.2.

Table B.2 IDirect3DRMDevice2 methods

Group	Methods
Buffer counts	GetBufferCount
	SetBufferCount
Color models	GetColorModel
Dithering	GetDither
	SetDither
Initialization	Init
	InitFromClipper

Table B.2 IDirect3DRMDevice2 methods (continued)

Group	Methods
	InitFromD3D2
	InitFromSurface
Miscellaneous	GetDirect3DDevice2
	GetHeight
	GetTrianglesDrawn
	GetViewports
	GetWidth
	GetWireframeOptions
	Update
Notifications	AddUpdateCallback
	DeleteUpdateCallback
Rendering quality	GetQuality
	SetQuality
Shading	GetShades
	SetShades
Texture quality	GetTextureQuality
	SetTextureQuality
Transparency	GetRenderMode
	SetRenderMode

The IDirect3DRMDevice2 interface also inherits the following methods from the IDirect3DRMObject interface:

- AddDestroyCallback
- Clone
- DeleteDestroyCallback
- GetAppData
- GetClassName
- GetName
- SetAppData
- SetName

IDirect3DRMDevice2::AddUpdateCallback

This method has the same definition as IDirect3DRMDevice::AddUpdateCall-back except, of course, that it calls the IDirect3DRMDevice2::Update method and not IDirect3DRMDevice::Update. Please see page 401 for details.

IDirect3DRMDevice2::DeleteUpdateCallback

This method has the same definition as IDirect3DRMDevice::DeleteUpdate-Callback except, of course, that you must have created the object using IDirect3DRMDevice2::AddUpdateCallback. Please see page 401 for details.

IDirect3DRMDevice2::GetBufferCount

This method has the same definition as IDirect3DRMDevice::GetBufferCount except, of course, that you must have set the value with a call to IDirect-3DRMDevice2::SetBufferCount. Please see page 402 for details.

IDirect3DRMDevice2::GetColorModel

This method has the same definition as IDirect3DRMDevice::GetColorModel. Please see page 403 for details.

IDirect3DRMDevice2::GetDirect3DDevice2

Description

This method is used to acquire a pointer to an IDirect3DDevice2 Immediate Mode device. This device will support the DrawPrimitive interface and execute buffers. It is also required for progressive meshes and for alpha blending and sorting of transparent objects.

C++ specification

```
HRESULT GetDirect3DDevice2(
    LPDIRECT3DDEVICE2 * lplpD3DDevice
    );
```

Parameters

lplpD3DDevice. The address of a pointer you wish to initialize with a pointer to an IDirect3DDevice2 Immediate Mode device object.

Returns

Successful: D3DRM_OK

Error: One of the Direct3DRM Retained Mode return values.

Example

```
LPDIRECT3DDEVICE2 lpd3dDev2 = NULL;
LPDIRECT3DRMDEVICE2 dev2;
.
.

if (dev2->GetDirect3DDevice2(&lpd3dDev2) != D3DRM_OK)
    // Handle error
    goto generic_error;
```

IDirect3DRMDevice2::GetDither

This method has the same definition as IDirect3DRMDevice::GetDither. Please see page 404 for details.

IDirect3DRMDevice2::GetHeight

This method has the same definition as IDirect3DRMDevice::GetHeight. Please see page 405 for details.

IDirect3DRMDevice2::GetQuality

Description

This method is used to acquire the rendering quality for your device.

C++ specification

```
D3DRMRENDERQUALITY GetQuality( );
```

Parameters

None

Returns

This method returns one or more of the members of the enumerated types from the D3DRMRENDERQUALITY type.

See also

IDirect3DRMDevice2::SetQuality

Example

```
LPDIRECT3DRMDEVICE2 dev2;
D3DRMRENDERQUALITY quality;
    .
    .
quality = dev2->GetQuality();
```

IDirect3DRMDevice2::GetRenderMode

Description

This method is used to retrieve the current transparency flags.

C++ specification

```
DWORD GetRenderMode( );
```

Parameters

None

Returns

The current transparency flags are returned. They can have the values:

Flag	Value
No Flag (The default)	0
D3DRMRENDERMODE_BLENDEDTRANSPARENCY	1
D3DRMRENDERMODE_SORTEDTRANSPARENCY	2

See also

IDirect3DRMDevice2::SetRenderMode

Example

```
LPDIRECT3DRMDEVICE2 dev2;
DWORD renderMode;
    .
    .
```

```
renderMode = dev2->GetRenderMode( );
if (renderMode == D3DRMRENDERMODE_BLENDEDTRANSPARENCY)
{
    // handle transparency
    .
    .
    .
}
```

IDirect3DRMDevice2::GetShades

Description

This method is used to acquire the number of shades in a ramp of colors which are used for shading.

C++ specification

```
DWORD GetShades( );
```

Parameters

None

Returns

The number of shades.

See also

IDirect3DRMDevice2::SetShades
IDirect3DRMDevice::GetShades

Example

```
LPDIRECT3DRMDEVICE2 dev2;
DWORD shades;
.
.
.
shades = dev2->GetShades( );
if (shades == 32)
{
    // handle transparency
    .
    .
    .
}
```

IDirect3DRMDevice2::GetTextureQuality

This method has the same definition as `IDirect3DRMDevice::GetTextureQual-ity`. Please see page 407 for details.

IDirect3DRMDevice2::GetTrianglesDrawn

This method has the same definition as `IDirect3DRMDevice::GetTriangles-Drawn`. Please see page 405 for details.

IDirect3DRMDevice2::GetViewports

This method has the same definition as `IDirect3DRMDevice::GetViewports`. Please see page 408 for details.

IDirect3DRMDevice2::GetWidth

This method has the same definition as `IDirect3DRMDevice::GetWidth`. Please see page 408 for details.

IDirect3DRMDevice2::GetWireframeOptions

This method has the same definition as `IDirect3DRMDevice::GetWireframeOptions`. Please see page 409 for details.

IDirect3DRMDevice2::InitFromClipper

This method has the same definition as `IDirect3DRMDevice::InitFromClipper`. Please see page 410 for details.

IDirect3DRMDevice2::InitFromD3D2

Description

This method is used to initialize an IDirect3DRMDevice2 Retained Mode device from an IDirect3D2 Immediate Mode object and an IDirect3DDevice2 Immediate Mode device. The IDirect3DRMDevice2 device which is initialized from IDirect3DDevice2 is required for progressive meshes and for alpha blending and sorting of transparent objects. It also supports execute buffers and the `DrawPrimitive` interface.

C++ specification

```
HRESULT InitFromD3D2(
    LPDIRECT3D2 lpD3D,
    LPDIRECT3DDEVICE2 lpD3DIMDev
    );
```

Parameters

lpD3D. The address of the IDirect3D2 Immediate Mode object you wish used to initialize the Retained Mode device.

lpD3DIMDev. The address of the IDirect3DDevice2 Immediate Mode device you wish to be used to initialize the Retained Mode device.

Returns

Successful: D3DRM_OK

Error: One of the Direct3DRM Retained Mode return values.

See also

IDirect3DRMDevice::InitFromClipper

IDirect3DRMDevice::InitFromD3D

IDirect3DRMDevice2::InitFromSurface

Example

```
LPDIRECT3DRMDEVICE2 dev2;
LPDIRECT3D2 myD3D,
LPDIRECT3DDEVICE2 myIMDev
.
.
.
if  (dev2->InitFromD3D2(myD3D,  myIMDev) != D3DRM_OK)
    goto generic_error;
```

IDirect3DRMDevice2::InitFromSurface

Description

This method is used to initialize an IDirect3DDevice2 device from the specified DirectDraw surface, using the IDirect3DRM2::CreateDevice method. This initialized IDirect3DRMDevice2 device will support the DrawPrimitive interface and execute buffers. It is also necessary for alpha blending and sorting of transparent objects as well as progressive meshes.

C++ specification

```
HRESULT InitFromSurface(
    LPGUID lpGUID,
    LPDIRECTDRAW lpDD,
```

```
LPDIRECTDRAWSURFACE lpDDSBack
);
```

Parameters

lpGUID. The address of the GUID which specifies the Direct3D device driver to use.

lpDD. The address of the interface of a DirectDraw object which created the DirectDrawSurface.

lpDDSBack. The address of the interface of a DirectDrawSurface back buffer onto which the device will be rendered.

Returns

Successful: D3DRM_OK

Error: One of the Direct3DRM Retained Mode return values.

See also

IDirect3DRMDevice2::InitFromD3D2

IDirect3DRMDevice::InitFromClipper

IDirect3DRMDevice::InitFromD3D

Example

```
LPDIRECT3DRMDEVICE2 dev2;
LPGUID myGUID,
LPDIRECTDRAW myDD,
LPDIRECTDRAWSURFACE myDDSBack
.
.
if (dev2->InitFromSurface(myGUID, myDD,  myDDSBack) != D3DRM_OK)
    goto generic_error;
```

IDirect3DRMDevice2::SetBufferCount

This method has the same definition as `IDirect3DRMDevice::SetBufferCount`. Please see page 411 for details.

IDirect3DRMDevice2::SetDither

This method has the same definition as `IDirect3DRMDevice::SetDither`. Please see page 412 for details.

IDirect3DRMDevice2::SetQuality

This method has the same definition as `IDirect3DRMDevice::SetQuality`. Please see page 413 for details.

You can set a Direct3DRMProgressiveMesh, a Direct3DRMMeshBuilder, or Direct3DRMMeshBuilder2 object's quality using `SetQuality`. The quality has a default value of `D3DRMRENDER_FLAT`. The quality of an object has three components: shade mode (flat or Gouraud), fill mode (point, wireframe, solid), and lighting type (on or off).

IDirect3DRMDevice2::SetRenderMode

Description

This method is used to set the transparency mode with a default value that renders transparent objects using stippled transparency. You should set the `D3DRM-RENDERMODE_BLENDEDTRANSPARENCY` and `D3DRMRENDERMODE_SORTEDTRANSPAR-ENCY` together to make sure that when two objects are rendered on top of one another, they will blend in the correct order so you get the desired effect.

C++ specification

```
HRESULT SetRenderMode(
    DWORD dwFlags
    );
```

Parameters

`dwFlags`. One or more of the transparent mode flags. Flags can have one or more of the following values:

- `D3DRMRENDERMODE_BLENDEDTRANSPARENCY` (dwFlags = 1) This flag sets the transparency mode to alpha blending.

- `D3DRMRENDERMODE_SORTEDTRANSPARENCY` (dwFlags = 2) This flag sets the transparency mode so transparent polygons in the scene are buffered, sorted, and rendered in a second pass. The flag will have no effect if `D3DRMRENDERMODE_BLENDEDTRANSPARENCY` is not also set.

Returns

Successful: D3DRM_OK
Error: One of the Direct3DRM Retained Mode return values.

See also

IDirect3DRMDevice2::GetRenderMode

Example

```
LPDIRECT3DRMDEVICE2 dev2;
DWORD renderMode;
HRESULT result
     .

     .
result == dev2->SetRender Mode
        (D3DRMRENDERMODE_BLENDEDTRANSPARENCY );
if (result != D3DRM_OK)
    goto generic_error;
```

IDirect3DRMDevice2::SetShades

This method has the same definition as `IDirect3DRMDevice::SetShades`. Please see page 414 for details.

IDirect3DRMDevice2::SetTextureQuality

This method has the same definition as `IDirect3DRMDevice::SetTextureQuality`. Please see page 415 for details.

IDirect3DRMDevice2::Update

This method has the same definition as `IDirect3DRMDevice::Update`. Please see page 416 for details.

The IDirect3DRMFrame2 Interface

The `IDirect3DRMFrame2` interface is an extension of `IDirect3DRMFrame` adding methods which allow the use of materials, bounding boxes, and axes with frames as well as ray picking. The `IDirect3DRMFrame2::SetAxes` method can be used with right-handed projection types in the `D3DRMPROJECTIONTYPE` structure and the `IDirect3DRMViewport::SetProjection` method to enable right-handed projection. You can obtain a Direct3DRMFrame2 object by calling `IDirect3DRM2::CreateFrame`.

Like all COM interfaces, this interface inherits the `IUnknown` interface methods. They consist of `AddRef`, `QueryInterfacem`, and `Release`.

The `IDirect3DRMFrame2` interface methods can be organized into the groups in table B.3.

Table B.3 IDirect3DRMFrame2 methods

Axes	GetAxes
	GetInheritAxes
	SetAxes
	SetInheritAxes
Background	GetSceneBackground
	GetSceneBackgroundDepth
	SetSceneBackground
	SetSceneBackgroundDepth
	SetSceneBackgroundImage
	SetSceneBackgroundRGB
Bounding Box	GetBox
	GetBoxEnable
	GetHierarchyBox
	SetBox
	SetBoxEnable
Color	GetColor
	SetColor
	SetColorRGB
Fog	GetSceneFogColor
	GetSceneFogEnable
	GetSceneFogMode
	GetSceneFogParams
	SetSceneFogColor
	SetSceneFogEnable
	SetSceneFogMode

Table B.3 IDirect3DRMFrame2 methods (continued)

	SetSceneFogParams
Hierarchies	AddChild
	DeleteChild
	GetChildren
	GetParent
	GetScene
Lighting	AddLight
	DeleteLight
	GetLights
Loading	Load
Material	GetMaterial
	SetMaterial
Material modes	GetMaterialMode
	SetMaterialMode
Positioning and movement	AddMoveCallback2
	AddRotation
	AddScale
	AddTranslation
	DeleteMoveCallback
	GetOrientation
	GetPosition
	GetRotation
	GetVelocity
	LookAt
	Move
	SetOrientation
	SetPosition
	SetQuaternion
	SetRotation
	SetVelocity
Ray Picking	RayPick
Sorting	GetSortMode
	GetZbufferMode
	SetSortMode
	SetZbufferMode
Textures	GetTexture
	GetTextureTopology
	SetTexture
	SetTextureTopology
Transformations	AddTransform

Table B.3 IDirect3DRMFrame2 methods (continued)

	GetTransform
	InverseTransform
	Transform
Visual objects	AddVisual
	DeleteVisual
	GetVisuals

The `IDirect3DRMFrame2` interface also inherits the following methods from `IDirect3DRMObject` interface:

- `AddDestroyCallback`
- `Clone`
- `DeleteDestroyCallback`
- `GetAppData`
- `GetClassName`
- `GetName`
- `SetAppData`
- `SetName`

IDirect3DRMFrame2::AddChild

This method has the same definition as `IDirect3DRMFrame2::AddChild`. Please see page 436 for details.

IDirect3DRMFrame2::AddLight

This method has the same definition as `IDirect3DRMFrame2::AddLight`. Please see page 436 for details.

IDirect3DRMFrame2::AddMoveCallback2

Description

This method is used to add a callback function to your object for special movement processing. If you use multiple callbacks on a frame, they will be called in the order they were created.

C++ specification

```
HRESULT AddMoveCallback2(
    D3DRMFRAME2MOVECALLBACK d3drmFMC,
    VOID * lpArg,
    DWORD dwFlags
    );
```

Parameters

d3drmFMC. Your application-defined D3DRMFRAME2MOVECALLBACK callback function.

lpArg. The application-defined data you want passed to your callback function.

dwFlags. Either:

D3DRMCALLBACK_PREORDER. Callbacks for a frame are called before any child frames are traversed when IDirect3DRMFrame2::Move traverses the hierarchy. This is the default value.

D3DRMCALLBACK_POSTORDER. Callbacks for a frame are called after the child frames are traversed when IDirect3DRMFrame2::Move traverses the hierarchy

Returns

Successful: D3DRM_OK

Error: One of the Direct3DRM Retained Mode return values.

See also

IDirect3DRMFrame::AddMoveCallback

IDirect3DRMFrame2::Move

IDirect3DRMFrame2::DeleteMoveCallback

Example

```
LPDirect3DRMFRAME2 floor_frame;
    .
    .
    .
if (floor_frame->AddMoveCallback (GroundCheck, 0,
        D3DRMCALLBACK_PREORDER) != D3DRM_OK)
    goto generic_error);
```

IDirect3DRMFrame2::AddRotation

This method has the same definition as `IDirect3DRMFrame::AddRotation`. Please see page 439 for details.

IDirect3DRMFrame2::AddScale

This method has the same definition as `IDirect3DRMFrame::AddScale`. Please see page 440 for details.

IDirect3DRMFrame2::AddTransform

This method has the same definition as `IDirect3DRMFrame::AddTransform`. Please see page 441 for details.

IDirect3DRMFrame2::AddTranslation

This method has the same definition as `IDirect3DRMFrame::AddTranslation`. Please see page 442 for details.

IDirect3DRMFrame2::AddVisual

This method has the same definition as `IDirect3DRMFrame::AddTranslation`. Please see page 442 for details.

IDirect3DRMFrame2::DeleteChild

This method has the same definition as `IDirect3DRMFrame::DeleteChild`. Please see page 443 for details.

IDirect3DRMFrame2::DeleteLight

This method has the same definition as `IDirect3DRMFrame::DeleteLight`. Please see page 444 for details.

IDirect3DRMFrame2::DeleteMoveCallback

This method has the same definition as `IDirect3DRMFrame::DeleteMoveCall-back`. Please see page 445 for details.

IDirect3DRMFrame2::DeleteVisual

This method has the same definition as `IDirect3DRMFrame::DeleteVisual`. Please see page 446 for details.

IDirect3DRMFrame2::GetAxes

Description

This method is used to acquire the vectors which are aligned with the direction (rvDx, rvDy, rvDz) and up (rvUx, rvUy, rvUz) vectors that are supplied to the `IDirect3DRMFrame2::SetOrientation` method. You can use this method and the `IDirect3DRMFrame2::SetAxes` method, to support right-handed and left-handed coordinate systems. You can specify that the negative Z-axis is the front of the object using `IDirect3DRMFrame2::SetAxes`.

C++ specification

```
HRESULT GetAxes(
    LPD3DVECTOR dir,
    LPD3DVECTOR up
    );
```

Parameters

`dir`. The frame's Z-axis with a default of `(0,0,1)`.
`up`. The frame's Y-axis with a default of `(0,1,0)`.

Returns

Successful: D3DRM_OK
Error: One of the Direct3DRM Retained Mode return values.

See also

IDirect3DRMFrame2::GetInheritAxes
IDirect3DRMFrame2::SetAxes
IDirect3DRMFrame2::SetInheritAxes

Example

```
LPDirect3DRMFRAME2 animated_wall_frame;
LPD3DVECTOR dir;
LPD3DVECTOR up;
        .
        .

animated_wall_frame->GetAxes(dir, up);
```

IDirect3DRMFrame2::GetBox

Description

This method is used to acquire the bounding box encompassing your DIRECT3DRMFRAME2 object. This bounding box holds the minimum and maximum coordinates of your model in all three dimensions. You must set a bounding box on the frame using IDirect3DRMFrame2::SetBox. You need to use the IDirect3DRMFrame2::SetBoxEnable method to set the enable flag to TRUE.

C++ specification

```
HRESULT GetBox(
    D3DRMBOX * lpD3DRMBox
    );
```

Parameters

lpD3DRMBox. The address of a D3DRMBOX structure you want filled with the bounding box coordinates.

Returns

Successful: D3DRM_OK

Error: Returns D3DRMERR_BOXNOTSET if a valid bounding box has not been set on the frame.

See also

IDirect3DRMFrame2::GetBoxEnable
IDirect3DRMFrame2::SetBox
IDirect3DRMFrame2::SetBoxEnable

Example

```
LPDirect3DRMFRAME2 animated_wall_frame;
D3DRMBOX Box
        .
        .

animated_wall_frame->GetBox(&Box);
```

IDirect3DRMFrame2::GetBoxEnable

Description
This method is used to acquire the flag to find out if a bounding box is enabled for your Direct3DRMFrame2 object. The `IDirect3DRMFrame2::SetBoxEnable` flag must be called to set the enable flag to TRUE in order for a bounding box to be enabled. The box enable flag is FALSE by default.

C++ specification
```
BOOL GetBoxEnable( );
```

Parameters

Returns
TRUE if a bounding box is enabled.
FALSE if it is not enabled.

See also
IDirect3DRMFrame2::GetBox
IDirect3DRMFrame2::SetBox
IDirect3DRMFrame2::SetBoxEnable

Example
```
LPDirect3DRMFRAME2 animated_wall_frame;
BOOL boxEnable;
   .
   .

boxEnable = animated_wall_frame->GetBoxEnable();
```


IDirect3DRMFrame2::GetChildren

This method has the same definition as `IDirect3DRMFrame::GetChildren`. Please see page 447 for details.

IDirect3DRMFrame2::GetColor

This method has the same definition as `IDirect3DRMFrame::GetColor`. Please see page 447 for details.

IDirect3DRMFrame2::GetHierarchyBox

Description
This method is used to calculate a bounding box which contains all of the geometry in the hierarchy contained in this Direct3DRMFrame2 object.

C++ specification
```
HRESULT GetHierarchyBox(
    D3DRMBOX * lpD3DRMBox
    );
```

Parameters
lpD3DRMBox. The address of a D3DRMBOX structure you wish filled with the bounding box coordinates.

Returns
Successful: D3DRM_OK

Error: One of the Direct3DRM Retained Mode return values.

See also
IDirect3DRMFrame2::GetBox

IDirect3DRMFrame2::GetBoxEnable

IDirect3DRMFrame2::SetBox

IDirect3DRMFrame2::SetBoxEnable

Example
```
LPDirect3DRMFRAME2 animated_wall_frame;
D3DRMBOX box;
    .
    .
    .
if  (animated_wall_frame->GetHierarchyBox(&box) != D3DRM_OK)
    goto generic_error;
```

IDirect3DRMFrame2::GetInheritAxes

Description
This method is used to acquire the flag specifying whether the axes for the frame are inherited from the parent frame. Axes are inherited from the parent by default.

C++ specification
```
BOOL GetInheritAxes( );
```

Parameters

None

Returns

TRUE if the frame inherits axes (the default value)

FALSE if the frame does not inherit axes.

See also

IDirect3DRMFrame2::GetAxes

IDirect3DRMFrame2::SetInheritAxes

IDirect3DRMFrame2::SetAxes

Example

```
LPDirect3DRMFRAME2 animated_wall_frame;
.
.
BOOL getInherit = animated_wall_frame->GetInheritAxes(&box);
```

IDirect3DRMFrame2::GetLights

This method has the same definition as `IDirect3DRMFrame::GetLights`. Please see page 448 for details.

IDirect3DRMFrame2::GetMaterial

Description

This method is used to acquire the material of the Direct3DRMFrame2 object.

C++ specification

```
HRESULT GetMaterial(
    LPDIRECT3DRMMATERIAL *lplpMaterial
    );
```

Parameters

`lplpMaterial`. The address of a variable you wish filled with a pointer to the Direct3DRMMaterial object which is applied to the frame.

Returns

Successful: D3DRM_OK

Error: One of the Direct3DRM Retained Mode return values.

IDirect3DRMFrame2::SetMaterial

Example

```
LPDIRECT3DRMFRAME2 animated_wall_frame;
LPDIRECT3DRMMATERIAL material
     .
     .
     .
if  (animated_wall_frame->GetMaterial(&material) != D3DRM_OK)
     goto generic_error;
```

IDirect3DRMFrame2::GetMaterialMode

This method has the same definition as `IDirect3DRMFrame::GetMaterialMode`. Please see page 449 for details.

IDirect3DRMFrame2::GetOrientation

This method has the same definition as `IDirect3DRMFrame::GetOrientation`. Please see page 449 for details.

IDirect3DRMFrame2::GetParent

This method has the same definition as `IDirect3DRMFrame::GetParent`. Please see page 450 for details.

IDirect3DRMFrame2::GetPosition

This method has the same definition as `IDirect3DRMFrame::GetPosition`. Please see page 451 for details.

IDirect3DRMFrame2::GetRotation

This method has the same definition as `IDirect3DRMFrame::GetRotation`. Please see page 452 for details.

IDirect3DRMFrame2::GetScene

This method has the same definition as `IDirect3DRMFrame::GetScene`. Please see page 453 for details.

IDirect3DRMFrame2::GetSceneBackground

This method has the same definition as `IDirect3DRMFrame::GetSceneBack-ground`. Please see page 453 for details.

IDirect3DRMFrame2::GetSceneBackgroundDepth

This method has the same definition as `IDirect3DRMFrame::GetSceneBack-groundDepth`. Please see page 454 for details.

IDirect3DRMFrame2::GetSceneFogColor

This method has the same definition as `IDirect3DRMFrame::GetSceneFog-Color`. Please see page 455 for details.

IDirect3DRMFrame2::GetSceneFogEnable

This method has the same definition as `IDirect3DRMFrame::GetSceneFogEn-able`. Please see page 455 for details.

IDirect3DRMFrame2::GetSceneFogMode

This method has the same definition as `IDirect3DRMFrame::GetSceneFogMode`. Please see page 456 for details.

IDirect3DRMFrame2::GetSceneFogParams

This method has the same definition as `IDirect3DRMFrame::GetSceneFog-Params`. Please see page 456 for details.

IDirect3DRMFrame2::GetSortMode

This method has the same definition as `IDirect3DRMFrame::GetSortMode`. Please see page 457 for details.

IDirect3DRMFrame2::GetTexture

This method has the same definition as `IDirect3DRMFrame::GetTexture`. Please see page 458 for details.

IDirect3DRMFrame2::GetTextureTopology

This method has the same definition as `IDirect3DRMFrame::GetTextureTopology`. Please see page 458 for details.

IDirect3DRMFrame2::GetTransform

This method has the same definition as `IDirect3DRMFrame::GetTransform`. Please see page 459 for details.

IDirect3DRMFrame2::GetVelocity

This method has the same definition as `IDirect3DRMFrame::GetVelocity`. Please see page 460 for details.

IDirect3DRMFrame2::GetVisuals

This method has the same definition as `IDirect3DRMFrame::GetVisuals`. Please see page 460 for details.

IDirect3DRMFrame2::GetZBufferMode

This method has the same definition as `IDirect3DRMFrame::GetZBufferMode`. Please see page 461 for details.

IDirect3DRMFrame2::InverseTransform

This method has the same definition as `IDirect3DRMFrame::InverseTransform`. Please see page 462 for details.

IDirect3DRMFrame2::Load

This method has the same definition as `IDirect3DRMFrame::Load`. Please see page 463 for details.

IDirect3DRMFrame2::LookAt

This method has the same definition as `IDirect3DRMFrame::LookAt`. Please see page 464 for details.

IDirect3DRMFrame2::Move

This method has the same definition as `IDirect3DRMFrame::Move`. Please see page 465 for details.

IDirect3DRMFrame2::RayPick

Description

This method is used to search the hierarchy starting at this Direct3DRMFrame2 object. It calculates the intersections between any visuals and the ray specified by the `dvPosition` and `dvDirection` parameters in the coordinate space specified by the `lpRefFrame` parameter.

You define the ray in the reference frame coordinate space. If the reference frame is NULL, the ray is specified in world coordinates.

Optimization flags will let you limit the search in order to speed it up.

Interpolation flags indicate what to interpolate if a primitive is hit. The three possible interpolation types are color, normal, and texture coordinates.

C++ specification

```
HRESULT RayPick(
    LPDIRECT3DRMFRAME lpRefFrame,
    LPD3DRMRAY ray,
```

```
DWORD dwFlags,
LPD3DRMPICKED2ARRAY* lplpPicked2Array
);
```

Parameters

lpRefFrame. The address of the Direct3DRMFrame object containing the ray.

ray. This parameter is a pointer to a D3DRMRAY structure holding two D3DVECTOR structures. The first D3DVECTOR structure contains the vector direction of the ray and the second D3DVECTOR structure holds the position of the ray's origin.

dwFlags. One of the values below:

- D3DRMRAYPICK_IGNOREFURTHERPRIMITIVES. Only the closest visual intersecting the ray is returned.

- D3DRMRAYPICK_INTERPOLATECOLOR. The color should be interpolated.

- D3DRMRAYPICK_INTERPOLATENORMAL. The normal should be interpolated.

- D3DRMRAYPICK_INTERPOLATEUV. The texture coordinates should be interpolated.

- D3DRMRAYPICK_ONLYBOUNDINGBOXES. Indicates you do not want to check for exact face intersections. Only intersections with bounding boxes of the visuals in the hierarchy are returned. The texture, normal, and color data in the D3DRMPICKDESC2 structure will be invalid.

lplpPicked2Array. The address of a pointer to be initialized with a valid pointer to the IDirect3DRMPicked2Array interface.

Returns

Successful: D3DRM_OK

Error: One of the Direct3DRM Retained Mode return values.

Example

```
LPDIRECT3DRMFRAME2 character;
LPDIRECT3DRMFRAME refFrame;
LPD3DRMPICKED2ARRAY Picked2Array
LPD3DRMRAY ray;
HRESULT result;
    .
    .

result = character->RayPick(refFrame,  ray,
        D3DRMRAYPICK_IGNOREFURTHERPRIMITIVES, &Picked2Array );
if  (result != D3DRM_OK)
    goto generic_error;
```

IDirect3DRMFrame2::Save

Description

This method is used to save a Direct3DRMFrame2 object to an indicated file.

C++ specification

```
HRESULT Save(
    LPCSTR lpFilename,
    D3DRMXOFFORMAT d3dFormat,
    D3DRMSAVEOPTIONS d3dSaveFlags
    );
```

Parameters

lpFilename. The address holding the name, which must have a .X file name extension, of the created file.

d3dFormat. The D3DRMXOF_TEXT value from the D3DRMXOFFORMAT enumerated type.

d3dSaveFlags. The value of the D3DRMSAVEOPTIONS type which specifies the save options.

Returns

Successful: D3DRM_OK

Error: One of the Direct3DRM Retained Mode return values.

See also

D3DRMSAVEOPTIONS
D3DRMXOFFORMAT

Example

```
HRESULT result;
LPDIRECT3DRMFRAME2 myObject;
.
.
result =myObject->Save("newObj.x", D3DRMXOF_TEXT,
        D3DRMXOFSAVE_ALL);
if (result != D3DRM_OK)
    goto generic_error;
```

IDirect3DRMFrame2::SetAxes

Description

This method is used to set the vectors defining a coordinate space by which the IDirect3DRMFrame2::SetOrientation vectors are transformed. You can use this method to set right- and left-handed coordinate systems.

C++ specification
```
HRESULT SetAxes(
    D3DVALUE dx,
    D3DVALUE dy,
    D3DVALUE dz,
    D3DVALUE ux,
    D3DVALUE uy,
    D3DVALUE uz
    );
```

Parameters

dx, dy, dz. The *Z*-axis for the frame, with a default of (0,0,1).

ux, uy, uz. The *Y*-axis for the frame, with a default of (0,1,0).

Returns

Successful: D3DRM_OK

Error: One of the Direct3DRM Retained Mode return values.

See also

IDirect3DRMFrame2::GetAxes

IDirect3DRMFrame2::GetInheritAxes

IDirect3DRMFrame2::SetInheritAxes

Example
```
HRESULT result;
LPDIRECT3DRMFRAME2 myObject;
    .
    .
D3DVALUE dx,  dy,  dz,  ux,  uy,  uz;
    .
    .
result = myObject->SetAxes(dx, dy, dz, ux, uy, uz);
if (result != D3DRM_OK)
    goto generic_error;
```

IDirect3DRMFrame2::SetBox

Description

This method is used to set the box you wish to use in bounding box testing.

C++ specification
```
HRESULT SetBox(
    D3DRMBOX * lpD3DRMBox
    );
```

Parameters

    lpD3DRMBox. The address of a D3DRMBOX structure holding the bounding box coordinates.

Returns

    Successful: D3DRM_OK

    Error: One of the Direct3DRM Retained Mode return values.

See also

    IDirect3DRMFrame2::GetBox

    IDirect3DRMFrame2::GetBoxEnable

    IDirect3DRMFrame2::SetBoxEnable

Example

```
HRESULT result;
LPDIRECT3DRMFRAME2 myObject;
D3DRMBOX box;
   .

   .
result = myObject->SetBox(&box);
if (result != D3DRM_OK)
    goto generic_error;
```

IDirect3DRM2::SetBoxEnable

Description

This method is used to enable or disable bounding box testing for your Direct3DRMFrame2 object. A valid bounding box must have been set on the frame or bounding box testing cannot be enabled.

The bounding box is transformed into model space and checked for intersection with the viewing frustum when it is ready to be rendered. If the entire box is outside of the viewing frustum, the frame's visuals, and any of its child frame's visuals, will not be rendered.

You can keep the frame from being rendered by enabling bounding box testing with a box of {0,0,0,0}

C++ specification

```
HRESULT SetBoxEnable(
    BOOL bEnableFlag
    );
```

Parameters

bEnableFlag. This flag should be set to TRUE in order to enable a bounding box. The default value is FALSE.

Returns

Successful: D3DRM_OK

Error: One of the Direct3DRM Retained Mode return values.

See also

IDirect3DRMFrame2::GetBox

IDirect3DRMFrame2::GetBoxEnable

IDirect3DRMFrame2::SetBox

Example

```
HRESULT result;
LPDIRECT3DRMFRAME2 myObject;
    .
    .
result = myObject->SetBoxEnable(TRUE);
if (result != D3DRM_OK)
    goto generic_error;
```

IDirect3DRMFrame2::SetColor

This method has the same definition as IDirect3DRMFrame::SetColor. Please see page 466 for details.

IDirect3DRMFrame2::SetColorRGB

This method has the same definition as IDirect3DRMFrame::SetColorRGB. Please see page 466 for details.

IDirect3DRMFrame2::SetInheritAxes

Description

This method is used to indicate if the axes for the frame are inherited from the parent frame. Axes are inherited from their parent by default.

C++ specification

```
HRESULT SetInheritAxes(
```

```
       BOOL inherit_from_parent
       );
```

Parameters

> `inherit_from_parent`. This flag specifies if the frame should inherit axes from its parent. If this flag is set to TRUE (the default), the frame inherits axes.

Returns

> Successful: D3DRM_OK
> Error: One of the Direct3DRM Retained Mode return values.

See also

> IDirect3DRMFrame2::GetAxes
> IDirect3DRMFrame2::GetInheritAxes
> IDirect3DRMFrame2::SetAxes

Example

```
HRESULT result;
LPDIRECT3DRMFRAME2 myObject;
   .

   .
result = myObject->SetInheritAxes(TRUE);
if (result != D3DRM_OK)
    goto generic_error;
```

IDirect3DRM2::SetMaterial

Description

> This method is used to set the material of your Direct3DRMFrame2 object.

C++ specification

```
HRESULT SetMaterial(
    LPDIRECT3DRMMATERIAL *lplpMaterial
    );
```

Parameters

> `lplpMaterial`. The address of the Direct3DRMMaterial object which will be applied to your frame.

Returns

> Successful: D3DRM_OK
> Error: One of the Direct3DRM Retained Mode return values.

IDirect3DRMFrame::SetMaterialMode

Example

```
HRESULT result;
LPDIRECT3DRMFRAME2 myObject;
LPDIRECT3DRMMATERIAL material;
    .
    .
result = myObject->SetMaterial(&material);
if (result != D3DRM_OK)
    goto generic_error;
```

IDirect3DRMFrame2::SetMaterialMode

This method has the same definition as `IDirect3DRMFrame::SetMaterialMode`. Please see page 467 for details.

IDirect3DRMFrame2::SetOrientation

This method has the same definition as `IDirect3DRMFrame::SetOrientation`. Please see page 468 for details.

IDirect3DRMFrame2::SetPosition

This method has the same definition as `IDirect3DRMFrame::SetPosition`. Please see page 469 for details.

IDirect3DRMFrame2::SetQuaternion

Description

This method is used to set a frame's orientation relative to a reference frame using a unit quaternion. You can use the function `D3DRMQuaternionFromRotation` to generate unit quaternions from arbitrary rotation values.

A quaternion is a four-valued vector that can be used to represent any rotation. It is useful when interpolating between orientations. A quaternion is a unit quaternion if `s**2 + x**2 + y**2 + z**2 = 1`.

C++ specification

```
HRESULT SetQuaternion(
    LPDIRECT3DRMFRAME2 lpRef,
    D3DRMQUATERNION *quat
    )
```

Parameters

`lpRef`. The address of a variable holding the Direct3DRMFrame2 object you want use as the reference.

`quat`. A D3DRMQUATERNION structure holding the unit quaternion.

Returns

Successful: D3DRM_OK

Error: One of the Direct3DRM Retained Mode return values.

Example

```
HRESULT result;
LPDIRECT3DRMFRAME2 myObject;
D3DRMQUATERNION quat
    .
    .
result = myObject-> SetQuaternion(&quat);
if (result != D3DRM_OK)
    goto generic_error;
```

IDirect3DRMFrame2::SetRotation

This method has the same definition as `IDirect3DRMFrame::SetRotation`. Please see page 470 for details.

IDirect3DRMFrame2::SetSceneBackground

This method has the same definition as `IDirect3DRMFrame::SetSceneBackground`. Please see page 470 for details.

IDirect3DRMFrame2::SetSceneBackgroundDepth

This method has the same definition as `IDirect3DRMFrame::SetSceneBackgroundDepth`. Please see page 471 for details.

IDirect3DRMFrame2::SetSceneBackgroundImage

This method has the same definition as `IDirect3DRMFrame::SetSceneBackgroundImage`. Please see page 472 for details.

IDirect3DRMFrame2::SetSceneBackgroundRGB

This method has the same definition as `IDirect3DRMFrame::SetSceneBackgroundRGB`. Please see page 473 for details.

IDirect3DRMFrame2::SetSceneFogColor

This method has the same definition as `IDirect3DRMFrame::SetSceneFogColor`. Please see page 473 for details.

IDirect3DRMFrame2::SetSceneFogEnable

This method has the same definition as `IDirect3DRMFrame::SetSceneFogEnable`. Please see page 474 for details.

IDirect3DRMFrame2::SetSceneFogMode

This method has the same definition as `IDirect3DRMFrame::SetSceneFogMode`. Please see page 475 for details.

IDirect3DRMFrame2::SetSceneFogParams

This method has the same definition as `IDirect3DRMFrame::SetSceneFogParams`. Please see page 475 for details.

IDirect3DRMFrame2::SetSortMode

This method has the same definition as `IDirect3DRMFrame::SetSortMode`. Please see page 476 for details.

IDirect3DRMFrame2::SetTexture

This method has the same definition as `IDirect3DRMFrame::SetTexture`. Please see page 477 for details.

IDirect3DRMFrame2::SetTextureTopology

This method has the same definition as `IDirect3DRMFrame::SetTextureTopology`. Please see page 478 for details.

IDirect3DRMFrame2::SetVelocity

This method has the same definition as `IDirect3DRMFrame::SetVelocity`. Please see page 478 for details. The frame will be moved by the vector [rvX, rvY, rvZ] with respect to the reference frame each time you call the `IDirect3DRM::Tick` or `IDirect3DRMFrame2::Move` method.

IDirect3DRMFrame2::SetZbufferMode

This method has the same definition as `IDirect3DRMFrame::SetZbufferMode`. Please see page 480 for details.

IDirect3DRMFrame2::Transform

This method has the same definition as `IDirect3DRMFrame::Transform`. Please see page 481 for details.

IDirect3DRMInterpolator Interface

To me, one of the most interesting interfaces is this new one which has a great deal of power. The interpolators allow you to store actions for objects and apply them so that the system automatically computes the in-between values.

These interpolators are actually a generalized `IDirect3DRMAnimation` interface with a much greater set of animatable object parameters. Remember that the `IDirect3DRMAnimation` interface only lets you animate an object's position, size, and orientation. This interface lets you animate colors, meshes, textures, and materials.

This capability can be applied to move objects, morph meshes, transform objects' positions, change an object's color, or blend colors.

Each of these animation steps is stored as a *key* which consists of a stored procedure call and an associated index. Whenever a key is recorded, it is stamped with the current interpolator index value, which never changes after it is set. The interpolator takes these key values and automatically computes the values between them.

There are a number of interpolator types to which objects can be attached. As an example, a Frame can be attached to a FrameInterpolator. You can attach one interpolator to another. If you do this, when one interpolator's index changes, it sets the indices of these attached interpolators to the same value.

The same interpolator can be used to store other keys (scale, etc.). These properties each exist on a parallel timeline. When you call Interpolate, the interpolated value for each of the properties are assigned to the attached frames. You can interpolate more than one method, and you store different keys in the same interpolator. You need to remember that you cannot interpolate between keys of different methods so they will be stored in Key Chains (parallel execution threads).

The available types are:

- FrameInterpolator
- LightInterpolator
- MaterialInterpolator
- MeshInterpolator
- TextureInterpolator
- ViewportInterpolator

The list of interpolation options are:

- `D3DRMINTERPOLATION_CLOSED`. The interpolation is cyclic so the keys repeat infinitely with a period equal to the index span. If a key has an index equal to the end of the span, it is ignored to allow for compatibility with animations.

- D3DRMINTERPOLATION_OPEN. The first and last keys of each key chain will fix the interpolated values outside of the index span.

- D3DRMINTERPOLATION_LINEAR. Linear interpolation between the two nearest keys is used for in-betweening on each key chain.

- D3DRMINTERPOLATION_NEAREST. The nearest key is used for in-betweening on each key chain

- D3DRMINTERPOLATION_SPLINE. B-spline blending function on the four nearest keys is used for in-betweening on each key chain

- D3DRMINTERPOLATION_VERTEXCOLOR. Indicates that vertex colors should be interpolated for IDirect3DRMMesh::SetVertices.

Finally, remember that an interpolator covers a span of index values. The start of a span is the minimum of the key index values and the current index, and the end of the span equals the maximum value.

Like all COM interfaces, this interface inherits the IUnknown interface methods. They consist of AddRef, QueryInterfacem, and Release.

The IDirect3DRMInterpolator interface method can be organized into the groups in table B.4.

Table B.4 IDirect3DRMInterpolator method

Attaching Objects	AttachObject
	DetachObject
	GetAttachedObjects
Interpolating	GetIndex
	Interpolate
	SetIndex

IDirect3DRMInterpolator::AttachObject

Description

This method is used to connect an object to your interpolator. The interpolator must be the same type as the object to you are attaching it. For example, a Frame can be attached to a FrameInterpolator. The type of interpolators are FrameInterpolator, LightInterpolator, MaterialInterpolator, MeshInterpolator, TextureInterpolator, and ViewportInterpolator.

C++ specification

```
HRESULT AttachObject(
```

```
          LPDIRECT3DRMOBJECT lpD3DRMObject
          )
```

Parameters

lpD3DRMObject. The address of the Direct3DRMObject object you wish to have attached to your interpolator.

Returns

Successful: D3DRM_OK

Error: One of the Direct3DRM Retained Mode return values.

See also

IDirect3DRMInterpolator::DetachObject

Example

```
IDirect3DRMInterpolator  myInterp;
IDirect3DRMFrame myFrameInterp;

// Create our frame interpolator
pd3drm->CreateObject(CLSID_CDirect3DRMFrameInterpolator, 0,
        IID_IDirect3DRMInterpolator, &myInterp);

myInterp->QueryInterface(IID_IDirect3DRMFrame, &myFrameInterp);
// Add a position key to our interpolator
// Set our interpolator's internal index using the
// IDirect3DRMInterpolator interface
// Record the position by calling the
// IDirect3DRMFrame::SetPosition
// Note:  The method is applied to our interpolator and not the
// real frame. The function call and its parameters are stored in
// the interpolator as a new key with the current index.
// You can add more keys by calling SetIndex to set the
// index and then following it with the desired object method(s)

myInterp->SetIndex(keytime);
myFrameInterp->SetPosition(NULL, keypos.x, keypos.y, keypos.z);

// Attach the frame to the interpolator to play actions back
// through a frame
pInterp->AttachObject(pRealFrame);

// Use the Interpolate method to set the position of the frame
// using the interpolated position.
// The attached frames SetPosition will be called by the
// interpolator and pass the calculated interpolated position
// between the nearest SetPosition keys using a B-Spline
pInterp->Interpolate(time, NULL, D3DRMINTERPOLATIONSPLINE |
        D3DRMINTERPOLATION_OPEN);
```

IDirect3DRMInterpolator::DetachObject

Description
This method is used to detach an object from the interpolator.

C++ specification
```
HRESULT DetachObject(
    LPDIRECT3DRMOBJECT lpD3DRMObject
    )
```

Parameters
lpD3DRMObject. The address of the Direct3DRMObject object you wish detached from your interpolator.

Returns
Successful: D3DRM_OK

Error: One of the Direct3DRM Retained Mode return values.

See also
IDirect3DRMInterpolator::GetAttachedObject

Example
```
IDirect3DRMInterpolator  myInterp;
IDirect3DRMFrame myFrameInterp;

// Create our frame interpolator
pd3drm->CreateObject(CLSID_CDirect3DRMFrameInterpolator, 0,
        IID_IDirect3DRMInterpolator, &myInterp);
myInterp->QueryInterface(IID_IDirect3DRMFrame, &myFrameInterp);

// Add a position key to our interpolator
// Set our interpolator's internal index using the
// IDirect3DRMInterpolator interface
// Record the position by calling the
// IDirect3DRMFrame::SetPosition
// You can add more keys by calling SetIndex to set the
// index and then following it with the desired object method(s)

myInterp->SetIndex(keytime);
myFrameInterp->SetPosition(NULL, keypos.x, keypos.y, keypos.z);

// Attach the frame to the interpolator to play actions back
// through a frame
pInterp->AttachObject(pRealFrame);
.
.
```

```
// Detach the frame from the interpolator
```

pInterp->DetachObject(pRealFrame);

IDirect3DRMInterpolator::GetAttchedObject

Description

This method returns an array of the objects which are currently attached to your interpolator.

C++ specification

```
HRESULT GetAttachedObjects(
    LPDIRECT3DRMOBJECTARRAY lpD3DRMObjectArray
    )
```

Parameters

lpD3DRMObjectArray. The address of an IDirect3DRMObjectArray object which contains the Direct3DRMObject objects that are attached to the interpolator.

Returns

Successful: D3DRM_OK

Error: One of the Direct3DRM Retained Mode return values.

See also

IDirect3DRMInterpolator::DetachObject

Example

```
IDirect3DRMInterpolator  myInterp;
IDirect3DRMFrame myFrameInterp;
LPDIRECT3DRMOBJECTARRAY myObjectArray;

// Create our frame interpolator
pd3drm->CreateObject(CLSID_CDirect3DRMFrameInterpolator, 0,
        IID_IDirect3DRMInterpolator, &myInterp);
myInterp->QueryInterface(IID_IDirect3DRMFrame, &myFrameInterp);

// Add a position key to our interpolator
// Set our interpolator's internal index using the
// IDirect3DRMInterpolator interface
// Record the position by calling the
// IDirect3DRMFrame::SetPosition
myInterp->SetIndex(keytime);
myFrameInterp->SetPosition(NULL, keypos.x, keypos.y, keypos.z);

//Attach the frame to the interpolator to play actions back
```

```
// through a frame
pInterp->AttachObject(pRealFrame);
.
.
.
//Get the attached objects
pInterp->GetAttachedObject(myObjectArray);
```

IDirect3DRMInterpolator::GetIndex

Description

This method is used to acquire the interpolator's current internal index (time).
Each key in an interpolator possesses an index value. When a key is recorded by
calling a method, the key is stamped with the current interpolator index value.

C++ specification

```
D3DVALUE GetIndex( )
```

Parameters

None

Returns

This method returns a D3DVALUE containing the interpolator's current internal
index.

See also

IDirect3DRMInterpolator::SetIndex

Example

```
IDirect3DRMInterpolator  myInterp;
IDirect3DRMFrame myFrameInterp;
LPDIRECT3DRMOBJECTARRAY myObjectArray;

// Create our frame interpolator
pd3drm->CreateObject(CLSID_CDirect3DRMFrameInterpolator, 0,
        IID_IDirect3DRMInterpolator, &myInterp);
myInterp->QueryInterface(IID_IDirect3DRMFrame, &myFrameInterp);

// Add a position key to our interpolator
// Set our interpolator's internal index using the
// IDirect3DRMInterpolator interface
// Record the position by calling the
// IDirect3DRMFrame::SetPosition
myInterp->SetIndex(keytime);
myFrameInterp->SetPosition(NULL, keypos.x, keypos.y, keypos.z);
```

```
// Attach the frame to the interpolator to play actions back
// through a frame
pInterp->AttachObject(pRealFrame);
.
.
.
// Get the attached objects
D3DVALUE newKeytime = myInterp->GetIndex();
```

IDirect3DRMInterpolator::Interpolate

Description

This method is used to create a series of actions by interpolating between keys you have stored in the interpolator. These actions are then applied to either the specified object, or if none is specified, the currently attached objects.

C++ specification

```
HRESULT Interpolate(
    D3DVALUE d3dVal,
    LPDIRECT3DRMOBJECT lpD3DRMObject,
    D3DRMINTERPOLATIONOPTIONS d3drmInterpFlags
    )
```

Parameters

d3dVal. A D3DVALUE holding the current internal index for the interpolator.

lpD3DRMObject. The address of the IDirect3DRMObject object which you want to be assigned interpolated values for all properties stored in the interpolator. If you set this to NULL, the property values of all of the attached objects will be set to interpolated values.

d3drmInterpFlags. You can set one of more flags to specify what type of interpolation will be done. The possible values are:

- D3DRMINTERPOLATION_CLOSED

- D3DRMINTERPOLATION_LINEAR

- D3DRMINTERPOLATION_NEAREST

- D3DRMINTERPOLATION_OPEN

- D3DRMINTERPOLATION_SLERPNORMALS

- D3DRMINTERPOLATION_SPLINE

- D3DRMINTERPOLATION_VERTEXCOLOR

Returns

Successful: D3DRM_OK
Error: One of the Direct3DRM Retained Mode return values.

IDirect3DRMInterpolator::SetIndex

Description

This method is used to set your interpolator's internal index to the specified value (time). Any other interpolators attached to this one will have their indices set to the same value.

C++ specification

```
HRESULT SetIndex(
    D3DVALUE d3dVal
    )
```

Parameters

d3dVal. The time which you wish to set the interpolator's internal index to.

Returns

Successful: D3DRM_OK

Error: One of the Direct3DRM Retained Mode return values.

See also

IDirect3DRMInterpolator::GetIndex

Example

```
IDirect3DRMInterpolator  myInterp;
IDirect3DRMFrame myFrameInterp;
LPDIRECT3DRMOBJECTARRAY myObjectArray;

// Create our frame interpolator
pd3drm->CreateObject(CLSID_CDirect3DRMFrameInterpolator, 0,
        IID_IDirect3DRMInterpolator, &myInterp);
myInterp->QueryInterface(IID_IDirect3DRMFrame, &myFrameInterp);

// Add a position key to our interpolator
// Set our interpolator's internal index using the
// IDirect3DRMInterpolator interface
// Record the position by calling the
// IDirect3DRMFrame::SetPosition
myInterp->SetIndex(keytime);
myFrameInterp->SetPosition(NULL, keypos.x, keypos.y, keypos.z);

// Attach the frame to the interpolator to play actions back
//  through a frame
pInterp->AttachObject(pRealFrame);
.
.
// Get the attached objects

D3DVALUE newKeytime = myInterp->GetIndex();
```

IDirect3DRMMeshBuilder2 interfaces

Retained Mode meshes can be controlled with the `IDirect3DRMMesh`, `IDirect3DRMMeshBuilder`, and `IDirect3DRMMeshBuilder2.COM` interfaces. This new interface has the same capabilities as `IDirect3DRMMeshBuilder` but also has the new `IDirect3DRMMeshBuilder2::GenerateNormals2` method which allows greater control over the manner in which these normals are generated and the `IDirect-3DRMMeshBuilder2::GetFace` method which lets you access a single face in a mesh.

Like the `IDirect3DRMMeshBuilder` methods, the `IDirect3DRMMeshBuilder2` interface provides the `AddVertex`, `AddFace`, and `AddFaces` methods. You can also get a single face using the `IDirect3DRMMeshBuilder2::GetFace` method.

You can obtain the Direct3DRMMeshBuilder2 object by calling the `IDirect-3DRM::CreateMeshBuilder` method.

Like all COM interfaces, this interface inherits the `AddRef`, `QueryInterface`, and the `Release` methods from the `IUnknown` interface.

`IDirect3DRMMeshBuilder2` interface methods can be organized into the groups in table B.5.

Table B.5 IDirect3DRMMeshBuilder method

Color	GetColorSource
	SetColor
	SetColorRGB
	SetColorSource
Creation	GetBox
Faces	AddFace
	AddFaces
	CreateFace
	GetFaceCount
	GetFace
	GetFaces
Loading	Load
Meshes	AddMesh
	CreateMesh
Miscellaneous	AddFrame
	AddMeshBuilder
	ReserveSpace
	Save
	Scale
	SetMaterial

	Translate
Normals	AddNormal
	GenerateNormals2
	SetNormal
Perspective	GetPerspective
	SetPerspective
Rendering quality	GetQuality
	SetQuality
Textures	GetTextureCoordinates
	SetTexture
	SetTextureCoordinates
	SetTextureTopology
Vertices	AddVertex
	GetVertexColor
	GetVertexCount
	GetVertices
	SetVertex
	SetVertexColor
	SetVertexColorRGB

The `IDirect3DRMMeshBuilder2` interface also inherits the following methods from the `IDirect3DRMObject` interface:

- `AddDestroyCallback`
- `Clone`
- `DeleteDestroyCallback`
- `GetAppData`
- `GetClassName`
- `GetName`
- `SetAppData`
- `SetName`

IDirect3DRMMeshBuilder2::AddFace

This method has the same definition as `IDirect3DRMMeshBuilder::AddFace`. Please see page 529 for details.

IDirect3DRMMeshBuilder2::AddFaces

This method has the same definition as `IDirect3DRMMeshBuilder::AddFaces`. Please see page 530 for details.

IDirect3DRMMeshBuilder2::AddFrame

This method has the same definition as `IDirect3DRMMeshBuilder::AddFrame`. Please see page 531 for details.

IDirect3DRMMeshBuilder2::AddMesh

This method has the same definition as `IDirect3DRMMeshBuilder::AddMesh`. Please see page 532 for details.

IDirect3DRMMeshBuilder2::AddMeshBuilder

This method has the same definition as `IDirect3DRMMeshBuilder::AddMeshBuilder`. Please see page 532 for details.

IDirect3DRMMeshBuilder2::AddNormal

This method has the same definition as `IDirect3DRMMeshBuilder::AddNormal`. Please see page 533 for details.

IDirect3DRMMeshBuilder2::AddVertex

This method has the same definition as `IDirect3DRMMeshBuilder::AddVertex`. Please see page 534 for details.

IDirect3DRMMeshBuilder2::CreateFace

This method has the same definition as `IDirect3DRMMeshBuilder::CreateFace`. Please see page 534 for details.

IDirect3DRMMeshBuilder2::CreateMesh

This method has the same definition as `IDirect3DRMMeshBuilder::Create-Mesh`. Please see page 535 for details.

IDirect3DRMMeshBuilder2::GenerateNormals2

Description

This method is used to process the Direct3DRMMeshBuilder2 object and generates normals for each of the vertices in a mesh. This is done by averaging the face normals for each face in the object that shares this same vertex. If the faces sharing a vertex have an angle between them greater than the crease angle, new normals are generated.

One handy thing about setting the `D3DRMGENERATENORMALS_PRECOMPACT` flag is that the precompact pass will search all of the vertices in the mesh and merge any of them that are the same. Since some meshes have multiple vertices if they have multiple normals at a vertex, this will remove these multiple vertices since they are not needed in Direct3D. Once the compacting is complete, the normals are generated. If the angle the faces make at the edge is less than the crease angle, the face normals are averaged to generate the vertex normal. If this angle is larger than the crease angle, a new normal will be generated.

C++ specification

```
HRESULT GenerateNormals2(
    D3DVALUE dvCreaseAngle,
    DWORD dwFlags
    );
```

Parameters

`dvCreaseAngle`. This is the smallest angle in radians that faces can have among them and still have a new normal generated.

`dwFlags`. One of the following values:

- `D3DRMGENERATENORMALS_PRECOMPACT` (dwFlags = 1). This value indicates that the algorithm should attempt to compact mesh vertices before normals are generated.

- `D3DRMGENERATENORMALS_USECREASEANGLE` (dwFlags = 2). This value indicates that the dvCreaseAngle parameter should be used. If this flag is not set, the crease angle is ignored.

Returns

Successful: D3DRM_OK

Error: One of the Direct3DRM Retained Mode return values.

See also

IDirect3DRMMeshBuilder::GenerateNormals

Example

```
HRESULT result;
LPDIRECT3DRMMESHBUILDER myMeshBuilder;
D3DVALUE creaseAngle;
    .
    .
result = myMeshBuilder->GenerateNormals2(
    creaseAngle,
    D3DRMGENERATENORMALS_USECREASEANGLE
    );
if (result = D3DRM_OK)
    goto generic_error;
```

IDirect3DRMMeshBuilder2::GetBox

This method has the same definition as `IDirect3DRMMeshBuilder::GetBox`. Please see page 537 for details.

IDirect3DRMMeshBuilder2::GetColorSource

This method has the same definition as `IDirect3DRMMeshBuilder::GetColorSource`. Please see page 538 for details.

IDirect3DRMMeshBuilder2::GetFace

Description

This method is used to retrieve a single face of your Direct3DRMMeshBuilder2 object.

C++ specification

```
HRESULT GetFace(
    DWORD dwIndex,
    LPDIRECT3DRMFACE* lplpD3DRMFace
    );
```

Parameters

dwIndex. The index of the mesh face you wish to get. This face must already be part of a Direct3DRMMeshBuilder2 object.

lplpD3DRMFace. The address of a pointer to an IDirect3DRMFace interface you wish filled with an address of the face.

Returns

Successful: D3DRM_OK

Error: One of the Direct3DRM Retained Mode return values.

See also

IDirect3DRMMeshBuilder::GetFace

Example

```
HRESULT result;
LPDIRECT3DRMMESHBUILDER myMeshBuilder;
LPDIRECT3DRMFACE face
    .

    .
result = myMeshBuilder->GetFace(3, &face);
if (result = D3DRM_OK)
    goto generic_error;
```

IDirect3DRMMeshBuilder2::GetFaceCount

This method has the same definition as IDirect3DRMMeshBuilder::GetFace-Count. Please see page 539 for details.

IDirect3DRMMeshBuilder2::GetFaces

This method has the same definition as IDirect3DRMMeshBuilder::GetFaces. Please see page 539 for details.

IDirect3DRMMeshBuilder2::GetPerspective

This method has the same definition as IDirect3DRMMeshBuilder::GetPerspective. Please see page 540 for details.

IDirect3DRMMeshBuilder2::GetQuality

This method has the same definition as `IDirect3DRMMeshBuilder::GetQuality`. Please see page 541 for details.

IDirect3DRMMeshBuilder2::GetTextureCoordinates

This method has the same definition as `IDirect3DRMMeshBuilder::GetTextureCoordinates`. Please see page 542 for details.

IDirect3DRMMeshBuilder2::GetVertexColor

This method has the same definition as `IDirect3DRMMeshBuilder::GetVertexColor`. Please see page 542 for details.

IDirect3DRMMeshBuilder2::GetVertexCount

This method has the same definition as `IDirect3DRMMeshBuilder::GetVertexCount`. Please see page 543 for details.

IDirect3DRMMeshBuilder2::GetVertices

This method has the same definition as `IDirect3DRMMeshBuilder::GetVertices`. Please see page 544 for details.

IDirect3DRMMeshBuilder2::GetLoad

This method has the same definition as `IDirect3DRMMeshBuilder::Load`. Please see page 545 for details.

IDirect3DRMMeshBuilder2::ReserveSpace

This method has the same definition as `IDirect3DRMMeshBuilder::ReserveSpace`. Please see page 546 for details.

IDirect3DRMMeshBuilder2::Save

This method has the same definition as `IDirect3DRMMeshBuilder::Save`. Please see page 547 for details.

IDirect3DRMMeshBuilder2::Scale

This method has the same definition as `IDirect3DRMMeshBuilder::Scale`. Please see page 549 for details.

IDirect3DRMMeshBuilder2::SetColor

This method has the same definition as `IDirect3DRMMeshBuilder::SetColor`. Please see page 550 for details.

IDirect3DRMMeshBuilder2::SetColorRGB

This method has the same definition as `IDirect3DRMMeshBuilder::SetColorRGB`. Please see page 550 for details.

IDirect3DRMMeshBuilder2::SetColorSource

This method has the same definition as `IDirect3DRMMeshBuilder::SetColorSource`. Please see page 551 for details.

IDirect3DRMMeshBuilder2::SetMaterial

This method has the same definition as `IDirect3DRMMeshBuilder::SetMaterial`. Please see page 552 for details.

IDirect3DRMMeshBuilder2::SetNormal

This method has the same definition as `IDirect3DRMMeshBuilder::SetNormal`. Please see page 553 for details.

IDirect3DRMMeshBuilder2::SetPerspective

This method has the same definition as `IDirect3DRMMeshBuilder::SetPer-`
`spective`. Please see page 554 for details.

IDirect3DRMMeshBuilder2::SetQuality

This method has the same definition as `IDirect3DRMMeshBuilder::SetQual-`
`ity`. Please see page 554 for details.

IDirect3DRMMeshBuilder2::SetTexture

This method has the same definition as `IDirect3DRMMeshBuilder::SetTexure`.
Please see page 555 for details.

IDirect3DRMMeshBuilder2::SetTextureCoordinates

This method has the same definition as `IDirect3DRMMeshBuilder::SetTexure-`
`Coordinates`. Please see page 556 for details.

IDirect3DRMMeshBuilder2::SetTextureTopology

This method has the same definition as `IDirect3DRMMeshBuilder::SetTexure-`
`Topology`. Please see page 557 for details.

IDirect3DRMMeshBuilder2::SetVertex

This method has the same definition as `IDirect3DRMMeshBuilder::SetVertex`.
Please see page 558 for details.

IDirect3DRMMeshBuilder2::SetVertexColor

This method has the same definition as `IDirect3DRMMeshBuilder::SetVertex-`
`Color`. Please see page 559 for details.

IDirect3DRMMeshBuilder2::SetVertexColorRGB

This method has the same definition as `IDirect3DRMMeshBuilder::SetVertex-ColorRGB`. Please see page 560 for details.

IDirect3DRMMeshBuilder2::Translate

This method has the same definition as `IDirect3DRMMeshBuilder::Translate`. Please see page 561 for details.

IDirect3DRMPicked2Array interface

The `IDirect3DRMPicked2Array` interface was developed to let you organize pick objects and return information beyond that which was available with the `IDirect3DRMPickedArray`. The `IDirect3DRMPicked2Array::GetPick` method lets you acquire data in the D3DRMPICKDESC2 structure. The data includes pick position, the vertex's horizontal and vertical texture coordinates, the vertex normal, the color of the intersected objects, and the face and group identifiers.

Like all COM interfaces, this interface inherits the `AddRef`, `QueryInterface`, and the `Release` methods from the `IUnknown` interface.

The methods of the `IDirect3DRMPicked2Array` interface are `GetPick` and `GetSize`.

IDirect3DRMPicked2Array::GetPick

Description
This method is used to acquire the Direct3DRMVisual and Direct3DRMFrame objects intersected by the pick.

C++ specification

```
HRESULT GetPick(
    DWORD index,
    LPDIRECT3DRMVISUAL * lplpVisual,
    LPDIRECT3DRMFRAMEARRAY * lplpFrameArray,
    LPD3DRMPICKDESC2 lpD3DRMPickDesc2
    );
```

Parameters
`index`. The index into the pick array which specifies the picked object for which you will be getting information.

`LplpVisual`. The address you want filled with a pointer to the Direct3DRMVisual object associated with the pick.

`LplpFrameArray`. The address you want filled with a pointer to the Direct3DRMFrameArray object associated with the pick.

`lpD3DRMPickDesc`. The address of a D3DRMPICKDESC2 structure which describes the face and group identifiers, pick position, horizontal and vertical texture coordinates for the vertex, vertex normal, and color of the objects that are intersected.

Returns

Successful: D3DRM_OK

Error: One of the Direct3DRM Retained Mode return values.

See also

IDirect3DRMFrame2::RayPick

IDirect3DRMPickedArray::GetPick

IDirect3DRMPicked2Array::GetSize

Description

This method is used to acquire the number of elements in the Direct-3DRMPicked2Array object.

C++ specification

```
DWORD GetSize( );
```

Parameters

None

Returns

The number of elements in the array.

See also

IDirect3DRMPicked2Array::GetSize

IDirect3DRMProgressiveMesh interface

The new progressive mesh is one which is stored as a base mesh along with a set of records which are used to progressively refine it. You can use this to set the level of detail at which the mesh is rendered. It also provides for the progressive download from remote sources.

You can define a minimum level of detail to be used for rendering and you can set the number of vertices or faces to render to control your detail. A progressive mesh is normally rendered as soon as the base mesh is available, but if you use the `Direct3DRMProgressiveMesh::SetMinRenderDetail` method you can require a greater level of detail before rendering. Another handy capability is that you can build a `Direct3DRMMesh` object from one state of your progressive mesh by calling the `IDirect3DRMProgressiveMesh::CreateMesh` method.

Finally, you can load a progressive mesh, synchronously or asynchronously, from a file, resource, memory, or a URL. If you use asynchronous loading, you must determine and handle loading progress with the `IDirect3DRMProgressiveMesh::Register-Events` and `IDirect3DRMProgressiveMesh::GetLoadStatus` methods.

Like all COM interfaces, this interface inherits the `AddRef`, `QueryInterface`, and `Release` methods from the `IUnknown` interface.

The `IDirect3DRMProgressiveMesh` interface's methods can be organized into the group shown in table B.6.

Table B.6 IDirect3DRMProgressiveMesh methods

Creating and Copying Meshes	Clone
	CreateMesh
	Duplicate
	GetBox
Loading	Abort
	GetLoadStatus
	Load
Setting Quality	SetQuality
	GetQuality
Managing Details	GetDetail
	GetFaceDetail
	GetFaceDetailRange
	GetVertexDetail
	GetVertexDetailRange
	SetDetail

Table B.6 IDirect3DRMProgressiveMesh methods (continued)

	SetFaceDetail
	SetMinRenderDetail
	SetVertexDetail
Registering Events	RegisterEvents

The `IDirect3DRMProgressiveMesh` interface also inherits the methods below from the `IDirect3DRMObject` interface:

- `AddDestroyCallback`
- `Clone`
- `DeleteDestroyCallback`
- `GetAppData`
- `GetClassName`
- `GetName`
- `SetAppData`
- `SetName`

IDirect3DRMProgressiveMesh::Abort

Description

This method is used to terminate the active download. As long as the base mesh was downloaded before the call to this method, the end effect is as if the progressive mesh has been loaded, the vertex splits are in a valid state, and the progressive mesh is renderable (plus the other progressive meshes will work).

If the base mesh were not loaded before the call to this method, and the progressive mesh has been added to the scene, the render will succeed but the progressive mesh will not be rendered!

If the base mesh is not downloaded, if you try to use the progressive mesh (such as creating a clone), you receive an error of the type `D3DRMERR_NOTENOUGHDATA` returned.

C++ specification

```
HRESULT Abort(
    DWORD dwFlags
    )
```

Parameters

dwFlags. This parameter must be set to 0.

Returns

Successful: DD_OK

Error: `D3DRMERR_INVALIDOBJECT` or `D3DRMERR_INVALIDPARAMS`.

IDirect3DRMProgressiveMesh::Clone

Description

This method is used to create a copy of the Direct3DRMProgressiveMesh object that is currently loaded. You must have the base mesh loaded for the progressive mesh being cloned. If the progressive mesh is being asynchronously loaded when you call this method, the cloned mesh will have the same amount of detail as the loading progressive mesh has at the time you clone it. Also, this method does not share any of the progressive mesh's internal data. If you wish to, use the `IDirect3DRMProgressiveMesh::Duplicate` method.

C++ specification

```
HRESULT Clone(
    LPDIRECT3DRMPROGRESSIVEMESH* lplpD3DRMPMesh
    )
```

Parameters

lplpD3DRMPMesh. The address of a `Direct3DRMProgressiveMesh` pointer you wish filled with a pointer to the generated Direct3DRMProgressiveMesh object.

Returns

Successful: DD_OK

Error: `D3DRMERR_CONNECTIONLOST`,
`D3DRMERR_INVALIDOBJECT`,
`D3DRMERR_ INVALIDPARAMS`, or
`D3DRMERR_NOTENOUGHDATA`.

See also

IDirect3DRMProgressiveMesh::Duplicate

IDirect3DRMProgressiveMesh::CreateMesh

Description

This method is used to build a mesh from the current level of detail.

C++ specification

```
HRESULT CreateMesh(
    LPDIRECT3DRMMESH* lplpD3DRMMesh
    )
```

Parameters

lplpD3DRMMesh. The address of a Direct3DRMMesh pointer you wish filled with a pointer to the Direct3DRMMesh object that is generated. This method will return the error D3DRMERR_NOTENOUGHDATA if the base mesh is not available or you request a level of detail that isn't available yet.

Returns

Successful: DD_OK

Error: D3DRMERR_CONNECTIONLOST,

D3DRMERR_INVALIDDATA,

D3DRMERR_INVALIDOBJECT,

D3DRMERR_INVALIDPARAMS, or

D3DRMERR_NOTENOUGH-DATA.

See also

IDirect3DRMProgressiveMesh::Duplicate

IDirect3DRMProgressiveMesh::Duplicate

Description

This method is uscd to create a copy of your Direct3DRMProgressiveMesh object. This copy will have the same geometry and face data as the original mesh, but you can set the detail level independently from the original. This allows you to use the same mesh data in different parts of the hierarchy but you can give them different levels of detail. This gives you the ability to have almost two instances of the progressive mesh in the frame hierarchy.

The base mesh data, the data which defines the current state of your progressive mesh, and the current level of detail are not shared among the duplicated meshes, but the vertex splits are. Remember that if you call this method on a progressive mesh which is currently being asynchronously loaded, the duplicate mesh will have only the amount of detail as the progressive mesh that was loading had at the time it was duplicated. The progressive mesh you are loading must at least have its base mesh loaded.

Also remember that a progressive mesh has a set of data that represents the base mesh and a set of data that represents the vertex splits.

C++ specification

```
HRESULT Duplicate(
    LPDIRECT3DRMPROGRESSIVEMESH* lplpD3DRMPMesh
    )
```

Parameters

lplpD3DRMPMesh. The address of a Direct3DRMProgressiveMesh pointer you wish filled with a pointer to the new Direct3DRMProgressiveMesh object.

Returns

Successful: DD_OK

Error: D3DRMERR_CONNECTIONLOST,
D3DRMERR_INVALIDOBJECT,
D3DRMERR_INVALIDPARAMS, or
D3DRMERR_NOTENOUGHDATA.

See also

IDirect3DRMProgressiveMesh::CreateMesh

IDirect3DRMProgressiveMesh::GetBox

Description

This method retrieves the bounding box containing a Direct3DRMProgressive-Mesh object. The bounding box gives the minimum and maximum coordinates relative to a child frame, in each dimension.

C++ specification

```
HRESULT GetBox(
    D3DRMBOX * lpD3DRMBox
    );
```

Parameters

lpD3DRMBox. The address of a D3DRMBOX structure you wish filled with the bounding box coordinates.

Returns

Successful: D3DRM_OK

Error: One of the Direct3DRM Retained Mode return values.

See also

IDirect3DRMMesh::GetBox

IDirect3DRMProgressiveMesh::GetDetail

Description

This method is used to acquire the current detail level of the progressive mesh normalized between `0.0` (the minimum number of vertices, e.g. the number in the base mesh), and `1.0` (the maximum number of vertices).

This method will return `D3DRMERR_PENDING` if the base mesh hasn't been downoaded. If the requested level of detail has been set, the return value will be increased on each subsequent call until the requested level has been met. If you do not request a level, the detail will be increased until all vertex splits have been downloaded.

C++ specification

```
HRESULT GetDetail(
    LPD3DVALUE lpdvVal
    )
```

Parameters

`lpdvVal`. The address of a D3DVALUE you want filled with the current detail level of your progressive mesh.

Returns

Successful: DD_OK

Error: `D3DRMERR_CONNECTIONLOST`,
`D3DRMERR_INVALIDDATA`,
`D3DRMERR_INVALIDOBJECT`,
`D3DRMERR_INVALIDPARAMS`, or
`D3DRMERR_PENDING`.

See also

IDirect3DRMProgressiveMesh::GetFaceData

IDirect3DRMProgressiveMesh::GetFaceData

Description
This method is used to acquire the number of faces in your progressive mesh.

C++ specification
```
HRESULT GetFaceDetail(
    LPDWORD lpdwCount
    )
```

Parameters
lpdwCount. The address of a DWORD you wish filled with the number of faces in your progressive mesh.

Returns
Successful: DD_OK

Error: D3DRMERR_CONNECTIONLOST,

D3DRMERR_INVALIDDATA,

D3DRMERR_INVALIDOBJECT,

D3DRMERR_INVALIDPARAMS, or

D3DRMERR_PENDING.

If the number of faces is not available, this method returns D3DRMERR_PENDING.

See also
IDirect3DRMProgressiveMesh::GetDetail

IDirect3DRMProgressiveMesh::GetFaceDetailRange

Description
This method is used to acquire the minimum and maximum face count available in your progressive mesh.

C++ specification
```
HRESULT GetFaceDetailRange(
    LPDWORD lpdwMinFaces,
    LPDWORD lpdwMaxFaces
    )
```

Parameters
lpdwMinFaces. The address of a DWORD you wish filled with the minimum number of faces.

lpdwMaxFaces. The address of a DWORD you wish filled with the maximum number of faces.

Returns

Successful: DD_OK

Error: D3DRMERR_CONNECTIONLOST,

D3DRMERR_INVALIDDATA,

D3DRMERR_INVALIDOBJECT,

D3DRMERR_INVALIDPARAMS, or

D3DRMERR_PENDING.

If the face count isn't available, D3DRMERR_PENDING will be returned.

See also

IDirect3DRMProgressiveMesh::GetDetail

IDirect3DRMProgressiveMesh::GetLoadStatus

Description

This method is used to check the current status of the load. If the base mesh has been downloaded and the data is not corrupt, and therefore it is renderable, the dwFlags member will contain D3DRMPMESHSTATUS_RENDERABLE. If the download was interrupted, the dwFlags member will contain D3DRMPMESHSTATUS_INTERRUPTED.

C++ specification

```
HRESULT GetLoadStatus(
    LPD3DRMPMESHLOADSTATUS lpStatus
    )
```

Parameters

lpStatus. The address of a D3DRMPMESHLOADSTATUS structure. This structure is defined as:

```
typedef struct _D3DRMPMESHLOADSTATUS
{
    DWORD dwSize;         // The size of this structure
    DWORD dwPMeshSize;    // Total size (bytes)
    DWORD dwBaseMeshSize; // Size of base mesh (bytes)
    DWORD dwBytesLoaded;  // Total number of bytes loaded
    DWORD dwVerticesLoaded;// Number of vertices loaded
    DWORD dwFacesLoaded;  // Number of faces loaded
    DWORD dwFlags;
}
D3DRMPMESHLOADSTATUS;
typedef D3DRMPMESHLOADSTATUS *LPD3DRMPMESHLOADSTATUS;
```

The dwFlags member can have the following values:

- D3DRMPMESHSTATUS_VALID. The progressive mesh object contains valid data.
- D3DRMPMESHSTATUS_INTERRUPTED. The download was interrupted either because the application called Abort or because the connection was lost.
- D3DRMPMESHSTATUS_BASEMESH. The base mesh has been downloaded.
- D3DRMPMESHSTATUS_COMPLETE. All data has been downloaded.
- D3DRMPMESHSTATUS_RENDERABLE. It is now possible to render the mesh.

Returns

Successful: DD_OK

Error: D3DRMERR_CONNECTIONLOST,
D3DRMERR_INVALIDDATA,
D3DRMERR_INVALIDOBJECT, or
D3DRMERR_INVALIDPARAMS.

IDirect3DRMProgressiveMesh::GetQuality

Description

This method is used to acquire a member of the D3DRMRENDERQUALITY enumerated specifying the rendering quality of your progressive mesh.

C++ specification

```
HRESULT GetQuality(
    LPD3DRMRENDERQUALITY lpQuality
    );
```

Parameters

lpQuality. If the call is successful, this will contain a pointer to the D3DRMRENDERQUALITY indicating the rendering quality.

Returns

Successful: D3DRM_OK

Error: D3DRMERR_BADOBJECT. The progressive mesh is invalid.
D3DRMERR_BADVALUE. The pointer to the D3DRMRENDERQUALITY member is invalid.

See also

IDirect3DRMProgressiveMesh::SetQuality
IDirect3DRMMesh::GetGroupQuality

IDirect3DRMProgressiveMesh::GetVertexDetail

Description

This method is used to acquire the number of vertices in your progressive mesh.

C++ specification

```
HRESULT GetVertexDetail(
    LPDWORD lpdwCount
    )
```

Parameters

lpdwCount. The address of a DWORD you wish filled with the number of vertices in your progressive mesh.

Returns

Successful: DD_OK

Error: D3DRMERR_CONNECTIONLOST,

D3DRMERR_INVALIDDATA,

D3DRMERR_INVALIDOBJECT,

D3DRMERR_INVALIDPARAMS, or

D3DRMERR_PENDING.

This method will return D3DRMERR_PENDING if the number of vertices is not available.

See also

IDirect3DRM::GetVertices

IDirect3DRMProgressiveMesh::GetVertexDetailRange

IDirect3DRMProgressiveMesh::GetVertexDetailRange

Description

This method is used to acquire the minimum and maximum vertex count available in your progressive mesh.

C++ specification

```
HRESULT GetVertexDetailRange(
    LPDWORD lpdwMinVertices,
    LPDWORD lpdwMaxVertices
    )
```

Parameters

lpdwMinVertices. The address of a DWORD you wish filled with the minimum number of vertices.

lpdwMaxVertices. The address of a DWORD you wish filled with the maximum number of vertices.

Returns

Successful: DD_OK

Error: D3DRMERR_CONNECTIONLOST,

D3DRMERR_INVALIDDATA,

D3DRMERR_INVALIDOBJECT,

D3DRMERR_INVALIDPARAMS, or

D3DRMERR_PENDING.

This method returns D3DRMERR_PENDING if the vertex count information is not available.

See also

IDirect3DRMProgressiveMesh::GetVertexDetail

IDirect3DRMProgressiveMesh::Load

Description

This method is used to load a progressive mesh object from a file, memory, a resource, or a URL. This loading can be done synchronously or asynchronously. The progressive mesh must be initialized to be used and if you use an asynchronous download, the API will return immediately and a separate thread will be spawned to perform the download. This method, IDirect3DRMProgressiveMesh::Clone, and IDirect3DRMProgressiveMesh::Duplicate will initialize a progressive mesh. You can initialize an object only once, so you cannot clone or duplicate a progressive mesh and then try to load into the cloned or duplicated mesh. You also can't load into a previously loaded mesh.

C++ specification

```
HRESULT Load(
    LPVOID lpSource,
    LPVOID lpObjID,
    D3DRMLOADOPTIONS dloLoadflags,
    D3DRMLOADTEXTURECALLBACK lpCallback,
    LPVOID lpArg
    )
```

Parameters

lpSource. The address of the source for the object you are loading. This source can be a file, memory block, resource, or stream, based upon the source flags in the dloLoadflags parameter.

lpObjID. The address of the ID of the DirectX file record that is a progressive mesh. This can either be a string or a UUID (determined by `dloLoadflags`). If `lpObjID` is NULL, then `dloLoadflags` must be `D3DRMLOAD_FIRST`.

dloLoadflags. The value of the D3DRMLOADOPTIONS type which define how you want the load performed. One flag from each of the following two groups must be included.

1 These values are used to determine which object in the DirectX file is loaded:

D3DRMLOAD_BYNAME	The `lpObjID` parameter is interpreted as a string.
D3DRMLOAD_BYGUID	The `lpObjID` parameter is interpreted as a UUID.
D3DRMLOAD_FIRST	The first progressive mesh found is loaded.

2 The following flags determine the source of the DirectX file:

D3DRMLOAD_FROMFILE	Interpret the `lpSource` parameter as a string indicating a local file name.
D3DRMLOAD_FROMRESOURCE	Interpret the `lpSource` parameter as a pointer to a D3DRMLOADRESOURCE structure.
D3DRMLOAD_FROMMEMORY	Interpret the `lpSource` parameter as a pointer to a D3DRMLOADMEMORY structure.
D3DRMLOAD_FROMURL	Interpret the `lpSource` as a URL.

You can also specify whether the download is synchronous (the default) or asynchronous. The `Load` call will not return until all the data has been loaded or an error occurs. You can request asynchronous loading with the flag: `D3DRMLOAD_ASYNCHRONOUS`. The `Load` call will return immediately. Your application must use events with `IDirect3DRMProgressiveMesh::RegisterEvents` and `IDirect3DRMProgressiveMesh::GetLoadStatus` to determine how the load is progressing.

lpCallback. The address of a `D3DRMLOADTEXTURECALLBACK` callback function you wish called to load any necessary texture. This will be called with the texture name as encountered by the loader and the user-defined `lpArg` parameter. A new thread is not spawned for the callback. If you want the application to download a texture progressively, it must spawn a thread and return with an LPDIRECT3DRMTEXTURE as normal.

lpArg. The address of the user-defined data passed to the D3DRMLOADTEXTURE-CALLBACK callback function.

Returns

Successful: DD_OK

Error: D3DRMERR_BADPMDATA,

   D3DRMERR_BADFILE,

   D3DRMERR_CONNECTIONLOST,

   D3DRMERR_INVALIDOBJECT,

   D3DRMERR_INVALIDPARAMS, or

   D3DRMERR_INVALIDDATA.

See also

IDirect3DRMMeshBuilder::Load

IDirect3DRMProgressiveMesh::RegisterEvents

Description

This method allows your application to register events with the progressive mesh object which will be signaled when the appropriate conditions are met. You can use this method to monitor the progress of your loads. Your application should always call the IDirect3DRMProgressiveMesh::GetLoadStatus method after being signaled since events will also be signaled if an error occurs.

C++ specification

```
HRESULT RegisterEvents(
    HANDLE hEvent,
    DWORD dwFlags,
    DWORD dwReserved
    )
```

Parameters

hEvent. The event you want signaled when the required condition is met.

dwFlags. Can be one of the following:

- D3DRMPMESHEVENT_BASEMESH. Signaled when the base mesh has been downloaded.

- D3DRMPMESHEVENT_COMPLETE. Signaled when all data has been downloaded

dwReserved. This value must be 0.

Returns

Successful: DD_OK

Error: `D3DRMERR_INVALIDOBJECT` or `D3DRMERR_INVALIDPARAMS`.

IDirect3DRMProgressiveMesh::SetDetail

Description

This method is used to set a requested level of detail normalized between `0.0` and `1.0` The normalized value `0.0` represents the minimum number of vertices (the number of vertices in the base mesh), and the normalized value `1.0` represents the maximum number of vertices.

C++ specification

```
HRESULT SetDetail(
    D3DVALUE dvVal
    )
```

Parameters

`dvVal`. The requested level of detail.

Returns

Successful: DD_OK

Error: `D3DRMERR_BADPMDATA`,
`D3DRMERR_CONNECTIONLOST`,
`D3DRMERR_PENDING`,
`D3DRMERR_INVALIDOBJECT`,
`D3DRMERR_INVALIDPARAMS`,
`D3DRMERR_IN-VALIDDATA`, or
`D3DRMERR_REQUESTTOOLARGE`.

See also

IDirect3DRMProgressiveMesh::GetQuality

IDirect3DRMProgressiveMesh::SetFaceDetail

Description

This method is used to set the desired level of face detail. It is not always possible to set the progressive mesh to the number of faces requested, but it will always be within 1 of the requested value. The reason for this is that a vertex split can add one or two faces. As an example, if you call `SetFaceDetail(20)`, the progressive mesh may only be able to set the face detail to 19 or 21. You can get the actual number of faces in the progressive mesh by calling the IDirect-3DRMProgressiveMesh::GetFaceDetail method.

C++ specification

```
HRESULT SetFaceDetail(
    DWORD dwCount
    )
```

Parameters

dwCount. The number of requested faces.

Returns

Successful: DD_OK

Error: D3DRMERR_BADPMDATA,
    D3DRMERR_CONNECTIONLOST,
    D3DRMERR_PENDING,
    D3DRMERR_INVALIDOBJECT,
    D3DRMERR_INVALIDPARAMS, D3DRMERR_INVALIDDATA,
    D3DRMERR_REQUESTTOOLARGE.

D3DRMERR_PENDING is returned if not enough detail has been downloaded yet, but it will be available. This error is informational and specifies that the requested level will be set as soon as enough detail is available. D3DRMERR_REQUESTTOOLARGE is returned if the detail requested is greater than the detail available in the progressive mesh.

See also

IDirect3DRMProgressiveMesh::GetFaceDetail

IDirect3DRMProgressiveMesh::SetMinRenderDetail

Description

This method is used to set the minimum level of detail which will be rendered during a load from 0.0 (minimum detail) to 1.0 (maximum detail). The progressive mesh will normally be rendered once the base mesh is available and the mesh is in the scene graph.

Any subsequent IDirect3DRMProgressiveMesh::SetDetail, IDirect3DRM-ProgressiveMesh::SetFaceDetail, or IDirect3DRMProgressiveMesh::Set-VertexDetail calls will override this value.

C++ specification

```
HRESULT SetMinRenderDetail(
    D3DVALUE dvCount
    )
```

Parameters

dvCount. The requested minimum detail.

Returns

Successful: DD_OK

Error: D3DRMERR_CONNECTIONLOST,

D3DRMERR_PENDING,

D3DRMERR_INVALIDOBJECT,

D3DRMERR_INVALIDPARAMS,

D3DRMERR_INVALIDDATA,

D3DRMERR_REQUESTTOOLARGE,

D3DRMERR_REQUESTTOOSMALL.

See also

IDirect3DRMProgressiveMesh::SetFaceDetail

IDirect3DRMProgressiveMesh::SetQuality

IDirect3DRMProgressiveMesh::SetQuality

Description

This method is used to set the rendering quality of a Direct3DRMProgressiveMesh object which defaults to D3DRMRENDER_GOURAUD (Gouraud shading, lights on, and solid fill).

Remember that an object's quality has three components:

- shade mode (flat or Gouraud, phong is not yet implemented and will default to Gouraud shading)
- lighting type (on or off)
- fill mode (point, wireframe or solid)

You can set the quality of a device with IDirect3DRMDevice::SetQuality which defaults to D3DRMRENDER_FLAT (flat shading, lights on, and solid fill).

Also, remember that DirectX Retained Mode will render an object at the lowest quality setting based on the device and the object's current setting for each individual component. So, if the object's current quality setting is D3DRMRENDER_GOURAUD, and the device is D3DRMRENDER_FLAT, the object will be rendered with flat shading, solid fill, and lights on.

C++ specification

```
HRESULT SetQuality(
    D3DRMRENDERQUALITY quality
    );
```

Parameters

quality. A member of the D3DRMRENDERQUALITY enumerated type which specifies the new rendering quality you want to use.

Returns

Successful: D3DRM_OK

Error: One of the Direct3DRM Retained Mode return values.

See also

IDirect3DRMDevice::SetQuality

IDirect3DRMMesh::SetGroupQuality

IDirect3DRMProgressiveMesh::SetVertexDetail

Description

This method is used to set the level of vertex detail.

C++ specification

```
HRESULT SetVertexDetail(
    DWORD dwCount
    )
```

Parameters

dwCount. The desired number of vertices.

Returns

Successful: DD_OK

Error: D3DRMERR_BADPMDATA,
D3DRMERR_CONNECTIONLOST,
D3DRMERR_PENDING,
D3DRMERR_INVALIDOBJECT,
D3DRMERR_INVALIDPARAMS,
D3DRMERR_INVALIDDATA, or
D3DRMERR_REQUESTTOOLARGE.

D3DRMERR_PENDING is returned if not enough detail has been downloaded yet, but it will be available. This error is informational and specifies that the requested level will be set as soon as enough detail is available.

D3DRMERR_REQUESTTOOLARGE is returned if the detail requested is greater than the detail available in the progressive mesh.

See also

IDirect3DRMProgressiveMesh::GetVertexDetail

IDirect3DRMTexture2 interface

The `IDirect3DRMTexture2` interface enhances the `IDirect3DRMTexture` interface by adding methods allowing resources to be loaded from DLLs and executables other than the currently executing file, generating a mipmap from a source image, and producing a texture from an image in memory.

In the older `IDirect3DRMTexture::InitFromFile` and `IDirect3DRMTexture::InitFromResource` methods, the textures were loaded inverted which many people thought was an odd thing to do. The new `IDirect3DRMTexture2::InitFromFile` and `IDirect3DRMTexture2::InitFromResource2` methods load the textures from BMP and DIB (device-independent bitmap) files right-side up!

Like all COM interfaces, this interface inherits the `AddRef`, `QueryInterface`, and the `Release` methods from the `IUnknown` interface.

An IDirect3DRMTexture2 object is created by calling `IDirect3DRM2::CreateTexture` or `IDirect3DRM2::CreateTextureFromSurface`.

The IDirect3DRMTexture2 interface methods can be organized into the groups shown in table B.7.

Table B.7 IDirect3DRMTexture2 methos

Color	GetColors
	SetColors
Decals	GetDecalOrigin
	GetDecalScale
	GetDecalSize
	GetDecalTransparency
	GetDecalTransparentColor
	SetDecalOrigin
	SetDecalScale
	SetDecalSize
	SetDecalTransparency
	SetDecalTransparentColor
Images	GetImage
Initialization	InitFromFile
	InitFromImage
	InitFromResource2
	InitFromSurface
Mipmap generation	Generate mipmap
Renderer notification	Changed

Table B.7 IDirect3DRMTexture2 methos

Shading	GetShades
	SetShades

The `IDirect3DRMTexture2` interface also inherits the following methods from the `IDirect3DRMObject` interface:

- `AddDestroyCallback`
- `Clone`
- `DeleteDestroyCallback`
- `GetAppData`
- `GetClassName`
- `GetName`
- `SetAppData`
- `SetName`

IDirect3DRMTexture2::Changed

This method has the same definition as `IDirect3DRMTexture::Changed`. Please see page 581 for details.

IDirect3DRMTexture2::GenerateMIPMap

Description

This method is used to generate a mipmap from a single image source. You can call this method after you create a texture. It is used to generate a mipmap of your source image all the way down to a resolution of `1x1` by using bilinear filtering between levels.

After a mipmap has been generated, it will always be available and will be updated whenever `IDirect3DRMTexture::Changed` is called.

You need to remember to change the texture quality to `D3DRMTEXTURE_MIPNEAREST`, `D3DRMTEXTURE_MIPLINEAR`, `D3DRMTEXTURE_LINEARMIPNEAREST`, or `D3DRM-TEXTURE_LINEARMIPLINEAR` using `IDirect3DRMDevice::SetTextureQuality` whenever you use mipmapping.

Extra mipmap levels will not be put into video memory for hardware devices unless the texture quality includes a mipmapping type and the hardware device supports mipmapping.

C++ specification

```
HRESULT GenerateMIPMap(
    DWORD dwFlags
    );
```

Parameters

dwFlags. This value should be set to 0.

Returns

Successful: D3DRM_OK

Error: One of the Direct3DRM Retained Mode return values.

Example

```
HRESULT result;
LPDIRECT3DRMTEXTURE2  myTex;
    .
    .
result = myTex->GenerateMIPMap(0);
if (result != D3DRM_OK)
    goto generic_error;
```

IDirect3DRMTexture2::GetColors

This method has the same definition as `IDirect3DRMTexture::GetColors`. Please see page 582 for details.

IDirect3DRMTexture2::GetDecalOrigin

This method has the same definition as `IDirect3DRMTexture::GetDecalOrigin`. Please see page 582 for details.

IDirect3DRMTexture2::GetDecalTransparency

This method has the same definition as `IDirect3DRMTexture::GetDecalTransparency`. Please see page 585 for details.

IDirect3DRMTexture2::GetDecalSize

This method has the same definition as `IDirect3DRMTexture::GetDecalSize`. Please see page 584 for details.

IDirect3DRMTexture2::GetDecalScale

This method has the same definition as `IDirect3DRMTexture::GetDecalScale`. Please see page 583 for details.

IDirect3DRMTexture2::GetDecalTransparentColor

This method has the same definition as `IDirect3DRMTexture::GetDecalTransparentColor`. Please see page 585 for details.

IDirect3DRMTexture2::GetImage

This method has the same definition as `IDirect3DRMTexture::GetImage`. Please see page 586 for details.

IDirect3DRMTexture2::GetShades

This method has the same definition as `IDirect3DRMTexture::GetShades`. Please see page 587 for details.

IDirect3DRMTexture2::GetDecalOrigin

This method has the same definition as `IDirect3DRMTexture::GetDecalOrigin`. Please see page 582 for details.

IDirect3DRMTexture2::InitFromFile

This method has the same definition as `IDirect3DRMTexture::InitFromFile`. Please see page 587 for details. You need to have created the `Direct3DRMTexture2` object to be initialized using the `IDirect3DRM2::CreateTexture` or `IDirect3DRM2::CreateTextureFromSurface` methods.

IDirect3DRMTexture2::InitFromImage

Description
This method will initialize the texture from the specified image which you must have created using the `IDirect3DRM2::CreateTexture` or `IDirect3DRM2::CreateTextureFromSurface` methods.

C++ specification
```
HRESULT InitFromImage(
    LPD3DRMIMAGE lpImage
    );
```

Parameters
`lpImage`. The address of a D3DRMIMAGE structure which defines the source of the texture.

Returns
Successful: D3DRM_OK
Error: One of the Direct3DRM Retained Mode return values.

See also
IDirect3DRMTexture2::InitFromFile
IDirect3DRMTexture2::InitFromResource2
IDirect3DRMTexture2::InitFromSurface

Example
```
HRESULT result;
LPDIRECT3DRMTEXTURE2  myTex;
LPD3DRMIMAGE image;
  .
  .
result = myTex->InitImage(image);
if (result != D3DRM_OK)
    goto generic_error;
```

IDirect3DRMTexture2::InitFromResource2

Description

This method is used to initialize a Direct3DRMTexture2 object from a specified resource. This IDirect3DRMTexture2 object must have been created using the IDirect3DRM2::CreateTexture or IDirect3DRM2::CreateTextureFromSurface methods.

C++ specification

```
HRESULT InitFromResource2 (
    HModule hModule,
    LPCTSTR strName,
    LPCTSTR strType
    );
```

Parameters

hModule. The handle of the specified resource.

strName. The name of the resource you want used to initialize your texture.

strType. The type name, which can be in RT_BITMAP, RT_RCDATA, or user-defined, of the resource used to initialize the texture. If the resource type is user-defined, this method will pass the resource module handle, the resource name, and the resource type to the FindResource Win32 API.

Returns

Successful: D3DRM_OK

Error: One of the Direct3DRM Retained Mode return values.

See also

IDirect3DRMTexture::InitFromReource
IDirect3DRMTexture2::InitFromFile
IDirect3DRMTexture2::InitFromImage
IDirect3DRMTexture2::InitFromSurface

Example

```
HRESULT myResult;
HModule module;
LPCTSTR mame;
LPDIRECT3DRMTEXTURE2  myTex;
.
.
myResult = myTex->InitFromResource2(module, name, RT_BITMAP);
if (myResult != D3DRM_OK)
    goto generic_error;
```

IDirect3DRMTexture2::InitFromSurface

This method has the same definition as `IDirect3DRMTexture::InitFromSurface`. Please see page 589 for details. This IDirect3DRMTexture2 object must have been created using the `IDirect3DRM2::CreateTexture` or `IDirect3DRM2::CreateTextureFromSurface` methods.

IDirect3DRMTexture2::SetColors

This method has the same definition as `IDirect3DRMTexture::SetColors`. Please see page 590 for details.

IDirect3DRMTexture2::SetDecalOrigin

This method has the same definition as `IDirect3DRMTexture::SetDecalOrigin`. Please see page 591 for details.

IDirect3DRMTexture2::SetDecalScale

This method has the same definition as `IDirect3DRMTexture::SetDecalScale`. Please see page 592 for details.

IDirect3DRMTexture2::SetDecalSize

This method has the same definition as `IDirect3DRMTexture::SetDecalSize`. Please see page 593 for details.

IDirect3DRMTexture2::SetDecalTransparency

This method has the same definition as `IDirect3DRMTexture::SetDecalTransparency`. Please see page 594 for details.

IDirect3DRMTexture2::SetDecalTransparentColor

This method has the same definition as `IDirect3DRMTexture::SetDecalTrans-parentColor`. Please see page 595 for details.

IDirect3DRMTexture2::SetShades

This method has the same definition as `IDirect3DRMTexture::SetShades`. Please see page 596 for details.

appendix c

CD contents

The CD accompanying this book contains *numerous* objects that you should find *very* helpful in the creation of your Direct3D applications. These include the following:

- The code for the examples in each chapter
- New Microsoft demos
- DirectX
- 3D objects—In both *.x* and *.3ds* format.
  - Meshes
  - Animations
- Textures
- Utilities
- Extras—Various projects and tools from other authors that are very useful for helping to explain D3D from other perspectives.

Code for each chapter's projects

The code for this book is stored in one large Microsoft C++ project, *Makefile1*, and the Immediate Mode code is stored in a smaller project, *ImmMode1\IMChapter*. The subprojects of the main *Makefile1* project each contain the files (code, resources, etc.) for one of the chapters. The project directory is organized as: tutorial\Chap2, tutorial\Chap3, and so forth. The code from each chapter creates executables as follows:

tutorial\Chap2   This project contains the code to generate the basic Microsoft Windows application we will use for all of our Direct3D Retained Mode applications. You can reuse the base code from chapter 2 for any Windows application you wish to build in the future. This code produces a blank window on the screen when the executable is run.

tutorial\Chap3   In this chapter's project, we add all of the set-up code necessary for us to build a basic, bare-bones, Direct3D Retained Mode application. Nothing is rendered to the screen yet, so this first Direct3D application produces a screen that looks exactly like the screen in chapter 2, but we now have the Direct3D foundation in our code.

tutorial\Chap4   We now will have a project that shows a Direct3D scene for the first time. The scene will display a point source light and a spot light in the middle of the screen. You can change the light types easily by requesting another type of light in the call CreateScene routine in the create.cpp file for this project. The code shows how to create a light using standard Direct3D call sequences and also by calling my CreateLight routine.

tutorial\Chap5   In the code for this chapter, we add the ability to load objects from files. We load a wall, a bucket, a well, and a guard tower to our scene.

tutorial\Chap6   We now add mouse and keyboard and mouse control to our code so we can move around our sparse 3D world.

tutorial\Chap7   In this chapter, we add the code which generates a landscape and a mountain wall. The most important thing we will learn is how to use a motion callback function to create a dynamic object level-of-detail capability. This very useful functionality allows us to create range bins where we can have a callback function automatically add or remove detail as we move closer, or farther from, respectively, to our objects. You will notice that things run a fair amount slower now, but we will optimize later, so don't worry too much about speed.

tutorial\Chap8   Next we add textures, materials, and colors to our objects. We also add an object for our background representing mountains at one side of our world. You will also notice that the optimizations made speeds things up about 80 percent from our untextured world from chapter 7!

tutorial\Chap8_Decal   This project demonstrates how to use the decal feature of Direct3D. It scales the texture up and down in size and moves the texture around the screen.

tutorial\Chap9   Although keyboard and mouse control may be all we need for some applications, others such as games will require joystick input. This will allow the user to control motion through, and manipulation of, the world and its objects. In this chapter, we add joystick control using DirectInput. You will learn all of the aspects of DirectInput necessary for you to add joystick control to your applications.

tutorial\Chap10   In this chapter we add one of the most critical capabilities you will need for any realistic 3D application: Collision Detection. We will learn about, and be shown code for, creating an overloadable collision class. This class provides collision shape abstraction objects for rectangle, prism, sphere, and cylinder. You can easily add any other shape you need by adding another collision class built from the base collision class.

tutorial\Chap11   We now add wave (.wav) sound files and MIDI (.mid) music files. I provide code to play multiple Wave files and a MIDI file all simultaneously. You will be able to use this code in your projects to play any sounds or music you desire.

tutorial\Chap12   In the main project for this chapter, I show you the code to create a shadow object. You can then take this code and add shadows to any objects in your world. All you need to do is add a shadow casting light that is focused upon the plane on which you wish the shadow to be cast.

tutorial\Chap122   In the second project for this chapter, I show you how to load and play an animation. You can take an object with multiple animation sequences in it—for example, your object can have segments with walking, transition from walking to running, running, transition from running to jumping, jumping, and so forth—and play each segment based on a user's actions. As an example, by playing each segment based on the user's joystick movement, you could control a 3D virtual character in a game.

tutorial\Chap14   In this project, I show you how to create a 3D terrain editor that allows you to vary parameters such as maximum and minimum height. You could easily modify this code to create a dynamic landscape modifier which you could use to create morphing landscapes.

tutorial\Chap15   This project shows you how to create a complete full-screen application. A full-screen application helps speed the program by removing window handling overhead, resizing issues, and so forth.

tutorial/Chap152   This project shows full screen project using an AVI file to generate an animated texture.

tutorial\ImmMode1 This project shows you how to set up an Immediate Mode program. The code discussed in chapters 16 through 18 is shown with the full screen debugging capability enabled in the Debug version of the project.

New Microsoft Demos

This directory contains several new excellent demonstration programs from the folks on the Direct3D team at Microsoft. The projects demonstrate the new DirectX 5 capabilities such as fog, mipmapping, lens flares, lighting, and a nice demo of a landscape with trees. Several of these utilize DrawPrimitive so you should look at the code in detail in order to learn this new aspect of D3D.

DirectX

The *entire* Microsoft DirectX SDK is contained on this CD. This includes Direct3D, DirectDraw, DirectSound, DirectPlay, and DirectInput.

3D objects

I have included numerous *public domain* 3D objects in both DirectX and 3D Studio format! These include both frame objects and animation objects.

3D object thumbnails

Black and white thumbnail shots of the 3D objects contained on the CD are shown below. The name of each file is shown below the object. I have supplied a wide range of object types, so there should be an object that fits in almost every category of need for your projects. Color plates of selected 3D objects are located in the color insert to this book.

The files were provided by the following individuals:

Lee Shapiro

Lee has provided an excellent female object. It has a high level of detail and is very realistic.

lady2.x

Web page: Please check my web site for the newest location of his web site.

Patrick Cady

Patrick provided the excellent female2.x object. He spent an incredible amount of time on this model and the detail shows it. This model should be useful anywhere you need a female model and will save you a lot of time modeling.
Email: 71361.2003@compuserve.com
Web page: Email him for his Internet web page information or check my web page for a link to his page.

Acuris 3d models

Acuris sells a wide variety of 3D models. The models they have provided are:

B17, corbu, destroyr, F-16, flowers, Porsche, rockhrse, roller, sofa

Web page: www.acuris.com

Animotion

Animotion sells a wide variety of models. The models they have provided are:

desk, plant, vrtblind, rosks, videowal, frame, lamp, rlngfile, clock

Web page: www.animotion.com

Cyberware

Cyberware produces a fantastic scanning system. The models they have provided are of very detailed scanned humans. They are:

bull, r96005a, r96012-2, r96025k, r96033, theo16

Web page: www.cyberware.com

Matt Harter

Matt has produced some fantastic street car models. These are as follows:

PCC11, type7, type8, wcar

Email: crew@flyingleap.com

Zygote

Zygote sells the nicest human models I have seen. They also do custom work. The models they have provided are:

abomsnow, viser

Web page: www.zygote.com

Mike Beals

Mike has provided a number of nice human models at several spots on the Internet. The following are included on my CD:

bridget, dominique, frank, gidget, mark

Web page: http://home.earthlink.net/~bacasino/

Platinum Pictures

Platinum Pictures provides a wonderful web site with hundreds of 3D models. If you need a great, free, 3D object, look here first. They also do custom work. The models they provided are:

55GALDRM.3DS	COUCH01.3DS
83ATC110.3DS	COUCH7.3DS
8FTFENCE.3DS	CURTAINS.3DS
ANVIL.3DS	DART.3DS
BANISTER.3DS	DARTBORD.3DS
BARN.3DS	DBLDOOR.3DS
BARSTOOL.3DS	DOOR2.3DS
BAT.3DS	DOOR3.3DS
BENCH.3DS	DOOR4.3DS
BICYCLE.3DS	DOOR5.3DS
BIG_F14.3DS	DOOR7.3DS
BLOTTER.3DS	DOOR8.3DS
BOOKSHL2.3DS	EDISON.3DS
BOWLBALL.3DS	ELIGHT.3DS
CAGE.3DS	EXCALIBE.3DS
CALIPER.3DS	FIREPLAC.3DS
CAN.3DS	FLPYDISK.3DS
CASKET.3DS	GATE02.3DS

CASKET2.3DS
CHAIN.3DS
CHAIR.3DS
CHAIR02.3DS
CHAIR03.3DS
CHAIR4.3DS
CHAIR05.3DS
CHAIR11.3DS
CHAISE.3DS
CHALKBRD.3DS
CHAMPAGN.3DS
CHERRY01.3DS
CHRFLWBR.3DS
CNDLHOLD.3DS
CORINTH.3DS
MALLET.3DS
MICROM.3DS
OUTLET.3DS
PAIL.3DS
PALLETTE.3DS
PINECON2.3DS
PROPANE.3DS
ROBOT.3DS
ROSES.3DS
SCISSORS.3DS
SCREWDRV.3DS
STONEBEN.3DS
STOOL.3DS

GAZEBO2.3DS
GUN.3DS
HANDBELL.3DS
HANDCUFF.3DS
HARP.3DS
HIGHCRWN.3DS
INDYCAR1.3DS
LADDER.3DS
LAMP01.3DS
LAMP02.3DS
LEAVES.3DS
LIGHT.3DS
LIGHT_FL.3DS
LITE01.3DS
LOUNCHAR.3DS
SKELETON.3DS
SPRING.3DS
SUNFLWR.3DS
TALLPLNT.3DS
TESTTUBE.3DS
TOILET.3DS
TOOLBOX.3DS
TRACTOR.3DS
TREE01.3DS
WAGON.3DS
WALLACES.3DS
WASHTUB.3DS

Web site: http://www.3dcafe.com/

Thumbnail images

The following thumbnail shots show the name and appearance of each of the DirectX (and the original 3D Studio) file on the CD. There should be something for almost every need!

55galdrm.jpg

83atc110.jpg

8ftfence.jpg

abomsnow.jpg

anvil.jpg

b17.jpg

banister.jpg

barn.jpg

barstool.jpg

bat.jpg

bench.jpg

bicycle.jpg

big_f14.jpg

blotter.jpg

bookshl2.jpg

bowlball.jpg

bridget.jpg

bull.jpg

cage.jpg

caliper.jpg

can.jpg

casket.jpg

casket2.jpg

chain.jpg

chair.jpg

chair02.jpg

chair03.jpg

chair05.jpg

chair11.jpg

chair05.jpg

chaise.jpg

chalkbrd.jpg

champagn.jpg

cherry01.jpg

chrflwbr.jpg

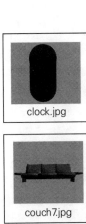
clock.jpg

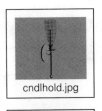
cndlhold.jpg

corbu.jpg

corinth.jpg

couch01.jpg

couch7.jpg

curtains.jpg

dart.jpg

dartbord.jpg

dbldoor.jpg

desk.jpg

destroyr.jpg

domini~.jpg

door2.jpg

door3.jpg

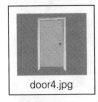
door4.jpg

door5.jpg

door7.jpg

door8.jpg

edison.jpg

elight.jpg

excalibe.jpg

f-16.jpg

female2.jpg

fireplac.jpg

flowers.jpg

flpydisk.jpg

frame.jpg

frank.jpg

gate02.jpg

gazebo2.jpg

gidget.jpg

gun.jpg

handbell.jpg

handcuff.jpg

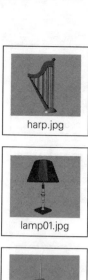
harp.jpg

highcrwn.jpg

indycar1.jpg

ladder.jpg

lamp.jpg

lamp01.jpg

lamp02.jpg

leaves.jpg

light.jpg

light_fl.jpg

lite01.jpg

lounchar.jpg

mallet.jpg

mark.jpg

microm.jpg

outlet.jpg

pail.jpg

pallette.jpg

pcc11.jpg

pinecon2.jpg

plant.jpg

porsche.jpg

propane.jpg

r96005a.jpg

r96025k.jpg

r96033.jpg

ringfile.jpg

robot.jpg

rockhrse.jpg

rocks.jpg

roller.jpg

scissors.jpg

screwdrv.jpg

skeleton.jpg

sofa.jpg

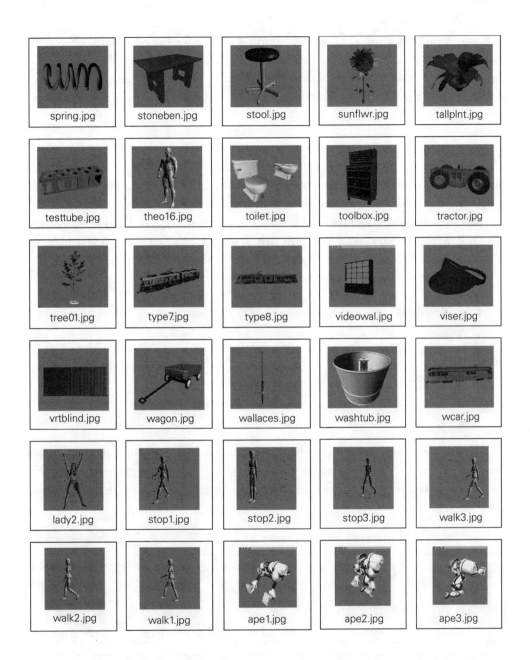

spring.jpg	stoneben.jpg	stool.jpg	sunflwr.jpg	tallplnt.jpg
testtube.jpg	theo16.jpg	toilet.jpg	toolbox.jpg	tractor.jpg
tree01.jpg	type7.jpg	type8.jpg	videowal.jpg	viser.jpg
vrtblind.jpg	wagon.jpg	wallaces.jpg	washtub.jpg	wcar.jpg
lady2.jpg	stop1.jpg	stop2.jpg	stop3.jpg	walk3.jpg
walk2.jpg	walk1.jpg	ape1.jpg	ape2.jpg	ape3.jpg

I have also included three DirectX objects with animation built in. The first two files are walk.x and stop.x. These were created by Doug Kelly, author of the book *Light-Wave 3D 5 Character Animation flx*. The third is the ape.x object which is courtesy of Matt McDonald and NewTek, Inc.

Screen shots of a few steps in each action sequence for these animated objects are shown above. To see them and to view all of their actions, please load the files into the DirectX object viewer (/dxsdk/sdk/bin/viewer.exe) which came as part of the DirectX distribution on this CD. Make sure you pick the 'Load Animation' selection so you will see them moving.

Textures

All of the textures on the CD have been provided by Correia Emmanuel, who also did the cover for this book! He is a very nice person and has incredible talent. He also has a fantastic web site where he provides hundreds of free textures and displays his 2D and 3D work. Make *sure* you take a look. His web page is at: http:\\axem2.simplenet.com.

The textures I have included on the CD fall into the following categories:

1 Barks

   2 Cobblestones

   3 Parquets

   4 Tiles

   5 Wallpapers

   6 Walls

7 Woods

Thumbnail images of each of the 52 textures included on this CD, along with their file names, are shown below in black and white so you can get an idea of what they will look like on your objects. You should be able to create some beautiful worlds using these textures.

| 2parq07.bmp | 2parq81.bmp | 2rarq13.bmp | 2rarq58.bmp | 2rarq59.bmp |
| 2rarq88.bmp | 2rarq93.bmp | all013.bmp | ark09.bmp | ark11.bmp |

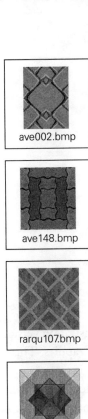
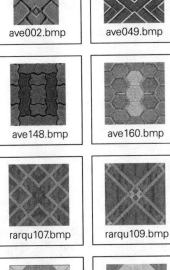
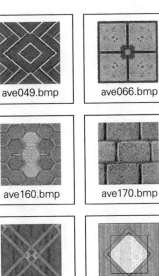

ave002.bmp ave049.bmp ave066.bmp ave123.bmp ave142.bmp

ave148.bmp ave160.bmp ave170.bmp parqu108.bmp parqu08.bmp

rarqu107.bmp rarqu109.bmp rarque22.bmp rarque42.bmp rarque52.bmp

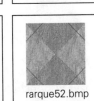

rarque57.bmp rarque60.bmp rarque61.bmp rellow12.bmp rellow14.bmp

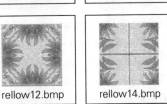

rk04.bmp rk34.bmp rk45.bmp rk53.bmp rlassi01.bmp

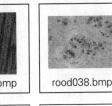
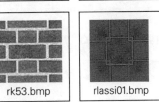

rlue55.bmp rlue80.bmp rood005.bmp rood010.bmp rood038.bmp

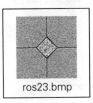

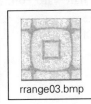

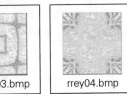

rood096.bmp ros23.bmp rrange01.bmp rrange03.bmp rrey04.bmp

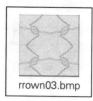
rrown03.bmp

S_rblue40.bmp

S_rgreen82.bmp

S_rgrey03.bmp

S_rpin~2.bmp

S_rpink50.bmp

S_ryello56.bmp

Utilities

I have also included three utilities I find very useful. The first is a demonstration version of the superb 3D conversion package PolyTrans by Okino Computer Graphics. This is the best software converter I have ever seen. Their web site is at: www.okino.com.

The other two utilities are HyperCam and HyperSnap. These two tools work wonderfully for grabbing screen shot stills (HyperCam) and screen shot videos (HyperSnap). The new version of HyperSnap supports Direct3D screen shots which is a very nice capability since it is very difficult to do a screen capture of a full-screen application!

Microsoft Immediate Mode/ DrawPrimitive Demos

I have included several new sample projects from the folks at Microsoft that do a great job of demonstrating some of the new DirectX 5 capabilities for Immediate Mode (including DrawPrimitive.) Since some features of Direct3D are not emulated in the software renderers, these examples need to be run on hardware and must have the right drivers to run properly. Because of this, some of the effects they are demonstrating may not work with all hardware configurations. All of these are self-extracting archives. I have also set up the contents of each of these archieved projects in seperate directories with it's out makefile.

ATEST (iatest.exe (137k))

The ATEST sample was created to let developers experiment with transparency effects using alpha polygons. The sample starts with a standard blue sphere and Src Alpha and Dest Alpha menus. Choosing Src Alpha=SrcAlpha and Dest Alpha=InvSrcAlpha produces the standard transparent effect.

BEES (ibees.exe (362k))

This project was written to demonstrate two effects—emissive materials and swarming behavior. The emissive material effect creates the illusion that an object is glowing. Swarming behavior is used to make individual objects appear to act as a group. I have used this effect in some virtual reality programs to simulate birds flocking overhead, fish schooling together, etc.

D_LIGHT (id_light.exe (142k))

The D-LIGHT demo shows how to animate colored light sources in real-time. The demo shows a sphere moving along a path over the viewport, which contains black dots. The black dots represent light sources. As the sphere approaches, the dots activate and color the sphere.

FLARE (iflare.exe (197k))

The FLARE demo shows how to use alpha textures to produce a lens flare. Lens flares can be used for a great number of effects to add realism to your programs. You can use it to create effects like sunlight reflecting off a window of a building, the canopy of a plane, or any other reflective object you can imagine.

FLIPA (iflipa.exe (138k))

The FLIPA demo was created to show how to use alpha textures. This demo is similar to ATEST but uses a spinning cube instead of a sphere. You can turn on alpha, specify an alpha texture, and then use the Src Alpha and Dest Alpha menus to specify alpha-blending modes. If you choose the standard Src Alpha=SrcAlpha and Dest Alpha=InvSrcAlpha, the cube will become transparent as a result of the use of the alpha channel in the textures.

FOG (ifog.exe (145k))

The demo shows how to use fog effects to hide the edge of a rolling fractal terrain. This allows you to remove the "edge-of-the-terrain" effects which cause "popping" if the edges are not "hidden" by fog or haze. You can also use alpha fade to hide edge effects.

MIPMAP (imipmap.exe (828k))

The MIPMAP demo shows how to use a texturing technique to provide multiple levels of texture detail. This demo shows the end increase in the visual quality by showing both views of the mipmapped and the un-mipmapped object.

TREES (itrees.exe (234k))

This demo shows how to simulate detailed 3D objects using color-keyed billboards. This demo also shows how you can create simple shadows by using a similar technique and combining it with alpha blending.

index

W

WaitMessage 309
Walk 229
WAV file 215
WAVE menu item 215
WAVEFILE 220
WAVEFORMATEX 215
WAVEMIX.DLL 214
windowed application 18
WindowProc 121, 311
WinMain 19, 22, 274, 293
WM_KEYDOWN 121
WM_PAINT 41

WNDCLASS 27
WNDCLASS structure 27
Word.Picture.6 170
world coordinates. 75
wrap 168
Wrapping Flags 169

X

x5.cpp 85

Z

Z-buffer 7, 278–279, 319, 335, 339

For details on the contents of the CD included
with this book, see the appendix starting on page 789.